HARVARD STUDIES IN BUSINESS HISTORY

III

EDITED BY N. S. B. GRAS

STRAUS PROFESSOR OF BUSINESS HISTORY
GRADUATE SCHOOL OF BUSINESS ADMINISTRATION
GEORGE F. BAKER FOUNDATION
HARVARD UNIVERSITY

LONDON : HUMPHREY MILFORD

OXFORD UNIVERSITY PRESS

THE JACKSONS AND THE LEES

Two Generations of Massachusetts Merchants
1765–1844

BY

KENNETH WIGGINS PORTER

AUTHOR OF
John Jacob Astor: Business Man

VOLUME II

CAMBRIDGE, MASSACHUSETTS

HARVARD UNIVERSITY PRESS

1937

PRINTED AT THE HARVARD UNIVERSITY PRESS

CAMBRIDGE, MASS., U. S. A.

HENRY LEE, 1782–1867, AT THE TIME OF HIS RETIREMENT FROM
ACTIVE BUSINESS, ABOUT 1840

CONTENTS

VOLUME II

DOCUMENTS

LIST OF ILLUSTRATIONS

VOLUME II

THE JACKSONS AND THE LEES

PART V

Second Generation (with a Glance at a Third): Joseph Lee, Jr., Henry Lee and Henry Lee, Jr.

1805-44

DIVISION XII

JOSEPH LEE, JR., AND HENRY LEE

BOSTON EAST INDIA MERCHANTS

1805-11

LETTER FROM HENRY LEE, BOSTON, SEPT. 24, 1805, TO JOHN
STILLE & Co., PHILADELPHIA, WITH TERMS FOR A VOYAGE
FROM EUROPE TO CALCUTTA [1]

Henry Lee had been absent from Boston for nearly a year, July,
1804–June, 1805, on a voyage to France. On his return he became
associated with his brother Joseph in the East India trade and assumed
the major share of the partnership's correspondence.

The plan, suggested in the letter below, of making a Calcutta voyage by way of Europe, stopping at Leghorn to get dollars, was not
carried out.

Mess John Stille &Co.   Boston Septr. 24th. 1805
    Philadelphia
        Gentlemen
                your reply to mine of the 13th. & 14th. is recd. I stated
Mr. Olivers acct. as it appears on his memo. — I was in error
in not noticing your remittance on 23rd. Ulto. of $1445 — it

1. Jackson-Lee Papers, "Letter Book. Clos'd on 19th. November 1806."

was occasioned by a wrong entry of our Clerks — The Voyage I think of — but have not yet fix'd upon will be from Europe say Leghorn to Calcutta to Sail in April next — Dollars have usually been bot, there at par probably if a large Amount should be Shipp'd they might Cost 1 per Cent advance — in case I conclude upon the Voyage & you Ship — I will agree to furnish you the Dollars. Charging nothing but what is Actually paid for them I will on my arrival in Calcutta deduct out 11 per Cent for freight & Commission the remainder invest in such piece Goods as you may direct Subject to your order at the port of Discharge in United States probably Boston — These terms are same we have had in Caravan, Pembroke &c being less by 2 per Cent I imagine than what you have paid in Ships from your port.

yours respectfully
Henry Lee

I mean by piece Goods. Gurrahs, Mamoodies, Sannahs &c. — Gunnys & Sail Cloth must not be Considered as included —

LETTER FROM HENRY LEE FOR JOSEPH LEE, JR., BOSTON, NOV. 8, 1805, TO EBENEZER STOCKER, NEWBURYPORT, IN REGARD TO INSURANCE FOR A VOYAGE TO FRANCE [1]

This letter does not indicate a departure from the previous practice of Joseph Lee, Jr., of trading only to the East Indies, since a large proportion of goods imported into the United States from Calcutta was later sent to markets in the West Indies and the Continent of Europe.

The brig *Perseverance*, 176 t., was on Oct. 22, 1805, owned by Joseph Lee, Jr., and Henry Lee, and commanded by Ralph I. Linzee.[2]

Ebenr. Stocker Esqr.   Boston Novr. 8th. 1805

  Sir

    I wish to know what you [received — stricken through] wd. take the following risque at — say $22000 — on Cargo

1. Jackson-Lee Papers, "Letter Book. Clos'd on 19th. November 1806."
2. Registers, Boston Custom House, 1805, no. 306.

Brig^t Perseverance Linzee from Boston for nantes — Cargo Sugar accompany'd with all the necessary documents including the English Consul's Certificate — there are [but — stricken through interlineated: only] 2 Shippers of whole on board & none of the Cargo imported by them except 20 Boxes Gums from Calcutta —

The [instruction — stricken through interlineated: intention] of the Shippers is that the Cargo be sold at Nantes & there is scarcely a probability of going to any other port with her Cargo, but I wish the liberty of going to one more port in france & to Holland if necessary — what insurance has been made in Town say 20,000 has been done at Mr Jones's office on the following terms — 4 p^{r}C^t. if Nantes only with addition of 1 % [interlineated: if to a second port in france & 2 p/c] if she goes to Holland Mr Welles office offer to take the Nantes Risque at 4 % but object to the additional prem. — if she goes to Holland as not being sufficient, I think it is as the Chance of proceeding to another port than Nantes is not more than 1 to 50 — will you have the goodness to let me know as soon as you can whether your office will take on above terms? —

yours &c

(Sign'd)   Henry Lee for
Joseph Lee Junr.

The P. is almost new this being her 2nd. V^o. is fine Vessel well found & Commanded — & has an intelligent Supercargo on board — let the policy be in name of Joseph & Henry Lee
Joseph Lee Jr p^r H Lee

LETTER FROM HENRY LEE FOR SELF AND JOSEPH LEE, JR., BOSTON, DEC. 5, 1805, TO JOHN BROMFIELD, NANTES, WITH INSTRUCTIONS FOR A VOYAGE TO FRANCE [1]

This letter seems to have been to the supercargo of the *Perseverance*, which had gone to Nantes with a cargo of India goods, probably

1. Jackson-Lee Papers, "Letter Book. Clos'd on 19th. November 1806."

from the *Caravan*, which, commanded by G. Lee, had left Calcutta for Boston on Dec. 22, 1804.[2]

John Bromfield, the son and namesake of Jonathan Jackson's first partner, was born in Newburyport, Apr. 11, 1779, and attended Dummer Academy; "at the age of fourteen he entered the counting-house of Messrs. Larkin & Hurd, of Charlestown, and afterward, during the period of his apprenticeship, that of Messrs. Soley & Stearns." The latter house failed just as he became of age and after several months, despairing of obtaining mercantile employment, he decided to become a carpenter. Happily, however, he shortly after this resolution obtained an engagement in the vocation originally chosen.[3] In a letter of Nov. 8 he was warned: "We hope you will not fall into an error very Common, I mean keeping a Cargo on hand when good prices can be obtained for chance of obtaining more, — when prices are beyond the usual ones the probability of a fall is greater than of rise." A century and a quarter later men could still, if they would, have profited by that advice. On Nov. 13 he was first advised that "if you can purchase 150 Dozen Champaigne wine at not more than 4 livres a bottle it will yield a freight" and then in a postscript was instructed to "send only 50 dozen." On Nov. 21 came the final injunction: "Wines & Brandy Continue very low & in no demand . . . — you will not send any Champaigne neither." A conscientious supercargo, such as John Bromfield, must frequently have despaired of being able to follow his employers' orders.

Robert Cabot, who was to go to Cherbourg as supercargo of the ship *Washington*, 192 t. (which on Dec. 4, 1805, was registered as belonging to Henry Lee, Joseph Lee, Jr., George Lee, and Robert Cabot; master, George Lee),[4] was the son of Andrew (1750–91) and Lydia (Dodge) Cabot and was born in Beverly, Aug. 24, 1784. He was thus a cousin to Joseph Lee, Jr., and his brothers.[5] The *Washington's* destination had been twice altered. On Nov. 13 she had been intended for Marseilles, on the 21st for the north of Europe.

2. *Ibid.*, "Vessels cleared and merchandize shipped from Calcutta, 1800–1812."

3. Hunt, *op. cit.*, vol. ii, pp. 470–472.

4. Registers, Boston Custom House, 1805, nos. 367, 369.

5. Briggs, *op. cit.*, pp. 169–170.

Boston
Decr. 5th 1805

Mr John Bromfield
Nantes
Sir

We last wrote you by the Sally for Nantes informing you that we had Changed the destination of the Washington from the Med^n. to North — we have now Concluded upon her going to Cherbourg or Nantes M^r. Robt. Cabot who is interested in the Ship &Cargo goes out Super-cargo — had we Contemplated a Voyage to Nantes we should not have put M^r. C. on board but consign'd her to you, from the engagement with him & the concern he has in the Ship we could not discharge him — we intend sending back the Brig^e. if the prospect should be good in which case if you remain behind, she will come to you — M^r. C. has on board some Bengal Sugars which the french Consul has refused to grant Certificates for — in Consequence of new instructions. — they are accompanyed with affidavits shewing that they were bot. of the Natives of Bengal & that no European has had any concern in the Sale or Shipment of them — we presume they can be admitted — we would thank you to ascertain whither that is the Case — & if they should not be admitted inform him, — [interlineated: by letters lodg'd at Paimboeuf —] if there is any thing to apprehend from having them on board & entering such part of his Cargo as is permitted, & generally any other information — you think will be usefull to him. —

Your friends & Ob^t. Serv^{ts}.
(Sign'd) Henry Lee for Self &
Joseph Lee Junr

The W. will probably go to Cherbourg — you will please to send a Copy of the letters you lodge at Paimboeuf —

Copy of above p^{r}Washington with following P S. Decr. 6 1805. The above is a copy of ours of yesterday via Nantes — the W. having on board India Sugar which possibly may not be admitted — we have given instructions to go to C. in preference to Nantes, as it will be more convenient to proceed for Hol-

land, Hamburg or Embden as may be necessary — notwithstanding if they find [the — stricken through interlineated:
from the] wind much more convenient to go to Nantes they
will — say Belleile — HLee —

LETTER FROM HENRY LEE, BOSTON, JAN. 15, 1806, TO JOHN STILLE & CO., PHILADELPHIA, SEEKING FREIGHT FOR A VESSEL TO CALCUTTA [1]

About a week before, Joseph Lee, Jr., had suggested that the Philadelphia firm might like to ship $100,000 in specie on the *Dromo,* in
which case he would be willing that the vessel should return to Philadelphia; or, if John Stille & Co. would ship $150,000 in specie, a
supercargo might be sent out from Philadelphia. It later developed
that it was "a Mr. Waln" whose offer of freight had been rejected;
this was probably J. S. Waln, who has recently gained literary im-
mortality in *The House of Exile* (Boston, 1933), by his descendant
Nora Waln. In a letter to Peter Remsen, the *Dromo's* owners boasted
that they felt "so much at home in the Trade" that they should "not
hesitate to warrant that the Cargo would be purchased in better terms
than any other at the same time." [2] The ship *Dromo,* built at Ames-
bury and registered Jan. 9, 1806, was owned by Andrew Cabot,
Joseph Lee, Jr., and Henry Lee. She was of 492 65/95 tons burthen
and was thus considerably larger than most American vessels of that
time.[3] She sailed for Calcutta early in Mar., 1806.[4]

Mess. John Stille &Cº   Boston Janʸ. 15ᵗʰ. 1806
   Merchants
      Philª.
         Gentlemen
         My Brother Mʳ. Jos. Lee Junʳ. wrote you on 9ᵗʰ.
Inst. respecting freight on board a Ship bound to Calcutta —
We have since learnt that some persons whose names we have
not been able to ascertain have offered the Owners of the Ship
Alexander Hamilton freight to a large Amount which those

1. Jackson-Lee Papers, "Letter Book. Clos'd on 19ᵗʰ. November 1806."
2. *Ibid.,* Henry Lee, Boston, Jan. 22, 1806, to Peter Remsen, N. Y.
3. Briggs, *op. cit.,* vol. ii, p. 794.
4. *Independent Chronicle,* Mar. 10, 1806.

Gentlemen have refus'd — will you be so obliging as to enquire who [those — stricken through] those persons are & let us know what they w^d. give to take out 100 or 150,000 Dollars to be brot back in piece goods, —

yours
Respectfully
(Sign'd)   Henry Lee for
Owners Ship Dromo

LETTER FROM HENRY LEE, BOSTON, MAR. 25, 1806, TO PETER REMSEN, NEW YORK, ON BUSINESS CONDITIONS [1]

In regard to the shipments to Rotterdam, John Bromfield, the supercargo, had something to say. On Mar. 16, 1806, he wrote to his mother: "I have been pursued by the most untoward and sinister events. Forty days on my passage to Nantes, — fifty-three days embargoed, — I could not arrive in Holland until the first of March. Fortune has pursued me, undeviatingly, with ill luck; I can not charge her with inconstancy. Existence is not worth possessing unaccompanied by independence of mind." Two of John Bromfield's salient characteristics were an almost morbid conscientiousness and a meticulous caution, the latter, he was accustomed jestingly to remark, being one of the reasons why he never married.[2] On Apr. 25, 1806, however, he succeeded in selling at Rotterdam, through Thomas & Adrian Cremer, his cargo of brown sugar, gum lac, sal ammoniac, and gum arabic for 40,766 florins and 8 stivers net,[3] a florin equalling 1s. 8¾d., and 20 stivers making a florin.

P. Remsen   Boston March 25th. 1806
    Dear Sir
    Since mine of the 19th. I have nothing from you — We want 30,000 Dollars — in Course of two Months 20,000 — & 10,000 immediately — if you can buy them at 1 % we wish you would do it & draw on us at Sight. or we will remit you post notes — I am anxious to hear what effect the last newes

1. Jackson-Lee Papers, "Letter Book. Clos'd on 19th. November 1806."
2. Hunt, op. cit., vol. ii, p. 472.
3. Jackson-Lee Papers, "Foreign Sales on acct. of J. & H. Lee From 1803 to 1810."

from Europe has had on business in your City — the Shipments of Sugar are ending sadly in Holland — the last prices hardly give the Cost &Charges — in Consequence — there is no Sale for this article — to day some Havannah Brown Sugars were offer'd & bid in by the owners, no offer having been made Exchange on London is now *at par* & in demand it is expected to be 1 @ 2 % above in Course of Six weeks — We expect a Ship of about 200 Tons in few weeks from Europe new &Coppered — do you think any kind of Contract can be made with Lennox & Maitland Wm. Neils &Co. or L. B. and McEvens. for Wine Voyage — I understood the Owners of the Hampton made the following terms — vizt. — to deliver a Cargo of assorted articles in Teneriffee at 33 1/3 % advance to receive a Cargo wine at 4 £ pr.pipe or Ton for freight to Calcutta 5 % on Sales — & a freight on the goods home of — perhaps something of some sort might be done again —

yours H, Lee

If you have any Cocoa on hand Sell — a letter in Town says — Barcelona 40 Days since — Carraccas Cocoa is worth 15 Cents pound on board — this is in consequence partly of the whole duty which is exorbitant being exacted Contrary to expectations of Merchants. —

H, Lee

LETTER FROM HENRY LEE FOR SELF AND JOSEPH LEE, JR., BOSTON, APR. 1, 1806, TO JOHN STILLE & CO., PHILADELPHIA, IN REGARD TO INSURANCE ON THE DROMO [1]

The supercargo, Andrew Cabot, so eulogistically described below, was the brother of Robert Cabot, the supercargo of the *Washington*;[2] he was born at Beverly, Nov. 23, 1780. He was accompanied on this voyage by his brother Sebastian, baptized Apr. 2, 1782.[3]

That portion of the *Dromo's* outward cargo belonging to her owners consisted of brandy, mahogany, glassware, coal, salmon, claret wine, deal boards, olive oil, bottles, rum, corks, and hats, which were sold at

1. Jackson-Lee Papers, "Letter Book. Clos'd on 19th. November 1806."
2. *Ibid.*, Henry Lee, Boston, Feb. 19, 1806, to Robert Cabot.
3. Briggs, *op. cit.*, vol. i, pp. 169–170.

Calcutta, Nov. 18, 1806, for sicca rupees 21,918, 7 annas, 3 pice, net.[4]
Twelve pice make one anna; 16 annas equal 1 rupee; the sicca rupee
was worth roughly 2 shillings or 50 cents.

Mess John Stille &Co   Boston April 1st. 1806
    Gentlemen
        yours of 24th. Ulto. are both recd. the latter Covering a
Draft for Eleven hundred forty two Dollars 86 Cents — We
wish you to have Insured Ten Thousand Dollars for Owners
Ship Dromo — Say Jos. Leejr for Self & Owners — on Specie
out & Merchandize home & two Thousand Dollars Specie out
& goods home for Joseph Breck — provided it can be done at
8 % — The Dromo is little more than year old Composition
fastened &Coppered — built of best materials & best manner
— in fact as good a Ship as can be built in this State — has
been one voyage to Europe only is Commanded by an experienced man — the Super-Cargo is an excellent navigator having
been Six times in & out Bay Bengal & once to China takes
Lunar observations & [interlineated: has] a Chronometer —
the Master is directed not to Stop unless under an absolute
necessity added to which the season both for going in & Coming
out Bay Bengal is favourable your offices may ask why under
these favourable Circumstances the offices in Town have not
taken the risk? — the reason is that the amot on Dromo is
larger than all our best offices together can take — we should
wish to be inform'd of the determination of the offices
                                    Respectfully
                                        your Obt. Servt.
                                    Henry Lee for Self
                                    and Jos. LeeJr

P. S. *Ship Dromo* Joseph Breck Master at & from Boston to
Calcutta at from thence to port discharge in United States of
America with liberty to Stop at the usual places for refreshment
— on Specie out & goods home till landed — Saild from Boston
10th. March — what can Dollars be obtain'd at with you?

4. Jackson-Lee Papers, "Foreign Sales on acct. of J. & H. Lee From
1803 to 1810."

— I would thank you to mention the Charge of effecting Insurance. — your ob[t] Serv[t].

Henry Lee

LETTER FROM HENRY LEE, BOSTON, APR. 5, 1806, FOR OWNERS OF CARAVAN, TO PETER REMSEN, NEW YORK, ON MANAGEMENT OF CARGO [1]

Although this letter is endorsed "not sent," it nevertheless probably gives an accurate idea of the shipowner's intentions at this time. Landing the *Caravan's* cargo at New York instead of at her home port of Boston was the idea of the captain, James Gilchrist, and was based on the inordinate quantities of goods being cleared from Calcutta for Boston and Philadelphia. The brig *Caravan* had left Calcutta Dec. 3, 1805, with a cargo of standard India goods — cottons, sugar, ginger, and gunny bags — [2] invoiced at 120,000 sicca rupees, two-eighths each on the account of Joseph Lee, Jr., and Timothy and John Williams, one-eighth each on that of Henry Lee and the captain.[3]

Mr. Peter Remsen   Boston April 5th. 1806
    Sir

By letter rec[d]. this day the Brig[e]. Caravan James Gilchrist was to leave Calcutta about the 5th. Dec[r]. — if not now with you she probably will be in Course of five days — when arrived you will please take the Consignment of her & sell the Cargo immediately for the Current prices being careful to receive in payment good notes — The Sugar & Ginger perhaps may be Sold on landing what goods are Stored have put in Safe Brick Buildings — The piece Goods we imagine will be of Coarse Kind such as are now *very* much wanted, are bot low & we think will Command great prices — the last Sales here 25th. february averaged 92 to 95 Cents p[r]Rupee — the Value of Calcutta piece Goods vary in advance from 80 to 110 Cents Rupee — you will not therefore be govern'd in Sales by the Rupee but

1. Jackson-Lee Papers, "Letter Book. Clos'd on 19th. November 1806."
2. *Ibid.*, "Vessels cleared and merchandize shipped from Calcutta, 1800–1812."
3. *Ibid.*, "Invoices," 1799–1812.

The Brig Caravan Leaving Salem

sell by the piece — for your government I have noted [another — stricken through interlineated: on the other] Side the last Sales of such goods as will Compose we presume — the Caravans Cargo — a Considerable number of Cargoes are destined for this place & Phil^a. — & some for your place we are therefore decidedly of opinion that prompt Sales will be best — As we shall want to send the Brig^t. away soon would it be agreeable to advance 20 or 30,000 Dlls

how soon could 60,000 be procured & at what premium — can a freight be obtain'd at Teneriffee & from thence to Madrass or Calcutta — After the observations made above with regard to selling p^r.Rupee you will not suffer the goods to be selected without ascertaining their full Comparative Value & you will Conceal the Cost from purchasers unless to ascertain Drawback in Certain Cases — Relying on your industry & exertions in making the most of the Cargo — We are

your Ob^t. Serv^{ts}.
Henry Lee for Owners
Brig^t. Caravan 3rd. V^o.

Sales of Calcutta Goods at Auction 25th. Feb^y. —

Boston Brig^t. Orient's Cargo —

	Cost p.C^o.	Sold at
Beerboom Gurrahs 35 to 36 by 2¼	69	— 355 @ 358
Mow Sannahs — 22 by 1⅜	36	— 1.75 to 1.80
Bandannoes Chocolate		4.25 —
D^o — Yellow		4.75 —
Chintz	10 by 1⅞ — 20 —	1.10 —
D^o	10 " 2 — 25 —	1.30 —
Mow Mamoody	20 " 2 — 40 —	2.— —

Those prices are high & we should not be disappointed if the Caravans should not bring so much — if not should arrive before her Cargo is sold I think you will obtain them besides the abov articles there will probably be Patnah Baftas — Patna Gurrahs Foolpore Mamoody & perhaps some low priced Jalalpore & Jannah Mamoody all which are worth about 90 Cents p^r. Rupee — Baftas — say Luckipores fine Chittabully, — Collapatty, & Putka, are not saleable — nor are Jal^a.poor Sannahs

— nor indeed any kind of fine goods — unless Long Cloths — (Rupee is Called 50 Cents, & a Corge 20 p^s) the Moses's will probably apply to you — they are good men I Suppose but will want to select the best goods at an average price of a Cargo. — H Lee   (not sent)

LETTER FROM HENRY LEE, BOSTON, APR. 12, 1806, TO JOSEPH LEE, JR., NEW YORK, WITH ACCOUNT OF VESSELS FROM THE ORIENT [1]

This account of vessels from India and China gives a hint of the scope at this time of American trade with the Orient. Joseph Lee, Jr., had gone to New York to assist in disposing of the *Caravan's* cargo. Of course, as Federalists, the Lees would rejoice at the re-election of Caleb Strong as governor of Massachusetts.

Boston April 12th. 1806

Dear Jos.

Since mine of yesterday — we have heard of the arrival at the Vine-Yard of Ship Mary Ann of Salem from Calcutta. — the Ship Adventure from Calcutta was spoken with on 8th. Inst. & if not now arrived will be here in 24 hours probably. — they both are owned by M^r. John Norris — have but small quaintity of piece goods — M^r. Francis has made Considerable progress in Sales of the Susan's Cargo at good prices. — The Asia is not yet in — China ships Continue to arrive — one in at Philadelphia — another spoken with on Coast — I should have mention'd yesterday that the 40,000 p^s. Nankeens were offered at 70 Cents Short price which is 5 Cents more than the last Auction Sales, should a parcel be offered at 72 Cents long price I should think it an object to purchase at long Credit on speculation. — From conversation with Grocers I think the Sugars p^r. the Susan of very good quality will sell at about $12 — I should like to know at what time you will draw for payment of Dollars you purchase that I may be prepared — Several persons besides those who wanted before you left us — are collecting — I know not from whence they are to come. —

1. Jackson-Lee Papers, "Letter Book. Clos'd on 19th. November 1806."

The Election stands well this morning by returns there were about Two hundred, more in favour of Strong than last year. —
Yours.

Mr. Jos. Lee Junr   Henry Lee
New York

I enclose a letter to Cap. Gilchrist
Exchange on London 1 % above par Cash
H Lee

LETTER FROM HENRY LEE FOR SELF AND JOSEPH LEE, JR., BOSTON, APR. 25, 1806, TO SAMUEL WILLIAMS, LONDON, IN REGARD TO TRADE WITH EUROPE [1]

This letter gives some idea of the scope of the Lees' trade with Europe at this time. "We have two vessels in Europe," Henry Lee had written to Peter Remsen, Mar. 25, 1806. These were the *Perseverance* and *Washington*, which had gone to Europe in the previous year. Shipments had also been made by two other vessels, not owned by them.

Francis Lee, another brother of Joseph, Jr., Thomas, Jr., (so-called in the family, although named for his uncle Thomas), George, Nathaniel Cabot, and Henry, was born June 24, 1784.[2] Jeremiah Lee of Marblehead was not related to the Lees of our special interest.

Boston. April. 25. 1806 —

Saml. Williams Esqr.

London —

Sir,

We have this day drawn on you in favour of Mess Stephen & Henry Higginson at Sixty days two Bills Seven & Eight hundred pounds each, Sterling money, — which you will please to Accept &pay for our Joint Account — Mr. Jeremiah Lee at Leghorn writes us Jany. that he had remitted you £ 1500. .. — .. Sterling & in few days should remit further 800 to 1000 £ — you will we think have recd. a Considerable portion of Proceeds of 22,000 ps. Nankeens in hands of Cremer —

1. Jackson-Lee Papers, "Letter Book. Clos'd on 19th. November 1806."
2. Briggs, *op. cit.*, vol. i, p. 155.

something from Washington &Perseverance's Cargo's — & perhaps a remittance on account of Shipment p^r. Elizabeth & Francis which sail'd in Feby. for Holland from these various sources we feel Confident you will be in funds for the amount we have drawn [on — stricken through   interlineated: upon] you — Our Brother M^r. Francis Lee Sails in few days in Brig^e. Eliza with Cargo Sugar &pepper for Cherbourg & Rotterdam — we shall feel obliged to you if you will address him a letter to each of those places — Containing any information you think may be useful to him —

We are Respectfully
your Ob^t. Serv^{ts}.
Henry Lee for Self &
Joseph Lee jr

Boston. April 28. 1806 — Wrote Jos Lee J^r. New York — Write ACabot — via New York — 28th April —

LETTER FROM HENRY LEE, BOSTON, SEPT. 9, 1806, TO PETER REMSEN, NEW YORK, WITH NEWS IN REGARD TO PROSPECTS FOR SALES [1]

William Oliver, who had been long closely associated with the Lees, had sailed for the Mediterranean, July 18, with a cargo in which the Lees had a concern of $15,000.[2] John Cabot, whose voyage looked so unpromising, was born in Beverly, July 31, 1782, the son of John and Hannah (Dodge) Cabot. He is said to have "had small aptitude for commercial life." [3] Robert Cabot, about the beginning of the year, had gone to Europe in the *Washington*, which on Mar. 13, 1806, had been stranded on the coast of Holland and converted into a brig at Rotterdam, and in which he had only recently returned; on Dec. 16 he became the owner.[4] Samuel Cabot, his cousin, had returned on the same vessel.[5]

1. Jackson-Lee Papers, "Letter Book. Clos'd on 19th. November 1806."
2. *Ibid.*, Henry Lee, Boston, Aug. 2, 1806, to Samuel Williams, London.
3. Briggs, *op. cit.*, vol. i, pp. 118, 268.
4. Registers, Boston Custom House, 1806, no. 306.
5. Briggs, *op. cit.*, vol. i, pp. 118, 268, 281–283.

Mr. Peter Remsen   Boston Septr. 9th. 1806 —
  Dear Sir

  I have recd. your favour's of 2nd & 3rd. Inst. with an Invoice [Invoice — stricken through] of Ashes — we thank you for the accommodation offered us in payment of them — from the low price Mr. Oliver's Cargo was purchas'd at, (Nankeens &Sugar) & the last amounts recd. from the Mediteranean we have reason to expect even if peace takes place he will make a saving voy. — John Cabots Voy. does not look so favourable — the Olive Branch's Cargo was offered at Auction — about 40,000 lbs. Java Coffee was sold at 27½ to 28 Cents 40 to 60,000 lbs. pepper at 17½ cents (principally to retailers) the owners refus'd to sell the remainder of the Cargo at these prices — I presume if they had been disposed they could not have obtained them for the whole Cargo — Sugars cannot be sold at any price — I hope you have been fortunate enough to have sold the Elisabeths Cargo even at 18 Cents — we recd. a Sale yesterday from Holland shipp'd at 17 Cents which gives only about 1 Cent pr. pound profit.

yours
H. Lee

Messrs. Robert &Saml. Cabot have arrived from Europe with a very good vessel of about 200 Tons will the agents for the wine houses offer them a good freight to take a Cargo Merchandize from this Country to Teneriffe or Madeira — a Cargo wine from thence to Madrass or Calcutta — or Ceylon or any other port in India?

H — Lee

LETTER FROM HENRY LEE, BOSTON, OCT. 14, 1806, TO JOHN STILLE & CO., PHILADELPHIA, WITH TERMS FOR FREIGHT TO CALCUTTA [1]

  On Oct. 6, 1806, Henry Lee had written John Stille & Co., trying to get freight for the "Ship now Building," the brig *Gulliver*.[2] The

---

1. Jackson-Lee Papers, "Letter Book. Clos'd on 19th. November 1806."
2. Registers, Boston Custom House, 1806, no. 313.

Lees' first Indiaman, the *Caravan*, had been sold in June to the "Messᶜˢ. Williams," [3] who had been associated with them in the *Traveller*. Their other Indiaman, the *Dromo*, was at Calcutta and would sail on Nov. 13.[4] In the earlier letter Henry Lee was particularly interested in the possibility of "a Contract for a Cargo of Merchandize from hence & from T[eneriffe] or M[adeira] a Cargo of Wine to Madras or Calcutta."

"Our none intercourse law," to which the writer refers, was the Non-Importation Act, approved Apr. 18, 1806, which provided that after Nov. 15 it should be unlawful to import into the United States certain enumerated goods of British manufacture. The law was thus not in effect at the time of this letter, and indeed its operation was finally suspended till Dec., 1807.[5]

Note the mention of failures. William Coleman Lee was a cousin of Henry, the brother of Capt. George Gardner Lee.[6] Francis Amory, who was born on Dec. 28, 1766, the son of John and Catherine (Greene) Amory, and who married Sarah Kirkland, July 4, 1804, was the brother of the merchants John and Thomas Amory.[7]

Messᶜˢ. John Stille &Cᵒ.   Boston Octʳ. 14ᵗʰ. 1806
    Gentlemen

I have recᵈ. your favour of 11ᵗʰ. & thank you for the trouble you have taken in endeavouring to procure us a freight — we hope that before our Ship sails say last of November you will be able to aid us, or perhaps you may yourselves be inclin'd to make an adventure, our terms are 11 % including Commissions to Super-Cargo to be invested in Silk &Cotton Goods or Indigo & we will undertake that they shall be purchas'd on as Good terms as any goods bought at same time — on their return as is usual — they will be sold at public Sale attended

3. Jackson-Lee Papers, "Letter Book. Clos'd on 19ᵗʰ. November 1806," Henry Lee, Boston, after June 4, 1806, to Peter Remsen, N. Y.

4. *Ibid.*, "Vessels cleared and merchandize shipped from Calcutta, 1800–1812."

5. Channing, *op. cit.*, vol. iv, p. 358.

6. Lee, William, *op. cit.*, p. 49. One of his account books, "Journal 1796 Wᵐ. Cⁿ. Lee. N. 1," Mar., 1796–Feb., 1800, is in the Jackson-Lee Papers.

7. Amory, *op. cit.*, p. 22.

with no other charge than Wharfage & Auctioneers Commission of ¼ % or ½ % or if 100,000 Dollars can be obtain'd we would take it at 10% with a Super-Cargo & order the Ship to Philadelphia These we presume are better terms than what your Ships take out money. — For the information you sent M^r.Cabot which cannot fail of being useful if he avails himself of it we are also extremely obliged [to you — stricken through] — It is not improbable that before December our none intercourse law will be repeal'd, in which case the shippers will the [interlineated: have] advantage of being the first to avail themselves of it. —

Yours with esteem &respect
Henry Lee. —

We have within a few days two failures to Considerable Amo^t. — I believe neither of them are correspondents of yours — vizt. — Francis Amory & W^m. C. Lee —   H.Lee
I w^d. be obliged to you to quote me the price of Dollars from time [interlineated: to time] as we may possibly find it necessary to send on to your place — H. Lee —

LETTER FROM HENRY LEE, BOSTON, ABOUT OCT. 16, 1806, TO PETER REMSEN, NEW YORK, ON BUSINESS CONDITIONS [1]

The Lees were naturally anxious to obtain, for themselves and the adventurers in their vessels, the specie which was the most valuable constituent of the outward cargo, without paying too large a premium. Consequently they usually wrote to their correspondents in a number of cities to obtain dollars in comparatively small quantities. On Nov. 7 the Lees sent Remsen "thirty Thousand Dollars in Baltimore Bills" to be used in purchasing specie "in small parcells . . . without alarming the holders of Dollars — Would it not be best to omit advertising?" On Nov. 12 Henry Lee wrote Remsen in these frank terms: "We are giving you a great deal of trouble in a business *which cannot afford a Commission* yet it is not without its advantages — as it makes you known to some of our most respectable and wealthy merchants & will procure you the Consign-

1. Jackson-Lee Papers, "Letter Book. Clos'd on 19th. November 1806."

ment of the returns, if by chance (*which is not great*) they should be discharged at your port — at any rate we shall probably make a shipment on the return of the vessel." The italics are mine.

The writer was of course wrong on this occasion in anticipating peace. Henry Lee's "friend Devereux" was probably Capt. James Devereux, in the service of J. & T. H. Perkins.[2]

Dear Sir

I was glad to learn by yours of 13th. recd this day that you have escaped from a loss in the misfortunes of our friend. — We shall certainly avail ourselves of your information in any business we may have at your place. — Mr. Walley will write you by mail to invest some funds of his in your hands in Dollars, he is a shipper in our vessel for Calcutta, I hope you will not therefore charge him much, if any thing, for collecting, he was recommended to you by Mr. Dudly Pickman I presume. — Th'o he may not a present have much business you may yet I am glad he is in your correspondence — as he is one our most wealthy &respectable merchants, — I wish you could find some house who would put the 100,000$ you mention on board our vessel we can take it on much lower terms than any Vessel has ever done from your port — your shippers of West India Goods are mad — we think peace will be made in this quarter — which will certainly ruin many of your no *Capital — dashing Merchts*.

I should myself not readly trust any one who would give 11 $ for brown Havanna & 30 Cents for Coffee — such a purchaser in this Town would ruin the Credit of the most wealthy man in it — I congratulate my friend Devereux on his expeditious &favourable Sales & hope he will not fail to charge his Concern'd especially freighters, with a round Commission. —

Yours

Henry Lee

Collect for me as it comes in your way all the information you can for our voyage,   *H .Lee*

2. Briggs, *op. cit.*, vol. ii, pp. 511, 531.

P, S, *I would not Credit* the person you mention with **One or Two Thousand Dollars** without an endorser

H. Lee

I would have you insert an advertisement to the following effect. —

— For Calcutta —

"A fast sailing [interlineated: Coppered] Vessel, any person desireous of shipping Specie will please apply to Peter Remsen " — on application you can say that she will sail in all November — goods will be return'd to this place where they shall be sold free of any charge except Commission ¼ % [interlineated: to] the Auctioneers — that if 100,000 — is offered they [interlineated: returns] will be deliver'd at N. York & Super-Cargo [interlineated: of their own] may be sent — *H. Lee* —

LETTER FROM JOSEPH LEE, JR., BOSTON, OCT. 22, 1806, TO RUFUS KING, JAMAICA, LONG ISLAND, SUGGESTING AN ADVENTURE TO CALCUTTA [1]

The vessel on which Lee suggested a shipment was the brig *Gulliver*, then building. It is curious that he mentions only the prospective profit but not the terms of shipment. Perhaps those had been mentioned "in May last" when Lee obtained permission to make the proposition below. They were probably 11% on the shipment, payable in Calcutta, for freight, the other usual alternative being one-third profits, payable in Boston. Joseph Lee could not have been accused of grandiose and overpersuasive exposition of the profits to be expected; he rather preferred to err by understatement. We have no record that Rufus King took advantage of this opportunity.

Rufus King at the time of this letter was, between two unsuccessful candidacies for the vice-presidency on the Federalist ticket, engaged in farming on Long Island. The Lees, staunch Federalists so long as that party endured, may, in making King this offer, have had the secondary motive of assisting one of the Federalist standard bearers to make a good profit.

1. New York Historical Society, Rufus King Papers, box 11.

Boston, Oct. 22. 1806

Honble Rufus King
   Dear Sir
   Supposing it possible from conversation with you while at
New York, that you may have funds unapropriated, I take the
liberty of informing you that I have a Vessel that will sail for
Calcutta early in December, in which you may ship, from five
to twenty thousand dollars, with a *moral certainty* of gaining
Six per Cent p Ann with a *reasonable expectation* of ten p Cent
p Ann & *a chance* for twelve p Cent p Ann with very little
hazard — if Calcutta goods are as high next year as this an
adventure will give a profit of 15 to 20 p Cent p Ann after
paying all charges including insurance — Shoud you have funds
that you are willing to adventure & you will cause the money
to be placed in the hands of Mr Peter Remsen for my Acot I
will take care & make every other arrangement without troubling
you & have as much Insurance done as you shall direct — I
cannot allow myself this liberty without reminding you that in
May last I had your permission — I pray [interlineated: you]
will do me the honor to make my respects acceptable to Mrs
King & accept my best wishes — respectfully
                              your very humb servt
                                   Jos Lee jr

      [Addressed]
      Honbl Rufus King
      Jamaica
      Long Island
      Care of Mr Peter Remsen
      [Endorsed]
      Mr Jos Lee
      Boston 22 Oct 1806

LETTER FROM JOSEPH LEE, JR., BOSTON, OCT. 27, 1806, TO AN-
DREW SMITH, CALCUTTA, WITH ACCOUNT OF SALES AND PRICES [1]

Andrew Smith, evidently an American merchant resident in Calcutta, was perhaps identical with the New York merchant of that
name to whom Joseph Lee had written Jan. 19, 1802, in regard to
abortive plans for a correspondence. He had shipped some India
goods to Boston by the *Rising Sun,* Capt. George Lee, to be sold
by Joseph Lee, Jr. The latter lays most of the blame for the low
prices at which they sold to the poor selection of the goods; in other
letters he also mentions the perennial prospects for peace as a de-
pressing influence.

The new vessel belonging to the Lees which was "to sail in about
a month" for India with Robert Cabot as supercargo was the *Gulliver,* a brig of 245 tons burthen, commanded by George Lee, for
which Henry Lee was trying to make insurance, Dec. 22, 1806.

This letter, though about three weeks out of its chronological
order, is by position the last in the letter book of Joseph Lee, Jr.,
and of Joseph Lee, Jr., and Henry Lee, 1793-94, 1797-1806. Although this letter book covers a period of more than ten years, as
many pages are required for the entries of 1805 and 1806 as for
all the other years preceding, which indicates something of the
comparative scope and intensity of the Lees' interest in commerce
during this general period.

Andrew Smith Esqe.   Boston Octe. 27th. *1806*
   Calcutta
     Sir

        your favors of 30th. Jany. 28th. Feby, 25th. March &
24th. May, have been recd. the two former have already been
reply'd to — I have now to inform you that the sales of your
piece Goods except a Muster Bale is Completed — at bottom
you have a note of the prices from which you can make estimation of the proceeds — the Account sales not yet having been
recd. from the Auctioneer cannot be sent till another opportunity — you could not have been more unfortunate in a choice
of Goods for this market than in your Invoice pr. Capt. Lee —

   1. Jackson-Lee Papers, "Letter Book. Clos'd on 19th. November 1806."

they were all of them of the most unsaleable Kind — The Baftas which on Comparrison with Capt. Lee's — were said to have been. considerably inferior in quality were Invoiced 5 Rps. pr.Corge higher, the checks were of much too good a quality & did not sell in proportion for as much as the coarse kind — Cossa's have for a long time been out of repute except the coarsest kind that are shipped from Bengal however such as they are, I have made the most of them — these observations are made that you may not be surprised at the low Sale of your goods while other Invoices by same vessel sold at near 90 Cents the Rupee — Capt. Lee's Cargo Consisting of Gurrahs Mow Sannas — Coarse mamoodies, Blue Gilla hdkfs, Coarse Checks Emerties &c, averaged $89\frac{1}{4}$ Cents prRupee — Drugs have been plenty from Mocha & Muscat of better quality & Cheaper than from Calcutta — not having been able to dispose of yours at any price, I have shipp'd them to Philadelphia I wd. not advise shipping any Gums or Drugs unless you can buy them of a very good quly. & as low as they Come Charged from Muscat — & even then our market is so small, that exportation must be resorted to for any considerable quantity — perhaps a small quanty. of Copal & good Senna when you have opportunities of sending at a low freight may Answer well — The coarse piece Goods the demand has been great during the season. — Rising Suns sold at 89 Cents — The Endeavours at 87 Cents — the Sally (Mr. Goodhues) sold at 81 Cents Ulysses at 85 Cents — since August there has been Imported in this State & at Providence 2500 Bales which being distributed among the retailers the demand has become supply'd, & a Cargo could not now be sold at more than 80 Cents — Sugars in consequence of State of things in Europe have been for several months past low — good Bengal wd. not now bring more 11 Dollars & if peace is made will fall below that price — Indigo Continues high, the last sales (Endeavours) which was not *good first quality* — was at \$2.15. — this price cannot be calculated upon — I should say the first quality wd now command from \$ 2, to 2.20 — with respect to goods suited to our market it is impossible to anticipate for 3 months what Kind will best answer

—I sh^d. generally say — Coarse goods, such as Beerboom Gurrahs, Catwah — Manickpore, Gurrahs — Patna Baftas —
Coarse Checks, Manickpore Mamoody, Foolpore D^o. Mow d^o.
—Boran & Jugdia Baftas, Coarse Gillas Mow Sannas, Blue
Cloths 36 by 2¼ not Costing more than 70 Rp^s — Chintz not
more than 20Rp^s. 10 by 2 & White Goods 40 by 2 under 75
Rp^s. p^rC^o. — at present all kinds of fine goods are out of repute, yet possibly 12 Months hence they may be wanted particularly if Cotton goods in England should from any cause be
higher — I shall remit the proceeds of your sales by a vessel of
my own to sail in about a month — Mr Cabot who goes out in
her will do himself the pleasure to call on you — & I hope will
be able to make some negotiation mutually advantageous, —
I pray you to offer M^rs. Smith my best regards, & believe me —
Sincerely —

your friend
(Sign'd) Jos, Lee j^r.

The remittance by my vessel will be insured — the premium
will be about 4½ % —

(Sign'd) Jos, Lee j^r.

LETTER FROM HENRY LEE FOR SELF AND JOSEPH LEE, JR., BOS-
TON, NOV. 1, 1806, TO SAMUEL WILLIAMS, LONDON, ON SHIP-
MENTS TO EUROPE [1]

This letter gives an account of shipments to Europe since the
Perseverance, which had gone to Europe the previous year and returned, sailed again for Cherbourg on June 18, 1806, with a cargo
of sugar and coffee. Capt. Linzee was master and Francis Lee may
have been supercargo.[2] The Lees "made a Shipment of $12,000 pr.
Helen to Nantes."[3] John B. Greene seems to have been the supercargo. On Sept. 10, hearing rumors of peace, of which, however,
they were skeptical, the Lees wrote him advising him that if peace

1. Jackson-Lee Papers, "Letter Book. Clos'd on 19th. November 1806."
2. *Ibid.*, Henry Lee for self and Joseph Lee, Jr., Boston, Aug. 3, 1806,
to Thomas & Adrian Cremer, Rotterdam.
3. *Ibid.*, Henry Lee for self and Joseph Lee, Jr., Boston, Aug. 2, 1806,
to Samuel Williams, London.

had taken place and "prices [were] so low as to leave Considerable loss" he should keep their adventure on hand but also that "you will do well therefore not to wait if a saving offer is made even tho. the war Continues." They had made a shipment to the value of $15,000 to the Mediterranean by William Oliver in July, so the shipment of $4,000 by the *Republican* to the same quarter of the world must have been an addition. John Cabot was the supercargo,[4] difficult though it may be to imagine a Cabot consenting to be associated with a vessel of such a name. The ashes shipped by the *Brutus* had been obtained in New York by Peter Remsen. The *Pedler* was doubtless the brig later famous on the North West Coast as an Astor vessel. The *Roxanna* was probably a Perkins vessel [5] and John Bromfield was supercargo.[6]

Samuel Williams Esqr.   Boston Novr. 1st. 1806 —
   London
     Sir

     your several favours down to Septr. 1st. have been duly recd. — since our draft in of Mess. Boott &Pratt the Acceptance of which is acknowledged in yours of 4th. August, we have drawn on you as follows. —

	August 2nd.	£1,000.	" — " 60 Days
	Septr. 16 —	1,500	" — " — Do.
	Octr. — 15th.	1,500	" — " —
1 Bill 416.1.10			
1 do. 370.16."	do. — 23rd.	1,086.17.10	
1 do. 300. " "			
	do. — 30th.	1,500. " — "	
	Novr. — 1	1000. " — "	
		£7,586.17.10. —	

from your letters & my Brother Francis's memorandum of advances made by Ridgway &Co. [& — stricken through] remitted before he left Antwerp — there must still be a balance

4. *Ibid.*, Henry Lee, Boston, July 14, 1806, to Peter Remsen, N. Y.; *ibid.*, "Letter Book Finished Decr. 1808," Henry Lee, Boston, Apr. 18, 1807, to Samuel Williams, London.

5. Briggs, *op. cit.*, vol. ii, p. 543.

6. Jackson-Lee Papers, "Foreign Sales on acct. of J. & H. Lee from 1803 to 1810. — "

due us which shall draw for immediately. — we presume before this (from /M^r. Greene's letters at Nants) you will have received something for Acco^t. of the Helen's Cargo — in July we made a Shipment to Med^n. in the Brig^e. Republican of $4000 Cost — in Septr. a Ship^t. of *Ashes* from New York in Ship Brutus for Nants Cost $4000 — Our adventure in Pedler, in Ashes Ivory & Sugar Cost $19,000, we made also a small adventure in the Roxanna, arrived sometime since at Amsterdam, the proceeds of these different shipments are directed to be remitted you except a small amount conditionally ordered in goods to this country — On examination of M^r. S Cabot J^{rs}. Accounts of 3 Thomas's Cargo — there appears a balance due you [interlineated: on] Henry Lees prop^{on}. of said concern — & also in M^r. S. Cabots concern purchas'd by us you will charge them to our joint Acco^t.

We enclose you mess^{rs}. S & H Higginsons order to transferr two remittances made you by M^r. Bromfield on their account £1260 .. & £1350, to our account — you will charge our account with one eight part of a Bill of exchange Drawn by Capt. James Gilchrist on you of the owners of Brig^t. Caravan — we remain —

with respect your Ob^t. S^{ts}.

(Sign'd)   Henry Lee for Self &
Joseph Lee J^r.

L**ETTER FROM** H**ENRY** L**EE FOR** S**ELF AND** J**OSEPH** L**EE,** J**R.,** B**OS-TON,** N**OV.** 13, 1806, **TO** G**OLUCK,** B**ANIAN,** C**ALCUTTA,** R**E-QUESTING** P**RICE** I**NFORMATION** [1]

A banian was a member of a Hindu caste of traders and merchants who frequently acted as bankers and brokers in foreign commerce. About the same time, Henry Lee also wrote letters of a similar tenor to various other Calcutta merchants — Ram Kissen Day & Ramchunder Mitre, and Ram Lochun Bonarjia. The Lees had apparently never before sent a vessel to Madras, their trade with India having been confined to Calcutta.

The ship *Susan* of Boston had sailed from Calcutta, Dec. 3, 1805,

1. Jackson-Lee Papers, "Letter Book. Clos'd on 19th. November 1806."

under the command of D. D. Pulsifer; Francis Lee was probably supercargo. The ship *Rising Sun*, Captain G. G. Lee, had sailed from Calcutta for Boston, Feb. 6, 1806.[2]

Goluck   Boston Novr. 13th. 1806 —
    American Banian
        Calcutta   pMinerva
            Sir
            The faithfulness with which you transacted the business of my Brother M^r. Francis Lee of Ship Susan & my relation Geo. G. Lee. of the rising Sun induce me to address you on this occasion &request that you would write M^r. [interlineated: Robert] Cabot Supercargo of a vessel of ours which will sail in few days for Madrass —
    the following information — Viz^t. price of Spanish Doll^s. Brandy, Rum, Claret wine, Madeira D^o. — Cheese, Salmon Hats Mahogany &Gin, also the price of Sugar, Indigo, &piece Goods, — M^r. C. will proceed from Madrass to Calcutta — & on his arrival if you will call on him — he probably will purchase your goods
    direct your letter to the care of your friend at Madrass who will find out M^r. C — as soon as he arrives — and a Copy of the same to Mess Lys, Satur & De Monte. —
                                                    your friends
                                    (Sign'd)   Henry Lee for self &
                                                    Jos. Lee Jr
[In margin: (two words illegible) to buy 2000 ps Brown Baftas — 2000 ps Mow sannas — 2000 ps Tookery —]

LETTER FROM HENRY LEE, BOSTON, NOV. 17, 1806, TO PETER REMSEN, NEW YORK, IN REGARD TO ARRIVAL OF DROMO AT CALCUTTA [1]

Since late in May all the letters from the firm of Joseph & Henry Lee had been signed either by Henry Lee or by a Donald Morrison.

2. *Ibid.*, "Vessels cleared and merchandize shipped from Calcutta, 1800–1812."

1. Jackson-Lee Papers, "Letter Book. Clos'd on 19th. November 1806."

Apparently the older brother was occupied with travelling, for the purpose of disposing of India goods to merchants in other ports and obtaining freights for the firm's vessels. It would of course be to the advantage of the Lees in seeking freight for the *Dromo* on another voyage to have the speed of her passage widely known among prospective shippers. The *Dromo* cleared from Boston, Mar. 11 and from Calcutta, Nov. 13, 1806.[2]

M[r]. Peter Remsen   Boston Nov[e]. 17th. 1806
   D[r].Sir

    Your Ans[r]. to my enquiries are very full & satisfactory — should you know of any thing that will be useful to us futher you will mention it in your letters from time to time — I presume ere this my Brother has arrived — if has not or has left Newyork for Phila. open the enclos'd letter to him which contains an order from M[r]. S. H. Walley on you to deliver what Dollars you have collected for him — M[r] Tim[o]. Williams will write by this mail to transferr to our account — due him from y[e] — to 15th. Dec[e]. — $6113.59 — this sum we must request you to be in advance for us in purchasing our Dollars when the sum already remitted has been dispos'd of — We shall not draw on you for Amount of your Draft in favour of Hurd as I mention'd in mine of 5th. Ins[t].

    We hope you have by this time Converted all our paper into specie as we shall want it as soon as it can be brought on — our Vessel will be ready very soon We had the pleasure on Saturday of learning the arrival of the Dromo at Calcutta in 107 days — a very short passage, We have no letters from M[r]. Cabot but presume he is well as the Cap[t]. who bro[t]. the information saw a letter at Madrass from him to his friends there — you will be kind enough to have the arrival mentioned in Langs Ship news — it is of some Consequence in establishing a reputation for the Ship to have so remarkable a passage known —

Yours
(Sign'd)   *H Lee*

   2. *Ibid.*, "Vessels cleared and merchandize shipped from Calcutta, 1800–1812."

LETTER FROM JOSEPH LEE, JR., AND HENRY LEE, BY DONALD
MORRISON, BOSTON, NOV. 20, 1806, TO JOHN B. GREENE,
NANTES, WITH EXPOSITION OF BUSINESS POLICY AND SCOPE
OF EXPORTS TO EUROPE [1]

The manuscript book in which this is the first letter follows without break the volume "Letter Book. Clos'd on 19th. November 1806;"
the character of the business revealed is consequently similar in both.

John B. Greene had gone as supercargo for the Lees in a vessel
to Nantes. From there on Dec. 9, 1806, he shipped Joseph Lee, Jr.,
and Henry Lee an invoice of 40,000 livres in gloves, handkerchiefs,
silk hosiery, umbrellas, taffetas, etc.[2] This letter reveals that, counting the cargo which Greene had accompanied, the Lees were at this
time engaged in no less than half a dozen shipments to the Continent.

Boston November 20th. 1806 —
Mr. John B, Greene (via New York)
  Dear Sir
    We have recd. your several favours to 26 September, —
the last informing of Sales of our adventure came to hand two
days since — in reply generally to your letters, we say with
pleasure that you managed the Sales of our shipment to our
satisfaction — It has been a maxim with us in foreign ports, to
sell when a saving price could be obtained, unless there was a
moral certainty of doing better by delay — it does not appear
to us in this instance that there would have been — & in doing
as you have done, you have acted on the spirit of our instructions & tho, upon calculation there is no profit, yet on the
whole under existing circumstances we are very glad to come
off so well, — We regret that you have determin'd on remaining in France, unless you have some other object in view than
what appears in your letters to us, — did we think the prospect encouraging or even prudent we should upon the strength
of information sent us make a shipment &Consign it to you —
but there is neither, Ashes, Cotton, or Indigo, unless at such

    1. Jackson-Lee Papers, "Letter Book Finished Decr. 1808."
    2. Ibid., "Invoices," 1799–1812.

high prices as forbid any hope of Profit. — As for Sugar it is no lower than the spring prices, & great quantities are going & already gone — besides we have now unsold in Europe (with our Brother T Lee) a cargo at Antwerp, another on the way to Cherbourg — part of Cargo in Rotterdam, and two adventures to Amsterdam under these circumstances & at the present war prices of Colonial produce — we do not see a shadow of hope for profit on the articles you name altho, prices quoted on were even higher — we shall show the information to M^rWinslow &M^r. Chandler, and endeavour to prevail upon them to make you a Consignment — which however we conceive there is a very small chance of their doing — Ashes are now at 200Dollars and none at market of any Consequence, should they fall to 180 Doll^s. which we presume must have been the price you calculated upon we will ship 2000, Dollars worth on your account, —

We are your friends

gave Prices Current in Boston ⎱   Joseph Lee J^r, and
at foot of letter forwarded — ⎰   Henry Lee — by
　　　　　　　　　　　　　　Don^d. Morrison (sign'd)

LETTER FROM HENRY LEE FOR SELF AND JOSEPH LEE, JR., BOSTON, DEC. 22, 1806, TO WILLIAM FARRIS, NEWBURYPORT, IN REGARD TO INSURANCE [1]

The Lees' offer of 8% premium for the *Gulliver's* voyage to and from India seems reasonable; at least a little later they made insurance at Newburyport at 4% [2] for the return voyage of the *Dromo*, which cleared from Calcutta, Nov. 13, 1806.[3]

The description of the vessel and equipment and of the experience of her captain, George Lee, is of interest. The *Gulliver* had already cleared for Calcutta at the date of this letter.[4]

1. Jackson-Lee Papers, "Letter Book Finished Decr. 1808."
2. *Ibid.*, Henry Lee for the Owners of *Dromo*, Boston, Dec. 27, 1806, to Samuel Cutler, Newburyport.
3. *Ibid.*, "List of Vessels clear'd for America from Calcutta."
4. *Independent Chronicle*, Dec. 20, 1806.

W^m. Farris Esqr.   Boston December 22^d. 1806 —
  Sir

We wish to know whither your Office will take a risk on specie out & goods home till landed on board Brig^t. Gulliver at and from Boston to Calcutta & back to port of discharge in United States at Eight p^rCent to return one if she goes only to Calcutta & arrives without loss — this is rate at which we have an insurance done on vessel &Cargo at Fire &Marine Office in Town & we will give you the same — the only public offices in Town except one which has not written at all — are full — we shall be glad of your reply by return of mail —

your Ob^t. Ser^{ts}.

P, S, — Gulliver is new-Cop-   Henry Lee for self &
per'd — & well found the   Joseph Lee j^r.
master has been 8 times in &
out the Bay Bengal — has
time piece & Sextant to ascertain Longitude — is order'd
not to stop unless through
necessity — H, Lee

LETTER FROM HENRY LEE, BOSTON, DEC. 26 OR 27, 1806, TO HAZARD & CABOT, PHILADELPHIA, WITH FATHERLY ADVICE [1]

Peter Remsen, New York, John Stille, Philadelphia, B. & G. Williams, Baltimore, had for several years been the agents of the Lee brothers in their respective cities. The relationship had on the whole been friendly, save for a controversy over commissions between Joseph Lee, Jr., and John Stille, which had not, however, resulted in the severance of commercial relations. But when in Dec., 1806, Samuel Cabot, Jr. (1784–1863), cousin to the Lee brothers, formed a partnership for seven years with Samuel Hazard of Philadelphia, each putting in $6,000,[2] family claims may have combined with memories of this difference of opinion to lead the Lees to transfer their Philadelphia agency to the firm of Hazard & Cabot.

1. Jackson-Lee Papers, "Letter Book Finished Decr. 1808."
2. Briggs, *op. cit.*, vol. i, pp. 281, 283, 325.

That the Lees were not entirely ingenuous in transferring the agency
from John Stille & Co. to Hazard & Cabot is revealed in a letter of
May 21, 1807, to the former firm, in which they lament that "the
Dromo was detain'd in Calcutta 6 weeks ['by an embargo'] — after
being ready for Sea which brings us in Competition in the sale of her
Cargo with all your most valuable importations — & has prevented
us from sending to your place a large amount of piece Goods —
which in Month of March & April woud have done well." The effect
of this explanation is somewhat weakened in the very next letter,
to Hazard & Cabot, which announces a shipment to Philadelphia,
even though a small one.[3]

Henry Lee, out of his four years' greater age, felt qualified gravely
to warn his less experienced kinsman against carelessness in making
out prices current.

Messrs. Hazard &Cabot   Boston. Dec^r.   1806.
  Gentlemen
          yours of 16th. & 20th are rec^d. the letter enclosing a Draft
on S. Cabot for $2862.49 & post note for $2,500 — I had made
an arrangement with M^r. S, Cabot to receive of him the Amount
of the two Drafts on Waln — presuming that I could inform
you of it before you had time to act upon my letter of 13th.
however it is well as it now stands — I am obliged to you for
this service &hope you will not sustain any inconvenience from
the transaction — I wish may have an opportunity to recipro-
cate the obligation — At present I presume there is no certainty of your river being open —if we had any goods to ship —
this will not be the case on the arrival of the Dromo — Ihope
from her Cargo to send you some valuable shipments if you
will Keep the Course of the Market for Bengal goods & inform
us from time to time we should be glad — I would remind [in-
terlineated: you] that in yours of 16th. the quotations of Aloes
&c were *blank* on this occasion it is of no Consequence — to
other persons who do not Know you it might have a bad effect. —
                              your friend
          (Sign'd)   Henry Lee

3. Jackson-Lee Papers, "Letter Book Finished Decr. 1808."

LETTER FROM HENRY LEE FOR SELF AND JOSEPH LEE, JR., BOSTON, DEC. 29, 1806, TO SAMUEL WILLIAMS, LONDON, WITH ACCOUNT OF SHIPMENTS TO EUROPE [1]

This letter gives some idea of the number and size of the Lees' shipments to the Continent. Both the south and north of Europe — Leghorn, Barcelona, Nantes, Cherbourg, mentioned in this letter, as well as Antwerp, Rotterdam, and Amsterdam, referred to in a letter to a supercargo — received consignments. None of the vessels mentioned, however, seems to have been owned by the Lees. In general their policy was to send goods to Europe as freight or in chartered bottoms but to trade with the East Indies in their own vessels, perhaps because of the greater danger of capture on the former voyage.

John Cabot, Jr. (1782–1855), one of the Lees' multitudinous Cabot cousins, had gone as supercargo on the *Republican* with a consignment for Italy.[2] From Leghorn he shipped silk hats and sewing silks.[3] It was probably Thomas and Francis Lee to whom Joseph and Henry Lee referred as "our brothers" in connection with a proposed shipment of sugar. Andrew Cabot (1780–1816), another cousin of the above, is said to have gone in 1806 "into a mercantile partnership at 65 India Wharf with his cousin Charles George Cabot," son of ex-Senator George Cabot. This association, it is said, "lasted only a short period," which would seem to be borne out by the fact that, late in the year in which the partnership is supposed to have been formed, Andrew was acting as supercargo in Calcutta for his Lee cousins.[4]

Boston December 29th. 1806 —

Saml. Williams Esqr. (London)

Sir.

We have received since our last your favor of 8th. October — we have now to advise that since the 1st. of November we have drawn on you as follows. —

1. Jackson-Lee Papers, "Letter Book Finished Decr. 1808."
2. *Ibid.*, Henry Lee for self and Joseph Lee, Jr., Boston, Apr. 18, 1807, to Samuel Williams, London.
3. *Ibid.*, "Invoices," 1799–1812, Jan. 2, 1807.
4. Briggs, *op. cit.*, vol. i, pp. 169–170, 275.

November 11th. — 60Days	—		£ 420.1.6
— " — 12. —	do.	—	1,200. .
— " — 17. —	do.	—	. 121.14.6
December 12. —	do.	£ 400. —	1,000. .
— " — " —	do.	— 600. —	
— " — 15. —	do.	—	1,600.4.
— " — 16. —	do.	—	. 584.5.2
— " — 27. —	do.	—	1,000. .
— " — " —	do.	—	1,500. .
— " — " —	do.	—	1,000. .
— " — 29 —	do.	—	. 500. .

9,726.5.2   we are

inform'd some months since of the arrival of the Juliana at
Barcelona & the Sales of her Cargo the whole of our concern
in it is order'd London — M^r. John Cabot J^r. will also remit
you from Sicily the proceeds of 5000 p^s. Nankeens — part of
which have been sold in Leghorn — M^r. Greene wrote he had
remitted on account of Shipments to Nantes & we expect soon
to hear of the arrival of the Pedler at Cherbourg & Brutus at
Nantes — the balance of Perseverances & Eliza's Cargoes —
the adventures p^r. Francis, Catharine Roxanna must have been
remitted or will soon be — we have made no further Shipments
since our last — in Company with our brothers we are now
loading. the *Ship Roxanna* with Sugar for France or Holland
our portion will be from 9. to 12000 $ and will be ordered to
you — M^r. Andrew Cabot Super-Cargo of the Ship Dromo
owned by ourselves jointly with him, writes us July 24th. 1806
Calcutta — that he may draw bills on you at 4 &6 months sight
— when said bills appear we request you to honor them & we
will provide in season —   with respect —
We are your Ob^t Ser^{ts}
(Sign'd)   Henry Lee for self and
Joseph Lee jr

LETTER FROM HENRY LEE, BOSTON, JAN. 19, 1807, TO ROBERT
CABOT, CALCUTTA, IN REGARD TO CALCUTTA BANIANS [1]

The standard by which business men in the Orient were judged,
curiously different from that applied to those in Europe and America,
comes out clearly in the remarks concerning Ram Lochun and his
rivals.

Robert Cabot (1784–1862) was supercargo of the *Gulliver,* younger
brother of Andrew of the *Dromo,* and, of course, a cousin of the Lees.
In Sept., 1807, he sold in Calcutta the *Gulliver's* cargo of bottles,
mahogany, brandy, wine, brandied fruit, marble tile, currants, corks,
and gin jugs on the account of the Lees [2] and purchased an extraordi-
narily miscellaneous return cargo of senna, sal ammoniac, asafetida,
sugar, gunny bags, buffalo horns, sago, shellac, ginger, cow hides,
tiger skins, deer skins, cassia, gum copal, nux vomica, and turmeric,[3]
invoiced at sicca rupees 10,636, 7 annas, 6 pice. (The rupee was approximately the value of 2s.; 16 annas equalled 1 rupee and 12 pice,
1 anna. By an act of 1835, one-fourth of an anna was described as a
pice and one-twelfth of an anna a pie, but before this act not pie but
pice was the word applied to one-twelfth of an anna.)[4] The *South
Carolina* and *China Packet,* both of Philadelphia, and the *Hector* of
Beverly had left Calcutta on July 25, Aug. 7, and Sept. 1, 1806, respectively.[5] "Mr. *Heard* of the *Hector*" was probably Augustine
Heard, later one of the greatest of Salem shipmasters and shipowners,[6] perhaps on this occasion acting as supercargo.

Mr. Robert Cabot   Boston, January 19th. 1807.
via New York ⎫ Dear Sir
Ship   ⎭
I wrote you on 6. Inst. by Java from Salem we have since
recd. letters from Andrew down to 1 Septr. he found goods both

1. Jackson-Lee Papers, "Letter Book Finished Decr. 1808."
2. *Ibid.,* "Foreign Sales on acct. of J. & H. Lee from 1803 to 1810."
3. *Ibid.,* "Invoices," 1799–1812.
4. Milburn, William, *Oriental Commerce,* 2 vols. (London, 1813),
vol. ii, p. 108; Balfour, *op. cit.,* vol. i, p. 779.
5. Jackson-Lee Papers, "List of Vessels clear'd for America from
Calcutta."
6. Morison, *op. cit.,* pp. 89–90, 101, 274, 277, 283.

scarce & high — partly from great quantities that had been shipp'd & were then shipping — but principally from the low rate at which they had been sold the last year which induced many manufacturers to divert their attention to other objects — he predicts that in six months they will again be plenty &low — I find on conversing with M^r. *Heard* of the *Hector* that *Andrew* thinks fine goods will answer judging from the few that have been shipp'd & from their Comparative Cheapness — I think Mr H. is mistaken — if he is not A's judgement will be unfortunate the fact as you know — is that fine goods are furnished from England on better terms than they can be made from India — dont risk the purchase unless of few recommended in my mem^o. — neither the *China Packet* (Cargo 1700 bales) South Carolina or Hector have brot any Bandannas of Consequence — they have become very scarce & will be more so — I am apprehensive Andrew will not bring many as they were high &Scarce — I recommend the whole quantity or more than what is put down in our mem^o.

Taffaties have been sold within these few days at $8. which Cost only 8/8 Rps. 1000 p^s. dark colours w^d. sell at that price — If you find you have not time to get as many silks as you wish have them shipp'd after you sail by some vessel bound to any port in U States — B, &G, Williams Baltimore, at Phil^a. & N. York you know who are our Correspondents Colourd Goods are at this time rather more in demand than white — your Chintz if bot under 20Rp^s. 10 by 1⅞ will do well — but you cannot buy at that price in the Bazar — Andrew has purchased his Cloths &had them printed in the way I pointed out to you the price is 20% lower than Bazar & he has actually sold some of his at 20% advance — Andrew made choice of *Ram Lochun* for his Banian & he gives the following Good reason — that his reputation was sinking so fast that he required some large Consignment to keep it up — & in order to effect this he made promises to A. which he will find it for his interest to perform — to buy his goods on better terms than any other Banian in Calcutta — Andrew writes that he has done very well — he says Dugespesand &Calisunken are great knaves — if you have employ'd them beware — C. &D. have business enough & to make them extravagant

I sh^d. therefore on the whole prefer Ram Lochun or some of the others — the China Packets Indigo has been all sold at 2^{40}/$_{100}$ the highest sale ever made in this Country — her p^s. Goods at 87 & 89¼ Cents a Rupee — the Hectors Cargo will be sold at Auction next week — Sugar Continues dull & no prospect of its being better — I think even better of Ginger than when I last wrote — if Sugar is high I w^d. advise 80 Tons of it whether much or little has been shipp'd — if Sugar is very low &Great deal of Ginger has come & is coming then I think 60 will be en^o. dont forget to write to Madrass as mentiond in the enclos extract —

yours
(Sign'd)   Henry Lee

LETTER FROM JOSEPH LEE, JR., BOSTON, JAN. 28, 1807, TO OLIVER WOLCOTT, NEW YORK, OFFERING TO SELL OR TAKE A FREIGHT FOR THE DROMO [1]

Oliver Wolcott (1760–1833), who succeeded Hamilton as Secretary of the Treasury, was at this time a leading figure among New York merchants.

The description of the *Dromo* is of interest. That vessel, of which Andrew Cabot was supercargo, left Calcutta in Nov., 1806, with a cargo of piece goods, invoiced at over 100,000 sicca rupees, sugar at over 50,000, and a few hundred rupees each in gum lac, gum copal, and twine;[2] she arrived at Boston the latter part of Apr., 1807.[3]

Oliver Wolcot Esqr.

Dear Sir

presuming from some observations of Colonel Humphries that he has left with you his papers I am induced to take the liberty of asking you to send me on a Copy of my receipt for money rec^d. by me of him, & which was shipped in the Dromo for

1. Jackson-Lee Papers, "Letter Book Finished Decr. 1808."
2. *Ibid.*, "Invoices," 1799–1812.
3. *Columbian Centinel*, Apr. 22, 1807.

Calcutta last winter — Knowing or rather believing that you have the management of the affairs of a Company that have large Concerns beyond Cape Good hope I am induced to state to you that I have a Capital Ship 500 Tons that sails extremely well, which will probably be here early in March, as Ihave no object for her at this moment — I shall be glad to engage to take a freight for her, or part of freight, upon terms that will certainly be for the interest of the shippers — or to sell her at a reasonable price if there is any probability that such a ship will be [interlineated: wanted] in the spring, I pray you will inform me

I am respectfully & with regard
your mo. Hble Servt.

Boston Jany 28. 1807   (Sign'd)   Jos. Lee J^r.

Oliver Wolcott Esqr.

New-york.

NB the ship alluded to is the *Dromo* copper'd to within 2 feet of her wales — sails well, she went from this to Calcutta up to Town in 107 Days — she cross'd the Equator in Long. 24 in 20 days from Boston — she is a thorough built ship as was ever built in New England. —

LETTER FROM HENRY LEE, BOSTON, FEB. 2, 1807, TO ROBERT CABOT, CALCUTTA, WITH INSTRUCTIONS FOR FACILITATING RE-TURN [1]

It was the writer's suggestion that the supercargo of the *Gulliver* should make arrangements with his banian, and with the supercargo of some vessel leaving later, to ship on the latter vessel "any colour'd goods" which should not be ready when the rest of the Lee vessel's cargo was, in return for taking to the United States part of the cargo of the vessel sailing later. In this way part of the latter vessel's cargo would reach a market earlier than would otherwise be the case, which would, as Henry Lee pointed out, be to the owners' advantage.

1. Jackson-Lee Papers, "Letter Book Finished Decr. 1808."

(this letter did not go it having arrivd too late)
Dear Robert   (via New York)   Boston Feby 2. 1807

 I wrote you yesterday — since then I have had a conversation with my Brother who as well as myself are more than ever impress'd with the importance of your making great dispatch & to be home before the numerous fleet that will be in Calcutta with you, any colour'd goods which may not be ready you can have shipped to any port in United States by your Banian after you leave — it will be well to agree with some of the Super cargoes for rate of freight before you leave — or you can make an exchange with any of the ships that are there — Ton for Ton Ipresume you will find no difficulty as the advantage will be on their side, on looking over the memo. given you I notice the article of Duck — blank N^o. p^s. — it is so very Scarce &high that I think 400pieces would not be too much — The Twine is an important article add some fishing lines, of the Sugar I would have 200 Bags of similar kind to that brot. home in Caravan 2^d. voy. I do. not recollect the name — George can tell you it is a Clean, Coarse grain'd [interlineated: white] Sugar & is lik'd by many families better than Havana white — From the great Sales lately made of Indigo — perhaps our Countrymen may run largely upon the article — we would not have you go beyond its usual price — & if very great quaintities have been Shipp'd & now shipping we would have only small quaintity say 2. or 3000 lbs come — unless you can purchase for a bill on London — M^r. Heard brot. home (in Hector) some Choppa Romals (Flag Hdkfs) that cost 70. @ 75 Rupees if you can buy at that price they will do well — I can think of nothing further —   yours.
                               Sign'd   (H. Lee)

 I understand the ship Superior stops at Madrass on her way to Calcutta she has 150,000 — or thereabouts — the Ceres about the same or more —

 The *China Packet* will be in Calcutta before you leave — your silk goods behind a we presume most of our stock will be in them — H.Lee —

In my letter of yesterday I mean by 100Rp^s. p^{r}Ton 40 Cubic feet & not ton weight which is a great deal more — H.Lee

Before you leave tell *Ram don* [interlineated: or] Ram Lochun or who ever may be your Banian to write us from time to time the prices of p^s. Goods & European goods, say Brandy, Claret, Coals Mahogany, &c a list of which articles you will leave with them — it is of importance that you collect all the information you can respecting what articles will be wanted in Calcutta next year

I am told that Cod Oil for Tanners is wanted in Calcutta make enquiries of the Europe Shoe makers Tanners &c, — Andrew sold an Inv^o. Glass ware (English) for 80% find out the purchaser & ask him what he will give for such another Inv^o. or a different one, such as he would be better pleased with — when you come away enquire of *Whetherell* the value of Sparrs — Tarr Turpentine &c — it may be peace when you return & such a Cargo may then do well —

Lungee hdkfs, have become very scarce, there having none been imported for several years 500p^s. of common ql^y. to cost 6 or 7 Rp^s. will do well & 200p^s. Sistersoy — if you do not find white Cottons at the prices you wish then @ 1000 or 1,500 p^s. or more will be safe — (H. Lee)

LETTER FROM HENRY LEE FOR SELF AND JOSEPH LEE, JR., BOSTON, MAY 30, 1807, TO RIDGWAY, MERTENS & CO., ANTWERP, DESCRIBING CARGO FOR FRANCE [1]

This mixed consignment, principally of sugar (valued at $25,000–$30,000),[2] by the ship *Reward,* seems to have been the Lees' first to the Continent since the cargo of sugar and pepper by the ship *Roxanna* "for Antwerp or Holland," Jan. 20, 1807, with which John Bromfield went as supercargo;[3] the *Reward's* cargo sold, Sept. 21, 1807, for 260,490 francs, which would seem to have been a good price. On June 3 the Lees announced "a shipment by Merimack for Leghorn

1. Jackson-Lee Papers, "Letter Book Finished Decr. 1808."
2. *Ibid.*, Henry Lee for self and Joseph Lee, Jr., Boston, June 3, 1807, to Samuel Williams, London.
3. *Ibid.*, Boston, Jan. 19, 1807.

of $7000;"[4] William Farris, the supercargo, on Oct. 23, 1807, sold the piece goods which made up the cargo for 9,180 pezzas, the pezza being worth about a dollar.[5] On the 27th the Lees notified Liquier, Bonhomme & Co. of Marseilles of a shipment in the brigantine "Neuterality" of "410 Bags Sugar consigned to M^r. William Oliver" or in his absence to the above firm; "another shipment of 700 bags to sail in four days on board the Brig Alice" was in preparation.[6]

Messrs. Ridgway, Mertins &C^o.

Gentlemen

We are loading in C^o. with our Brother M^r. Thos Lee j^r. & M^r. Tim^o. Williams, the ship Reward — with Coffee, Sugar, Ashes &Logwood — for — Cherbourg & a market — should the Super-Cargo, M^r. *John B. Greene* find it inexpedient to sell at C, — he will wish to be inform'd of the prices at your port — I would thank you immediately on recipt of this to address him in Triplicate — to the care of Messrs. Preble Spear &C^o. informing him of prices of Havannah. White & Brown, Muscovado — Java & Bengal Sugars — Coffee, — Ashes, and Logwood — and of Exchange —

with respect — we remain

your Ob^t. Serv^{ts}.

Boston May 30th. 1807 —   (Sign'd) Henry Lee — for self &

Joseph Lee — Junior

LETTER FROM HENRY LEE, BOSTON, JUNE 2, 1807, TO HAZARD & CABOT, PHILADELPHIA, IN REGARD TO TYPES OF BRANDY [1]

Since Cette is on the Mediterranean, Henry Lee seems to intend to say that the brandy of Cette, which he had sent to the Philadelphia firm, was not the product of Cette but had merely been shipped from that port.

4. *Ibid.*, Boston, June 3, 1807.
5. *Ibid.*, "Foreign Sales on acc^t. of J. & H. Lee from 1803 to 1810. — "
6. *Ibid.*, "Letter Book Finished Decr. 1808," Henry Lee for self, Joseph Lee, Jr., and Andrew Cabot, Boston, June 27, 1807, to Liquier, Bonhomme & Co., Marseilles.

1. Jackson-Lee Papers, "Letter Book Finished Decr. 1808."

Messrs. Hazard &Cabot   Boston June 2nd. 1807
    Gentlemen)
        since mine of yesterday I have recd. yours of 30th Ultimo
— we are not yet determined upon our voy to Mediteranian
when we have we shall apply for Insce.
    In speacking of Brandy, you say Brandy from Mediteranian
giving us the Idea that no distinction in price is made — with
us Cette is always worth 2 or 3 Cents more than any Medn. —
& 5 to 10 more than Alicant, or Barcelona — the fact is the
Brandy we have sent you is *Armagnac* — brot. down the Canal
of Lancguedoc to Cette — & is of about the same quality as
that from Bordeaux — that which is imported from Marseilles
is inferior — in the Newyork price Current it is quoted 5 Cents
higher than Spanish — these observations are made that you
may estimate it at its value & not confound it with alicant or
any other Medn. Brandy — we shall be content with whatever
you can git — after having try'd the market
        the purchase was consider'd here as a good one — the same
kind could have been retail'd at 82 Cents — since mine of yesterday a vessel has arrived from Calcutta, from her Cargo I
expect to get what Blue Cloths I want — you will therefore not
purchase at present — unless you can find some Cloths 38 by
2 — at $ 3. — I notice there are many advertis'd in your papers
— If you can buy nankeens at 80 Cents 6 Months — you may
send me 10,000 ps.
                                        Yours
                        (Sign'd)   Henry Lee
N,B. If Bandanna shd. rise to $6. I will send you 2000pieces —

LETTER FROM HENRY LEE FOR SELF AND JOSEPH LEE, JR., BOS-
TON, JULY 30, 1807, TO SAMUEL WILLIAMS, LONDON, WITH
ACCOUNT OF SHIPMENTS TO EUROPE [1]

Here again we have a complete list of shipments, their amount,
destination, and those concerned therein. The "present difficulties"
referred to, which furnished a burden to the Lees' correspondence

    1. Jackson-Lee Papers, "Letter Book Finished Decr. 1808."

until the Embargo Act of Dec. 22, 1807, provided a new refrain, resulted from the attack on the United States frigate *Chesapeake* on June 22 by the British ship-of-war *Leopard*; when the American vessel declined to yield up certain deserters supposed to be thereon, the *Leopard* fired on her, killed or wounded 21 men, and took from her four alleged deserters. Henry Lee informed a correspondent that the President intended "to do every thing that can be done consistent with the honour of the Country to keep at peace," implying as much approval of Jefferson's action as could be expected from such a bred-in-the-bone Federalist. Despite the belief of "the best informed men" that the affair would "be amicably settled," [2] insurance rates doubled, and on Aug. 1 the writer mentioned that "our offices that are considered safe will not write yet." [3]

On Feb. 17, 1808, it was announced in another letter to Samuel Williams that "Mr. Greene arrived three days since and bro't with him the proceeds of Reward's cargo," instead of remitting them to London as had been hoped. Thus a year had elapsed between the *Reward's* sailing from America and the return of the proceeds of the cargo.

Boston. July. [29th. — stricken through interlineated: 30th.] 1807.
Samuel Williams Esqr.
    London
        Sir,
            Since our last respects of the 8th. inst. — we have recd. all the accounts relating to the 3 Thomas s voyage & have been able to give your accounts a final examination — they are correct except (according to Vanbaggen & Parker's Account) an over Credit of £1 — 0 — 0 — they charge us with £362 — 3 — 8 —your account says £ 363 — 3 — 8 — you will continue our account as it stood the 17 February jointly — we will adjust here any separate interests we may have — we have been very particular to direct our agents to state our proportion of any remittances they may make — but in order to prevent any mistakes we state to you the shipments we are interested in & the

2. *Ibid.*, Henry Lee for self, Joseph Lee, Jr., and Thomas Lee, Jr., Boston, July 9, 1807, to John B. Greene, ship *Reward* for Cherbourg.
3. *Ibid.*, Henry Lee, Boston, Aug. 1, 1807, to Peter Remsen, N. Y.

proportions in which they are own'd — exclusive of the Rox-
anas which M^r. Bromfield has the direction of —

Ship Merrimack for Leghorn wholly to Jos. Lee j^r. & Henry
Lee —
Cost $7,500 — .. —
Ship Reward — for Cherbourg 4/8^ths. on accot. Thos. Lee j^r.

$3/8$ — D^o. — Jos. Lee j^r. & H^y. Lee

Cost $7,500 — .. — $1/8$ — D^o. John B Greene —
Super cargo

There is besides on board the Reward an Adventure —

$2/3$^rds. on accot Jos. Lee j^r. & Henry Lee
Cost $17,000 $1/3$ — — D^o. — And^w. Cabot —

Brig^t. Neuterality for Marseilles — $2/3$^rds. on accot. Jos. Lee j^r. & H^y. Lee
Cost $7000 $1/3$^rd. D^o. And^w. Cabot

Brig^t. America $\big\}$ ½ on accot. Thomas Lee Junr. $\big\}$
for Rotterdam $\big\}$ ½ — D^o. — Jos. Lee j^r. & H^y. Lee $\big\}$ Cost $2000 — ..
Brig^t. Alice $\big\{$ $2/3$^rds. on account Jos. Lee J^r. & H^y. Lee
for Marseilles $\big\{$ $1/3$ $14,500 Cost D^o. And^w. Cabot —

The
proceeds of the above are unconditionally ordered to you —
the Alice sail'd on the 16th. ins^t. — we shall suspend any further shipments to Europe till we hear of the result of our present
difficulties we have not drawn since the 8th. — nor shall we till
we are inform'd of remittances on account of some of the Shipments made — Messrs. Preble, Spear &C^o. inform us they remitted the 12th. Ult^o. £28.10.10 — the Amount of an error in
accounts of 3 Thomas's —

you will divide it — $11/16$^ths. on accot Jos. & H Lee

$4/16$ — D^o. — Thos. Lee j^r. & P. Dodge

$1/16$ — D^o. Saml. Cabot J^r.

Should they remit further on that account you will divide — in
the same proportions — we remain with respect

your Ob^t. S^ts.

(Sign'd) Henry Lee — for self &
Joseph Lee — j^r.

LETTER FROM HENRY LEE, BOSTON, AUG. 25, 1807, TO PETER
REMSEN, NEW YORK, ON BUSINESS CONDITIONS [1]

The apprehensions of war caused by the *Chesapeake* episode had
in two months produced upon business in the ports of New England
the effect described below.

Peter Remsen, to whom this and many other important letters
were addressed by the Lees, was probably their favorite among commercial correspondents. In recommending him to George Crownin-
shield & Sons, Salem, Joseph Lee, Jr., wrote: "M[r]. Peter Remsen . . .
is you may be assured both able and willing to execute any business
you may think proper to confide to him — he is punctual — industrious — honest — Capable & perfectly safe." [2]

M[r]. Peter Remsen   Boston. August. 25. 1807.
    Dear Sir,
        I have your favour of the 20th. Aug[t]. although I approve
of the Sale of 45 p[s]. of Bandannas yet I would not have you
offer any more till 15th. Sept[r]. they must rise at that time —
unless there should be importations from England — there are
not 500p[s]. in this place besides those we have — I have 15 Bales
Gurrahs on hand of an ordinary quality — I shall send them to
Philadelphia where they are more in demand than with you —
one of the Shippers in the Dromo has 51 Bales I will try to prevail upon him to send them to you There are not many coarse
Goods except in the hands of one or two persons who hold them
up not expecting to sell till October — I regret that my exertions to procure you business have not been more successful
your Credit stands as well as I could wish it — & when from any
course whatever those who do business with your neighbours
wish to change I shall find no difficulty in adding many of them
to the list of your correspondents — I have given your address to
Gilman Langdon &C[o]. & Phineas Adams they are Comm[n].
houses respectable but not doing much business — but probably
they may in the course events be instrumental in procuring you

1. Jackson-Lee Papers, "Letter Book Finished Dec[r]. 1808."
2. *Ibid.*, Joseph Lee, Jr., Boston, Jan. 23, 1808, to George Crownin-
shield & Sons, Salem.

some — Mess Hall & Lovering are already in correspondence with you They are a new house but safe & may in time do considerable business — I am glad you have seen M^r. Bromfield I was apprehensive he w^d. have left your place before the arrival of my letter introducing you to him — I should judge by the clearances you were not so timid as we are — shipments are almost entirely suspended — Sugars &Coffee are considerably lower than with you many failures are taking place every day in small Sea ports to Eastward & if the present stagnation continues or war is made 1/3rd of the Merchants will certainly fail & half the others be embarrased —

yours

(Sign'd)   Henry Lee

LETTER FROM HENRY LEE, BOSTON, OCT. 17, 1807, TO WILLIAM OLIVER, C/O LIQUIER, BONHOMME & CO., MARSEILLES, WITH INSTRUCTIONS [1]

Early in the previous month Henry Lee had written: "few shipments have been made since 1st July & none are now making." About the same time, writing to a European firm on behalf of himself, his three brothers, and John Bromfield, Jr., he remarked: "The fears of approaching hostilities between our Government & Great Britain we hope have caused a favourable change in the state of your Markets," and early in October, to a New York merchant, "Our Politicians are more apprehensive than ever that a war with England will be the result of our negotiations." [2] In the present letter, though stating "the general opinion that our [?] with England will eventually be amicably adjusted," he still expressed the resolution that "we would not be engaged in any voyage whatever." This determination would have been confirmed and the prospects of an amicable adjustment dimmed had he known that on the very date of the letter "the British government issued a proclamation . . . directing officers of the royal navy to exercise the right of impressing British subjects

1. Jackson-Lee Papers, "Letter Book Finished Decr. 1808."
2. *Ibid.*, Henry Lee, Boston, Sept. 9, 1807, to John B. Greene, ship *Reward* for Cherbourg; Henry Lee, etc., Boston, Sept. 8, 1807, to Thomas & Adrian Cremer, Rotterdam; Henry Lee, Boston, Oct. 8, 1807, to Peter Remsen, N. Y.

from neutral merchant vessels to its fullest extent."[3] On Nov. 13, Lee wrote to Peter Remsen: "Business is entirely at a stand in consequence of the news from England." On Nov. 18, he wrote Oliver that he had given up any intention of sending a vessel to Oliver loaded with sugar and had resolved upon selling both vessel and cargo; Lee accordingly advised Oliver to come home.

"The new Brig[t]." which was "still on the stocks" in the middle of November was the *Gipsy* and was intended for Calcutta.[4]

M[r]. William Oliver   Boston. Oct[o]. 17th. 1807.
    care of Mess Liquier, Bonhomme &Co
      Marseilles —   p Rattle snake saild 18th forLeghorn —
      D[r]Sir,
           Your several favors to Aug[t]. 12th have been rec[d]. — I am sorry you did not follow our instructions pNeutrality — we have drawn on S Williams & fear that he will not be in funds inseason to meet our bills — the rate of Exchange in the country or in Europe is never any object to us — if our remittances are no regularly made — our credit in London must suffer which is more important than the whole amount of property consignd you — should it so happen that the whole proceeds have not been remitted on rec[t]. of this have it done immediately both of Alice & Neuterality Adventures

In ordinary times we sh[d]. have no objections to take a Concern in any small speculation with you which might promise well — but in the present state of Europe & particularly while our affairs are unsettled with England we would not be engaged in any Voyage whatever — the few articles I desired you to ship in mine of 10th. Ult[o]. I wish you to omit shipping — It was not our intention to place any business under the Controul of M[r]. Winslow unless the Neuterality proceeded further up & he went in her — but we hoped you have made the acquaintance of Mess[rs]. Liquier Bonhomme &C[o]. — because we think well of their solidity which is the only Consideration in selecting a

3. Channing, *op. cit.*, vol. iv, p. 373.
4. Jackson-Lee Papers, "Letter Book Finished Dec[r]. 1808," Henry Lee, Boston, Nov. 18, 1807, to William Oliver, c/o Mess. Liquier, Bonhomme & Co., Marseilles; Registers, Boston Custom House, 1812, no. 3.

Merchant & because they will have the means to aid us in our Contemplated Voyage to Bengal — we shall indeed feel Chagrined if you have not Consign'd both our shipments to them — The proceeds of your Minerva Voyage are still on hand your Brother has inform'd you minutely of that adventure when the most favourable moment arrives we shall sell the Sugar — at present not more than \$12¾ @ \$13 — can be obtain'd for the best Sugars — yours are but common quality — I sh^d. not have shipped any thing to you had your orders been ever so positive — as no Insurance that I considered good against all events could be obtain'd — now the prospect in Med^n. is so indifferent — the probability is we shall sell at all events — I have made insurance @ 7 % on wine & oil on b^d. Maria — perhaps the latter article may give a profit — I never knew wine in bottles to do well scarcely — If you were well acquainted with value there & here of Italian Manufactures I sh^d. advise you to make a small shipment of Crapes, Sewing Silks, Italian Silks &c — but as you are not I think you cannot make any thing by such a shipment — you execute better than any man I ever knew — but you Certainly are too Sanguine to plan Voyages

The new Brig^t. is now ready to be Launch'd but affairs with England are so unsettled that we dare not now & I fear we shall not be able to for some time to come — if an Europe peace sh^d. take place or if our difficulties with England are adjusted I shall come out this winter in such case we may make an arrangement with you to on to Bengal on this subject I will write when any change take's place which influence's it — If we can establish a Credit with Bonhomme &C^o. which we shall do — if you do business with them I hope to negotiate 4 @ 10,000 £ Exchange on S, Williams at 6 M^os. Sight or in this Country — your information respecting Ginger &c is satisfactory — I wish you to extend it to other places & not confine it to that article alone

you are not aware how important it is to be inform'd of every kind of Merchandize which it is possible for us to deal in course of our lives — The Gulliver has arrived in Calcutta — she will be back in December our prospects are not flattering — It is the general opinion that our with England will eventually be amicably adjusted — our Congress meet 28 inst. after which we shall possibly know more — I will write you after as I have done since you sail'd — altho it is probable you will not get half the letters your Brother A — has promis'd to write you Public & private affairs he has already written several times —

Yours
(Sign'd)   Henry Lee

I wish you to ship me 5 Doz. Hermitage wine
½ "   white
½ "   Red

LETTER FROM HENRY LEE, BOSTON, NOV. 28, 1807, TO ARTHUR SPEAR, NANTES, CRITICIZING LATTER'S CONDUCT [1]

The controversy between Lee and Spear originated in a shipment to Cherbourg by the *Three Thomases* to be disposed of by Preble & Spear, which firm, in Henry Lee's opinion, made "errors and over-charges . . . and Gross ones too;" Lee particularly objected to a charge of ¾% interest per month on advances, feeling that 6% per year was sufficient.[2] In a letter of the same date to John B. Greene, the latter was ordered to "place the consignment of the 1000 bags shipped by Jʰ Lee Jun H Lee & A Cabot in the hands of Hottenguer & Co. in Homberg" if Preble & Spear "refuse to allow" the "errors and overcharges" in their statement.

Mʳ. Arthur Spear   Boston. Nov. 28. 1807.
    Sir,   origˡ. pBrutus — Cherbourg
                Copy pʳ Sally — for Nantes —
    I did hope that my last letters which you acknowledge in yours of the 6ᵗʰ August & 2ᵈ. Octᵒ. wᵈ. have terminated this tedious & unpleasant discussion — but since you have chosen to revive it I will take a short view of the points we have been contending about — which I hope will conclude our correspond-ence upon a subject which must give you pain whenever you reflect upon it — I will commence with your Mʳ. Preble's

---

1. Jackson-Lee Papers, "Letter Book Finished Decʳ. 1808."
2. *Ibid.*, Henry Lee, Boston, June 16, 1807, to Arthur Spear, Nantes.

letter on which you observe in yours of the 17th June 1807 "But if I wish to say anything in extenuation of such a letter 'tis upon the principle, that he must have been very much vex'd & griev'd that nearly a year after every acct had been clos'd & every penny paid that could be claim'd on 3 Thomases' Cargo that we shd. be call'd upon peremptorilly to settle that business" Your next paragraph informs me of a deduction of an overcharge (on examination of the Accts) of F686.57 how does this agree with Mr. Preble's letter to Mr. Bromfield & your extenuation of it — I am now to presume after your Mr. P's letter & your examination in consequence of our peremptory demand that the accts are correct — your letter of the 6thAugust acknowledging on reexamination the further overcharges of —

Guaranty on Loyseau's indemnity 10267 @ 2%   205.34
Int on 24821.38   2 M   — —   248.21
                                                    ─────
                                                    453.55

Shall be the only comment I will make on yours of the 17th June in which you extenuate Mr. P's letter, with this observation that the Accts. previous to this last correction, according to your own confession had undergone a review by you & no doubt had been look'd into by Mr. Preble before he wrote Mr. Bromfield. — I will now ask you what Conclusions I am to draw from such proceedings?

The queries & observations which relate to the transfer of part of my business from Hottinguer &Co. are address'd to a Child — you must have forgot yourself & me when you wrote them — I will therefore spare them — The reasons which operated upon me on that occasion I did not intend to say any thing of, but since you Compel me I will say that it was from a desire to promote your views that led me to Consign Cargoes &pledge myself to others for your good Conduct — with an expectation that at least you would act with the same liberality & justice toward me as I have hitherto experienced from others. — The Comparrison with H &Co. (which I am sorry appears so odious to you) was made merely to show you that I was not unreasonable in my demands upon you — you will not pretend that your services are more valuable than theirs, or that their charges of interest &c ought to be less than yours, —

My letter of the 10th. June was not intended to deceive you — you could not think it was — when you reflect that we could have had no motive so to do — we have no favours to ask unless you think our just demands are favours, — it was written before a final examination into your accounts & before I had with Mr. Greene an explanation of your Conduct in the management of the Helens Cargo — your reasoning in defence of retaining the Amount saved in the Duties carries in my mind no force. —

I do contend that you had no right to deviate from the ordinary Course of proceedings with the Cargo without the Concurrence of my agent

the very defence of that principle wd. in my mind be an objection to trusting you on the Score of safety — because the penalties attach'd to such offences in case of failure in a number of instances wd. destroy your responsibility — but setting this aside & supposing you to be out of the reach of such consequences — you are bound to inform my agent of the advantages of such a proceeding & then if he agrees to it — you can stipulate for your [selves — stricken through] services — As a proof of my Correctness I will cite Mr. Randeux — Mr. S, C Jr. has credited in his account with me F1539.23 if it were necessary I could quote other instances

Your suspicions of of Mr. G's ingratidude or injustice are entirely without foundation — his Statement of your Conduct in the Helen Adventure corresponds with yours — for the hospitality he received from you he is obliged — As for any information you gave him — you were bound to do it by every motive — but no obligations he could be under of whatever nature could have justify'd his desertion of our interest —

If you had [have been in — stricken through interlineated: written] to C. he no doubt wd. have had an explanation — altho. it appears by your letters he wd. have only lost time in so doing, — but at the distance you were at — it was not expedient —

nor w^d. have been had he have presum'd you w^d. have yelded him his rights —

If [interlineated: you] regret the opp^y. of doing me justice it is not now too late. — I do not wish to reduce your rate of interest but I see no reason why you should charge me more than others — had M^r. Cabot agree'd to have paid you 12% p^r. Annum I should not have refus'd — as you would have a legal advantage over me, which I could not have surmounted — I am only surpris'd that you complain of my giving your Credit a "stab" by withdrawing my business from your house when you acknowledge you cannot do it [interlineated: on] as favourable terms as my friends H. &C°. — you would have no right to Complain had I given you no reasons for my changing — but I believe I have now satisfy'd you with unanswerable reasons that it is not my Caprice but your own Conduct which has compelld me to seek my own interest by employing those persons whose Acco^t. are always Correct & whose Charges are according to your own acknowledgement more reasonable than yours — With wishes that you may find you other friends better satisfy'd with your management than I am — I remain

Yours

(Sign'd) Henry Lee

I wave my claim to any further demand on you rather than keep open the acco^{ts}. any longer — tho' it would be difficult for you to prove why you should not refund a Commission [interlineated: in] Loyseaus indemnity on a purchase given up for your Accommodation — thus the 2 % guaranty which we pay is of but little use — unless to fill your purses — it is the only instance however in which I have been so awake to the unreasonableness of this Charge. —

P. S since writting the above I have yours of the 15th. Sepr. I am oblig'd by your Congratulations but wish you to recollect that our trade with France is of as old a date as your establishment & that our information was not taken from Mr Greene's notes or your letters India, Muscovado & Havanna Brown Sugar

have always been our Cargoes for Fecamp Cherbourg &c — I congratulate you on your discovery of this information & hope your correspondents will profit by it —   Yours H, Lee
If Mr Greene has not already paid you the Balance on your Acco^t. I w^d. thank you to draw on me at sight & the Bills shall be duly honour'd — I am not dispos'd to [give — stricken through interlineated: do you] an injury — every thing which comes from me calculated to injure your feelings is forc'd by you — I am on the defensive — you on the offensive — I am injur'd — you only Complain (while you admit my rights) that I demand them — with good wishes for yourself &family — I remain

Yours
(Sign'd) H Lee

LETTER FROM HENRY LEE FOR SELF AND JOSEPH LEE, JR., BOSTON, DEC. 5, 1807, TO RAM LOCHUN BONARJIA, CALCUTTA, ANNOUNCING PROSPECTIVE VOYAGES [1]

The *William,* by which this letter went and on which were adventures belonging to the Lees and to Oliver, was one of the last vessels to get away from the United States for Calcutta before the embargo prevented such voyages as, we learn below, had been planned. The Lees' adventure on board consisted of wines and liquor which on May 30, 1808, brought net proceeds of rupees 8,114, 2 annas, 9 pice in Calcutta.[2] The Calcutta piece goods shipped to the Lees on the *William* the same day by Augustine Heard and N. Emery, Jr., were invoiced at sicca rupees 10,203, 3 pice.[3]

Boston Decr. 5th. 1807
Ram Lochun Benorgee.
(p^rWilliam via Salem) Dear Sir
It is now a long time since we have been favoured with a letter from you; we look daily for our Brother & M^r. Cabot & hope to hear them speak as well of you as M^r. A Cabot does —

1. Jackson-Lee Papers, "Letter Book Finished Decr. 1808."
2. *Ibid.*, "Foreign Sales on acc^t. of J. & H. Lee from 1803 to 1810."
3. *Ibid.*, "Invoices," 1799–1812.

We have however to complain that you did not execute our Orders for Bandannas per Capt Beckford or some other vessel a number having arriv'd that bro't silk goods which would have taken them. —

This will go by the William Consigned to the Capt & M^r. Heard whom you have seen, we hope they will give you their buisiness. at any rate they will call on you to invest two adventures belonging to us & M^r. W^m. Olliver & have no doubt you will furnish him with cheaper goods than any Banyan in Calcutta. — We have a vessel we shall probably send out in the course of a Month & another in 3 or 4 months. You must write us by every vessel. — Send us a list of the goods exported since the Gulliver sailed & let us know how goods are & the price of Europe Merchandize. We shall continue to speak well of you & hope you will continue to deserve the good Character you now sustain.

                    (Signed) Henry Lee for self
(Calcutta)   Jos Lee J^r)

P S. M^r. Olliver is now in Europe; it is not impossible he may again visit Calcutta

LETTER FROM HENRY LEE, BOSTON, DEC. 15, 1807, TO BENJAMIN & GEORGE WILLIAMS, BALTIMORE, IN REGARD TO THE BRITISH ORDERS IN COUNCIL [1]

There are many letters of the general tenor of the first part of the one below, relating to East India goods sent by the Lees to commission merchants in other ports, such as Peter Remsen, New York City, and Hazard & Cabot, Philadelphia. The American Non-Importation Act of Apr. 18, 1806, here mentioned, provided that after Nov. 15, 1806, certain manufactured articles should not be brought into the United States from within the British Empire. The time for this act to go into effect was later extended to July 1, 1807, and then to "not later than the second Monday in December, 1807, at the discretion of the President." The British Orders in Council, Nov. 11, 1807, declared all ports of France and her colonies to be subject to such

---

1. Jackson-Lee Papers, "Letter Book Finished Decr. 1808."

restrictions as if in a state of blockade, save that neutrals might still provide themselves with colonial produce and carry on trade between British dominions and ports not actually blockaded.[2] The United States replied with an embargo, which went into effect a week after the date of the letter below. Since the Lees' trade consisted almost entirely in sending vessels to Calcutta for goods which, after arriving in the United States, were reshipped to the Continent of Europe, it is not difficult to understand why Henry Lee felt that there would be "a cessation of business unless it should turn out that we are to be allow'd to go to france, Holland, &c under some restrictions." [3]

Messrs. Benja. &George Williams.   Boston Decr. 15th. 1807 —
   Baltimore,
     Dear Sirs,.
      Since my last I have your favour of 4th. instant — I am glad to hear there is a probability of your getting off the Hdkfs @ $5,50 — should the non Importation law be enforc'd they would become excessive high & if it is relaxed still I know of few expected — I have sold within 15 days 3000ps. $5.30 @ $5.50 — & have left only 1000ps. you will please to close at the best prices you can obtain all the Sales but the Bandannas — when you can buy bills at 3 Months or shorter sight I would thank you to remit — The last newes recd. from Europe has caus'd great Consternation — Vessels that are ready to sail are detain'd & no Sales can be made of any thing. —
      If it should turn out that all Europe which is under the Controul of france, is blockaded by the English — there must be an end to our commerce — West India Goods as well as all others for exportation must sink in value — those Vessels now on their way to Europe must return or go to England, in consequence, many bills will be return'd & some very rich Houses will be ruin'd — I cannot but hope that such a constrain'd situation of things will end either by a relaxation of Decrees on the part of france & England, or by a general peace — 'till one of

2. Channing, *op. cit.*, vol. iv, pp. 375, 377.
3. Jackson-Lee Papers, "Letter Book Finished Decr. 1808," Henry Lee, Boston, Dec. 16, 1807, to Benjamin & George Williams, Baltimore.

those two events occur our trade will be in a dreadful state —
Pray what effect has the newes produc'd with you —
Yours,
(Sign'd)   Henry Lee
the Goods p^r. G. Lovell are rec^d. in good order

LETTER FROM HENRY LEE, BOSTON, JAN. 13, 1808, TO PETER
REMSEN, NEW YORK, WITH INSTRUCTIONS FOR MEETING THE
EMBARGO SITUATION [1]

The Embargo Act, presented to Congress as a bill on Dec. 18, 1807,
was signed and went into effect Dec. 22. On Jan. 1, 1808, Henry Lee
remarked: "My friends are more gloomy to day than I have yet seen
them they think the chance of War much greater. . . . Gent^n. seem
to calculate very cooly upon the ruin of us Merchants." [2] But by the
time of the letter below, the writer had become somewhat more
optimistic as to the effects and continuance of the embargo.

The Lees' brig *Gulliver*, Capt. George Lee, which had sailed from
Calcutta, Aug. 31, 1807, arrived in America, Dec. 31, with an assorted cargo.[3]

M^r. Peter Remsen.
Boston Jany. 13th. 1808

DearSir.

I have yours of the 7 th. I am so strongly impress'd with the
beleif that the Embargo will not continue that I would not purchase any thing at higher prices than if it had not been laid on —
I had hoped that prices of Gin &c would not have risen so
[much — stricken through interlineated: soon] with you but
since they have already gone up higher than they are worth
I would not have you buy for me at any price the holders here
as I expected find them selves deceiv'd and prices have fallen
several cents — if sales should be forced they would decline
still more — we have not yet had but one failure nor do I think

1. Jackson-Lee Papers, "Letter Book Finished Decr. 1808."
2. *Ibid.*, Henry Lee, Boston, Jan. 1, 1808, to Humphry Devereux,
Salem.
3. *Ibid.*, "List of vessels clear'd for America from Calcutta." See also
Columbian Centinel, Jan. 20, 1808.

for some time to come we shall have any of consequence — yet even tho the Embargo should be repeal'd soon our Commerce must be in that state as will cause in the course of the year great embarrassment — I intend to sell only on short credits and to safe men — Pray are the purchasers on our sales good [men — stricken through] against probable events — if they are not I wish you to change away their notes for any Merchandize or money

Italian sewing silks are worth 5..50 assorted colours. Broad Diapers 5..50 — Ivory of large sizes entitled to Debenture 85 cts Havanna B. Sugar 8 $. Blue Nankins 190Cts. yellow 88 Cts. China Lutstring's 19 yds (black only) 19 $ — Bohea Tea 32 Cts. — Mahogany Bay large logs (grain of less consequence 7½ cents — I would not wish to speculate in these or any other articles but I should like to have suspicious notes exchanged for them I have directed Messrs. Hoppin &Son. to send you from Providence some Bandannas which you will sell on short credit only — inform me if 3 or 400 pieces can be sold at 5..50 well assorted for 60 day notes they must be scarce I should think — The Gulliver is still at the vineyard but we look for her every hour. — Havanna White Sugar bot yesterday on Speculation @ 12 $ no other sales of Merchandize since the Embargo — The holders of Exchange on London demand from 3 % to 5 %.

New YorK —   Henry Lee

LETTER FROM HENRY LEE, BOSTON, FEB. 9, 1808, TO BENJAMIN PICKMAN, JR., SALEM, ABOUT A LOAN [1]

By Feb. 8, "accounts from Washington" had modified the writer's earlier optimistic opinion and impressed him "with the beleif that the Embargo will be continued, and that our differences with England will not be settled by Mr. Rose." Cut off from foreign ports by Orders in Council and the embargo, Joseph Lee, Jr., decided to engage in speculation, and to that end attempted to borrow money from various merchants, including Benjamin Pickman, Jr. The conditions laid down by the borrowers are clearly expressed in the present letter. Pickman, however, wrote Henry Lee, claiming that "he understood

1. Jackson-Lee Papers, "Letter Book Finished Decr. 1808."

you were to take it on the following terms 'the money to be invested as you chose if any profit ½ to be paid him with interest if no profit then he was to loose the interest' thus We take the whole risk — he only the risk of interest on his money and receives the same share of profits." [2]

Benjamin Pickman Jun[r]. Esqr —   Boston Feb[y]. 9. 1808
    Dear Sir
        I find noted in a memorandum left me by my Brother the following — "M[r] B Pickman Jr lends me 10,000 $ If I gain I give him one third of the profits if I loose return him the amount loan'd without interest in five months;" the terms you mention differ so essentially from the above and from my brother's agreement with the other Gentlemen, from whom he receiv'd loans — that I must decline receiving your money — I remain —
                              With respect
                                    Yr O[t]. S[t].
    Salem   Henry Lee —

LETTER FROM HENRY LEE, BOSTON, FEB. 10, 1808, TO PETER REMSEN, NEW YORK, WITH OPINION OF GOVERNMENT [1]

As far as business policy is concerned this letter is largely a repetition of what has gone before. Its importance lies in its revelation of Henry Lee's opinion of the Jefferson administration. The embargo had completely reversed his previous attitude of tepid approval, tentatively adopted at the time of Jefferson's pacifistic policy in the crisis caused by the *Chesapeake* affair. Though the attitude described below was to be expected of a Federalist from Essex County, it has been pointed out that even among Federalists it was not universal, inasmuch as, among others, William Gray, "a Federalist, and the largest individual shipowner in the United States," regarded the embargo "as a necessary measure of self-protection." [2] Even more sur-

2. *Ibid.*, Henry Lee, Boston, Feb. 8, 10, 1808, to Joseph Lee, Jr., c/o Hazard & Cabot, Philadelphia.

1. Jackson-Lee Papers, "Letter Book Finished Dec[r]. 1808."
2. Morison, *op. cit.*, pp. 190–191.

prising, John Bromfield, Jr., another Federalist, who in Oct., 1807, was going to Europe as supercargo with a consignment of sugar belonging to Joseph Lee, Jr., Henry Lee, and Andrew Cabot,[3] and who in April wrote one of his customarily disconsolate letters from London to his mother,[4] nevertheless described the embargo as "a very well-timed restriction upon our commerce."

As an example of the "embarrassed state" of commerce at this time, Henry Lee, in a letter of a week later, informed Remsen that "we have two failures Low dii [Lowden?] and Rogers 65 000 $. Henry Cary Jr. [?] 35,000 Dlls." [5]

Mr. Peter Remsen.   Boston feby. 10. 1808.
   DearSir.

   Since mine of yesterday I am in receipt of yours of 6th. instant — Molasses cannot be bo't under 38 Cents Havanna but even was it lower I should decline a speculation, there are many others more safe. and more profitable — Gin has fallen to 105 cents and will not for the present be higher I should like to have any notes that you think are not perfectly safe exchang'd for that article @ 106 or even 108 cents but I would not go beyond 97 on speculation and then for not more than 100 Pipes — I can purchase 150 pipes 4 th proof french Brandy @ 118 cents 4 Mos. 115 Cash — but I have no faith in it at that price it is worth 5 % to guaranty sales on and it even for 60 days —

   I wrote you some time since that you might exchange my Notes for Merchandize I would not have you go higher than 7 50/100 for Havanna Brown Batavia [interlineated: Sugar] or 20 Cents for Coffee — I agree with you in opinion that Sugar will be lower and I think even less than 7 $. should the embargo continue 3 months our accounts from Washington are so contradictory that we do not Know what to think of our affairs with England — I beleive our government have no wish to settle

   3. Jackson-Lee Papers, "Letter Book Finished Decr. 1808," Henry Lee, Boston, Oct. 17, 1807, to John B. Greene, ship *Reward* for Cherbourg.
   4. Hunt, *op. cit.*, vol. ii, p. 472.
   5. Jackson-Lee Papers, "Letter Book Finished Decr. 1808," Henry Lee, Boston, Feb. 15, 1808, to Peter Remsen, N. Y.

affairs yet they cannot mean to have a war. I rather think it is their cowardly policy to Keep things in their present State to avoid the displeasure of Napoleon whether the English will forever bear it is another question at all events I think prudence dictates to us to prepare for the worst — Under the impression that our Commerce is to continue for some time in an embarrassed state — I have not been active to procure you business — for in all probability either one of these two things must happen — that you make no sales that would be satisfactory or that you make bad debts.

I notice the Bandannas have arrived — Messrs. Hoppin &Son of Providence informed me they shipp'd you some which should sometime since have been received — I would not have you sell them unless for notes that will be good in all events   Yours

/ Signed /   Henry Lee

New York

Letter from Henry Lee, Boston, Mar. 18, 1808, to Peter Remsen, New York, in Regard to Purchasing Brandy [1]

Henry Lee in the previous month had suffered another fluctuation of opinion as to the continuance of the embargo. Though still "of opinion . . . that the Embargo is to continue some months — yet," he wrote, "I doubt whether it will be beyond June." [2] Cotton, he had written his brother, was "too high to purchase" [3] and taking everything into consideration he had decided that brandy was the most proper object of speculation. A few days after the date of this letter he wrote: "I do not think I am too sanguine in saying that $ 2, will be obtain'd before October." [4] A reason for the place liquors took in the "speculation" in which Henry Lee was "so much engaged" [5] comes out in a letter of Apr. 21: "Liquors are the only Merchandize of consequence of which we have not an annual supply at least — of Teas,

1. Jackson-Lee Papers, "Letter Book Finished Decr. 1808."
2. *Ibid.*, Henry Lee, Boston, Feb. 26, 1808, to Peter Remsen, N. Y.
3. *Ibid.*, Henry Lee, Boston, Mar. 2, 1808, to Joseph Lee, Jr., c/o Peter Remsen, N. Y.
4. *Ibid.*, Henry Lee, Boston, Mar. 29, 1808, to Hazard & Cabot, Philadelphia.
5. *Ibid.*, Henry Lee, Boston, Apr. 19, 1808, to Peter Remsen, N. Y.

Nankins, Pepper, Coffee, Sugar, & Bengal Goods, we are supply'd with two years stock." [6] In a letter of the same date he mentioned that "so many vessels have gone out to Jam[a]. & S[t]. Croix that if they return loaded with Rum there will be no scarcity till the fall if there is then." [7]

Joseph Lee, Jr., was making a tour to the southward of Boston and was at this time in New York City. He had been in Philadelphia the previous month. The "Med[n]. Duty" was an ad valorem duty of $2\frac{1}{2}\%$ levied for the purpose of warfare against the Barbary pirates. The law establishing it expired on Dec. 31, 1807, and was restored later in January. The *Gulliver* arrived at midnight Dec. 31, and her manifest was delivered on Jan. 1. The contention of the importers, now confirmed as this letter reveals, was that this duty was not due, since the manifest had not been delivered till after the expiration of the law.[8]

M[r]. Peter Remsen   Boston March 18. 1808 —
    D[r].Sir

I have just return'd from Gloucester where I have been endeavouring to make a purchase of 250 pipes Cette Brandy — but in vain — the holders refuse to sell believing it will get up to 150. Cents I have offer'd for 50 Pipes Bordeaux 135 Cents & am refus'd —

three more vessels have arrived since my last — one only with Brandy which was shipp'd before news of Blockade reach'd the port at which it was shipped — other vessels will come in Balast or be detain'd &Condemned — so that not much more can be rec[d]. — I have bo[t]. with Hazard &Cabot 100. pipes —the whole that has been imported in the last arrivals Cette 4th. proof @ 120 Cents — 90 Days with liberty to Bond the Duties — I am one half in the above purchase — &you will join me or not as you think expedient — it will bring a profit tomorrow — there is little or none in hands of retailers — & they will soon be obliged to buy at our own prices — Will you

6. *Ibid.*, Henry Lee, Boston, Apr. 21, 1808, to B. & G. Williams, Baltimore.
7. *Ibid.*, Henry Lee, Boston, Apr. 21, 1808, to Peter Remsen, N. Y.
8. *Ibid.*, Henry Lee, Boston, Feb. 10, 1808, to Joseph Lee, Jr., Washington.

purchase Bordeaux @ 140 Cents? — Sewing silks are selling at $8 — buy what you can (Italian) at $6– Cash or $6–25 — the holders of Band^s. ask $6. — I would not advise you to make any sales till you write M^r. Pickman — tell my Brother that M^r. Weld has rec^d. orders to remit the Med^n. Duty —

yours

(New york)   (Sign'd)   Henry Lee

LETTER FROM HENRY LEE, BOSTON, MAY 4, 1808, TO BENJAMIN & GEORGE WILLIAMS, BALTIMORE, ON THE PRICES OF EAST INDIA GOODS [1]

On May 24, Henry Lee acknowledged sales of drugs by the Baltimore firm and announced a consignment of "Copal, Tumerick & Lac," also 500 pieces of bandannas to be sold at $6. Removing the embargo would "help coloured goods because they will be wanted for W Indias — I see no relief for coarse white goods — they *never were of so bad a quality* or *so high charg'd*."

The "last Supplement to the Embargo" which made the "Sale of flour . . . no longer possible" was doubtless the Additional Embargo Act of Mar. 12, 1808, which extended the embargo to apply to "inland waters and to exportation by wagon or sleigh," [2] thus making illegal the trade with Canada.

Mess Benj^a. &Geo. Williams   Boston May 4. 1808 —
    Baltimore
        Dear Sirs
            I am in rec^t. of your esteem'd favour of 28th. the Insurance I wish'd to have effected has been done in New york at 6 % — I am not surpris'd that the East India Company refuse having their Inv^o. Selected — perhaps M^r. Tracy who must have arriv'd in your City some days since may be able to purchase some goods at Auction — Calcutta fine Cottons sell here at 85 @ 90 Cents by the bale slowly — Coarse Goods are not worth more than 80 Cents on a long Credit — I sold an Inv^o. at that rate a few days since & w^d. gladly sell more — the

---

1. Jackson-Lee Papers, "Letter Book Finished Decr. 1808."
2. Channing, *op. cit.*, vol. iv, p. 399.

fact is the last Cargoes are purchas'd high & badly Chosen there being too many Goods of a Kind & almost wholly Coarse — if the Embargo continues 12 m^{os}. they will rise but should it be taken off in Octr. the Goods now on hand will be sold in Competition with Goods that will probably Cost 20 % less & of better quality — 7 or 8000 p^s. yellow Nankins 1st. Chop have been sold here this season for Consumption — at 85 Cents & perhaps 10,000 p^s. or 20,000 more can be sold at that rate — the value of what remain on hand (of which the quantity must be very large) must depend on the General opinion of the Continuance of the Embargo & our nonintercourse with Europe — in any event I think they will not be beyond 87 @ 90 Cents & with my apprehensions of the continuance of the Decree's even if the Embargo is off I w^d. not give over 70 Cents — yet as the principal amount of the article is in the hands of Capitalists I do not believe they will fall below 75 Cents. — Blue Nankins are selling in small parcels @ 190 Cts @ 194 Cts — but the demand for Consumption will soon be over & they will decline to 175 or less — Teas [interlineated: are] a Drug — 2 years stock on hand — almost every kind of Merchandize for Consumption has been forc'd up by speculation beyond the price which can now be realized — I have been more convinced of this from witnessing the attempts that have been made some days past to get off Rum &Brandy both these articles are 10.% less than what they have bought up at on speculation — The Sale of flour is no longer possible since the last Supplement to the Embargo — it must decline here to $5 — or less — your Draft on J Allen has been accepted & will without doubt be paid — be pleas'd as soon as convenient to send me on my Acco^t. Current & if there is any thing on hand except of the last shipment sell at Auction

I drew on you yesterday in favour of C. Coolidge &C^o. @ 60Days for $1,600 — I wait for an opp^y. to ship you some Bandannas — in mean time you may venture to Engage 500 p^s. @ 6 $ — of the same quality as those you receive from Mr. Francis —   yours

(Sign'd)   Henry Lee

LETTER FROM HENRY LEE, BOSTON, MAY 7, 1808, TO HAZARD &
CABOT, PHILADELPHIA, ORDERING PURCHASE OF EUROPEAN
GOODS [1]

So much liquor — rum and brandy — had unexpectedly arrived in
the United States that the Lees decided to dispose of their investments in these articles and turn their attention to other objects of
speculation.

Messrs. Hazard &Cabot   Boston 7th. May 1808 —
    Gentlemen
    We wish you to invest for our Account *Ten Thousand Dol-
lars* in Dutch Black Crapes they are manufactured in Swither-
land but being imported from Holland are call'd *Dutch* at
the following prices. — No. 32 @ $42. —
                          No. 34 @   43. —
                          No. 36 @   44. — pr. ps. of 4 packets
a packet contains about 12½ yards — they must not be below
these numbers nor any colour but blacks. —
    you may ivest also half that Amount say $5,000– in Italian
Crapes No. @ $50 — *black* but be certain they are Italian —
there prices are excessive the Germans Cost only $18 @ 22 &
the Italians not more than $25. — we presume you will be able
to get them for less — no time should be lost in purchasing &
you may draw for the payment on us at 60 Days or on longer
time if you can get a credit — Ship them on board the first good
vessel for this port — write immediately what you have done
& by what vessel you shall ship them. — your Obt. St.
                                                    Henry Lee.

LETTER FROM HENRY LEE FOR SELF AND JOSEPH LEE, JR., BOS-
TON, MAY 28, 1808, TO RAM LOCHUN BONARJIA, CALCUTTA,
WITH INSTRUCTIONS FOR A SHIPMENT TO THE UNITED STATES [1]

The vessel by which this letter went presumably sailed with a
license from the President, perhaps under the section of the Additional Embargo Act, Mar. 12, 1808, which allowed vessels to sail in

1. Jackson-Lee Papers, "Letter Book Finished Decr. 1808."

ballast to bring back American property from foreign ports.[2] The Lees were somewhat too optimistic in regard to the Embargo Act, which was taken off not in six but in well over nine months. Consequently the banian did not see his "old friends" in Feb., 1809, though the *Gulliver* had gone to Calcutta and was ready to return to Boston by Sept. 19.[3] The goods were ordered shipped by a vessel which had left the United States before the Embargo Act, lest they be endangered by proceedings for infraction of the law.

The prices of the handkerchiefs are given in rupees per corge, of the taffetas and lungees in rupees per piece.

Ram Lochun Bonarjia   Boston May 28th. 1808 —
   Dear Sir   p(Margaret)
      You will without doubt feel surprised at the long suspension of our intercourse with your place occassioned by an Embargo laid on by this Government to prevent our being engaged in the war which has now become general in Europe — at the moment of its commencement we had a new vessel preparing to sail for Calcutta & we intended also to have sent back the Gulliver — these Vessels are now at the wharves & one of them as soon as the Embargo Ceases (which we expect in 6 months) will sail for Calcutta with our usual stock — Government have prevented our remitting you the balance of account on Gullivers Cargo — we regret that Mr. Cabot accepted that Credit as the interest is almost double what is paid in this Country — The Gullivers Goods are very high charged — yet her Voyage will be tolerably fortunate which we know will afford you pleasure. — Have patience we hope you will yet see in Feby. some of your old friends — send me by any opportunity a price Current of piece Goods, European Goods & Dollars, — we should have made a shipmt. of Specie by this vessel to purchase a few silk Goods but are prevented by our laws. — we request you therefore to ship us by any Vessel that left this Country before the 14th December last 10,000 [interlineated: ten thousand] Rupees in Taffaties @ 9/8 — flag Hdkfs @ 90/ — Lungees @

2. Channing, *op. cit.*, vol. iv, p. 399.
3. Jackson-Lee Papers, "List of Vessels clear'd for America from Calcutta."

8 @ 9 — Band^s. @ 100/ — for the freights you may go as high
as 175 Rupees per Ton. — we shall be disappointed if this order
is not executed — on a former occasion you neglected following
our directions which we never have yet been able to account
for —   yours

(Signd)   Henry Lee for
Self & Jos Lee j^r.

LETTER FROM JOHN TRACY, JR., BOSTON, JULY 16, 1808, TO
HENRY LEE, NEW YORK, WITH A REPORT OF HIS ACTIVITIES [1]

John Tracy, Jr., born at Newburyport, Jan. 2, 1786, was the son of
John Tracy and Margaret Laughton; his father had been the junior
member of the firm of Jackson, Tracy & Tracy. He was thus a
nephew of Mrs. Jonathan Jackson. It may be that the privilege of
managing the Lees' commercial interests during the six weeks of
Henry Lee's absence accrued to him from the fact that a year later,
June 16, 1809, Henry Lee was to marry Mary Jackson, a cousin of
John Tracy, Jr. "Uncle Faris" was William Farris, who seems to
have married a cousin or sister of Mrs. John Tracy, Sr.[2] This letter
is of value in that the writer, reporting on his activities as clerk in the
absence of the heads of the firms, tells more of the minutiae of business than either of the Lees would see fit to mention and more than a
veteran employee would think it necessary to recount.

Dear Sir.   Boston July. 16. 1808
   Yours. of 11th. has come to hand, and the sales of rum [in-
terlineated: were] forwarded M^r. Remsen yesterday no charge
of freight, as advised — the goods you direct to be shipp'd to
New York will be sent by Capt. Canterbury a regular trader,
which vessel sails on Tuesday next. — I have written to Ports-

1. Jackson-Lee Papers, "Letter Book Finished Decr. 1808."
2. Currier, *Ould Newbury*, pp. 579, 584; Currier, *Newburyport*,
vol. ii, pp. 202–203; Lee, Thomas Amory, "The Tracy Family of Newburyport," *Essex Inst. Hist. Colls.*, vol. lvii, p. 67. Mrs. William Farris
(Elizabeth Laughton) was the daughter of Joseph Laughton; Mrs. John
Tracy, Sr. (Margaret Laughton), was "perhaps a daughter of Henry
Laughton." She was undoubtedly closely related to Mrs. Farris, as one of
her daughters was named Elizabeth Farris Tracy, and it is possible that
she was Joseph Laughton's, rather than Henry's, daughter.

mouth & Newbury port on the subject of Duck., the uncertainty of obtaining this article among those merchants who hold Russia goods, is very considerable, and Morrison is still unable to attend to business or I would have gone on. and tried to do something. but as the Cash payments of the Mº are considerable, and some sales may be made; my being at the Store is forwarding your interest perhaps more than to leave — no change whatever has taken place in the market since my last —

I have thot best to accept Mr Walley's offer, as there is considerable money coming due the begining of the mº. the paymᵉ. of the Dft is therefore deferred till 15/18 Aug. on the terms mentioned in my last.

a letter from Robt. Bach &Cº. on the subject of Cochineal, Quicksilver, &C. — I opened, and after enquiries, reply'd to it.

Uncle Faris tells me you have concluded to go on to Philadelphia whh. I am very glad to hear, and hope the weather will not be [interlineated: so] warm[er — stricken through] as to be unpleasant to you — as it is growing much so with us —

The notes of Mr. Swett who from the books, appears to be a good Customer have been punctually attended to, 2 or 3 have fallen due within a short time —

Your brother Jos. endorsed R Cabots draft from Simpson as your Attorney, and it is to his credit — his brother having funds prefers paying the Bonds to having the note Discounted —

I received and acknowledged upon interest from this day of Mr. John B. Greene 2000 $ and he has left town. Mr. Oliver regrets not meeting you at New York.

It will not be so easy for me to advance on goods, as they will be persuaded of obtaining a better bargain from you — I shall however do my best, and wish you to continue yr. present pursuits in confidence thereof

Your friends are all well, and with the priviledge you left me, am still reaping the benefits — which I wish may be reciprocal

Y. H. St.

John Tracy Jr

Mr. Henry Lee
    New York —

LETTER FROM HENRY LEE, BOSTON, OCT. 4, 1808, TO SAMUEL
PRICE, PHILADELPHIA, IN REGARD TO DAMAGED GOODS [1]

The response of the most respectable New England merchants in a
case of this kind is here well brought out: a disclaimer of any responsibility, followed by the expression of a willingness, in view of
the complainant's undoubted honesty, to make an allowance. Perhaps we see here one of the tendencies which developed into the retail maxim, "The customer is always right."

Saml. Price Esq. Phila   Boston Oct 4. 1808.
    Dear Sir
        Your favour of 29.th Ult is received, I certainly did not
intend to sell your Nephew damag'd goods — I tho't he examined them when he made the purchase, as is the custom of
this place; and I presume of yours — Were claims for damages
allowed after goods are transported by water, or even after a
removal from the place in which they are purchased, it would
lead to great difficulties and give opportunity, for exercise of
great injustice to the absent party — in this instance the character of yourself and Nephew does not admit of a suspicion of
this Kind — yet I do not think / according to the usages of
this place you can have any claim on me for damage if however
you are well assured, the damage did not arise to the goods
after their delivery from my store I am willing to make an allowance —and I request you to call on my friends Messrs. Hazard
& Cabot, who will adjust the business no doubt to our mutual
satisfaction — be pleas'd to present my regards to Mr. R. E
Price —

                        I am &c Henry Lee —

    1. Jackson-Lee Papers, "Letter Book Finished Decr. 1808."

LETTER FROM HENRY LEE FOR SELF AND JOSEPH LEE, JR., BOS-
TON, OCT. 6, 1808, TO FREDERICK CABOT, LONDON, WITH AN
ORDER FOR EAST INDIA GOODS [1]

The Lees, dealers in East India goods but cut off by the embargo
from direct contact with Calcutta, had to resort to other devices to
obtain a supply. A letter of similar tenor had gone on Sept. 1.

Frederick Cabot, born in Salem, Feb. 20, 1786, was the son of
Francis Cabot and of Anna Clarke. He is said to have "in 1807
started in business in Boston in company with his own cousin,
Francis Lee," brother of Henry, Joseph, Jr., etc., but evidently did
not carry on his part of the activities of Cabot & Lee entirely in
Boston.[2]

Mr. Frederick Cabot   Boston. Oct°. 6. 1808.
    London
        DearSir,
            Ihave made an arrangement with M^r. Tim°Williams for
a credit on his brother of £3000 stg say *three thousand pounds*
this sum with what Ihave remitted (945£) you will invest in Cottons as before directed — if you cannot buy the Bengal Cottons
at my limits you will not make use of the Credit & only invest
the 945£ in any goods you may think proper — if you buy cottons
I sh^d. prefer having them sent to this place — if you buy other
goods you may ship to this place or New York as may be most
convenient I repeat my request that you w^d. send me the most
particular information you can collect of the prices of Bengal
goods & if possible samples also — it is quite possible they may
be low en°.to make it an object to import a large amount — As
our countrymen are very much disposed to follow each other
particularly persons whose information they might think better
and more extensive than their own I would recommend a con-
cealment of your intentions — If you can buy any Baftas 24
by 1⅞ as low as 6/ sterling no matter how ordinary the quality
provided they are free of damage or any of the other goods I
have ordered one shilling less than my limits you may encrease

1. Jackson-Lee Papers, "Letter Book Finished Decr. 1808."
2. Briggs, *op. cit.*, vol. i, p. 279.

my shipment to 8000 £ taking care to have the full amount insured

Brandy and almost every other article which has been high can now be procured you will not make any purchases for my account — at foot I have noted the prices of Russia goods — it is probable they will not be any lower till we have an inter-course with the Baltic you may ship some for our account if they can be bot to answer.   Yours.

Henry Lee for self and
Jos. Lee Jr

Bengal goods now in demand —

Baftas 25 by 2 ⎫
  do.   24 " 1⅞ ⎬ to Cost 6 to 7/ Stg.

Gurrahs 36 to 2¼ 8/ @ 9/.

Jalalpore Sannas 39 " 2¼   13/ to 14/6

  do   Mamoodies 39 " 2.   12/ —

Meergunge or any other Mamoody of about the quality of the enclosed sample not to cost more than 9/6. 10/ Stg. for 39 by 1⅞ Cubits

Russia Sail cloth 1st. quality 33 prps.

   Ravens do — "   do — 18   "

    do   do   2   — — 16.50

   Broad Diapers   6. "

   Narrow. 4.50 Crash 11 Cts p lb.

   Sheetings 23 pr ps.

LETTER FROM HENRY LEE FOR SELF AND JOSEPH LEE, JR., BOS-TON, OCT. 17, 1808, TO JUDAH TOURO, NEW ORLEANS, IN RE-GARD TO THE POSSIBILITIES OF TRADE WITH THAT PORT [1]

The North Atlantic ports being plentifully supplied with East India goods, and the Continent closed to American vessels through the Orders in Council and the Embargo Act, the Lees were forced to seek a market among ports of the United States with which they had previously had but slight connection. They had already, on Apr. 30, 1808, "made a shipment of Bengal Goods" to New Orleans, con-

1. Jackson-Lee Papers, "Letter Book Finished Decr. 1808."

signed to the supercargo, who had instructions to leave them with the commission house of Kenner & Henderson if he could not sell them, but nothing came of this.

Judah Touro (1775–1854), born in Newport, R. I., settled at New Orleans in 1802, where he later became famous as a philanthropist.[2] Evidently he had already become well known as a merchant, or the Lees would not have selected him as their correspondent when they decided to push the trade with New Orleans.

M^r. Judah Touro   Boston Octr 17 1808
    Sir

    Enclosed you have an Invoice and Bill of Lading of India peice goods and N. E. Rum shipped by me on board the Brig Sally Capt. Richmond consigned to you — The rum I beleive to be of a superiour quality — you will sell it as you may judge most for my interest preferring immediate sales the piece goods are well calculated for yours and the W. I. Markets they are extremely scarce here and have risen within a few weeks 10 or 15 %. the prices they are invoicd are such as I had them at and less than what might be obtain'd was there no Embargo

I have shipd as much with a view of obtaining information as from any other motive and I would thank you in the Sales to note any observations as to the particular Kinds of Bengal goods most wanted in your Country. and the quantities that will generally sell I have constantly on hand a large assortment of those Kind of goods and may find it for my advantage to ship when they are in demand at New Orleans — I leave it to your judment to remit the proceeds either in Merchandize to this place or New York or in good bills — if you remit to New York either in Bills or Merchandize consign to M^r. Peter Remsen — I wish you to write me on the arrival of the Sally and from time to time as you may have any thing to say respecting the Sales &c   I am &c.
                          H. Lee for self
                      and Jos Lee. Junr —

2. Hunt, *op. cit.*, vol. ii, pp. 441–467.

LETTER FROM HENRY LEE, BOSTON, OCT. 19, 1808, TO PETER
REMSEN, NEW YORK, ON PRICES AND THE POLITICAL SITUA-
TION [1]

Late in March, Henry Lee had confidently anticipated that brandy
would reach $2 by October. We now find him deciding to sell what
he can at $1.30–$1.35.

Mr Peter Remsen.   Boston Octr 19. 1808
   Dear Sir.
      I received your favor by mail I am glad you have pur-
chased the Allum I have no doubt it will sell well in course of
some weeks the price is now 6 $. to 6 25/100 or rather it would
readily bring that price if there was any offered
      I have concluded to hold on my Brandy selling what I can
at 130 to 135 cts. the Bayonne is principally sold I have remaining with Mess C. 50 pipes Cette — of my own 120 pipes
of Barcelona and Alicant their is besides mine in this place &
Salem [and — stricken through] about 50 pipes Valentia 100
Barcelona 100 Alicant — 150 Cette and 200 Bayonne — of
Bordeaux and Rochelle there may be about 400 Pipes principally in hands of persons who will not sell unless at very high
prices — Should the French meet with any success in Spain
or should it be apprehended that Madison will attempt to throw
the Country into war with England as is by many expected it
may take a favorable turn and be up to 150 cts again. your
sales of Bandannas have given great satisfaction. it seems
Mess. Stille &Co. & H &Cabot have both sold at 5 75/100. I
would have you hold mine at 6 $. I have no doubt they will
bring that price cannot you sell 200 Ps. Company Bands. at
6 50/100 in nine months to some safe person. interest after 6
Mos. they are certainly well worth the difference — Mr. D L
Pickman asked me to day what Commission you charged in the
sale of Bills of Exchange — I informed him that it was ¼ % or
the same as the Brokers Commission aCargo of teas was sold

      1. Jackson-Lee Papers, "Letter Book Finished Decr. 1808."

to day prices went beyond the expectations of any one I am told there is no Kind of teas that are not plenty. principal quantity in Philadelphia — Since it has become almost certain that we are to have Madison for President — people have become apprehensive that we shall have war with England or that the Embargo will not be rais'd I have no doubt prices of many articles will be considerably affected very shortly.

I want to purchase 15 to 20 Logs Mahogany that will measure 2 feet 6 inches or if possible 3 feet — can they be found in your City   Yours

                                                Henry Lee —

LETTER FROM HENRY LEE FOR SELF AND JOSEPH LEE, JR., BOSTON, NOV. 4, 1808, TO "RAMLOCHEN BANYAN," CALCUTTA, ANNOUNCING A PLAN FOR IMPORTATION OF EAST INDIA GOODS [1]

Although the embargo forbade vessels to leave the United States for foreign ports, there was nothing to prevent foreign vessels, or American vessels which had sailed before the embargo, from bringing goods, not forbidden by the Non-Importation Act, into the United States. The embargo was lifted Mar. 15, 1809, a little over four months after the date of this letter.

"Ramlochen" was probably the banian Ram Lochun Bonarjia.

Ramlochen Banyan.   Boston Nov⁰ 4, 1808
Dear Sir,   Mr. Oliver who will deliver you this. and with whom you are acquainted, is going out with commercial views to your place — He is entrusted with full authorities to act for us in purchasing either peice goods, or others articles or to pursue such speculations as he may think will be for our advantage and we pray you to render him such services and to give him such advantages; as you would feel dispos'd to render to [others — stricken through interlineated: either] of us where we in calcutta. —

It is [possible — stricken through] probable Mr — Oliver will be desirous of receiving a considerable advance from you to promote our interest and should you enter into his views we

1. Jackson-Lee Papers, "Letter Book Finished Decr. 1808."

engage to be held responsible for whatever engagments he may mak with you.

Sence ours of 28th. May. Per margarett from New york we have yours of 30th. april per Traveller. We hope Mr. Heard follow'd our directions and purchased Mr. Olivers and our Investements of you, The embargo continues the most sanguine expectations are entertain'd however of its removal as soon as congress assemble which [soon tak — stricken through] will very soon take place The Gulliver and a new vessel will be ready to sail for Calcutta within seventy two hours after permission is granted by our government and I hope Mr. Oliver will be able to [come out — stricken through] concert measures to Purchase both their cargoes of you, We shall remit the balance of our account By Mr. Robert Cabot who will come out in one of our vessels.

The William is expected evry moment when we promise ourselvs the pleasure of Hearing from you.

We remain your friends Henery Lee for
self & Joseph Lee jr

LETTER FROM HENRY LEE, BOSTON, NOV. 21, 1808, TO WILLIAM OLIVER, [PRESENT], WITH INSTRUCTIONS FOR A VOYAGE [1]

The original intention in sending William Oliver to England was that he should proceed thence to India or, failing that, should purchase East India goods in England. In this letter Henry Lee at last prophesied, after many failures, the exact time at which the embargo would be lifted.

Mr. Wm Oliver   Boston Novr 21st 1808
    Sir

If from any cause you should determine to leave the Schooner & proceed for England Iwish you in your arrival to find Mr Frederick Cabot — from him you can learn the prices of India goods there perhaps you may consider it to be the interest of the concern'd to invest the amount you may be able to raise in English, India or any other goods you may find in

1. Jackson-Lee Papers, "Letter Book Finished Decr. 1808."

London rather than proceed on to India in which case you can remain in England — if you   to go on & [remain in England — stricken through] you can procure permission to go out in care of the E. I Company ships I wish you to raise ten thousand pounds Sterling in as much money as you can & I will remit to your order as early as possible I should think this mode of going better than any other less expensive probably less risk & more expeditious — if however you canfind a vessel well fitted that will probably sail fast & has American papers you may purchase and proceed in her — I rely however very strongly upon your being able to procure a passage in an Indiaman — perhaps you may find some house in London willing to join you in the speculation upon terms that will be advantagious at any rate you may get letters that will be of use — I cannot expect a war between this Country & England neither do I believe the Embargo will be taken off till March next should you fail in the Primary object in your voyage to England — it may be expediant to make a voyage to some port of the Continent — say to Spain. Portagal, Italy & c —I shall write you by the vessels to go to England more paticularly

Yours &c

LETTER FROM HENRY LEE, BOSTON, DEC. 4, 1808, TO FREDERICK CABOT, LONDON, WITH INSTRUCTIONS FOR PURCHASE IN ENGLAND [1]

Although the letter book does not end till Dec. 31, the letters which follow add little to our knowledge of the commercial situation at the end of 1808.

Nearly all the letters in this volume are signed by Henry Lee for himself or for himself and brother.

Mr. Frederick Cabot /by Constance/. Boston Dece. 4. 1808
    London
        DearSir.
            I wrote you yesterday to go per Packet which will sail from New York 7 th inst. copy of which is enclosed Should you

---

1. Jackson-Lee Papers, "Letter Book Finished Decr. 1808."

not succeed in purchasing Bengal goods I wish you to invest
1000 £ in silk goods mentioned in the inclosed memorandum and
in English or Italian Sewing silks those best suited to our market
and ship to the house of Messrs. Storrow and Brown in Canada
where they can be sold to a great profit my brother F informs
me Cotton has fallen and the Calicoes have advanced only five
per Cent if so it is probable low pric'd prints may be the best
article to import whatever you buy for me let it be cheap and
ordinary I believe they will give more profit than good goods
particularly as I calculate upon selling at Auction I wish you
to make use of the credit of 3000 £ on Mr. Williams I have no
doubt goods will pay the ensuing season. a very handsome advance there are many goods among which are prints that the
Importers will not sell at 75 %. Should a Non-intercourse act
be passed they certainly will advance and if the Embargo is
removed there will not be eno. for the encreas'd demand which
there will be on the revival of commerce. Should you think it
expedient you may encrease our purchases to 20,000 £ say
Twenty thousand pounds and either draw on us or request Mr.
Williams to advance which without doubt he will do you
despositing with him Policy of Insurance and consigning the
goods to Timothy Williams here, or Mr. Peter Remsen New
York,

The Non Intercourse Act is still before Congress. &c —

                    Yours   Henry Lee

LETTER FROM HENRY LEE, BOSTON, JULY 25, 1809, TO JOHN
BROMFIELD, JR., CANTON, ANNOUNCING RENEWAL OF NON-
INTERCOURSE WITH GREAT BRITAIN [1]

In the Lee letter books there occurs an unfortunate gap of more
than 19 months, covering the entire year of 1809 and to Aug. 19
in 1810. There are, however, in existence other scattering letters
which contain information upon Lee business activities, most of these
letters being either from John Bromfield to Henry Lee or vice versa.

The Non-Intercourse Act of Mar. 1, 1809, raised the embargo after
Mar. 15, except as to Great Britain and France, and interdicted both

1. John Bromfield Papers.

the importation of goods from those countries and the entrance of vessels sailing under their flags, or owned in whole or part by their citizens, into United States waters.

With the repeal of the embargo, American foreign trade, which had been suspended for more than a year, commenced to revive, and American vessels were once more permitted to clear for all ports save those belonging to Great Britain or France. Merchants specializing in trade with the East Indies dispatched their vessels to such ports as Canton and Sumatra; Calcutta, Madras, and other ports belonging to Great Britain were still under the ban.

The Lees, prior to the embargo, had specialized in the trade with Calcutta, and it was difficult for them to turn their attention to other less familiar centers of commerce. Nevertheless, for the first time in their commercial history, they began in a limited way to trade with Canton. On Apr. 17, 1809, Henry Lee shipped by the *Atahualpa*, commanded by William Sturgis,[2] John Bromfield supercargo, $2,000 to be invested half in yellow nankeens "@ forty five cents pr pᶳ. & one half in China Hdkfs."[3] On Apr. 13, Bromfield had bought 10,000 Spanish dollars from Henry Lee, paying a premium of 1½%.[4]

But while non-intercourse had forced Henry Lee and his associates to turn a portion of their funds and interest in the direction of Canton, it had not deprived them of all hope that they might still be able somehow soon to do business with Calcutta despite governmental restrictions. This hope was not without basis, for negotiations were then in progress between David M. Erskine, British minister at Washington, and President Madison, having as their aim the renewal of mutual commercial intercourse between the two countries. As a result of these negotiations, Madison, on Apr. 19, 1809, issued a proclamation renewing trade with Great Britain on June 10. This proclamation naturally caused a rush of American vessels to get to sea, avowedly clearing for some non-British port since the trade with Great Britain was not yet formally open, but actually intending to get to some British port so as to be ready to clear for the United

2. Jackson-Lee Papers, "Memoranda, Prices Current E. I. Goods — Imports & Exports &c &c."

3. John Bromfield Papers, Henry Lee, Boston, Apr. 14, 1809, to John Bromfield, Jr., Canton.

4. *Ibid.*, bill of sale from Donald Morrison for Henry Lee to John Bromfield, Apr. 13, 1809.

States with a cargo of British goods as soon as possible after June 10. Between Apr. 19 and June 10 at least a dozen United States vessels cleared for ports in Sumatra and Burma, actually intending to take a return cargo from some British port in India.[5]

A vessel belonging to Joseph Lee, Jr., Henry Lee, and Patrick Tracy Jackson, the *Gulliver*, on Mar. 28, 1809, three weeks before the proclamation, "saild . . . for Calcutta via Sumatra with $70,000." [6] The owners were doubtless aware of the negotiations and may have decided to chance a vessel to Calcutta, on the possibility that non-intercourse would shortly be raised. Should the negotiations prove abortive, and Henry Lee described their successful conclusion as "a most important and to me unexpected event," [7] there would be a choice of several possibilities. The captain might be notified of the situation in time actually to take a cargo at Sumatra, or perhaps he might even load wholly or partially at Calcutta, despite the Non-Intercourse Act. British customs officials, realizing that it was to the interest of Great Britain to maintain an exchange of commodities with the United States, sometimes assisted law-breaking American captains to conceal the origin of their return cargoes; an illegal cargo might even be smuggled into the United States. In any case the funds sent in the *Gulliver* were unusually small, which indicates a desire on the part of the owners not to risk too much in so uncertain a voyage. Fortunately, however, the *Gulliver's* captain did not find it necessary to circumvent the Non-Intercourse Act in any of the above ways. The daring of the *Gulliver's* owners was rewarded by the fact that their vessel (which cleared from Calcutta, Sept. 19, 1809) was the second in nearly six months to leave that port for the United States and the first for Boston in over fifteen months.[8]

On May 30, 1809, the month after the proclamation announcing the prospective end of non-intercourse, the *Gipsy*, another vessel

5. Jackson-Lee Papers, "Memoranda, Prices Current E. I. Goods — Imports & Exports &c &c;" *ibid.*, "List of vessels clear'd for America from Calcutta."

6. John Bromfield Papers, part of letter from Henry Lee, Boston, Apr., 1809, to John Bromfield, Jr., Canton; *Columbian Centinel*, Mar. 22, 1809.

7. *Ibid.*, Henry Lee, Boston, May 4, 1809, to John Bromfield, Jr., Canton.

8. Jackson-Lee Papers, "List of vessels clear'd for America from Calcutta."

owned by the Lees and P. T. Jackson, sailed from Boston for Pegu in Burma, but duly cleared from Calcutta, Nov. 1, 1809.[9]

Unfortunately, the British government disavowed the actions of its minister at Washington, and President Madison was consequently forced to resume non-intercourse against Great Britain by a proclamation of Aug. 9, 1809. The inevitability of this result was, however, known as early as the date of the letter below.

The short-lived arrangement with Great Britain had convinced many shipowners that France as well would be forced to make terms with the United States. According to a letter of May 27, 1809, "200 vessels have (at least) gone to Holland & other countries under her controul with very valuable cargoes." [10]

Mr John Bromfield Junr.   Boston. July. 25th. 1809.

Dear Sir,

In compliance with your request rather than any expectation of affording you pleasure or information — I avail myself of the politness of M^r. Dorr to write & send you a bundle of newspapers — the latter will contain all the political news both domestic & foreign — You will See on reference to the newspapers that the English Minister has disavow'd the — Settlement made by M^r. Erskine — the disappointment here is great — people are very angry & talk of Non Intercourse war &c — yet intelligent men are of opinion that it will not occassion a war between the two countries tho' it is now generally believ'd that the orders in Council will not be withdrawn — The new Minister M^r. Jackson has not arriv'd 'till then it is impossible to imagine what measures our gov^t. will take — at present it has not affected prices of Merchandize underwritters demand more premium upon large risks — The vessels thathave sail'd for France, Italy, Holland, Denmark, Russia &c have not been heard from except one in france she was seiz'd & fate left to the decision of the Emp^r. — The Danes have captur'd 7 &

9. *Ibid.*, "Memoranda, Prices Current E. I. Goods — Imports & Exports &c &c;" *ibid.*, "List of vessels clear'd for America from Calcutta."

10. John Bromfield Papers, Henry Lee, Boston, May 27, 1809, to John Bromfield, Jr., Canton.

it is fear'd they may be condemn'd — Should the property be admitted into Europe generally there will be a rise in the various products in our market suited to European markets — onthe other hand sh^d. they be refus'd there will not be any sale 'till commerce is again free — the exports have been great, but there is still an immense stock in hand & the next year's importation will be very great. — The following are the prices of China goods — but small sales only can be made — the holders are hoping for a demand for exportation — if there sh^d. not be any — they must fall —

Hyson Tea   110 @ 112 cts
Do Skin do — 75 @   77
Souchong —   65 @   67
Bohea —   40 —
Short yellow Nankins   80¢. ⌠ I am of opinion they will keep
    Blue —   1.90 ⌡ to these prices & if any exportation they will be higher — If you buy Nankins let them all be second chop if you can have the fair difference — We have not yet rec^d. any silks from Italy & it is very uncertain whether we shall have any — I am inclin'd to think they will be the safest articles for the bulk of your shipment — I put down Nutmegs in your Mem^o. for returns there has been a very great supply from England which has reduc'd the price from 10$ to $4 @ $5 for the best — Do not buy over $2.50 for the best or $1— for ordinary — The [only — stricken through] voyages that have terminated since the raising ofthe Embargo prove losing — The W. I. Islands are sinking under the weight of American produce — Cotton, ashes &c are lower in England than they have been for many years — At foot I have noted the prices of goods which may gratify your curiosity if nothing more — I inform'd you in my former letters that the Meridian's Cargo was sold — your case is not yet decided with Underwritters — my impression is that you will not losse much if it goes against you — Mess Tim^o. Williams & Co have sent off a vessel to Holland loaded with ashes M^r. Greene is in her she will probably discharge in England — They have also made

ashipment of Coffee to Holland — I send you with this a letter from your sister & remain

Yours
HLee

Sugars Hav^a. White	$12	Ashes $170 —	
Browns	8.50	Cotton 12 @ 13	
Green Coffee —	22¢	Rice — 3.—	
ordinary —	20	Tobacco — 5 —	
Brandy Spanish	100	Flour 6.50	
Rum Jam^a.	105	Wheat 125¢ @ 150¢.	
S^t. Croix —	45		
Sherry wine	120		
Salt $2 @ 3 phh^d —			
Russia goods no sales held — high —			
Bengal Indigo $1.75 @ $2 —			

[Endorsed]
Henry Lee.
Boston
25 July 1809.

LETTER FROM HENRY LEE, BOSTON, AUG. 29, 1809, TO JOHN BROMFIELD, JR., CANTON, IN REGARD TO RESULTS OF RENEWAL OF NON-INTERCOURSE [1]

The merchants who had already sent vessels to British ports were rather pleased than otherwise by the revival of non-intercourse, because it reduced competition in marketing their goods.

Dear Sir,   Boston. August. 29th. 1809.
    Annex'd you have a copy of my last p^r. Rapid — this goes by the Brig Ganges intended at first for Calcutta — but prevented by renewal of Non Intercourse with England an event to me wholly unexpected — many are of opinion that this act was a necessary consequence of Mr Erskine's agreement not being ratify'd &that President was oblig'd to issue his proclamation — the merchants do not appear to be at all displeas'd — indeed it rather aids them than otherwise particularly all who have made

    1. John Bromfield Papers.

shipments to England &her colonies — the new envoy is daily
expected it is not tho't he can have any new propositions to
offer & since it is understood the English Gov^t. will not deviate
from theirsystem no one can conjecture how we are to have a
settlement. The vessels that have sail'd for countries under the
controul of France have all been seiz'd except afew to Tonnin-
gen — the only hope that now remains of free & safe trade to
the Continent — is the defeat of Buonaparte by the Arch Duke
— opinions are quite balanc'd as to the issue of the wars —
God grant Austria may prevail —
It is probable the Non Intercourse Law may rather injure the
Canton voyages than otherwise — by diverting a portion of the
capital destin'd to other parts — I am quite confident that *silks*
will be the safest and most profitable article — the supplies
formerly from Italy & France were very great — We have not
rec^d. a piece since you left us & for 12 months before — the
Derby that arriv'd few days since bro't 60 @ 100 cases for
which many applications have been made & one thro' me —
they will sell at a great advance of *Teas* I think Hyson & Hyson
Skin will do the best but they must all be low — at present
they sell in small quantities at the following prices —

Hyson   110¢   Cassia 40¢ @ 45¢ — very scarce
Skin — 80 @ 85   Short yellow nankins no sales —
Souchong   70   Blue — 185 @ 190 do —
Bohea —   45   Long yellow no demand I have but
an indifferent opinion of nankins unless we can go to the Continent — that w^d. raise them to 85 cts or higher unless the
quantity shipp^d is great — If you remain behind after the Ships
have left I sh^d advise you to purchase for your own acc^t. a quantity of such articles particularly silks & nankins as fall the
lowest you will have an opportunity of selling or shipping next
year — as there will be a great many ships out — if we have
no war — I must congratulate you on the wise determination
you made when you resolv'd upon your present voyage — had
you gone to Europe or any other quarter your prospects w^d
not have been so fair as they now are for profit — besides the
vexation in being captur'd or detain'd — I think you may in-

dulge a reasonable expectation that your voyage will prove under all circumstances a fortunate one for you if not for your owners — I have written W^m. Oliver [interlineated: & RCabot] by this conveyance but as it is possible the letter may never reach them — I w^d. thank you to write RC to care of Ram Lochun Bonarjia Calcutta — inform him of the Non Intercourse & that it is the wish of [the — stricken through] his [own — stricken through] concern — that he & Mr Oliver sh^d. purchase up goods when they have fallen — as they no doubt will when it is known that no more americans can go to Calcutta — please to send Triplicates &say that I have written via England & Madeira — I have given your friends notice of this opp'y — they will no doubt write — if not they are well — I have not engaged in any voyages but to Calcutta — All most all kinds of Merchandise except German French & Italian goods are very abundant and low — I have nothing more to add but that I remain with esteem

Yours —
HLee

P S. Septr 1st. 1809. I enclose you a letter from your family nothing new —

> [Endorsed]
> Henry Lee.
> Boston
> 25th July & 29th. August
> 1809.

LETTER FROM JOHN BROMFIELD, JR., CANTON, NOV. 27, 1809, TO HENRY LEE, BOSTON, WITH A CONSIGNMENT OF SILKS [1]

The *Atahualpa* (Theodore Lyman, Sr., owner; William Sturgis, master; John Bromfield, supercargo), which cleared from Boston, Apr. 17, 1809, arrived at Canton, Sept. 11.[2] The voyage had not been without incident, for on the morning of Aug. 22, while lying about seven miles off Macao, the ship's company, which was depleted by the absence of the first officer with a boat's crew, had been forced

1. John Bromfield Papers.
2. Jackson-Lee Papers, "Memoranda, Prices Current E. I. Goods — Imports & Exports &c &c."

to beat off an attack "by twenty-two large Ladrone junks, some of
them twice the tonnage of the ship." In this action both the captain
and the supercargo highly distinguished themselves for coolness and
courage.[3]

When the *Atahualpa* sailed for the United States, Dec. 2, 1809,
among the invoices shipped by her were the silks mentioned below,
purchased instead of nankeens because of the latter's high price, and
20 boxes of nankeens and 5 of silks on Bromfield's own account, to
be sold by Henry Lee. Bromfield himself remained behind as a
factor for the owner of the *Atahualpa*.

Canton 27th Novr. 1809.

Mr. Henry Lee,
    Dear Sir

The william being upon the verge of departure, I have time
only to confirm my respects of 7th & 20th instants, & to say that
no material change has taken place in this Market — The
Atahualpa is loaded & will be ready for sea Tomorrow or the
day afterward — I enclose duplicate [Invoice & — stricken
through] Bill Lading of the Goods shipped by her for your account, [interlineated: As p note at foot] which hope [inter-
lineated: will] reach you in Safety. I remain Sir your mo
obt.Servant

J.Bromfield.

HL
1 @ 7 . 7 Boxes Contg
      45 ps Blk Sinchaws   16.25   731.25
      80 ps Blk & cold Crape 7.50   600 —
      86 ps. Blk & chkd Hkfs 7.75   666.50
                                                ———————
                                                1997.75
                        Certificates   2
                                                ———————
                        Dolls   1999.75

[Endorsed]
Letters to Henry Lee — Copies —
27th & 28th Novr. & 1th & 7th Decemr. 1809.
Wrote H. Lee under date of
7th & 20th Novr.

3. Hunt, *op. cit.*, vol. ii, pp. 475–476, 485–487, 493.

LETTER FROM JOHN BROMFIELD, JR., CANTON, JAN. 12, 1810, TO HENRY LEE, BOSTON, WITH ACCOUNT OF PRICES [1]

John Bromfield, from about the time of the *Atahualpa's* departure from Canton, frequently wrote Henry Lee concerning the prices in Canton of merchandise, both imports and exports. The price of short yellow nankeens ranged from $50 per bale of 100 pieces late in Nov., 1809, to $53 near the middle of December; late in November blue nankeens were $124, company $92, superior company $107. Sinchaws (silks) early in December were $15 per piece. Hyson tea was "49 Tales" per picul, a tale being 6s. 8d. stg. and a picul 133 1/3 lb.[2] Among goods for which there was a market in China was cotton — South Carolina upland cotton @ "13 @ 13½ Tales p picul" or "about 13 Cents here p American lb, all Chinese charges in Canton deducted." "Bombay & Bengal Cotton" would "not bring above 1 Cent plb more." Ginseng of good quality, if "put on board at 30 @ 33 Cents plb," would be "a safe article." These prices should be compared to those below; a decline will be seen. The reason for the decline lay in international trade restrictions. On Dec. 1, 1809, Bromfield had written "if the ports of the Continent should not be opened I think they [nankeens] Can hardly pay any profit." Similarly, on Dec. 7, he wrote: "The Dromo has just arrived, I do not know what kind of a Voyage she is likely to make, but believe little more than a saving one, the news of a peace between England & Spain having reduced the prices of Goods very materially on all parts of the Spanish Coast." The *Dromo*, formerly owned by the Lees, was engaged in illicit trade with Spanish possessions in South America.[3] The "peace between England & Spain" doubtless refers to the alliance between England and the popular movement against Napoleon. On Dec. 1, 1809, Bromfield received word of the supposed settlement between England and the United States and on Dec. 12 he mentioned "the abridgment of the orders of Council, whereby some North-Sea & the Baltic ports are opened, as well as some Mediterranean ones — this helps

1. John Bromfield Papers.
2. *The Oriental Navigator* (Philadelphia, 1801), p. 565; Milburn, *op. cit.*, vol. ii, pp. 471–472.
3. Little, George, *Life on the Ocean* (Boston, 1844), pp. 27–28, 33, 54–181.

our Stay in some particulars." [4] But the Order in Council of Apr. 26, 1809, reduced the prospects of an outlet for China goods and lowered their prices.

Canton 12th Jany 1810

Mr Henry Lee
   Dear Sir
   I wrote you under date of 12th Ultimo, and am just favoured with yours of 25 July p the Rapid, with enclosure &newspapers; for all of which am muchobliged — I lament to learn that the prospects we had of a free trade are nearly obscured & that markets should be so low, [should — stricken through interlineated: if] no European ports [be — stricken through interlineated: are] opened before this reaches you I presume Canton Goods must suffer a still greater depression in our market, as the quantity shipped this year will undoubtedly equal that of any former one, already we have had 35 Sail american Ships & several are yet to come. Should many more arrive they will hardly be able to procure Green or Black Teas of very good quality, as the gathering ofboth has been rather short this Year — [as — stricken through] the Eng: Compy Ships are [interlineated: now] nearly loadded, the prices have [if any rather — stricken through interlineated: somewhat] declined & may [now —stricken through] be [said at — stricken through] quoted Hyson 50 Tales. Young Hyson 42. Hyson Skin 27 — Souchong 28 @ 33 — Campoi 25 @ 26 — Congo 23 @ 24 & Bohea 11 @ [14 — stricken through] Tales. Short Yellow Nankins may be bought at about 47½ $ Compy do 84. Superior Compy 103. and first Chop Blue nankins at 120 $ — I observe your note on Nutmegs, I have not shipped any, they might have been bot on arrival here at 1¾ @ 2$ plb of good quality, but upon the whole do not regret having omitted them, as some have gone from hence direct to America and all that remined in the Market [bot up — stricken through inter-

   4. John Bromfield Papers, John Bromfield, Jr., Canton, Nov. 28, Dec. 1, 7, 12, 1809, to Henry Lee, Boston.

lineated: purchased] for the English Ships, part of which may probably find their way to our country also.

If no silks should arrive with you from france & Italy, I have [some — stricken through interlineated: yet] reason to hope your investment shipped by the Atahualpa, may prove in some measure profitable.

In my last, of which Copy herewith, I [quot — stricken through] quoted you the probable price of Cotton according to this year's Sales. —

I now find it has much fallen with you, as the [interlineated: Rapid] has some on board, which is said to cost [only — stricken through] but about 10 Cents. Should large quantities be shipped the [next present — stricken through interlineated: ensuing] year I do not think it would bring 13 Tales, as the quantity from Bengal &Bombay has been unusually small this [year — stricken through interlineated: Season.] [& will probably be greater the next — stricken through] I cannot close without again testifying to you my sincere thanks for [the — stricken through interlineated: your] kindness [you have shown — stricken through] in writing me, as I have received no letters but from you — let me ask a Continuance of your favors.   I remain DearSir

Your mo ob^{t}Servant

NB wrote H. L. 12th Feb^y.

RESPONDENTIA BOND FROM JOSEPH LEE, JR., HENRY LEE, AND PATRICK TRACY JACKSON, BOSTON, MAY 11, 1810, TO SAMUEL PICKERING GARDNER FOR PAYMENT OF A LOAN UPON THE CARGO OF THE GIPSY [1]

A favorite device of merchants who wished to load a vessel and who themselves did not possess adequate funds was to induce others to lend them money on respondentia; this method was one of simultaneously financing and insuring a part of the cargo, for if the vessel's lading were lost nothing was due to the lender, while if the returns arrived safely only the principal of the loan with specified increment

1. Jackson-Lee Papers.

was to be paid. In the case below the increment amounted to 24½%
on the original plan. If the borrowers were able to utilize the sum
for the full term of twenty-four months, the increment would amount
to only about what would be normal interest in Calcutta, but it is unlikely that more than a year would elapse beween the date of the
bond and the return of the vessel. As a matter of fact, the *Gipsy* returned directly to the United States from Calcutta, arriving about the
last of Feb., 1811. Thus the bond with increment became due within
a year from date.

Know all men by these presents that we Joseph Lee jun^r,
Henry Lee, & Patrick Tracy Jackson all of Boston in the Com-
monwealth of Massachusetts, merchants, are holden & stand
firmly bound & obliged unto Samuel Pickering Gardner of said
Boston merchant in the full & just sum of Ten thousand dollars
to be paid unto the said Samuel, his Executors, administrators
or assigns to the which payment well & truly to be made we
bind ourselves our heirs, executors & administrators firmly by
the presents witness our hands & seals. — Dated the Eleventh
day of may in the year of our Lord one thousand eight hundred
& ten. —

The condition of this obligation is such that whereas the
above named Samuel hath on the day of date above written lent
unto the above bound, Joseph, Henry & Patrick the sum of
Five thousand silver dollars, upon, specie, merchandise &
effects, laden, or to be laden on board the brig called the Gipsy
— Pulsifer master. — Now if the said brig shall with all convenient speed proceed to Calcutta, & from thence back to the
port of discharge of the said brig in the United States without
deviation, or any unnecessary delay, the dangers of the seas
excepted, and if the said Joseph Henry & Patrick, their Executors or administrators do or shall within sixty days after the
said brig shall be arrived at her port of discharge within the
United States from the voyage aforesaid, or at the end of
twenty four calendar months from the day of the date above
written (which of said times shall first & next happen) well &
truly pay or cause to be paid unto the said Samuel, his executors
administrators or assigns the sum of Six thousand, two hundred

& twenty five dollars. — Or if in the aforesaid voyage & within the aforesaid twenty four calendar months to be accounted as aforesaid, an utter loss of the specie, which the said Joseph, Henry & Patrick have sent out in said brig from the united States; and all other the merchandise & effects which they shall have acquired during said voyage, shall either by fire, enemies, danger of the seas or other casualties such as are commonly insured against unavoidably happen — or if a partial loss on the said specie merchandise & effects, from any of the perrils aforesaid should unavoidably happen, and to an amount for which insurers would be answerable. And if the said Joseph, Henry & Patrick, their Executors, or administrators, pay or cause to be paid unto the said Samuel his Executors, Administrators or Assigns such a just proportional part of the said sum of six thousand two hundred & twenty five dollars, as the whole amount of the said specie, merchandise & effects, may bear to the whole amount of the partial loss on the same. Then the within written obligation to be void & of no effect or else to stand in full force & virtue.

Signed sealed & delivered ⎫   Jos Leejunʳ
in presence of   ⎬   HenryLee
Francis C Lowell   ⎭   P. T. Jackson

[Endorsed] Respondentia bond

LETTER FROM HENRY LEE, BOSTON, AUG. 21, 1810, TO WILLIAM OLIVER, LIVERPOOL, IN REGARD TO TRADE WITH CALCUTTA [1]

There is, as has been mentioned, an unfortunate gap in the Lee letter books between Dec., 1808, and Aug. 19, 1810, a period of nearly twenty months during which many events of the utmost significance to commercial life took place. The Enforcement Act, Jan. 9, 1809, had prescribed severe penalties for violation of the Embargo Act of Dec. 22, 1807, but the Non-Intercourse Act, Mar. 1, 1809, had raised the embargo except as to Great Britain and France and repealed the Non-Importation Act, while both public and private vessels of Great Britain and France were forbidden the waters of the United States;

1. Jackson-Lee Papers, "Letter Book," Aug. 19, 1810–May 30, 1811.

BOSTON, 1810

this act was to end with the next session of Congress. On Apr. 19, 1809, accepting the assurance of the British minister that after June 10 the British Orders in Council would be withdrawn as respects the United States, President Madison had issued a proclamation renewing trade with Great Britain after that date, but the minister had exceeded his instructions and, after a brief revival of trade with Great Britain, new Orders in Council, "declaring a blockade from the River Ems to northern Spain and of the Mediterranean ports of France and northern Italy," forced Madison to revive non-intercourse. On May 1, 1810, "Macon's Bill No. 2" substituted for the Non-Intercourse Act, Mar. 1, 1809, an interdiction of the waters of the United States to British and French armed vessels and provided that should either Great Britain or France cease to restrict the neutral commerce of the United States, and should the other belligerent, within three months, not follow her example, the President should revive the Non-Intercourse Act against the latter nation; while the restrictions against the nation modifying her decrees should cease from the date of the President's proclamation announcing said modification. In the meantime, Napoleon, enraged by the Non-Intercourse Act of Mar. 1, 1809, which banned the waters of the United States to public vessels of France as well as of Great Britain, had by the "Rambouillet" Decree of Mar. 23, 1810, ordered all United States vessels entering French ports after May 20, 1809, to be seized and sold. In the summer of 1810, then, trade with the world was free to United States vessels as far as any law of the United States was concerned, but was nevertheless greatly restricted by the British Orders in Council and by Napoleon's punitive decree that American vessels entering French ports should be confiscated. Despite these serious restrictions, however, the period following the repeal of the embargo was one of great activity in American commerce,[2] something of the character of which will be developed in the letters which follow.

The letter immediately below reveals the Lees as still intensely interested in the trade with the East Indies. As soon as the embargo had been raised, two brigs, the *Gulliver*, 247 t., and a new vessel, the *Gipsy*, 283 t., had sailed for Calcutta, whence they were ready to clear under the command of C. Dutton and R. I. Linzee on Sept. 19 and Nov. 1, 1809, respectively, with the usual cargo of cottons, sugar,

2. Channing, *op. cit.*, vol. iv, pp. 400–413, 426–427; Morison, *op. cit.*, pp. 192–194.

drugs, goat skins, etc. The *Gulliver* seems to have been the first vessel from Boston to leave the United States after the lifting of the
embargo, and the second from any United States port to sail from
Calcutta; [3] her cargo, shipped by Robert Cabot as supercargo, was
invoiced at only sicca rupees 135,380, 4 annas, 3 pice. William Oliver,
however, who had gone out as supercargo on one of the Lee vessels,
had in addition, on Oct. 6, 1809, made a large shipment on the *Sally
Ann* of piece goods, invoiced at sicca rupees 246,910, 5 annas, 5 pice,
and indigo, shellac, gunny sacks, and pepper, invoiced at sicca rupees
37,677, 2 annas, 9 pice. William Oliver and Robert Cabot, acting
jointly as supercargoes for the *Gipsy*, shipped on her, Nov. 1, 1810,
a miscellaneous cargo of piece goods, sugar, spices, drugs, gums,
gunny bags, twine, etc., invoiced at sicca rupees 22,115, 13 annas,
1 pice.[4] At the time of this letter the Lees were actively engaged in
East India voyages in the same two vessels. The *Gipsy* had already
returned to Calcutta with a cargo of iron hoops, port wine, corks,
gin, bottles, fish, glassware, ale, demijohns, pipe-staves, cheese, tables,
tartar, saffron, and lignum-vitae, which Robert Cabot sold for sicca
rupees 31,391, 7 annas, 4 pice, net.[5] The revival of the Non-Intercourse Act in Aug., 1809, had caused Robert Cabot to anticipate a
fall in the price of goods in India, as restricting the re-exportation
of goods sent to the United States; but the presence of the *Euphrates*,
which sailed from Calcutta for New York, Apr. 21, 1810, with large
quantities of piece goods, temporarily kept up the price. Doubtless
Robert Cabot was later enabled to load the *Gipsy* at a low rate, for
nearly five months elapsed between the clearing from Calcutta of the
last ship sailing in the spring and the departure of the *Gipsy*, Oct.
10, 1810.[6] In the meantime everything was being done to facilitate
the loading of the *Gulliver*, which was making the voyage to India
by way of Liverpool whence she was expected to "sail for Calcutta
about 15 Sept[r] to 1 Oct[r]. with Bottles, Pale Ale & Glass Ware." [7]
William Oliver had apparently gone on the *Gulliver*; in England he
was to attempt to interest a "M[r] Richards" in the voyage in order to

3. Jackson-Lee Papers, "List of Vessels clear'd for America from Calcutta."

4. *Ibid.*, "Invoices," 1799–1812.

5. *Ibid.*, "Foreign Sales on acc[t]. of J. & H. Lee from 1803 to 1810. — "

6. *Ibid.*, "List of Vessels clear'd for America from Calcutta."

7. *Ibid.*, "Letter Book," Aug. 19, 1810–May 30, 1811, H. Lee, Boston,
Sept. 4, 1810, to George Lee and Joseph Hall, Jr., Calcutta.

get a credit from the Barings, and was also to obtain some funds from Henry Higginson, to whom Henry Lee had written the same day; the letter to Higginson reveals that those interested in the *Gulliver* were Joseph Lee, Jr., Henry Lee, and the latter's brother-in-law, P. T. Jackson. It was also hoped that some of the goods purchased for the *Gipsy* would be left over and could be used for loading the *Gulliver*. George Lee and Joseph Hall, Jr., had, apparently, gone out in the *Gipsy* for the purpose of having a loading ready for the *Gulliver* when she should arrive at Calcutta. How Henry Lee expected, even by these measures, so to expedite the *Gulliver's* voyage that she would reach Boston before both the *Reaper* and the *Caravan* is hard to see when we consider that the latter vessel actually left Calcutta, Dec. 20, 1810, or only a couple of months later than the *Gulliver* was supposed to leave Liverpool on her outward voyage; to be sure, the *Gulliver* did get away from Calcutta, Mar. 9, 1811, only a few days after the *Reaper,* which sailed Feb. 26.[8] The identity of the "Mr Stewart" against whom the Lee agents in Calcutta were warned is unknown; his first name was Thomas and, in the Lees' opinion, his intentions were always the worst. This whole letter is fairly charged with the enthusiastic determination of the Lees and their associates to push the India trade to the limit, now that they were no longer hampered by restrictive laws passed by their own government.

Boston August 21, 1810

Mr William Oliver   origl. per Brig Standard
    Liverpool
    Since my last to you of the 16th. inst. I have letters from Calcutta down to 26, March — Mr Cabot had recd. my letters written after the NonIntercorse commenced in August and had determined to buy goods to great extent when they fell — they were then low — but as there was one American Ship /the Euphrates/ & a Sp Ship from Manilla buying they did not fall so low as he expected & he concluded to wait a little while — he will no doubt make very great purchases as the natives were very much alarmed & he was very cool & determined — our letters will come in upon him every week in all of which we direct him to buy to a *great* extent — I believe there will be a

8. *Ibid.*, "List of Vessels clear'd for America from Calcutta."

large surplus after the Gipsy is Supplied which makes me more anxious to increase the Gullivers Stock to 130 @ 140,000 if a credit can be obtain'd in England — I cannot but believe you will find Mr Richards dispos'd to get you thro' the Barings 5$^£$ to 10000$^£$ or more ½ on your acc^t. & ½ his — he to pay ⅓ profits — he w^d. do well as he can meet the payment now at a saving Exchange being 4% to 5% discount It w^d. answer if you could get of Mr Higginson 5000.0.0$^£$ for which you might draw upon us — at 60 days — payable in Bills on London say pound for pound or which w^d. be better give us 6 or 12 M^o. to pay it in — we shall certainly do well in the Gulliver — sh^d. it [so — stricken through] happen as I cannot but hope that more goods have been bot than will be wanted for the Gipsy — the Gulliver may make great dispatch and be with us before the Reaper and Caravan — Should the Brig not have left hurry her off as soon as you can — Write Geo. & Hall how they associate with M Stewart — he intended to remain there & may do them some injury particularly in the sale of their outward Cargo —

We have remitted by this Conveyance to Mr Higginson £6600 — 0 — 0 to pay for 300 Bales R. C. has shipped us p^r. Euphrates — I wish you w^d. let him know what you have p^d for your Bills — No more vessels have sailed as yet for Calcutta — nor is there any more expiditions talked off — If you can find vessels coming home empty and can get Bottles brot to this place or NYork at 1$ p^r. Groce I wish you w^d. send us 1000 Groce say ¾ Wine ¼ Porter Bottles — we shall want to ship them by the Gipsy when she returns

Yours

It is not my intention you sh^d take from Mr Higginson the funds in his hands say the am^t. remitted from the Continent and proceeds of a Cargo of lumber — You are only to remit the Am^t. Sent you for the acc^t of the owners of the Gulliver

H Lee —

Duplicate via New York [written across face of letter]

LETTER FROM HENRY LEE FOR OWNERS OF GIPSY AND GULLI-
VER, BOSTON, AUG. 21, 1810, TO GEORGE LEE AND JOSEPH HALL,
JR., CALCUTTA, IN REGARD TO GOODS FOR THE GULLIVER [1]

This letter to the Calcutta agents for the *Gulliver* supplements
the preceding to the vessel's agent at Liverpool and is in the main
self-explanatory. The instructions not only to load the *Gulliver* but
to purchase goods for a vessel to be sent in December or January
are typical of other injunctions indicative of the intensity and extensive character of the Lees' interest in the India trade at this time.

Messrs. Geo. Lee   Boston August 21. 1810
Jos. Hall Junr
     Dear Sirs   orig^l. p Standard for Liverpool
                            Dup & Triplicate via New York
Quadruplicate via Madeira
    p^rCalisto —   Since my last of   ins^t. via London
I have letters from Mr Cabot p Union & Dolphin — I find he
was determined to buy as soon as goods fell low enough & as he
had before him 2 or 4 Mo^s without any arrivals from this country, we cannot but hope he will go to a great extent — the more
so since all our letters (a short one only which was rec^d) recommend strongly to buy without fear — Under this impression
we think there will have been a surplus after the loading of
the Gipsy — for the cargo of the Gulliver — at any rate a considerable quantity which together with what may be bot after
the rest of our letters p Charon & Reaper will have enabled you
to get off the Gulliver with more dispatch than we at first contemplated — We find M^r C had engaged freight in the Euphrates
and contemplated further shipments — not knowing the State
of his acct' we have remitted to Mr Higginson £6600.0.0 which
may go for the payment of any money taken up for the purchase of goods on credit, or if our acc^t. is balanced then it may
be invested if goods are quite low and shipp'd for the acc^t. of
J & H Lee & P T Jackson in the Gulliver, or retained and sent
home on freight in other vessels as goods can be bot to advan-

1. Jackson-Lee Papers, "Letter Book," Aug. 19, 1810–May 30, 1811.

tage — it is not impossible we may remit further — You will notice, this sum is not for the acc^t of the owners of the Gulliver, but for the owners of the Gipsy

We calculate Mr Oliver will send you 200,000 Rupees from England which was all we intended to have shipp'd by her, but if goods are lower than my limits you may take up a credit of 50,000 Rp^s — say fifty thousand Rupees — you may also draw on Mr Henry Higginson for £ 500,0,0 — at 4 to 6 Mo^s — perhaps it may be possible to buy some large lots of goods at 12 M^o credit, when the Americans have done buying —

You may commence your purchases as soon as goods are low for the vessel that will come after the Gulliver — both Gruff goods & piece goods — We may dispatch a vessel in Decr or Jan^y — & sh^d Exchange on London keep down so as to [interlineated: enable us to] remit to advantage, you will have further remittances from us — I find Mow Sannas & Meergunga Mamoodies were very low in March when Mr Cabot wrote p Dolphin & Union — I think it not improbable those two articles will continue down as they have been low here — in which case buy all you can get — say at 31/ for Mow Sannas & 62/8 for any Mamoodies however bad the quality — they will do for Chintz & to dye Blue for the worst & the others be pack'd in the White Cloth — We w^d recommend again & again as much Chintz as you can get @ 20/ for 9½ by 1¾ ⅞ also Long Cloths — Taffaties, Lungees — Sistersoies — low pric'd Seersuckers — Flags, & other articles of which the Americans do not generally buy much of —

Among the Gruff goods you must secure Ginger, Tumerick, Senna, and 40 to 50 Tons twine of various sizes as pMem^o — We shall always calculate upon 100 to 150 tons of those articles — & they cannot be had at short notice — get also as many Goat Skins as you can, they are very much wanted and will always do very well — even Gunny Bags sh^d not be neglected but 20,000 bo't when they are low — 500 p^s of cheap Bazar Duck @ 8/ to 12/ will do well — the 2 thread is preferred to the single tho' it cost less in Bengal — you cannot send too many Taffaties no matter what the colours are — for the prices

I refer you to the many Memorandums upon this article —
Bands & other Hdkfs will also do well — I give you no limits
because it is impossible for me to conjecture how many will be
bro't by the vessels out this year — but they will certainly do
at 100/ for Bands. ½ or more shd be chocolate, the remainder
scarlets & yellows — 1000 ps of all Blue wd do well — Lungees
and Sistersoies will do at the prices named in Memo. send 5 or
6000 ps — 2 to 3000 ps of Compy Flags & Twill'd Bands will do
well & 2000 ps of the Cora Cloth — We have nothing new —
Write us every oppy & very particularly — We shall continue
our advices via England —

Yours
H Lee for owners of
Gipsy & Gulliver

LETTER FROM HENRY LEE, BOSTON, AUG. 28, 1810, TO THOMAS
S. BEALE, WILMINGTON, ORDERING TURPENTINE [1]

This letter gives an idea of the relations of the Lees with the smaller
ports of the United States. The reference to turpentine indicates that
this Wilmington was the one in North Carolina.

Mr. Thomas S. Beale   Boston Aug. 28 1810
   Wilmington
      I hope as the fall approches you will be able to get rid of
my goods —
   I am in want of 3000 Gallons Spirits of Turpentine I wd.
thank you to procure me that quantity, & Ship it by the first
opportunity in double Barrel or Cased to prevent leaking — You
may draw on me or charge it to acct. to be deducted from the
proceeds of my Cottons —

Your Obt St.
H L

1. Jackson-Lee Papers, "Letter Book," Aug. 19, 1810–May 30, 1811.

LETTER FROM HENRY LEE, BOSTON, SEPT. 12, 1810, TO WIDOW POEY & HERNANDEZ, HAVANA, IN REGARD TO EAST INDIA GOODS [1]

The first letter in this letter book was to another Cuban firm, Antonio de Frias & Co. At one time the Lees had shipped their East India goods to such continental ports as Leghorn, Bordeaux, Nantes, Amsterdam, Antwerp, etc.; now shut out from their old markets by Orders in Council and imperial decrees, they found an outlet for Calcutta cottons in the West Indies, particularly the recently opened ports of Cuba. Between Dec. 22, 1809, and Nov. 22, 1810, we know of the sale of nearly $25,000 worth of India goods, principally piece goods, in Havana.[2] The comment on the characteristic Latin dilatoriness of some Havana traders, in making returns, furnishes an explanation for Henry Lee's relations with more than one Havana firm. In a letter of Oct. 14, 1810, however, to Gorham & Lawrence, Havana, he mentioned "the practice of Commis[n] Merchants in your place to make an immediate remittance of a portion of probable proceeds of consignments;" perhaps this alleged custom was more honored in the breach than the observance or, more likely, Lee restricted his Havana consignments to those who followed this convenient practice.

Widow Poey & Hernandez
  Havana   (p[r].Harriett)   Boston Sept[r]. 12th. 1810
Madam & Sir
  I enclose you with this an Inv[o]. of Seersuckers consign'd you — they are of very good patterns & colours being principally Check'd — I understood that Checks bring $17 — but I give you no limits persuaded you will obtain for them the most they are worth — my wish is that they be sold and the returns made either in White or Brown Sugars by the first opportunity —
  I have rec[d] your favors of 14th July. 3[d]. 9th. & 13th Ulto — with the Inv[o] & the Traveler has arrived — I thank you for your prompt attention in making returns — it is an objection generally to the trade with your Island — that returns are very often long delay'd.

1. Jackson-Lee Papers, "Letter Book," Aug. 19, 1810–May 30, 1811.
2. *Ibid.*, "Foreign Sales on acc[t]. of J. & H. Lee from 1803 to 1810. — "

BORDEAUX, 1804

I hope before this reaches you will have sold all my goods if not you may dispose of them as you think best — I w^d observe however that all kinds of Cottons have advanc'd 5 to 10 % & Blue Goods still more — While your place continues to be a market for Calcutta goods I shall be glad to be inform'd of the prices & probable demand for 6 m^o to come — in the months of Feb^y & March I expect to receive 1000 Bales of Madras & Calcutta goods among which there will be Blue Gurrahs — Blue Guineas — Cambrics — Niccanies — Salempores — Manilla Ginghams, Seersuckers — Blue Gillas — Sooty Romals — Chintz — Checks — Custers & White Cottons of all kinds —

I shall make no further shipments of White Goods until I have advices from you of there having become more in demand — which may be soon the case as shipments will be suspended now it is known your market is overstocked

Yours,

H Lee

LETTER FROM HENRY LEE, BOSTON, SEPT. 12, 1810, TO WILLIAM H. SAVAGE, KINGSTON, JAMAICA, ENQUIRING CONCERNING A CAPTURED VESSEL [1]

Either the brig *Albert* and cargo or the cargo alone evidently belonged to the Lees and had been captured by a British vessel on the way to Jamaica. Nothing further appears concerning the ultimate fate of the vessel and property.

W^m H Savage Esqr   Boston Septr 12, 1810
   Kingston Jamaica,   via N York
                                 orig^l & duplicate
       Sir
       I have been expecting for some time with great anxiety intelligence of the fate of the Brig Albert and Cargo — I presume so long a time as 7 Mo^s could not have elaps'd without your having written upon so important a subject — your last

1. Jackson-Lee Papers, "Letter Book," Aug. 19, 1810–May 30, 1811.

letter rec^d is dated 30 Jan^y — if you have written since the letters have been lost — I pray you to let me know in triplicate letters the State of the business — you appear'd to think the captors w^d not prosecute the appeal — I hope this has been the case & that before this the proceeds will have passed into your hands & shipments have been made either to me in this place or Mr Peter Remsen New York — Rum at present will do well for returns — I must again repeat my earnest request that you w^d let me know as quick as possible what has been done —

> I am Your Obt Servt
> Henry Lee

LETTER FROM P. T. JACKSON FOR SELF, JOSEPH LEE, JR., AND HENRY LEE, BOSTON, OCT. 15, 1810, TO GEORGE LEE AND JOSEPH HALL, JR., CALCUTTA, WITH INSTRUCTIÓNS FOR PURCHASING INDIA GOODS [1]

The unparalleled length of this letter makes it valuable for detailed description of the quality and prices of the many goods characteristic of India. Particularly worthy of note are the injunctions to purchase inferior goods and to increase the selling appeal of overfamiliar types of merchandise by the use of new names.

To "dammer" and "chunam" are Anglo-Indian expressions meaning to coat with resin or a short plaster, respectively.

Mr George Lee & Joseph Hall Jr   Boston Oct^o 15th 1810
    Dear sirs
        Our last was of 4th ulto via England & copy via Madeira. We write this under the expectation of sending it by the vessels that will sail from here in about 15 or 20 days. If we cannot get it on board any of them it will go by the Brig Vancouver for Madras, own'd by ourselves & Mr Newton, Mr John Tracy goes out in her, & should Mr Newton not have arrived he may come on to Calcutta, but of this Mr T. will inform you on his arrival.
        We have remitted for the account of the owners of the Gipsy

---

1. Jackson-Lee Papers, "Letter Book," Aug. 19, 1810–May 30, 1811.

thro' Henry Higginson Ten thousand two hundred Pounds sterling which sum is to buy goods which may be shipped at 100
Rupees p Ton freight or reserv'd for the Gipsy or which ever
vessel we may next send. we wish you however to ship all the
fine Cottons & Silks on freight as fast as you buy them even at
120 Rupees p Ton. the freight upon such goods is very small
charge & we shall always have funds for the vessels we send
out, if any deficiency a credit may be taken up even if you give
12% p annum, it is probable we may continue to remit further,
as Exchange on London is now low, but whether we do or not,
we wish you to make purchases at our limitations to the amount
of three or four hundred thousand Rupees in such goods as we
have reccommended and do now reccommend, it is our determination to pursue the Calcutta trade at all hazards & we think
we shall always do well even if others lose. because you will
have so much more time to make our investments, we shall
certainly send back the Gipsy & one other vessel next season,
& should the Gipsy not appear in season we shall buy a vessel
you will therefore provide *Gruff goods & Peice goods* & have
them pack'd. It would be well always to keep on hand a large
quantity of Ginger & Tumerick as they are sometimes difficult
to be had & rise very much. we always want more or less of
these articles to fill up with. if you cannot buy the sound —
then take the worm-eaten, we have suffer'd very much from not
having these articles shipd because the very best could not be
had, it is certainly safest to bring the best, but when good
cannot be had take the best you can get, *Tumerick* as well as
ginger may be stowed among the bales in bulk without any
injury to the goods, & it is profitable that we prefer to Ginger,
if the Gulliver should not have sail'd when you get this you
may take all Tumerick instead of Ginger as was directed. it is
often very low say 2/8 to 3/ you should then buy 100 tons &
store it and also 100 Tons Ginger when it is low, if it is not
wanted sell it, it often advances when there are several who
want. *Twine* will be a very profitable article & cannot be had
at short notice 50 Tons of the sizes reccommended p Memo
handed Mr Lee should be purchased, in invoicing it put some

mark against the various sizes that we may be able to tell the different qualities, without opening each bale, as we were obliged to do in the Gipsy's last voyage. I would have the bales uniform in weight and the tare marked on each bale. *Nut-Galls* is a very safe article & 20.000 to 50.000 lb may be purchased and kept as you may want to make up our cargoes, if you cannot get the blue, take the gray & white, *Goat Skins* will always do well, they are now worth 40¢ and will not be below 30¢. get all you can and pack them in bales of 500. mix powder'd Tobacco among them which will preserve them from moths, get the fairest you can. but buy them even if they are small, they are a certain article, *Sal Ammoniac* if you can get it as low as 12½¢. buy 10.000 lb if at 16¢ buy 5,000 and 2000 at any rate, *Shel Lac* is now an article of great use, buy 10.000 lb. @ 12¢, if as low as 8¢ as it sometimes is then 20.000 lb, it is best to pack this as well as other gums in *pine boxes* and not country wood as they break to pieces in opening them, this article comes from

and that quarter and is often very abundant. *Senna* you may buy 5000 lb even at 15¢, if as low as 8¢ to 10¢ as it often is, then 15,000 have it pick'd and screen'd into bales, the more the better as it saves room & keeps it sound, Gum Copal if you can get the large at 15¢ you may send 3000 lb, but that is high for it, 12¢ is common price at which you may send 7000 lb @ 10,000 lb but if that which is good cannot be had send only 3 or 4000 lb. *Crude Borax* will do well as ballast to put into bottom, buy 20 Tons if you can get at 8¢. p lb. but if at 10¢. then only 10.000 lb. above that price only 2000 lb it may commonly be had at [about that price — stricken through] 5¢ to 8¢ and sometimes lower. I do not know whether it is a production of Bengal or imported from eastward, *Asa Foetida*, if you can buy it like the samples sent out to mr Cabot at even 15¢. 5000 lb would do, and if at 8¢ or 10¢ then 10.000 lb @ 15,000 lb it costs very little in Persia and is sometimes cheap in Calcutta, great care is necessary in buying it as there is much deception. *Sago*,2 or 3000 lb will do at 2¢ p lb. *Block Tin* 20 Tons will do as Ballast if it can be bought at 14¢. p lb and 2000 lbs even at 16¢. *Colombo Root* if it can be bought at 10¢ p lb for that which is sound 4000 lbs would do well *Cassia* from Ceylon we have had one importation from Calcutta which cost only 8¢ p lb it was of a very exelent quality and was much liked, if as low as 15¢ 20.000 lb would do well, if at 10¢ any quantity might be bought even if it was not of the best quality, *Cinnamon*, you may possibly find, if real 2000 lb would be safe at 75¢ to 80¢ p lb, *Bastard Nutmegs* which are sometimes brought from eastward would do at $1 p lb say 3 or 4,000 lb. but no good nutmegs or Mace, they are very abundant and low, four cargoes having been imported this year from Batavia, *Crude Camphor* can sometimes be bought in Calcutta, if it can be bought at 45¢ p lb, 2000, and would be safe if as low as 35lbs then buy 4.000 lb. it is imported I believe from the eastward the cases should be dammer'd or chumand to prevent the air from penetrating *Gunny Bags* you will always want a certain quantity to stow among the Bales to prevent damage say 10.000 in each vessel, we do not want any on cargo besides, unless it should so happen that you cannot buy *Tumerick or Ginger* to fill up with. *Duck* there is now an abundance of Russia and considerable India in Market. yet it sells well, we estimate the two threads more than the single thread because it weighs more, that is the mode of rating the Russia and therefore the India — we understand the durable thread is lower than single thread in Calcutta, if Kemps can be had at 15/ p piece of 37 yards you may buy 300 pieces, but the most profitable is the *Bazar Duck* that costs 8/ to 12/ if it can be had at these prices even if very ordinary you buy 1000 peices or 500 at 14/, it will certainly do, there are many purposes for which it is wanted, and Russia Duck cannot be imported under 20$ even of the worst quality. it sells very well in South America & West Indies we do not want any more of Jones' than will serve for our own vessels say 100 to 150 Pieces if good at 17/ not higher, Gunny Cotton Bagging we hope a shipment has been made, if not send us 200 Pieces, we think it may prove a very profitable article, as the consumption is very great, *Dungaree* 100 ps may be sent at 6 Rupees p Piece it is not used here much but still at 6/ it would do say 100 Pieces and no more, *Coir Rigging* it is always an object to have a few tons in each vessel for our own use, and every vessel should be amply [supplied — stricken through] furnish'd, it now pays a duty of 2 or 3 Cts p lb, what is wanted [therefore — stricken through] for the use of the vessel should not therefore be invoic'd, but put among the stores, a quantity of *white rope, bed cords, log lines, deep sea lines* &c as p memorandum handed Mr Lee in Gipsy will always do, *Hemp* as it is possible we may at some future day be shut out of Russia, it becomes important to ascertain whether this article will not do to import, a very great quantity is now used in England and it is found to do well, we wish you to send us done up in bundles 5 tons as an experiment find out what it can usually be purchas'd at and give us all the information you can collect relative to it. our Country Hemp has been up to $400 this year and should there be a suspension of our trade with Russia it would go up to $500. we state these facts that you may understand why we want the 5 tons. *Skins* we have before mentioned, Goat Skins, they are very much of an object we hope you may be able to collect 20 or 30,000, but as you will not probably be able to find as many as you want make up the quantity with *Sheep Skins*. we want them as well as the Goat with the hair upon them, you will remember that we would not have you stow them in bulk, but pack them in bales and press them very hard, we want nothing to come in bulk but Tumerick Ginger and Gunny Bags as every other kind of merchandize is injured by stowing them loose, and if they were not, there would be no object as every crevice may be fill'd with these articles, *Sugar*, this article can never be an object worth your attention any further than 100 to 200 bags to put into the bottom of a vessel. It would be worth your while to keep on hand 2 or 300 bags of the cheapest you can find say 6 Rupees p hd. *Pepper* you must never ship this article higher than 4c p lb at that price it would do when Ginger or Tumerick cannot be had, These are the principal gruff articles which are to be found in Calcutta, perhaps we may mention some others before we close this, they are partly productions of Bengal and other provinces of India & partly imported from Arabia, Persia, Ava, Eastern Islands &c&c, the Banians know but little about them

& are never inclin'd to trouble themselves much to obtain them, you must find them yourselves which you will by going into the Bazars, Custom house yard, Auction Rooms &c &c and to the Armanian & Persian Merchants we do not calculate upon your being able to obtain the whole of the quantities or all the varities we have order'd, but you will many of them. it is a great object to have as many as you can get. as we shall calculate upon 300 Tons for the next vessel after the Gulliver & indeed every vessel we shall send will want a considerable quantity most of these articles the Americans have but little knowledge of & we hope they will not add to it by any thing you can communicate, many of them do not believe they are worth bringing & indeed the importers have often lost and commonly find much trouble in selling them. it is therefore the more object for us to attend to them, do not allow any of your samples to be seen nor give any information to any one. what you buy have stored in some distant part of the city. that they may be ready for the first vessel that appears. great care is necessary in selecting the Drugs as there is much imposition. Senna, Gum Copal must be pickd ever after you buy it. both of these articles in the Gipsy were very good last voyage, we do not calculate upon your being able to get such excellent qualities always, but get the best you can. The Twine will require great care and a long time to have it made, we think Mr Lee is so good a judge that there is no danger of your being deceived, it is no matter about the qualities of the coarse, the most important is to have the sizes correspond with the samples sent out in the Gipsy. we mean by Bazar Duck that which is made by the natives & which is very inferiour to Jones' Kemps and other European manufacturers, this article as well as the twine we suppose you will have to contract for. Twine is sometimes bought for Philadelphia & New York but the Northern vessels hitherto have brought little of it. we calculate very much upon it in fact we shall be very much disapointed unless you should be able to buy many of the gruff articles. they are certain at all events to give a good profit *Indigo*, when good merchantable Indigo can be bot at 140/ p M^d we think it would be worth while to buy 10,000 lbs and it might be shipped on freight as the Silks and fine Cottons are order'd to be, we would have you at any rate buy 10.000 lb of ordinary at 100/ to 120/ p m^d., which may be ship'd also on freight we know this kind will do very well for our home manufactures, pack all of a quality in a box and do not put several qualities into same box, this article must not be bought by sample, but every box should be open'd & examined. if at any time you find good Indigo at 130 Rupees p m^d, it would be worth while to buy 20 or 30.000 lb on speculation provided a credit can be obtain'd upon it, so that it will not prevent your purchase of Piece goods, You will also send us on trial 3000 lb of the most inferiour Indigoes you can buy say a Box of each kind to cost 50 to 100 Rupees p maud, it may be found to answer for some of our home manufactures which are becoming very extensive in Cottons, Good merchantable Indigoes have found very good market in Russia this year, it is convey'd from thence to Germany. Italy & even France first quality such as come charg'd at 150 Rupees in Bark Mary's cargo is now selling at $2 p lb and very little in market. we presume the vessels now out will bring home large quantities, yet there will be a demand it is very much lik'd all over Europe. we wish you to make yourselves judge of this article, because sometimes when piece goods are high it may be an object to invest considerable funds in it. but you must not be too nice in selecting for this country as the buyers are not at all judges and would not give any more for the very fine qualities than for merchantable, the middling qualities only should be sent to this country, it is quite probable you may at some time or other find this article so dull that it could be bo^t on 6 or 12 months credit, it such case you might venture to buy 20.000 lb at 150/ or if very fine 160/ and ship in any vessel you could get it on board at 100 Rupees p Ton of 40 feet. this article we presume goes by same measurement, as piece goods.

Contrary to our expectations there will be dispach'd this season 6 or 8 vessels, some of them with large stocks, so that the prices of goods in Calcutta will be kept up and prices on the imports here go down particularly upon the Staple Cottons, by which I mean those which our Countrymen run upon, it becomes therefore more necessary than ever that you should buy as many of those kinds of Goods that are not sought for by the americans or that they have not time to collect, as you can find at our limits, there is such a great variety of goods made in India and such great changes in the value of the different articles that an immense field is opened to an intelligent resident at all times, even when goods are ever so high, you must not therefore ever be for a moment inactive, but buy such goods, as you can find in the Bazar and contract for, the contract price for many articles, say for a 3 month contract is 10 to 15/, less than the Bazar Price, *Hum-Hums* are not usually purchased by the americans a few are shipped for Philadelphia, we think they will do well, the following are the name of some of the most common and the prices they have usually been sold at

Luckipour	24 x 2¾ 3.	sometimes only 22 Cubits	70/ to 80/
Hurrial	" "		70/ @ 90/
Dacca	22x2½ ¾		55/ " 70/
Serrapour	22x24x2¾.3		70/ " 80/

they are not a very common article in the Bazar, but no doubt you will find them from time to time we would have you buy 3000 pieces of the most ordinary you can find at 55/ to 70/ & 2000 pieces 70/ @ 80/ if they cannot be bought at these prices, then 1000 pieces at such prices as you can get them at, if you can get them as low as 60/ you may increase the quantity of ordinary ones to 6000 pieces, you will divide 1000 pieces into two parts. the regected ones will do for Chintz. to be divided into three parts, the figures should be large, they are wanted for Bed Curtains Coverings &c, the colours should be bright, Invoice them palempores Chintz, there are several other kinds of Humhums you will find out what they are, our object is the low pric'd ones. they will certainly do well. *Seersuckers*, you will have remark'd in all my letters, that I have strongly reccommended this article, it is now more than ever an object because the common white Cottons will be for a year to come very abundant. this article when it is low in this country can be exported to various ports, we wish to be particular in getting the kinds we order. the cheapest kind is the *Blue & Purple Stripe* of which there were some in Gipsy & Sally Anns cargoes that cost 8/12, they can usually be bought at 8/ to 9/8 at which 5000 Peices may be ship'd if you can have a portion of them (say ½) check'd it would be better even at 5% higher price, ¼ should be wide stripes say from ¼ to ½ inch wide, if you can get such patterns you might go to 7.500 Pieces, but if you cannot get any but common patterns then take only 5000 Pieces it is no matter what the quality is, get the cheapest you can find, *Check'd* are the next cheapest, say yellow, purple, green, red. Chocolate &C like the patterns I sent you out by the Charon & Reaper, the coarser they are the better, provided they are cheap in proportion, if you can get ¼ large checks say ½ inch to an inch wide, the remainder various patterns, we presume they may be bought at about 9/8 to 11/, we would have you send us 3000 pieces @ 11/8, if at 10/8 then 7,500 Pieces, if as low as 9/ then all you can get, you must take great pains to get these goods, & if you contract describe the patterns you want, and keep samples of every different figure say ¼ yard that they may serve another time, *Chandercowah* are the higher priced if you can get the above we want none of them unless @ 11/8, then only 1000 Pieces, and at any rate none higher than 12/, if you buy no Chandercowah, then you may have of the ordinary Kind 2000 pieces yellow striped common patterns, *Large stripes* say ½ inch to one inch wide are now very much wanted & as the other supercargoes from this quarter will not have time to look them up they will be a very profitable article, we want 3000 pieces no matter how coarse, of yellow, purple, red, green &c principally yellow, purple & red if they can be had, and for which you may go as high as 12/ and even 13/ for 1500 pieces, if they can be had at 10/8, then 5000 pieces. they ought not to cost any more than the others patterns, but I give you great latitude. because they are now scarce and will continue so, we do not want any seersuckers at higher prices than what we put down and remember that the coarser they are the more profitable, those which are very fine and cost 16/ bring no more than those which are ordinary and cost 11/.

pack them in bales of 50 p^s each and put a good wax covering on them, say double wrappers, because they are apt to get damaged by the least dampness, this article, as well as Silks, Long Cloths & other very fine Cottons, should be shipd as you can find oppertunity and never detain'd for our vessels, You may even go as 120 Rupees p Ton (100 is the common) they are so valuable that the freight is no charge upon them and it is an object to get them as soon as possible, indeed we prefer having our property divided to having it all come in our own vessels. You may divide 2000 pieces of the longest Seersuckers, say make them 15 x 1⅞ and 1000 pieces into three parts so as to have them 10 by 1 ⅞ always pack the rejected Seersuckers and invoice them with an R so that we may know them,

Karradery 28 to 30 x 1⅞ @ ¾ usually cost less than Seersuckers of the most ordinary kind. you may ship 3000 pieces at 8/8 and if you do not get all the Seersuckers order'd, then you may send 5000 pieces as high as 9/ get ¼ of them check'd and ¼ large stripe say ½ inch wide if you can, but send them at any rate let the patterns be what they may, it is probable you may get them at 7/ to 8/, it is of less importance when they are ship'd than the *Seersuckers*, divide 1000 pieces into two pieces and 500 pieces into three pieces, and pack them in the wax Cloth, remember that in Seersuckers and Carraderries that the figures are of great importance. the demand now is for Broad Stripes & large checks, you must take some pains in contracting for these articles to explain what figures you want, *Custers*, is always a good article at or under 30/, ¼ of the quantity may be broad stripes say ½ to inch wide, they can[not — stricken through] as well be made that pattern as any other, but if more is demanded you may go as high as 32/, the remainder various patterns, 10,000 pieces Custers are not to many as an experiment. I should like 500 pieces made large checks, we do not want any higher priced Custers pack 150 pieces in a bale. *Sooty Romals*, are a very staple article, for the ordinary ones you may go as high as 33/ and at that buy 10.000 pieces, part of them should be large checks, you may buy also 1000 pieces of company ones, large checks at 40/ or 500 pieces @

42/8, they must be much better than the others and Invoic'd Company. *Blue Gillas* are a very safe article the most ordinary are the most profitable. You may buy 5000 pieces at 30 to 32/8 and 2000 pieces 32/8 to 35/, but none above these prices, if they are as low as 30/ you may increase the quantity to 10.000 pieces. *Factory soy Handkerchiefs*, 8 in piece, any quantity may be ship'd at 21/. if at 23/ then 2000 pieces, but none above, it is no matter how bad the quality is, as they are not much sought for by the Americans, I think they may be bought on contract for about 20/. 20.000 pieces would not be too many. *Madras Pattern Handkerchiefs*, 8 in piece, if they can be bought for 45/ p C^o 2000 pieces will do and if very good bright patterns they will do say for 1000 pieces @ 55/, but none higher, *White Gillas* will do at 40/ say 2000 pieces. *Red Gillas* at 35/ say 2000 pieces. but not higher. it is no matter how bad the quality is they must be cheap or will not sell. *Kermitchee Handkerchiefs* 10 in piece if they can be bought at 50/ 2000 pieces will do. should be deep blue, with a broad white border for 1000 pieces you may go as high as 60/ if good quality and broad white border, if they should be as low as 45/ you may increase the quantity to 4000 pieces. *Chandsoy Handkerchiefs* are part silk and part Cotton you will find a sample of them among some that were sent out by Mr Cabot if they can be bought at 45/ 2000 pieces will do. *Checks* say small and ordinary 15 x 1⅝ will always be a profitable article at 30/. at that price 20.000 pieces or more may be shipped, & 5.000 pieces at 32/8. *Long Checks* 19.20 @ 1⅞ will do well at 40/ 5000 pieces, but if they cannot be bought at that you may go as high as 42/8 for 2000 pieces but no higher, 500 pieces of the long checks may be divided into two parts so as to make them 10 x 1⅞ Checks have done well & will always continue to do, do not buy any intermediate ones betwen the 32 and 42/8. 1000 pieces of large figured would do well, they should be pack'd in bales of 100 and 150 pieces.

Kirwah. if it can be bought for 22/. 3000 pieces would do very well or 1000 pieces at 25/. but none higher. it is seldom bought by the Americans and is sometimes low, it measures

13.14 x 1⅝ and is the Cloth of which the scarlet coverings to
Pelanquins are made, *Soosey* 11 x 1⅝ it usually costs 15/ p Co,
at which price 2000 to 3000 pieces would do very well or 1000
pieces at 17/ but none higher. *Long Cloths,* none of this article
have come out except a few bales in the Gipsys cargo for some
years, they are made near Calcutta and can always be contracted for. if you can buy them even very ordinary ones at
9/8 you may send 2000 pieces, they would do better if cheaper
say 8/. if they cannot be bought at that you may send 500
pieces at any price. 12/ should be pack'd very carefully in bales
of 30 pieces. *Chintz* is a most excellent article, it can always
be laid in cheap by selecting the lowest white goods and having
them printed the best dimensions are 9½ to 10 by 1¾–⅞ @ 2.
say mer gungee and other ordinary Mamoodies, divided into 4
pieces. the best colours are red and yellow. black and purple
will also do. Cloth should be well cover'd for the principal part
[in — stricken through] some large figures and some small, it
is important to have them well wash'd that they may appear
bright, they look better for being glaz'd. they can almost always
be laid in at 20/ p Co 9½–1⅞ at which price any quantity
will do, say 100,000 pieces one hundred thousand pieces 10,000
Pieces 7½ @ 1⅞ will do at 15/. if you cannot get any or as
many as you want at 20/. you may give as high as 22/ for 20,000
pieces, but there is no doubt you may in the course of a few
months collect what you may want at or under 20/. it is a very
safe and a very profitable article, and as it requires more time
than can be spar'd by those who remain only three or four
months in Calcutta to get any quantity, there is no danger of
our market being overstock'd with it, you must take great pains
in making your contracts for printing and visit the factories
very often, to see that the figures, colours &c are what you have
agreed for, and to contrive new patterns, you must make new
figures and the printers will have them cut into blocks, 4000
pieces printed Mow Sannas divided into two parts may do at
40/ for the whole piece, but in general Mamoodies are the
best kinds of goods to print on account of quality and dimensions. many of the Chintzes sent home are Mizapoor a very

muddy colour and sleazy cloth, they do not answer, a few may do if you can get no others, at 20/, remember that 11 to 12 by 1⅞ bring but little and sometimes not any more than 9½ by 1⅞, *Patna Chintz*, if good bright colours can be had at 24/ for 9 to 20 by 178. to 2 2 or 3000 pieces would do well. *Lucknow Chintz* of same dimensions, if it can be had at 27/8, 1000 pieces would do, but what we rely upon for one of the best and largest articles is the Calcutta Chintz as above described to cost 20/ no pains must be spar'd to get a very large quantity and pack it in bales of 200 pieces each, in buying Cloth for Chintz it is more important that it be stout. than for Blue Cloths, the best should be printed and the sleazy and very coarse may be dye'd blue. in receivᵍ Chintz from the factories when you have it printed. it is common to regect a small portion for bad printing, they may be pack'd seperate and invoiced rejected and not turn'd upon the printers as is usually the case an allowance will of course be made by them, *Blue Cloths*, we presume a great many will have been ship'd by all the Americans on account of the high prices they have sold at this year, but still they will be a good article, the best dimensions are *Gurrahs* and the most ordinary Cutuah, 33 34x2⅛ should be taken to dye. if you cannot get them for less than 82/8 you may buy only 3000 pieces. but if at 80/ 5000 pieces would be safe, if at 75/. you may buy 10.000 pieces. *Blue Mamoodies* or any other cloths of the same dimensions will do at 70/ to 75/. if you can get as many Gurrahs as you want, we do not want many Blue Mamoodies unless at 70/. at which price they will be very cheap. but if you cannot get *Blue Gurrahs* at the limits. then make up the quantity by Mamoodies @ 75/ if there is any other low pric'd white Cottons of 34 to 36 x 1¾ @ ⅞ that can be laid in at 65/ to 70. you may have dyed 5000 pieces. *Blue Mow Sannas* 5000 pieces will do at 40/. but when you can get them as 35/ you may buy 20.000 pieces, it is probable that white ordinary Mow Sannas will be low as they are very dull sale here and have been thro' the year, if so you will have a good oppertunity to buy, select the coarsest to have printed and dyed. Perhaps you may find *Tockeries Patna Baftas Maharaz Gungee Manickpore*

Gurrahs &c very low, in which case they will do well to dye and would be cheap at 45/, at that price any quantity might be ship'd, or any Cloth 30 x 1⅞ to cost 50/. there is always some cheap ordinary Cloth in the Bazar which will do no matter how bad the quality. it is as we have before observ'd of much less consequence than in Chintz, The Chintz printers. dyers ought to be engaged if they are not when you receive this, because the fleet that will arrive about the time this reaches may want considerable of Blue Cloth and some Chintz, but you must not be deter'd from buying for us when it can be done at our limits, as well this article as all the others, *Boglepours* 19 @ 1⅞ and Sooty *Carraderies* the same dimensions, the best colour for Boglepour is plain yellow, but any will do, Carraderies some broad and some narrow stripes and some checks cost 60/ to 70/ at which 3000 Pieces would do well, these goods are made at Dhunnakhally and are call'd Chickerre, Carradery, Sooty Carradery, are not generally bought by the Americans and are sometimes very low. In consequence of the Non Intercourse with France and Italy all kinds of Silks have been very high which makes it important to think of every kind of Silk goods made in India, we wish you to try at what you can obtain them at 1000 pieces *Cuttanies* partly Silk and partly Cotton, broad stripe cost usually 5/8 to 6/ p piece 28.30 x 1½ if they can be bought under 8/. you may buy 2000 pieces and if at 5/8.3000 pieces, they are made for Eastern markets and may be found among the Silk Merchants, hitherto very few have been imported here. they are not known at all by the Americans we shall send you a sample by some oppertunity, we hope you may be able to find them, as we anticipate doing very well 'till the article becomes generally known, which will not be the case for some time, *Cora Cloth,* or Bandannas before they are colour'd we have before describ'd this article and hope we have now on the way enough to give it a fair trial, we think it would be safe to try 2000 pieces at 80/ p Corge, they are wanted for linings &c, it is possible ordinary ones may be bought at 60/ to 70/ if so buy 4000 pieces. You will not find this article in the Bazar, but the Silk Merchants know what it is and can furnish it. you will send us 500 pieces let it cost what it may. if it has not already been shipped that we may make an experiment. we hope to find it in future an important article among our cargoes. *Choutars* (silk) 14 x 1½ ¾ we think a full piece is 28 Cubits but it would be better to have them divided 1000 pieces would do well to cost 50/ to 60/ for 14 by 1½, if as low as 45/ then 2000 pieces or more might be safe, *Mooty Coers* (Silk) are some what similar we understand 500 pieces would do well at 55/, *Mugga Duties* 10 x 2 are very thin and ordinary goods cost 25/ to 45/ buy 500 pieces and if as low as 25/, then increase it to 2,000 pieces. *Cookelah* (silks) 12 x 1½ 1000 pieces will do at 45/ to 50/ these four articles are made we imagine for the Persian or some other Asiatic Market and also for the use of the natives of India, you must take some pains to find them, as your Banians either know but little about them or are not inclin'd to trouble themselves to look them up. you must apply to the Silk Merchants, we want a small [quantity — stricken through] portion of these as well as other new goods send immediately, but for what others you may want, perhaps they may best be bought on contract. they should be packd in Bales and wrapp'd with double wax Cloth, and screw'd, all Silks as well as fine Cottons should be pack'd in wax Cloth, there are also some other new articles of Silk manufacture of which we want a bale of to make a trial, we will put down their names, *Soosey* 11 x 1⅛ ½ thin, ordinary cloth Silk or Silk and cotton, usually cost 16/ to 17/ p C⁰. at that price 5000 pieces would do very well or 1000 pieces @ 20/ should be pack'd in bales of 250 pieces each. *Phatas* 28.29 x 2¼ usually cost 80/. send us 1000 pieces on trial if not above 80/ of which ⅓ part may be divided into two parts. send 200 pieces at any rate they are we believe a check'd Cotton. dark Colours, Ginghams 10 x 1⅞ cost usually 25/ if they can be bought at that 1000 pieces would do, at any rate send us 200 pieces on trial cost what they will. *Carpets Patna* &c have done remarkably well this year and will continue to the dimensions wanted are 4 Cubits long and usual width, say ⅔ of this length, the remaining ⅓ᵈ may be 3½ to 3¾ long, you may also have a small portion longer or shorter as you can find them, we expect the quality will be ordinary, but no matter how bad they are if they can be bought at 45/ p cº. you may buy 20.000 pieces if at 50/ then 10,000 pieces if as high as 65/ only 5000 pieces and above that only 2000. the colours should be bright, if you can find them so, but get such as you can find, pack them in bales of 50 pieces to 100 pieces each and screw them very hard. we calculate much upon this article, and we do not think others will run upon it much as it is not easy to be had in short stay, and takes up much room, *Straw Carpets* you may send us 500 Rupees worth and of Bed Mats of the largest size 250 Rupees, they will sell in West Indies, *Curtain Cloth* we have before order'd this article, we wish much to make an experiment and think it must answer, if none has been shipp'd send us 2000 Rupees amount and at any rate the amount of 100 Rupees. pack it up in small packages, as we want to send it to various places to ascertain its value, green will be the best colour, but you may have a portion of purple, white, yellow, blue &c. send various qualities, *Taffaties*. this article always did well even while we had Silks in the greatest abundance from France, but since the intercourse has been interrupted they have been very much wanted. we have been disapointed in not receiving any & the more so because our orders were very particular about this article and the last ship brought a considerable quantity which sold very high indeed, we wish you to buy and contract for all you can get, provided you can get the most ordinary quality *of any colours* at 8/ and of those of middling quality at 10/ and the company at 12/. if they cannot be had at these prices you may go as high as 9/ for 3000 pieces of ordinary and 11/ for 1000 pieces of middling and 13/ for 500 pieces of company for the ordinary and middling no matter what the colours are. the high colours will do as well as the dark, formerly they would not, for the company or very fine ones the best colours are plumb, white, green, blue, yellow, fawn slea [?], purple, brown, slate, black &c, with some scarlet. it would be well to pack the high colours by themselves as they are wanted for exportation. *Striped* ones will do very well, rember that for the ordinary ones, never reject on

acc^t of the quality. they can generally be bought at 6/ to 7/8
p piece and they are very profitable, we have extended the
limits in this article because we wish very much to have a large
quantity, they are made at Cassimbazar and Mizapour and any
of the Silk Merchants will furnish them. you can very often
pick up small lots in the Bazar, you must not leave a piece because it is probable many of the Americans may want them, and
you will find it difficult to made up the quantity, take care that
those you contract for be not deliver'd to others, you must
draw up your contracts with great care and with all the forms
proper. perhaps it would be well always when you are in doubt
to consult a lawyer. *Bandannas* we hardly know what to say
about your purchases of this article, any you can ship in the
Gulliver will certainly come to a good market [any — stricken
through] you may go as high as 100/ for any quantity of the
most ordinary kind or 105/ for 5000 pieces if they have not
been much lower and many have not been shipp'd, this we
leave to your discretion whether to go on higher or not for
the Gulliver, for any you may b[uy — stricken through interlineated: ought] to ship home on freight or for the next vessel
we may send, we should say if you can get ordinary ones at 95/
a large quantity should be bought, say 10 to 15,000 pieces, if
lower any quantity, if they are higher then 5 or 10.000 pieces
as you may think best, the fact is it must depend on quantity
shipped whether it will do to go higher, this country will consume 150.000 in a year, we hope you may be able to get them
something under the Bazar prices by sending to Cassimbazar,
you will recollect that ordinary Bandannas sell as well as the
good for instance the most ordinary which cost 90/ will bring as
much as those which costs 102/ @ 105/ no difference is made
except for company ones and twill'd which cost 150/ to 180/.
the best assortment would be ¾ Chocolate and Scarlet and ¼
yellow, if there is any blues pack them seperate. this is the best
assortment of colours, but take such as you can get, never let
any rejected Bandannas go out of your go downs but pack them
all whether coarse or short measure, in our own vessels you
may pack part of the Bandannas in bales of 100 pieces as in the

Euphrates and part in boxes of 240 pieces, when you send on
freight they had better be pack'd wholly in boxes on account
damage, remember to put down the assortment in the Invoice
otherwise we have to open them here which is expensive and
troublesome. those which are put into cases should be first
put into bales of 30 pieces and very much screw'd, *Twill'd
Bandannas.* about 1000 pieces will sell but they must not cost
above 160/ p Co. *Company Bandannas.*asample of which I
shall send you, it is not often they can be found in the Bazar.
1000 pieces like the pattern sent will do at 170/. but we do
not want any between these and the common Bandannas as
they bring no more than those [that — stricken through] which
only 100/. *Ordinary Choppa Romals or flaggs* should cost 10/
in Corge less than the common Bandannas say 90/. at which a
large quantity would do more or less according to the quantity
of Bandannas that have been shipp'd, at any rate however you
may ship 3000 pieces at 90/, and if at 80/ to 85/ as many as
you can buy. it is no matter how ordinary they are provided
they are low in price, you may sometimes find some very coarse
at 70/ always take all you can get. *Company Choppas.* such
as cost 130/ in Sally Ann and Gipsy 2000 pieces will do at 130/
provided they are as good as those were, we shall send you a
sample if we can procure one, so that there may be no mistake.
Lungee Handkerchiefs, the good ones made at Cassimbazar we
believe and containing 16 in piece will do well at 10/8 which is
higher than formerly cost, 1000 pieces may be ship'd at that
rate and 2000 pieces at 9/8 but the most profitable are the
Mizapour Handkerchief (Lungees) very indifferent qualities
and much *congeed*, they cost 6/8 to 8/8 at which prices you
may buy 5000 pieces, no matter what the patterns or qualities
are. *Ordinary Sistersoies* 15 in piece may be bought at about
the same but we only want 2000 pieces. *fine Sistersoies*, may be
bought at 9/ say 500 pieces if lower then 1000 pieces. of late
years very few Sistersoies have been ship'd to this country, it is
not probable you will find many in the Bazar, but you can contract for them with the Silk Merchants. one quarter part of
the best Lungees may be divided into two parts and invoiced

Cassimbazar Romals they will be more saleable in that size than for a long piece you may also divide 500 pieces of the fine Sistersoies. *Dury Handkerchiefs* 16 in piece usually cost 10 to 11 piece if they can be bought at 10/8, 2000 pieces would be safe, if as high as 11/ then 1000, and at any rate 500 pieces. they should be divided into two parts, this is not a common article and it is doubtful whether you will be able to get many immediately but in course of some months you will collect 1000 to 2000 pieces should be pack'd in bales of 100 pieces of 8 Handkerchiefs in piece. *Inchey or Ringa Handkerchiefs* 15 in peice 500 pieces may be bought if to be had at 10/8. if at 9/ then 1000 or 1,500 pieces. you will not allow any rejected Silk goods to leave your go downs when you can have a deduction made, the allowance made there for rejected goods is always greater than the difference made here in the sales. of course they are always more profitable than the good goods, *Blue Baftas,* in mentioning Blue Cloths I forgot this article, it is a very saleable one you may have 5000 pieces dy'd, selected from the rejected and the coarsest Baftas 22 @ 25 by 1⅞ .2 it is no matter how coarse they are as they sell almost wholly by the name as do Blue Gurrahs and other Blue Cloths. perhaps you may buy them already dy'd, it that case it would be better to pack those which you otherwise would dye, provided the dy'd ones do not exceed 65/ for the major part get the best dye you can but take such as you can get, pack them uniformly 100 pieces in a bale, we have now particularized all the Silk and colour'd goods we can think of and proceed to the White Cloths. of which the most promising article is Baftas 22 to 25 by 1⅞.2. the more ordinary the more profitable. we have been very much disapointed hitherto at receiving so small a portion of this article when we have always been so earnest and positive in our orders for it. we wish you to attend particularly to our instructions respecting this article and follow them, *Ordinary Baftas,* have been this year very profitable and they will no doubt be very much sought for, but the demand is principally for Boran and the series up to Patha. they go together often, but besides these there are about 10 to 25 different kinds of 22 to 24 x 1⅞.2

which cost 40/ to 70/ which will do as well nearly. the following are among the most common of them. the prices annex'd perhaps are not accurate you will by comparing them with Boran, Jugdea, Luckipour & Chittabilly be able to judge of their value, these You may pack all Baftas except blue, in Wax Cloth and have the folded side of the Cloth placed in the right side as you face the mark that

Dacca Baftas	22 to 24 x 1⅞	40/ to 50/		
Brown do	24	1⅞	40 " 50	
Saib Gungee do	24 " 25 x 1⅞.2			
Morekee do	" " "			
Hurrial do	" " "			
Commercolly do	" " "		50/ to 70
Rangpore do	" " "		
Cusba do	" " "		
Gonuckpore do			
Sundiff do		50 to 70	
Seapour do			
Chittaging do			

when we open a bale the selvage may not appear the same must be observd in Chandpour Cossas and other fine goods we wish you to buy the above together with Boran, Luckipour, Jugdea, Chittabilly as many as you can find from 40/ to 65/. the rejected coarse and narrow ones you will have dy'd Blue, as they will sell for as much as Callipatty would dy'd, the remainder should be packd get as many as you can of the very ordinary and the remainder 60/ to 65/ we should not be sorry to hear you had purchased One thousand bales of this article as it will be the most profitable for some time to come, perhaps you may contract for some to be deliver'd in 4 to 6 months from the time you receive this, which will do for next year. this article will be very much sought for by all the Americans particularly the low priced Baftas you must be very much on the alert for it. *Narrow ordinary Baftas*, 24 by 1½ ¾, say Jannah. Tilpa & c will do to dye say 1000 pieces if it can be bought at 35/. *Fine Baftas* say Callipatty and Pathas, if you can get them very fine at 80/. 2000 pieces would do, and if you cannot get ordinary ones without a portion of these thin 3 or 4000 pieces may be bought but you must be certain of the qualities. those which came in the Sally Ann and Gipsy were no better than the Chittabilly. we want no intermediate qualities because they sell for no more than Chittabilly you need not invoice the ordinary Baftas by any other name than Baftas. the fine ones and the Chittabilly and also any other costing more than 60/ may be Invoic'd by name, you must not have any of this Cloth made into Chintz nor any of the rejected when you can have an allowance upon them go from your go downs. the average sales of low pric'd Baftas have been for three years past 100¢ to 120¢ p Rupee and some that came this year sold at 150, it is probable they will continue to be the most profitable article, *Beerboom Gurrahs*, will always do to purchase in very large quantities when they can be bot at 60/ for the most ordinary, indeed those are the ones we calculate most upon say *Catuah 34 to 36 x 2½ to 2¼* they are very often avoided under the idea that very ordinary gurrahs will not sell. we can only repeat what we have always said in our various memorandums that there is no Cloth too ordinary for this country, at least for the profit of the importer you will not ever refuse goods for bad quality, but seek out the worst goods if you can buy ordinary Beerboom Catuah Gurrahs at 60/ any quantity would be safe. but if they are above that then only buy 4 or 5000 pieces at 67 and no higher for very common ordinary Gurrahs. if you can get Company or very white and fine Gurrahs 36.37 x 2¼ 2 or 3000 pieces would be safe at 75/ but we want no intermediate qualities. the most ordinary and all the rejected Gurrahs should be dy'd, they are not profitable to be printed as Chintz is not wanted over 1⅞ wide. you will reccollect when you are looking for a lot of Gurrahs to have dy'd, that it is no matter how bad the quality is, nor how short the dimensions are always take the cheapest you can find, 500 Pieces of Fine Beerboom Gurrahs may be divided into two parts as an experiment. *Mow Sannas* this article has never been so low as it has this year. the sales have not been above 130¢. it is probable that it may be avoided by the Americans, we hope it will and calculate you will be able to make great purchases, it is no matter how bad the quality is, you may buy any quantity at 30/ and if other goods are higher than your limits than you may go to 31/8 for 20.000 pieces. but if other goods are as low as your limits then only buy 5000 pieces above 30/. we think they may be down to

28/ to 30/ as they are very unsaleable and low. everywhere, you will buy every piece you can at 30/ and have the coarsest and all the rejected dy'd blue, but no other colours. they did not answer this year nor will they ever do so well as blue, perhaps 2000 pieces made into Chintz not to cost more than 40/ would do well, and 1000 pieces divided into two parts to cost 20/, you will have that quantity printed if you can [interlineated: have] an abundance for your other purposes say to blue and pack with, *Remember* that we are not apprehensive of having too many goods of one name when they are cheap, *Ordinary Narrow Mamoodies*. these goods cannot be designated by names because they are very often chang'd, we mean ordinary goods 37 x 1⅝ ¾ such are Meergungee, Gudgepour, Mugga, Gauzepour, ordinary *Meergungee* gives the best idea of what we mean or goods of these quality and dimensions let them be call'd by what name they may, these goods have been very low this year probably on account of the great quantity brought here this year, and partly because the dimensions are not popular. we refer to the width principally — it is probable therefore that many Americans may avoid them. and that they may be low they will be safe at 60/ for any quantity however ordinary. and should other white Cottons be above the limitations then we would advise 20.000 pieces at 62/8, the most ordinary and the rejected should be made into Chintz, the staind will do to dye Blue. of those which you pack in white Cloth divide 5.000 pieces into two parts, do not invoice these goods by the name of Meergungee. but call them Shazard poer, Tilpah, or some other name, the buyers are sick of the sound of Meergungee. and it really affects the value of the article, we expect the Mamoodies we are now describing will be very ordinary. you must not be alarm'd at that, even if they are worse than was ever before seen. there are ten different kinds or more of narrow and coarse Mamoodies which go sometimes by one name and sometimes an other. *Ordinary Mergungee* or any that are inferiour are what we mean. *Ordinary Mamoodies*, 38 to 39 x 1¾ to 1⅞. say *Jannah*, this article does not exactly give an idea of what we mean perhaps if we say of the quality of Meergungee but rather

longer and wider it will be as near as we can describe, goods of
these dimensions will be cheap at 65/ to 70/ p Cº. we imagine
that the following are the kinds we mean perhaps some of them
may be rather better but we would not have you go higher than
70/. Khyrabad. Fulpour, Ande, Joyadpour, Tanda *Jalalpore
Mamoody. 39.40 x 1⅞ 2* in consequence of the great abundance of this article now in this Country and the very ordinary
qualities of those which have been sold thro' the years, they have
declind below their usual prices, we would not have you go higher
than 82/8 for the ordinary ones. and 85/ for those which are
very white and well glaz'd, you may pack the rejected ones
they are not good length for Chintz nor will they sell for any
more dy'd Blue than the ordinary narrow ones, *Tookeries Manickpore & Alligungee Gurrahs, Maharaz gungee, Patna Baftas,
Patna Cossas, Patna Gurrahs, 28 to 30 x 1⅜ 1½ ⅝* or goods of
this description, they are and have [interlineated: been] thro'
the year. very much out of fashion on account quality and width
being to narrow, it is probable they may be divided by our
countrymen. they will be safe to buy at 32/ for the most ordinary, and 35/ for the best say 10.000 pieces but if you can get
the ordinary at 30/ and the best at 33/ then any quantity you
can buy will be safe, the rejected may be dy'd Blue. *Alliabad,
Mow, Cannapour, Chandly Besurah, &c Emerties, 29.32* by
2⅛ or goods similar 3 or 4000 pieces at 67/8 would do very
well. if at 65/ than a large quantity unless they are very much
run upon by the Americans, in which case only a moderate
quantity say 4 or 5,000 pieces even at 65/. we would have you
divide into two parts the longest ones and Invoice them by some
other name, they should be over 2 Cubits wide because they
are valued for their width, we would advise to have the rejected
of this article pack'd in the White Cloth they are too good to
dye Blue or to make Chintz. there are many other goods of
these dimensions and about the same quality say Jannah Sannas Cawripour do you will of course consider them the same
as Emerties. *we would have you pay no regard to names but
only quality and dimensions* Emerties formerly came 28 x 2
we presume they now make them wider because wide goods

of late years have been more in demand among the Americans for the 28 to 30 x 2 we think you should not go higher than 60/ for a large quantity and 62/8 for a small. the quality should be as good as Alliabad, the most common name for Emerties besides those abovemention'd are Joyadpour, Nabob Gungee, Tanda, Khyrabad, Lawkerpour, Fulpour, for any that are inferior to *Alliabad* we think 50/ to 55/ is high enough. *Armegar, Banily, Alliabad Baftas* 35.36 x 1⅞.2 or goods of that discription if they can be bought at 60/ we would advise any quantity if at 62/8 we think 5 or 6000 pieces should be bought and if other white goods are higher than our limits, then we would advise that a large quantity be bought even at 65/. the most ordinary of goods of these dimensions and the rejected should be printed they are of the right length and breadth, *Jalalpore Sannas* 40x2⅛ ¼ will do at 102/8 for a moderate quantity if they are at 95/ to 100/ and not run upon very much, then a very large quantity would do. should be white and glaz'd for the fine ones, we would advise 1000 pieces divided and invoiced Jalalpore *Addies* the rejected should be pack'd. *Chandpore Cossas* 40 x 1⅞.2. this has been a very profitable article the present year and will always do well at 100/ for any quantity if they are 105/ then buy only 2 or 3000 pieces and none over that, unless it may be a few bales by way of assortment, pack all the rejected of this article. *Long & Wide Mamoodies, Alliabad and Chondilly,* 40 to 43.2 2⅛ or goods of that description, they will do well @ 82/8, when they are over 41 Cubits long they should be divided into two parts, the rejected will do for Chintz divided into five parts. *Mow Cossas* 40x2⅛ or any other thin and rather ordinary Cloths of the same dimensions will do well at 80/ and if other white Cottons are above the limits at 82/8. *Jannah Cossas* 38.40 x 2⅛. *Tanda* ditto. *Fulpour* do, or any other coarse and thin Cottons dimensions will do well at 75/ to 80/. there are several other names which you will find out by enquireing. names are so often chang'd of all kinds of goods that we only put down the most common and of those goods which we know you to be familiar with. *Tanda Sannas,* 39 40 x 2⅛ are sometimes no better than Tanda Cossas and sometimes 10 to 15% finer they should not be bought over 85/, if ordinary only 80. *Gurrah Sannas* are about the same. *Chandilly, Azmegur, Gauzepour, Alliabad. Sannas* 40 to 42 x 2⅛ @ 2¼ goods of these names sometimes are very fine and sometimes ordinary, they would be cheap from 90/ to 105/ according to quality, if you are at a loss to know their value, compare them with good Jalalpour and you will be able to decide whether they are better or worse and of course which will be the cheapest, they are at present very saleable and probably will continue to be. when they measure over 41, it would be well to divide them into two parts, pack all the rejected. *Fine Mow Sannas*, when those of very fine qualities can be had at 50/ p C⁰ 2 or 3000 pieces would do, but not unless they are very fine and white. we want no intermediate qualities *Chandegungy Mamoodies*. 40.41.2 @ 2⅛ are very good Cotton and will do well at 90/. we think 1000 pieces divided into two parts would be well disposed of. *Mow Mamoody*, 36 x 1⅞. say very like those in Gipsys Cargo they were very white and fine and will do at 80/. *Mamarackpore*, 39 x 1⅞ are worth little less than Jalalpore. they will do @ 75/. *Malda & Beerpour Cossas*, 38. to 40 x 2¼ ⅜. these goods have not done well for some time past, but as it is possible they might now answer, *we would have you buy 500* pieces even at 135/ p C⁰ if at 120/ then you may buy 2000 pieces. we have now made our observations and fix'd what we consider as the relative value of goods, by which you will be govern'd in your future purchases of the very great variety of White Cottons in Bazar. we have mentioned only a portion and in doing it we have selected the most common kinds and such as we presume you are acquainted with of the value of others you must judge by comparing them with these, and *we again repeat in earnest request that you will not allow yourselves to be led away by names, but judge only by qualities & dimensions*, names often change and goods are depreciating and appreciating in qualities as well as changing in dimensions every year. the colour'd Cottons & Silks (there being less variety) we have been able to be more definite, but there are some others of these also that we may have forgotten. We enumerate some of the names of other Cottons. you must see them all and as many more as you can hear of and examine and compare them with the standard goods and you will never be at a loss to know whether they are cheap or dear *Cossas*, Jugdea, Luckipore, Sugapore, Rungpore, Commercolly, Beran Hurrial, *Mamoodies*, Tanda. Lucknow, Cawnpour, Besurah, Unda Fulpour, Shazardpour, Khyrabad, Lawkerpour. Joyadpore. Nabob Gungee Barilla Maharaz Gungee, Tilpa, *Sannas*, Nabob Gungee, Khyrabad, Lawkepour. *Baftas* Nabob Gungee. Tilpa, Tanda &c besides the above (many names of which probably are fictitious, it having been the practice among the natives as well as Americans Supercargoes of late years to make new names) are the following goods of various discriptions, Sutena Guzzenah Salem Cossas, Tegry, Banisparty, Sallgatchee, Guzzenahs of various kinds. Bengal Bengal Natty, Gorackpony, Gocul Natty, Mohunpore and Balagore Sannas many of which you will not find but it will be well to ask for them all.

Terrindams.   38.2 cost 80/ to 90/⎫
Tanjebs   35.2 "   60/.   70/⎬ these articles have
never been imported, but we think they will do well. you may send us on trial 1000 pieces, and if lower than the limits and you think them cheap, then 2000 pieces, at any rate 200 pieces of each. the following goods have not been shipp'd to this Country, but we wish you to send us 2 bales of each on trial and particular memorandums respecting the cost and quantity that may be obtain'd. Addaties, Seerbands Seerboties, Sullimes, Doosaties, Lacouries, Elachees, Halassies, Tepays Allachans Seerhandcannies, Jaspees, Alliabannies, Chaucannies, Percaulas, Penniascoes Janniars, Jamdannes, Nillies &c, these goods are made for shipping to various parts of Asia and many of them to England. we wish to make an experiment of them, if you think any of them cheap you may ship 500 pieces and at any rate two bales of each. You will have remark'd on looking over the above memorandums that the quantities of goods order'd will more than take up the funds you may think proper to invest for us, we do not calculate upon your being abe to get every article and

we have therefore given you as great limits as to the quantities that you might be able to make up the amount in some articles, if one fails an other will not we rely very much upon the colour'd goods generally, particularly the Chintz Blue Cloth, Seersuckers, Checks and cheap Handkerchiefs, upon Silks say Taffeties, Bandannas, Lungee and other Handkerchiefs. & upon low priced Baftas, Long Cloths, Humhums, and those goods which may be very low from whatever cause. do not be afraid of too large quantities. we have no objection to a 1000 Bales of one article provided it is cheap. should you find it difficult to get away the Gulliver for want of goods, you may venture upon 20,000 lb Merchantable Indigo @ 150/ p maud at 10.000 lb of ordinary at 125/. but if you have low priced goods enough then we would not have you send any unless you can get a credit for it. any goods you may have left or that you may may buy after the Gulliver sails you may ship @ 100 Rupees p ton for Cottons of the common kind or 120 Rupees for Silks. fine Cottons, Seersuckers, if you can find any one who will take very coarse Cottons at 11% you may then ship them at that rate, but you must select those as coarse as Gurrahs, ordinary Mamoodies Blue Cloths &c. our freight will then come as low. if not lower than 8%. you may send to any part in U S but we prefer Boston New York or Baltimore. keep nothing on hand except very ordinary goods, that you can get freighted @ 100 Rupees p Ton — and the Silks and Seersuckers 120/ We repeat our requests that you would write us very particular letters by by every oppertunity. let your information extend to everything, you will find in the box with this a sample of the Company Bandannas I refer to, and also a piece of Company Choppa, we send also samples of Seersuckers that cost 11/. if 20% coarser they would do, the figures would be better if larger, I only send them that you might see the quality the Bandannas and Choppas must be as fine as the sample sent you we send also a sample of *Cuttanies*. we would have you divide our piece goods into several Invoices. say the Silks into one, the colour'd goods into an other. and the Cotton divide into Invoices of about 25.000 Rupees, in this way they are more convenient to sell, mark one Invoice A, one B, and so on. we request you to keep our business as much to yourselves as possible as much of our success depends upon it. We have now only to add our wishes that the above directions may be follow'd as nearly as possible. we are confidant no exertions will be wanting on your part to obtain our ends and we feel sanguine of success the returns of $4000 we ship by Union you will make in the coarsest goods you have on hand, say Gurrahs. Blue Cloths &c and if the Supercargo is willing and you have the goods, you may make up the shipment to $15.000. you will find the freight on coarse goods say Gurrahs @ 65/ does not amount to more than 80 Rupees p Ton, as there is so much reluctance at taking letters and as you will want to send duplicates of long and important letters after the Gulliver has left. we would suggest to you the plan of putting them into a Bale of Cottons p Union, which you can refer to in a short letter. tell us the No of the Bale &c. we shall expect letters by every vessel and hope you will continue to get them on board,

We are with regard & c

(signd) P T Jackson for self & Jos Lee Jr

Henry Lee

original pr Union from Salem enclos'd with specie

Copy pr Vancouver via Madras [written across face of letter]

LETTER FROM HENRY LEE, BOSTON, OCT. 19, 1810, TO EDWARD A. NEWTON, MADRAS, ON THE INDIA TRADE IN GENERAL [1]

The Lees had already sent two vessels, the *Gipsy* and the *Gulliver*, to India in 1810, both to Calcutta where all previous Lee vessels to the East Indies had gone. They were now introducing an innovation into their trade with India and sending the ship *Vancouver*, 250 t., which Patrick Tracy Jackson had purchased Aug. 31, 1810,[2] from T. H. Perkins, but in which the Lees were apparently concerned, to Edward A. Newton at Madras. The Lees had apparently also had goods shipped them from Madras on the brig *Charon*, 238

1. Jackson-Lee Papers, "Letter Book," Aug. 19, 1810–May 30, 1811.
2. *Ibid.*, Henry Lee, Boston, Aug. 31, 1810, to Peter Remsen, N. Y.; Registers, Boston Custom House, 1810, no. 396; 1807, no. 168.

t., built by Thatcher Magoun and registered under P. T. Jackson's ownership, June 29, 1810, and the brig *Boston*, 146 t., belonging on Feb. 2, 1810, to Edward A. Newton, Henry Lee, and P. T. Jackson.[3]

Under "gruff goods" were apparently classed almost all goods from India not piece goods, such as drugs and goat skins.

Madras   (p Union from Salem for Calcutta)
Mr Edward A Newton   Boston Oct° 19. 1810
    Dear sir

    The ship Atlas for Calcutta was the last vessel that went direct, I forwarded to Philadelphia a letter to go by her but it was refused & return'd, I have put a letter on board the Francis that will probably reach before this, M J. & myself were not particular in our letters because we were not certain of our conveyance this will go by the Union to sail in 5 to 15 days now waiting only for her Dollars —
I leave to Mr J to inform you of the purchase of the Vancouver to sail in a month for Madras her cargo &c — The ship Pilgrim of Salem sail'd in July for Madeira, Teneriffe, & Bombay, her object I imagine is Surat piece goods, It would be worth your while to write over to Bombay and ascertain what her outward cargo sells at and what her homeward costs, which you can send us and we shall be enabled to know when the cargo is sold here how her voyage results, it is possible the goods made on that coast may be cheaper & better suited to the African trade than the Madras goods, & that at some future day, we may wish to extend our views to that quarter, — at present there are no persons in this country who have any knowledge of the cost of goods obtain'd on Malaber coast, & the supercargo of the Pilgrim is a young lawyer who cannot posess every information whatever.

    The ship Java own'd by J Prince Derby &c saild 8th August from Teneriffe for Madras, I cannot find out her object, but I imagine it is to get some profit on her wines, she will probably go on to Calcutta but of this you will know. — No other voyages that I can find out have been undertaken that can in any way

3. Registers, Boston Custom House, 1810, nos. 27, 247.

interfere with ours, nor do I hear of any expeditions — Calcutta
seems now to be the object of the India traders, and in addition to the ships I sent you the following are preparing to sail
in course of two months —

Ship Francis   Salem $175,000⎫
  "   Union   do   100.000⎭   to sail in 10 to 20 days
                                              1 month
Brig Leader Newburyport 80.000

two ships at New York and probably more will sail in two
months. I think it not improbable one of them may stop, it is
conjecture only Northern Liberties Boston $60.000 and cargo
of merchandize, which I shall find out & write you. Mahogany
is one article. One ship is talk'd of from Providence and one
from Philadelphia, so that our next years importations will be
greater than the last. these ships will not probably return till
November and December 1811 and some of them Jany. 1812,
so that the Vancouver will have a chance to anticipate them, We
calculate she will return by Oct^o & if possible earlier — for the
fall sales.
The market continues in a very favourable state for Madras
goods particularly Blue guineas, Camboies, Niccannies, Mouilla
Ginghams, Salempores punjums &c the importation of color'd
goods from Calcutta has been considerable, but not sufficient
to supply the demand, which has been greater than was ever
before known — there has been sold in months of August &
September 400 bales of Blue Gurrahs & Mamoodies &c at 4.25
to 4.50 which are very inferior to Blue Guineas. more so than
the difference between the prices still however Blue Guincans
of 7 call will have always a preference of 25 to 50 Cents
in a piece over Blue Gurrahs and generally more than that will
be made. The Baftas sold at 3.25 to 4.50, 12½ yards by 1 —
notwithstanding, this large supply they are still worth 4.52 in
Philadelphia and 4.75 here for the most ordinary kind which
cost 80/ in Calcutta — I have sold myself which I received
by last ship from Calcutta twenty bales to one man at 4.50.
and 300 more could now be sold at 4.25 to 450. Calcutta checks
20 & 1⅞ cubits are now worth $2.25. they cost 40/ they have

never been more in demand nor ever so high, I imagine Cam-
boys would now sell at $4.50 for a large quantity, and I see no
reason why they should not as well as Blue Cloths be as high
in the spring, there is not a single Calcutta vessell out, except
those that sail'd since May, and the only one expected before
june is the Gipsey and one to Baltimore, the latter may be here
in May the Gipsy in March. *Custers* are as much in demand as
Guineas and very scarce. Fine Gurrahs have done better than
ever I knew them to of course punjums and salempores may
be consider'd as high, Byrampauts Benjudipauts, Negonipauts,
Topsails, Nunsarees and other Surat goods are very often enquired for, and no doubt would sell very high. — in fact our
prospect for a great sale of the Charons cargo. (and the Bostons
if she should have any) is almost certain. The Sales of Bengal
goods this fall have been very great, and notwithstandg. the
importation has been very large and goods cost very low, yet
prices are higher than usual, The exportation to Africa, Spanish
Maine. South America &c has been very great. I cannot but
believe that the prohibition of the slave trade by England has
encreas'd very much our exports to Africa, because it is no
longer an object to carry goods from England since the traders
are deprived of their most profitable returns, which were slaves
to the English Islands the slave trade is now in the hands of
the Americans, who carry it on under the Spanish flag, This
trade will continue and the traders can only supply themselves
with India Goods in this country the relax'd state of commercial
laws of the Spanish colonies serves to encrease the exports to
that quarter, because, the duties are diminsh'd and prohibitions
which formerly existed, taken off, the demand in North Europe
is very great but as yet no exportations have been made, nor
will there be for the present, except of Indigo, Ginger, Tumerick, Sugar, &c &c. the importations of color'd goods will, I have
no doubt be very large from Calcutta this year, but at the prices
you contemplated upon buying at, there is nothing to apprehend in sales of the return cargo of the Vancouver, As for the
Charons we expect to sell the whole in a month from her arrival,
Of the gruff goods I promise myself more from goat skins than

any other article because they cannot be had in Calcutta in sufficient quantities to over stock the market, & because they are better than the Bengal skins, I should advise you to collect them as fast as possible, you cannot send too many. *Tumerick* We now think better of than Ginger, *Cassia* will be a very good article, as will also Cinnamon it is very much wanted, I recommend to you with confidence these, and also the other gruff goods mention'd in our memᵒˢ and letters, and should advise you to buy them as you can find them cheap [that they — stricken through] that they may be ready for some future shipment, You will be particular in the information you send us relative to the outward cargoes that are wanted, We can get Pale Ale at about $5 or $6 charge p barrel from London in course of 4 or 5 months, We should want that time in order to avail ourselves of the taxes & rate of freight from London to this country bottles can usually be had at about $8 p groce. Casks country gin &c you know the cost of, I think country gin may be a good article it sells as well in South America as the Hollands and in fact the quality is very little inferiour to that, the price this year has been high on account of high price of grain, it may be down to 60¢ next year We shall have no Brandy to ship 'till we have an intercourse with France, an event which at present is very uncertain.

Our political situation is the same as it was when I last wrote, Napoleon has made some continental premises respecting the repeal of his degrees, but whether with a view to relax them entirely to make us the more ill humored with England, is very uncertain, at present but few people are sanguine as to a renewal of our trade with France.

The voyages to North of Europe have been very good particularly to Russia. many captures & condemnations, but yet on the whole much money has been made, the trade to West Indies as usual. Sᵗ Domingo at present is well stock'd with goods, they are very low and many of the houses in England who traded there have stop'd payment among which are Sharp, Graves & Fisher, the houses upon whom D. D. &Co gave you £ 20,oo.o.o bills. it is very fortunate for us that we sent our

Mr T and that his exertions have been able to get so large a portion of our property, I am apprehensive we shall yet have some difficulty with these men, I fear the outstanding debts will never be credited as if received We shall expect to see the Boston in February, when we shall be able to judge what you can do, and whether it will be expedient to continue the business, If you are able to buy goods as low as you were confident you could when you left us, we shall immediately send off a vessel.

Yours

(signd)   Henry Lee

Copy pr. Vancouver — original p Union [written across face of letter]

LETTER FROM HENRY LEE, BOSTON, OCT. 20, 1810, TO PETER REMSEN, NEW YORK, IN REGARD TO THE HAVANA MARKET[1]

Piece goods sent to Havana were largely used for clothing the Cuban slaves or for use in the African slave trade. The Lees very rarely sent goods direct to Africa. One case which comes to hand is of a consignment of blue guineas sold for $4,593.74 2/3 by William S. White of the *Manchester*, Feb. 20, 1810, at Prince's Island, a Portuguese possession in the Bight of Biafra, Gulf of Guinea, West Africa.[2]

The "repeal of Decrees" refers to the declaration of Aug. 5, 1810, revoking Napoleon's Berlin and Milan decrees against trade with Great Britain, so far as the United States was concerned, after Nov. 1.[3]

Mr Peter Remsen   Boston Octr 20. 1810
  DrSir

I have yours of 15 & 16th. You may Consider the Sale made to the New Yorker as comprising R C's goods that remain unsold I wd. hold the Bands @ 575 & take 5.60. they are good ones — the Jala. Mamoodies if they are good will bring $4 — Calcutta goods will not be any lower & you have now

1. Jackson-Lee Papers, "Letter Book," Aug. 19, 1810–May 30, 1811.
2. *Ibid.*, "Foreign Sales on acct. of J. & H. Lee from 1803 to 1810. — "
3. Channing, *op. cit.*, vol. iv, p. 427.

5 M⁰. to sell them — they have advanced 5% in Phila. Schott & Yorke wrote me — I wd. advise you to hold on Phillips goods & to sell those of R C's that are wanted & the remainder hold — The Havanna Market has been a good one for me because I have got off my unsaleable goods such as Mow Sannas & Meergunge Mamoodies — but most of the shippers have not made any thing out — upon the returns there has been a great profit — Some Shipments have lately been made from here and there was a good supply on hand at the last accts. so that I do not think there is much encouragement to ship — I always have sent the worst goods I had say Meergunge Mamoodies, Mow Saunas together with some particular kinds of Seersuckers — If you wish to make a shipment I wd. advise Meergunge Mammoody @ 2.70. @ &280 Mow Saunas @ 130. B Gurrahs 3$ — or any other goods that may be as low Sugars have advanced ¾ to 1$ & it is thot when the news of the repeal of Decrees gets out they will go higher — they may again decline when it is known that no exportations have been made   Coffee is rather advancing here 21¢. & scarce — Rum and Molasses high — Sugars scarce but do not advance beyond $12 for Hava Browns — Hemp has risen since the last sales to $360 Iron holds its own — & will not be lower   Sheetings 20 Heavy Duck 22 — Ravins 12 — I am expecting 30000 Yds Crash ordinary kind what is the best you can do with it I am offerd 12½¢. — P T J wants his Dollars as soon as they can be Collected if you cannot get them send to Yorke & S —

Yours

LETTER FROM HENRY LEE, BOSTON, OCT. 30, 1810, TO WIDOW POEY & HERNANDEZ, HAVANA, ON TRADE WITH THE WEST INDIES [1]

This letter indicates Henry Lee's interest in trade with islands in the West Indies other than Cuba. The "Spanish Maine" refers to the coasts of Spanish colonies bordering on the Caribbean Sea; Sisal is a port in Yucatan. It is hard to tell what is meant by the state-

1. Jackson-Lee Papers, "Letter Book," Aug. 19, 1810–May 30, 1811.

ment that "some goods sold very well at Sisal" but "are not admitted."
Perhaps the goods were sold by sample; perhaps they were smuggled
in, and Lee was interested in learning how they could be imported
legally.

In a letter of Oct. 26 to Antonio de Frias & Co., also of Havana,
Henry Lee stressed that by "Brown Sugars" he always meant "those
of the cheapest kinds without any reference to quality they answer
my purpose better than the high chargd ones;" urged greater care
in shipping by seaworthy vessels even "giving $\frac{1}{4}$ more" if necessary;
and requested minute information on the value of and demand for
India piece goods, particularly for the "African trade." Shipments
from Cuba — we know of at least five between Sept., 1810, and Feb.
19, 1811[2] — were doing well.

Widow. Poey & Hernandez   Boston October 30, 1810
    Havanna   via New York
    Madam & Sirs
        Since my respects of 17. inst. I have none of your favors.
the late arrivals bring me nothing from you which I regret
because I am waiting for information that will enable me to
make up for the shipments of Cottons. I must request you wd.
be as particular as you can in quoting the last Sales of India
Cottons & the demand — also any variation in prices of Sugars
— My friend Mr Peter Remsen shipped you on 15th. int. 5 Bales
goods which you will sell for the most you can obtain & ship
him the proceeds — I shall send you in 10 or 15 days 10 to 15
Bales more and some further small shipments — I wish returns
made as you have hitherto done promptly — Should Brown
Sugars of any ordinary quality have risen above 10r. you may
go higher for Whites — if both have risen above that then send
me the cheapest browns you can find at the prices you can buy
at — there is at present no prospect of an intercourse with
France — but Sugars will continue up for consumption tho' not
at the present prices — I am often without advises for a long
time on acct. of the long passages our vessels have at certain
Seasons

2. Lee-Cabot Papers, 1810–12, Sept. 10, Nov. 12, Dec. 21, 1810, Jan.
1, Feb. 19, 1811.

I wish you to write me via Charleston S C. Baltimore & New York copies of the letters to this place — it is a great Satisfaction to me to hear often & I sometimes save my insurance by it — Is Cinnamon say real from Ceylon an article that is much in demand with you? — what is the prices & how much w^d. Sell? Is there not a demand for it for the Spanish Maine? —

I have had some goods sold very well at Sisal which is I believe in the Bay of Campeachy — the Super Cargo who sold them sayd they are not admitted Pray can you give me any information upon this Subject as to the mode of obtaining permission to send them there? Be good en^o. your next to let me know the value of Coffee & what rate you can buy me 50.000 of the small Kernal very green & almost round —

Yours
H Lee

LETTER FROM HENRY LEE, BOSTON, OCT. 31, 1810, TO HARROD & OGDEN, NEW ORLEANS, IN REGARD TO A BRIG TO THAT PORT [1]

The connection with New Orleans which had originally been instigated by the embargo was now being pushed, because of the blockade of ports under the control of France from the River Ems southward. The Lee correspondents at the Louisiana port were now Thaddeus Mayhew [2] and Harrod & Ogden. An innovation in the Lee relations with this port was the sending of a Lee-owned vessel to New Orleans to take on a cargo for England. This vessel was, however, "lost in the Oct^o gale in the Bay of Hunda," [3] probably Bahia Honda on the northwestern coast of Cuba.

Messrs. Harrod & Ogden   Boston October 31. 1810
New Orleans   p Mail
I trust before this comes to hand the Brig Buffalo will have arrived & made some progress in her loading for England —

1. Jackson-Lee Papers, "Letter Book," Aug. 19, 1810–May 30, 1811.
2. Ibid., Henry Lee, Boston, Aug. 26, 1810, to Thaddeus Mayhew, New Orleans.
3. Ibid., Henry Lee, Boston, Dec. 4, 1810, to Harrod & Ogden, New Orleans.

I w^d. not have you sell the Brig at $12000 — if you can get a freight to New York or this place (I prefer NY) of 3 Cts p H [lb.] for Cotton in square bales —

If freight to G. Britain are low — & 8 Cts pr H can be had to Gottenburg or any other port as safe — you may accept it — but I hope & trust you will be able to get our limits & more for a freight to Liverpool which we prefer to any other port — If you sell the Brig my wish is that you ship the proceeds of her & cargo in Cotton at 14¢ or Sugar at 9$ on board to Mr Peter Remsen New York — or to me in this place If neither can be had I wish you to invest the am^t. in Doubloons which I understand can be had at about $15.25. to $15.40 and ship them to Havanna consigned to the house of Widow. Poey & Hernandez who will have instructions what to do with the proceeds you will have the am^t. Insured at some Safe Office you will do the same with the proceeds of my goods or any Advances you may make upon them which I w^d. thank you to make as large as you can conveniently — as it is an object to get returns as soon as possible — I notice the N^o. Liberties has arrivd I presume also the goods from Phil^a. have also been rec^d. before this & I hope are sold I wish this year to give your market a fair trial & I cannot but hope the result will be such as will induce me the Coming year to make further shipments — I am expecting in 4 m^o. a considerable quantity from Calcutta and Madrass among which are great variety of coloured goods — write me via N York & by land — passages to this place are always long — Should the Buffalo go to Liverpool as I hope you will consign her to John Stewart Esqr. to any other part in Great Britain to Henry Higginson Esqr. & direct Capt. Greely to write him as soon as he arrives —

Yours

LETTER FROM HENRY LEE, BOSTON, OCT. 31, 1810, TO EDWARD
A. NEWTON, MADRAS, ON EXCHANGE AND ON EAST INDIA IM-
PORTS AND EXPORTS [1]

This voluminous and detailed letter reveals both the ambitious
plans of the Lees in regard to the East India trade and the care with
which they intended to carry them out. "Mr Tracys Mem° Book,"
mentioned near the end of the letter, contained all the information
concerning Madras goods, instructions as to their purchase and requests for further information, which the employers of John Tracy,
Jr., could think of; to this was added a copy of a similar memorandum book furnished to George Lee for a Calcutta voyage, May 7,
1810.[2]

The means of remitting funds to India was always a problem, as a
sufficient quantity of ordinary merchandise could not be sent out in a
single vessel to pay for the return cargo of India goods. American
merchants, accordingly, resorted to shipments of specie, which it was
a difficult and tedious task to procure and for which a premium was
charged, and also purchased bills on London to be exchanged in the
latter city for bills on the various ports of India. The Lees were
taking advantage of the comparatively small need to remit funds
from the United States to London, because of restrictions on commerce, to obtain bills on London at a discount; with these bills,
through their London agents, they purchased bills on Madras, from
which fewer importations were made than from Calcutta and on
which exchange was in consequence lower. Their knowledge of the
state of exchange on Madras gave them an advantage over merchants who, not so well informed, made remittances in specie or purchased bills on Calcutta. Henry Lee seems to intend to write that
"you may perhaps wonder that," under the circumstances, "we did
[not] convert the specie we are sending you into Exchange & remit
via London." The answer was that the specie was shipped "on
respondentia," that is, given as security for a loan made upon a high
rate of interest, which loan was to be cancelled if the goods did not
reach their destination.

1. Jackson-Lee Papers, "Letter Book," Aug. 19, 1810–May 30, 1811.
2. *Ibid.*, "John Tracy Jr's Book 1810."

Mess Edward A Newton   Boston Oct⁰ 31. 1810
    Madras.

    Dear sir

      My last was dated 19th. inst by the Union from Salem which vessel is still detain'd for specie, the owners of the Francis refus'd our letters. I mention this least you might think we neglected any oppertunity, you may always conclude when you do not get letters by a vessel. that either we did not know of the oppertunity or that our letters were refus'd. this will go by the Vancouver. Captn Gardner detain'd for specie, it is very scarce on account of a considerable exportation within a few weeks to China, India and even to W Indias & Spanish Maine, she will however be ready 10 days earlier than Mr J calculated or wish'd when she was purchas'd. We had several objects in view in buying the V. one of the most important was, to have a vessel at Madras to take home the cargo bought for the Charon, should any accident have happen'd to prevent that vessels reaching her destination this is a contingency which is certainly worth providing against, if it can be done without any sacrifice, of this you will judge on her arrival at Madras & act accordingly. another motive was to get home [all the — stricken through interlineated: whatever] goods you may have bought or be able to buy after she appears, before the arrival of the ships that have sail'd lately & are about to sail for Calcutta & Madras, We hear of only one destined for Madras, but it is possible & probable that there may be others that will stop there of which we know nothing. We think it very much of an object to get back the Vancouver by October next, because goods must come down when all the goods are in from Calcutta. we have no fear but we shall do well, even should the V. not return 'till winter or spring, but should do much better to return earlier, because there are many Calcutta Goods particularly colour'd goods that come in competition with Madras goods should the Charon not have arriv'd you have funds & a vessel to carry on that voyage, should she have arriv'd, you then have to decide upon the expediency of loading the Vancouver at Madras on account of yourself, P T Jackson & myself, or allowing her to proceed to Calcutta on acc^t of P T Jackson & J & H Lee. we hope you will find it for your interest and ours to determine upon the former, at any rate we hope you will see in it our inclination & ability to enter heartily into your plans. & a proof of the great confidence we feel in your judgment & abilities.

Until lately we have not been able to find out the course of Exchange between London & Madras, we now have the pleasure of know^g from an agent J & H Lee have in England (who sent out for the purpose of remitting funds to Calcutta) that bills on Madras can be bo^t at 7/4 st^g p Pagoda. I presume this the *Star Pagoda*, & if so the rate is very favorable, estimating Dollars at 163 p Pagoda, which I am told is the average when bills on London are at par. the premium of insurance would be sav'd, the premium on Dollars will be about balanced by the expence of purchasing Bills & the time lost. besides the certainty of getting out our funds is an important consideration to us. as in case of capture of the vessel they can be reserv'd for the next. bills on London are now at 5½ to 6 p Ct discount, so that at this moment the gain would be 8 to 10 p Ct. you may perhaps wonder that we did convert the specie we are sending you into Exchange & remit via London. Our reply is that it is on respondentia, & we should not wish you to be without a portion of V^s's funds even if it was on our own account, we are told that there is some uncertainty whether bills can always be procur'd in London on Madras. we shall know when our remittances to Mr Higginson get to hand, & by that time or soon after we shall hear something from you & be able to judge whether it is expedient to send you more funds, this mode of getting out funds to India is not known to any one but ourselves, but the low rate of Exchange on London if it continues may enduce others to adopt the plan, but not to Madras. Calcutta is the place to which the attention of persons is turn'd, but few people here know what is a favorable remittance to Madras, so that we shall not be injured by competition of any one at present, The remittance from London to Calcutta is not so favorable by 3 to 4 p Cent. The Rupee which is worth only 48¢ or 208 Rupees p 100 Spanish Dollars, costing in London 2/4ᵈ or 52¢. We do not wish anyone in Madras to know the advantages of remitting, because they would write out to their friends — & thus we should be injured. it is now a very convenient as well as profitable operation, but should there be another Non Intercourse or any other impediments to our visiting English settlements, we should be able to derive great advantages — & have them to ourselves. it is probable that Bills on London in this country will continue down for 6 months to come 'tho not so low as at present. because one reason why exchange is now so low is a very great scarcity of money among the most enterprizing Merchants it may continue to be as low as 3 to 4 p Cent discount. this will aid us in any Bills you may have drawn on London, we find that bills on Bombay were at same time at 2/2ᵈ p Rupee, which is not so favourable, as the Bombay Rupee is not worth more than 44 or 45¢ estimating Dollars at 220 to 225 Rupees p 100 still it would answer very well should we at some future day wish to make any voyages to that coast & want funds. you must let us know what is the rate of Exchange between Madras & Calcutta and Ports on the Malabar coast, say Bombay, Goa, De Maun &c &c. we then can tell the best mode of remitting there, we have taken measures to get the best information of the rates of Exchange between England & India and shall be able to know at once, when we hear of your arrival at Madras. & what you are like to do, whether we ought to send you more funds or not, this business of Exchange we presume is as interesting to you as to us and will be worthy your attention, let us know what you think on the subject and whether you can suggest any thing new.

The outward cargo of the V. has been collected with care and comprises all the articles we thought safe to send, The Iron and Bottles are low, the Naval Stores, Corks, Salmon &c as usual. the Gin is high it may appear to you extraordinary we should send so much *Turpentine & Tar*, we did it because it is the only chance we shall have of sending these articles &Spars. because generally shippers & underwriters object to Naval

Stores, 'tho not contraband, in this instance we have no shippers to consult, and we prevail'd upon the underwriters not to
charge any extra premium, part of the Turpentine & Tar we
presume you will send to Calcutta, where it will do well, the
remainder you can do as you think best with, the last sales of
Spt^s Turpentine in Calcutta was 8 Rupees p gallon, Spars also
will do well in Calcutta, & also Salmon if you have more than
is wanted at Madras. *Gin* we wish you to be very particular in
your enquiries relative to this article because we are of opinion
it will be a profitable one for some time to come. American Gin
sells for as much nearly as Hollands in many foreign countries,
& the quality is very similar to Hollands, that which we sent
last year to Calcutta sold for a higher price than Brandy & it
was consider'd as Hollands. I find on looking over some Mem^o
Books that 1805 there were several cargoes of liquors sold at
the various ports on the Coromandel coast besides at Madras,
among which 13,000 Gallons of Gin at Porto Novo at 1 Pagoda
per gallon. a great price as at that time there must have been a
very great stock of Brandies &c at Madras, you can judge best
whether it will ever be an object for us to have a vessel stop at
any of those & barter or sell for Cash, or whether those places
can be furnished from cargoes landed at Madras, this article
of Gin may be purchased commonly at 60¢. & as grain is now
falling it will probably be at that rate 6 or 8 mo^s *Iron* is now
very abundant but will not be lower than $100. If it will answer
you must let us know what sizes are best, *Brandy* is out of the
question. Spanish 4th proof is now at 1.75 & none here of any
consequence. 100 Pipes could not be bought at that, we are
not like to have any intercourse with France, & if we do it
will be some time before the article will get down low enough
to ship. *Teneriffe* Wine is very high at Teneriffe, & will continue so as long as Spain remains in its present state, we use
Teneriffe instead of Sherry. *Madeira* is also high in the Island,
so that a Wine voyage is out of the question, indeed as far as
my information goes they were always hazardous, we can always
I imagine collect a cargo in this country that will give some
profit, perhaps a cargo might be sold at some port in Ceylon,

We can always have liberty to stop there by paying 1 p Ct additional premium, which will be but little since we shall send a portion if not all our funds via London in Exchange. you will please to write us fully on the subject, Perhaps Allum may by some management be obtain'd at some of the little ports on the coast, it will always be an important object 200 tons have been imported from C. G. Hope, cargo own'd by Mr Boyd and by mere accident has found its way here. Mr Tracy can explain the voyage &c. it has not produced any effect. we shall obtain as much as we expected for any that may come in the Boston. ──

With regard to homeward cargoes, I would recommend you send a few Cases of the various kinds of Indigoes from the worst to the best, & if any of middling quality can be had as low as 60¢. I would venture upon 10,000 lb. it will do for our home manufactures, which are becoming very extensive, it is true we get this article from Calcutta very cheap, but still it is worth while to make an experiment upon Madras Indigo, get it in cases if you can, but if not then take lumps or broken pieces, the boxes should not contain more than 200lb they. are more convenient of that size than of any other, Bengal Indigo has done very well this year in Russia &c. the whole is shipped off & the demand next year will be great. the present price of Bengal is $1.90 @ $2 p lb & probability of remaining as high. *Cassia*, the more I hear of this article, the more I am enclined to think it will afford a great profit from Madras. I am quite certain it is abundant & cheap in Ceylon, & this is one of the greatest Cassia markets in the world, the consumption is very great, We now get it from China, but the price has increas'd there 50 p ct within 5 years & it now costs 15 to 17¢ p lb & far inferior quality to Ceylon, it will be worth your while to send down to Ceylon & know at what it can be bought. if you cannot find any in Madras. 500 lb of Buds would also do well on trial, they are worth 60¢ p lb a small quantity of oils of Cassia & Cinnamon would also do well.

Cinnamon still continues high, as it must always be while we get it thro' England, a very considerable amount of this article can be sold during a year for consumption & I imagine a quantity can be disposed of in the Havana & on the Spanish maine, we have sent out for information, I would certainly send out a quantity even if I gave 90¢ and 1000 to 2000lb at any rate, we shall take care in the disposal of this article, & Cassia, to conceal from every one from whence it came. which we can easily do what may be wanted in Havana we can send there ourselves. as the duties in that Island have been reduced to 15 p Ct & it has become a place of very great trade, *Cardamams*, I believe are produced in Ceylon as well as in Bengal. 2000 lb would do well, I do not know what they cost, they would sell here at $1.50 p lb. 500 lb might be sold at 2$, but I would not go higher than 75¢ for 500 lb or 60¢ for 2000. should they prove of good quality we might at some future time. venture upon a larger quantity. *Colombo Root* produce of Ceylon & can be bought there very low. 2000 lb would do well at 12¢ p lb & if very sound & fresh at 15¢, if it can be had as low as 10¢ I would advise 5000 lb. I advis'd in some of my memos that this article should be avoided, but since then I find the old stock has either been consumed, or has become so worm eaten, that it will not sell, there is great deception in this article, get that which is new & sound, it is almost always a little eaten, but still it will answer. *Gum Benzoin* sometimes calld Benjamin is very much used, it is produced in Sumatra & probably in some other parts of India. that like the sample is worth 60¢. I would venture upon 2000 lbs @ 25¢. if as low as 20¢ then 4000 lb. send a small quantity even at 35¢ on trial, *Gamboge* is produced in Ceylon. if you can get it at 60¢ 1000 lb would do, if as low as 40¢. I would advise 3000lb, you may find many other kinds of gums & Drugs. I would send a few hundred pounds as samples, & we will return you an account of their value, & how a larger quantity would sell. We used formerly to get many of our drugs from Persia & Mocha while our trade continued to that quarter but now that source is stopped, as we have not a vessel gone to Arabia or Persia, nor is there any inducement for one to go there, this makes it the more important for us to pick up such kinds as we can find at Madras *Goat Skins,* this is so prom-

ising an article that every thing relating to it is interesting. I
would advise you not to stow any loose, because they get very
much injured & you save no room, as spaces between the Bales
may always be fill'd with Tumerick. Ginger. or Gunny bags, I
would mix Tobacco, very fine, with Spirits of Turpentine & draw
a brush ½ dozen times across the hair side. & then pack 500 in
a bale. & screw them very hard, in this way they will come
out very fair & not moth eaten, as they often are stow'd loose,
I think you ought to secure as many as you can of whatever
size, they will certainly sell at a great advance for any quantity. the consumption of them is encreasing. As for Piece goods,
I can think of nothing to add to my former letters, there are
no Madras goods in the country. & we can only estimate them
in comparison with Calcutta, of which all kinds simalar to
Madras are in great demand particularly *Fine Sannas, Checks,
Blue Cloths*, which answer to niccannees & Manilla Ginghams,
these goods have all been exported. say 1500 to 2000 Bales &
by the time the Charon appears they will be very much wanted,
I think it would be better to devide 1/2 or 2/3 the Camboies &
also the Niccanees that measure 24 Cubits Bengal white goods
have thro' the year sold very well, but they are now dull &
rather low. the fall sales having principally been made the
stocks sent out this year to Bengal amount to a very large sum,
& will produce a return of 15 to 20,000 Bales but they will
come high and many of the importers will be obliged to hold
them. We have no apprehension but what we shall do well with
the Vancouvers cargo, if bought at the prices you calculated,
The African trade is now immense and the Madras goods will
certainly have the preference. besides they will be cheaper than
the Calcutta can be afforded at. I think Camboies the safest
article & that 500 bales would not be to many. I would advise
you to send us a Bale or two of all the various kinds of Goods
that can be found at Madras, that we may have an oppertunity
of ascertaining how they will do, it is no matter if we lose upon
some of the bales. we more than make up the loss in the experience we acquire, send enough to make a fair experiment, I am
inclined to think there are several kinds of goods that may do

for this country that have not yet been tried, or if they have
been the buyers in India gave too much, the fact is. that the trade
to Madras has never been carried on by any persons who have
had much knowledge of the mode of buying there, or of the
kinds of goods our country requires, the general result of the
trade to that place has been a losing one. & adventurers have
been driven out of it before they had an oppertunity to become
acquainted with it. We have a fair chance to keep to ourselves
for a time at least, all the advantages which it offers, should our
voyages terminate successfully, no doubt others will follow, but
I trust we shall be able to do much before that time. you may
depend upon it we shall keep to ourselves as close as possible
every thing which relates to it, & that we shall not admit any
adventurers at profits as we at first thought of, least they should
become familliar with the cost & profits on the goods. we except some of our friends who will give us the entire controul
of their shipments and never ask for an Invoice or an account
of any kind.

Persons who have [interlineated: some time] been in India
& examined a great many goods, whose nice discriminations are
made in qualities are apt to grow particular as to the qualities
& refuse many goods under an idea that they are too bad. I
have myself suffer'd from this when I thought myself certain
of judging right, let me repeat what has been before said I
believe in my letters, that it is impossible to manufacture any
goods to ordinary for this market, there is always a greater
difference made there than here, I would make an observation
with respect to large quantities of any one article, almost every
one that goes out to India are alarm'd at the idea of 500 or
even 3 or 400 Bales one article in a Cargo. they would not buy
so many at half price — any one may see the absurdity of this
fear, when it is known that this country imports 15 to 20.000
Bales in a year, and among them 3 or 4000 Bales of some of the
staple articles. they come in different vessels to be sure, but
they come to this country and are sold I have seen goods so
low in Calcutta that I would have bought 5000 without hesita-
tion. do not be alarm'd at buying a large quantity of an article

when it is below its relative value. we think you are furnished with the best information it is possible to collect, no doubt there will be changes. & that in some articles we may be disapointed. We have taken infinite pains to collect every kind of information relative to the trade. we have devoted time & thoughts to it & shall continue to & will write as we have oppertunity — When your letters come to hand you may depend upon immediate and particular answer to them. in mean time we shall have little or nothing new to say to you, in fact in turning back to my long letters I find them in the main little more than a repition of my memorandums & first letters, perhaps the greatest satisfaction they will afford will be to convince you that we have you and your business constantly in our thoughts, & that we feel more and more interested in your plans & more & more sanguine that they will succeed. We feel a most perfect confidence in the information we send you. and the data upon which our voyages are predicated. we feel no less confident of your ability to purchase cargoes and of our skill in disposing of them on their return. Money from various causes is now very scarce. Mr J & myself have made great efforts to carry on our plans. we hope & trust the Boston & Charon will appear in good time to put us again in funds & eneable us to send out another vessel, among the information we want from you will be a memo from Custom House of all the exports & imports from Madras this year to U States. this would be useful in the disposal of the Cargo and eneable us the better to judge how much of each article can be sold in this country. the more particular this the better. and if you could obtain a memo of the cargoes for 10 years past. such a Document would be valuable to us. notwithstanding the rigid system which has been adopted in all countries un the controul & influence of France & the various other difficulties which Commerce has had to encounter, the country has been prosperous during the past year, the produce of the country has been bery high & our ships have found employment at a very high rate, whether this will continue no one can tell. from appearances one would imagine that for the coming year our trade would be confined to Russia alone. but the world is in such a strange situation that all calculation is vain. we must go on with our projects and trust to providence for their success. I do not believe our political situations with France & England will change much for the present it is now thought that the offer on the part of France to repeal her decrees is not sincere but merely to embroil us with England, & indeed should the orders in council be repeal'd (as they will be when the decrees of France are) there would be some other obstacle in the way to a settlement with England. it is the plan of our government to keep in ill humour with G Britain that France may not be offended, the administration have higherto and will continue to act upon it.

Congress will meet next month. there will be many fiery speeches made resolutions pass'd & perhaps some restrictions on commerce, or any thing else that is ridiculous that you may imagine. but we shall have no war with England. the interests of the *people* are too much opposed to it do not be affected by any reports you may hear, but rely upon us — we will send you information from time to time of any changes, as you will always want something to fill up the vessels with we reccommend your buying when it is low 50 to 100 Tons Tumerick, & as much ginger, as they will always be the best article for that purpose, should you have more than you want and be obliged to sell the surplus at a loss it will be no consideration compared with the advantage of having enough of those two articles on hand, I would also buy large parcels of the other gruff articles reccommended. most people believe they are not worth attending to, indeed those who have made the experiment upon drugs formerly have suffer'd as much loss upon some articles as they gain'd upon others. we have advis'd nothing but what we have experience to justify, formerly we received many drugs & gums from *Persia &* Arabia, so much so as to reduce their value very low here, but not a ship has gone this year to either of those countries, we have found it very convenient to have a cargo divided in several invoices of $10,000 to $20,000 each as sometimes we can sell an Invoice of that amount when we could not one of 50.000, & as it will never do to break an Invoice we often lose a good sale. sometimes New York requires one kind of goods Boston or Philadelphia another, now as we may have to resort to several places for sales of our goods, I would advise the cargo be divided into Invoices of $10 to $20.000 some of which I would have composed of assorted goods & others of two or three articles of the cheapest goods and such as it will not do to offer at an advance, because a high rate always alarms the buyers. let the goods be bought ever so low. I would mark 1st. Invoice A 2 Invoice B & so on to C.D. &c this may give you some trouble but may be of a great advantage particularly as J Lawrence. Moses. Heards. Haggerty & Austin. Mason &Co and other speculators in New York always want to buy at the Invoice. and when goods can be sold in that way it is a great advantage & it is impossible to retail a cargo except at auction the charges of which as you know in New York are great. I would advise that you do not put the dimensions on the tickets you put into the bales. because if they should differ from the Invoice, even tho' the Cloths measure as much as they are sold for. it occasions difficulty, there is no convenience in it. I would pack the white Cottons except the very coarse ones, in wax cloth, they appear better for it, send home a certificate that your cargo was bought of the natives of India, as I presume it will be, this enables us to export to Russia &c otherwise we should have difficulty and no one would buy to export, I can think of nothing more indeed it is not necessary, as you will take a much more comprehensive view of our plans than we can give, our letters may serve to suggest some things to your mind & at any rate will serve to show that we are alive to the business, as much so as when we parted. I shall add a Price Current of staple articles either to this or Mr Tracys Memo Book & also the vessels that have sail'd or are about to sail for East Indies. Mr Tracy will furnish anything you may require that we have omitted. He is intelligent and zealous in the business & from his having so long been with us knows what we wish & think, his knowledge of qualities & value of piece goods is very considerable & he is furnish'd with samples & Memorandums.

Yours

(signd)　　Henry Lee

Original p^r. Vancouver [written across face of letter]

LETTER FROM HENRY LEE, BOSTON, NOV. 8, 1810, TO JOSEPH HALL, JR., CALCUTTA, WITH INSTRUCTIONS [1]

The importance of these detailed instructions is as clear as their meaning. The emphasis laid upon constantly furnishing commercial information to the owners in the United States should be noted, as in this respect both Robert Cabot and Joseph Hall, Jr., were evidently negligent.

Henry St. George Tucker (1771–1851) was at this time in Calcutta as secretary in the public department of the East India Co. He had previously at various times since 1801 been accountant-general; managing partner in the house of Cockerell, Trail, Palmer & Co.; again accountant-general; a prisoner for six months after conviction of attempted rape; and supernumerary member of the board of revenue. It is unlikely that Joseph Hall's father's letter was ever presented to Tucker, who left Calcutta for England in Jan., 1811. He returned in about a year and on Aug. 8, 1812, was made secretary to the government in the colonial and financial department.[2]

(per Vancouver via Madrass)

Mr Joseph Hall Jr　　　　　　Boston November 8th. 1810

　　Dear Sir

My last to you was by the Union & agreeable to what I promised I have purchased for your account One thousand pounds on London to be remitted from thence on your account — this will serve to pay for any goods you may have shipped in the Gipsy on credit on your own acc^t. or may be appropriated to a shipment in the Gulliver — I have done this without any authority from you because it is more advantageous than any other remittance could be — & because you may not have a

1. Jackson-Lee Papers, "Letter Book," Aug. 19, 1810–May 30, 1811.
2. "Henry St. George Tucker," *DNB*.

high rate of interest to pay for any long time — you will see in the letters of the owners by this vessel what are their orders I hope & trust nothing will be found wanting on your part to fulfill them —

After all that has been said about letter writing I shall add nothing more — except that a neglect of it disqualifys in my opinion any man from being an agent — I w^d not trust any one however much confidence I had in his talents who w^d refuse to comply with so important a duty — Let your information extend to every subject & be minute — We wish to know as much as possible what the kind of goods & the quantities the Americans are shipping — this aids us in disposing of our Cargoes —

You will find it difficult no doubt to keep from your countrymen a knowledge of what you are doing — at least entirely so, but we rely upon your address to prevent their knowing so much as to be able to follow you — I cannot but think that when the present fleet all get out — goods will be high — still however there will always be something in the Bazar that comes within our limits — buy if only one Bale — goods will come down when the vessels have left but not so low as they were last year, while the ships were in Calcutta — Put as little trust as possible in your Banians or Sircars pay the latter well for any services they may render — a few thousand Rupees in a year may do well thus disposed of, but do not place much confidence in any one — I have send Newspapers to Mr Newton if he has any opportunity he will forward them — Send me Calcutta Register — & other Books of that kind & also the Newspapers —

I want from the Custom House in Calcutta a list of the Cargoes exported to this country since 1800 & also the specie imported there & Merchandise from U States — this document w^d be worth 500 Rupees — let it contain if possible a Mem^o of each cargo — Remember the Book which I requested you to keep — I depend upon it for the best information upon trade to Calcutta which has ever yet reached this quarter of the world — Do not limit your inquiries — but let them embrace every thing which can have the most distant bearing on trade to India — and send me copies & extracts from it —

I suppose the Gulliver will have saild before this reaches if not hurry her off as fast as possible — We must not sell her return cargo before the fall fleet returns — When she is dispatch'd you will commence purchasing another cargo according to Memorandums — never stop for want of funds while your credit is good eno' to borrow — We shall continue to remit via England as long as Exchange continues down — We shall certainly send back the Gipsy — shd she be lost or captured, then some other vessel — We shall send also another vessel in two or three months after the Gipsy — We rely wholly upon the Calcutta & Madras trade & shall carry it on at all hazards —

Your father has sent you a letter to St. Geo Tucker he was a man of great consequence & shd you want any aid or advice he may do you great service — I wd. explain to him that you wished his permission to call upon him in any such cases — as to any attentions he may be inclined to pay you I wd avoid them when I could without violation of good breeding — his occupation will not admit of his devoting any time to you if you were in situation to remain there —

The Vancouver by which this goes will afford you an oppy to send home a copy of your Memo. Book — your accounts & particular letters — she will no doubt return from Madras and we hope will not be detained there more than a month — When you make a shipment — it wd be worth while to put some of your papers into a Bale, they wd come safe — you can refer to it by some notice in the letter — in this way — look at Bale No — there are some choice goods in it — I shall know what it means — It is so important to get our letters Accts. &c. that it might be worth while to pay 150 Rupees a Ton for 2 @ 3 Tons for the sake of safe conveyances you can also send to us Mr. Newtons letters in this way —

We believe we have omitted to put down Table Cloths & towells — you may buy 1000 Rps worth of the cheapest kind as an experiment as we have before observed a bale of any other goods you may see that we have forgotten to mention The vessels now preparing are Ganges to sail 15th. Decr. with some merchandize & a small sum in Specie say 30 or 40.000$ the

Caledonia from Phil^a about same time with 350 @ 400.000$ —
600 Tons — Mr Chamberlain who was out last year goes in her
& will remain in Calcutta 6 Mo^s. — he is very clever at buying
piece goods you must take care he does not take away your
bargains — One more will go I think from New York & perhaps some one or two in course of winter from this quarter —
You will not get any letters by the Ganges we shall try to get
some on board the Caledonia — but you must not be disappointed if you do not receive any — I cannot close this without
reminding you again of the great trust that is [opened —
stricken through interlineated: repos'd] in your industry & strict
attention to the directions your owners have given you — I will
not doubt for a moment of the strong interest you take in our welfare nor of your abilities to do all we expect or wish — from
[interlineated: your] not writing as I so earnestly desired you
— I sometimes feel some degree of anxity — but I attribute it
in part to your not feeling responsible while Mr C. remained
in Calcutta — we have now placed our reliance upon you &
hope we shall not be so sadly disappointed as we have been M^r
Cabot — who has litterally given us no information of what he
was doing —

Yours with regard —

Original p^r. Vancouver [written across face of letter]

LETTER FROM HENRY LEE, BOSTON, NOV. 8, 1810, TO GEORGE
LEE, CALCUTTA, WITH ACCOUNT OF PLANS FOR THE INDIA
TRADE [1]

The jealousy and rivalry prevailing among traders with the East
Indies comes out clearly in this letter. The *Francis* refused the
Lees' letters, while the character of the owners of the *Leader* and the
Ganges made the Lees unwilling to entrust letters to these vessels.
Thomas Stewart, owner of the *Ganges*, was Henry Lee's particular
bête noire among merchants trading with India. The Lees intended
to return good for evil, heap coals of fire, etc., by offering volun-
tarily to take any letters and papers which masters and super-

---

1. Jackson-Lee Papers, "Letter Book," Aug. 19, 1810–May 30, 1811.

cargoes wished sent from India. The intention of the Lees to push the India trade to the limit is more clearly expressed below than anywhere else.

Mr George Lee   Boston Novr 8th 1810

My last to you went by the Union, the letters excepting two or three were put into the boxes with the specie, as were also some newspapers. We did not do this on account of any suspicions we entertaind of the honor of the Captain or owners of the Union. they behaved to us with great politeness and voluntarily offer'd to take any letters we might wish to send, We did it because the letters were important, and we wish'd to secure them a safe passage. We wish you to be particular in sending word if the Gulliver leaves before the Union, that you will take charge of any letters or papers they may wish to send, We wish you also to send to other Masters and supercargoes and take all their letters & papers, We prefer this civility to refusing letters tho' we are often refused — You got no letter by the Francis for reasons stated, The Leader is the next vessel she got away in about 10 days. We do not write by her because *We know the owner of her*, as it happens it is of no importance, because the Vancouver will arrive at Madras before her, and you will get your letters by her as soon as the Leader arrives, she has $80,000, partly on freight & partly on account of the owner, she must take part gruff goods, sugar and ginger probably. The next vessel will be the Ganges, bought by Joseph Head for Mr Stewart, she will carry out some Mahogany and other Merchandize, no bottles, Glassware or pale ale, nor any iron hoops this vessel is the one that went to Canton (Captn Ingersoll last year she is 260 tons, the Northern Liberties that was charter'd is given up Mr S will probably have small funds and will want gruff goods we have already said what we thot of this man, and how much, We hoped you would avoid him. we suffer'd formerly from a connexion with him and know what he is. You may depend upon it he is a mischievious fellow, If you should have any quarrel with him or if he should excite any suspicions with the government against you on acct of your long residence there. You can only let him know that he is carrying on a trade thro Mr Head which is illegal, he being a British subject, we shall not send by this vessel, Indeed we do not at present know of any oppertunity that will occur for sometime I shall insure for you $8500 on board the Gulliver at and from Calcutta to port discharge in U States. I do it now because the premium is low and should any captures be made and we hear of them, as will probably be the case. it would advance. it will be done at 5% we wish you in all cases where you ship property of your own to have a seperate Invoice & not involved with the cargo. we.wish Mr Hall to do the same otherwise in case of loss we should lose our demand upon the Underwriters We shall get no permission to transfer your $8500 from Gulliver to any other vessel you had better therefore ship it in her if possible Let us know what amount you wd. have returned you by every vessel that may be sent — It is our intention as I formerly mentioned to you to do nothing but in the Calcutta trade — We shall send back the Gipsy, as soon as she appears shd. she be captured we shall buy another vessel —

We have also a vessel 330 tons building at Medford which will be ready in June — she will probably go — We put up her upon the calculation that one of the Brigs might be taken or we might sell one if a good offer is made —

it is not improbable all three may come out — The business perhaps next year may be bad on acct. of the great stocks sent out this year — but we shall do well eno. if the goods can be bot according to our Memorandums. [if piece goods are too high — stricken through] — if piece goods are too high you will have collected eno. gruff goods to fill them up when the present fleet shall all have left it is not improbable goods may again get down at any, rate if Calcutta [interlineated: business] is bad next year at this time as it may be — then but few vessels will be dispatched and it will be good again the year after —
We wish you to buy as you can find goods at our limitations to any extent & we will take our chance — do not be alarm'd at the extent of our plans we can provide you with funds & the means to get home the goods — When goods are so high that

you cannot buy invest your funds in Companys paper so that you may always have them at Command when an opp^y presents of buying — you will always be able to find something within our limits piece goods as well as Gruff goods — Should the Gullivers outward Cargo be unsold — we advise you to dispose of it at your leisure — the speculators of combine to put down goods, & it is probable that Mr Stewart may be one of them —

I w^d. not deal with him on any terms — he has given me some history of his life & which I doubt not is true which fixes [interlineated: him in] my mind as man who sh^d. be avoided — Bottles, Ale & Glass ware are staple articles & will no doubt find purchasers — Let us know what we can calculate upon for such an other cargo —

Yours &c

H Lee

[Original p Vancouver via Madras — written across face of letter]

LETTER FROM HENRY LEE, BOSTON, NOV. 10, 1810, TO GEORGE LEE AND JOSEPH HALL, JR., CALCUTTA, WITH INSTRUCTIONS FOR THE PURCHASE OF EAST INDIA GOODS [1]

The "Mr Tracey," going out on the *Vancouver,* was doubtless John Tracy, Jr., cousin to Henry Lee's wife, whom we have met before. Evidently the Lees were not impressed with the old adage about a superfluity of cooks or they would not have confronted with equanimity the prospect of adding another to the two agents they already had in Calcutta. The necessity for chintz having "a lively appearance" was that it might be better adapted to the African trade. The repeal by Napoleon of various imperial decrees affecting the commerce of the United States had been acknowledged by a proclamation of the President declaring that, according to Macon's Bill No. 2, the Non-Intercourse Act would within three months be renewed against Great Britain unless she similarly revoked her edicts. Federalists, with good reason, regarded Napoleon's alleged revocation of his decrees as not to be taken seriously. "Cassimbazar" (variously spelled) was an important silk-producing center

1. Jackson-Lee Papers, "Letter Book," Aug. 19, 1810–May 30, 1811.

of Bengal. A *lac* is 100,000 of anything; a *lac* of rupees would amount to £10,000.

Boston Nov 10th 1810

Mess George Lee & Jos Hall Jr
 Gentlemen
  our last a copy of which we now enclose you went by the Union for Calcutta, she sail'd about the 3d of this month & has on board for our account $4000 for which you have directions for its disposal. This goes by the Brig Vancouver for Madras, we expect she will take her cargo on board there and return, It is possible however that Mr Newton may not be able to buy a cargo there, it which case she will proceed on to Calcutta and load with such goods as Mr Tracey (who goes in her) and you may think for our interest.
It is Mr Tracys expectation that Mr Newton will want him to remain in Madras. should he [not — stricken through] not he has engaged to join you in Calcutta and manage our business jointly with you, and we wish you to consider him in that light, He has good information generally upon business and from his long experience in India piece goods and having liv'd with us. He is well qualified to carry into effect our plans. If Mr T should remain at Madras, We wish you to keep with him a correspondence which will be mutually convenient. The Gulliver saild at the time we calculated 10th Septr, we trust she will either have sail'd or be on the point of it when this arrives. it is very important indeed that she should return as soon as possible, because goods will be low when all the vessels that are now out return. after she sails you will commence purchasing according to the Memorandums sent you, We have bot £3000.0.0 since our last to remit making together 13200.0.0£ stg part of which will be remitted in bills on Madras, We shall continue to remit while Exchange on London continues down so that you will have funds and credit enough to buy all the goods you may probably find within our limitations which may be shipd if opperty offers or if none offers than kept for the return of the Gipsey or the vessel we may send next, We have some articles

to add to the list of drugs, gums &c which will appear at foot of this. The Chintz sent home in Euphrates that cost 16/8 was very good quality and the figures were good, but too many dark colours, there should have been more red and yellow they are much the best colours as they have a lively appearance, *as this is a very important article*, particular attention must be given to patterns and colours. as well as to the quality of Cloth and demensions, as for other piece goods our Memos are so minute that we can think of nothing to add,

Our political situation remains the same — The [President — stricken through] President has issued a proclamation restoring the intercourse with France to its former footing, and we are told by goverment that if English orders in Council are not repeal'd in Feby our intercourse with Great Britain will be interdicted, We consider many of the acts of this goverment as tricks to amuse the mob, nothing can be infer'd from this act as to any speculations that are made, they are not worth consideration, no one can calculate what will be the conduct of goverment for a year to come. but of this we are confident that we shall have no war with G Britain — do not listen to any reports you may hear, but follow your instructions, we will send you information if any great change is likely to take place. We wish you to add to the memo of Drugs 3000 lb *Arsenic* if it can be bought at 7 Cts p lb if higher say at 10¢ then 1000 lbs and above that none, *Glin gun* or Gallingal you may send 500 lb at what you can buy it at, and if as low as 7¢ then 2000 lbs, *Gamboge* produced in Ceylon send 200 lb at any rate and if as low as 40¢. 2000 lbs should be sent. *Cardamons* produce of Patna send 500 lb at any rate and if you can buy them at 30¢ to 50¢ then 1500 lb. We wish you to send us samples of any other drugs you may meet with and let us know all you can respecting them. perhaps you may induce some of the Persian Merchants to import them for the next year. You will observe in looking over our letters and memorandums sent Mr Cabot, that we have said much on the subject of sending or going to Cassimbazar to buy silks. We are of opinions something like 10% could be saved in that way and that permission would be granted. at any rate if you have leisure we advise that it be attempted. If practicable it would be an immense affair, and a large amt might with safety be invested in Silks, say one or two lacs of Rupees. You will see also what can be done in way of contracting for other goods. Colour'd goods can always be had in that way to great advantage & perhaps some white ones may be, leave nothing untried. you have time, funds, experience and the best information before you that any men ever had who went from this country. — We have a letter from Mr H Higginson giving us notice of the receipt of £ 6600.0.0 part of the remittances refer'd to above, we find it better to remit bills on Madras and have sent out orders to that effect, part of the amount therefore may be remitted to you in bills on Madras which you can negotiate in Calcutta or send down for collection to Mr Newton you must ascertain from him therefore how remittances can best be made from Madras to Calcutta, whether by selling the drafts in Calcutta before they are accepted or send them down for collection and have the funds remitted by Mr Newton Let us know to whom to address our letters whether or what Banian. You had better write out in Memo Book our various orders and memorandums that none of them may be lost

We are &c

sign'd P. T. Jackson

H Lee for self &Jos Lee

Sent the proclamation & Gallatins Circular — not to be alarmed at any report of War with England or Non Intercourse — but to buy according to our instructions — Whether it is necessary for a vessel going from England to India to stop at Madeira? — to ask the Collector at Calcutta that question that GeoLee's insurance was done @ 5% — $8500 in the Gulliver & $3000 for P. Remsen — which must come in his name — notice of the Caledonia, Ganges & Meridian — that we shd. send back the Gipsy or some other vessel by 18th March —

Original pr. Vancouver for Madras [written across face of letter]

LETTER FROM HENRY LEE, BOSTON, NOV. 12, 1810, TO EDWARD
A. NEWTON, MADRAS, WITH PLANS FOR TRADE WITH THAT
PORT [1]

Between the last long letter to Edward A. Newton (Oct. 31) and
the letter below (Nov. 12), President Madison, Nov. 2, 1810, had
issued a proclamation declaring that all restrictions on commerce
with France were removed in consequence of the revocation of her
edicts "violating the neutral commerce of the United States;" and
that if Great Britain did not within three months similarly modify
her edicts the Non-Intercourse Act should be revived against her.
It was the wish of Henry Lee that Newton, by a partial report of
these circumstances and an exaggeration of the potential effects,
should so alarm the Madras merchants as to lower the price of goods
and induce the American merchants to decrease their shipments.
Henry Lee also regretted to inform Newton that another vessel had
adopted the Lee method of remitting to India via England by bills
of exchange on London with which to purchase drafts on Calcutta,
instead of remitting in specie; but he did not think anyone knew
yet that it was more advantageous to remit to Madras. Lee requested Newton to find out the possibilities for trade with the Malabar Coast in case American merchants should be barred from ports
controlled by Great Britain. He also advanced the possibility that,
instead of importing goods next year, the Lees and their associates
should furnish funds to other merchants in India if a large advance
could be obtained — say 50% to 65%, as had already been offered;
in such a case it would pay to send out funds borrowed on respondentia even at 23% to 25% interest.

William Coleman, "man of information and . . . correct politician," was the leading Federalist journalist of the time and editor of
the *Evening Post*.[2]

Mr Edward A Newton   Boston Novr 12th 1810
  Madras
    Dear sir
      The Brig being detaind gives me an oppertunity to add
a little to the long letter you will receive from me, It is fortunate for us that the Vancouver has been detain'd, because

---

1. Jackson-Lee Papers, "Letter Book," Aug. 19, 1810–May 30, 1811.
2. "William Coleman," *DAB*.

it has given us an oppertunity of writing you a word about the proclamation & guarding you against any effect it might produce upon your operations. I think you may turn it to great advantage by selecting from the Papers such remarks as may alarm the merchants in Madras, and thus reduce a little the price of goods, or if any American should be at M, and trying to make an arrangement with some of the houses to take home goods. You may destroy their confidence in the safety of property in this country. this is very important, so much so that it would be better to admit some other house to ship in the V. rather than have any rivals we really hope that there may be as great an alarm this winter as there was last, it would help our sales in the spring, but let what will happen. I shall never act upon the calculation of war with England, Mr J has sent you files of Boston Papers, I have sent you the Evening Post, I think the remarks of Coleman as worthy of some attention, He is a man of information and a correct politician. and remarkably careful to collect as many facts as possible, I have sent you also 2 gallons of pickled Nuts and will put on board some Cyder if I can find any that will keep, Mrs L, has put on board a jar Cranberry sauce, understanding from me you were fond of it, and hopes it may arrive in good order. I could think of nothing else this Country affords that you cannot get in Madras, I have omitted in the list of vessels that Brig Phoebe cleard about a month since from Baltimore for Ceylon, I think she is on the same voyage as the Dolly went upon last year, say to Ceylon & Madras, she probably has a small stock, and if she will take freight low and comes away before the Vancouver, I would put on board her 50 or 100 bales say at $40 to $50 p ton paid in Madras, you will see in the papers the ship Meridian for Calcutta via England, her object is to take out Bills of Exchange and invest proceeds in drafts on Calcutta, I am very sorry this mode of remitting is like to become known, but unless the consern have an agent to receive their funds in India should the Meridian be taken, they will be awkwardly situated, I trust no one will find out that it is better by 5% or 6% to remit thro' Madras. Indeed I know of no one who can tell what is a favorable remittance to Madras. I hope you will conceal from the Madras Merchants the advantage of sending Exchange instead of Dollars to India, we may yet derive great advantages from our information. besides enabling us to increase our speculations without any great sacrifice in interest or credit, It becomes of great importance now there is any degree of probability of another Non Intercourse to find out some port on the Malabar coast belonging to the Porteguese or natives, that we may resort to in case of such an event at present no one but ourselves would think of such a thing. they do not know that there are any goods on the Malabar Coast that would answer even if they could go there, we want to know what is the best port. the Export duties inward do. what kind of goods would sell there & what we can procure in return, what siz'd vessels may be sent, how long it might require to collect a cargo, the season that is safe, the best mode of getting funds there, whether to remit in Exchange or Spanish Dollars the best house to call upon, the terms of doing business & any other information you think may be useful to one sent on such a voyage there. If this business of sending vessels to Madras is one that we can continue it would be worth while to let us know whether it would be expedient to send a vessel via England for a cargo of Pale Ale. Glass Ware &c, we can usually get a freight out that will pay all the expences in England & sometimes more, you had better let us know what advance you could procure on $50 or 100.000. If we should think best to do that next year instead of importing on our own account, as we may if piece goods should be excessive low. if you could get 50%, it would be very well, as there is no doubt we may obtain 40 to 50000 in respondentia at 23% to 25% & we could put in the balance ourselves. I do not mean by this to advise our friends there to engage in a speculation that would be losing to them, I would not certainly abuse the confidence they might be disposed to place in us but I refer to any houses that may have goods on hand with which they can do no better. I know this has been given in some instances where there was no prospect of the goods giving more than the cost & duty in this country & it has been repeated by the very men who we think would be almost ruin'd by it, 65% was offerd for the specie of the *Financier* and 50% for specie and merchandise together, which was very well, this was the lowest rate I have ever known. You know more upon this subject than I can I only mention it by way of reminding you of what you probably have contemplated a 1000 times. I mean also to say that if such terms can be obtain'd and we think it better than importing on our own account we can send you $200,000 p annum if our vessels return in due time.

Yrs —

pʳ. Vancouver [written across face of letter]

LETTER FROM JOHN BROMFIELD, JR., CANTON, NOV. 18, 1810, TO HENRY LEE, BOSTON, WITH ACCOUNT OF PRICES AND PURCHASES [1]

During the remainder of his period of factorship in China, where he had arrived Sept. 11, 1809, Bromfield continued to make frequent reports of prices in Canton to Henry Lee, as well as to purchase and ship merchandise ordered by his friends in the United States, as indicated below.

The "difficulty in shipping off the Goods of *outside men*" probably related to some effort on the part of the Hong, the Canton merchants' gild, to prevent sales to foreigners by non-members of their organization. Some project or other to build up an effective monopoly was usually in process and had been for nearly a century. By Dec. 11, the "stoppage in shippᵍ the Goods of *outside men*" had, however, "been got over with a great deal of difficulty, and only as it regards the Ships now here — the Hong merchᵗˢ appearᵍ resolved to let no goods hereafter be shipped *for* outside dealers." [2]

Mʳ HenryLee   Canton 18ᵗʰ Nov. 1810
My dearSir
    Your numerous &obliging favors of april & may by different conveyances have safely reached me; and If I do not answer them at so much length as they so justly merit, I hope

    1. John Bromfield Papers.
    2. *Ibid.*, John Bromfield, Jr., Canton, Dec. 11, 1810, to Henry Lee, Boston.

you will not charge it to a want of thankfulness, for the very marked attention to me & my interest; but to a lack of anything interesting to Communicate.

The shipment by Hazard &Cabot from Philad^a p Atalanta, came safe to hand for ^a/ct of yourself. Mr P.T. Jackson & Mr Eben^rFrancis — it appears that you had been impressed with the idea almost to a certainty, that Silks would have been as low this year as they were the last, and you will be surprized at the prices hereunder quoted for them — This difference is principally owing to a loss of a considerable portion of the Silk Worms & to an unexpected & great demand by a Spanish Ship from Manilla (for the Acapulco market) both in raw and manufactured Silk. — Sinchaws have been up to 19¼ & even 19½ $ Blk Sarsnet 15¼ & 15½ col^d Sarsnets 16¾ @ 17 $ & Sew^g Silks 6½ to 7¼ doll^s. Thereis not even now a difference of more than ¼ to ½ a dollar from these prices, altho' the demand for all the american Vessels has been contracted for some time ago — In conformity with your instructions, Ipurchased a few coarse ready made Sarsnets at 12½ and have since contracted for some good ones at 15½ — some very common Crapes at 8 $ & some better at 9 $ of 16.yards. As Sew^g Silks were so very high I omitted them altogether & have purchased some ponjees at about 6$ nearly sufficient to compleat the investment of $10,000. shipped by Hazard &Cabot. These Goods could not be got ready for the *first* ship — There is also a difficulty in Shipping off the Goods of *outside men*, which is not yet arranged & if they were in readiness could not at this moment be shipped.

I cannot but regretthat you & your friends should have adventured in this Shipment at so unlucky a moment, the more, as I know you were induced to it through the intention of benefiting my interest, and I fear both you &them will suffer by this renewed instance of your desire to Serve me. As to the shipment of theGoods, I shall send them by the first Vessel on which I can ship them after they are ready & the difficulties attending the exportation of them are removed — I think they will be sent in the [Pekin — stricken through interlineated:

George] to Philad^a, as I fear no opp^o will offer for Boston or newyork — but on this point will write you in a few days by another opportunity. Notwithstanding the high prices, the quantity of manufactured Silks will be very considerable in the American Ships, principally to Philad^a. — The quantity of Sew^g Silks however very small. The prices of Teas have not yet so much fallen as might have been expected & will not probably be very low, until after the lading of the English Ships. The American Ships now here (9, in all) are most of them taking a large supply of China Ware. —

Young Hyson is now selling at 42 @ 45 Tales, but all Teas must at the end of the Season decline very much — The quantity of Shortnankins taken by the Ships now here will not be very great — they can now be bot at about $45 [interlineated: @ 46$] — common Comp^{ys} say 87 @ 88 — best d^o 99 @ 101 — best Blues 122 @ 124 $. but these will likewise probably fall, unless more Amerⁿ Ships should come than are now expected — It is not thought that Silks can be much lower, as there is a want of the RawMaterial & the Worms produceno more until the Spring renews the cultivation of the Mulberry-Leaf. At the advanced prices ofSilks, I have not thought it prudent to invest so largely for myself as you recommended me to do, if they were low — and hitherto have only purchased about $5000. for myself, which I am to ship with the like sum for the joint a/ct of Captⁿ Sturgis & myself.

Your order for ChinaWare is already executed & I shall ship it by the Atahualpa — The 3 ps [interlineated: Blk] Crape I shall not fail to send or bring with me. — It is yet uncertain whether I return in the Atahualpa — Some other opportunities will shortly offer of addressing you, which I shall not fail to avail myself of, in interim remaining with Sentiments of true regard

Sir your affectionate & ob^t Servant
J Bromfield

P.S. Let me ask thefavor that you communicate to Messrs. P. T. Jackson & E. Francis, that part of these Contents which relates to their interest. —

LETTER FROM HENRY LEE, PATRICK TRACY JACKSON, AND JOSEPH LEE, JR., BOSTON, NOV. 29–DEC. 14, 1810, TO GEORGE LEE AND JOSEPH HALL, JR., CALCUTTA, WITH INSTRUCTIONS FOR PUSHING THE TRADE WITH INDIA [1]

The burden of this letter, as of others to the same port, is to buy largely of the goods specified and within the limits set, without regard to non-intercourse or fear of war. The specifications in regard to the color and the quality of piece goods indicate that they were intended for the African trade.

The disorganization of the British government, resulting from internal conflict in the cabinet and George III's final attack of insanity, had made it impossible for William Pinkney, minister to England, to procure an admission that the French decrees had been revoked and that, consequently, the British government should consider the revocation of the Orders in Council. Losing patience, Pinkney decided to come home, which action made the revival of non-intercourse almost inevitable.[2]

Mess George Lee & Jos Hall Junr   Boston Novr 29th 1810
   Calcutta
     Gentlemen
       Our last was dated   inst by the Vancouver for Madras, she sail'd on   inst. a copy of the most important part of our letter went by the Union that sail'd about a month since direct for Calcutta by which we shipp'd $4,000, the letters were put into the boxes with the money except one or two short ones. We adopted that mode on account of greater certainty of our [of our — stricken through] letters reaching you. the present is intended to go by the Ganges. Mr Stewarts Brig, or rather Ship she having been alter'd since her last voyage she has no cargo that can interfere with the sale of the Gullivers. except perhaps a few Iron Hoops. knowing the disposition that prevails among the traders to India & China to refuse letters, I wrote you some time since that you would not hear from us by this vessel. but we have been agreeably disappointed as Mr

---

1. Jackson-Lee Papers, "Letter Book," Aug. 19, 1810–May 30, 1811.
2. Channing, *op. cit.*, vol. iv, pp. 419–420.

Head has offer'd to take letters and newspapers. you will receive a bundle of the latter.

The Caledonias voyage which we mentioned would commence in Decr. or January, is abandoned for the present. it is given out that shippers are not willing to hazard a violation of the Non Intercourse Law, that will take place as Stated in the Proclamation on 2^d February 1811. provided the Orders in Council are not repeal'd by British Government. we cannot believe that this is a reason that will prevail with many, because it now being legal to go to Calcutta, a vessel would not be liable unless the law has a retrospective operation in that case she would be on the same footing that vessels now out are, for all that arrive after February will violate the letter of the law, but no one believes but what Government must and will consider them innocent, to do otherwise would be so gross a violation of justice, that even our government, stupid and wicked as it is would shrink from it. It is not improbable however that after 2^d February our intercourse with England may again be prohibited for a time, but at present no effect is produced by the expectation of that event, you will of course make the most of it, if such an apprehension should exist in Calcutta, but do not be prevented buying any goods you can get at our limits we will take care and provide conveyances for any that may remain over and above what you may be able to freight from time to time at the limits we have fixd.

The next vessel for Calcutta is the Ship John Adams, 220 Tons own'd by F H Walley. the Meridian that was intended to go via England having been given up. Mr Webb goes out supercargo. she will have $120. to $150,000 Stock. she is expected to leave about 15th January, by her you will receive letters if we are permitted to send them. her object will be principally Piece goods, and 50 to 60 Tons Gruff goods to fill up with, probably Sugar and Ginger, with regard to your conduct towards the Supercargoes, Master &C, who come out to Calcutta we have already told you what we wish'd, we would further observe that there is considerable jealousy existing towards us among some of our neighbours, who think we influence the Calcutta Market to their disadvantage, absurd as this may appear to you, it is true, we would therefore by all means caution you against doing or saying any thing that may have that appearance there is much prudence necessary. but we feel confident that you will do all that our interest requires without giving any just cause of offence to any one. The Super-cargo of the John Adams is a worthy young man but we imagine not very particularly acquainted with Piece goods, he of course would be likely to follow you in them as well as gruff goods, the effects that would have on our sales here and purchases there, you can judge of as well as we can One vessel was talk'd of from New York for Madras or Calcutta, but we have learnt that it is suspended for the present. we do not know of any voyage besides the J Adam's that is thought of, indeed prices of Cal-cutta goods are so low that it requires some courage to think of importing Calcutta goods and to come in after the immense cargoes that are now on the way and collecting in Calcutta. we shall do very well with the Gipsy's and also Gullivers, if our orders have been follow'd but we imagine that some of the traders to Bengal this year will hardly realize their capitals, a considerable demand for goods continues for exportation but we hope to supply with the Gipsys and Charon's cargoes the most urgent demand of the Exporters.

Should there be no prohibition to go to Calcutta on the ar-rival of the Gipsy, she will be dispatch'd in three or four weeks after she appears. you may calculate upon this, but do not be prevented from shipping on freight on that account. we will take care and provide funds enough for any cargo you may have collected for her, or may be able to buy after she arrives back, we never wish for any goods to be kept where they can be freighted on our terms, the Calcutta trade is becoming more than ever an object with great capitalists. they have gone deeply into it this year and will continue to while they can get a mod-erate interest, we must therefore make all we can of it while we have the start of our neighbors. the year after next it will probably be better than the coming year but it will always be safe and profitable when such goods can be bought as we have sent you Memorandums of and at our limitations. while we think of it we would again repeat that in getting Chintzes made the principal colour should be *Bright Red* and not Mud Colour, there should be also a due proportion of yellow and very few pieces of Black, one colour, black and red or black and yellow look well, but coarse Cotton with only a black colour looks very badly and will not sell, Chocolate should likewise be mix'd in some pieces with yellow and red and not be put alone upon a piece, The thin *Mizapour Chintz* of ever so ordinary quality is sometimes low in the Bazar, if you cannot get as much *Calcutta made Chintz as you want*, then this miserable stuff may be bought at 20/ for 9½x1⅞. but we are persuaded an abundance of the other can be had if you adopt the plan we reccommended, too much attention cannot be devoted to it and we reccommend your reading often the Memorandums upon this very important article. We wish you to buy 4000 pieces *Cuttanies*, instead of the quantity mention'd in ours of   if they can be had at 6/8, and if as low as 5/8 then 6,000. We think very well of all Silk goods, go to the extent of our limits and let them be as bad as you can find provided they are cheap. — We have just heard that the S⁰ Carolina will go about the 10ᵗʰ Decʳ from Philadelphia with Mr Chamberlain Supercargo, and $200.000 stock, being part of the funds destin'd for the Caledonia whose voyage is now abandon'd. we shall try to get a short letter on board the S⁰ Carolina.

It is not improbable you may receive a small shipment p John Adams, say $2000. you will open them as soon as you receive them for our letters which may go inclos'd.

Yrs

(sign'd) Henry Lee

P T Jackson for self

& Joˢ Lee Jr,

Boston Dec 8. 1810

Since the above the apprehension of Non Intercourse with Great Britain after 2ᵈ February has become much more prevalent than it was, and indeed we think it not improbable, we would

not have you suspend your purchases in consequence but buy
when you can get goods at our limitations. ship home as many
as you can get freighted on our terms, and the remainder we
will find conveyance for if there is really a Non Intercourse.
this cannot be determined at present but may be by and by —
if you cannot have much *tonnage*. then you must ship only silks
and valuable goods, so as to get on board as large an amount as
possible. do not be alarm'd at any reports. but when there is a
panic buy with confidence and follow our memorandums.
We shall write you via Madeira, England, Canton &c. you will
write us also via England, Cape of Good Hope &c when no
oppertunities offer direct,

Yr^s

H Lee for P T J & J Lee Jr

We send to your care letters for Mr Newton, forward them and
also some News Papers if you have oppertunity. this we send
to George Tyleer Esqr for safety. the letters that are directed
to you contain nothing you must remark whether they have
open'd.

H L

P. S. Decr 14th 1810. We have just heard of the arrival of the
Boston at Madras and that Mr Newton had gone on to Calcutta,
should he be there when you receive this shew him your Memorandums, his interest and ours is one, Do not be alarmd by any
thing you may hear respecting Mr Pinkneys recal we shall have
no war with England. tho' a non Intercourse is expected remit
all the goods you can, we think Indigo @ 150 to 160 Rupees p
Maud will be a good article. send us 30.000 lb and more if you
have but little tonnage. Bandannas and all other Silks will be
high, send us as many as you can find and go high for them.
we shall have no Silks from France or Italy, we may possibly
send out a vessel, but you must send all the goods you can on
freight. we will provide funds for her cargo if she goes.

Yr^s

H Lee for owners

original p^r Ganges for Calcutta [written across face of letter]

LETTER FROM HENRY LEE, BOSTON, NOV. 29–DEC. 14, 1810,
TO EDWARD A. NEWTON, MADRAS, WITH ACCOUNT OF THE IN-
TERNATIONAL SITUATION [1]

This detailed description of the way the international situation
affected foreign commerce is interesting, both in itself and from the
light it throws on the opinions of the Boston merchant who was the
author. Similarly significant is his exposition of the advantage he felt
a small specialized trader had over the large general merchant.

The "Charons cargo," shipped from Madras by E. A. Newton,
Jan. 5, 1811, was invoiced at 43,945 star pagodas, each worth 7s.
5½d.; it consisted chiefly of piece goods, but contained some spices
and "Japan Copper." [2]

The "Eastern Islands," to which vessels are noted as having gone
for tin and sandalwood, were doubtless the chain east of Java.

The sicca rupee, containing approximately 176 grains of silver, was
proportionately more valuable than the Bombay rupee, containing
only 165 grains.

Mr Edward A. Newton   Boston Novr 29th 1810
  Dear sir

    My last went by the Vancouver, she sail'd on the   inst
for Madras, Mr Tracy Supercargo, I trust she will be with you
sometime before this reaches, which goes by the Ship Ganges
via Calcutta. When we wrote you about the Unions voyage we
did not know that she had any Naval Stores. I have learnt
within a few days that she has a quantity of Spirits Turpentine
and Tar on board. this is a consideration for you in the disposal
of the Vancouvers cargo, we do not know of any more on the
way or intended, but as there is an expectation that the Isle
France will be captur'd, and that there will be a demand for
Naval Stores. I think it not improbable that in course of some
months there may be some cargoes dispach'd for Cape Good
Hope and market and would therefore advise a sale when good
prices can be realized, but I would not be alarm'd into a sale

1. Jackson-Lee Papers, "Letter Book," Aug. 19, 1810–May 30, 1811.
2. *Ibid.*, "Invoices," 1799–1812.

at low prices, as there will not be any reach Madras for many months if at all.

The voyage I mention'd as being contemplated from New York for Madras, Mr Remsen writes is abandoned for the present. nor do I hear of any vessel that is even talk'd of for Madras as from any quarter, the arrival of the Charons cargo, if it should be known that it sells well, may put some one in motion, but we have so much the start of our neighbours, that for a year to come at least we have nothing to fear, the impression still continues that no one can make any thing upon Madras goods and indeed such has been the fact hitherto. the Pilgrim destined as I wrote you for Bombay for *Surat Goods,* has not yet left Teneriffe that I have heard of, so that she cannot possibly return 'till after the Vancouver, Wines have advanced amazingly in Madeira and still more in Teneriffe, the situation of Spain and Portugal is such that considerable quantities have been carried to those countries, this will explain to you the cause, Sherry here is now $1.75 and Nidonia $1.60 and very little in the country the Pilgrims prospect, if Wine is her object is but indifferent, the *Caledonias* voyage from Philadelphia to Calcutta is abandoned, it is said on account of the Non Intercourse that will take place 2d February 1811 agreeable to the Presidents Proclamation, (provided the British Order in Council are not repeal'd) I cannot believe that is the reason, because ships sailing before 2d February cannot be liable unless the act has a retrospective operation which would be too gross a violation of justic even for our government to be guilty of. It is thought by many that on 2d February we shall have a suspension of our Intercourse with England at present the expectation produces no effect on the minds of anyone that I can perceive, if it does take place it will have effect on India goods if no other, it will induce the importers of them next summer and fall to demand more for them, because it will be too late for the Spring fleet (that will sail when the intercourse is renewd) to return for the next years Spring sales I am supposing in that case that it may continue three or four months but it will have little or no immediate effect on prices, every one knowing that before the supplies now on the way can be dispos'd of that a change will take place, or at least every one will calculate so, because that has been the case hitherto, and those who have gone upon the calculations of War with England as permanent Non Intercourse have suffer'd most severely in their speculations.

We think you may make use of the expected Non Intercourse to depress goods a little in Madras, but we think you ought to continue to buy when you can get goods at such prices as you calculated upon when you left us. The Ship *John Adams.* will sail 15th January for Calcutta, before that time Congress meets, and we may be able to conjecture better than we now can what will be the conduct of this government, but you must not expect to have any clear views upon the subject, because it is impossible for any one to calculate upon the measures of a government that have no fix'd principles to govern themselves by. You know as well as we do their mode of amusing the people with projects they never intend to act upon. we are fix'd in this opinion that let what will happen we shall have no War with Great Britain it is very easy to see that Government intend to keep alive the hostile feelings of the Mob towards the English, but a war with that nation is so oppos'd to thro' interest. not to say safety of this country, that I cannot for a moment believe that it will ever take place in the present state of Europe, indeed no administration however popular could preserve their places for a month under the sufferings and disgrace such an event would produce, the probability is they would lose both their places and their lives notwithing the repeal of the Berlin and Milan Degrees, or rather the promise of their repeal, there is no evidence that we shall have any safe intercourse with France or her provinces, on the contrary all the letters down to middle of October, say that the new duties alone would be destructive of all trade, and besides that the system generally of restrictions & anti commercial laws is becoming more and more severe, some few shipments have been made to France and Italy, but they are consider'd as enterprizes to ascertain what can be done rather than as rational plans that will result profitably. Insurance cannot be done at any rate, the exportation to Denmark continues but is very limited, the voyages up the White Sea and to St Petersburg have been very profitable, and should the French be repuls'd in Portugal, and be compell'd to retreat, as I trust they will be, no doubt but what American Property may be safe in Russia the coming year, at all events large shipments will be made and the Cargoes introduced there will be transported from thence to Germany and even to France, say those that are made up of very valuable articles.

The trade to Portugal and Cadiz in provisions still continues, and will continue while the English remain in Spain and Portugal. this has been a source of great profit to the country and has taken up a very large tonnage. The *Spanish Colonies* are in great confusion. there being two parties one for Old Spain and Ferdinand 7th. the other which is the most numerous for independence, each petty District has a plan of its own, so that it will require many years for them to settle down in some permanent state, still however their severe laws against the trade or foreigners are ameliorating, and our trade increases in that quarter, both parties are friendly to the British and to us. this country (Sp America) must become a great mart for India piece goods, as well for the consumption of its inhabitants as for cargoes of the slave traders, I presume that this year the exportation has not been less than 2000 Bales from the United States. I have been able to ascertain this fact with more certainty from having myself exported upwards of 300 Bales, which has led me to make most minute inquires they are very satisfactory as relates to our concern. we keep up a very extensive and active correspondence with every market that is like to require piece goods, that we may be prepared for the most advantageous disposal of our cargoes, our plan is always to sell here when we can, but if any time we happen to have some goods that cannot be sold at their fair value, either from their not being known, or from any other cause, we sometimes export, we flatter ourselves we shall not be driven to that in selling the Charons or Boston's Cargoes.

The vessels that went to the Mediteranean have not been able to introduce their cargoes any where except in Turkey where they have done very badly. some cargoes have been return'd as they were ship'd, so that with the property that has been sequester'd, the losses there have been very great, at present no one thinks of adventuring, except some small vessels for Coast of Africa, four or five cargoes of Silks and Brandies have been brought to this country since the raising of the Embargo, but at immense hazard and expence. we cannot calculate upon large supplies either from France or Italy, tho' it is probable we may have some even if the English do not repeal their Orders in Council. *India Piece goods* are very high in the North of Europe, but while Sugars Cottons &c remain so high there will be no exportation, because piece Goods are consider'd more obnoxious to French power than Sugars &c. and therefore more liable to confiscation, it is not improbable however that some of the rich importers next year may ship some should they be very low in this market, as they must be in the summer, after the spring sales have been made such an exportation even if only 500 Bales would relieve the market very much there is also one other cause that I always calculate upon to favour us small traders, which is that most of the *India traders* are *rich*, and when goods get down to the cost and charges say 80¢ p Rupee they will store them. this leaves the market to those who must sell, and who perhaps by retailing may make 3 to 5% more than those who calculate upon selling by the cargo. we have always found that we could retail a considerable quantity of goods at saving prices when Calcutta goods were at the lowest. we can do it better now because we confine our whole time and attention to that business, you have seen this in the case of your Madras goods that Mr Jackson sold, for while L & Whitney and even Remsen with all his industry could not in a year sell $20.000 at any price, Mr J sold a much larger amount at very handsome prices. there is nothing extraordinary in this. it is an advantage which a man who deals wholly in one article has over a general trader.

We have given you not only a Memorandum of all the vessels for Calcutta but generally those which have sail'd for any part of India, at present the John Adams is the only vessel that we know of for Bengal, she is a freighting vessel and will load in Calcutta, her stock will be $120.000 @ 150.000. this vessel takes the place of the Meridian that was intended to go via England. the undertakers found so many difficulties that they prefer a direct voyage with Specie, The Brig *Phoebe* which I mention'd to you have cleard from Baltimore for Ceylon has put back in distress, she will probably proceed on again, and I think is destin'd for the same voyage that was made last year by the Heart of Oak and Dolly, they return'd with Coffee and Skins, the first taken in at Ceylon, the latter I presume at Madras There has not been the usual number of vessels to Sumatra this year, but we have a sufficient supply of Pepper. about six vessels have arrived this summer, and so many more are now out and will arrive here in course of six months the article of pepper if forced in the market would not keep up higher than ✔ 16¢ or 17¢ but it happens that the trade is carried on principally from Salem by men who prefer exporting it unless they can sell at 19¢ or 20¢, and thus the price is supported at about 18¢, at which a moderate quantity can one time with another be sold in short time say 50 to 100 Tons, it cost for the last cargoes about 4½ to 5 Cts p lb. we led you into a belief that Malabar pepper might bring more than Sumatra, I doubt if a difference of a cent p lb or even ½ a cent would be made. The trade to Mocha has ceas'd wholly nor have I heard of any vessels to the Persian Gulf, two have clear'd for Bombay, three or four have gone to Batavia or rather to Java for Nutmegs and Mace, of which we have an abundance for many years, two or three have gone to the Eastern Islands for Sandal Wood and Tin. from thence they go to China.
Notwithstanding the low prices of Teas and Nankins, very large stocks have gone out to Canton this year, but principally with a view of obtaining Silks which have done very well this year, and which promise to do equally well the coming year, we now

shall have to resort to China for the Silks we received formerly from Italy and France, and should our Non Intercourse with these two countries continue we shall require three or four Millions of Dollars from that country. Teas and Nankins we have an abundance of for a year at least. Cassia is scarce and high, it has done well in North of Europe and is now wanted for that quarter.

The season of business for India piece goods is now over, the last sales of Bengal goods were very low except for coloured goods and *fine Gurrahs* which are both wanted. we dare not encourage ourselves with the hopes of getting such prices as a cargo of colour'd goods would have sold at any time since you left, because they have been very high, but we have not the least doubt but we shall do remarkably well with the Charons cargo come when it will. but more especially should her voyage not be more than nine or ten months. the gruff articles are also wanted, some of them very much indeed.

Should the Ganges be detain'd as long as I think she will be, I may add something more.

Yours
H L

December 8th 1810.

Since writing the above applications have been made to Mr Gallatin to know how vessels that arrive after 2d February will be affected by Non Intercourse Law should it be reviv'd, he has said, "that all vessels will be seized coming in after that time, no matter when they sail'd, but no one believes that government will think of doing that, indeed should they do it, the United States Supreme Court would clear them, some people however are apprehensive that vessels sailing after the Proclamation will be liable, but this I very much doubt, for besides the injustice of it, it would involve so many as to make the execution of it impracticable it has been the cause of some voyages being suspended, but in general vessels continue to go as before to Great Britain, and we think you ought to send back the Vancouver without regarding it.

I now think it not improbable that we may have a Non Intercourse sometime the present session, but I would by all means advise you to continue buying goods after the Vancouver sails, when they can be had at such prices as we have always calculated upon.

It now becomes very important to ascertain how a cargo of piece goods can be obtain'd at a Portuguese or native port on the Malaber coast. we have ascertain'd how we can get out funds and stated to you in our last the rate. we have since learnt that the Rupee is the *Sicca Rupee*, if so it is very favourable, but I rather think it is only the Bombay Rupee. We now want to be informed 1ˢᵗ what *port* we can go to on the Malabar Coast or any other quarter, what size vessel, the season when it is safe, the best Merchant to call upon &c. 2ᵈ what kinds of piece goods and the prices, to be obtain'd there, the duties upon Exportation and the time required to collect a cargo, also what gruff goods can be had, their prices &c. 3ᵈ the value of Spanish Dollars what kind of Merchandize would sell, the prices, and the duties on imports, if this expected Non Intercourse should take place, and continue one year or even six months, a great voyage may be made to a port when piece goods can be had at about the Madras and Bengal prices. we shall not be able to know what measures Governᵗ. intend to adopt relative to England for some time, we shall write you from time to time via Madeira, as no more direct oppertunities will offer after the John Adams sails.

The Brig South Carolina sails about this time from Philadelphia for Calcutta she takes part of the funds destin'd for the Caledonia, her voyage as I mentiond having been abandoned, her stock is $200.000.

I have nothing more to say except to repeat my request that you would write us very often and very minutely. Give my regards to Mr Tracy and your Brother. tell Mr T. his friends are all well. You will receive letters from yours.

I am with regard

Yours

(sign'd) Henry Lee

P. S. December 14th 1810 We have just heard of your arrival
by the Clarissa and that you had gone on to Calcutta. we fear
you have been disappointed in prices of goods at Madras, but
we hope you may find them low in Calcutta should it turn out
that you have remain'd at Calcutta for the Charon and Vancouver, the latter vessel may be in Calcutta when you receive
this. if so I would not be impatient to dispach her, because if
there is a Non Intercourse goods must go down, there will at
any rate be a suspension of it for some months, if you should be
at Calcutta we reccommend you to send down to Madras for
Cassia and Cinnamon. Mr Jackson has written you under cover
to Harrington &Co at Madras. you can stop the letter, he did it
for safety. if you are in Calcutta and find Cottons high or indeed unless they are very low. we would advise you to send
home in the Vancouver 20.000 lb of Indigo @ 100 Cts p lb. and
also a considerable quantity of Bandannas. there is a great
quantity of Indigo wanted for Europe.

   pr Ganges for Calcutta — saild 17th Decr. [written across
face of letter]

LETTER FROM HENRY LEE, BOSTON, DEC. 2, 1810, TO PETER
REMSEN, NEW YORK, ANTICIPATING A RENEWAL OF THE NON-
INTERCOURSE ACT [1]

   Non-intercourse with Great Britain — the prohibition of United
States waters to the vessels of that nation and banning the importation of British goods — was scheduled for Feb. 2, 1811, and actually
began on Mar. 2. We are not told to what port the Lees intended
"to send out a cheap vessel in Jany" in anticipation of that event —
perhaps to Calcutta, as later on Henry Lee writes: "such a measure
[non-intercourse] would of course affect the value of piece goods
from Calcutta, as no more vessels could be dispatch'd." [2] But on
Mar. 2, he urged his Calcutta agents "to ship as many goods as
you can get freighted" as "it is generally thought that a vessel sailing after the proclamation" of Nov. 2, 1810 "would be liable to

   1. Jackson-Lee Papers, "Letter Book," Aug. 19, 1810–May 30, 1811.
   2. *Ibid.*, Henry Lee, Boston, Dec. 4, 1810, to Harrod & Ogden, New
Orleans.

seizure." Nevertheless, "if there is actually a Non Intercourse we will continue in some way or other to get out a vessel." [3]

"Mr Lowell" (Francis Cabot Lowell), who had married Hannah Jackson, a sister of Henry Lee's wife, was travelling in the British Isles for his health.

Mr. Peter Remsen   Boston Decr. 2d. 1810
New York

I have yours of 27 & 28 Ulto. with the acct. Sales & Invo. of Corp. Ellis & Shaws goods they are very high charged & we could not afford to give them more than 82½ on 5. 6 & 9 mo credit — The time may come this winter when they may be worth more — or if we shd. have reason to apprehend the capture of the Gipsy they wd. do for an early Spring sale here — the assortment is very bad & there are no coloured goods of consequence nor any Baftas — I think it not improbable we could afford to give Kane 90¢ for 400 bales of his say ½ his Invo. but if he does not want to sell — it wd. not be worth while to speak to him — You may assure C. E & S that no one shall see there Invo. — nor will we make any use of the confidence they place to injure there sales It wd. be well to sell the Bristles for the most you can get say not under 60¢ — which is about the cost & charges the crash is very bad sell it @ 8cts if no better can be done. I enclose you 2 Deb. Certificates one for 59.19 & one 107.11 — I also enclose you 2 letters for Scotland which put on board the first vessel for that quarter — I hope you have forwarded all the letters I have sent for Mr Lowell — I always wish them sent to the nearest port by first vessels going — Sugars have risen to 13r/17r for Whites & Browns equel to 12 & 16$ all charges paid in U States — I hope you may be able to send me considerable amt. in course of a month — my payments from some of my customers are very slack & I do not wish to push any that require indulgence — I think we shall have some failures — & that in Phila. & with you there will be still more — if you are doubtful about any of your Correspond-

3. *Ibid.*, Henry Lee, Boston, Dec. 6, 1810, to George Lee and Joseph Hall, Jr., Calcutta.

ents send me the names of such & I will let you know how they stand — Sh^d. there be a Non Intercourse we may want to send out a cheap vessel in Jan^y — with a quantity of Bottles &^c. the stock we have remitted — for a cargo of 500 bales or more — See if the Mt Hope can be bot & what state She is in — or any other burthensome & cheap Ship of 250 @ 350 Tons — Copper'd or not —

Yours
H Lee

LETTER FROM HENRY LEE, BOSTON, DEC. 14, 1810, TO THOMAS LEE, JR., HAVANA, ON THE INTERNATIONAL SITUATION [1]

The "distress'd situation" of Spain, whose legitimate king had been ousted in 1808 in favor of Joseph Bonaparte and which was now the scene of the Peninsular War, had resulted in the relaxation of laws forbidding her colonies to trade with non-Spanish vessels. On Oct. 27, 1810, President Madison by proclamation had included in Orleans Territory the piece of Spanish territory known as West Feliciana — in which American settlers had already set up a revolutionary government.

If the price of cochineal in Russia is expressed (as it appears to be) in dollars, this, combined with Lee's opinion of the maximum price in New York, gives some idea of the profits made in the Russia trade by those lucky merchants whose vessels safely made the voyage out and back.

The "Chs" to whom Henry Lee asked to be remembered was Charles George Cabot, son of the well-known statesman "Mr G Cabot," also mentioned below. Charles George Cabot was born in Beverly and baptized there Sept. 14, 1777, attended Phillips Andover, and was graduated from Harvard in 1796. He "embarked on a career in commerce, starting as a mariner," became a captain in the East India trade, was a mercantile agent on the Isle of France about 1801, and was concerned about 1806 in a brief partnership with his cousin Andrew Cabot. In 1810 he went to Havana for his health and died there of tuberculosis in Jan., 1811, the month after this letter was written.[2]

1. Jackson-Lee Papers, "Letter Book," Aug. 19, 1810–May 30, 1811.
2. Briggs, *op. cit.*, vol. i, pp. 275–276.

Mr. Thomas Lee Junr.   Boston. Decr. 14th. 1810
   Havana

    I wrote you yesterday via New York. this I shall send by the first vessel from this port which will probably be the Gleaner — Mr Gowen's vessel — by which you will receive 9 bales cottons, being part of purchase made before you sail'd, and a few Bales Colour'd Goods bought since to make an assortment, they go consign'd to you, but we made a promise to Mr G that he should sell them. I also made a small shipment of linens belonging in part only to me, which I have not consign'd to you, because I wish'd a sale at any rate, and immediate returns, the 9 Bales we insur'd for $2000 out and home @ 5% at Broker's, if you have no property to ship on our joint Account, ship the amount from mine, the Insurance is made, P T Jackson for himself and others.

    You will have seen the President's message before this arrives, it has produced less sensation among the people generally than we would have suppos'd, our friends think they can discover in it a determination on the part of government not to be on good terms with Great Britain. they are of opinion that should the Orders in Council be repeal'd still some pretence will be found why a Non Intercourse Law should be pass'd, and they fully [expect ?] it in course of the session. something it is thought will depend upon the fate of Portugal, should Lord Wellington be defeated our government will be more insolent than they would be otherwise. some voyages have been suspended on account of the apprehension of seizure for having sail'd after the Proclamation The seizure of Florida has caus'd some alarms least the Spanish Colonies should retaliate in some way or other, I have myself felt some anxiety and on conversing with Mr G Cabot I found he thought there was some chance perhaps less in Cuba than in some others, on account of the intimate connexions between that Island & this country, He thought it worth while however that it should be mention'd to you that you might be guarded against any measures that might be taken, most people have never thought upon the subject because of the little importance to Spain of West Florida and also of her present distress'd situation, if you think there is the least danger of the sequestration of American property. I wish you to sell any goods of mine that may remain unsold in the hands of De Frias &Co, Gorham & Lawrence & Widow Poey & Hernandez and remit the proceeds in any way you think best, it is certainly consider'd as a very serious thing by reflecting men, and even if that part of Florida should have been paid for in the Louisania purchase still taking forcible possession can only be consider'd as a very gross attack upon Spain, if not a declaration of War. I am told the Spanish Minister and Mr Morier view it somewhat in that light. I shall be glad to find our fears turn out to be unfounded and I think they may, but it is worth your consideration, and it will certainly be prudent to place your property out of the reach of any measures which may be adopted by the government of Cuba

We have bought some days since in Philadelphia $12.000 amount of Seersuckers, say 1/3 like those we ship'd by the Roxana Markd G No 11 the remainder broad stripes, checks and narrow stripes of very good patterns, the 1/3 cost about $7.50 a piece, the remainder will average $11.50, if there is any demand, and every thing is safe, we can send them to you in season for the spring demand, at present we shall make no farther shipments and we fear from the accounts we received lately that you will find it difficult to get rid of those you carried out, they are as cheap as can be afforded and if they bring as much as those which have sold the worst hitherto, there will be a profit. I do not believe any more shipments will be made, because those made from Philadelphia they write me have been very losing, and it is now known that there is a loss upon the returns, Sheetings do not now sell I imagine they will come down to $18 to $19 but cannot now be bought under $19. Sugars remain @ $1150 @ $13.50 they will rise here unless they fall in the Havana, there are not many more than will be wanted for consumption 20,000 Boxes will be wanted in February to make up the cargoes for the Baltic and Archangel, some few vessels are now loading, and P Dodge Gray & c, buy when they can find them low, Coffee is very dull, I cannot sell 30.000 lb Carracas for more than 18½ Cts. some small fine green will be wanted in Spring, there will no doubt be large exportations to the North for prices were very high in Russia at the last accounts, and every one has done well with Dye Wood, Sugar, Cotton & Rum. Exchange on London is lower than when you left, it cannot be sold for Cash for more than 7% to 8%. this however arises in part from the very great scarcity of money. the credit price is about as when you left, it cannot be any better for the present, because the importers are countermanding their orders for spring goods. at any rate will not be inclin'd to remit so much as they would if there was no appearance of Non Intercourse.

I desired Mr Remsen to send you Langs Gazette regularly by every vessel that sail'd, he wrote me he should do it and that he would write you from time to time.

Vessels have fallen in New York and they will here, freights are as low at Charleston and New Orleans as they have been for some years, no shipments are making to England of Cotton, or indeed any other produce. Nor will there be 'till it falls. Cotton is expected to go down to about 13 Cents in Charleston and lower if there is a Non Intercourse. If you cannot buy Sugars as low as you expected, I think some Cochineal would be a safe remittance. it is now very scarce, the consumption is very small, but I imagine 500 lb would soll for Russia where it is worth $[?]14 $6 is as high as I should think would be prudent to go.

Vessels are falling fast, so that if you should want one for any purpose towards Spring, I imagine one may be bought on reasonable terms.

Mr T Williams has letters from J B Green down to the last of Octo, which preclude all hope of his doing any thing he has promis'd to write you.

Should you find Cottons very low in Havana perhaps you may send some to St Jago, I am told it is a considerable port, and probably not a Bale has been sent to this country. Bengal goods of all kinds from present appearances will be low in the spring.

and if the African trade is continued I cannot but think Colour'd goods will be wanted in the Havana. Remember me to Ch[s], I hope by this time you will have found comfortable quarters.

Yours

(sign'd) Henry Lee

p[r] Gleaner [written across face of letter]

LETTER FROM HENRY LEE, BOSTON, DEC. 20, 1810, TO JOSEPH L. BROWN, RIO DE JANEIRO, IN REGARD TO TRADE WITH SPANISH AMERICA [1]

This letter reveals that the Lees were not confining themselves to shipments to the West Indies but were also carrying on a trade with the recently opened ports of South America, in this case with Brazil. On Apr. 23, 1811, Samuel W. Balch & Co. shipped to Henry Lee from Rio de Janeiro sugar invoiced at some 3,000 reals.[2]

Joseph L Brown Esq[r]   Boston Dec[r] 20th 1810
    Rio Janerio
        sir

I trust before this will have been received, you will have sold my goods p Baltic and remitted the proceeds. Should they be on hand when this reaches, it is my wish they be sold for the most they will bring and the proceeds remitted in sugars, either to Baltimore Philadelphia New [interlineated: York] or this place, indeed to any port in United States to which you can have them freighted on the best terms.

The taking possession of Florida I hope will not produce any retaliatory measures by Spain or her Colonies. if it should the risk of capture &c by privateers of that nation might be great. I must in such an event trust to your prudence and good management to escape as many dangers as possible, I am expecting a very large supply of Madras and Calcutta goods and shall be glad to ship to you if you can furnish me information that is satisfactory. I wish it to be very particular and that you

1. Jackson-Lee Papers, "Letter Book," Aug. 19, 1810–May 30, 1811.
2. *Ibid.*, "Invoices," 1799–1812.

would send me patterns, whole pieces if they cannot be had otherwise Your country is becoming every year more and more important to us, and as we are not like to have a secure trade to any part of Europe, not even to England, the attention of our enterprizing Merchants will be turn'd towards S° America, you cannot therefore but be benefited by sending to your friends the most extensive and particular information I wish to be inform'd among other things of the Rate of Exchange on London the facility of selling bills, or buying them, also the value of gold, and whether specie can be exported without a duty, if one should stop there on the road to China. send me also the general cost of Sugars, the expences of shipping them &c.

Yours

(sign'd) Henry Lee

p^r. Tyger   (Duplicate p Vigilant) [written across face of letter]

LETTER FROM HENRY LEE, BOSTON, DEC. 20, 1810, TO SAMUEL YORKE & JAMES SCHOTT, PHILADELPHIA, IN REGARD TO GOODS ALLEGED TO HAVE BEEN DAMAGED [1]

Although still keeping up a correspondence with Hazard & Cabot, the house with which their kinsman Samuel Cabot was connected, the Lees had evidently transferred a large share of their business with Philadelphia to the firm addressed below. This firm had evidently sold a parcel of goods for the Lees to a "Mr Hunt," merchant in Havana, who had claimed that the goods were damaged.

Thomas Stewart, mentioned in this letter, was doubtless the Stewart against whom Henry Lee had warned his Calcutta agents.

Messrs Samuel York & James Schott   Boston Decr 20th 1810
    Philadelphia
        Dear sirs
            I have yours of 13th. inst, I am very much obliged for the service you have done me in getting my letters on board the South Carolina, I now enclose you a letter to Thomas Stew-

---

1. Jackson-Lee Papers, "Letter Book," Aug. 19, 1810–May 30, 1811.

art Esqʳ, Calcutta, handed me by a gentleman who is very solicitous to get it on board the Sᵒ Carolina I should esteem it a great favour if you will use your influence to have it sent in her, it contains nothing that can injure the voyage of Mr Chamberlain and if it will be any satisfaction you can open it and read it to him or the owners.

I am not disposed to make any allowance for damage on the goods sold Mr Hunt. it is certainly the business of the buyers of goods to examine them in this Country, the estimation of damage is very different here, to what it would be in the Havana, besides a Certificate can be obtain'd for any purpose for $20. I do not mean by this to impeach the intentions of Mr H. I have no doubt he thinks the goods were damaged but only to give my opinion of W I Certificates. The cargoes of the Gipsy and Sally Ann contain'd 2000 bales of goods out of which there were not more than 20 bales damaged, and those not 5%, it is therefore altogether improbable there could have been so much damage in the small parcel sold Mr H if there had have been it could not have escaped the notice of so many persons thro' whose hands they have pass'd, I am sorry for Mr Hunts loss but I have no doubt the representation is incorrect upon which the Certificate was made.

We look for a non Intercourse, but such is the scarcity of money that no one will buy goods of any kind however low.

Yours
(sign'd) Henry Lee

LETTER FROM JOHN BROMFIELD, JR., CANTON, DEC. 25, 1810, TO HENRY LEE, BOSTON, IN REGARD TO GOODS AND CARGOES [1]

In a letter of Dec. 11 Bromfield had refused to advise George Lee to ship saltpetre to Canton, "as traffic in it is forbidden, altho' the Country Ships have sometimes brought it round & transhipped it Whampoa, by bribing the Mandarins, But the difficulties attending it are every day increasing, this Governᵗ looking with an unusually jealous eye at all foreigners ever since the Attempt of the

1. John Bromfield Papers.

English on Macao in 1808 & any article remotely relative to War or
Gunpowder is most strictly watched." [2]

Canton 25 December 1810

Mr Henry Lee
  Dear Sir

    I wrote you last p the George, Jas. Wickham Master for
Philada. under date of 11th [Decr. — stricken through interlineated: inst] handing Invoice &Bill Lading your Goods
shipped p that Vessel, which left the River on the 17th. Notwithstanding the high prices of Silks there have been pretty
large investments made for the Philadelphia Ships — [The
Pacific, Pekin, Atalanta &South Carolina — have all considerable the George has some — stricken through] The Atalanta
Pekin & Pacific have the most, the George & South Carolina
have likewise some Silks, — The Chinese for Newyork & the
Hope — [a small ship from the Fejee Isles with Sandal Wood
— stricken through] — have little or none — I should think the
Newyork market the best for your Silks pthe George If one
can judge from the trifling quantity destined to that port —
[Notwithstanding Although there is no demand for Silks, yet
the contract prices remain very nearly the same, although
though — stricken through] new contracts [interlineated: for
Silk] might [interlineated: now] be a little lower, yet as the
raw material is really Scarce they [cannot be — stricken
through interlineated: are not] expected to fall much until the
new Silk comes in the next year, — [indeed — stricken through
interlineated: &] should several ships arrive now for Silks, it
is thought they [must — stricken through interlineated: would]
again rise immediately. —
[interlineated: Short] Nankins have somewhat declined, some
[interlineated: few] have been sold as low as 42 @ 43$ but the
respectable dealers refuse to sell them under 44 @ 45$ — The
[interlineated: best] Blue nankins remain at $120 — & the
Canton Dyed nankins whh cost last year 98$ — are now at

109 — which is too high to expect any profitable advance upon — Teas are now falling & might [now — stricken through] be had considerably lower than my former quotations, but the great quantity Sent to America the last year, [leads — stricken through] deters allmost every one from Shipping them — The Chinese [interlineated: however] took a full Cargo &the Hope likewise for Newyork will be laden with them, the Trumbull will also take Teas — The Philadelphia Ships have taken [a pretty large a considerable quantity of — stricken through interlineated: principally] Young Hyson [& some — stricken through interlineated: with a few] other Teas — [& with — stricken through] & a pretty large proportion ofChina Ware. —

I have again written your Brother George a few days since as to Saltpetre, [I do not think — stricken through] under so many restrictions here, it is rather a troublesome article, as it [canno — stricken through] must be smuggled — The only shipment of it this year which has come to my knowledge, was about 100 peculs pthe Margaret-Francis from Bengal, which was sold to be smuggled at 12$ ppecul.

Hitherto I have not yet made any [further — stricken through] purchases pr my own account, excepting the shipment p the Trumbull [in con — stricken through] jointly with W. Sturgis, my half of which will be about 5100 — to $5200 — he has insured for me 10000 Dolls out & home, and I have written him to cause an additional sum to be insured in my name &for my account to the amount of 7000 Dollars more, — which may probably be shipped in some very late Vessel — I trouble you with this, requesting that in case of his absence you will please get the same effected for me [interlineated: to any port in the United States] — & if [interlineated: he is] in Boston I have requested him to speak to you on the subject. — I remain Sir

Your mo obtServant

LETTER FROM HENRY LEE, BOSTON, DEC. 28, 1810, TO ZADOCK
GILMAN, CHARLESTON, S. C., IN REGARD TO FAILURES [1]

For a month comments on the stringent financial situation had
mingled in the Lees' letter book with enthusiastic orders to buy
more and more India goods. In a letter of Dec. 13, 1810, to Peter
Remsen, Henry Lee had written: "the greatest want of money pre-
vails among those who are among our richest men, who have such
good credit that they have calculated upon getting what money
they wanted, as indeed they may in common times, but credit avails
nothing now, nothing will produce money." However, he had prefaced
these gloomy remarks with the optimistic if illogical assurance: "No
failures yet, nor do I think we shall have any for the present." On
Dec. 24, writing to Samuel Yorke & James Schott, Philadelphia,
Henry Lee remarked: "the only thought now is how one is to pay
his notes, as they come round." Two days later he notified Hazard
& Cabot that Barker & Bridge had "stop'd and will make little or
no dividend it is thought," requesting that the Philadelphia firm
attach "whatever balance may be due them." The present letter
mentions the failure of other houses, one of which owed money to the
firm of which one of Henry Lee's brothers was a member. In a letter
of the same date to Peter Remsen, Henry Lee wrote: "we have two
failures today. . . . I lose . . . $500."

Mr Zadock Gilman   Boston Decr 28 1810
    Charleston (S C)
original via New York
Copy per Mail —   Dear Sir
    I wish you immediately on rect. of this to attach Mr John
Smith as trustee to Augustus Story Merchant of this place who
stop'd payt. this day — for money due Frederick Cabot and
Francis Lee as pr. acct. annex'd he is a dealer in dry goods. I
wish you also to attach Mr Wm Mooney if you find he has ever
received any goods from Mr S. or any other persons who have
been in the habit of doing business for Mr S. Be good enough
to do what you intend immediately as other orders may go on.
do not sell any goods of mine unless for very short credit and

1. Jackson-Lee Papers, "Letter Book," Aug. 19, 1810–May 30, 1811.

good security. W^m M *perhaps* is connected with Caleb Hawyard, M H has fail'd.

Yrs

(sign'd) Henry Lee

Augustus Story to Cabot & Lee Dr
Dec 28th 1810.   Goods p Bill & to notes due . . . $5.000

LETTER FROM HENRY LEE, BOSTON, JAN. 4, 1811, TO CAPT. CHAUNCEY DUTTON, LA GUAYRA, WITH INSTRUCTIONS FOR PURCHASES [1]

On Oct. 15, 1810, Capt. Samuel Foster of the *Chance* had sold at La Guayra (in what is now Venezuela) India goods to the amount of $4,901.81, paid for in coffee.[2] Capt. Chauncey Dutton, in the *Resolution*, apparently owned by the Lees and P. T. Jackson, had made sales in the same place and had sent his vessel, with the returns, to Boston, where she arrived Jan. 2, 1811,[3] Capt. Dutton himself remaining behind with the unsold goods. On Nov. 26, 1810, Henry Lee had written Robert K. Lowry, of La Guayra, requesting commercial information. In the days before wireless telegraphy and rapid steamship communication it was a serious dereliction for a captain or supercargo to fail to write his owners "by every opportunity," as the phrase was. Just what it signified is brought out clearly in this letter. On Dec. 31, 1810, P. T. Jackson, for Henry Lee, had written: "If you cannot procure Indigo or Coffee — you may if possible Send Dollars." [4]

Dutton had commanded the *Gulliver* in 1809.

Captn Chauncey Dutton   Boston Jany 4th 1811
  La Guayra   forwarded via Phil^a.
    Dear sir   Copy via New York
    Your letter p Resolution to Mr Jackson and myself is received. we think you did right in remaining behind with the goods and we trust you have before this made sales. if not

1. Jackson-Lee Papers, "Letter Book," Aug. 19, 1810–May 30, 1811.
2. *Ibid.*, "Foreign Sales on acc^t. of J. & H. Lee from 1803 to 1810. — "
3. Lee-Cabot Papers, 1810–12, Jan. 2, 1811.
4. Jackson-Lee Papers, "P. T. Jackson — Letter Book A," p. 159.
P. T. Jackson, Boston, Dec. 31, 1810, to Chauncy Dutton, Laguira.

sell all that remain and invest the proceeds in Indigoes of any kind, prefering the best and middling say @ $150 @ 2 pr lb, which is higher than what yours cost by 20¢ to 50¢, p Resolution. if Indigo cannot be had you must send Coffee upon which there is a Loss unless it can be shipp'd @ 11¢ on board, you may go as high as 3¢ p lb freight for Indigo because it is so valuable that the freight is nothing. You may ship to New York to Mr Peter Remsen, Baltimore to Mess B & Geo Williams and to any other port to my order and Mr Jacksons.

Complaints have been made from every quarter of your not writing. it is not sufficient to send one or two letters, you ought to write by every vessel to any part of U. S. even to Charleston, and your letters ought to be very particular. we did hope your letters would have contain'd some information that would have induced us to send you out a vessel, but they say nothing only in general terms, collect all the information you can and bring home patterns of such goods as will be wanted next year.

the Resolution is sold and no vessel will be sent you of course you will lose no time in shipping on goods by any vessel that may offer leave nothing of ours unsold or unsettled, but close our sales and remit as soon as you can.

Yours

(sign'd) H Lee

LETTER FROM JOHN BROMFIELD, JR., CANTON, JAN. 20, 1811, TO HENRY LEE, BOSTON, WITH A SHIPMENT OF SILKS [1]

Bromfield on Mar. 25, 1811, was planning to sail for Boston on the following day in the *Derby*, like the *Atahualpa* a Lyman vessel.

Mr Henry Lee   Canton 20th. Jany. 1811.
   DrSir/   Duplicate

I enclose you the 2nd of Exchange drawn by Daniel Stansbury in my favor, on Minturn & Champlin ofN. York for 2500 — 60 days sight, to which please do the needful — I also en-

1. John Bromfield Papers.

close Invoice &Bill lading 17 Cases Silks J.TB N°s 1 @ 17 —
shipped for my own account & risque on board the Ship Trumbull Benj: Page master for Providence — consigned to your care — They are a parcel of ready made goods, which I picked up in a hurry — I should think it best to sell them by the peice at auction — The [interlineated: 24 p^s] shawls are of many different colours & have 20 in a p^s — the price of them is much lower than they could [interlineated: now] be manufactured at. I enclose patterns of the Sinchaws & Col^d Sarsnets — but of the Ponjees I have taken no patterns — This Invoice, with my half of Invoice in Comp^y with W.Sturgis, also shipped by the Trumbull, just about makes up the sum insured for my a/ct by W.Sturgis of 10,000 $ out & home — and I have written him & you to cause $5000 — more to be insured for my account &in my name to be shipped hereafter — if any freight can be obtained. Short Nankins have been sold as low as 40 $ Comp^{ys} 82 &bestBlues 118 — Teas say Hyson 44 — Souchong 26 @ 34 Campoi 22 @ 23 Congo 20 @ 21 — no young Hyson in the market — Silks on new contracts would now be lower, but the quantity sent this year to U.S very large, say to the amo^t of 1,000,000 of Dollars.

I regret that I cannot return in the Atahualpa, but the arrival of the Derby *from* NWCoast, makes it necessary to remain & attend to the business of that Vessel, in which I shall probably come home. —

You will excuse my troubling you with this Shipment of Silks — and I beg that you will take no other pains about them than to send them to auction, or to such market as may be preferable to that of Boston — If you should think it best to sell them in Providence, B & T Hoppin have requested they may have the agency there, and if you judge it best & safest, you will please give them the consignment, should you sell them in Providence.

Ingreathaste

Yours most truly

J.Bromfield.

LETTER FROM HENRY LEE, BOSTON, FEB. 5, 1811, TO OCTAVIUS
PLUMMER, SUPERCARGO, BRIG CORNELIUS, WITH INSTRUCTIONS
FOR PURCHASE OF GOODS IN NORTHERN EUROPE [1]

In a letter of Jan. 31 to G. W. Erving, Minister to Denmark,
Henry Lee mentioned the capture of certain property on board the
brigs *Cygnet* and *Cornelius*, doubtless by some of the Danish privateers then preying on American commerce. On Sept. 15, 1810, Henry
Lee had referred to the "capture of 15 to 20 sail of the homeward
bound Russia ships" and on the previous day had stated that the
"fleet of homeward bound Russia ships together with outward bound
vessels lately carried into Norway are estimated at 2 Millions of
Dollars & principally owned in Mass^a." [2] Early in Nov., 1810, Henry
Lee was offering for sale cloth "received from Russia," doubtless on
the *Sally* from Archangel.[3] Henry Lee seems to have had no doubt
that his property would be returned on the proper representations.
His belief was doubtless strengthened by the fact that the Czar was
growing more and more willing to use his influence in favor of
American vessels captured en route to Russia; this attitude was one
of the reasons for Napoleon's break with his erstwhile ally and for
his fateful invasion of the Czar's dominions in 1812.[4]

M^r. Octavius Plummer   Boston Feby 5 — 1811 —
    Supercargo of Brig Cornelius
        Dear Sir   p Trim
                         Copy p^r Mr. Erving Minister at the
                         Court of Denmark —
        We have heard of your arrival at Copenhagen & pre-
sume long before this reaches you will have been cleard at the
high court — The concern have generally sent by Mr Erving
our Minister to the Court of Denmark copies of their Invoices &
Bills of Lading to substantiate their claims — in case the property sh^d still remain under seizure —

1. Jackson-Lee Papers, "Letter Book," Aug. 19, 1810–May 30, 1811.
2. *Ibid.*, Henry Lee, Boston, Sept. 15, 1810, to Samuel Yorke and
James Schott, Philadelphia; *ibid.*, Henry Lee, Boston, Sept. 14, 1810, to
Peter Remsen, N. Y.
3. Lee-Cabot Papers, 1810–12, Nov. 12, 1810.
4. Channing, *op. cit.*, vol. iv, pp. 450–451.

Russia manufactures are very low — you need not at any rate send me any Diapers or Linens of any kind — but remit as directed heretofore — in case that cannot be done — then send me Russia Sheetings of the most ordinary quality — or ordinary Duck — (Sail Cloth)

I trust you did not discharge at Gottenburg — as there is no possibility of making sales at any rate —

If on receipt of this any goods of mine remain on hand sell them at once — Have your remittances guarantied

Yours —

Henry Lee

LETTER FROM HENRY LEE, BOSTON, FEB. 6, 1811, TO SAMUEL CABOT, JR., PHILADELPHIA, ON FINANCIAL STRINGENCY [1]

Since the first of the year Henry Lee's letters had revealed a steadily increasing difficulty in raising money. On Jan. 2, 1811, he wrote to Peter Remsen, "I wish you to make the arrangement with Prime [Nathaniel Prime, the famous money lender] if possible for a continuation of the whole — we shall want all you can spare besides as we have Respondentia Bonds to meet in 60 days after the Gipsy appears — if he will not renew the whole then agree to pay him ½ 10th to 15th of this month & continue the bal^a. as much longer as we pay this in advance." On Jan. 21 he sent Samuel Yorke & James Schott of Philadelphia a list of failures in Boston in return for a similar list furnished by them, and commented "no business doing." The following day, writing to B. & G. Williams of Baltimore he remarked cheerfully, "we have had only one failure of late." On the same day he wrote more at length to Peter Remsen: "we have got thro' the most pressing time and not one failure has happened, but thro' their overtrading excessively and having no credit to keep themselves up, most of them have been suspected for three years, at least, thus far I lose only $8 to $10,000, at most. I do not hold any bad paper but still I make up my mind to losses." On Feb. 5 he informed Zadock Gilman, Charleston, S. C., "there have been many bankruptcies in this place." All the time he was urging his correspondents to sell his goods they had in their hands, but only for cash or on short-term credit to safe people. It is evident from this letter

1. Jackson-Lee Papers, "Letter Book," Aug. 19, 1810–May 30, 1811.

that he was now himself feeling the sharp financial pinch, apparently in part because he had indorsed some paper for the firm with which his cousin Samuel Cabot, Jr., was connected.

Mr Saml Cabot Junr   Boston Feby 6th 1811
    Dear Saml
        I am glad to hear thro' A Cabot that you have such favorable accounts from Mr Hazard. You ought to convert every thing you can into money, our Banks do less and less every day and I find it difficult to keep along your notes at the Banks — Mr H should get an advance if possible on the Coffee, that article has fallen here to 16¢. and no sales at that Your presence will be useful here as soon as you can leave Philad^a your father is too sick to aid us, and will not even allow his name in way of renewing the notes. we have one at Massachusetts to morrow as my name and J Lee's are in there as much or more than they ought to be we find it difficult to get names. the Cash payments are also very heavy balance due me $4000 and $4000 more to pay in day or two, I am so situated that my ability to aid you will be diminished, unless business should be better than I can calculate upon.

    Sell by all means any of your German Goods or any other indeed you may have on hand.
The *Rachael* has been spoken with or arrived at Heligoland I wish before you leave Philadelphia you would ascertain what the state or City duty on wholesale Auctions is, and also the Auction^{rs} Commission on a Cargo, and whether there are any who guarantee sales and the premium demanded.
                                Yours
                            (sign'd) H Lee
Exchange on London will sell here @ 9% Cash or 6% 60 days perhaps Mr Hazard may pay his balance in that way, say by furnishing a good Bill of Exchange on London, it should be drawn by some house that is known.

LETTER FROM HENRY LEE, BOSTON, FEB. 9, 1811, TO S. & C. HOWARD, SAVANNAH, GA., WITH A TRIAL CONSIGNMENT [1]

This letter is another evidence of Henry Lee's determination to push the sales of his India goods even in ports of the United States with which he had not previously been in commercial relationship.

Mess S & C Howard   Boston Feby 9th 1811
    Savannah
       Dear sirs
          Mr Zadock Gilman informs me he has shipped you 8 Bales Cottons on my account from Charleston S.C. I have done this to make trial of your market, and hope I may find it an object to ship larger quantities, I have now on hand, and am expecting a great variety of all kinds of Cottons and shall be glad to be kept inform'd of their value from time to time

It is my wish you sell the 8 bales for the most you can obtain, if there is no demand at private sale offer them at auction.

I shall draw on you at 30 or 60 days for $1500 on account of them as soon as I hear of their arrival.

With regard
Yours
(sign'd) Henry Lee

LETTER FROM HENRY LEE FOR SELF AND JOSEPH LEE, JR., BOSTON, FEB. 13, 1811, TO GEORGE LEE AND JOSEPH HALL, JR., CALCUTTA, WITH INSTRUCTIONS TO USE CAUTION IN PURCHASING [1]

In the two months intervening between the Lees' last letter to their Calcutta agents and the one below, the commercial situation had changed and the Lees had perhaps also found time for a few sober second thoughts. Their tone, at any rate, had undergone a marked change; they now urged caution, even contraction, in purchases. The letter arrived too late to affect the purchases of the

---

1. Jackson-Lee Papers, "Letter Book," Aug. 19, 1810–May 30, 1811.

---

1. Jackson-Lee Papers, "Letter Book," Aug. 19, 1810–May 30, 1811.

Gulliver's supercargoes in any way; the vessel cleared from Calcutta, Mar. 9, 1811, with a cargo in which the piece goods alone were invoiced at more than sicca rupees 264,000.[2] The new policy was undoubtedly the correct one, had it come earlier; but not because they were right in thinking that non-intercourse would fail to take place, for it did go into effect almost within a fortnight. The Lees were, however, correct in thinking that but few vessels would leave the United States for India during the remaining months of 1811; the lists of those vessels leaving Calcutta for the United States in 1811 and 1812 contain at the most no more than eight which could have left the United States in 1811 after the date of this letter, while during the same period in 1810 there had been probably twice that number.[3]

Messrs. Geoe. Lee & Jos Hall Junr.   Boston Feby 13. 1811
    Calcutta   Dear Sirs
        Our last was of 14 Decr. p Ganges since which there has been no opportunity of writing —
    The voyage of the John Adams having been abandon'd in consequence of the apprehended *Non Intercourse*. It is not yet settled upon what footing our relations with Great Britain are to be — it is probable however that we shall not have any interruption of our Intercourse at all certainly not for a long time — In consequence of the great Stock of Calcutta goods expected in this Country this year & the quantities of the old Stock that remain on hand — they are not like to be high again for a long time — It is our wish therefore that you invest no more funds than what we have remitted via England & that in your purchases you take the cheapest you can find, taking as a standard of value — our Memorandums dated Octr 15. 1810 we think better of [the — stricken through] Silks generally than almost any Cottons — You cannot get too many Taffaties if they can be had 7/ @ 10/ *Blue Cloths* we think will not do very well not only from the [interlineated: great] quantities that will have been shipped but because the trade

2. *Ibid.*, "Invoices," 1799–1812.
3. *Ibid.*, "List of Vessels clear'd for America from Calcutta."

to Africa has diminish'd — we w^d. not in fact have you buy any unless @ 70/. or under for 35 x 2¼ & then only a moderate quantity — we wrote also too favourably of seersuckers 2000 p^s. of all kinds will be enough & let them be of the cheapest [qualitys — stricken through interlineated: kind]

Among the Gruff goods we w^d. have you avoid Duck — altogether go largely upon Goat Skins & buy considerable quantities of all the other gruff goods — Indigo we consider as too precarious unless it sh^d. fall to 130/ @ 140/ for very good then buy 10,000 lb. — Do not speculate in goods under the idea the Americans will come out in great numbers as last year & rise the prices — there will be but few despatched this year not en^o. to make goods rise in Calcutta — we repeat we do not want any more goods bot than you have funds for

If Mr Tracy sh^d. be in Calcutta he will of course be connected with you & follow the instructions we give you — Sh^d. he remain at Madrass you will write him & say that his owners do not wish him to make any further purchases than he may have funds for & that they advise him not to buy many *Blue Cloths* but to go more upon Comboies Salempores, Niccannies &c. — We w^d. not have you on any acc^t. draw on London as we some time since recommended nor borrow any money in Calcutta — Do not make any contracts if you can get what goods you want in the Bazar & when you do — have them drawn up by a Lawyer — Do not in your purchases go beyond our [interlineated: lowest] limits in the letter of Octr 15 & unless the Common White Goods are lower than these limits buy only a small quantity but take of Chintz, Silks, Long Cloths, Seersuckers & such other goods as are not commonly run upon by the Americans — Ship by every vessel Silks & fine Cottons at our Freight say 120 Rp^s p^rTon —

The coarse goods keep unless you can send them at 60/ or 70/ Rp^s p^rTon —

Yours
H Lee for Self & Jos Lee J.

Duplicate original & Triplicate to Newton Gordon &C^o. Madeira via New York

LETTER FROM HENRY LEE, BOSTON, APR. 1, 1811, TO THADDEUS MAYHEW, NEW ORLEANS, ANNOUNCING FAILURE [1]

There are unfortunately no letters between Mar. 1 and the date of this to reveal the details of Henry Lee's failure. The reason for it, however, was clearly that which he himself gave as explanation for earlier failures at a time when he did not anticipate adding to their number; namely, too enthusiastic overexpansion. With this letter temporarily ends the record of Henry Lee's career as a sedentary merchant, which had begun in the summer of 1804 when he entered into partnership with his brother Joseph. Since Henry Lee's return from Europe early in 1805 he seems to have taken the leading rôle in the partnership, if the number of letters signed by him or on behalf of himself and associates is of any significance.

Thaddeus Mayhew Esqr Boston April 1st 1811
  New Orleans
    sir
      I find in looking at your acc^t Current, I am indebted a balance $192.47, &that the sales of Seersuckers fell short $258.60 of what I drew for, it was not my intention to have been in your debt & I tho't I was safe in drawing for ¾ am^t shipped, when the sales were rec^d. I did not think it worth while to remit, because I contemplated further shipments of Cottons this season. I understand from Mr Andrews there will be another dividend upon Wells' estate. I hope it may be enough to discharge my balance, if not you will have the misfortune to become a Creditor of mine. my situation perhaps is known to you or will be made known by your friend, I have assign'd my property for the benefit of all my Creditors & I hope the loss will not be great, I wish you to send on your demand & instruct your agent to come in with the other Creditors. a limited time will be allowed by my assignees, but I should be gratified with having your signature thro' your attorney as soon as you have made up your mind to come in as the others have done.
          I am your Ob^t Servt
          (sign'd) Henry Lee

1. Jackson-Lee Papers, "Letter Book," Aug. 19, 1810–May 30, 1811.

I suppose a Power of Att^y will be requisite to eneable your agent to sign

Mr Mayhew has made an attachment on Mess H. & Ogden New Orleans for Bal^a. of A/C Due him which is $452.07

DIVISION XIII

HENRY LEE, CALCUTTA SUPERCARGO AND AGENT
1811–16

LETTER FROM STEPHEN HIGGINSON & CO., BOSTON, AUG. 16, 1811, TO HENRY LEE, BRIG REAPER, WITH INSTRUCTIONS FOR PURCHASES IN CALCUTTA [1]

After Henry Lee's failure early in 1811 he found it necessary to look about for employment. In August, he was given the opportunity of going to Calcutta via England as supercargo of the brig *Reaper*, of which Andrew Cabot was the sole owner. In England, it was reported, exchange on Calcutta could be obtained at a discount; about a score of merchants and firms joined to place in Henry Lee's hands credits on England totalling £40,000. Each adventurer in the *Reaper* of course submitted to Henry Lee, the supercargo, a letter of instructions. That below is typical of the instructions given by the larger investors. Some of the adventurers merely told the supercargo to invest their funds "in Merchandize, at your discretion" [2] or in such "Cotton & Silk goods as shall appear to you most for my interest." [3] Others gave detailed lists of acceptable (or unacceptable) goods with price limits, possible substitutions, etc. Piece goods of various kinds and indigo were the goods commonly specified.

Andrew Cabot was one of Henry Lee's many cousins, and the *Reaper*, a brig of 284 tons, had been built in 1808 at Medford by Thatcher Magoun.[4]

1. Jackson-Lee Papers, "Bristol letter Book, orders from Shippers in Brig Reaper 1811 — voyage to Calcutta," pp. 28–29.
2. *Ibid.*, John C. Jones, Boston, Aug. 19, 1811, to Henry Lee, brig *Reaper*.
3. *Ibid.*, Joseph Tilden, Boston, Aug. 17, 1811, to Henry Lee, brig *Reaper*.   4. Briggs, *op. cit.*, vol. i, pp. 169–170; vol. ii, p. 794.

CALCUTTA, 1792

Henry Lee Esqr Boston August 16th. 1811 —
  Dear sir
      The enclosed letters you will please to take charge of &
deliver according to their directions. They relate to a shipment or rather an investment which I contemplate making in
Calcutta thro' your agency &to be brought home in the Brig
Reaper of which you have the control. If my friends should
determine to engage with me they will inform you accordingly
&make the necessary provision for that purpose. I have directed
three, five, or ten thousand pounds to be furnished you, either
in drafts on Calcutta or good credits which will enable you to
draw there on H Higginson of London with equal advantage,
if they determine to engage for the smallest sum only, say
three thousand pounds sterling, it will then be for my sole
acc^t, &not for the account of S H &Co. but, of the particular
parties interested you will know more when you arrive in London. If the appearances of a rupture between this Country
& G Britain are such as to alarm my friends in E. they will
not ship or invest any sum whatever, either for my A/C or
their own, but I have requested them in case of fair prospects
of a continuance of Peace with this Country to furnish you
with from three to ten thousand pounds in bills or Credits
as they may think proper. If the investment exceeds three
[interlineated: 3] thousand pounds, you will follow the directions you may receive from M^r H as to the Kinds of goods to be
brough home, but if it is confined to three thousand pounds,
you will consider the enclosed Mem^o as the one by which you
are to be govern'd, so far as you can comply with it, But if
you should be compell'd to deviate from it. your own excellent judgement &information in this business must be your
guide &my protection. I need add nothing to these lines but
that I wish most sincerely you may be able to accomplish your
voyage to your satisfaction &benefit &that you may return
in health &happiness to your family &friends among whom I
have the pleasure to subscribe myself with great sincerity being

my Dsir with great esteem &regard your ob^t Servt. £ 5000 stg
will invest say S^a Rps 40000

to be invested in good Gurrahs from 25 to 70 Rps .. Rps	10.000	
Baftas, if you can have your choice, w^d prefer ⎞		
Callipatty &fine & Bogdia, Boran &Lucki- ⎬ ..	10.000	
pore .... ⎠		
Common Checks not to cost over 25 Rps	10.000	
Chintz not to cost over 15	2.500	
500 p^s Common Taffaties @ 5	2 500	
Bandanna flag Handkerchiefs	5 000	40.000

I would have you avoid Mamoodies of all descriptions unless
25 pCt cheaper than they were bot last year, Mow Sannahs must
also be avoided unless to be bot at 20 Rp^s for good common
kinds. Blue Goods of all kinds (except Checks) we w^d have
you *avoid*. If any of the above kinds are not to be got, 2500
Rp^s Chadpore Cossas might answer &the quantity of Taffaties
may be increased &2500 Rs of the finer Kinds not to cost over
10 R^s may do. There is a certain quality of Indigo which can
be got at 120 Rp^s pm^d which w^d bring here from 150 to 165
ct^s but every thing depends on the quality &purity of it as
great deceptions are practiced in both. I have fixed in this
Mem^o on £ 5000 but it may be increas'd or diminishd according to the sum invested in like proportion &you may if the Shipment sh^d be increased to £ 10,000 invest ½ or 1/3^d of it in
Indigo if to be got on the terms & quality discribed. It will
pay perhaps better than any other article if it is of real good
quality for its price & I should like it as well as any thing I
have named say for my own a/c one thousand pounds or one
third of my investment —

LETTER FROM EDWARD A. NEWTON, BOSTON, AUG. 18, 1811,
TO HENRY LEE, BRIG REAPER, WITH INSTRUCTIONS FOR PUR-
CHASE OF GOODS IN ENGLAND FOR SHIPMENT TO INDIA [1]

Newton seems to have been the only adventurer on the *Reaper*
who preferred to use his credit in England for the purchase of goods

1. Jackson-Lee Papers, "Bristol letter Book, orders from Shippers in
Brig Reaper 1811 — voyage to Calcutta."

for shipment to India rather than for transfer in the form of bills of exchange or drafts on Calcutta.

Mr Henry Lee   Boston 18th. August 1811
     Dear sir

     Herewith I have the pleasure to hand you Shimmin &Colmans draft on Thomas Dickason &Co London at 60 days sight for Five hundred pounds sterling with which I request you to do the needful on my account.

If you determine to prosecute your intended voyage, I wish you to invest the whole amt in good french Brandy if to be got at 7/6d Sterling a gallon on board &ship the same for a/c my brother Mr Wm, A, Newton now at Madras, If this cannot be done & Brandy is as high as 8/6. I would prefer investing only have the amt therein &the other half in Small Window Glass as described if to be got at fifteen shillings sterling pr Box of 50 feet, together with 2 or 300 pieces of Sponge. Should your stay in England be too short to enable you to get these things from London where probably you will have to look for them, or should you find it difficult to obtain them, then I request you to do with this adventure as with your own funds, laying out the money in articles Easy to be obtain'd & offering in your opinion the most profits. —

On your arrival in Calcutta, if you find you can dispose of the adventure to good advantage I wish you to do so at once, but if otherwise, I wd have you communicate with my brother at Madras.

This adventure being for a/c my brother Wm, A, Newton I wish you to hold the proceeds subject to his order, & in case you leave Calcutta before your hear from him, deposit the amt in the hands of Messrs Alexander &Co for his account.

If you give up in London your Calcutta voyage, leave the money with Henry Higginson to my credit, I have agreed with Mr Cabot to pay him five per Cent of the proceeds in Calcutta in lieu of freight.

            With sincere regard I remain Yrs &c
               / sign'd) Edwd, A, Newton

You will oblige me by purchasing a piece of plain Dacca Muslin of 20 yards, Very fine, to cost 70 or 80 rupees, take en⁰ to pay for it from my funds, If I am not at Home when you return please to send it in my name to Mrs Saml G Perkins.

LETTER FROM ANDREW CABOT, BOSTON, AUG. 19, 1811, TO HENRY LEE, BRIG REAPER, WITH GENERAL INSTRUCTIONS FOR THE VOYAGE [1]

The cargo shipped on board the *Reaper* for England seems to have been principally lumber, though Samuel Cabot, Jr., consigned to Henry Lee "3 Boxes german quils," [2] invoiced at $2,789.09.[3]

Mr HenryLee   Boston, Augt 19th. 1811.
    Sir,
       You being SuperCargo of the Brig Reaper, Captn Spooner, on yr arrival at Bristol you will dispose of what cargo she has on board of which you have herewith Inv⁰ & Bill of lading. If you find it practicable to prosecute the voyage proposed by the freighters, you will proceed immediately on it, & if you think it for my interest to load a cargo on board the Reaper at Bristol, you will purchase such a one as you think best, for which purpose I herewith hand you a letter of Credit on Saml Williams for £5000 stg (Five thousand pounds sterling). my agreement with the freighters is to deduct (13½) thirteen & one half pCent. from the amt shipped by each individual which is to be in full for freight of goods home & your commission for investing, this amt will therefore be pass'd to my cr together with the proceeds of the cargo, &which you will invest for my acct in such goods as you think most for my interest, & ship on board the Reaper for my acct. you will forward me from Bristol a note of the amt belonging to each

1. Jackson-Lee Papers, "Bristol letter Book, orders from Shippers in Brig Reaper 1811 — voyage to Calcutta," pp. 24–25.
2. *Ibid.*, Samuel Cabot, Boston, Aug. 17, 1811, to Henry Lee, brig *Reaper*.
3. *Ibid.*, Henry Lee's account book, London, Sept. 30, 1811–Calcutta, Mar. 1, 1816.

Freighter together with the Inv⁰ of the cargo on board that I may make Insurance here.

Should you not be able to prosecute the voyage proposed you are at liberty to employ the Reaper in any way you think most for my interest, taking care to keep me advised of what she may be doing that I may make Insurance.

If you should load on board the Reaper a return cargo for this country which may be interdicted by the present Non Importation act, you will observe by the orders to Captⁿ Spooner of which you have copy, that he is instructed not to enter any port of the United States, but to hoist a signal off New York &wait further orders. Altho' there is hardly a *possibility* of its continuance untill your return to this country, it is still an event we ought to guard against.

Wishing you success, I am your friend &c
(sign'd)   Andrew Cabot.

LETTER FROM ANDREW CABOT, BOSTON, AUG. 19, 1811, TO NATHANIEL SPOONER, JR., BRIG REAPER, WITH INSTRUCTIONS FOR HIS CONDUCT AS CAPTAIN [1]

The intricacy of commercial operations during the unsettled period of the Napoleonic Wars is graphically brought out by the instructions as to the signals to be employed should the vessel return to the United States while the Non-Importation Act was still in effect. Note the suggestions for increasing cargo space and the provisions for the captain's compensation. A ton (measurement) was 40 cu. ft.

Boston Augt. 19. 1811.

Capt. N. Spooner Jr.
    Sir
        The Brig Reaper [interlineated: under] your command being ready for sea, You will proceed with all possible despatch to Bristol in England, where you will deliver your cargo in conformity to your Bills Lading — As it is at present uncertain what voyage may be undertaken from thence. I leave it to

1. Jackson-Lee Papers, "Bristol letter Book, orders from Shippers in Brig Reaper 1811 — voyage to Calcutta," pp. 25–26.

Mr Henry Lee who goes out in the Reaper, as Supercargo to give you such instructions, as he may deem neccessary as to the further prosecution of it, and to whose directions you will conform as implicitly as to my own — You will be extremely careful that on whatever voyage you may proceed, no law of any place you may be at, nor any law of nations be violated by any person under your control — If you should load a Cargo at any foreign port the importation of which is interdicted by the present Non Importation Act, you will recollect that it can not be imported into the United States during its continuance, and although the probability is, that every difficulty of this nature will be removed before you reach the American Coast yet it is possible, such may not be the case — You will not therefore enter any port of the United States untill you have good assurance of its repeal — But on your arrival off the port of New York (where you will proceed on your return to the country) You will hoist as a signal a white pendant forward and an American Ensign aft, standing off and on until you receive further orders — That the vessel may bring as much Cargo as possible you may if necessary build a Coach House on deck as on the last Voyage, and have as much water stowed on deck, as can be done with safety — You will not fail to write me by every opportunity the particulars of this voyage —

Wishing you a successful voyage —

I am   Your friend &c.

(Signed)   Andrew Cabot

For your services during the voyage you are entitled to Sixty Dollars per Month & Eight Tons /measurement) priviledge on board —

Note — In addition to the Signal mentioned in the above you will have a piece of Blue Bunting or Blue Cloth stitched to the middle of the Fore Top Sail —

STATEMENT BY ANDREW CABOT, BOSTON, AUG. 21, 1811, OF
HENRY LEE'S COMPENSATION AS SUPERCARGO OF THE REAPER [1]

As stated in earlier letters, 13½% of the funds furnished by each
adventurer was to be deducted at Calcutta "in lieu of freight, Commissions &c" [2] and the remainder invested by the supercargo for the
benefit of the shipper. We learn from the memorandum below that
2½% of the funds handled was to be for the benefit of the supercargo. These funds, of course, would be invested by him in merchandise, and for the purpose of transporting these goods to the
United States he was allowed a "priviledge" of ten tons. It is evident that a few fortunate voyages as supercargo would do much
toward achieving or restoring financial independence. The supercargo's commission, privilege, and expenses may be compared to the
captain's $60 per month and eight tons.

Agreement for Compensation for voyage in the Reaper to Calcutta

As compensation of Mr Henry Lee for transacting the business of the Reapers voyage he is entitled to 2½% on the proceeds of forty thousand Pounds in Calcutta — Ten Tons
measurement priviledge on board the Reaper — his neccessary
shore Expences in England and Calcutta paid —

If the Reaper should return from England, and not proceed to Calcutta no expences paid —

Boston Aug. 21. 1811   (Signed) Andrew Cabot

LETTER FROM ANDREW CABOT, BOSTON, AUG. 22, 1811, TO
HENRY LEE, BRIG REAPER, WITH FINAL INSTRUCTIONS FOR A
CARGO FROM BRISTOL FOR INDIA [1]

Cabot's suggestion that Henry Lee should "never sign in Calcutta,
but as agent for the R[eaper]" was probably inspired by a fear that
some of Lee's creditors might seize the goods under his charge.

1. Jackson-Lee Papers, "Bristol letter Book, orders from Shippers in
Brig Reaper 1811 — voyage to Calcutta."
2. *Ibid.*, Samuel Cabot, Jr., Boston, Aug. 17, 1811, to Henry Lee, brig
Reaper.

1. Jackson-Lee Papers, "Bristol letter Book, orders from Shippers in
Brig Reaper 1811 — voyage to Calcutta," p. 23.

Mr HenryLee   Boston. Augt. 22d. 1811.

Dear Henry,

For a Cargo from England, you will take Pig iron and perhaps 5 or 6 Tons Iron hoops for ballast — Sea Coal 20 or 30 Tons — Empty Bottles — & such other articles as you think best not to exceed in all £2000 — including the proceeds of the Cargo now on board.

In remitting your Exchange to Calcutta (say to Alexander&Co/ perhaps it will be as well to endorse the Bills "Pay Alexander &Co for account of the Freighters of the Brig Reaper, Spooner —

HLee agent for freighters

Enclose them at the same time a Schedule of the different sums to be plac'd to each man's account in case of the R. not arriving.

On your return to this country, have two Manifests without the place of destination that we may insert some other place in case of the Non Importation continuing — one withthe destination Boston. —

I think you shd never sign in Calcutta, but as agent for the R — & have your account with your Banian in Spooner's or some other name — Yours

(sign'd)   A. Cabot

LETTER FROM HENRY LEE, LONDON, SEPT. 28, 1811, TO ANDREW CABOT, BOSTON, WITH AN ACCOUNT OF THE DIFFICULTY IN COLLECTING FUNDS [1]

Henry Lee had left Boston on Aug. 22, 1811; Col. Thomas Handasyd Perkins was a fellow passenger.[2] On Sept. 22 the *Reaper* arrived at Bristol, where Henry Lee found an unfortunate situation awaiting him. Several of those who had placed in his hands credits on London had considerably overestimated what was due them, or else had been drawn on for other purposes without the fact having

1. Jackson-Lee Papers, "Bristol letter Book, orders from Shippers in Brig Reaper 1811 — voyage to Calcutta."
2. Briggs, *op. cit.*, vol. i, p. 410.

come to their attention before Henry Lee's departure. As a result, instead of being in possession of funds totalling £40,000, he found himself with only a little more than three-eighths of that amount. The difficulty of carrying on business under such uncertain conditions and the need for rapid decisions and vigorous action on the part of a business man involved in them are brought out clearly in the accompanying letter.

The impression among certain elements in the United States at this time was that the danger of war with Great Britain had been considerably increased by the clash on May 16, 1811, between the American frigate *President* and the British sloop-of-war *Little Belt,* in which the latter was put out of action. Almost the first news Henry Lee had received on landing in Bristol was that the *President* had been captured by the British frigate *Melampus* after a battle in which the American vessel had lost 60 men. Henry Lee correctly believed this report to be the product of wishful thinking on the part of some disgruntled Britisher; he went on to assure his correspondents that, though the British had been at first annoyed by the treatment accorded one of their war vessels, after a few days "it excites no more attention than a quarrel with the Sandwich Islanders."

Mr Andrew Cabot   London, Septr 28. 1811.

   Dear A,   (Galen)

    Since writing you this morning by the Louisa via New York, Ihave ascertain'd that there will be a great falling off in the freight — Mr Higginson has no funds of Mr Cleveland's they having been employ'd by a brother of that gentleman in some other way — Mr Sawyer has no funds & Mr H thinks he shall not be able to advance — Touro has only a balance of 20£ or 30£

I am apprehensive some of my letters on Williams will not be answ'd — I shall go on with the voyage however if there is £ 20,000 — you must have remittances follow me — perhaps I may take up the £ 5000 on T. Williams & you will dispose of it to Mr Sawyer & those persons whose funds fail — in the meantime get them to remit as soon as possible & write me that I may know what &how much to expect — You need not calculate upon my getting funds from Dickason &Co or any other sources — I shall try but no probability of succeeding with such short funds I shall invest for you to the extent you have allow'd me particularly as I hear the Vancouver got up early (& if she sold as you told me the Capt was order'd to) she must have done well — There is strong probability of war between Russia & France — this will depress still lower the prices of W. I & American produce which are now very low in Russia as you will have heard before this —

I can give you no information on political subjects — the general impression is there will be no war — at least that there is no more probability of it now than there was before the Little Belt affair — Ihave not seen Mr Williams yet — shall call on him Monday or perhaps meet him on 'Change to day.

Ihave just presented my letters of credit to Mr Williams the following he will answer — vizt

Jos Tilden	£1200.0.0	
P. C. Brooks —	2000.0.0	(increas'd as the Tartar does not go)
R. Hooper &others —	3375.0.0	
W & A Hooper —	1000.0.0	
C. Coolidge &Co —	1000.0.0	
R. G. Shaw —	1350.0.0	
Saunders —	300.0.0	
SamlCabot Jur —	1000.0.0	11225.0.0

To which add Grenough in Leeds	600.0.0		
S. Train & B & Valentines Bills	1104.4.0		
S. Appletons — do —	1125.0.0		
Jno Cabot Jun — d —	1400.0.0	4229.0.0	£15454.4.0

this is all the stock I am certain of — if T. H. Perkins concludes upon his £ 10,000.0.0 Mr Higginson upon £3000.0.0 for S. G. Perkins & I get $6000 from English & £1000 from De Tastet for Jones — Ishall make up say £31000.0.0 — this is the most I fear I shall be able to collect from the letters — I am in hopes Mr Williams may conclude to advance for Jona Amory the amt of his letter — it seems T. Clements has drawn out his balance from the Cape Good Hope, yet as MrA is an old correspondent of Williams's & is well known to him — I shall be surpriz'd if he does not advance for him — S. Cabots' Balance

is only £1000.0.0 & J. Cabots £836.13.1 has be drawn out by
F. Cabot — Ihave not yet presented my letter of credit on
Mr W. for £5000.0.0 in your favour — If I cannot get M^r H
to advance for W. Sawyer — Ishall take up the amount which
he has authoris'd MrHigginson to advance me, in case he sh^d.
have no funds in hand vizt £1500 from H. Higginson by virtue
of your letter in my favour on H. H there being about that
am^t. remitted by J. Williams of the Independence, if M^r S.
makes provision (as I suppose he will do as soon as he hears
that his funds upon which he calculated to make up his investment have been appropriated) to meet the advance of £1500 —
o.o — there will then be to your credit again the am^t. I borrow
as it were from you tobuy Mr S's bills — perhaps I am not
clear — but you will understand what I mean — I may do the
same withregard to Amory out of the funds I get upon the
£ 5000 letter

As to Cleveland &C^o their orders were to buy bills out of a
particular remittance made by J. W. Smith — the amt. has
been taken up by a brother of M^r C's — so that I am inclin'd
to think Mr H will not feel authoris'd to advance for them,
persuasion shall not be wanting however on my part — Should
Ifail in prevailing on Mr H — to advance for Cleveland I may
appropriate the amt they agreed for or so much as I may have
after making up the £ 2000.0.0 for the outward Cargo & Amory's
sum, to the purchase of Bills for them, they of course will make
provision for it & then the am^t. may be return'd to Mr Williams — but of this I cannot speak with certainty for the
present, nor indeed do I know whether Mr W — will answer
this letter from T. W — I did not think it prudent to present it,
'till I settled about Amory's letter — upon which subject he
is to give me an answer on Monday —

I feel very sorry that the stock is not like to come up to
£ 40,000 — I never contemplated any considerable deficiency
— sh^d. M^r H not engage any either for himself or Mr Perkins,
there will be a great falling off — but Ihave made up my mind
toproceed with £ 20000.0.0 if no more can be obtaind — I see no
alternative — to return in ballast w^d. be runinous & I do not

hear of any employment in this quarter that w^d. not be worse — £20,000 w^d be a small stock — but Ish^d. calculate you w^d. have remittances follow me & upon getting some freight in Calcutta — I hope therefore that such a decision, sh^d I be driven to it will not be thought imprudent —

Sunday. 29 Septr. I gave Mr P. notice yesterday that Ish^d. be ready to buy my bills as soon as he had made up his mind — he reply'd that he had resolv'd or nearly so upon shipping the £ 10,000 — but prefer'd waiting to see Mr Higginson who may be expected in a few days — Ihave no objection to the delay otherwise than I can do nothing about the outward cargo 'till this point is settled — another reason why I wish^d a decision is that I am afraid old Mr H. will discourage his engaging in it — upon the idea that eventually we shall have war with England — there is no help for it & I must wait with patience the motions of Mr P. as I cannot even make up the smallest sum Ish^d. feel authoris'd to proceed with without him — I know you did all you could to fix this matter before sailing but you have taken a great risk in leaving it at his option, if he chooses to say the danger of war is too great for him to adventure — Ihave not one word to say, tho Iknow in his opinion it is much less than when we sail'd — Iknow too that he has not met a single individual who apprehends war any more now than for two years past — The exchange I hit is all not for acceptance an answer will be given on Monday, it is the practice here to leave bills a day, before an answer is given — I dare say comparisons will be made between the dispatch the Restitution has made & the delay that will necessarily attend us — the shippers may settle that among themselves as they please, it is no fault of mine or yours — I am ready to pay & gave Mr P. notice to that effect in 6 hours after I ascertain'd what I could raise out of my Bills & Letters — I have the sanction of Mr Williams & every one will allow he is not a very rash man — be that as it may the shippers have made him my counsellor & they no doubt will give due weight to his judgment —

I w^d. not have you understand from anything I have said that there is yet anything pass'd between Mr P & myself that induces me to think he will violate his engagements — Indeed very little has been said at all — he intimated that he had rather not decide 'till he saw old M^r H & I thought it both impolitic & unreasonable considering the am^t. he adventures to press the subject any further — it w^d. only give offence & not effect the object

About the trade of Russia, markets &c you know more than I can tell you — M^r H tells me the Independence did well having sold early & that Whitney must have also done well if he sold on arrival — which I presume he did, I mention this because you seem'd to lay some stress upon it in the amt of cargo you intended to invest for India I feel justifyd in going to the extent you limited me say £ 2000 — including the proceeds of the outward cargo

My 1st. sent p. Lydia — via Liverpool
  Copy of do — G. Hamilton do
  2 letters p Louisa — others goes by Galen

Yours

HL

LETTER FROM HENRY LEE, LONDON, OCT. 1, 1811, TO ANDREW CABOT, BOSTON, ANNOUNCING THE OBTENTION OF THE NECESSARY FUNDS [1]

By the date of this letter, Henry Lee had succeeded in obtaining from other sources funds sufficient to replace in part those of which he had been disappointed and to make possible his voyage to Calcutta.

The "Bills @ 2/2^d. @ 2/2½" were bills on India purchased at from 2s. 2d. to 2s. 2½d. per rupee. Since the rupee was worth about 2s., exchange on India was not at a discount, as had been reported. Perhaps the reference below to "the Broker who buys all the Exchange on India" explains why exchange on Calcutta was at a pre-

---

1. Jackson-Lee Papers, "Bristol letter Book, orders from Shippers in Brig Reaper 1811 — voyage to Calcutta."

mium. Henry Lee succeeded in obtaining bills at the upper limit of the above-mentioned rates and insured some of them with Samuel Williams against non-payment for a premium of 1%.[2]

Mr Andrew Cabot,   London — Octo. 1. 1811.
    Dear A,   (pr New Galen)
    I wrote you under date of 28th & 29th Utop Galen — she being detaind gives me an opportunity to say that Mr Perkins came to a decision last evening to invest £10000.0.0 — so that Ihave no fault to find with that gentleman — considering the amount it was not to be expected he wd. take less time to make up his mind — Mr Williams has engag'd to advance £ 2500.0.0 on acctof Jona. Amory & H. Higginson funds to the credit of Geo. Cleveland £ 1450..0..0 the amt of Co C's letter — I shall transfer the amt. remitted by J. Williams to H H to Wm Sawyer — if he replaces the amt. as I suppose he will — then you will have the amt. still in Higginson's hands & I may leave an order in such case to pay the amt. to J. Williams on acct of money he may advance upon T. Williams letter — Mr Williams was mistaken in saying he had a balance of £1000..0..0 to the credit of S. Cabot Jr. he has not recd. anything tho he is in expectation of something
    Nothing can be done about Touro's letter, because it is an order for a balance, of course Mr H has no authority to invest anything more — Today I call on De Tastet for Jones English for F &C & J T. C & on Thos Dickason &Co in behalf of Shimmin & Coleman —
    MrWilliams bot the Restitutions Bills @ 2/2d. @ 2/2½ Ihave seen the Broker who buys all the Exchange on India hesays I shall not do better than 2/2d½ & perhaps not better than 2/3d — several inquiries have been made from other quarters — the Shippers did an injury to the concern in making so many agents — Ihave united Mr H & Mr Williams but the other persons Ihave not seen —

    2. *Ibid.*, Henry Lee's account book, London, Sept. 30, 1811–Calcutta, Mar. 1, 1816.

If old M^r. H ships he will furnish me with a letter of credit, but I do not calculate upon more than £3000..o..o from him, which will be for Mr S. G. Perkins — Mr H. not yet arriv'd —

You will not fail in writing me direct & via Mad^r. and send Triplicates of your letters — be as explicit & decided as the nature of things will admit — the meeting of Congress will enable you to form some conjectures as tothe Non Intercourse, probability of war &c — at present I do not conceive it to be your intention to leave any property behind or have any remitted to China on acct of apprehension of war with England if you have any such wish write me — I shall act with more confidence knowing the opinions of the concern'd — I can get Glass ware, iron hoops, coals & crates in Bristol on good terms — to which I shall add some cheese, herrings & hams

Oct^o. 2^d Mr English is in Manchester — Ihave applyd to M^r. Wilson for J. S. C he has not decided what to do — Ihave no doubt but what I shall F &C^o's from Mr Bromfield — De Tastet has given no answer — Ihavegiven directions to M^r H & MrW. to go as high as 2/2½^d. & I suppose they will buy tomorrow it is lower than the average rate & there is danger in waiting because there are other buyers — no news — business here in a bad state & many articles of Merchandize without value —   Yours

HLee

LETTER FROM HENRY LEE, LONDON, NOV. 12, 1811, TO THOMAS LEE, BOSTON, WITH SUGGESTIONS FOR SPECULATIONS IN ENGLAND [1]

The detailed discussion of goods, prices, and possible operations gives a clear picture of the international commercial situation, as Henry Lee saw it. Note the reference to a return of part of an insurance premium in case of safe arrival; also to insurance on the payment of insurance in case of loss.

1. Jackson-Lee Papers, "Bristol letter Book, orders from Shippers in Brig Reaper 1811 — voyage to Calcutta."

Dear Thos,   London Nov 12th, 1811

I have written you two or three letters, but as most of the Ships in this Kingdom have been wind bound I suppose they will all come to hand together, I understand from C W, you have about £3000 in the hands of S W. which I hope you have not drawn for while the present unfavourable rate continues, S W has been shipping Iron from Gottenburg for his brother Tim @ £13..10..0 pton & \$18 freight, I hope you are not engaged in that speculation, it must be a loosing one, besides the very long time it requires to convert that article in to money — The little time I have had to spare in this place, I have endeavoured to obtain what information I could generally as to any speculations that one might engage in who had funds, my means have been very limited, for not one of the men I have had intercourse with knew any thing out of their own line of business, indeed that is the case you know with all English Merchants &more especially those of London — there are many kinds of merchandize excessive low, but principally articles which we do not want in U. S. Sugars &Coffee have risen a little, but still foreign Sugars are much lower than with us. & if the American flag with W. I. produce from this country w^d be safe in Russia, it w^d be a good speculation to ship Coffee &Sugar there next spring, but I presume from the premiums demanded here it is not safe, [here — stricken through] [interlineated: in London] they do not make the difference between the Baltic &White sea that [they do with us — stricken through] we do in U. S. as the Vessels go to both under convoy, I suppose to Archangel they w^d demand 25% & 30% to St Petersburgh, some return if safe arrived, in case of loss it w^d be worth 20% to insure your demand, for many of the U Writers are failing &others dispute their losses — if you look into the London papers you will see an immense number of trials, this business of simulated papers. fgⁿ flags &c is very hazardous, & ruins all that engage under them almost, — There are considerable shipments making to the Medⁿ. but I am told without much prospect of success, freights, insurance, & indeed every thing relating to commerce is much more expensive than with us, & as for dispatch we make an India voyage in about the time they do one to the W Indies or the Med^n.

There is one thing which I think from the best information I can obtain might be done to great advantage, there has been you know about half dozen vessels captured bound from Bordeaux to U S, within 2 mo. some of there cargoes have not yet been disposed of, the Brandy &Wine both are allowed to be sold for consumption & are very high, but the silk manufactures must be sold for exportation & there is now a cargo (the Catherine Augusta's owned by L'^{y} B'^{d} &Co) that cost 400,000 livres in Silks suited to our market, that may be bot for about the cost in France, some persons tell me for less. I suppose certainly for a small advance, these goods might in such case be sent to Lisbon at an expence of not more than 5% or 6% & from thence w^d be readily admitted, Mr Perkins I think will buy them & it is certainly a very promising speculation if they go at the prices I think they will, besides this cargo there are one or two others & every month one two or more captures are made — if you are not engaged in any business &have the controul of your funds, I really think you w^d do well to come out in the month of Feby with £10,000 or more — if bills get above 15 or 16% disc^t, take with you Gold, it is worth 19% or 20% more than it costs with us. Spanish dollars 2% @ 3% less than the gold, if on your arrival you cannot find any french goods which perhaps you ought not to calculate upon, then you may invest that sum or more at the India Ware Houses, in the following articles which will certainly pay a very handsome profit in the U. S. when the intercourse is renewed, or if that should not take place you might sell them again at a small or perhaps no loss, or send them to Canada, this to be sure you w^d think a bad resort, but the chance of a continuance of the Non I Law is certainly Very little — I did not get my information which I send you second hand or thro' any of my friends, I found out the Brokers & as I am very familiar with the names of all the Company goods. I gave them a list of what I wanted to see, &they took me to the Warehouses

where I examined the Goods 'till I was satisfied of their qualities they are principally *private trade* somewhat inferior to
Company Goods but better than those we bring from Calcutta
the following are the cheapest for our market, the brokers gave
me a list of what they had for sale, I saw only two of them,
perhaps other brokers may have more, but probably it w^d be
difficult to find many if any more [interlineated: of similar
qualities &prices] &the prices have been so low for a year
past that the next fleet is not expected to bring very large quantities, should they have many so much greater your chance of
getting them still lower than they now are.

Dimensions

			no of ps	Prices they w^d sell for
Bandannas Chocolate, 14x2 ordinary &little spotted,			14/6.400,	$4.75 @ 5
do	do	" " little better	15/6.500	5.—
do	do	" " very good	16/6.700	5.25

Do yellow & Scarlet 14 x 2 little better than those 16/6 but
as the price is increased on acc^t of the colours which are not any
more valuable with us than the Chocolates they w^d not do so
well, there are 3 or 4000 p^s or more &may be bot from 18/ to
19/6.

There is a better quality still which they call Company for
which they demand 20/ to 25/ but they never have done as
well nor never will — sometimes a few cases will bring the
difference, but often they will not sell at 50¢ p p^s more when
they ought to bring $2 higher.

Choppa Romals 14 x 2 about equal to those we import from
Calcutta at 130/ p^r Corge, I think some of the lots are rather
better than the last importations into Boston — there are 6 or
8000 p^s & can be purchased @ 19/ to 20/ they go here under
the general name of Bandannas, but the brokers will understand you if you ask for Choppas or flowered Bandannas, they
consider this as the cheapest article in the market, formerly
great quantities of them were sent to the continent & oflate
many of them have been smuggled after they were shipped —
for home consumption, 12 months since they sold at 26/ to 30/,

I have before me a Catalogue of the sale — &now many of the
holders are not willing to part with them at the present prices,
tho' there is no doubt 2 or 3000 ps may be purchased, I wished
very much to have sent you a sample, but it is impossible to
get a piece from the India House P T J can tell you what they
are & how much they are worth, there is not the least doubt in
my opinion that they will bring $5.75 & if Handkfs advance as
is [possible — stricken through] 6 @ 6.50 they have always
brot' above $6 'till the Gullivers sale &those were ordinary.

Lungees 16 in ps such as usually cost 7/ @ 7/8. 800 ps
offer'd at 23/ I think 400 ps wd sell at $7. 5%/₁₀ perhaps it would
be hazardous to buy more, there are 150 ps @ 21/ which would
do still better, these goods have been on hand 5 years &few
only remain out of a great quantity imported. There are some
very fine Company's @ 40/ but they come too high for our
market.

Dury Romals 16 in ps. such as cost usually 9/8 to 10/, very
good quality &patterns. they demand 31/, I think 1000 ps
might be sold at $9 & 300 400 ps @ $10. I have sold 3 or 400
ps @ $11 @ $12, but that was when they were first introduced
&the buyers were pleased with the novelty of them. P, T. J,
knows very well what they are, there are 2000 [2000 — stricken
through] ps or more to be had at this price, There are Taffaties, Cuttanies &many other Silks that are low but will not
answer so well as the Hdk Handkfs. Should you come out I
wd reccommend all the Bandannas under 17/. 3·or 400 ps of
the Lungees if you only make a small investment, if a large one,
then the Whole say 1000 ps the balance of your investment in
Choppa Romals, so as to make half at least of the amt in that
article, the expence of buying is ½% to the Broker & something for shipping them I suppose that might be done for a
few pounds. Should you think well of this speculation you
ought to come out, because it cannot be done thro an agent.
G W knows nothing about such business &wd make some mistake, if you will come out you will have no trouble but to call
on the Broker & after getting his best terms try another 'till
you have ascertained the market.

Should you be here at a sale of the Companys you must employ a Broker to bid for you, one will take place in February or March, but if it is over when you arrive you will find the goods, the owners buy them in, or else the speculators buy & will sell to you for 2 or 3½ advance more or less as the market may be, there is no duty on exportation &the freight to U. S. w^d not am^t to more than 1%. If you cannot come out yourself — perhaps F Cabot or Frank may do the business if either of them are coming over, in that case your best way w^d be to give them a sample of the Choppas, the Dury's &the Lungees. the Bandannas every one knows, if you are not coming out, nor can get any one to buy for you who may be coming this way. you can employ S Williams giving him such directions as he cannot mistake. India goods are sold for Cash, or acceptances 60 days on interest, any bills you bring with you can be discounted with the person they are upon generally, but always with some of the Bankers, if you find the above mentioned goods have advanced, perhaps you will think Indigo (Bengal) low en^o to ship, it is certainly nearly as cheap as in Calcutta. I have examined a great many lots, the article has advanced within 2 mo^s a little particularly the fine kinds which have been sent to France & Russia &the Coarse which has been so low that the Dyers [interlineated: here] have bot' largely, the middling qualities are abundant, & of the ordinary there is as much as you w^d want. I have samples of 30 Chests 10,000 lbs which is offer'd @ 3/6 plb, & also a sample of a larger quantity at 4/4 to 4/6. I intend to send them by the first conveyance & you will be astonished when you see them, the annual sales have averaged 20,000 Chests, in April there will be a sale of 14000 Chests & I have no doubt some of it will go at 2/9, which is the price the 3/6 lot I send you was bot at some 2 or 3 months since. I believe the 3/6 Indigo I send you w^d have brought last spring $1.40, the 4/6 $1.60 @ $1.65, the first is much the cheapest, the middling qualities are 5/6 to 7/ &the first Indigoes 10/ to 11/6. they will not do in our market — the ordinary Indigo is call'd in the price Currents "Copper" that being the appearance of it when rub'd — The Broker who

appear'd to know the most about piece goods was Jos Cohen
&Co N⁰ 27 New Broad Street — I left with him P. T. Jackson's
address &desird Mr C — to write him every month on the subject of India goods which he promis'd he wᵈ — The other Broker
I saw was Ripley, Wiss &Co N⁰. 6 Lawrence Pountney Lane —
he appeared to be more acquainted with Indigo & there I got
the samples — if you come or send an agent to London — you
need not communicate to Mʳ Williams or any one else your
business every thing can be done & must be done by the Brokers
— it wᵈbe well to see two or three more besides Ripley &Cohen
to get the lowest prices in the market —

In Feb'y the Company have a sale of 8 to 10,000 Bales of
piece goods & in April 14000 Chests of Bengal Indigo — Shᵈ
therenot be any more intercourse than at present exists between this Country &the Continent — no doubt prices will go
[interlineated: low] particularly if the low qualities & such
as suit any market the best — the mode of buying goods at
the India ware houses is very satisfactory because you can see
every piece goods — & the qualities in general are uniform —

Bristol — Novʳ. 20ᵗʰ. 1811 — I sent the samples of Indigo
refer'd to in the above by Mʳ David West of Boston passenger
in the Galen — shall send duplicate samples if I have opportunity.

Should you not incline to do anything as recommended —
I wᵈthank you not to communicate to any but our friends the
information sent you — I expect Mʳ F. C. Lowell will have his
funds invested in silks & I think it not improbable on my return
I may be able to make as cheap an investment in London as I
can in Calcutta & if no one engages in the business — there may
be an opening for me — You perhaps may conclude if India
goods are low — all importers will buy them — it is not probable any ofthem will think of it for many reasons — one of the
best is the calculation of being able to better — in buying
Manchester goods —

I find some people here & in London have an idea that Mʳ
Perkins' visit to this country was on acct of the situation of
H H — this I know to be a false supposition — Mʳ P. knew no

more about than I did or any other person — 'till within 48 hours before H. H stop'd — MrP. has behav'd with great honour & good feeling — they are losers £31,000..0..0 & took no steps to get a £ from him after he had concluded to stop

Nothing new —   Yours

HL

LETTER FROM HENRY LEE, BRISTOL, NOV. 20, 1811, TO PATRICK TRACY JACKSON, BOSTON, REQUESTING INSURANCE [1]

Henry Lee was intending to ship his merchandise in his father's name lest it be seized on by his creditors. In another place, he wrote: "Give the preference & an additional prem^m even, to the Suffolk or marine, do not trust the N° American or the Union, if any other will write." [2]

On Nov. 3, Col. Perkins had announced "the failure of Mr. H. Higginson" which had resulted in his having "no less a sum than 30,000 pounds sterling locked up, if not lost, in a foreign country." However, he had succeeded by the 11th in rescuing "between 40 and 50 thousand dollars," which was the amount he had promised Henry Lee to send to India.[3] The H. Higginson referred to was Henry Higginson, son of Stephen and Susanna (Cleveland) Higginson, born at Boston, Feb. 5, 1781, who had married Nancy M. Cushing in 1803. From the birth-dates of his children it is probable that he had come to England in 1807 or 1808 and had divided his time thereafter between that country and Boston.[4] He has already appeared as a London correspondent of P. T. Jackson and the Lees.

John Lowell (1799–1836), mentioned below, apparently was reputed to possess an unusually enquiring mind. His aunt, Mary Lee, about this time, in a letter to her sister, his mother, pictured to herself "your husband satisfying John's inquisitive mind by explaining to him the motions of the heavenly bodies, etc., etc." By his will he left half his fortune, $250,000, to found and sustain the Lowell Lectures.[5]

1. Jackson-Lee Papers, "Bristol letter Book, orders from Shippers in Brig Reaper 1811 — voyage to Calcutta."

2. *Ibid.*, Henry Lee, *Reaper*, Jan. 7, 1812, to P. T. Jackson, Boston.

3. Briggs, *op. cit.*, vol. i, pp. 416–417.

4. Higginson, T. W., *Descendants of the Reverend Francis Higginson*, p. 31.   5. Morse, F. R., *op. cit.*, pp. 88, 223.

Dear P   Bristol Nov 20th. 1811

I have not written you since the several letters about the 1st inst informing you of the failure of H. H. I hope you are not affected by any consequences resulting from that event. I was anxious to get you early information least you might be making engagements with S H, I am told H H's failure is on account of advances made some of his correspondents &that of himself [interlineated: he] is solvent, I know but little about it as he has not talk'd with me since it happened. — he owed me a balance of £157 or rather A C which is not lost because A C owes him &of course will deduct out the balance due me as A C's agent, — W Sawyer's funds wd have been involved if H had not behaved with great honor & firmness, the Broker in whose hands W. S's funds were placed tho't he must hold the amt to the disposal of H's assignees, but after a while gave them up. my stock is reduced from £50,000 which it wd have risen to, to £35,000,

Before leaving London I desired Mess H & F Vignes to write you once in 2 months the rates of Exchange on Calcutta, Canton, Bombay &Madras, they promised to do it, I wish you wd reply to their letters (direct to London to save postage) &thank them for their civility, they are respectable, intelligent &worthy men &may be rely'd on & as long as we have any thing to do with India, it will be useful to us to correspond with them.

I have also left your address with Joseph Cohen &Co Brokers in India piece goods & desired them to write you, my motives you will have explain'd in my letter to T. Lee junr. White goods particularly, *Salempores &Gurrahs* are higher than with us. large shipments have been made to the Brazils, Spain, Malta, Sicily &South America. Cold goods are low on acct of the state of the African trade, there is no danger however of being unsold from this country except in some few particular articles upon which the freight is small. Silk Hdkfs are low, the prices I have sent T. L as also of Indigo, I hope he will follow my advice & come out.

I write [interlineated: you] Geo & Hall had drawn £5000

on H H on a/c of J & H L. W O & Yourself, I trust the Assignees will make provision for it, they cannot get rid of it if they w^d. as you & W O w^d be held &they thro' you, the bills will become due on 2^d April 1812. — You have now heard from Tracy & can tell what he will do. Give me definite instructions how to act under all circumstances.

My funds are invested in Merchandize &will be *shipped in the name of my father*, I wish you to make insurance for that sum say $4000 out &home & as much more home only, in addition, if you cannot get the $4000 out done against all risks, then except ags^t English War &leave the home insurance 'till it can be done ags^t all risks, I w^d not have it done at the North American nor any other office that writes very freely, I w^d rather pay more prem^u &be safe than take any hazard of not getting my money in Case of loss. perhaps some private writers may be found for so small a sum that are undoubted in such case I w^d prefer them to an office it w^d be best to agree for a prem^u from Bristol to Calcutta to touch at madeira & from Calcutta to port of discharge in U. S. giving an addition for permission to go to Amelia Island or some other port in case the Non I Law Continues, You Know what I want — Security. — We are now ready &waiting for a wind. I left Mr Lowell in London, getting passports for france. Mr Russell Charge d'Affaires has promis'd him dispatches, this week — they will get away in 10 or 15 days

M^rs L, Harriot &the two Children are at Clifton from whence they go to Bath &meet M^r L on his way to Plymouth, they set out in a few days, all of them well, tho' I am afraid M^rs L will fall off since she has return'd to School Keeping again, John is en^o indeed to pull down the stoutest constitution, it w^d require ½ dozen men to answer his questions & dispute with him

Yrs
H Lee

M P. T. Jackson

[written across face of letter:]
via Liverpool — Novr. 20th
Duplica^t do — Novr 27th

LETTER FROM HENRY LEE, BRISTOL, NOV. 22, 1811, TO WILLIAM
OLIVER, [BOSTON], ON GENERAL BUSINESS MATTERS [1]

William Oliver, who had for long been connected with the Lees, had
evidently been involved with them in some business venture at the
time of their failure. George Lee and Joseph Hall, Jr., had been and
still were in Calcutta as agents for the owners of the *Gipsy* and the
Gulliver. Judging from the reference to "R. C.," Robert Cabot, who
had also been in Calcutta the previous year, had not, in his cousin
Henry Lee's opinion, distinguished himself by his business efficiency
on that occasion.

A portion of a letter to P. T. Jackson written from Calcutta in
1813 more than amply confirms this impression. "You perhaps may
have conceiv'd it hazardous, from the transactions of R C's in which
we suffer'd so much, to deal in this article [indigo], this is not the
case, unless as in that instance the purchaser takes the quality on the
faith of a Bengallee, without even examining the musters, it is not at
all surprizing that R C should have been imposed upon, perhaps there
never was another instance in which an agent abandon'd himself to
the influence & controul of men, whom he knew were villians, he as-
sented to every thing propos'd by his banions, & I consider it as a
wonderful piece of good fortune, that ofthe immense property which
pass'd thro' his hands, we should have rec^d back so large a portion as
we did, it is impossible for you to imagine how totally he neglected
all our plans &instructions &with what wantonness he wasted the
property entrusted to his charge. M^{r}Hall had, I imagine a very im-
perfect idea ofthe effects which his conduct produced upon our concerns, the advantages he was favour'd with by his being first here
after the Embargo & afterwards by being furnish'd with funds during the Non Importation Law, when there was not a buyer in the
market, were greater than I had imagin'd, &if he had been merely a
sober man of common capacity, we could not have fail'd of realizing
an immense profit, on all the funds we sent to this Country, the de-
pendance upon his Banion, was thro' his own fault, he only consulted
his convenience in the induldence of his intemperance, & thus committed every thing to the direction ofone of the greatest villians in
Calcutta, the purchase of 2000 bales in which Newton was concern'd,

1. Jackson-Lee Papers, "Bristol letter Book, orders from Shippers
in Brig Reaper 1811 — voyage to Calcutta."

was managed by a fellow of the name of Richards from New York, who had neither funds nor Credit, Duloll was the Banian, & as nearly as I can Judge the prices were about 25% higher than the common market prices, or than they would have been had he been a sober man & gone alone into the Bazar, but enough of this — When we meet I shall have much to tell you, &tho it is painful to go back to events which have been follow'd by such mortifying effects to me, &so much loss &vexation to you, &others, yet there is a satisfaction in being able to trace the causes ofthese misfortunes, to the failings &vices of others, rather than our own imprudence, I do not deny that we acted upon too large a scale in our business to this place, yet as events turn'd out, we could not have fail'd of great success, had our agent been simply a sober man & acted with common industry &Judgment." [2]

The bitterness engendered by Robert Cabot's conduct was still operating at least as late as Mar. 3, 1816; in a letter to his brother Francis when on the point of sailing from Calcutta, Henry Lee mentioned his intention of having certain goods consigned to the Philadelphia merchant Samuel Archer. He went on: "You will I imagine be strongly solicited to employ some relations ofours settled there, but I beg to be excused from having any ofmy concerns entrusted to them, or any ofthe name, with the exception ofone or two — I have made sacrifices en° in that way, &have no mind to be ruin'd a second time for the pleasure of serving my Cousins." [3] The relation settled at Philadelphia was Samuel Cabot of Hazard & Cabot; the favorable exception to Henry Lee's opinion of his mother's family was probably Andrew Cabot.

"Mess F & S" were Ebenezer Francis and William Shimmin, two of the Lees' assignees. The *Gipsy* was sent next year to Havana with a cargo of flour and was wrecked on the return voyage. Henry Lee's "Cargo of about £35000" did not entirely consist, of course, of the "Bottles, Iron hoops, Glass Ware, Ale & small quantity of Hams & Cheese" immediately after mentioned, nor of the porter, perry, arrow root, tin plates, rum, crockery, shoes, corks, and coal which he might have added to the list. Their total invoice price at Bristol was less

2. *Ibid.*, "H. Lee's Letters from Calcutta from August 1812 to June 1813," Henry Lee, Calcutta, June 10, 1813, to P. T. Jackson, Boston.

3. *Ibid.*, "Letters written in Calcutta by H. Lee from July 1813 to March 1816."

than £5,000. Included in the £35,000 were the bills "bo^t . . . thro'
the Vignes." It is of interest to note that in most of these invoices the
brig *Reaper* is described as "bound for Madeira" though the cargo
was actually intended for Calcutta.[4]

Mr William Oliver   Bristol Nov 22^d 1811
    Dear sir   via Liverpool. Novr. 27th
        I wrote you on the 8th. inst in reply to yours of the 22^d
Septr. I have no doubt many things have passed between our
Assignees & you that have given you a great deal of vexation,
but your suspicions of their intention to make you liable for
Geo & Halls engagements, I believe to be unfounded, but if
I am not mistaken there are ways en^o to avoid any attempts
they may make, but as it w^d require some time to explain, I
will defer it till we meet, be as moderate as you can with Mess
F &S & remember the difficulties they have to contend with.
        I cannot in conformity with your request do anything to
detain Geo & Hall in Calcutta, neither does your interest require it. but if it did surely they must not be sufferers, they
have already borne their share &we are all of under infinite
obligations to them for saving the property which had it fallen
into R C's hands w^d have been lost, if it is necessary any one
should be detain'd in Calcutta, I am the person, they must
come home.
        I made an attempt to get something from Hibbert for the
Ale, but he w^d not listen a moment. he says it is a common
thing for Ale to perish Hodgsons as well as that made by other
people. he appears to be a vulgar fellow who cares but little
what may be tho't of his honor or his morality provided he can
save his money. pretty much like most of us merchants.
        I am sorry you have not been able to sell the Gipsy. I fear
she is a burthen to you. if she should be still unsold, perhaps
you might get a freight of Wheat or flour, there will be large
shipments of both to this Country from U States.

    4. *Ibid.*, Henry Lee's account book, London, Sept. 30, 1811–Calcutta,
Mar. 1, 1816.

I am now ready for sea, but no prospect of a wind, Cargo of about £ 35000..0..0 Bottles, Iron hoops, Glass Ware, Ale &small quantity of Hams &Cheese, they are rather lower than what the Gulliver cost.

I bo^t my bills thro' the Vignes, they are the most respectable men I met with in London &very intelligent, this business of getting bills on Calcutta is somewhat uncertain but generally one may get £ 20,000. you know there are only 4 or 5 houses & they will not usually go beyond 5 or £6000 at once. I gave 2/2½^d. if there had been one other purchaser, I could not have bot under 2/3^d, &perhaps sh^d have been obliged to wait for some time to make up what sum I wanted.

This place is better on some accounts to buy a cargo for Calcutta than Liverpool, but as for dispatch there is no such thing the Custom house & Excise Regulations are such that it is impossible to get on fast.

There is some expectation that there will be a brisk trade with licences between this Country & France, if that should be the case, Sugars Coffee Ashes & cotton will rise a little.

I shall not leave Calcutta earlier than Sept^r, I wish you w^d write me &let me know what you have done with the Gipsy.

I am very glad to hear you intend to remain at home with your family, it will be better for your health &necessary for them, they require your care, give my regards to them.

Yrs with regard.

LETTER FROM HENRY LEE, BRISTOL, NOV. 24, 1811, TO PETER REMSEN, NEW YORK, ON GENERAL BUSINESS CONDITIONS [1]

This letter is very similar to others written at the same time but goes perhaps a little more into detail.

The reason why the owners of the *Reaper's* cargo to England "did badly by our lumber" is told in a letter of Nov. 22 to Francis Lee: "the lumber is the worst that has ever been seen in this place. besides the dimensions were very unfavourable for the duties. I am afraid it will not produce en° to pay the duties, should it not Gov^t will not allow

1. Jackson-Lee Papers, "Bristol letter Book, orders from Shippers in Brig Reaper 1811 — voyage to Calcutta."

us to abandon it to them nor will they make any deduction for bad quality you were imposed upon in the cargo, most of the oak boards are outside slabs & all of them refuse, there is not a clear & sound one among the whole lot."

In a letter, of the same date as the one below, to Edward A. Newton, Henry Lee referred to "James Russell Esqr a Bostonian" as "one of the most worthy men I have ever met with. . . . I never knew a man so disinterested in serving his friends."

An interesting comment in the same letter is that in Bristol "the business is too much confined to capitalists to admit of good bargains being made. there is also a very great delay, but I suppose no worse than at all other places in England."

Mr Peter Remsen   Bristol Nov 24th. 1811
Dear sir   via Liverpool Novr. 27th
     (Duplicate via Plymouth p^r Mr Perkins) with P.S
     to Decr. 10th

Since I wrote you last I am favour'd with yours of the 29th. Sept^r, your letter contains much information, I hope to find at Mad^a others for me with the Catalogues promised, I shall not reach that island till the 15th Decr as the wind is now ahead &it will remain so for 10 days in all probability.

As I have got over my fears of War, I begin to be very apprehensive the Non Importation law will continue, we shall not get away from Calcutta 'till Sept^r, it will be dangerous cruising on our coast, you must keep a good look out as we shall be directed to you for advice.

I have been detain'd here longer than I expected, our cargo is now on board &cost about £ 3500.0.0, we did badly by our lumber but hope to make it up in the cargo to Calcutta, it consists of Glass Ware, Iron hoops, Ale, Coal, &c

I am glad to hear you did so well with your adventure in the Gulliver &c. hope you have got rid of all J &N's goods &made no bad debts but that is not to be expected, I was sorry to hear he & M^r N had been buying at auction in Boston. the risk of selling is too great for any profit that can be made, I hope the Vancouver is in & her cargo sold to safe men, J will not be easy 'till all his large concerns are terminated, I trust they will soon be & profitably. I have bo't my bills @ 2/2½ p Rupee which is favourable. Bills cannot always be had & the amt is uncertain, large sums, say beyond £ 30 or 40,000 cannot usually be purchased.

I agree with you that there will not be any war 'till some new events turn up, little or no interest is taken in our affairs, & even the suspension of exports to our country excites very little conversation. our trade no doubt is important to this Country, but when you consider what a small portion of the revenue is derived from that source, you will perceive it is not of so much moment as our people imagine. The trial of Rodgers is considered as a mockery & issued as was expected, but no one is either sorry or glad they wish Captn R might have a battle with some one a little inferior in force, but they have no notion of making War about it.

W. I. goods have been down very low, started of late a little in consequence of an expected licenced trade to france, they want Brandies &to sell Sugars &Coffee, in France they want the revenue & a sale for wine &Brandy. Nothing from U. S.tates but Wheat & Flour will sell. Wheat is worth 115/ @ 120/ &rising, but Visgoth has written you. Cotton little better on account of the cessation of imports from U. S. but it cannot rise much 'till the stock is diminished.

Cotton Goods are low in Manchester, Woolens (fine) are on the rise. Spanish Wool looking up, Tin Plates & Copper very low, I have seen your friend Mr Visgoth often. he is an intelligent man &has what is not common here, good general information. he is quite respectable in point of Character but I know nothing of his credit — I do my business with James Russell Esqr a Bostonian.

I have tho't that some of Pierpoints best Gin wd sell well here, while there is no trade with Holland. the Country Gin is intolerable &high. Hollands is 15/ net of duty, certainly ours ought to command 7/ which wd do. I am not certain but what it wd pass as Hollands as it does in many other parts of the world this is a new idea, I wish you wd make the experiment with two pipes for my acc^t & charge me with the loss, send two pipes to James Russell Esqr of this place &two more to London to some man there in the small way, I am quite certain it will do.

I visited the India Warehouses, but it is very difficult to get much information, White Cottons are higher than with us particularly salampores & Gurrahs, which two articles have been in demand for S^o America & the Med^n. Silk HandKfs are lower, upon that subject I have written T Lee Junr & am in hopes he will come out and purchase, perhaps he will advise with you, I could send you a printed Catalogue of the last sale of the Company's goods but you w^d, not understand it. the qualities & dimensions differ so much from our goods that it is not easy to make a comparison, from the samples I saw, I know they are higher than with us.

I spoke to Chas Williams upon the subject of agency. he told me S W had rec^d a letter from you & that he w^d try to get you the Powder Agency, it is impossible in such a place as London to find out who wants agents, but you are in the confidence of all the Williams &they will do all they can, your best way is to find out what business is desirable &let him know where to look for it. if G &Lovett have fail'd, as I hear they have, you can add some Salem men to your correspondents, but I hope you will not make advances without ample security to any one. you never ought to place yourself at the mercy of chance in any considerable degree.

I will venture to predict many (unexpected) failures in Boston & New York this winter. I suppose you have heard of H Higginsons, it has been caused by advances made to various correspondents who have not reimbursed him as they ought to have done.

There have been a vast many failures all over England but there is not half the distress there is with us. the capitals are so large that they can sustain heavy losses. the American Merchants in England are in bad repute in consequence of the ruin of several who have done the business of the Americans, the last H H & Potter & Page.

People still talk of War between France & Russia, quite uncertain I think. Bullion continues high, Paper money is not now talk'd about so much as it was, entire confidence in it among all commercial men, if you have business here do it with S Williams, he is good against all events, his credit is better than almost any man's who goes into the London Exchange. Remember me to M^r & Mrs Lawrence I hope they &your neice are well.

Yr^s with affectionate regard.

POSTSCRIPT TO A LETTER FROM HENRY LEE, BRISTOL, DEC. 11, 1811, TO THOMAS LEE, JR., BOSTON, WITH AN ACCOUNT OF THE POLITICAL SITUATION AS AFFECTING BUSINESS [1]

It is of interest to read this New England Federalist's opinion of the British statesmen who were Napoleon's contemporaries.

Andrew Cabot had ordered Henry Lee to remit part of his funds to Canton from Calcutta "if there is a probability of a Non Intercourse" with Great Britain,[2] which would shut out from the United States British goods from Calcutta but not Chinese goods from Canton.

Poscript to *letter to Thos Lee jun^r of* Novr 12th. 1811 Bristol Dec 11th. 1811. The above is a Triplicate, the Original & Duplicate being detain'd at Liverpool. I have sent a third that you might be sure of having one, 'tho it is probable the information may be of no use to you. I hope however you will come out & I have no doubt you will find something to be done which w^d not be hazardous. I have just return'd from London having been there about a passport from the Portuguese Ambassador, I have it &shall meet with no more difficulties, I have seen papers & letters to 10th. Novr. the Message was expected with some eagerness because it was supposed from letters rec^d of late from America, that the Intercourse w^d be renew'd, it is consider'd as hostile, but the tricks of our Gov^t are becoming so well known that no inference [that no in-

1. Jackson-Lee Papers, "Bristol letter Book, orders from Shippers in Brig Reaper 1811 — voyage to Calcutta."
2. *Ibid.*, Henry Lee, London, Oct. 3, 1811, to Andrew Cabot, Boston.

ferences — stricken through] are drawn as to what Congress will do — it is tho't here our Gov^t. will continue the restrictions & that this Gov^t. will retaliate by prohibiting everything but wheat & naval stores from U S — I wrote some time since this was Mr Jackson's opinion & from the correspondence between Sec'y Munro & M^r. Foster Ihave but little doubt it will prove correct — this Gov^t. w^d. never throw out such a threat without meaning to act — it is not their mode of negotiating You will notice reports in the papers of a change of Ministry — no reliance can be placed upon them, they are the conjectures of Editors to amuse their readers, it is not improbable however that the Prince Regent may introduce some of his friends, but *Percival* will continue to lead &probably the M^s of Wellesley, the former is certainly more in the confidence of the nation than any man *since Pitt* he is as much devoted to business &is said to be in favour with the prince, at any rate he is with the house of Commons &the nation. Marquis of Wellesley has very powerful connexions is not obnoxious to any party &is rather popular, he has they say great talents, but wastes much of his time in pleasures he gives energy to the Cabinet & I have no doubt united with such an industrious man as Percival, he is useful, Parliament will do nothing 'till Feb^y, they meet for business about the last of Jan^y.

Reinforcements of men & ammunition are going off, constantly for Portugal &Spain, the conduct of the Spaniards of late, has given more confidence in their eventual success, Lord Wellington stands higher in the estimation of the nation than any General since the Duke of Marlbro'. the officers are very eager to be employ'd under him &so are the soldiers, it is not uncommon for the principal part of a regiment of militia to volunteer into the line to be sent to Portugal.

I found some persons in London quite sanguine that there w^d be some modification of the orders in Council, Mr Perkins seems to be of that opinion, but I find no one who can assign any better reason for a change than has existed for a long time, I do not myself believe there will be a repeal of them.

The merchants at Liverpool & common Council in London

are making a noise about them, but they have very little influence, no do they represent any great proportion of the Mercantile interest. Business is better than it was, though bad enough, Sugars have advanced very much. Cotton 2ᵈ p lb but will fall as soon as there are any considerable arrivals, Coffee not quite so low, but no demand, Indigo risen a little, Rums are high, Brandies falling under the expectation that there will be some trade with France, which I look upon as quite uncertain, Govᵗ will not allow it unless W I produce is admitted into France, of that you can judge as well as they can here.

Exchange on India remains at it was. I could now place some few thousands of pounds in Canton @ 4/9ᵈ @ 4/10ᵈ pʳSp Dollar Mʳ Perkins is remitting thro' Calcutta, as it is pretty certain I shall be able to buy for him bills on Canton in Calcutta at about par, one of the India merchants in London told me it could sometimes be done @ 5% gain. such an operation wᵈ be very profitable now Exchange from U S to this Country is so low, I intend to remit part of the owners stock &part of my own to Canton, if I do not hear of the repeal of the Non Intercourse, Should Bromfield go to Canton & you have no better mode of getting your funds from this Country, why not have remittances made to him & in his absence to Perkins &Co, you can remit in bills on Calcutta direct to Canton, where I am told they will always sell, or remit to Canton via Calcutta, or direct to Canton if bills can be had.

I mentioned to you in my last that Mʳ Perkins wᵈ buy the Catherine Augustas (Le Roy Bayard &Cos Brig/ he & Mʳ Higginson Senʳ have bot' the vessel &Cargo for £ 15000.0.0. the silks on board cost 400,000 livres &she has 60 pipes Cognac. the Brig is worth £1500 she cost £ 5000.0.0. valuing the Brandy @ 15/ short price (last sales 21/) &the Brig @ £1500.0.0. the silks will stand them about 12ˡ the livre. they have besides a quantity of Wine worth £1000 to 2000 or more, it is a great speculation & I think they will get the Traveller on better terms, she has 200,000 livres, they will send the silks to Lisbon &from thence to   , I recᵈ this information from T, H, P, under a promise not to mention it to any one, it is indeed important *on one* account that it should not be known I request you therefore *not to* communicate what I write to *any one*. You are the only person I write to on this subject, & do to you because I hope you will be induced to come out, there are several other prize vessels &more coming in every week or 10 days, the silks are not allowed to be consumed here &therefore they will always go low besides the Captors are always willing to make great deductions when they can get rid of vessel &Cargo & get the Cash, it will not do to open packages &so ignorant are the agents of the value of goods that they sell them in the gross so much per package, in some instances they have sold without the Invoices, you may imagine perhaps that you can make a speculation of this Kind thro' an agent. you cannot, you must come out yourself & go to the outports or bargain with the prize Agents in London. Perkins bot his in London, the Captain & Prize Agent came up to town for the purpose. I do not imagine that French prize goods coming from England w^d be seized by our Gov^t. certainly not if from Lisbon, but of this you can ascertain before you leave home.

Do not be afraid of Bills of Exchange on account of the depreciation of paper money, the alarm is over & it is as safe as specie, should bills rise above 15% disc^t bring gold with you it is worth 18% to 20% Spanish Dollars cannot be bot' for less than 5/4^d but the value of them is uncertain. gold is sure sale, the high price of Indigo in Russia will clear the U States of that article next spring, which is in favour of a purchase of the lowest quality I have sent you whatever may be said about the finest quality being wanted. I know that the ordinary gives more profits. I reccommend therefore the *Copper* or the lowest priced. Mr Lowell will make a purchase of Silks in the spring unless he is persuaded the Non Intercourse will be continued, but it will not amount to more than 2 or £3000.

Tell Andrew we have some prospect of a change of wind.

Yours

(sign'd)   H Lee

LETTER FROM HENRY LEE, BRIG REAPER, JAN. 9, 1812, TO AN-
DREW CABOT, BOSTON, WITH ACCOUNT OF PLANS [1]

It was not until Dec. 29, 1811, that the wind shifted so as to allow
the *Reaper* to sail from Bristol. Henry Lee's original intention had
been to sail by Nov. 5. The unfavorable winds which prevented this
were the last and most persistent of the unfavorable influences of
varying importance which had afflicted him ever since his arrival —
the difficulty of raising funds, the poor quality of his cargo, Henry
Higginson's failure, etc. Among the minor difficulties was the desertion of part of the crew. On Nov. 26, Henry Lee wrote to Andrew
Cabot: "Capt S. had a great deal of trouble with his men. at least
part of them. Brown deserted & we think enticed away 4 others. We
prevail'd upon him on account of his worthy father to return, he did
return & deserted a second time & is now lounging the streets, he is a
worthless fellow & will I fear prove a vagabond, it does not do to take
gentlemen Sailors, they spoil others."

In the letter below, Henry Lee's meticulous care to avoid the slightest suspicion of padding his expense account is worthy of note.

Amelia Island, off the coast of Spanish Florida and just to the
southward of the United States boundary, was the center of the
southern trade with the enemy during the War of 1812 and, at
the time of this letter, of trade with Great Britain in violation of the
Non-Intercourse Act.

Mr Andrew Cabot   Reaper Jany 9th. 1811 [1812]
    Dear sir
        We are now by our account nearly up with Madeira, we
expect every moment to make the land; we left our Pilot off
Lundy Island on the 29th. ulto, have been boarded three times
by English Ships of War & treated with great civility, I trust
we are now out of danger from French privateers
I enclose you the following papers, the Vouchers for the Disbursements MrRussell will send you viz

Memo Cost of the Cargo of the Reaper amtg to	£2913..13..10
Jas Russells A/C disbursements Reaper do	" 530. 5. 7
Nathl Spooners do do "	" 32.. 9.. 6

---

1. Jackson-Lee Papers, "Bristol letter Book, orders from Shippers
in Brig Reaper 1811 — voyage to Calcutta."

Acc^t of Sundry disbursements p'd by me including my own
   Expences ....   " 104.. 0.. 7
Do Expences p'd by me for S Cabot ....   " 68..11.. 8
My Acc^{ts} Current balance in your favour
part of this arises from a balance due me from   " 130..18..10

Captⁿ Spooner assumed to my own account. for this balance
I have sent you a draft on my father, the rate of Exchange to
be the same as you remit M^rWilliams, with the Charges of
Commission &c I have already stated to you the reasons that
induced me to exceed the am^t limited for the outward Cargo. I
hope they will be approved of, I shall make a seperate Inv^o
for the £ 1329..7..0, presuming you will either sell out, or take
it to your own account, in either case there will be a convenience
in not having it involved with your Cargo.

I have charged agreeably to your orders S Cabots expences,
he has expended more money, which he will settle with Captⁿ
Spooner in all I imagine about £ 100.0.0

In making up the account of my expences, I have taken the
Tavern bill where I paid the lowest price, I shall send it with
the papers that you may see I lived with all the economy possible I have charged 10/6 p day which is about 2/3^{ds}. of what
my eating &lodging cost. for travelling expences I have charged
Coach Hire only. With regard to the disbursements of the Brig
I have no remark to make, Captⁿ S will give any explanation
you may want, I imagine they are as low as usual, if there
should be any items either in the A/Cs now render'd or in
any that may be in future, that you think extravagant. I wish
you not to consider me as having any agency in the business,
I w^d further add that I have not nor do I mean to add 1/ to
the already enormous expences of the voyage for my own personal accommodation — I w^d not have you infer any thing
more from these observations than that I mean to disclaim all
responsibility where it is not my business to direct or advise.

I occupy much more than my privilege, it was my intention
to have shipped £ 300.0.0 in Glass Ware & as much more in
Hats & other valuable goods, but the cargo costing so much
more than I contemplated in consequence of being obliged to

ship so many Hoops & of a misunderstanding with the Glass manufacturer he having dl^d £1600 & upwards worth instead of 6 or £700 as we calculated & finding I had gone £ 1000.0.0 beyond your limits, I took a larger share in Glass, Iron &c for the freight of which I expect to pay the same as Mr Newton. Mr Russell has an interest under me of ⅓ the Glass Ware paying for the freight out ⅓ the profits & home 13½% on the am^t invested. Mr Russell has also furnished me with a letter of credit for £ 1500.0.0 to £ 2000.0.0 to be return'd in my name. I have already sent you instructions to insure it, let it be done in a safe office & as it is doubtful whether I shall be able to negotiate the Bill, you had better say in the Mem^o you give the office, that it is uncertain whether there will be any shipment & then when you call for a return of prem^s. there will not be so much explanation as otherwise, you will let M^r R know what you have done in this business by Duplicate letters.

The Charge for guarantee on £ 1350.0.0 will appear in Mr Williams A/C with you & also some small charges for postage & passports

You will notice I have charged you with the whole balance due from H Higginson to me, I did this because I knew you were indebted to him, it is to be divided among several persons, M^r H overpaid you he ought before he sent on your A/c to have transfer'd this balance to your debit. it was never my intention to have taken up from him more than the am^t remitted by Williams on acc^t of the Independence I did not see your A/c 'till he had stopped &then it was too late to make any alterations. I understand the balance due from you to Mr Higginson has been diminished by a subsequent remittance from Williams, in which case there will be something due after you have adjusted your A/c with him, whatever it may be I am accountable to you for my proportion & Mr Newtons also. when we meet I can settle it in a moment to your satisfaction.

I do not calculate upon our Congress doing any thing about the N I Law 'till the close of the session, you will have time to let me know what has been the result, upon this depends my

disposition of your funds in Calcutta, I shall wait 'till the last
moment before I remit to Canton, because I conceive it much
more for your interest the returns sh^d be made from Calcutta.
Ships will be touching at Madeira every month for some time to
come, send qu a [?] duplicates & to different houses, I shall
then be certain of hearing from you — Write also via Batavia
Isle France, Cape Good Hope & England, As I before said I
think I shall go upon Indigo, because I think it will be low in
Calcutta & in demand in U. S. I am confident Band^s will be
high, because the raw Silk is all wanted in England, still I think
well of them at 119/. I think fine Goods will be higher in proportion than Coarse & if so I shall avoid them, because tho' they
are now high in U. S. yet when the Intercourse is renew'd the
market will be fill'd with Manchester Cottons 20% lower than
they have ever been Am I right in my conjectures? —

Some persons imagine if the N I Law is continued, our Gov^t
will seize any vessels that may be found on the American Coast
from British ports Mr Higginson when I last saw him in London
thot it w^d be imprudent to call off New York, if there is any
danger of that kind you must have known it long since, because numbers of Vessels, must have been found in that situation within the last 6 mo^s. if we cannot be admitted on our
return I suppose Amelia Island will be our destination. if so
when you send off your orders, send with them a good chart
of that port. I believe it is a dangerous place to enter & we
have no information on the Subject. I repeat again my wish
that you wd be explicit under what circumstances I shall remit
part of the funds to Canton & what am^t on your own private
acc^t &how much for the owners — Suppose I should not be able
to get bills on Canton or that the rate of Exchange is unfavourable, what is to be done with the retain'd Stock? I suppose
Alexander &Co will allow 6 & perhaps 7% or 8% interest —
I should consider property lodged with them or Palmer &Co
as perfectly safe.

Should I find goods plenty &low &no Americans, [& no
Americans — stricken through] in Calcutta we may get away
in 2 to 3 mo^s, but it is probable We may be there 3½ to 4 mo^s.

I notice in the papers that additional duties are as usual, proposed upon Cottons, should there be any imposed, I ought to know what they are upon every article, that I may calculate them on the returns to be made for you, in such case I should have an additional inducement to buy Indigo. —

Besides the above mention'd papers I send you the particular Invo. of Crokery & Glass ware & 1st. of my Exchange on J Lee for Balce. of Acct. due you £ 130..18..10 — We have just made Porto Santo which lies 15 leagues from Funchal — we shall be there tomorrow — Funchal Jan'y th16 & 17th — P. S. In answer to his letters of 8th & 12th November — That I shd. send part of his funds toCanton — desir'd him to write me via Madeira & the India fleet wd take the letters — to direct Cathcart to forwd. the letters by different conveyances — to let me have the proceedings of Congress — I shd. wait till the last moment before remitting toCanton —

      [written across face of letter:]
      original pr. Independence for Boston
      Duplicate — Edward — New York
      Triplicate Shipped p — Cape de Verde

LETTER FROM HENRY LEE, MAY 20–22, 1812, UPON ARRIVAL AT CALCUTTA, TO ANDREW CABOT, BOSTON [1]

Henry Lee began this letter the day he arrived at Calcutta, where he found low prices for his cargo, India goods higher than he had expected, and restrictions on Americans.

He remarked in a letter of the following day to James & T. H. Perkins, "The duties on goods imported & exported in American vessels have been doubled, while the Portuguese pay the same as the English. There is every appearance that before long we shall either be excluded altogether from this Country or charged with such heavy duties as will amount to the same thing."

The intricacy of the trade with India was greatly increased by the lack of any consistent standard in weights and measures. The maund, for example, in which weight was ordinarily expressed in

1. Jackson-Lee Papers, "Letters written in Calcutta from May to August 1812."

wholesale transactions, varied according to the commodity involved, the locality, and whether the merchant was buying or selling. It might be as little as 7½ lb. or as much as 116. "Every town has a different maund." [2] Usually, however, the maund of southern India was between 25 and 30 lb. while that of Bengal was not far from 80 lb. A prices current of Bangalore, capital of Mysore in southern India, in which prices are given both in maunds and in hundredweights, reveals, for example, that here a maund was something over 25 lb. [3] However, the maund, according to which the price of the hoops mentioned below was given, was probably the Bengal maund of a little more than 82 lb.; confirmation of this appears in a letter of July 7, 1812, to Andrew Cabot in which Henry Lee says that "no sales have been made even as high as 9 Rps, which is 10% below the price of Iron." As iron for India was about this time invoiced at approximately $100 per ton and of course usually sold at a considerable advance, it is clear that, with rupees at about 2s. 6d., a maund of 82 lb. would approximate the above description.

The reference to "bills on Canton @ 30 days sight for 87 Sicca Rp^s" would be utterly unintelligible if divorced from the other letters. "87 Sicca Rp^s" will buy *what* in exchange on Canton? The answer appears in a letter of May 21 to J. & T. H. Perkins: "Rps 86 . . . 2 [annas] . . . 6 [pice] . . . for which you receive in Canton $44." The sicca rupee was worth roughly half a dollar; an anna was worth one-sixteenth of a rupee; and a pice, one-twelfth of an anna.

In Henry Lee's letters from India one is forced to adjust one's mind to a new set of values and symbols. In statements of price in the Jackson-Lee Papers, the oblique line (/) in most cases signified a shilling; in reference to India goods, it means a rupee, while the numerals immediately following the sign are annas (16 annas = 1 rupee) rather than pence. In referring to the price of cloth, also, when no quantity unit is mentioned, the reference is almost always to the corge, that is, a score of pieces. This is brought out by "Invoices of all the goods ship'd by Henry Lee during his stay in Calcutta from May 1812 to March 1816."

The same invoice book introduces another confusion into our idea

---

2. Balfour, Surg. Gen. Edward Green, *The Cyclopaedia of India*, 3 vols. (London, 1885), "Maund," see also "Weights and Measures."

3. Jackson-Lee Papers, "Memoranda, Prices Current E. I. Goods — Imports & Exports &c., &c."

of the maund. The letter below refers to "estimating the price [of indigo] @ 100 Rp^s. per factory maund." The invoice book above mentioned invoices various consignments of indigo both by the English hundredweight (112 lb.), quarter, and pound, and by the maund, seer, and chittak (16 chittaks = 1 seer, 40 seers = 1 maund). A comparison indicates that in this case the maund (specified as factory weight) amounted to slightly less than 75 lb. whereas the Bengal maund was a little over 82 lb. It is quite probable that the East India Co. bought indigo by the larger Bengal maund and sold it again by the factory maund; weight juggling of this type was common in the commercial world of India.

A lac in Indian commercial parlance meant 100,000 of anything; in T. Stewart's case it doubtless meant 100,000 rupees. Three lacs of rupees would indeed be an excellent return for a voyage to the Isle of France (Mauritius), which had been recently captured by the British.

pr Restitution   Calcutta May 20th. 1812.

Captn Pulsifer

Dear A.

I closed one letter to day & sent it on board the Restitution. I fear I shall [not ?] be able to send you by Captn P such satisfactory information as I could wish, shall add to this from time to time till the R gets to Hedexee, [Kedgeree ?] she is now at Fultah.

The bills are all accepted including M^r F C Lowells by Alexander &Co for the honour of the drawers. I am apprehensive I shall not be able to negotiate S H &Co^s letter of Credit. I told M^r H so when I rec^d it, but *he* thot his credit was as well established here as in U States. There is a letter, M^r H told me to Alexander &Co reccommending him, but nothing short of a guarantee from some London house known here, will answer the purpose. I shall try all I can, the new duties on Merchandize which now amount to 20 to 25% will destroy the outward voyage, I can tell you little or nothing about the value of the articles, hoops are low say 12 Rp^s p maund Bottles 28 to 30/p 100, the new collector is very arbitrary & unjust. I expect to have some difficulty with him.

I found no letters later than 18th. Oct⁰ they came by the Derby. I hope in two months to have acc⁻ᵗˢ to the last of Janʸ or Febʸ.

I cannot possibly determine what amount of your stock I shall invest here & what amount remit to Canton, remittances to China are not easily made, it is probable however I shall be able to get bills on Canton @ 30 days sight for 87 Sicca Rpˢ which is very [un — stricken through] favourable, but much caution will be requisite in the choice. Alexander &Co have promised to aid me & so have Palmer & Co, but such general promises do not come to much. Money is scarce which renders it more difficult to sell Bills on London than formerly The supercargo of the Francis I am told has not met with same facility as formerly in selling Peabodys Bill, the rate is 1[?]ᵈp sicca Rupee 6 moˢ sight.

A Bond is exacted of 24000 Rpˢ penalty that the cargo on board every vessel shall be landed within 2 years I or Captⁿ S will have to sign it with our Banian, the duties on Bandannas have been [interlineated: raised] to 7½% upon the new and at price say 6½% on the shipping price, this will not prevent me from buying a considerable quantity if they can be shipped at about 120 Rpˢ including the export duty, there are few in the Bazar & those held at 115/ — I shall see the silk merchants & know what can be done on contract, the very high price of the raw article will keep the prices of Silk goods from falling. Our non Intercourse has no effect, because Band annas are never made in great quantities except to order.

Indigo is by no means so low as I expected the quality of most at market very indifferent, but as yet I have not seen any samples. I shall be quiet for some days, 'till the natives get rid of their *patience* [written over: patients] of which you know they have a large stock, they are looking for more Americans. I shall keep possession of my own funds & employ Ramdon as a Banian. I am well satisfied he will serve me well. Indigo pays 5% duty, no drawback, estimating the price @ 100 Rpˢ per factory maund.

May 21st. Thursday

The Brig is now moor'd. We shall not be able to begin to discharge for some days. I must look into the new revenue laws &prepare to fight the new Collector. I understand he puts what value he pleases on goods, without reference to the cost, perhaps I may get Downie &Co or Palmer &Co to aid me.

Raw Silk has almost doubled. Bands will not be any lower — I shall buy for you some very low priced Indigo, but not very bad quality, there is a good deal of broken I am told in the Bazar, which will do for our retailers.

Money is scarce. Bills on London 2/5d to 2/6d no American Bills will sell without being well endorsed by some one here or guarantyd by some known house in England.

The rate of Exchange on China as you will perceive is favourable. Bills cannot all [interlineated: ways] be had & great care is now requisite in buying, the failure of Harrington &Co Madras has shaken the confidence of the Mercantile world, but their affairs are not very bad I am told —

I shall defer remitting to Canton 'till the last moment because I am quite sure your goods from this place will give much more profit than Canton Silks.

I send you a Memo of the Restitutions Cargo, pray do not allow any one to see it. Captn P's feelings would be hurt perhaps the sale affected. Do not incourage any extravagant expectations of the shippers for they will be disappointed. *goods are* not remarkably low, especially fine ones.

The affairs of J & H Lee are all settled as you will long since have heard, so that your interest will sustain no injury from that cause, nevertheless, I have directed that the accounts be kept with me as agent for the shippers &owners of the Brig Reaper.

May 22d.

I shall send off this letter to day as the Restitution is now at Diamond Harbour, nothing to add —

T Stewart arrived this morning from the Isle of france he has done an immense deal of business &worth 3 lacs or more —

they say — the Derby will make a good voyage Ellery's Brig will do well with her wine. I am on the look out for goods but shall not make any purchases for a few days.

I am sorry I cannot be more particular, but it is impossible to learn anything in the short time I have been here, by the Francis, I shall write fully & also via Isle of France. —

Y^{rs}

H Lee

LETTER FROM HENRY LEE, CALCUTTA, JUNE 4, 1812, TO WILLIAM H. TRANT, SECRETARY OF THE BOARD OF REVENUE, DEFENDING HIMSELF AGAINST A CHARGE OF ATTEMPTED SMUGGLING [1]

As he had anticipated, Henry Lee speedily came into conflict with the custom house, though not in the connection which he had expected. His appeal in this letter was successful.

A peon is a Hindu term for a native foot soldier, messenger, footman, or similar functionary; a sircar, in the sense used below, is a native employed by a European as a writer and accountant, and occupies a position of considerable importance.

W^m H Trant Esqr   Calcutta June 4th. 1812
   Sec^y of the board of Revenue
      Sir
         I beg leave respectfully to submit the following statement relative to a quantity of Spars belonging to the Cargo of the Brig Reaper, which have been seized by the officers of the Customs, &to request you w^d lay it before the board of Revenue. —

On Friday the 29th. ulto I sold to Captⁿ J L Stewart of the Hon^l Companys service (thro' his Sircar) 15 Spars then on board the Brig Reaper, giving him a note at the same time directed to the 1st. Officer of the R. to assist the bearer in the examination of them, a Copy of which is enclosed.

On Saturday morning I made application for permission to

   1. Jackson-Lee Papers, "Letters written in Calcutta from May to August 1812."

land them at Kidderpore. I applied for that place instead of the Custom H⁰ to accommodate Mᵣ Kidd for whose yard I understood they were destined

This was refused & an order endorsed on my application, to land them at the Custom H⁰. a fact I was unacquainted with 'till Monday morning when I learnt that they had been seized by a Custom H⁰ peon in possession of a sircar of Mᵣ Kidd, who was in the act of transporting them to Kidderpore.

On inquiring into the circumstances, I found that the 1ˢᵗ Officer at the Reaper without any orders from me, my Banian, or any one connected with me, had, (late on Saturday) delivered them to 2 of Mᵣ Kidds Sircars.

On demanding from him his reasons for so doing, I recᵈ a note which I herewith enclose, together with a receipt from one of the Sircars of Mᵣ Kidds.

As Mᵣ Bancroft is a stranger in this place & wholly unacquainted with the Custom House regulations, I hope the agency he had in this business will be attributed to the misrepresentation of Mᵣ K's Sircars or to a misunderstanding between them, rather than to any improper motive.

The spars were manifested agreeable to the Custom H⁰ regulations & application made to land them in the usual form previous to their delivery. these facts are known at the C H⁰ &will go far. I should hope, to prove that I could not have had any intention of defrauding the Honˡ Companys revenue.

I further add, that the whole cost of the Spars in the U S as admitted at the Custom H⁰ was 18 dollars, the duties upon them amount to Sᵃ Rpˢ 4..0..9, admitting therefore that I was disposed to defraud the Revenue, & that from a cargo contᵍ several valuable articles I should select this bulky one, I believe it will be apparent to every one, that the expence of Smuggling the Spars would have amounted to a larger sum than the duties.

I wᵈ beg leave further to direct the attention of the board to this fact — that every person engaged in this business except the 1ˢᵗ. Officer of the R. who acted without orders, & under the directions of Mᵣ K's Sircars, were people in the service of Mr Kidd or Captn Stewart &wholly unknown to me.

I trust this explanation will be satisfactory to the Board of Revenue & that they will give orders to have the Spars delivered to me on payment of the duties.

Should it be required, I can furnish evidence corroborate the truth of the above.

I am Y^r

(Sign'd)   Henry Lee

Supercargo of the American Brig

Reaper

LETTER FROM HENRY LEE, CALCUTTA, JULY 7–10, 14, 1812, TO ANDREW CABOT, BOSTON, WITH AN ACCOUNT OF GOODS AND PRICES [1]

The few specimens of India piece goods mentioned below give but a slight idea of the complexity of the trade as a whole and the intricate knowledge which the successful supercargo must have at his very finger tips. There were literally hundreds of types of India piece goods in the market, some known by more than one name; pieces of each variety differed widely in dimensions, quality, and color. Just as, in his letters from Calcutta, Henry Lee expresses the prices of India piece goods in rupees instead of in shillings, so in expressing their dimensions he employs the cubit instead of the yard — the India cubit "invariably exceeding the English cubit of 18 inches by 1½ or 2 inches." [2] This is confirmed by entries in "Directions to C. D. Miles 1817 for purchases Piece goods Indigo &c &c," which, after giving dimensions of India piece goods, express the number of square yards per piece, thus revealing that the unit employed in describing the length and width is about 19 in.

In other words, the "foolpour Cossas . . . 38 to 39 by 2 @ 1/16 @ 48/ p Co," which Lee on May 23 mentioned having purchased, was a type of cotton cloth, each piece of which was from 38 to 39 cubits long and from 2 to 2 1/16 cubits wide, and the price of which was 48 rupees per 20 pieces. Part of this lot was to be printed for chintz, and the inferior grade dyed for "blue cloths." Among the "Contract

1. Jackson-Lee Papers, "Letters written in Calcutta from May to August 1812."
2. Balfour, *op. cit.*, "Weights and Measures."

goods" were "500 pˢ long cloths to be dlᵈ in 45 days at 8 Rpˢ pʳ pˢ." Lee had also purchased "1500 pˢ Chittabilly Baftas @ 52/ [per corge]."

The "heavy goods for ballast" were only less varied than the piece goods which were the staple of an India cargo. These "heavy goods," with goat skins, gunny sacks, drugs — in fact almost everything but piece goods and indigo — were frequently lumped together as "gruff goods." Conspicuous among Lee's purchases for this purpose was about 20,000 lb. of sal ammoniac @ 11 cents per lb.

The "Godown" in which the goods were to be stored was, as the use of the word would imply, merely a warehouse.

The manuscript volume, "Invoices of all the goods ship'd by Henry Lee during his stay in Calcutta from May 1812 to March 1816," reveals that the prices of turmeric and ginger were estimated in bazaar maunds of a little over 82 lb. rather than in factory maunds of something under 75 lb. The price given for the "Gunny bags" was per hundred.

A "chow Chow Cargo" is one of a miscellaneous nature; the *Monticello's* at the Cape of Good Hope probably consisted of assorted provisions.

Original pr Francis
Mr ACabot   care ofMr Kemp   Calcutta July 7ᵗʰ. 1812
  Dr Andrew   Duplicate p Calcutta
               say as far as "Sharcadder &c &c"

Enclosed you have a Copy of my last. since then the Tartar has arrived &brought me duplicates of the letters pʳ Caravan.

I have now before me yours of 12ᵗʰ. Febʸ: it was my wish that you would be explicit in your orders for the disposal of owners stock and you have been so. I wish I could feel warranted in following them. I then should only have to collect my cargo with all possible haste &proceed to U States. I presume when you wrote your last letter, you did not contemplate our being so late in Calcutta or at least being so long detain'd as we are like to be, & as I have thought it expedient we should be, both for the interest of the shippers & owners, my contracts & other arrangements are calculated for a stay of four months from the time of arrival, previous to the expiration of that period, we shall have advices of the termination of the session of Congress, provided their sittings close on the 1st. May. I have therefore concluded upon reserving the whole of the owners stock [interlineated: excepting the ¼ which will be ship^d at all events] & your private adventure 'till the last moment of our stay. I do this for several reasons 1st. the investment I shall select for owners of piece goods & Indigo, will at the lowest prices: goods have ever sold at, produce 90¢p rupee, 2^d. the prospect for Canton goods from all the accounts I can collect is very bad, & your funds will not reach you so early by many months as by the Reaper.

3^d. Our stock is not great enough, if so large a portion should be withdrawn. & the amount on account of the owners would only buy gruff goods en^o. at least there would hardly be anything left for piece goods & Indigo.

I think if you place yourself in my situation you will approve of my determination. if I remit to Canton the voyage is ruin'd, if I ship in the Reaper I am morally certain your investment will sell very well. I calculate upon Bengal goods being low. perhaps lower than when I sail'd, but that I allow for. it w^d be a sad business to remit &have your returns perhaps delay'd 'till next summer &then make nothing & in mean time the N I Law should have been repeal'd, it makes me sick to think of remitting & I shall not do it 'till the last day.

It is even possible. I may remain behind to see whether the law is repeal'd, but of this I will think more, there is no need of deciding upon it 'till the time of our departure approaches.

I shall have opportunity of informing you of what I may do in this respect. [hav — stricken through]

Having always in view this remittance to Canton, I have engaged of Palmer &Co exchange on Baring &Co Canton to the amount of Rp^s 50,000 at [interlineated: SaRps] 190 p^r 100 Spdollars, being the rate I have bought for Mess^s Perkins it is I believe the lowest rate that has ever been sold, being 5% under par valuing the Rupee @ 2/3^d. bills at 30 days, my agreement is conditional, I may take or not, these gentlemen have been very liberal & discover'd a confidence in me, considering the situation in which I appear to them, that astonishes me, I shall hereafter shew a proof of it.

It is unfortunate for us, that the Caravan Monticello Tartar arrived so soon, goods were falling, I was in treaty for large lots on the day they were reported & closed immediately at some Rp^s p Co more than I should otherwise have had them for.

I have added perhaps 100 Bales since then, of those goods which others avoid, for the remainder of what I want I shall wait till Heard has done, he seems to be in great haste to buy, 'tho I understand he does not intend to sail immediately, there is besides a Portuguese ship with 9 lacs rupees, she produces more effect than all of us together on the market, from the large amount of stock &the manner in which they do their business.

Alliabad goods, I thought high even at the prices paid by Captn Pulsifer & did not buy, they have advanced a little. Mr Heard I am told has bot largely, he may be right, but I do not believe Emerties at 64/ Chondogerrys @ 85/ will do, they are coarse & uneven. I shall take more Col^d goods than I expected before my arrival, but they will come very low, the Cossas (blue) I could not avoid. they were too coarse to pack white & could not be sold, so the best I took for Chintz &to pack white & the coarse for blue Cloths. You will perceive a small portion of fine Cottons, there are no more in market, there are *fine* names but no fine Cloth. My *Gurrahs* (say the C^o) are uncommonly good & cheap, no coarse & narrow ones in the Bazar. I hope to get some however *Baftas* are also of excellent quality & very cheap, the *Mamoodies* are some of them good & some bad but cheap, as you will see by the mem^o.

My Contract goods are certainly low, for some of them I have been offer'd 10% advance, I trust they will all be deliver'd, the rains which have been excessive are against the contractors, & Chintz Printers, & also delay our shipments, but as we stay so long, that is of little consequence we shipped 24 bales yesterday for the first & have 100 more at the Custom house waiting for dry weather.

I am very glad to find *Indigo* low, on your account as well as the Shippers most of them have left me to buy such goods as I may think most for their interest, it is a thankless business to be cloth'd & to act with such powers. some of the gentlemen will be dissatisfied, let the result be what it may, but I have accepted the Charge & shall discharge it according to my best abilities.

You will have accompanying my letter a Schedule with the amounts to be invested in piece goods & Indigo, the quantity requir'd will be 900 maunds, 500 of which is agreed for at 104 Rp^s (sicca p factory maund) in this lot are some chests of broken, the quality of which is good, but I shall sell part of it. the loss upon them will bring the price to 108/ this Indigo I am of opinion (& so are those who judge better than I do) is equal to the Reapers last voyage. The owner has been offer'd within 6 mo^s 130/ — 125 — 110/ Rp^s pmaund & parted with it now at the pressing solicitations or demands of a man who had made advances upon it & wished to have his money again, it is in the hands of Baretto who assures me it is of good quality & free from mixture of bad kinds, I do not depend upon him however I have compared it with all the samples I brought from England & all I have seen here, &further I have taken the opinion of Dr Bruce &some other Europeans say Palmer &Co. they all assure me it is good.

The lot I refer'd to in my last, is not yet bot' it is superiour to this & if I am fortunate enough to secure it, will make up the quantity I want & I shall feel confident that in going so largely upon this article I have done what will be for the interest of the shippers. — I feel more confidence in my judgements because it concurs with that of some of the principal shippers. S H &Co order 1/3d or more in that article if as low as 120 Rp^s. I imagine the quality of what I have bot' & shall buy will be equal if not superiour to what they refer to in their orders. J & T H P. R Hooper &Sons & W N Hooper, Ge^o Cleveland &Co order 1/3d. J Cabot jr the whole, the other shippers except three give me no orders, for them I shall take ¼ and perhaps more, especially should not I get the Bandannas I am searching for, either in the Bazar or at Cossimbazar it appears to me unless we are shut out of every port of the Continent that this article must do well, the U. S. must by this time be clear'd of the principal lots, indeed there can be no debenture Indigo even now, of the old stock; & I find on looking at the list of Cargoes expected this year (1812) that only 152 Chests are among them, the Ganges & S⁰ Carolina have in addition   Chests more, the Francis has none, the Montecello has no stock & will only take a small quantity, that goes on freight, the Caravan I imagine will have little or none, the Tartar has no funds except sufficient for her voyage Mr Thorndike has $10,000 which may come in that article, if she (the Tartar) goes to U'S. or be shipped on some other vessel the vessels that are yet to come from Isle of France.Madras Penang &c with cargoes of Gin. Tar &c have all small stocks & will be more likely to invest their funds in Sugar & piece goods than one so valuable, it is true should the Intercourse be renew'd there will be ships out with large funds, but they must be here late for the old Indigo, &the new will be 30% higher for the same quality, besides the R's Cargo will be the first & arrive in good time for the Russiamen. —

I shall collect some cheap for the owners & if I must remit to Canton, sell again, every body says it will rise when the Indiamen arrive. I do not mean to speculate, but only secure you a quantity while it is low: in fact, if not now done I shall not be able to buy at all, for there is very little good Indigo, or even merchantable in Calcutta. I believe I have examined all the principal lots & I know of only two large ones or three or four small ones that can answer for me & some of those in hands of Europeans, who will not sell now the arrival of the fleet approaches.

The Article I was most desirous of obtaining after Indigo [was — stricken out] is *Silks*. I did not expect to find it low; because the raw material is in such demand for England, but the new duty is an additional charge & makes them very high; I made an attempt 'thro Alexander &Co to get a quantity of an English Gentleman at Moorshdebad & offer'd him 98/ for ordinary & 107/ for fine, 2500 p^s each, he return'd me for answer that he could not think of making them at that: I afterwards sent up Country 10,000 Rp^s &have secured 3000 p^s of ordinary at 104/ to be dl'd in 2½ months, say the 5th. Sept^r., this was all I could procure. I have sent up another agent & have hopes of adding 4000 p^s more of fine & coarse @ 103/ & 113/ to be deliver'd 15th. Septr. I think at these prices they promise better than Cottons, more especially as they have hitherto been 120/ to 125/ & few shipped. I trust too, the vessels now here will not take many &that what they do buy will come considerably higher, the Francis I am pretty certain has none, the Montecello I know will not have on cargo, nor do I know of any freight going in her except the Indigo mentioned above, they demand 118/ in Calcutta for fine, of the ordinary only 1000 p^s in market of which I have bot 750 p^s & hope to get the other chest @ 105/, there are no Lungees. I have bot 500 p^s of Durys @ 8/8 to 9/8 & shall buy any small lot of Sistersoies or Lungees that may offer. Flags are lower than last year but I am afraid of a large quantity of them. I have purchas'd 1000 p^s @ 110/ about equal to Captn P's & may get them reduced to 108/, they are of the Gulliver quality, if more can be had at this I shall buy 2000 p^s, they will answer, *Taffaties* I can get @ 5/ to 6/ but in my opinion this article will never answer, the Canton silks are cheaper, I shall buy some for one of the shippers, because he has order'd them, but none for you, or any other person.

As it is somewhat uncertain whether I get my Silks, I would not have you mention any thing to the shippers, they may be disappointed & I have a long story to tell how it happen'd, if they should be high on arrival; in fact I hope you will not communicate any particulars of my proceedings, or what I am like to do, they will be satisfied when their Invoices come to hand, that their interests have been taken care of, & that is all they ought to know.

With regard to gruff Goods it is impossible to say what quantities we shall take till the Cargo is pack'd. I did not wish to take much, or indeed any Sugar, because it takes up much room & will not give so much profit as either piece goods, Indigo or many gruff goods more valuable. Captⁿ S. seems so much afraid of her being crank (the Brig) that I have put on board 175 bags, the wood is partly under the platform, which hitherto we supposed had stones plac'd there, but on taking it up turn'd out otherwise, the remainder is in the wings. I have taken more Sal Ammoniac than otherwise to avoid Sugar, it is very low & must do well. I shall not buy any Ginger at the present price of 6/12 p^r maund, nor much if it falls to 5/ of which there is no chance & even then it w^d be uncertain whether it sold so well as Turmerick. I shall take the quantity of Turmerick you order, if there is room without excluding Goat Skins & some other Gruff articles, which I am confident will do well, at any rate 300 to 400 m^{ds}., at my particular request, Captⁿ S has turn'd as much loose among the boxes, bags & bales as can be stow'd, he was very averse to it because he felt confident it would damage the Bale goods & that the shippers w^d blame him. I know this is a common opinion. Ge^o thought so in the Caravan, but I know by experience that the peice Goods will not be injured & that we should sustain a great loss of room if it was not done, I therefore told him that I consider'd *myself responsible for any bad consequences that might arise in* so doing, the Tumerick therefore will be started among the Cargo. I have bot' 300 md^s @ 2/8 to 3/ it is scarce in the Bazar. I have persons collecting, they have already sent me 150 md^s. & will procure what more I may want. I do not find any has been ship'd in 1812, except Pulsifers, nor are any of the ships now in port buying, questions have been ask'd me about it. I got rid of them by saying Ginger is too dear, & we want something for dunnage &c. I have been afraid the Francis as she will not be full, w^d take a a large quantity & also the Monticello in the same condition, but I believe neither of the agents of these vessels are acquainted with the article & I hope it may escape their notice.

Goat Skins, I fear will be plenty in U. S. &tho' the quantity gone from hence is not great yet the consumption is so much increas'd &still increasing that I consider them a staple article. I have shipp'd 3500 of large ones, engaged 2500 more, &hope

to get a further quantity from the [quantity — stricken through]
Country of good sized ones, the whole at 20/ which is only
double the price of good Gunny bags. I trust they will never
go below 25¢. I put them in bales, loose they w^d occupy more
room & get injured, the whole quantity will be 10 to 15,000 all
with the hair on.

Gunny bags, I have engaged 10,000 of rice bags @ 6/12, prefering them to new Gunnies at 10/, shall take as many more
as we can dispose of to advantage. I have bot 20 Md^s. of
Assafoetida of good quality at 20 Rp^s pm^d. & 25 md^s Borax
@ 19/ which is all of these two articles I shall take. I find no
other drugs or gums that are low en^o. the Arabs, (20 to 25
Ships) are expected in a month, from their cargoes I hope to
get some, *Copal galls and Senna*, a small quantity of each will
be as much as we can find room for. I had some thoughts of
taking 200 md^s of ordinary *Java Coffee* at 3 Rp^s pm^d. thinking
you might enter it as triage & have an allowance on the duties,
in which case it might stand you in *something less than 5 cts
long price,* provided 1/2 or 1/3d of the duty should be allow'd,
but our room is so valuable that I shall not take it unless I
get more Silks, Indigo &fine Cottons than I have at present
any prospect of, there is no *Mocha* in market. Capt P has a
small quantity in the Restitution but it is of bad quality, I am
told, &most of it not in original packages, a most important
point as otherwise it w^d not be consider'd as genuine Mocha.

My outward cargo I am sorry to say will turn out to a loss,
the Glass Ware is sold at about 45% but the duties are so great
as take of all the advance, the *Crockery* at 150% but so much
is broken, (from what cause I cannot imagine as the Crates
were shipped in good order) that not more than the cost will
be realiz'd. the *Cheese Perry & Ale* sold high, but great deductions are made for the damaged, ulaged &c. The Rum on
hand, the abundance of Gin & ordinary Brandy (american
made) prevents a sale. I shall try to get it off by bottling. the
Hoops which considering the low cost I had reason to hope
much for, are on hand & if I get 9 Rp^s pm^d. it will be the top
of the market, the nominal price on my arrival was 12 Rp^s

but no sales have been made even as high as 9 Rp^s, which is 10% below the price of iron. I w^d hold them, but the Indiamen will have such large quantities as to depress prices still lower than the present ones, it is a most grievous disappointment to me to have such a result from a Cargo that at any time within 5 years 'till now w^d have yelded a great profit, but it is the fortune of trade & I must bear the chagrin & you the loss as well as we can, the new duties alone make a difference of 4 or 5000 Rp^s, none of my sales are made up, I cannot therefore make any estimate of what will be the proceeds of the outward cargo, the most I can hope for is the prime cost, the market is fill'd with every kind of European goods & 20 ships are now on the way from London to this place &madras, most of which will have cargoes of merchandize, the 4 ships that have arrived at Madras sold their investments at 30% to 32 advance, the buyers rejecting about ¼ of such articles as they saw fit, leaving on hand goods that will not bring anything like prime cost, from this you can form an idea what the other cargoes will come to, now the market is fill'd with more than is wanted for the season, the difference in the duties paid by us & the English will exclude valuable merchandise in American ships, the Portuguese are only liable to half the duties we pay, so much for Non Intercourse Law, the increas'd duties having been laid entirely upon the principle of retaliation, so says the Collector, the duties on exports are heavy, about half the goods we buy come from the Nabobs territories & by law are chargeable with an export duty of 7½%, by management they are shipp'd at an expence of 1% but this cannot be expected to continue, &then we can no longer take Nabobs goods, which comprise some of the best articles for our market. Silks of all kinds & all articles of which silk is a material used, say Seersuckers, Carraderies &c pay 7½% &no way to avoid it, unless by smuggling, which some may undertake, but I will not. Indigo pays 5% on the value of 160 Rp^s pm^d. & gruff articles from 2% to 7½%.

The new Collector is unaccommodating tyranical & unjust, we have all of us had to fight every inch we go. I have endeavourd to propitiate him by sending newspapers &paying him other attentions, but his *strong sense of duty* to his masters the Company, &what is still more operative, his duty to himself, that is, his intentions to fill his own pockets which have been empty for a long time, will not allow him to desist from imposing upon all Who fall under his powers, he indeavoured to have our Spars confiscated, but was overrul'd by the board of Revenue to whom I sent a memorial, which prov'd the charges upon which he reccommended confiscation, so utterly groundless that they were restored. I am however on good terms with others & I hope to meet no more difficulties as I mean to be fair & regular in all my transactions, the business of the Custom H⁰ has become very intricate &troublesome. My Banians (Tillock) is very clever & gets on better than any of the others, he & Ramdon are both very intelligent &industrious & are with me from 6 in morning 'till 9 at night, not a day have they been absent.

I perceive you have been anxious least we should have been refused an entry with our merchandize from England, your fears were not without reason, the Collector told me I had no right to come here, & actually refused for one day to receive our papers, we finally thro' the assistance of MʳSnice [?] who translated our Madeira papers, made it appear that our voyage commenced at that Island &that we could not be consider'd as coming from England, &were admitted. I do not imagine even had we been direct from Bristol that we should have been turn'd off, because hitherto our vessels under like circumstances have been admitted we should have been stop'd at the C H⁰, but the Govʳ wᵈ have overrul'd the proceedings of the Collector, Revenue Board &c, &for this reason, that we had not any notice nor could have been expected to have had it: of the new Regulations, but henceforth I am of opinion it wᵈ be hazardous to come here from England via Madeira, or any port except some one in U. S. I should not have taken any merchandise had I known of the Increas'd duties or the new regulations.

I mention'd in my former letters, the apprehensions I felt

that I Should not be able to negotiate S H &Co⁵ letter of Credit. Messʳ Alexander &Co refus'd having consider'd of the proposal for some days, as this was the house Mʳ H rely'd upon, having procurd letters to be written as H H told me by Porcher &Co to Alexander strongly reccommending S H &Co, which they seem'd to think wᵈ certainly be sufficient, such letters were written & recᵈ. but A &Co told me that in the present situation of Affairs, political as well as commercial, they had rather not take my Bills; I despair'd after this of selling them, more especially as the Company's [interlineated: interest] was about being paid, &that the receivers could either take Cash or drafts on the Company in London @ 2/6ᵈ. p SᵃRpᵉ 6 moˢ. added to which the scarcitty of money is great & every one wants to draw rather than sell; under these circumstances I thought it wᵈ only injure S H &Coˢ Credit, to run hawking their letter of Credit (which had been refus'd by the only house [that — stricken out] who could know any thing [about — stricken out] of them) about Calcutta the only hope I had left, was, that news might arrive previous to my departure of a repeal of the Non Intercourse &some sort of settlement of difficulties between the two countries which might give confidence to A &Co & induce them to take the Bills, as to Palmer &Co I knew they had refus'd Mʳ Mansfields bills, tho' he had on former voyages sold to a large amount in Calcutta, &tho' his owner was as well known here as any man among us, except his honor The Lᵗ. Govʳ. I therefore never supposed it possible to do anything thro' them, tho' I meant eventually for forms sake before my departure, to have made them & Downie &Co the offer, while I was lamenting the ill success attending my application to A &Co, I was inform'd by a gentlemen intimate with the house of Palmer &Co, that Mʳ Maitland (who is one of the house & now in the absence of J Palmer the acting man) had in conversation with him, express'd considerable interest for the success of my voyage; &from the confidence he felt in me, was disposed to afford me all the aid that was in his power in any business where I might require it: I consider'd this as I do all such general professions, merely com-

plimental, as a kind of return for some little attentions I had
paid him, such as sending him my latest papers English &
American, delivering his letters without the delay usually attending those that go into office, & accommodating him in the
payment of their acceptances &c &c I thot' it well however to
put him to the test: &the next day call'd upon him with my
letter: to my surprize he offer'd to take my bills, saying that
he w^d wait for letters by the fleet & if they brought no bad
news about war &c &c he w^d give me the money at once, the news
by the fleet, was rather unfavourable to me, but the Tartar
brought me some letters, particularly one from Uncle Cabot,
which by reading to him did away the Eng^h news, in fact it
had made no great impression, he concluded to take my bills
@ 2/7^d p rupee 6 mo^s sight which is their full Value. I drew
them on the 2^d inst & am now in possession of Sa Rp^s
66967..11..11 on acct of S H &Co, the freight of which Rp^s
10451..9..9 being deducted an addition to our stock that is
very desirable more especially should I be compell'd to remit
the ¾ of your property to China S H &Co will be disappointed
I fear at what may strike them as a very unfavourable rate,
but if a calculation of interest be made, allowing from the time
the shippers bills were bought 'till July 1813 when my bills
will probably become due in London, the difference will be
found to be only 1^d. &they have avoided the risk of having
funds here without any one to take care of them, as w^d have
been the case had the R been left, & also that of nonpayment
of Bills, but whether they are satisfied or otherwise, I have
follow'd my orders & should have felt myself liable to censure
had I even refused 2/8 @ 2/9 had these been the market price
I send you an extract of their orders, you can judge for yourself I have been thus particular, perhaps you will think heed-
lessly so, that you may understand all the difficulties I have to
encounter & that I have not acted without reflection &without
using all the means in my power to promote the interest of
H &Co. I w^d further add that Indigo upon which they count
the most in their mem^o of returns is 15% lower than their
limits, & that some other articles they have added, are also as

much below the prices named. Should there be any observations made to you, make the best defence you can, &when I arrive I will do what remains. I consider myself as having follow'd the letter, as well as the spirit of my orders.

They will perhaps hear that Mr Mansfield even sold @ 2/6d. &it is I believe true; but he forced his bills upon his Banian, by threatening to withdraw his present business &the future patronage of Jos Peabody, while at the same time another Banian stood by with his Bags of Rupees to loan the sum required 40 to 50,000 Rps. upon the condition of having the business of Mr M. (what remain'd unsettled), & a secret resolution I presume to get back a part in good round *dustaye* I had no such means to use, nor should have used them, had they been within my power, it wd have been better for M. to have sold his bills for Cash @ 2/7d. &bought the goods, he could not sell them at all. I believe I can easily prove to H &Co that there is more difference between my good & the Francis', but I do not mean to say it as a boast, only as an explanation of this transaction, this is all uninteresting to you I know, but it may be of importance to me, in order to prevent bad impressions which might be more difficult to remove than after my arrival.

I have not negotiated Mr Russels letter & do not feel warranted in doing it, unless I should hear of the repeal of the Non Intercourse

F C Lowells remittance which was left to my discretion, I have concluded to send in the Reaper. I cannot calculate upon any other addition to our stock.

I have had no offers of freight or passengers, Captn Hinckley if he goes on his voyage will have some remittances to make & I should suppose wd give us the preference, our vessel being the best in port, but I shall not accept less than 100 Rps pton &perhaps not have room to take it at that, but of this I can judge better when our Cargo is pack'd. I shall try for passengers, but without any expectations of getting any except poor vagabonds &these we shall decline taking, no gentleman will imbark in our vessels, we have a bad character among Englishmen, a 1000 Rp^s w^d be profitable, more so than goods; any that can pay that sum we shall gladly receive.

My opinion is that we shall be deep, quite so, & that from the state of our Copper we shall sail heavy do not therefore expect us too soon, you should give us 5 mo^s I am reserving for you some of the goods purchased in case I sh^d not remit to Canton, but your investment will not be so well chosen as it w^d if I had now resolv'd to ship the whole in the Reaper. I cannot keep in reserve so large a quantity, either of piece goods or Indigo as ¾ of the stock will amount to, because I am apprehensive goods will rise, &then I sh^d have to pay higher for what w^d be wanting for the Shippers: indeed the uncertainty of what I shall do embarasses me very much. I have bot some small lots of Indigo at 90/ to 105/ for the owners, upon the hazard of Repeal of the N Intercourse, if that does not take place I must sell it again, for this you will have to take the chance of loss or gain.

I take the rejected goods when a large allowance is made & I shall place them to your acct. I should give the shippers a portion, but on arrival they will sell there for good, the buyers will complain & I shall be call'd to an account for putting up damaged goods, from you I have nothing of this kind to fear, you will sell them for what they are.

If the Non Intercourse is repeal'd you will have no risk to encounter but the market. I hope you will not sell out, either the Cargo or your adventure. I shall take a vast deal of pains that your investment be well selected &it w^d mortify me to find I had been laboring in vain, more especially as the voyage to B. was so unfortunate, &the cargo out has come to so poor a market. I depend upon the returns to make out a saving voyage, should the restrictions be removed I trust something better than that will be the result.

The latest accounts from England are to   March, they came by the fleet to Madras a Month since in the short passage of   days, judging from the papers, they seem to think our stupid, blustering Congress are in earnest in their ridiculous resolutions &measures I am quite certain the B

Gov^t will not take any steps in relation to us 'till they know the final doings of our miserable Congress, the fleet for this place is look'd for in August, by it I shall have letters from the Williams' & Mr Lowell if our N I Law is not done away I hope we shall be excluded from the ports of this nation.

Captn H met with an accident &put into Teneriffee, he arrived on 30th ulto he has confided to me & advised with me, as to the object of his voyage. I cannot therefore communicate to you tho' it is known to half the inhabitants of the City, when he commences it I shall write you upon the subject, he will not interfere with us. A Heard has pack'd most of his goods, he takes no Indigo or Silks, his stock not admitting, indeed he told me he had not funds en^o to fill her, he brought Bills on London &has met with the same ill success as others in the like situation. I believe he raises nothing upon them, he did intend to go to Brazils for orders &perhaps his still the intention, the time of his departure uncertain on account of his merchandize, most of which comes to a bad market. — Montecello came on from Cape G Hope where she sold a chow Chow Cargo just before our vessels were excluded, $6000 produced $ with which she came here as Bills on London were 50% advance, she will have 200 bales piece goods & 100 tons Sugar 15,000 Goat Skins, a quantity of Gunny bags, the Caravan will have say 500 to 600 bales, Sugars, 1000 bags more or less, 20 tons of Sanders. The Francis 500 bags Sugar more or less &   bales, some Goat Skins, &Gunnies. Pulsifer has a better cargo than the Francis. Mansfield has a great quantity of *Alliabad goods* which he thinks will do well. I do not, tho' I have express'd great mortification that I did not buy largely before they rose about 5%. I can now get them at M's prices, but should think them high @ as much below. P & M have both some good Gurrahs of the same dimensions as my C^o. only mine are selected &the coarse & short p^s pack'd seperate @ 4% less. I bot' at the same time with Mansfield. Pulsifer had the Bazar to himself. I have bot since the Caravan arrived at about former prices, some goods are much higher however.

The arrival of three Americans & a Portuguese all at one time together with information that 5 more of the latter were on the way, as many more of the former, rais'd prices, but since M^r H^d has nearly finishd & they have discover'd what small stocks they all have except the Portuguese, they are declining again, &sh^d there be no more ships here for a month will be lower than when I bought was low, indeed I think my purchases made within a few days are as favourable as any, perhaps there has scarcely ever been a time when there were so few good goods &such a little variety as now in the Bazar. My Cargo will be badly assorted in that respect. I am very desirous of getting some fine Sannas 40 x 2¼, fine & coarse mow Sannas, Humhums, Chandpore Cossas Coarse &narrow Gurrahs, Jal^a Mamoody (fine) Meergungee Mam^y, coarse &many others, but there are none here. I sh^d imagine there might be in market   bales &there is expected for the following months   bales more, should the N Intercourse have been repeal'd &numbers of vessels from U S dispatch'd with heavy stocks, I think they will have to pay considerably more than present prices, the last vessel that sails so as to be after the *fleet*, that will leave America will do the best, as by that time the market will be well fill'd with Cottons, there is an abundance of brown Cloths up Country, which will not be prepared 'till there are more buyers in Calcutta.

Silks will not be any lower, the raw material is all wanted in London & much more, price 10/ to 14/ p seer, when you was here in Dromo it was about 8/, you can easily account for high prices of Silk manufactures &their bad quality.

Sugar, Duloll says will fall to 6/8 for such as we have paid 8/4 say good Benares. I do not believe it will go so low, nor do any of the Banians. *Ginger* is kept up by high prices in the Country, it seems some new markets have been found nearer the places where it is produced than Calcutta. *Indigo*, is low in England yet as there is nothing else for returns, the Indiamen must take it, last year it was high, every one says it will not be so this season, but that it will advance from its present price, none of 1st quality in market, new will be down in 3

months to 4 mos. mine is of the quality usually shipped to
U S, none of the best of any consequence has ever been shipped
to America, last year it sold @ 180/ to 200/ &this will be
160/ to 180/. I have seen all the *Indigoes* in the City natives
& Europeans shall bring samples of some of the lots, that you
may compare with one I have bought. M & Fulton have a
parcel they hold @ 163/. I should say it was about 10 to 15
Rps better than my lot. Fairley, Alexander Downie &Co.
Palmer &Co. McDonald & others also have parcels, all of which
I have carefully examined & taken the opinions of others upon,
the Captns of Indiamen are their men, it is with that article
as with piece goods, we never can do any thing with them, they
have the reputation of selling nothing but good pure Indigo
&the natives that of selling nothing but bad, but the fact is
many of the parcels they sell, are put into their hands by
natives merely to raise its value. I have traced many parcels
to their makers & owners, 'tis a difficult article to manage
few even here, pretend to know the very nice distinctions which
increase or diminish its value.

I have given you a *concise* & as clear a view as I am able, of
all my proceedings &intentions I close now that I may get my
letter on board previous to her dropping down. I mean to confide this to the 1st officer Mr Kemp, the Captn & SCargo offer
to take letters, to them I shall give others, but after the con-
fessions I have heard them make about keeping back letters,
&from the well known practices of the Middletown teamsters
I am not willing to rely wholly upon them. I shall write again
at the last moment before the F departs, in mean time I remain with great regard

Yrs

(Sign'd)   H Lee

Commencd 7th. ended 10th. July

P. S. 14th July — sold 1000 Mds hoops @ 9 Rs — enclosd the
following papers — List goods packd

    Vessels cleard in 1812

    Memo Restitution's & M's Cargoes

Copy of S H &Co Letter Credit
Duplicate of Letter 19th June
Memo Ship news —
Schedule of shippers — enclosd the whole with a letter to
my wife to O. Goodwin Jr. — & deliv'd the packet to Mr.
Kemp —

LETTER FROM HENRY LEE, CALCUTTA, AUG. 12, 1812, TO
THOMAS LEE, BOSTON, ON RATES OF INTEREST AND EXCHANGE,
PRICES, ETC. [1]

In addition to the information concerning interest, exchange, prices,
and the influences affecting them, the description of the trade carried
on by the Arabs is of interest.

The "Whabees" who were disturbing the trade with Arabia were
the Wahabis, a fanatical and puritanical Moslem sect, who had gained
control of most of the Arabian Peninsula but were at this time beginning to yield to the power of the Turks. The East India Co.'s
monopoly of British commerce with India was abolished in the year
after this letter.

Mr T. Lee   Calcutta Augt. 12th. 1812
    Dear Thos.   Original pr Monticello via N York
Dup. pr. Tartar
    I have recd yours of 10th Feby by the Tartar, it is perhaps
fortunate (since the Non Intercourse has probably been continued) that you did not engage in the speculations I advised,
when I wrote it was under the full expectation the intercourse
with GBritain would be renew'd in the spring, shd you by chance
have sent out to England & imported from thence Indigo &Silk
Hdkfs, sell them, particularly flags that article in consequence
of low price in England, has fallen here, & I shall have 3000
ps @ 109/. of Ordinary Indigo most of which goes to U. S. this
season will be of this discription &some of it very bad indeed
Silk Goods in general here are very high &will continue so
'till the English get raw Silk from the Continent, they buy that

1. Jackson-Lee Papers, "H. Lee's Letters from Calcutta from August
1812 to June 1813."

article now @ 12 Rp^s pseer of 2lb which formerly sold at 7 Rps which accounts for the high price of Bands for three years past. M^{r}Perkins writes from Boston to M^{r}Newton that old M^{r}Higginson has made a great profit on the french goods he bot' & of which I wrote you.

In some of my letters I said much of the advantage sometimes to be made of Exchanges in remitting to India &China. I have done very well with M^{r}Perkins' funds which he remitted by me on Calcutta as you will perceive by the following statement. M^{r}Perkins gave me S^{a}R^s 100,000.0.0 which I invested in Bills at 30 days on

Canton at 190 S^{a}R^s p 100 Sp Dollars deduct^g my Com^{ns}
  of ½% for Collecting, buying &c ⎫
100,000 R^s cost in England 2/3^d p R^{pe} say $50,000 ⎬   52,368½
Ded^t gain on Exchange from U S. say 20% .... 10,000 ⎭   40,000
                                                       Nt gain $12 368½

the premium of Insurance on Dollars is Saved, which will pay the interest on the difference of time between this & a direct remittance, I bot' to be sure at a very favourable rate on Canton, it may not ever be done again, the houses here are very much disappointed at having such large drafts upon them from London &they all agree that from the present state of trade &particularly the large am^t of goods unsold in England, that no one will have bills next year to sell in London. I mention this least some of our friends might be undertaking the voyage I came upon, there is great revolution here in money matters, last year it was @ 5% int, now the best men in the place are giving 10% @ 12% & collateral security, I have loan^d for a month part of Andrews funds @ 11½% & could do it for 6^m @ 10%, last year the Companys 6% paper bore a premium of 2% to 3%, now it is at a discount of 4½% &may go down to 8% @ 10%, there are many causes assign'd among them the remittance of large sums to England; when interest fell from 8 to 5%, every one of course prefering money at home, interest being the same 2^d formerly the Canton agents for the Company bot' dollars there &remitted them to this place, last

year they sent them home. 3ᵈ non importation of Dollˢ from
U S. &Portugal, most of the funds this year having come out
in Bills instead of Specie, I find they view the loss of our trade
on that account as a great evil. The failure of Harrington &Cᵒ
whose affairs are bad, has also contributed to embarrass the
merchants by shaking the confidence of Civil & military gentlemen & causing them to withdraw their funds. when I was in
London S Williams wᵈ guaranty for 1%, now I imagine he wᵈ
not do it at any rate. I have made particular inquiries about
Mocha Coffee of Merchants of Muscat, Mocha & Bussarah.
they all agree in stating the price to be from *20 to 25 Cts plb*
& say it will continue so while the Country is distracted with
Civil wars between the Whabees &other sects of the Mahomet-
ans, the cultivation is nealy suspended &transportation from
the interiour to Sea Coast unsafe. some small lots of ordinary
Mocha Coffee were in the Bazar &offer'd me @ 15¢ plb, but not
in *original packages*, Captⁿ Pulsifer bot' a quantity at about
that price in bags. Some of the Persian Merchants inform me
SaltPetre can be had at Muscat, but others say not, I imagine
the latter to be correct, however I have written over, or rather
some one has for me, but I do not expect any satisfactory information.

The Arabs now carry on a great trade here. 25 Ships look'd
for Indigo is an article they take largely of, they send it over
land to Turkey & even into Greece Italy &c. they bring to this
place drugs, fruits, horses, specie &c.

They expect here that there will be a modification of the
Compʸˢ Charter, so as to admit the merchants in England to a
parcipitation of the trade. but under such restrictions as will
prevent any one from succeeding, if any thing is done vessels
will leave England about this time &those who bring Cargoes
of merchandize will meet with a total loss, the exports on the
other hand will be enhanced, so that inevitable ruin must attend
the first enterprizes, as was the case in Sᵒ America, if we are
in competition with English merchants, our trade must diminish,
particularly in Gruff articles which we export to Europe, say
Tumerick Ginger, Red Wood &c & also in piece goods, at least

we shall have rivals in the sale of them at the Havana &c. Considering the great quantity of piece goods that has been taken out of the market the last year for U S &other quarters, I think my Cargo well charged, &many articles particularly the Gurrahs &Baftas of very superiour quality. I take a large quantity of Indigo of middling quality, &50 to 60,000 R^s in Silk Hdkfs.

Should our affairs with England be settled &we have any Commerce left, there is much to be done with advantage in the trade to this place & especially if an intelligent &sober agent can be found, either to reside here one or two years or only 4 or 5 mo^s which is necessary to invest a large stock to advantage, a residence here of two or three years if we were certain of continuance of peace w^d certainly afford great advantages to a concern who could send two vessels annually, but every thing is so uncertain that it is not worth while to look forward to anything.

If you engage in a voyage to this place before I return, take care what merchandize you send here, more especially ifthe Charter ofthe E I Company is alter'd so as to allow the merchants of Liverpool &c to send out their vessels, & at any rate whether that takes place or not, it is hazardous to to make any more shipments of Merchandize —

Septr. 3^d Wrote H. Jackson p^r Tartar

" 4 Mrs Lee from Augt. 4 to this date p^r d^o. —

" 3 Jas. Lee — that I sh^d retain ¾ of my funds if I remaind behind —

" 3 W. Oliver — Osias Goodwin J^r. —

" 2 John Bromfield —

LETTER FROM HENRY LEE, CALCUTTA, AUG. 20, 28, 31, 1812, TO PETER REMSEN, NEW YORK, ON CARGOES FOR THE UNITED STATES [1]

Henry Lee's opinions as to the comparative futures of the textile industries of Bengal and of Manchester, and as to the respective abili-

1. Jackson-Lee Papers, "Letters written in Calcutta from May to August 1812."

ties of the East India Co. and of individual merchants, are worthy
of notice.

Mr Peter Remsen   Calcutta Augt 20th. 1812
                         original p^r. Monticello
  Dr Remsen   Dup — Tartar

 I wrote you on the 5th. inst &sent the letter to Newton at
Madras, who writes me he shall sail about this time for New
York I think it not improbable he may be detain beyond this
period, on account of the surf which has interrupted his business one third of the time, he has done very well with the outward Cargo & I imagine his returns are well purchased, they
consist of 200 tons Sugar, a quantity of Tumerick, 300 bales
p^s goods, & Indigo a large parcel, he negotiated his Bills on London at a very fair rate, what no one else could have done at all,
even with better credentials than he had. I mention these few
particulars knowing how much you feel interested for M^r N,
& as it is quite probable this may reach before his arrival.

 This is my 4th letter to you. I have rec^d yours of 4th. Feb^y,
with a file of papers principally of old dates. You thought I
suppose that a month or two could make no difference, especially
as I sh^d within the year arrive, &then could see them all, as it
happen'd I had the papers down to 19th Feby so it was of no
consequence. I am glad to learn from so good an authority
as you are, that there was like to be so considerable an exportation of Cottons, still however the market will be overstock'd,
especially if the N I sh^d have been removed of which I am in
great doubts. I never had a favourable opinion of fine Cottons
from Bengal knowing as I do that they are actually cheaper
at Manchester than here *indeed this Country will one day be
supplied from England with the finer Calicoes*, at present there
are importations of shirtings, the [interlineated: use] of which
is confined however to Europeans. I have bot the Common
staple goods Gurrahs, Baftas, Mamoodies, Cossas, Sannas,
Checks, Gillas &some blue Baftas, Cossas &Gurrahs, but very
low indeed, in all white &Col^d Cottons 200,000 Rp^s. I have
bot' all the low priced *good* Band^s I could get, they were too

high in Bazar, so I sent up Country they will cost 107/ &the export duty of 7½%, 6000 p^s. Flags such as the Gullivers 3000 p^s @ 109/ very cheap, & 1000 p^s Durys &Lungees @ 8/8 @9, 15 @ 16 in p^s. I consider my Silks as certain, because none have gone, nor can any quantity be had without going to 115/ for Band^s &the same for flags, am^t in Silks 60,000 Rp^s. Of Indigo I have as yet only bot' 35000 lbs @ 108/ pm^d of quality which cost last year 130/. I shall have of Gruff Goods, Drugs, a little Sugar, Gunny bags, Goat Skins, & 40,000 lbs Tumerick, my cargo I consider as the lowest charged of any that has been shipped since the Gullivers that came into your hands, the Colour^d goods lower. I don't say this by way of boast but only as a piece of information for you, presuming that some part of it may get into your hands &if it does pray do not sell by the Inv^o prices.

I will before I sail send you a Mem^o of my Cargo &the others that have been ship'd this season, that you may compare them together. Goods have risen 10% on account of the arrival of 6 portuguese *Ships with 1600,000 Doll*! Sh^d the Intercourse between England &the U S have been renew'd &ships dispatch'd in May for Calcutta, they will pay high, as will those who are buying now, the ships now here are Monticello by which this goes for N York with 1000 bags Sugar 10,000 Goat Skins, 200 bales Goods, & 20,000 lbs of of very ordinary Indigo, some of it broken &some refin'd it will injure the sale very much, unless it be explain'd to the buyers. The Tartar for Boston with *Rice* & 20,000 lbs Indigo & a quantity of Tumerick to sail in 15 days, the Caravan with 500 bales p^s goods, Sugar, Ginger, Tumerick, Skins, &small quantity of Indigo, she is own'd by P Dodge, the shippers are most of them your correspondents say T Williams, D L Pickman, Walley & Foster W Pratt Jr, write them, your place will be the best market as Boston will have been fill'd with the Cargoes already gone to Salem & ours which must be landed in Boston on a/c ofthe shippers.

The opening of the trade to the Merchants of England will injure us, we cannot come in competition with individuals, with the same success as with the E I Company, all the voyages from England the year on which the trade is open'd will be ruinous in a greater degree than the S⁰American.

Andrew very prudently has order'd me not to send home more than ¼ of his funds without knowing the N I Law is repeal'd. I cannot 'tell what I shall do with the balance, whether to remit to Canton or remain behind with it 'till I hear what will be done about the N I Law. All kinds of American merchandize low, the voyages to Isle of france &Java will be loosing, there ✓ are no returns. *Pepper* at Sumatra is only $3 pᵣ picul of 133 lbs. Coffee at Java $4 pᵣ picul. I have sold my outward Cargo at a small gain, the Cargoes of the indiamen will prove loosing, all Kinds of English goods very low indeed.

Calcutta Augᵗ 28th. the Indigo I refer'd to in mine of 20th. is own'd by a passenger in the Monticello, there is another parcel belonging to Mᵣ Thorndike of Boston, which is better, there are also afew Cases of Bandˢ belonging to Mᵣ T, they cost 115/ & duty of about 7/ to 8 Rpˢ more pCo, say in all @ 122/ @ 123/, mine cost 106/8 they were bot' up Country. I trust they will do well, &yet they come high.

There are now 7 Portuguese Ships, they want 8000 bales, have rais'd prices 10 @ 15% &upon some articles more, they will not finish for 3 or 4 moˢ. till then goods will remain high, especially Good Gurrahs & Alliabad Goods.

the Philᵃ Ship (the Harmony) has a small stock say 250,000 Rpˢ she will remain 4 moˢ. no other vessel look'd for unless the N I Law shᵈ have been repeal'd, of which I begin almost to dispair, if it had been repeal'd last session, we shᵈ have had arrivals from U. S. I am rather inclin'd to think I shall remain behind to take care of my owners property.

I send you a Mem⁰ of the cost of the Cargo of the Ship Francis of Salem, bot' in April &May. Andʷ will send you the prices of mine if you are desirous of Knowing them.

MᵣNewton I imagine sails about this time, & I hope will have arrived when you receive this, remember me to him, if with you & also to your brother.

Yrs
(Sign'd)   HLee

P.S. 31 Aug^t.

Sent a File of Newspapers to Mr R. & requested him to forward them by private hand to Mr Cabot — Mem^o of cost of some of R's goods — Cargoe of Monticello — Tartar

Septr. 3^d Dup. p Tartar — Enclos'd R Invoice — price Current —

LETTER FROM HENRY LEE, CALCUTTA, AUG. 26–27, 1812, TO FRANCIS LEE, BOSTON, IN REGARD TO INDIGO [1]

Previous letters on quantities and qualities of goods in the Calcutta market, prices, purchases, etc., had dealt chiefly with piece goods. The letter below is principally concerned with the other great staple among Indian exports, indigo.

Calcutta Augt 26th. 1812

Mr F Lee   orig^l. p Monticello
Dr Frank   Dup. p Tartar

I send you a Copy of mine p^r Francis. I have nothing since the date of that from you except an old letter p^r Favourite via Madeira, it is rather singular that of so many letters by circuitous routes, not one should have been lost. I have rec^d all that you & And^w have written & all those of my wife except one by a Newport Ship. I hope to hear from you once more via Madeira, vessels w^d leave that island in May & June & after what I said about forwarding letters then, I trust you did not fail to do it, if the N I Law was repeal'd the last session, direct conveyances will have offer'd. I am not without hopes that in course of 20 days we may have intelligence of that wish'd for event, our last news is via Isle of France, p^r Talbot, a letter from S Cargo says nothing had been done by Congress when he sail'd on 10th. March, but this does not make me dispair, because I never imagined they w^d act 'till the last moment, my fears are however stronger than my hopes.

So large a sum is depending upon the repeal of the N I Law,

1. Jackson-Lee Papers, "Letters written in Calcutta from May to August 1812."

& which cannot be invested 'till I hear of it, that my business is necessarilly embarrass'd by the uncertainty I am in. I shall not go beyond the am^t order'd by Andrew to be shipp'd for owners, but as to what I shall do with the balance I am undetermined &must remain so, 'till the time of the departure of the Reaper. I am inclin'd to think however I shall remain behind with it in preference to remitting to China, in which case I shall loan it for the most I can obtain, taking collateral security at present I am receiving 10% for what stock you have, but money is becoming less scarce, & interest falling. I have goods for 10,000 Rp^s &Companys paper for the remaining sum loan'd so that you are as safe as possible.

I have not added a pound to the quantity of Indigo bot' when I last wrote. I do not expect to complete my purchases at so low a rate I w^d buy some of fine quality if to be had, but there is no new in market nor expected 'till Octr. I send you a sample, or rathe[?] Andrew of the 500 mds bot' by me, there are 13 boxes 5 fine, 11 boxes of the B the remainder of the fine & A, it is better than the Reapers which you gave me samples of, somewhat inferiour to the Caravans which cost 165/, perhaps it may be consider'd as equal certainly to Geo^s adv^e which you sold at Auction, in every lot of Indigo there are three &sometimes more distinct qualities &the difference in value very great, say 20% to 40%, it is all important therefore, that in selling you do not allow a lot to be selected without paying in proportion, it offten happens in U S. that persons holding a parcel will allow it pick'd at a very small difference, or even at the average price. Broken Indigo sells at 2/3d price of the whole Cakes, the quality is not injured, but the natives mix in with the good a great deal of ordinary especially when the prices are small, there is in every lot more or less broken especially of fine qualities, every time a box is moved, more or less Cakes break, no allowance is made on the broken unless the proportion is large &then the price of the whole lot is reduced.

None of the 1st quality Indigo is sent to U. S. the difference between that &what We buy is greater than you have any idea of, such as you had in the Susan w^d now cost 175/, certainly it w^d not bring in that proportion above the 120/ to 130/ Indigo which we buy.

In the box of Samples there is one of parcel bot by Mr Hinckley mark'd Alexander &Co, 200 m^{ds} @ 130/, it is a good lot, perhaps rather better than the Reapers, also a sample of Mr Heards @ 104/. I think the quality ordinary. I examined the parcel when I first arrived.

There are likewise two Cakes mark^d Crittenden &Co, who have 200 md^s @ 120/, from these musters you will have a good idea of the prices of Indigo, or rather what they have been, the old is now pretty much clear^d off &the new when it comes down will be higher Mr Hinckley has besides one parcel @ 104/, considerable broken among it, &he will also buy more @ 120/ to 130/, but the Alexander lot is the best. I know it very well, having examin'd & compar'd it with all my musters. Pulsifer had 50 boxes of same lot &paid 130/ for it.

The S Cargo of the Harmony has bot' he informs me all he wants, say 400 md^s more or less, it is old Indigo & about the same as mine, he probably gave 130/, that was the price the holder demanded of me, the Indiamen Capt^s &officers are buying all the new as it comes in by Sample, sh^d the NI have been renew^d & &the usual number of Ships dispatch'd, they will not get good merchantable Indigo at less than it was last year, not till the Indiamen have saild.

The Harmony remains 4 mo^s, her funds do not exceed 250,000 Rp^s partly in dolls & partly in Bills on London drawn by W &Francis, they have not yet sold. Ramdullol I hear does not like to indorse any bills.

Do not rely in any voyage you may undertake upon Bills of Exch^{ge}. American never will sell as well as those drawn here &when they do the Banian must endorse, &thus you are placed in his power, & goods cannot be bot' so low as they otherwise could. Letters of Credit will not enable any one to draw unless they are back'd by some well known house in London, there is not a house in U S. which is known here, or if it sh^d be no one will take bills when the Company draw & also houses of Agency.

Captⁿ Woodward is at Madras, to claim $183,000 deposited in the Admiralty Court, taken from the wreck of the Rapid, Mr Newton writes me they will be deliver'd to him after deducting a Salvage, from thence he returns to Java &China.

The Diomede sold at Isle of France, she has gone to Manilla, the Talbot will probably sell at Isle of france or proceed to Java. I like my Banians very well. I am certain your interest as well as that of the shippers has been benefited Considerably by taking them in preference to any others, if you & And^w sh^d send out a vessel, or any of our friends, by all means direct the S Cargo to employ them.

Augt 27th. Captn Hinckley takes about 120 to 150 md^s more of Indigo making in all 450 Md^s. the parcel he purchased last was 120 md^s of Alexander &Co. he paid 128/ &it is very ordinary indeed, I sh^d think not better than Mr Heards @ 104/ of which you have a sample, he bought contrary to the advice of his banians. I mention this to clear them from any blame which may be thrown upon them, Sh^d complaints be made by the owners of this Indigo, the sample mark'd H is of a parcel of 40 Md^s bot' on my account & the owners, it is middling & cost about 70/ @ 75/ Rp^s pm^d. cannot tell [?],purchased by the box &they have not been weighed. I have also bot for you &myself some other small lots, in all say 90 Md^s. at various prices under 100 Rp^s. if I do not Ship I shall sell again.

I have sent the musters of Indigo to give you an idea of the market, & also to aid you & any of our friends who may want to purchase that article, but I trust Andrew will not shew them, nor make known the opinions I have express'd the sale might be injured, besides I may be mistaken. I have sent also by the Tartar samples of my White Cottons, their prices I gave & also what they are now selling at, goods will not be lower 'till the Portuguese have done buying say 3 to 5 mo^s. they want 6 or 7000 bales. Gurrahs & Alliahabad Goods they are now buying but they cannot get more than 4000 Bales, for the remainder they must take other kinds, if the N I is continued I think it not improbable that in Feby goods may be very low, the present prices will cause the merchants to bring large quantities to market. Silk goods will not be lower 'till the raw material falls which will not happen this year, no one will now contract at less than 112/ for ordinary Bands. &same for flags, when I engaged mine there were no Indiamen in, at present they want raw Silk & Hdkfs, tho' of the latter much fewer than heretofore.

I was wrong in saying to Andrew that the Ships of private Merchants were expected this year, they will not have permission 'till March 1814, at which time the Companys Charter expires.

Yrs

HL

LETTER FROM HENRY LEE, CALCUTTA, SEPT. 20, 1812, TO P. T. JACKSON, BOSTON, WITH DESCRIPTION OF A CARGO SUITABLE FOR INDIA [1]

In a letter to his wife about this time Henry Lee declared that it was not his "intention to hazard against the [Non-Intercourse] Law more than $2,500." He estimated that he would "make by the voyage, when all my property is shipped in goods and has arrived, something like $1,000, and if the Law was repealed, . . . should . . . be able to do better." [2]

Caravan arriv'd
16th March. —

Mr. P. T. Jackson,   Calcutta, Sep. 20th. 1812

I put letters on board the Monticello & Tartar for you — this goes pCaravan & is the last time save bythe Reaper, that I shall have of writing you direct for some months —

The proceeds of W. A. Newton's advr. more or less Sa. Rs. 5000..0..0 transferd' to your account as agreed' upon with E. A. Newton will be shipd' you in the Reaper —

Having now no expectation ofthe repeal ofthe N. I. Law, Ihave come to the determination of remaining behind with my owner's property & ¾ of my own — the shipment in the name

---

1. Jackson-Lee Papers, "H. Lee's Letters from Calcutta from August 1812 to June 1813."

2. Morse, F. R., *op. cit.*, pp. 114–115.

of my father will comprize M^r. Russell's adventure say R^s. 4500 — & 5000 R^s. more or less on my acc^t. which I shall consign to you — the two concerns in separate Invoices — how long my stay will be here must depend on circumstances — it may be long enough for you to write me after this comes to hand — which I most earnestly hope you will do — give me particular information as to the value of India goods & upon any other Subject that can in any way be useful — hitherto I have to complain of your neglect — I suppose you tho't I sh^d. learn from others all I wanted & spard' yourself the trouble — I pray that nothing will now prevent your complying with my wishes — write fully —

I consider my cargo as low charg'd — I think taking any article into consideration lower than the Gulliver's her 2^d voyage — my outward cargo disappointed me but I do not consider I was imprudent in taking it from England — there never was a time 'till now that it w^d. have fail'd giving a great profit —

Should no vessels have been despatchd' during the past year with merchandise for this place — an assorted cargo would do, but not a Sufficient object to found a voyage upon — the best articles w^d. be say 400 Barrels Tar — 1000 Gall^s Sp^ts. Turpentine — 10,000 feet Bay and S^t. Domingo Mahogany — for which 12 annas p^r. foot could be obtaind' — 300 kegs Salmon — sounds & tongues — 50 do Mackarel — 2000 Groce Corks — 100 — Spars or more — 20,000 feet of clear Boards — 20 pipes white 4^thproof Gin, in casks that will not stain the liquor — as all new casks will — casks sh^d. be well Secur'd with iron hoops — Brandy 25 Casks at 150 pGallon french — White Champaign wine at 12$pDoz. Sweedes Iron if to be had at 70$ pTon — pig copper at 20¢. plb a moderate quantity — No Madeira or any other wines unless very low — Sicily did well in the Francis' Cargo — but no more than 250 R^s can be safely calculated upon 22 @ 30 R^s. p 100 — with a breakage of 10% — Send Rum, cheese, cyder, Salt fish, or Iron hoops — a vessel with Such a cargo might stop at Madras & land Such articles as w^d. Sell there — but Calcutta is commonly by far the best market for everything

You will have consign'd to you about R^s 20,000 ofthe Reaper's Cargo — I hope you will not Sell an article by the Inv^o. price — M^{r}Russell's goods & my own I wish you to Sell on short Credit to undoubted men — I am of opinion an auction w^d. be best & if Jones does not ask too much — have the sales guarantied —

If you continue to speculate in Bengal Goods — I think you may venture to buy the Reaper's Invoices at the current rate of goods —

Indigo — the old is sold — new held @ 125/ @ 170/. — but few lots in market sh^d. the May Sale in England prove tolerable — it will rise & at any rate not be lower — crop short & Comp'y expected to buy 15000 M^{ds} — as much more will be wanted for India Captains & private traders — In your investment & F. & L's there will be some broken Indigo — the quality is good being mostly A pieces —

M^r. Newton seems to have manag'd your affair's at Madras with great address & good judgment & Ibelieve he feels rejoicd' that he has it in his power to render you a Service — he has been very communicative to me & given much information —

Sugar & ginger high — Gurrahs & Alliabad goods do — cottons will fall when the Portuguese have done buying — but not very low for some months —

Letters pCaravan —

Sep. 26th. J^{os} Lee — that I sh^d. remain in Calcutta — amount
          5000 R^s. —
          Shipd' & bal^n. retaind' —
"   M. Lee — Sep — to 27th —
"   O. Goodwin J^r. — in aswer to his p Union of March
     Caravan arrivd' in Salem, 16th March 1813.
     35 days from Pernambucca, at which place she touched
     for advice — she was taken possession of at the entrance of that place by a British ship, & recapturd' by
     some boats mand' by Americans from Ship Francis &
     other American ships at P. —

LETTER FROM HENRY LEE, CALCUTTA, SEPT. 22, 24, 1812, TO
ANDREW CABOT, BOSTON, ANNOUNCING PLANS IN CASE OF AN
EMBARGO [1]

On Oct. 12, Henry Lee wrote in similar terms to P. T. Jackson,
describing the cargo he intended to ship on the *Reaper*.

The anticipated embargo, to last for 90 days, had gone into effect
on Apr. 4 and had been followed on June 18 by a declaration of war
against Great Britain.

The "Estate of Sebastian" refers to the property left by Sebastian
Cabot, Andrew's brother, who died at the age of thirty on the *Reaper*,
May 17, 1812,[2] just before she reached Calcutta. Curiously, this is
the first reference to that event we encounter in Henry Lee's letter
books, but there is in the Patrick Tracy Jackson Collection a group
of papers relating to the "Estate of S. Cabot," 1813–17, and also
several references in the account books to P. T. Jackson as an
executor of the estate.

Caravan arriv'd 16th March

Mr Andrew Cabot   prCaravan   Calcutta Septr 22d 1812
  Dear Sir   *Dup pr Reaper*

I am still without any advices from you later than what
the Caravan brought.

The Frigate President arrived last night in 18 days from the
Isle of France, by this conveyance letters to the 4th. & newspapers to the 8th. April have been recd by Messs Alexander
&Co, who were obliging eno to send for me this morning &read
such part of their letters as related to politicks, under Date 4th.
April their correspondents says, "an Embargo was expected immediately &he apprehended a War with GBritain wd follow,"
I recd from them at the same time a file of papers from the
5th March to the 4th April which contain'd the debates in Congress upon Navy Bill, New taxes &c &c, the speeches are full
of wars, but I see no serious preparations on the part of the
Govts nor any diminution of the number of clearances or any

1. Jackson-Lee Papers, "H. Lee's Letters from Calcutta from August
1812 to June 1813."
2. Briggs, *op. cit.*, vol. i, p. 170.

other indications on the part of the merchants, of an expected war. An Embargo appears to be more probable. I think such men as Emott, Lloyd & Quincy w^d not have sent the information they did to the merchants of New York; unless they had good grounds for believing such a measure was in contemplation. I did hope that we should have had the last acts of our Legislature, for now I am as much perplex'd as ever to imagine what will be the final measures of government if an Embargo is imposed, some of the political speculators in the American papers seem to think the N I will be repeal'd, I hope to God their conjectures may turn out right.

After an anxious &mature consideration of what is most for your safety &interest &what I conceive you would do in my situation, I have resolved to dispatch the Reaper as soon as the remainder of her Cargo can be collected, &to remain behind myself with three quarters of the owners funds, one half of the funds belonging to the Estate of Sebastian &the whole of your private adventure say £1329..7..0. these several amounts (the whole of which I am not yet in Cash for) will be invested in notes with Company paper as collateral security, at the highest rate of interest that can be obtain'd, at present I am receiving 11 @ 12% &hope to be able to continue my loans at that rate. if peice goods should become dull sale, which they will do after the Portuguese sail, I may do a little better by advancing upon Cottons deposited as security, in which case I shall be careful that the value of the goods, if put up at Auction, exceed the amount advanced, I shall enter into no speculations nor make any engagements but such as will enable me at a days notice to have the command of my funds in case the N I should be repeal'd, or I should have further orders from you relative to the disposal of them.

In deciding between this alternative &remitting to Canton, I trust you will believe I cannot have been govern'd by any motive but a regard for your interest &that however it may result, I shall have the satisfaction of having my conduct approved of.

Your orders to remit to Canton were rec^d about the middle

of June, I deviated from them for reasons assign'd in my letter of July 7th. — when I bot. the Bill for Messs Perkins of Messs Palmer &Co. they agreed verbally that in case I shd want 50,000 Rps more within 30 or 40 days I might have it @ 190 Rs. since then they have sold @ 193/, &of late have refus'd to draw at any rate, of course as I did not apply within the time agreed upon, I can have no claim for the 50,000 Rps. there is no probability therefore [that — stricken through] at this moment that if I was disposed to remit, I could do it under 200 Rps pr 100 Sp Dolls &perhaps not at all — there is also another reason why I feel reluctant to making this remittance &that is the uncommon pressure (for money) among the best houses; many [interlineated: good] reasons are assign'd &perhaps they are the true ones, but I should be unwilling to Venture so large an amount as I have now at my disposal in the Bills of any house here that wd be likely to draw, the failure of Harrington &Co has alarm'd me &taken very much the confidence I shd otherwise have in five or six houses here. — if MrNewton shd have arrived you can learn from him what impression Harringtons failure produced at Madras, &what the thinks of the credit of India Houses. — that many of them are solid I have no doubts, but just now it is extremely difficult to seperate the secure from the doubtful. How long I shall remain here must depend on circumstances, especially upon the letters I may have from you written after the termination ofthe session of Congress, when I conclude to return I shall remit to Canton to Perkins &Co to whom no doubt you have written on the subject.

I have kept in reserve for the owners a selection of ps goods, in case I should have such intelligence as wd induce me to ship all their funds in the Reaper — I shall now distribute them among the shippers, it is with great regret circumstances compel me to do it, certain as I am of their selling at a great advance I shall hardly be able I fear to replace them in the event of my hearing of the repeal of the N I Law. certainly not for several months to come. The amount ship'd on account of the owners will be as near one quarter oftheir funds as circumstances will permit, say Twenty thousand Rps. the principal part of which will be in gruff goods as p^r memo forwarded, I cannot yet ascertain what room will be left after the shippers goods are on board, whatever there is, will be fill'd with such [(goods) — stricken through] drugs as I can get, &in addition Tumerick, Coffee &Gunny bags. I have been disappointed in many gruff articles, the Arabs did not bring large quantities, they hold them high. I shall add to the memo, some Copal &Galls if to behad.

The Union is expected to come on to Calcutta, by her I trust I shall receive letters. The Harmony will not get away in less than 4 mos, unless there sh^d be a great change in prices of goods for the better. The Portuguese confine themselves for the present to the purchase of Gurrahs &Blue Gillas &Alliabad goods, which has rais'd those articles very high. I think other Kinds are falling, but still prices high except for ordinary Baftas, Old Indigo has become Scarce &for new much higher is demanded, good merchantable quality such as the best we take home will not be less this season than 130 Rp^s. say some what inferiour to my 500 m^d lot. I think that parcel w^d bring 130 Rp^s just now. I shall ship you a few boxes of Indigo, some of it broken, but the quality good, the remainder say 120 M^{ds}. more or less which I have been collecting for the owners & myself one half each, I shall sell, presuming it will bring a profit.

It is very uncertain how long I remain here, but you had better write me by various channels how I am to act under the various circumstances I may find myself in on the receiving of your letters. Sh^d a permanent Embargo or War have taken place, what will you have me do? — there is no doubt of my being able to remit to Canton, somewhere about par, what funds I have.

Septr 23^d. I have just rec^d a packet of letters that came by the Union to Isle france, from thence in the Frigate I mention'd yesterday. I am sorry to find none from you — from the opinions express'd in the several letters, I have some little hopes that the N I Law may on this have been repeal'd &that I shall hear of it in season to ship the Property I retain behind in the Harmony or the Union, either of which vessels no doubt will be glad of freight atthe usual rate. I know the Harmony is in want of it, but am not certain at what rate they would take, nor w^d I put the question, least they should suspect I should want some, — India goods I see had risen, they will fall again before I arrive, but Still the R's Cargo must do well, the peace between Russia &GBritain will reduce Tumerick but still it must answer, in price in London is never less than what we can afford to sell at in Europe. I shall therefore depend principally on that article to fill up the Brig, if there sh^d be any room left. Septr 24th. 1812. M^rMaitland of the house of Palmer &C^o sent me word this morning that he had letters from LeRoy Bayard & McEvers of 4th. April, they give it as their opinion that an Embargo w^d be imposed, but no immediate danger of War. Robert Lenox has written to the same effect, this corresponds with my letters, & gives me hopes, tho' not very strong ones, that the N I may be repeal'd. I cannot hear of it however 'till after the departure of the Reaper. The expectation of an Embargo in U S produces no effect for the present because while ships continue to arrive they give no credit to any intelligence, no doubt when the Portuguese have completed their Cargoes goods will fall but not very low, unless there sh^d be a cessation of arrivals for some months. Gurrahs, Sooty Romals, Gillas & Alliahabad goods are higher than when I wrote last, other Kinds are on the fall, but not so low as I fear'd, Baftas excepted which are excessive bad. I shall keep myself inform'd of the state of the market to be ready to act as circumstances may require, but this is a place in which one cannot do much in piece goods without being observed, &the moment any news is rec^d every one is on the alarm. We have no later dates from England than the 10th. April, at that time there was no appearance of war with U. S. if our Gov^t make a permanent Embargo, one of the most powerful inducements they have had to keep the peace with us will [be — stricken through] have been done away, yet I do not beelieve they will revenge themselves in that way. I trust not.

The Talbot 20 days since was at the Isle of France, from whence she was going to Batavia, the James of Phil^a is at Batavia, she does not come this way, the Meridian I suppose is still at Madras. I hear of no other American Ships in this quater.

I have not yet purchased what more of Indigo I want, shall not wait, but make up the investment in Cottons. I have nothing to add to the list of Goods purchased, therefore do not send any.

Enclosed is a Memo of Gruff goods, to which some additions will be made. All my merchandize, Rum excepted, sold, that I shall keep on hand, the result will not vary from what I have stated say the cost of charges, sales not yet made up.

Spanish Dollars 210/ Bills on London 6 mos sight 2/6½ to 2/7d for best bills. the S Cargoes of the Harmony sold @ 2/6 .4 mos sight on 3 mos Credit, which estimating interest @ 1% pmo. is not quite equal to 2/7d 6 mos, the rate I sold for S H &Co — never rely upon American Bills in any voyage you undertake this way.

New Indigo comes down slowly, there is no doubt the Crop is quite short say less than 50,000 mds. the average crop may be call'd 70,000 mds, ifthe May sale in England is tolerable, the new will sell rather high, & at any rate not be less than 130/ to 140/ for merchantable American market Indigo — & 165/ @ 170/ for fine, Barettos Crop has been sold to the Captn of the Bengal (Companys Ship) at 170/ &several parcels are held at that price, it wd I imagine in our market bring 25₵ plb more than what I have purchased, unless the buyers as was the case of the Charons which sold so well in Russia, shd suspect it was not genuine — if you are an exporter of the article you may find among the Reapers if they will allow you to select, Indigo that is worth 160 Rps, the low Nos in each lot are the best, the whole is assorted.

P. S. Sunday 27th Nothing new —

LETTER FROM HENRY LEE, CALCUTTA, OCT. 1, 12, 21, 1812, TO
ANDREW CABOT, BOSTON, MENTIONING BANIANS' FRICTION
WITH CAPTAIN [1]

The training of the banians employed by Henry Lee, and that of
their sircars, is revelatory of certain inner aspects of the trade with
India. "Jepare," where the banian Tillock had acquired his knowledge of indigo, was undoubtedly Japara or Djapara in Java. The
identity of *"Prankissen* the Japender" is less easily determined. It
would seem at first glance that this man's title was an eccentric form
of "Japanese," and that he might have been a native of Japan who had
settled in India despite the Japanese prohibition of emigration. Since
the Japanese surpassed all oriental nations in textile manufacture, a
man trained in Japan should be "a good judge of piece goods." On
the other hand, though Prankissen does not sound entirely unlike a
Japanese name, it can be demonstrated to be definitely Hindu. The
possibility that Prankissen's title was a national designation is mini-
mized, and a new problem introduced, by a later reference to him as
a "Jessendar." Evidently there was a copyist's confusion between
"p" and "double s" (one long, one short). "Jessendar" was probably
the form most nearly correct, since "-dar" is a Bengali suffix expressing agency. Application to natives of India, skilled in Bengali, Hindustani, Hindi — even Gujerati and Andhra — brings no information as to the word in question, save that it is probably a Bengali
word so badly Anglicized as to be unidentifiable. At any rate a
"jessendar," from the context, was undoubtedly some sort of superior
specialized functionary in a Calcutta mercantile establishment.

Henry Lee's high praise of his banians' commercial ability did not
extend to their social qualities. In a letter to his wife he commented
that he saw "no one but my banians, who never had, nor ever will
have a thought except on business. Were the natives as well informed as they are civil and well bred, one would receive great
pleasure from their society, but their opinions are so confined, that I
can truly say I never derived half an hour's gratification from any
one I have been acquainted with. Nothing can be more uninteresting
than their characters." [2] Apparently the Babbitt, in some of his aspects, is not solely indigenous to twentieth century America.

The jealousy which sometimes existed between captain and super-

---

1. Jackson-Lee Papers, "H. Lee's Letters from Calcutta from August
1812 to June 1813."   2. Morse, F. R., *op. cit.*, p. 117.

cargo [3] comes out in this letter. Sometimes a supercargo was ordered not to give the captain any information as to goods and prices lest the captain, in filling up his privilege on board, might interfere with purchases and sales on behalf of the owners; this would always be a fruitful source of irritation. In the case of Capt. Nathaniel Spooner, Henry Lee laid most of the blame on "his intemperance" by which he had been "ruin'd forever," but went on to remark, "indeed without that vice he was unfit for any important charge." [4]

The "Holydays" here mentioned were the Dasahara, a Hindu festival in honor of Durga, which took place at the autumnal equinox.

Miss F. R. Morse assumes that the "Charles," whose care of Sebastian Cabot during his last illness is commended, was a Cabot,[5] but no one of that name can be discovered who seems to fit these circumstances. He was evidently a kinsman or close acquaintance of Andrew Cabot and Henry Lee. The strong probability is that he was Charles D. Miles, who later went out to India as supercargo for Henry Lee in the spring of 1817.

On July 7, Henry Lee had written to Andrew Cabot: "My outward cargo I am sorry to say will turn out to a loss." [6] The profit which he now discovered the outward cargo had brought must indeed have been a small one, since most of the consignments had fallen somewhat short of the invoice price and charges, and only the glass, bottles, ale, perry, and porter had fallen on the right side of the ledger.[7]

pReaper
Dup pr Harmony

Mr Andrew Cabot   Calcutta Octo 1st. 1812
Dear Andrew,
            Copied
    Annexd you have Copy of my last pr Caravan Captn. Heard, who left us three days since, I am told he is bound for

3. Hunt, *op. cit.*, vol. ii, p. 474.

4. Jackson-Lee Papers, "H. Lee's Letters from Calcutta from August 1812 to June 1813," Henry Lee, Calcutta, Mar. 21, 1813, to Francis Lee, Boston.   5. Morse, F. R., *op. cit.*, p. 161.

6. Jackson-Lee Papers, "Letters written in Calcutta from May to August 1812," Henry Lee, Calcutta, July 7–10, 1812, to Andrew Cabot, Boston (see above, pp. 1017–1035).

7. *Ibid.*, Henry Lee's account book, London, Sept. 30, 1811–Calcutta, Mar. 1, 1816.

Rio de Janeiro, thence as order'd. this is good news to me, because the Reaper must arrive before her, & give you an opportunity of selling such articles as will be likely to be affected by the large quantities on board the Caravan I suppose the Gum & Tumerick are intended for Russia; the Skins must of course be sold for consumption, the quantity in all the vessels together is great but as there must be a cessation for some time of further importations, I am in hopes they may do well. I imagine from the eagerness ofthe southern gentlemen to get them, that they are wanted in Phil^a & New York. The gums in the R are good. *Cassia* ordinary. Assafoetida middling, Sage good. Sal Ammoniac &Borax better than common, the first much lower than any I ever imported, the Indigo for the owners is of good quality, do not imagine otherwise from the price it is charged at, it was by mere chance I met with it. the Benares Sugar is new &of good quality, but I am persuaded it is the worst article in Cargo. I thought so when I bot it, but there seem'd nothing else that could be put in as ballast, the wood took up more room that we could afford, & of Sal Ammoniac I was afraid to increase the quantity. had I however thot' of retaining so large portion of the owners funds, I w^d have taken ballast, &it would have been more for the interest of the Owners than what I have now done, the gunny bags are ordinary, the goat Skins I imagine from their having been [plenty — stricken through] purchased while plenty, are rather better than the others shipped since, tho' they cost about 10% less. part were collected by one of our Sircars in the Country, the Tumerick is chiefly new & collected by a sircar, the quality I think you will find is good.

I am striving to get away before the Holydays which commence the 10th. have to day repack'd a parcel of Indigo & after rejecting about 1/3d. made a tolerable lot, tho' not so cheap as Barettos, there are 70 to 80 m^ds. I hope to add 50 or 100 more, but shall not wait for it.

I have not been able to get any freight nor have any passengers offerd except such as were too poor to pay us for taking them. Mr Russels letter of Credit has not enabled me to negotiate my Bills upon him. I was desirous of doing it because we have not stock enough especially since so large asum has been withdrawn, it was fortunate I got rid of those upon S H &C°, but it was a mere chance & you must never rely again upon Bills. let who will be the drawers.

Oct° 12th 1812 I was in hopes to have finish'd before the Holidays but we are interrupted by them, business commences again on the 19th. when every package will be ready, indeed they are now except a few bales to complete Higginson &Perkins' Invoices, tho reserving a large quantity of goods for the owners &the delay in receiving the contract goods, have been the cause of a months detention, but I never consider'd it for your interest we should make great dispatch, because I consider'd it as all important your property shd be return'd in the Reaper. & I thot' there was some chance Congress wd have repeal'd the N I Law the last session &that we shd have heard of it sometime early this month.

We have no later news than what came in Union to Isle of France, she has not yet reach'd this place, but is daily look'd for. I hope to hear something from England later than our present accounts from U. S. but not before the R sails. we are now six months without any thing from England. the probability of Russian war &the successes of English in Spain, I look upon it will have some effect on the present conduct of our Govt. which together with opposition at home will be sufficient to prevent a war with England.

The Harmony is the only vessel here besides the Reaper, she will remain two months at least, as yet they have pack'd only 30 bales. the Portuguese have not yet finished buying, when they have left Calcutta goods must come down to the prices I paid &fore some articles lower, unless a number of Americans in mean time shd arrive with heavy stocks, there are not many goods in market, but from the high prices paid for Gurrahs &c for 2 mos past, I am inclin'd to think large orders have been sent up Country for manufacture of Goods. &that in three or four months the market will be Well fill'd. Cotton has fallen & will go still lower which will operate to reduce prices.

Ginger is higher than I have ever known it. price 7/8 Sugar 8/4 this article will never answer, it is better to take stones for Ballast. *Gums* are not plenty except Copal, the Arabs brought large quantity. I w^d have shipped more but I Knew they are difficult to sell &while Indigo could be purchased at the average yours cost, I doubt if any gums or gruff articles will pay a greater p^rCentage than that article.

Cottons are so low that they occupy 50% more room than when I was here last. we sh^d have had very little room for gruff goods, unless I had gone largely upon Indigo &silks, of the latter I could have obtain'd only a small portion if our stay had been less than four months this is some consolation for so long a detention, I consider 20 tons of room saved, which will turn out worth $60 to $70 p^rton. I trust.

Oct^o 21st. 1812

The Holidays are over, we are ready, but the Pilot will not move till the 24th. on account of the tides. I have already given you the reasons which have operated upon me to remain behind, to which I have nothing to add but my sincere wish that the decision may result to your benefit. I have on hand 120 m^ds Indigo, half on your account & half on my own, a memo^o of which I shall send you. this lot I am now endeavouring to dispose of, &believe I shall be able to do it at a profit, tho' just now there is little doing in the article. the remaining funds of the owners are in notes of hand, &Cash, a payment of R^s 30,000 having been made me yesterday, the borrower refusing to renew the loan @ 11½% they borrow only for short periods at high rates of interest, but I have little doubt when at leisure to look up those who are in want of money of being able to loan all the funds now in hand at about 11%. still interest may fall & I may not four months hence be able to Get more than 8 or 9%. the natives, such men as Duloll tell me there are no subscribers to a loan lately open'd by Gov^t @ 6% &that in their opinion no one will subscribe 'till they raise the rate to 8%. I judge from this there is not much probability of rate of interest being much lower than it now is, besides there are several great houses who are yet in want of money &who pay 1% @ ¼% [1¼%?] pmo.

I have kept Chas with me because I thought it imprudent to be alone with such a large sum of money, in case of accident happening to me, Chas will be able to act under my directions, the expence of living will be very little more for two than one, indeed nothing but clothing & washing. it is my intention to take a small house unless I can let my go downs so as to reduce my present rent to 100 Rps pmo. in that case remain where I now am, the whole expence of living will be small.

I have already in my letters to Frank made all the observations I thought might be useful in the goods purchased for you, the quantity of Tumerick is greater than I wish'd to take, I was deceived in the room that wd remain after the shipment of the last piece goods, it was not my intention to have gone beyond 60,000 lbs. but there was room to be occupied & nothing offer'd but Tumerick or gunny bags, the latter are high & I have a great quantity, the last Tumerick which cost 3/7 is of better quality than either ofthe other lots, it is from Patna, most of it is in bags if you ship to Europe take this (it is between decks) &sell that which is in the hold, I have put into a muster box with the Indigoes a sample of the best kind.

I have no doubt Ginger will be wanted in U. S. but I do not believe it can rise so high as to make it profitable at the cost of 7/ @ 7/8 which would stand you duty paid $5 75/100, supposing it to be worth $11 pCwt & Tumerick 6 cts plb. the latter will be the most profitable. I thought at one time of taking 2 or 300 mds of Coffee, but I was afraid to hazard it, tho' I am inclined to think that article will be higher on the return of the Reaper than when we sail'd. I shall send you my Declaration before a notary, relative to the purchase of the goods from the natives, it will serve to make certificates &by lodging it with a notary you will be saved the trouble of going to the CuHo or notarys &swearing continually as to the origin of the Cargo.

With regard to the estate of S. C. I have retain'd the same portion that you advised shd be remitted to Canton, his Clothing I have sent an inventory of & also of his books, the Sextant

&many of the Books, or all of them, Captⁿ S. claims as his own. I do not therefore take possession of them. they are under Captⁿ S's charge, who no doubt will explain every thing relating to them, there is nothing of much value among them excepting your Sextant & Encyclopaedia. the Sextant is an excellent instrument &if you feel rich enᵒ to give away so valuable a thing I wish you wᵈ bestow it upon Charles, whose attentions to S while sick were unbounded &who contributed more to his ease & comfort than all the rest of us together.

The Bond for landing Cargo in US is sign'd by my Banians &Captⁿ Spooner, the time allowed is 5 years, the cargo actually on board consists of more packages than what are included in the bond, but the Certificate you send here to cancel it must be made conformable to the Bond.

I have been perfectly well satisfied with my Banians &have I think promoted your interest as well as that of the shippers by employing them in preference to any ofthe others. I have myself a good opinion of the characters of Tillock & Ramdon. I think them much more capable in their business than any ofthe others &they have every motive that can operate upon men desirous of establishing a reputation & acquiring wealth; to serve me faithfully, & I am satisfied they have done so &that you will be convinced of it equally with myself, there are somethings which make greatly in their favour which cannot be explain'd till we meet. In mean time I am exceedingly desirous you should do all you can to recommend them &that in any future voyages you undertake to this place, give your S Cargo orders to employ them, when I depart from the Country I will impress still more strongly than I have already done, the importance to their future success to serve you faithfully, they have to money to loan to Captˢ or S Cargoes, &this will operate much to prevent their employing them, some ofthe Banians &S Cargoes on my arrival indeavour to persuade me that as they were not rich the merchants wᵈ not bring goods into our godowns, so far from it that we had the preference, &for this reason, we made our payments punctually while it is the practice of others to delay 10, 20 or 30 days that they may have the benifit of the

interest. the address with which Tillock has mentioned the
C H° business has pleas'd me greatly & convinced me among
many other things ofthe great superiority of these two young
men over the other American Banians. Indigo they understand
particularly well. Tillock having lived 2 years in Jepare. &had
the charge of several factories.

In the purchase of Piece goods they rely principally upon
Prankissen the Japender that Ramchander Benerjia & after
him Lucknaut employd you remember him I dare say, he is
an exceeding honest fellow & a good judge of piece goods, their
other Sircars are Ramchanders old ones & as good as any in the
City. Tillock does the out door business, buys the Indigo &
takes charge of the C H° business. Ramdon Keeps the accounts
with me &with the Banker, & aids *Pran* in purchase ofthe piece
goods. he has not quite energy en°, but makes a good associate
with Tillock who has more of this rare quality than I have ever
seen in a Bengallee, he has excellent manners, &manages with
great address the natives who come to the Godowns — they
seem to rely upon you as one of their patrons & I hope they
will not be disappointed for they are deserving of your confidence in a much greater degree than you wd venture to place it
in any native of this Country. Captn Spooner they inform me
has threatend to use his influence to prevent their getting any
more business, how much may be ascribed to the passion ofthe
moment, or how much to a deliberate intention to put his threats
into execution, I cannot tell, but I really believe the greatest
&only charge Captn S can bring against them is their refusing
to neglect my concerns to attend upon his, &those too which
it was the business of a sircar to manage. I trust therefore any
thing he can say to their prejudice will be wholly disregarded,
when I assure you that ever since my arrival they have both
been occupied from an early hour in the morning till 10, 11
& 12 oClock, & that there has been every possible exertion
made by them to promote their interest &that ofthe concerned
generally. I shall furnish you with the proof ofit but without
the explanation which would do them the most credit, if it
could be made in a letter. In the purchase of my Cargo I con-

sider my chance as not having been so good as those of Captn
Pulsifer &Haskell they had no competitors part of the time,
some of my goods were bot' at the time ofthe Francis', part
during the time Mr Heard was purchasing &part after he had
done, I think we all of us had a better chance than he had I
have before sent you a memo of the cost of the Francis & Restitutions, & I now send that ofthe Caravans, which I must request
you to keep out of sight &not allow it to be known I sent it
to you. by comparing these several Inv^{os} you can judge whether
my Banians have done me justice, I w^d observe that I consider
my Gurrahs as the best that have been shipped &my Chintz
superiour to common kind, I imagine also the Baftas are better
than most [others — stricken through] that have been ship'd,
&that the colourd goods in general are better [than — stricken
through] because most of them were contract goods, the Band^s
are like the Bazar @ 112/, except some few cases that cost
less than the 104/12 ones.

I find there is a profit on the Cargo brot' from Bristol tho'
a small ones. I am exceeding sorry it is not greater, but we
have had 5000 @ 6000 R^{ps} more duties to pay than formerly
&we came to an overstock'd market, in addition to which most
ofthe cargo came out in bad order. I do not know whether it
was tho' any fault in stowing, or whether the goods were not
well pack'd, the Cheese perished in great measure for want
of air. I requested the after hatches might be left open, but
Captn S refused giving as reason that he was apprehensive
she w^d take in water. you are as good a judge as I am ofthe
sufficiency of such a reason, this article was taken upon the
particular reccommendation of Mr Newton, whose information
I consider'd as better than my own &it w^d have done well had it
come out in usual order, the Rum is still unsold, one cask
&little more has been used at sea &in port. the remainder I
shall keep on hand for better prices than can now be obtain'd.
I send you two boxes of Indigo musters, they contain those ofthe
Reapers Cargo as part of Captn Hinckleys, &some new Indigoes,
to give you an idea ofthe present prices. the article is dull
&probably may fall unless the Company soon commence buy-

ing. piece goods are falling fast, I shd not be surprised if the Harmonys cargo shd be lower than any purchased since I arrived, especially shd She remain here three months.

With regard to the Disbursments, those for the ship come of course under Captn Spooners direction he can give you such explanations as may be required, those for house I have indeavourd to make as small as possible, the wine bot at Madeira for the ship &house I was in hopes wd have lasted as long as my stay is like to be, but I am disappointed. I shall indeavour that my expences when the Brig has sail'd shall be small.

The interest due you cannot be adjusted at present, it shall appear in my next account Current, you will bear in mind that ofthe Cargo it was principally sold on credit, &that about 16 to 18000 Rs are still outstanding. I shall also have some other items to carry to your credit, for which I will give an explanation when we meet, in mean time I wish you to consider yourself as in great measure indebted to the zeal &intelligence of my banians for these savings.

The house rent which amounts to Rs 1400 is charg'd in prices of goods — I send you a price Current &c

LETTER FROM HENRY LEE, CALCUTTA, DEC. 23–25, 1812, TO ANDREW CABOT, BOSTON, DESCRIBING SITUATION AFTER NEWS OF THE REPEAL OF THE ORDERS IN COUNCIL [1]

Henry Lee, as soon as he heard of the embargo of Apr. 4, 1812, concluded that such a measure "just at this time wd distress the English considerably" by cutting off the supplies they would need for their armies in Spain and Portugal.[2] It now seemed that the repeal of the British Orders in Council had confirmed both his opinion of the effects of the embargo and his frequently expressed belief that war would not result. Henry Lee took advantage of this favorable turn in the international situation to ship some indigo by the *Harmony*, which cleared for Philadelphia, Dec. 28, even though he had heard nothing of the non-intercourse law's having been repealed.

1. Jackson-Lee Papers, "H. Lee's Letters from Calcutta from August 1812 to June 1813."
2. *Ibid.*, Henry Lee, Calcutta, Sept. 26, 1812, to Francis Lee, Boston.

THE WHARVES OF BOSTON, 1829

The letter below gives some idea of the various sources from which India goods were obtained, and of the persons involved. There is mention of the banians, the native merchants through whom the American supercargoes transacted most of their business; the silk merchants, with whom Henry Lee was trying to make contracts to furnish him goods on commission; the native weavers, with whom Lee intended, if necessary, to deal directly through his sircars, without intervention of silk merchants or banians. Henry Lee also refers to the bazaar where the native merchants displayed their goods and to the auctions by the East India Co. of goods rejected as unsuitable for the London market, which would, however, be quite satisfactory for the southern United States, the West Indies, or Africa. Then, too, there were the European houses of agency, which the East India Co.'s monopoly did not entirely exclude from the trade with India.

Henry Lee was always apologetic about his expenses. He had evidently been forced by the claims of hospitality to entertain lavishly other captains and supercargoes and perhaps resident merchants as well, to the great increase of his house expenses in the items of rum and wine. The remark that "of Saltpetre too the quantity used is excessive, but . . . had there been less, the quantity of Rum & Wine w^d have been greater" is at first perplexing until we learn that in Calcutta at this time saltpetre was used in cooling wine and other drinks, "which is rather expensive." [3] Henry Lee meant either that his guests would have consumed more wine had it not been cooled or else that by the use of cooling non-alcoholic drinks, such as sherbets, he diverted the attention of some from the rum and wine to which they would otherwise have devoted themselves.

Note that the *Union's* captain was also her owner.

Mr Andrew Cabot,   Calcutta Decr 23^d. 1812
   Dear Andrew   p^r. Harmony
        My letters of Novr 8th. & 19th & Dec 11th copies of which I send by this conveyance together with Copy of one to Frank, will inform you of the state of the market since the Reaper sail'd, on the 16th. inst we rec^d by a vessel that left Cadiz on 1st. Augt. the Orders in Council of 23^d June repealing those of 1807 &1809, which I presume was follow'd by a repeal on our

3. Roberdeau, Henry, "A Young Civilian in Bengal in 1805," *Bengal: Past and Present*, vol. xxix, pp. 114, 144.

part of the Non Int & Embargo laws. I am not sanguine that it was done immediately, but however much disposed our Gov^t may be to keep up a hostile disposition among us towards GBritain, I conceive it so much for the interest of the country not to go to war that we shall at all events have a temporary settlement, &I think it very probable the President issued his proclamation soon after receiving notice of the repeal &that in 20 or 30 days there will be arrivals from U S. I am sorry this event had not been delay'd for 2 or 3 mo^s, in which time Cottons w^d have fallen they had began to come down in their prices, but this news which the natives understand very well, together with the arrival of 2 Portuguese &one Spaniard, making in all 6 buyers besides Captn Chardon, rais'd prices 3% @ 6 @ 7%, & I see no chance of their falling unless our N I Law. should be continued some months longer. the natives are at the Banks hall constantly waiting for the report of an American, & as soon as one appears the holders of piece goods will raise the prices, &should the usual number come buyers must pay at least 10% higher than goods are now held at. I hardly know how to act, I am afraid to buy least the Law should not be immediately repeal'd, in which case I loose the Interest, &pay more for goods than I should to wait, on the other hand if I wait 'till the Americans arrive I shall have to give higher prices than I think the prospects will warrant. I am of opinion Cottons will be low in U S. from the moment the N I Law is repeald, & continue so 'till our importations are diminish'd, I have ventured to offer 51/ for 10,000 p^s Meergungees 38 + 1 ¾ ⅞, which is the cheapest article by far on market, &52/ for Baftas, but the former are held @ 55/, the latter at 53/ I am somewhat apprehensive the last article will be low in U S. so many have been carried home in the Boston & Salem Ships & also in the Harmony, there is no other cloth that I w^d venture to buy even if I was sure the Americans w^d arrive, unless it was with a view to sell again, &that is difficult from the obstacles the Banians would throw in the way, as to Super Cargoes they really have little to do in their business, &indeed the mode of doing business is such that one must necessarilly be very dependant, tho' not so entirely as most of my country-men are.

I mention'd in some of my letters of which you have Copies by the Harmony, that Raw Silk had fallen &that consequently Bands. wd be lower, this is the case, & I have been in treaty with the Silk Merchants for 3 or 4 days, they will agree to buy on Commission & think they can deliver at about 92/ pCo. but I wish to enter into a contract that I may not be disappointed, but if they will not do that, I shall send a sircar into the Country &buy of the weavers &hope to have them bot' at 91/ to 93/, there is some uncertainty as to the time & quantity that may be had in this way, but I have a good opinion of the article &no other way can be found. it will not do to get them in the Bazar indeed they are not to be had there in any quantities, &the price 10 Rps pCo more. I shall also get some Sistersoies & Lungees if the time required to make them should not exceed two &half months, I hope before the Harmony sails to let you know the result of my negotiations with the Silk Mer-chants, I purchased on the 17th. 400 ps of Company Bands. at auction of Companys rejected goods, they average 115/ &if they should turn out equal to the musters I had an opporty of examining, I shall think them very cheap. I intend to ship them by the first vessel that sails after I hear of the repeal of the N I Law, &that no doubt will be the Union for NYork.

I have ventured upon shipping your part of the Indigo of which I sent you an Invo pr Reaper. it is cheap & I hope will sell readily either at NYork or Phila. I shd advise you to push off all the Indigo you may have on hand, it is low &without doubt the Americans will go largely upon it. & I think the houses of Agency will make some shipments, &perhaps to a considerable extent, none will come cheaper however than that of the Shippers in the Reaper. you may rely upon it, &those who want better must pay 140/ @ 165/ the fine qualities are higher in proportion than the ordinary.

I paid freight on the Harmony at $75 pton & drew on Mr Remsen to whom the Indigo is consigned, for the payment, they demanded Rs 125 payable here, or $75, in U S. I think it probable I may invest a considerable amount in Indigo &ship on the Union Captn Chardon now demands 150 R^s paid here, but he will come down unless Palmer &C^o sh^d load him as he has hopes.

I w^d not give more than R^s 100/ unless for Indigo &Silks. & I think it so important to get them early to market, that I w^d go to 125 R^s rather than lose the opport^y of shipping. the Indigo in the H'y is in your name, (& I shall use no other because the ships papers, Inv^o &c are so) but for the account of the owners of the Reaper.

With regard to insurance, whether for yourself, owners, or Sebastians Estate, you had better say ship or ships, as it is uncertain by what ones I may send the goods, probably in two or three different ones. I believe there have been no french Cruisers, since the capture of the Isle France to the eastward of the Cape GHope.

I send duplicates of all my accounts, I have not yet come to a final settlement with my Banians, nor shall be able to for some time, as they have not settled with their contract merchants &c, but you may calculate upon 3 or 4,000 R^ps more to your credit for interest &c. The Ships Expences I leave Captn S to explain, those of the house I indeavour'd to have as small as possible, but I must confess those for wine, I sh^d be ashamed of had it been in my power to have controul'd them, the consumption of that article was enormous, but I could not prevent it without adopting measures which w^d have been extremely unpleasant of Saltpetre too the quantity used is excessive, but I am not sure but there was economy, had there been less, the quantity of Rum & Wine w^d have been greater. I shall make some deductions when I come to a final adjustment with the owners, the House expences & Ships Disb^ts. differ from the originals as charged in my acc^t. I shall have occasion to alter them again.

I have already sent you Inv^o of all the Cargoes that have been pack'd since my arrival, I now send a Mem^o of the cost of the Harmonys as far as I have been able to obtain, the Alliabad Goods are lower than the R's, but not so much as they appear to be. those in the Harmony are not the real Alliabad, the lowest charged are rejected. I do not myself think they will be very profitable, formerly Alliabad Mamoodies, Emerties &c were of an excellent fabric now they are coarse &uneven, the Band^s. @ 110/ are somewhat better than the R's but will not sell for any more, the Baftas are inferiour, I have seen them, the Col^d goods are all higher, as are the Tandas. the S Cargoes of the H could not get any Gurrahs, the article is still high &will continue so 'till the Portuguese are out ofthe market.

Dec 24th 1812

The Harmony has no Tumerick, about 40,000 Goat Skins 20 to 30,000 Gunny bags, a quantity of twine, on the shippers &owners account 400 M^ds Indigo, & as much more on freight for persons here no gums of any kind, nor ginger which .still continues high, as does Sugar.

The Union is now in dock, I do not think it possible she can get away sooner than the 10th. to 15th. Feby. I shall certainly send some Indigo in her. & all the Silk goods I may have purchased & rec^d in season, &if the freight sh^d not exceed 100 R^s pton, I shall ship some Cottons, part of the balance & perhaps the whole due to the Estate of Sebastian I shall ship in her & some on your private account, she is a good vessel, Copper'd, &sails well. the owners is Captain & is an excellent navigator, the Union is Now in Dock *for new Coppering*, she has new suit of sails & a new Cable, &may be consider'd in every respect as good a risk as the Reaper, better in some respects.

I have had the Silk merchants with me to day, but done nothing. they will not consent to make a contract 'till they hear from the Country, from whence they expect letters in two days. I have also been examining some Baftas, the quality is bad &price 2 R^s higher than I will give. I cannot get any Meergungees under 55/. I w^d go as high as 53/ for 5 or 6000 p^s, part of which I sh^d make into Chintz I shall look round for some Indigo, but not purchase 'till I hear of the repeal, as that article will not be rais'd much, if any, by the arrival of the Americans.

Decr 25th. 1812

I have seen the Silk Merchants to day, one offers to contract at 98/ or buy on Commission at 94/, this will not do. I hope to do better with another who has written to his principal in the Country &expects an answer tomorrow or next day. I have also had the Barnagore merchants, to see if I could make a contract for Checks &Sooty Romals, they offer 22/ for what I paid in R's Cargo 20/ & 26/ for Sooty Romals that cost 22/4. Gillas & Custers in proportion, I shall do nothing in these articles. I have also look'd at three lots of Baftas for which 53/ is demanded, the quality is so bad, &such great quantities have gone, that I am afraid of them. I shall buy Meergungees at 53/ if they can be had, this article has been down in price so long, that no more will be manufactured 'till it rises. I think it the cheapest Cotton in market, &the reason it has not advanced is, the Portuguese will not touch narrow goods, &the SCargoes of the Harmony have avoided it. I know it is now down in U S, but those now in Calcutta are wider &finer than the ones shipped last year &will be more likely to sell at $2.75 than some other goods that cost 65/ to 75/. the bulk they occupy makes the freight come high, that applies to all Cottons now in market, there are no fine ones.

LETTER FROM HENRY LEE, CALCUTTA, JAN. 20, 1813, TO ANDREW CABOT, BOSTON, ANNOUNCING ARRIVAL OF THE DECLARATION OF WAR [1]

It had taken nearly seven months for news of the declaration of war by the United States against Great Britain to reach Calcutta. This fact illustrates the necessity for the frequent urgings to "write by all opportunities" found in the commercial correspondence of the day, to which counsel Henry Lee evidently himself conformed, judging from his list of letters and routes.

On hearing the unanticipated news of war Lee seems to have given himself up to despair, so far as the goods he had recently shipped were

---

1. Jackson-Lee Papers, "H. Lee's Letters from Calcutta from August 1812 to June 1813."

concerned. "The *Reaper*," he wrote to his wife, "will be captur'd in all probability." Assuming that she would be captured, he announced, "The *Reaper's* voyage will be a bad one unless Andrew has made insurance, and even then it is probable the offices will not be able to pay more than 10/ in the £ — even the best of them." Again he wrote, Apr. 21, 1813: "The *Reaper* has long since, I doubt not, been in the hands of England. She was taken in the West Indian latitudes or off our coast." [2] But Lee was too pessimistic as to the fate of vessels from Calcutta which were at sea at the time of the declaration of war; all the vessels which sailed from that port for the United States during 1812 seem eventually to have reached a home port in safety.

> pLady Carrington arrived 10th Nov
> Dup pr. Portuguese Brig Invega
> — via Rio de Janeiro or Lisbon —

Mr Andrew Cabot   Calcutta Jany 20th. 1813
   Dear Sir,
   On the 14th. inst a vessell arrived from England with accts to 6th Augt. by her we have the Declaration of War by U. S. against GBritain & Ireland, an event very unexpected by me. I have never been wholly without fears that war wd eventually be the result of our hostile conduct towards England, but I did not suppose the time yet arrived, nor can I imagine now what end our Govt can hope to accomplish, certainly nothing but a revolution in our own Country, &there appears too large a party opposed to them to give much chance for the success of such a project. I see by a statement of votes in Congress, that the minorities in both houses are large, &we are told the news exicted very general &mark'd disapprobation in New York &Boston. I cannot but hope therefore, considering all things that on the news of the repeal of the orders in Council reaching, a negotiation will be open'd, which will terminate in a settlement.
   Should war have been continued it is probable the Reaper will be captured as well as most of the other Ships I have written by, some of my letters however I hope will reach. I have sent

2. Morse, F. R., *op. cit.*, pp. 126, 131, 147.

3 or 4 via London, 4 via Rio Janeiro, 2 Isle of France, 1 via Batavia, besides the direct conveyances. I annex a statement of the amt of Invo ship'd on acct ofthe owners in the Reaper & Harmony, it is unfortunate I did not adhere to my resolution of making no further shipments after the R sail'd 'till I heard of the repeal of the N I Law, but I cannot reproach myself with acting imprudently, when every thing concurr'd to induce a belief that a settlement wd certainly follow the repeal of the orders in Council, & I presume from letters down to the last May which have been recd here sometime since from Phila. that the measure was as unexpected with you as it was to me.

Soon after the San Fernando arrived, which vessel brought us the repeal of the orders in Council, I contracted for 3000 ps Bands @ 95/ & forother 2000 ps @ 91/ to be bot on Commission, I purchased 4000 ps Mamoody @ 51/8, the mamoody had not been paid for, the merchants consented to take it back, &the Silk merchants have agreed to annul the contract except for such as may already have been bot' when notice reaches their agents in the Country. I am in hopes there will have been only a few hundred ps engaged, the only goods I have on hand are 400 ps Bands bot' at Companys sale ½ on my acct & ½ on owners, & a few hundred pounds of Nutmegs, both can be sold again without loss, the goods I bot' & contracted for were cheap, in the event of a settlement I doubt if I shall do so well, unless some time elapses before the Americans arrive, all the merchants have an idea that as soon as things are settled a great number of ships will come out & of course they raise their goods upon the slightest rumour of such an event.

There are three Portuguese & one Spaniard purchasing Cottons, they want together 3000 bales, as soon as the news of war arrived they suspended buying unless at a reduction of 10% in prices, this the natives refuse doing, so that just now nothing is going on in the Bazar. the holders of Cottons are very much depress'd & will no doubt in few days come down 4 or 5% &should the war be continued &no hope exist of a settlement, they will fall very low, this will not continue however for a long time, because the present prices are below what the goods cost.

Raw Silk is not affected by the cessation of our trade nor Indigo, tho' the latter article w^d rise a little, especially the ordinary Kinds sh^d three or four Americans arrive, at present the fine Kinds are more in demand than for some time past, the accounts from England are more favourable than was expected, I shall do nothing till I hear from England or America the effect produced by the news ofthe repeal ofthe orders in Council, I am afraid that will be some time first.

There is only one ship here (American) the Union of New York, she is seized, no Cargo on board, the Harmony left her pilot the 1st Jan^y, Reaper 1st. Novr. the Caravan for Brazil about 1st. Oct^o. Tartar in Septr. Monticello &Calcutta in Augt. Francis in July, Restitution 1st June.

I am under no apprehensions at present that Gov^t will sequester property on shore, our Gov^t I fear will that of British property, &in that case the Eng^s Gov^t I suppose w^d retaliate, I shall however guard myself if possible

Should the war have been continued you will of course write me via Eng^d & Rio Janeiro, Maderia &c. I shall continue to write via London, but the letters will be 7 or 8 mo^s on their way.

The enclosed Acc^t Current will present to you the state of the owners concern at the departure of the Reaper, to the balance you may add 3 or 4000 R^ps for interest &c &c. on the back of the account I have stated the balances due your private account &the Estate of S Cabot.

Money is still scarce, I am getting 1% &something more for part of your funds. my expences however will reduce the rate to 6% or 7%, have so small a capital the charge is heavy, I live with all possible economy, my table expences do not exceed 1 R^pe p^r day, but house rent you know is high, &one cannot do without a certain number of servants. I w^d go into private lodgings if it was possible to find them, but I have tried without success to get a place. Charles will remain with me. I have sold the Rum at an average of about 2/8 p^r gall^n. there is nothing from our Country much in demand, Naval Stores there is an abundance of tho' they will rise after a while should there be no settlement.

The amount of Shipments p^r Reaper will be seen in the enclosed A/C, as also those p^r Harmony for A Cabot &the Estate of S Cabot, there is on board the Harmony for the owners 15 Chests of Indigo, cost S^a Rp^s 6202..13..0

There are no American ships at Madras, the Meridian sail'd 3 mo^s since for Canton, Captn Woodwards Clerk remains at Madras with Captn W^s property, he having been appointed one of his executors by Captn W previous to his death, the freighters property is consignd to Perkins &C^o Canton.

As it is possible none of my letters have reached, I w^d observe that your various letters down to March & Franks to April 8th. have been rec^d. &that I have not remitted any thing to China, nor do I intend to do it. The Reapers cargo is low charged. I think your Inv^o will sell @ 100$\cent$ @ 110 ^{cts}. the Rp^e I mean Indigo &Cottons, there is 80,000lbs Tumerick cost 2/8 to 3/4 pm^d. a quantity of Skins Gums &c all low charged, the Brig leaks & I am afraid will damage. I w^d not be in haste to abandon the Cargo, the vessel is much out of repair &worth not more than half what you estimated at when she sail'd, this for your government in case of detention &c

Say to Mess^s Perkins I wrote their house in Canton via Penang it is probable however the news will reach sooner than my letters.

You will no doubt long since have heard of the loss of the P Adams of Boston, in the China Seas.

Yours as ever
(Sign'd)   H Lee

James Russell

Jan'y 31st. 1813 — Wrote him p^{r}Lady Carrington in answer to his of Ap^l. 14th. 1812 —

Postscript to letter to A Cabot of 20th. Jany 1813
pLady Carrington
Jany 30th. 1813   arrived 10thNov^r
Dup. p Portuguese Brig Triunfo deInvege
via Rio de Janeiro —

An opport^y offering by the Steward ofthe Reaper who was left in the Hospital, I avail my self ofit to send with this the

Invoices of shipments made in the Reaper &Harmony, for owners, yourself &the Estate of Seb^n if the war is continued I shall send a dup^t sett of accounts with the sett of Bills Lading via London.

We have nothing from England since I wrote on the 20th. in the course of a month I expect to hear what effect the repeal of the Orders in Council produced in U. S. I have heard from the Silk Merchants, only 2 or 300 p^s of Band^s had been purchased &those I am in hopes they will not oblige me to take. Goods have not fallen much, they will however if the war should continue. Indigo is low, I shall not buy any for you however till I know every thing is settled. I have paid the Steward his wages.

Thos Williams is indebted for some expences incurr'd in his sickness which I shall send you an account of, with the files of accounts I intend to send via London.

I pray you to write me in the event of the wars continueing, I am apprehensive my health will not admit my remaining for a long course of time in this hot climate.

Yours

(Sign'd)   H Lee

LETTER FROM HENRY LEE, CALCUTTA, JAN. 30, 1813, TO P. T. JACKSON, BOSTON, EXPRESSING HOPE FOR A DISRUPTION OF THE UNITED STATES [1]

Nothing can more strikingly illustrate the animosity of the Federalist merchants of New England against the South and West, the Republican Party, and the War of 1812, than this desire for secession on the part of one of their representatives, apparently not a man of conspicuously fiery temperament. In a letter of Feb. 22, 1813, to his wife, Henry Lee wrote: "If we were united in New England, and New York w'd join us heartily, the Western States might have the war to themselves. We must one day or other separate and since things have gone so far, the sooner it takes place the better. The Northern section w'd soon have the ascendancy and control over the

---

1. Jackson-Lee Papers, "H. Lee's Letters from Calcutta from August 1812 to June 1813."

others, and thus govern instead of being governed by a people half civilized." [2]

Calcutta Jany 30th. 1813

pLady Carrington

M^r P T Jackson   Saild from Madras
March 15th.

Dear P,   and at London
10 Nov

On the 14th. ins^t we rec^d the Declaration of war by U S against GBritain, much to the surprize of every one in this quarter, &to none more than myself I never imagined any decided measures w^d be taken 'till the session of 1813, &the repeal ofthe Orders in Council (which we rec^d 6 weeks since) I concluded w^d open the way to a settlement or at any rate prevent hostilities, but it seems I have been mistaken &our wise Gov^t have at last brought us to the desired point, miserable wretches! what can they expect to accomplish but their own &their Countrys ruin? I have Strong hopes that on the arrival of the repeal of the Orders in Council, the peace party will be strong en^o to compell the Gov^t to negotiate & that every thing captured on both sides will be restored, this was the expectation in London the 7th. Augt. to which time our acc^{ts} extend.

Should the war have been continued God only Knows what may be the consequences, you & all other commercial men largely in trade I suppose will be ruin'd, the only good effect which can result will be the seperation of States, &that is quite uncertain. I hope with all my heart it may happen, the evils attending such an event cannot be greater than being subjected to the controul of the Southern &Western States.

My situation is unpleasant, but on the score of interest I am better off than if I embark'd in the Reaper
I hope &trust Insurance was made on my property &M^{r}Russells, tho' you write in such a way as to leave me in doubt if all was done, I made a shipment unfortunately on board the Harmony which I fear will be uninsured. mine as well as the owners.

2. Morse, F. R., *op. cit.*, p. 132.

I send you Invoices of my Shipments &also yours. E A Newton has with him all the bal^{ce} due you in Madras, save the shipment in the R. he saild from Madras 26th or 27th Augt for NewYork. I suppose the Reaper will be captured &the Harmony also, in which case you will have no Bill Lading, I suppose however the Inv^o I now send will be sufficient proof of property to claim ofthe U Writers. the am^t for J Russell is S^{a}R^{ps} 1605..1..10 & S^{a}R^{ps} 1766..8..5. this is in J Lees name & included (if my instructions were observed) in policy with J L's, I have on my acc^t in J Lees name in the Reaper as follows.

Inv^o piece goods	S^{a}R^{ps}	2595..12..1	
Indigo		4059.. 7..7	
Gum Copal		226..10..6	6881..14..2
p^r Harmony Inv^o Indigo			2091.. 3..3
		S^{a}R^{ps}	8973.. 1..5

If war is continued I shall send Duplicate accounts for owners & Shippers via England, including one sett of bills Lading which remains with me.

You will of course write me via England &c &c any thing which may be interesting or useful, for if the war continues. I do not see but I must remain here, I have a few thousand R^{ps} of goods on hand for owners & about 100 M^{ds} of Indigo on my own account which I shall sell. Goods have not fallen much, but they will be low in 6 mo^s if the war is continued.

LETTER FROM HENRY LEE, CALCUTTA, FEB. 14, 1813, TO P. T. JACKSON, BOSTON, WITH SUGGESTIONS FOR BUSINESS IN CALCUTTA DURING THE WAR [1]

On Mar. 6, 1813, Henry Lee wrote to his brother Francis on the same subject, mentioning some additional details. "If you engage in this project," that is, send an agent to India to loan funds during the war and invest them at its close, "by all means direct your agent to employ Ramdon & Tillock Bonerjia, who are doing my business, it

1. Jackson-Lee Papers, "H. Lee's Letters from Calcutta from August 1812 to June 1813."

is to them I owe my success in getting so cheap a cargo. . . . I mention these things that my Banians may have some little credit for their fidelity to me & to your interest." The virtue of these banians stood out in even brighter colors than life, against the gloomy background furnished by the conduct of some of their colleagues. "Do not send any one this way relying upon a credit from the natives," Henry Lee warned, "& give positive orders that he should not take any from any one if offer'd. Pat has a great opinion of Duloll, but he does not Know him, or he has changed his character, the other banians are still worse, they have imposed greatly upon every S Cargo that ever came here, & will continue to do it."

p^r Castle Huntley
care of Ch^s Williams.
Sail'd from S^t. Helena June
arriv'd Portsmouth August 8th

M^r P T Jackson   Calcutta Feby 14th. 1813
D^r P

By an arrival yesterday from London we have acc^{ts} to 29th. Septr I have indulged very sanguine hopes hitherto that when the repeal of the Orders in Council was Known in America, a negotiation w^d be open'd & follow'd by a settlement. I did not suppose the Gov^t desirous to make peace, but I thought the people w^d be clamorous especially at the northward, &that Madison would feel himself compell'd to abandon his plans. the dates from America are to the last of Aug^t. &it appears the repeal was Known, but was not follow'd by a cessation of hostilities, still however, I do not dispair of a speedy termination to the war, tho' my fears are greater than my hopes.

I enclose you with this copies of the Invoices of Goods shipped by me in the R for yourself (J Lee for J Russell) J Lee for H L, & also an Invoice of Indigo ship'd in the Harmony, these documents will be sufficient to enable you to recover from the Underwriters, should none of the sett, I forwarded direct be received. My remaining behind with so much property proves to be a fortunate thing &it w^d have been still more so, but for a shipment made in the Harmony, after hearing the repeal of the Orders in Council.

I shall remain here at present, but if the war is like to continue it is probabe I shall deposit my funds in the hands of some house here & proceed to England, the climate does not agree with my health, Otherwise I sh^d have no objection to remain 'till the war was terminated.

If you or any of our friends should have money in England & can do nothing else with it, or if it should not be safe in U States, you might get 8% p^r annum &perhaps 10% or 12%, by remitting it here &when the war is at an end make a profitable investment, in such case a prudent agent sh^d be sent out with orders to live at not exceeding 150 R^ps pm^o. a passage may be obtain'd in England, on board the private ships if the trade is open'd, otherwise in some of the extra Ships. I pray you to write me via England, Madeira, Rio Janeiro, Isle of France, or any places to which conveyances may be found.

I have made $2 or $3000 upon purchases of liquors &c &sh^d have done still better, but I sold out before the war was Known, thinking the repeal of the Orders in Council w^d certainly make way for an adjustment.

There are no vessels in this quarter but the Union, she will of course be condemn'd as soon as orders are rec^d from England.

Y^rs truly

(Sign'd)   H Lee

LETTER FROM HENRY LEE, CALCUTTA, NOV. 14, 1813, TO FRANCIS LEE, BOSTON, ON GENERAL BUSINESS MATTERS [1]

This letter to Henry Lee's brother Francis, who was acting as his agent in Boston, was written at a time when Henry Lee was at once cheered by the arrival in the United States of two cargoes in which he was concerned and rendered somewhat less hopeful of peace by the news of Napoleon's invasion of Russia. He had, however, determined to remain in Calcutta till peace. This raised the question of how his stay should be rendered profitable. He had tentatively considered investing in coffee and in baftas, but the uncertainty of the international situation had prevented him from going further. In the meantime he

1. Jackson-Lee Papers, "Letters written in Calcutta by H. Lee from July 1813 to March 1816."

had lent his available funds at an interest of 1% per month. This high rate and the possibility of profitable investments in case of peace made him anxious to increase his funds, which accounts for the request below that his returns from the *Reaper* and *Harmony* should be remitted. A bill on London for £10,000, at first refused, had been finally paid, but fifteen days before he received word of this fortunate result (Sept. 15) his banians, in whom he had expressed the utmost confidence, having involved themselves in unfortunate speculations absconded with funds to the amount of 25,000 or 30,000 rupees, though they later endeavored to make restitution.

"Dustory" is one form of a word meaning "commission."

p^r H.M. S. Sterling Castle
Arriv'd at C. G. Hope
18th February.

M^r F Lee   Calcutta Novr 14th. 1813
    Dear Frank
        I have had the satisfaction of learning, within a few days, the Safe arrival of the Reaper &Harmony the latter vessel is mentioned in a letter 'from Lisbon of 29th. May, the writer says he saw the fact mention'd in a New York Paper of 20th. May. The R's arrival comes in a letter from S Williams to Palmer &C^o. he says the Caravan &Reaper arrived in Boston 16th. March. I am almost afraid least he should have meant the Tartar, as I have seen a Boston Paper to 27th. March, & there is no advertisement of R's Cargo. tho' several of the shippers have long advertisements, and it is usual on such occasions to put in every thing. I shall be most happy to have a confirmation ofthis unexpected good news, for I never indulged a hope she would escape.

I am disappointed at being so long without letters, more especially as I was very urgent in my letters p Caravan, to have you, Pat &others write, tho' I had not at that moment Scarcely [written across face of the letter:] Arriv'd in England May 1814. any expectation of remaining here long enough to receive them. — Our accounts from America come down to May 15th. @ 20th. but the extracts from our papers are so scanty &there

are so many rumors & conjectures afloat, that I can form no opinion as to the actual State of things with you, &prospect for the future. I am extremely desirous of letters. I am less sanguine than I was, of a Peace some time, next Session of Congress, yet I do not dispair, the defeat of the Allies will no doubt encourage our Government to go on with the war. I shall remain here 'till there is a Peace. You will of course continue to write me, &send duplicates. write via Madeira, nearly all the ships from England &Portugal stop there. write also via Pernambuco & Rio de Janeiro & *Bahia*.

If it is true that the R has arrived, &her voyage should prove a saving one. You may be inclined to undertake an enterprize this way, as soon as Peace takes place. I should advise you to remit your funds thro' London in Bills, and as it is possible I may not be here when they arrive, direct Mr Williams to send them to Mess^s Cruttenden & MacKillop, with orders to hand them over to me, should I be here. in that case the amount will remain in their hands 'till the arrival of your vessel, to the SCargo of which, you can give an order, to receive, or if you do not send a vessel of your own, then to any other SCargo you may think best. they will allow a fair interest, say from 6% @ 8%.

This may perhaps strike you as a scheme of too much hazard for you & our friends, but I do not view it in that light. the Money will be safe, &there will be an interest accumulating at as high or higher rate than is obtain'd in America. You will gain upon the Exchange with London, & if I am here, you may calculate upon a better investment than can be made after the ships arrive. I have mentioned C &M because they are remarkably prudent & their concerns are smaller &more within their Controul than those of some other houses Alexander &C^o and Palmer &C^o are also safe. &so are the other houses which I have mentioned in my letters. Do not fail in your letters to give me the most minute information upon India goods of every discription, whether you remit or not. it will be useful to me. I think there are many articles from the

Country which ours will be bare of, if the war continues 2 or three years, and that the first Cargoes which arrive, if properly selected will do well.

The long expected Portuguese have arrived. there are 5 Ships here & two more on the way. I have not been able to ascertain their funds, but I do not imagine they have more than 12 or 15 lacs of Rupees. they have made but few purchases. Piece goods have not risen, but the quantity in market will be reduced very much, unless new goods Come down. as yet very few have been imported. the Arabs will take away 1000 or more bales, and small parcels are purchased for the Eastern trade.

Raw Silk has fallen still lower than my last quotations. I suppose Bandannas might now be contracted for at 85/ pC^o. like those of the Reapers. there are a few thousand pieces in the Bazar for which they ask 100/ or more. — Colour'd goods might now be obtain'd on contract something less, than what I paid for the Reapers, except Chintz I should find it difficult to get such cheap Cloth as I did last year, the Meergungees are all sold for Consumption.

Indigo of fine qualities is higher than last Year, but the middling and ordinary Kinds may be had for 100 to 130/ pm^d. & I might collect among the natives some small parcels at 80/ to 100/. the Crop turns out better than was expected, but still 20,000 M^{ds}. short of the average.

I should like to have the proceeds of my shipments in the Reaper &Harmony remitted to me, in my absence to go into the hands ofCruttenden &McKillop. in that case you can agree with some of the SCargoes that may be coming this way, to invest them for a Commission &ship them at 100/ p^{r}ton or whatever they can get them freighted at. I shall lose the whole benefit of my stay here without I have a larger capital of my own. I have no means of borrowing here. My Banians of course cannot do anything to aid me. I am settling my affairs with them, selling their lands & collecting their debts. they will have no means of paying my balance of say 6 or 8000 Rupees unless there should be a vessel sent out to me, since no other person besides myself or Mr Hall would employ them. Notwithstanding their imprudence in trading. &loaning money without my Knowledge &consent and consequently involving themselves in a loss which must fall upon us, I still consider them as better able &more disposed to serve their employers than any of the other Banians. tho' from their poverty &past imprudence, they should not be trusted with money. I shall continue to do business with them, by which means I shall diminish the debt they owe, by keeping the Dustory. This must be a consideration with you in undertaking a voyage to Calcutta. they are perfectly competant to the transaction of business, &I have not been able as yet to find anything dishonest in their Conduct. at least they have not intentionally wrong'd me. & they are ready to abandon to me in payment of their balance, every thing but the Clothes upon their backs. I have possession of their houses &lands, which they might easily have prevented my taking, since they stood in the name of their Children &Parents.

Sugar, Ginger, Tumerick &other Gruff goods remain as before quoted. *Goat Skins* are plenty &might be bought low, because they are a perishable article. *Pepper* has fallen to 8/ , the last cargoes from the Coast of Sumatra cost $3 ppicul. it will probably be lower next Season. if our war continues &the Continent should be shut to the English. *Coffee* is low at Java, but I do not know the Price. *Sugar* is purchased there by the Arabs. the quantity for exportation is small, the Cultivation of it being confined pretty much to the Chinese.

Mr Stark has not done any thing in Piece goods of late. he made a contract for some Checks two or three months since. I sent you the prices of all his goods, as obtain'd from the brokers. I think his goods are well bought, but the interest will bring up the prices &make them high, if the war continues much longer. I have not been able to sell the Band^s. or the Piece goods which were on hand when I heard of the War.

There is very little business going on, less than last season. Some shipments of Cotton &Rice are making for England. the second fleet have all reached in Safety, the first homeward bound fleet will sail in all next month, &the Second in the month of January.

Almost every article of Europe goods is low. there will be a loss upon the India officers investments. wines are plenty & in no demand. Brandy &Gin from England sell at 6/ prGalln. but the Sale is very slow. the Consumption of these two articles is extremely Small. there is nothing wanted from our quarter but Naval Stores. Spars & Tar would answer well. There is a great deal of ship building going on, more than 20 have been launched since my arrival & 3 of them 1200 tons.

Companys Paper is again down, it sells at a discount of 7% & has been bought at 10% within a Month. Dollars 208/ Bills on London 2/6d @ 2/7d. 6 months. It is difficult to Sell American Bills. Still, if you send a ship this way after the Peace, you may as well furnish the SCargo with a letter of Credit to draw upon you &upon London.

The Messs Perkins continue to remit to Canton thro' this Place & I think they judge well in so doing. You will perceive the advantages by a statement in my letters to Tom &Pat. Bills on Canton can now be purchased at 190/ to 195/ for 100 SpDollars at 30 days sight. I do not know of any funds remitted to this place, besides those Mr Stark brought & about 150,000 to Duloll from R Lenox &Sheaffe of Portsmouth. The Perkins' have an Agent on the way to this place he is on board the Country Ship Barrossa for Isle of France. he is expected here in few weeks, from whence he goes I am told to Canton. it is a young man by the name of Payne, his object in going to London was a passage to China, which being refused, he embarked on a Country Ship for the Isle of France.

When you send your letters to London for me, desire Charles Williams to put them on board different ships, not all one board one vessel. desire him also to prefer those which are bound direct for Calcutta, which he can know by refering to the printed list, published every Season

There will probably be Some new Custom Ho regulations on the opening ofthe trade. I shall give you the earliest information upon the Subject. I have nothing to add but my repeated request, that you would write often &be particular in Sending me information of every kind that may be useful.

Yours

(Signd) HLee

LETTER FROM HENRY LEE, CALCUTTA, JAN. 24, 1814, TO FRANCIS LEE, BOSTON, ON PRICES AND EXCHANGE [1]

Although handicapped by lack of funds, Henry Lee had begun to make investments. He continued to urge his correspondent to make remittances. In letters of the previous month he had warned Francis Lee in the case of peace not to ship out any merchandise except naval stores, since other goods would be supplied from England, and not to "rely upon letters of Credit, for the purpose of negotiating Bills on London," since the exchange was unfavorable and it was hard to sell such bills even with the reluctant endorsement of the banians; "beside this uncertainty, you are placed entirely inthe power of the Banians, provided he will endorse." [2] Bills on London were low — 2s. 7½d. to 8d. per rupee; while Spanish dollars were, on the other hand, worth 208–211 rupees per hundred. Although previously convinced of the safe arrival of the two vessels by which he had made shipments, Henry Lee had now, in the general uncertainty, come to wonder whether his early information was correct.

The "Mr. Stark" mentioned in this and many other letters had arrived at Calcutta on the American schooner *Alligator*, May 6, 1813, and was engaged in large-scale buying, presumably as agent for some American firm or firms.

p Lady Flora

Mr Frank Lee   Calcutta Jany 24th. 1814
    Dear Frank,
Copy p Northumberland   You have above, a Copy of my last letter. I tho't at the time I wrote that, we should not be many days without accounts from Europe, either by Sea or land, but my expectations have been disappointed. The over-

---

1. Jackson-Lee Papers, "Letters written in Calcutta by H. Lee from July 1813 to March 1816."

2. *Ibid.*, Henry Lee, Calcutta, Dec. 14, 18, 22, 1814, to Francis Lee, Boston.

land dispatch has been due a month &more, it must Soon Come. &I hope to hear Something favourable relative to our affairs with GBritain. if Mess.^s Gallatin &Bayard have been sent on a mission to Russia for the purpose of opening a negotiation for Peace, we must at least hear of their arrival there. — The accession of Austria &the Victory of Lord Wellington, will probably have a tendency to make our Gov.^{t.} more pacific than they otherwise would have been. — If the Allies Succeed in expelling the french from Germany, I shall Consider a Peace between our Country and England as certain, & at any rate I am pretty Confident the present Session of Congress will not end without an armistice having been declared.

There has been nothing to alter the market for Piece goods materially, I think since the Portuguese closed their purchases. Alliabad goods &Gurrahs have rather fallen, but the arrival of the Portuguese Ship Rosalia, now at Madras may raise them again a little should she have large funds, she remains there to dispose of a Cargo ofWine. Mr Stark has done nothing within a few days, he pobably suspends buying with the hope of a further fall in prices of Chondogurry & Gurrahs. I imagine he has pack'd in all about 7 or 800 bales, & they are very Cheap, as I am inform'd by the brokers.

I have purchased to day 800 p.^s Alliabad Chondogurry at 54/ for the purpose of making Chintz which I shall try to sell if the war Continues, it will Stand me in about 18/8 pC.^o 10 + 1⅞ 2. of better quality than the Reapers. I look upon it as the most certain article that can be purchased, it is only when white Cottons are very low that it will answer to print them. I think you will have found the Chintz in the R's Cargo one of the most profitable kind of goods in it, this I am now about to make will be of greater dimensions &better Cloth, besides, as I have more leisure to attend the printing, I think the Colours will be better. M.^r S is getting a large quantity made from his rejected Cloths, which must come Still lower than mine, but I cannot get any rejected, the buyers now take all &make wrapping Cloths of the rejected or get it printed or dyed. — The price I have paid for Alliabad Chondogurry is

50% less than the Reapers Cost, as you will see on Comparing them together. &Mansfield &others Paid more than I did for that article, & the Portuguese Still higher, however I did not think it Cheap at 80/ tho' I do at the present price. I imagine it to be 20% at least. less than the prime Cost &Charges. I suppose I might collect 10,000 p^s at this rate, but I shall not at present make any further purchases. Gurrahs are equally cheap. I could buy 10,000 p^s 34 + 2⅛ at 51/ @ 52/ which would in the worst of times Sell at $2.90 @ $3, &of better quality at 60/ such as I sent in the Reaper at 68/. I am afraid these two articles will advance again when the Portuguese Come, which may be in four or five months. More new goods have come down within the last two months than was expected by me, — according to the information received from the persons I rely upon, & considering the little incouragement the prices for 6 months has afforded, the merchants — From 1st. May to 1st Decr. there were enter'd at the Custom H^o 4200 bales, from the 1st. Dec to this date, the importations have amounted to 2000 bales, the following purchased have been made in the Bazar since the 1st. June.

Larkin &C^o (Armenians) on Speculation &now
 on hand .... say 1000
Nilmoney (native) " " " 300
5 Portuguese Ships .... " 2500 perhaps 3000
For County trade to the Easter^a. Isle France, Jan 9 " 1000
By Spanish Phillipine Companys Agent for Manilla 500
Mr Stark .... Say 100 6000

besides which a quantity of Coarse Cloths for the use of the natives, say Meergungees. Foolpour Cossas, Coarse Jannah Mamoodies, &rejected cloths of all kinds to the extent of 500 bales or more. — The manufacturers have suspended making most of the kinds of goods, which formerly we found here in abundance, &the reason why All^d. goods are so abundant now is the high price paid for them just after I arrived in the Reaper. Say July to Oct^o 1812 when they were 83/ @ 85 for Chondogerry, 75/ for Emerty. The Same thing applies to Gurrahs, such as I sent in the R at 65/ @ 68/ rose to 75/ & 80/ & continued so 'till Decr 1812 &even later. If you will look over the Invoices of the Harmonys Cargo which I sent you by that Ship, you will find only one parcel in the whole Inv^o. — The SCargo was extremely desirous of having a large quantity, but was deter^d buying by the high price. Chondogurry & other Alliabad Goods had fallen at that time, & Mess^s Burr & Foster tho't them so very Cheap that they made up nearly their whole investments in them & checks & Tonda goods. The Alliabad Chondogurry which I have bo't at 54/ are Similar to Harmonys at 74/ & 77/ but I take the rejected at same rate, &such as are too coarse to pack, or injured by damage &c, I make into Chintz, they are indeed exceeding cheap. I can hardly keep from buying & taking the risk of a Speedy Peace, but you have kept me so intirely in the dark by neglecting to write me that I am afraid, perhaps the next accounts will be that a negotiation is open'd &then up they go to 60/ @ 63/ again. The holders are very unwilling even now to sell, & it is only the most needy that offer their goods at these extreme low prices. Gurrahs are not so much below the Common prices as Alliabad Goods, yet they will do nearly as well. & that is what I meant by Saying they were equally cheap.

I most ardently hope that the next arrival may bring me letters from you, with orders to invest your funds, & also that you have, or intend to increase them by remittances from London. My Stock is now so small, that the expence of living makes a heavy charge, whereas had I $50,000 more, It would not be felt. Since there would be no further expence, I have always Supposed Some of you would be glad to avail yourselves of my being here, to make certainly the most profitable, & at same time, safe adventure, that ever before offer'd. I am Sorry I had not made up my determination to remain here earlier than I did, & yet you will have had time en^o unless my letters miscarry.

I have not yet Settled my accounts with my Banians, there will be a loss to us in spite of all I have done, which cannot be got back unless you should send a vessel out, &they should buy the Cargo, in that case. they would give up their Comm^{ns}. I still employ them in Conjunction with Ramkissen Day, &they do my business better than any other Banians could or would. — My misfortun has been in trusting them with too much, & their fault, in trading upon my funds &spending more freely than they ought to have done. I have not found in them any intention whatever to defraud me, on the Contrary when I was intirely in their power, they willingly surrender'd themselves & all their effects, & are now making every exertion in their power to make up my loss. I am much mortified in this affair, yet I think I had taken all the precaution that was necessary, it was my eagerness to make the utmost of my little capital which led me into difficulty I cannot say what will be the extent of our loss, but not less than 6 or 8000 Rps to be divided between us. Should there be a ship sent out consigned to me, I shall get back the whole, if her stock is 250,000 Rps.

There is no change in the price of Indigo, the fines are all ship'd &now the middling qualities begin to Sell. The 2d fleet is loading, it will take off the principal part of the Crop, leaving on hand a quantity of ordinary, which the Americans must take, if they arrive in four or five months, at 110/ @ 125/. We have no advices relative to this article, or any other from London later than June 1st. that being the date of the sailing of the last ships that arrived. We have had however ships from Lisbon Madeira &Brazil. &by those *I ought to have had letters from* you. I mentioned all these places in my letters &had you written by the *frequent Conveyances* which offer'd in neutral ships &Packets. I should have heard from you down to June & July, but you did not write even by way of England, or the very few letters you did write, have been lost — It will be very mortyfing to me & equally so to you, to find when your Invoices come to hand that the goods are 15 @ 20% higher charged than they might have been, had I been inform'd of events in season, in this respect my neighbour has an advantage over me, in the vigilence of his employers, which he will not fail to turn to their profit &to his own reputation. I never wd have remain'd here had I imagined there was any chance ofwar &when I heard of that event, should have embarked for England if it had not been for the almost certainty in my mind of a Speedy Peace. My Situation is extremely disagreeable on many accounts, & being without letters, adds much to my anxiety & impatience. I not yet know whether the Reaper has arrived, I have heard thro Mr Williams that she reached Boston, the same day with the Caravan but as no mention was made of her or her Cargo in a paper of the 31st.March, I am fearful of a mistake, it appears to me almost impossible I should not have heard from home, if he had arrived on 16th. March, since you could then no longer doubt of my remaining behind. The Harmony I know had arrived. You must when you are thinking of my unlucky decision in staying behind, take into view the profits on that shipment, since the same funds would have gone to China had I return'd in the R. &it is probable they would have been ship'd on the Derby &the whole been lost to you, or at any rate, if on any other Ship & arrived Safe, the profit on Silks must have been Small, according to my conjectures of the value of China Silks. You tho't it unfortunate I should have sent Indigo in the Harmony, so it may have been, but if there had been no war, Indigo would have done better than Cottons, especially as I had a freight to pay. If the R has arrived I think you will have done well with the goods I sent you. I regret I did not send some Ginger, but it is the War which has rais'd the price, it never was more than $8 @ $10 for many years previous, & at $12 @ 13 Tumerick is a better article reckoning upon the Sale of the Tartars which I took from the Repertory of March 31st it was quoted 13 @ 14 Cts N &Bonds Sales. The limited amount which I had to ship on your account was an additional reason for prefering the Tumerick, especially as I found your shipments had exceeded the amount you order'd me to invest.

Should you send a ship out you had better give the SCargo a letter of Credit to draw on London, he may be able to Sell for money, if he cannot do that some of the houses may give Indigo, but I do not think that article will be so low in future, because of the open trades Now the only buyers are the India Captains, but the private traders will go largely upon it, probably take the whole Crop, which amounts only to 3 or 4

millions of Dollars, not much in the trade with England. —
The private traders will come with letters of Credit, the Consequence will be a fall in value of Bills on London they are
now 2/8 pRupee 6 Mo. — I should not be surprized to see
them at 2/9d to 3/ when the ships arrive, remember this in
your Calculations. The opening the trade will raise the price
of Bills on this Country in London. I hope you may have remitted while they were at 2/2d @ 2/3d.

The English no doubt will trade to Sumatra, Mocha, Java   ✔
&c. but perhaps not immediately to the former, since they
cannot get dollars in England without giving too much, however they can get Opium &ps goods from hence which will
answer the purpose. — There is an abundance of Coffee in the
Compys Stores at Java @ $3 @ $4 ppecul, it will rise if things
go well in Europe, pepper was $5 the pecul some four or five
weeks ago, at Sumatra, but it will be at $3 when the Crop
Comes in. There are 40,000 Mds. here, the price 6/12 to 7/
pmd (83 lbs) The ship this goes by carried part of a cargo,
she is own'd by Thos Stewart, he has sent 500 tons to London,
& others have also sent largely, we shall no longer have so large
a portion of the trade, in this article as we formerly had.

The trade with the Mauritius &Bourbon has fallen to nothing
since the conquest of those Islands. Do not engage in any
voyage there, they are Supplied with every thing that is wanted,
from England, &the produce is very high, if you want to get
funds away in Bills you must pay a premo of 15%, either on
London or this place, it is the case also at Batavia Bills on Calcutta are at a premo & Dollars not to be had, on any terms nor
Bills on London. Our Ships now pay double duties at every
port in India. — I have [continued — stricken through] caution'd often against sending Merchandize here, except some
few articles mention'd by me. The India Officers have almost
all of them lost upon their investments, &it will be still worse
next year, when the private ships arrive. The Portuguese too
have lost upon their Wines tho they pay only half duties.

There has been no alteration in the duties this year, tho' it is
expected there will be when the new Charter comes into opera-

tion. I shall inform you of the changes, it is possible we may not be so much favour'd as we are now, but it will be Settled in the treaty when peace is made, &of that you must Send me information.

[written across face of letter:]
Northumberland Sail'd from Table Bay, May 1st. 1814.
arriv'd in England August 8th. 1815
Lady Flora arriv'd in England early in July

LETTER FROM HENRY LEE, CALCUTTA, FEB. 24, 1814, TO WILLIAM OLIVER, [PLACE UNKNOWN], ON PROSPECTS FOR TRADE AFTER PEACE [1]

William Oliver was presumably, from the first sentence of the letter below, a British subject; the same was also apparently true of Edward A. Newton, another associate of long standing, judging from a letter of Mar. 12, 1813, to his brother William A. Newton, condoling with him over the death of a third brother, killed fighting in Spain under Wellington.[2] The lack of nationalism and the emphasis on party spirit, strikingly brought out by this letter, are in direct contrast to developments in the century which followed. Imagine an American, even an opponent of participation in the World War, congratulating a friend on being employed in constructing German submarines!

The privateers which were "so much complained of" were probably the "three letters-of-marque, the brig *Rambler*, . . . ship *Jacob Jones*, and schooner *Tamaamaah*," which had been dispatched by a group of Boston China merchants to carry instructions to their blockaded vessels at Whampoa. "All three reached Canton safely, and took a few prizes off Lintin."[3] The *Jacob Jones* took the cargoes out of two vessels on the coast of Borneo and allowed the vessels to proceed; the *Hyder Ali*, her sister ship, was captured.[4] But these vessels were letters of marque and not strictly privateers; their main function was to carry orders to their owners' merchant vessels and to

1. Jackson-Lee Papers, "Letters written in Calcutta by H. Lee from July 1813 to March 1816."
2. *Ibid.*, Henry Lee, Calcutta, Mar. 12, 1811 [1813], to William A. Newton, Madras.   3. Morison, *op. cit.*, pp. 204–205.
4. Morse, H. B., *op. cit.*, vol. iii, pp. 217–218.

bring back part of their cargoes. American privateers pure and simple would have little reason for seeking the Pacific when prizes could so easily be picked up in West India waters and off the British Isles, nearer to a base of supplies, prize courts, and a market.

p.Marchioness   Exeter

Mr William Oliver   H. C. S   Calcutta Feby 24th. 1814

copy pBarrossa P S of 22^{d}April

Dear Sir

    It is only within a few days I have heard from my friends since April 1812. I was glad to learn that you were well &had found Some employment, in building ships for the use of his Majestys Service. Your Tom Thumb is highly praised by John Bull, &will probably be found useful in clearing the seas of those yankee privateers, that are so much complaind of. — We have been alarm'd in this quarter several times with reports of their being on the Coast, Sumatra &in the Bay, but they have vanish'd without doing any mischief. I do not imagine any will venture beyond the Cape, indeed I presume by this time there are few out, since the business proves unprofitable. The fleets go from hence with strong convoy, the last with 2.74 & a frigate. — My wife says there was no one of my friends that express'd more regret at my not returning in the R than yourself, I doubt not you were sincere, but I should have Consider'd a letter from you as a much more Satisfactory token of your friendship than a thousand such Speeches. — Why did you not write? — You knew in Jany that I should remain in the Country. A letter from you would have been extremely gratifying and useful, especially as my other correspondents have all fail'd me, except my wife & Frank. — Had my friends written frequently, some of the letters would have Come to hand four months ago, & I should have embarked on the fleet for England, but I cannot go now because of my health. I am afraid to encounter a winter in England or on the Atlantic, which I must do if I embark before next Nov^r. &before then I hope to hear of Peace. Pray write me via Madeira & England. I may be here for two years to Come. —

Your information will be useful to me. — Mr Jackson, upon whom I counted with certainty, has not written me, &probably will not often if I remain ever so long. — I therefore look to you for the best statements of markets for India goods &c. — direct my letter to Palmer &C^o. I have written quires to Mr Jackson &others relative to prices of goods. no material changes have taken place of late. Mr Stark has made the best purchases that were ever made in this place, &his concern will make a good business. I should think 100% if the war ends in two or three years. — I have given you all good advice, if you had follow'd it, Your funds could now be loan'd at 12%. — Money will not be below 9%. A gentleman offer'd to guaranty me 9% for two years for 5 lacs, &he belonged to one of the most solid houses in India, the opening the trade will tend to our disadvantage by bringing into competition with us, traders that can supply the Continent with Gruff goods cheaper than we can, freights to England will not be higher than £15, for 50 feet, paid in England, we cannot do it so low, besides they are nearer the Consumers, &will have less duties to pay on exportation from hence. — The private trade will be here in Aug^t., they will find plenty of Pepper, Cotton, Peice goods, &Drugs, & at Java an abundance of Coffee, they will also be in time for the new Crop of Indigo, they are laugh'd at in London for their projects, but I see no reason why the should not do well, if there is a trade between GB &the Continent. The goods they bring out will sell badly, but after the warnings they have had, I imagine most of them will be in ballast. Europe goods have been low for 3 years past, there is nothing wanted from our quarter but a few articles I have mentioned in my letter to Mr J. —

The Country ship after 10th. April will be allow'd to take from hence what Cargoes they wish. — the new Charter takes effect on that day. — It is not improbable some of the Cargoes may find the way to US. should Peace have taken place on their arrival in Europe, they could not do better than go there with Peace goods &c &c. The trade in Saltpeter is free to the mer-

chants, which will reduce the price of this article in Europe.
Bills on London will be lower than formerly, the traders will
come out with letters of Credit, & as there are only few houses
that can furnish the funds they will be obliged to draw at
2/9^d. @ 3/ pRp^e I do not know whether British ships will be
allow'd to go from hence to U. S. if they are, you will have some
no doubt as soon as the war terminates. Several ships are preparing to load as soon as the Charter expires. Thomas Stewart
will probably have one &he talks of going in her, if there is
Peace on her arrival, she may proceed on to UStates. I do
not think she will have any Piece goods, he has Pepper &Coffee
& will ship largely. The former is selling at 7 Rps p 3 lbs, the
latter 7/ @ 8/ for Java, they will both answer if Bounaparte
is beaten out of Germany, & at any rate, probably there can be
no loss.

It is probable you may when Peace takes place, engage in a
voyage here, I think a freighting voyage will always be certain,
when you can get 150,000 dollars at 11% — You ought in such
case to have a burthensome vessel, more so than the Caravan,
sailing is no object, besides, the difference between the dullest
&swiftest vessel is not more than thirty days in each passage,
&oftentimes not half that time, the difference in burthen is as
3 to 2, &you must reckon 100 tons freight at 8000 doll^s. The
ships employ'd in this river carry much better than ours, for instance a ship 400 tons will store 600 @ 650 — Mr Stewarts ship
that Sail'd from hence a few days ago for London, measured
700 tons. She had in her hold 850 tons, & I suppose 250 more
between decks, she sails as well as the Reaper. — Do not think
of employing your Lark, or any such constructed vessel, nor send
her here with an expectation of Selling her, no vessel of that
kind is wanted. — An American Privateer Sch^o. was sent out
from England 250 tons &is now in the River, they wanted to
sell her but no one would have given a thousand Rupees for
her. —

The Gov^t have been thinking for some time past of making
Dock yards & a naval depot at Trincomalee, it is now resolved

upon, &the works are Constructing, all the ships of war will be repair'd there, I think a ship coming this way might dispose of the following articles to advantage at any time, viz

    3 to 400 bbls Tar in good Iron bound barrels
       50 " Pitch
       20 " Turpentine
      500 Gallons Spts Turpentine

A few tons of large Lignum Vitae, & a quantity of Spars, the best you can buy of sizes for ships Topmasts, Yards & of 300 to 1200 tons a ship might call there, & if the navy agent would not buy them, they would find a market at this place, nothing could be lost upon them, the Spars should be selected with great care, &not a bad one allow'd to pass, a good Spar costs but little more than a defective one in America, but the difference here is immense. A few pipes of Pure white Gin & 200 Kegs of Salmon might be added &100 doz Champaigne at $12 p doz, it will sell for 50 Rp^s. I do not know of any thing besides of which the English will not bring in abundance. — of T. and Ramdon, that they have & w^d. continue to be in dbt, that if employ^d it w^d. be imprudent to trust them with money — characters of Banians — Kissen still had the reputation of gambling &c — prices cottons — P. S. March 5th. —

[written across face of letter:]
    Rec^d in U. S. March 1815

LETTER FROM HENRY LEE, CALCUTTA, MAR. 12–APR. 15, 1814, TO FRANCIS LEE, BOSTON, ANNOUNCING PURCHASES IN ANTI-CIPATION OF PEACE [1]

The uncertainty of communication at this period, particularly in time of war, is illustrated by the fact that at the date of this letter Henry Lee had only just received his first letter from home since his arrival at Calcutta nearly two years before.

On the *Kent,* by which this letter went, Henry Lee shipped to

1. Jackson-Lee Papers, "Letters written in Calcutta by H. Lee from July 1813 to March 1816."

London, on his own account, indigo invoiced at sicca rupees 11,522, 14 annas, 6 pice.[2]

It will be remembered that Henry Lee had long suffered from ill health, which was not likely to be mitigated by a sojourn in the tropics; but despite this handicap he attained, as is frequently the case with persons of delicate constitution, to the fairly ripe old age of eighty-five.

Calcutta March 12th 1814

Mr F Lee   ⌈ p. Kent
  Dear Frank,   ⟨ Left pilot 18th May.
             ⌊ Copy p Barrossa

[Left pilot 11th. May. — stricken through] I have at last letters from you, it is unfortunate for me, &may perhaps turn out so for you, that you did not write me earlier, &that when you at last wrote, you had not sent Copies of the letters, in either case the intelligence which I received only a few weeks ago, would have reached me in Octr or Novr. had it come even in December, I should now be on my passage to England, with your funds invested in Indigo &Bands. the former at that time could have been purchased for 110/ such as sold last year in London at 6/ to 7/. & which will this year do still better if Germany remains open, the Band's would have cost 80/ &might in event of a long war have been sold in London for 20/, or if a peace should have taken place, ship'd to America, where they would have Stood you in 100/ all charges paid, which is lower than they will cost in this place on the return of Peace, but now it is too late for either of these articles, the first has been ship'd off &the latter are in hands of Mr Stark, & I know of nothing else, I would venture upon to England, besides such is the indifferent state of my health, that I am unwilling to encounter a winter in England, or on the Atlantic, which I must do, if I embark earlier than Octo. before which time, notwithstanding the fears entertain'd in Boston to the Contrary. I think we shall hear of an Armistice, upon this Subject however, I am

2. *Ibid.*, "Invoices of all the goods ship'd by Henry Lee during his stay in Calcutta from May 1812 to March 1816."

less Confident in my hopes than formerly. — Should I not hear of Peace by Oct°. it is probable I may embark in some of the private ships for England, but as this is uncertain, I wish you to continue writing, 'till you hear of my actually having embarked, I have already suffer'd much unnecessary anxiety, the loss of a year & great Injury to my health for want of a letter, which ought to have been written two months earlier than it was, &when written to have been forwarded by half a dozen different routes. — I have no possible means of getting political or Commercial intelligence, except thro' you. I hope hereafter to have frequent advices. You mention having desired CWilliams & F. Cabot to write from London, neither have done it, nor do I expect they will — *All the Ships* from England &Portugal stop at Madeira, send letters to Mr Cathcart & desire him to forward them by a ship for Calcutta or any other port in India, & direct them to Palmer &C°., any remittances you may have occasion to make to me, or for any other purpose, Direct to Alexander &C°. a safe house, they will give you credit for the Current rate of interest. In case of my going to England, it is my intention to take my own property with me in merchandize, &probably yours too. Our passages will Cause a heavy deduction from my stock, in the regular ships they demand '6000 Rps for 2persons.' I hope to go for less in the private ships.

The Cassia you Complain of turns out very different from my expectations. I knew the quality was inferiour to China, but I thought it might do for our Country, the loss on the ton of the Indigo is occasioned by the drying of the boxes, they were made of green wood, those which contain'd the owners portion, they should have been weigh'd &not sold at the mark'd ton. — I am sorry to find this article has not been rais'd by the war, that which you sold at 178^d. [?] w^d have done better in England, it was broken to be sure, but the quality was equal to the best of the Shippers at 106/8.

I have Converted 400 p^s. of the Alliabad Chondogurry into Chintz which stands me in 18/8 for 10 by 1⅞ the remainder I shall pack in white Cloth. I have made no further purchases except 70 M^{ds}. of Indigo at 65/ which will do well if Peace

is made, otherwise Can be sold here without loss, there have
been no changes in piece goods, nor will there be any till the
Portuguese arrive, or there is Peace with U. S. M^rS goes on
with his purchases.

The private Ships will not arrive earlier than Oct^r. &will
Sail from hence in Dec^r. — I shall not have an opp^y of sending
this for some weeks, should any thing in mean time occur, I
will add to it. —

March 25th. I have sent 4000 Rps up to Cossimbazar for the
purpose of buying Band^s. I expect they may be procured at
about 80/ to 85/ pC^o. if so, I shall buy some thousands of pieces.
April 5th. We have just rec^d overland accounts to Decr. informing us of Buonapartes disasters &retreat into old France,
every one thinks there will be a general peace, the natives seem
inclined to hold on &raise the prices of their goods. I shall
probably make some purchases. I think there is Peace by this
time between GBritain &America. Goods will be high when the
American Ships Come, for it is probable some Portuguese ships
will arrive in Aug^t. &the English private trade will want some
piece goods, Indigo will be high & so will Ginger, Pepper
&Coffee

April 15th. I am investing your funds, the holders of goods
are not willing to sell. I hope to make some purchases however
in a few days, but they will not be so low as they would have
been two mo^s. since. I have purchased 1500 M^ds. Coffee &Pep-
per, which I shall sell again &probably get a Small profit, it is
on our joint account, I have no doubt there will be a Peace
following the Successes of the Allies, between our Country
&GBritain, but I am afraid there will be much time lost, in
Communicating between the two [Gov^ts. — stricken through]
Countries. It is my intention to embark for England in August,
unless by that time I can ascertain that the Americans will be
here by Septr. or October, my health will not admit of my
remaining any longer &if I stay beyond Octr. I shall not reach
America 'till cold weather, it requires almost a year to get home
via England. Your goods I shall leave with Mr Stark or some
of the houses here to be shipped on first vessel for America.

Several vessels are expected from England in the Course of a month, but I am afraid there will be no letters for me, indeed you seem all of you so remiss in writing, that I do not expect to hear further while I remain, unless from my wife. I repeat my regret that you had not written often when you knew I remain'd, as events have turn'd out, your interest would have been greatly promoted by a shipment of Indigo to England, it has advanced 30% to 40% there.

Every thing will be high in this place as soon as the private ships arrive, the Americans can take nothing but p^s. goods &those at the old prices, the quantity in market is small, the manufacturers I suppose will resume their works, but if the English take p^s. goods &the Portuguese Come in usual numbers, there will be a great demand.

Yours
Sin   HLee

Dollars 206 @ 208/

Bills on London 2/8^d @ 2/9^d. will be 2/10^d. @ 3/. You may write me in London but no longer in this place.

Coffee has advanced in Batavia from $3 to $14 the picul, Pepper will be high on the west Coast, enough for the Supply of Europe has been sent to England. Indigo will be 30% to 40% higher next year than it has been for 3 years

LETTER FROM HENRY LEE, CALCUTTA, JULY 23–AUG. 11, 1814, TO FRANCIS LEE, BOSTON, WITH AN ACCOUNT OF THE EFFECT OF NAPOLEON'S OVERTHROW UPON BUSINESS [1]

Peace between the United States and Great Britain did not take place as soon after Napoleon's abdication as Henry Lee had expected. He was right, however, in expecting the United States to put a high duty on cottons.

It is interesting to discover that Henry Lee's knowledge of India goods was recognized by his being "employ'd . . . in making purchases of Sugar for a house here."

1. Jackson-Lee Papers, "Letters written in Calcutta by H. Lee from July 1813 to March 1816."

On Aug. 6, Henry Lee began to make contracts with natives for seersuckers, advancing them, as was the custom, three-fourths of the total price.[2]

Of the vessels mentioned near the end of the letter, the reference to "The Hunter, Rogers . . . at Madras for condemnation" may throw some light on the identity and fate of the *Huntress,* a vessel in which John Jacob Astor was concerned, which sailed for the "S Seas" in 1809 and which her owner, in 1813, feared was "gone." Gov. Baranov, writing from Sitka in 1811, referred among other vessels to one named "Interess" (probably an error for *Huntress*) which was going to Canton, and mentioned in a list of captains a certain "Rodgers;" he gives the name of the captain of the "Interess" as "Davison," probably meaning William Heath Davis, but vessels in the Pacific frequently swapped captains and Baranov could easily have erred in some details of his information. Henry Lee does not seem to have known that the Capt. Porter he mentioned was the captain of the schooner *Tamaamaah,* which was from Boston, not New York.[3]

Copy p. Novo Destino — Rio deJaneiro —
p^r Trowbridge

Mr Frank Lee   Dup p^r. Edinburgh

Dear F   Calcutta July 23^d 1814

Enclosed is a copy of my last, I yesterday rec^d yours of 2^dOct^o. I find my letters recommending a remittance for the purchase of goods during the war, had been received. You Say not a word in reply upon that Subject, I presume therefore, you did nothing subsequently. Peice goods have continued to advance, &most of the holders refuse any prices, two Portuguese are in the market &want most of the goods in the Bazar, besides which there is expected to be a demand for Eng^d when the Ships arrive. We have Lord Castlereagh's Correspondence with our Gov^t. proposing to treat for Peace at Gottenburgh & Mr Madisons reply, accepting the offer. I conclude there will be a Peace, indeed I never doubted it, since having the Battle of Leipzic, it cannot be ratify'd earlier than 1st. July. I expect

2. *Ibid.,* "Henry Lee's Calcutta Memorandum Book. — 1814 & 1815 — ."

3. Porter, *op. cit.,* vol. i, pp. 151, 237–238, 472.

American Ships by the 15th Novr. the prospect is very bad for them. Indigo is out of the question unless prices should be much higher than the Reapers brought, the London price is much beyond it, allowing for the duty, they talk of 200, some 225. I think it will be higher still. Piece goods will probably go 10% to 20% beyond the Reapers Cargo, if our ships come in four or five months.

As there is a certainty of Peace before this reaches, I am no longer afraid of getting you into difficulty with the Govt. by writing on business. Your funds are invested in Chondogurry, Baftas, Checks, Chintz, Gurrahs, Flags, Bandannas, &Some Blue Goods, they were mostly bought after I heard the Leipzick Battle, &when they had advanced. Still they are Cheap. I have besides a 1,000 Mds. Coffee, which I shall sell if a profit can be obtain'd, otherwise ship to Engld. I trust I shall be able to do the former, as it has advanced in Batavia & there is none here. I had sold it for 12/ but the buyer refused, having met with a difficulty in finding the Security I demanded. It cost 10/ and it is certainly worth 12/ I have besides 400 Mds. Pepper, in which you are half Concern'd, this I can at any time sell for some profit. I have no intention of entering into any speculation on your acct. I would however if an advance on the peice goods can be obtain'd, exchange them for ordinary Indigo, if by chance it should be low, but of this I have Scarcely any hope. I have a letter from SW to 31st. Decr. Andrew was in London, but has not written. Mr W says Bayard was expected then. I suppose he will hear of the New Negotiation &remain in the North. I hope he will not go to America as it would cause great loss of time. It is not my intention to remain here longer than the Coming Season. If the Americans do not Come, I shall go to Engd &take with me my Coffee &Some Piece goods, if they should again fall. A House here has offer'd me a Lac of Rupees to be repaid in London, the goods to be consigned to their Agents as is usual. I prefer however to Sell, should the article rise, as it ought, unless the prices in London fall, which is not expected. I have 1,500 Maunds. I tried some weeks ago to get it on board Some ship for London, but freight was so exorbitant that I prefer'd waiting, now I am more inclined to Sell.

July 27th. I have purchased 40 M^ds Nutmegs on your account, @ 4/4, they are of an excellent quality. It is my intention to Substitute them for an equal amount of Peice goods, which I hope to sell to advantage, this article has risen in London &will go yet higher. I do not know any place from whence we can be supplied but England, before these will get to market. I have bought the Same quantity for myself which I shall take to England, or Sell. Peice goods advance every hour, indeed every thing is on the rise, accounts from England to Feby 18, which Came by the fleet at Madras, are extremely encouraging. Pepper 20^d lb. Indigo 16/ Sugar 110/ &c Peice goods risen in London 50% the prospect for Americans is worse &worse, there will be a demand for more goods than can be made in a year, the market was never so naked. You have lost a fine Speculation by not following my plan of remitting. If you had sent me orders only, without the funds, or only intimated that on return of Peace, you should send a ship, I would have bought, &sold again, or kept, as events might render expedient. I was afraid to do it on my own account, or rather, I prefer'd Coffee, because I Knew it would do in Eng^d. — I find most of my letters had reach'd England, but my wife does not acknowledge any but the Rio de Janeiro ones. I imagine some of our impertinent Marshalls have stop'd those via London, I desired CW to send them by private hand.

July 30th.

I have received yours of 26th Decr. You say nothing of prospect of Peace, the ruin of Buonaparte which was anticipated in Novr in England, in consequence of the entire overthrow of his troops &the defection of all his allies, seems to have made no impression in America, SW writes me 18th July that the negotiations for Peace with America would not Commence 'till May, &that if every thing goes on smoothly, the ratification will be made in Nov or Dec. I think his calculation cannot be correct. Our Gov^t must in Feby have determined upon Peace, upon any terms, it is too late to talk of Neutral rights or impressment, such nonsense will be no longer tolerated notwithstanding your brilliant feats by Sea in Canada.

We had an express overland this morning with the account of Buonapartes abdication. This event as you may imagine, has produced a strong effect upon Commercial affairs, but I cannot tell to what extent. Peoples minds are not yet tranquil enough to think of business. I have been employ'd all the morning in making purchases of Sugar for a house here. Every thing will rise. I shall venture upon Some articles for my own Account, but not to any great extent.

August 1st.

For twenty four hours after the news, not much was done, but Speculation rages furiously now. I have Securd about 10,000 M^ds Sugar. It has not advanced much. I tried Pepper for my own account, but while I was bargaining at 10/8 it rose to 14/ &to morrow it may go to 20/. No one will Sell Peice goods. 80/ is offer'd for Chondogurry &for other goods in proportion. I try'd to get some cheap Cloths for you, that I might sell my Baftas, but the news prevented me. 230/ is offer'd for the Coming Crop of Indigo by Sample, they talk of 250/ @ 275/ there are large orders for p^s goods from London, &the Danes, French, Portuguese &c are expected, there are not 3000 Bales in the Bazar. Coffee has not started a pice but I imagine it will. I shall sell yours at any rate, but my own I shall ship unless the price advances to 15/. It will be well for our Countrymen if they Should not get here for 9 M^o to come, by that time Peice goods may be reasonable, for 6 mo^s prices must keep up. I should not be Surprized to see them 20% @ 30% higher than the Reapers.

I told you I might venture on my own account, a Small Speculation. I have bo't some Sugar, Ginger &few drugs. I hope to Sell them at some advance, do not be alarmed, it is not my intention to adventure far. I have had great temptations &but for my timidity could have made myself rich. I have no want of funds, but in my situation, I feel bound to be prudent. I lament every hour that you had not sent me orders to buy. — I should sell now, for I do not think goods will answer in U.S.

(unless the first Cargoes) at more than the old rates. I have some expectation our Gov^t may prohibit, or add to the duties, as an encouragement to home manufactures. Remsen encourages me in this Opinion, M^{r}S's purchase is worth 150,000 Rp^s. I would sell were I in his place &had authority, there are no Ships loading for America. I am trying to get some one to go, that I might send your goods, but they are afraid the war will continue. A cargo of Gruff goods would do well, Peice goods cannot be had.

August 6th. I am in treaty for your Chondogurries (700 p^s) @ 83/ there will be a profit, after deducting Dustory, Int &c of 1500 Rps, I shall sell my Baftas (6000 p^s) when they will afford 10 Rps pC^o profit. If there is no loss on the Coffee, I shall make up the loss Sustain'd by my Banians. — An American Came in the Feby fleet from London, he is a Philadelphian with 5 or 6 lacks he is invisible & I do not know his name, he is trying to contract for Silk, Checks &c to a great amount, as to White goods they Cannot be had in that way except a few Gurrahs. The Phil^{an} is too late, there are buyers in the Bazar for three times as many goods as are, or will be in Calcutta for months. All the English Houses are shipping to England, &the Portuguese have not finished. I shall be able to replace the goods I sell, for others which do as well. Indeed I am now in advance to the Owners 15 to 20,000 Rp^s. It is said 40 ships are coming from London private trade, besides those from the outports. Cotton is the only article which they can fill so much tonnage, & if it keeps up above 12^d in England, there will be a profit. Sugar is advancing I think a Cargo would now do in our Country, as this article must double in price in West Indies. I expect it will get up here to 12/ &perhaps 15/ @ 16/ pm^d. there is no Coffee at Batavia but what is bought up for London. Pepper is cheap on the W Coast, but agents are going from hence to buy it. Raw Silk is the only article which will continue low, but tho' it is only half the price of 1812, there is such demand for Hdkfs for London &c that manufactures are nearly as high as the Reapers Cargo Cost. Some Kinds, say Choppas 20% higher. As yet the Silk Merchants will not enter into Contracts. I have purchased a 1000 ps on Comsn. I am trying to get some Checks on Contract, but there is some danger in advancing from the poverty of the cloth merchants. Our war has ruin'd many of them, especially those who live in this vicinity, &who are the only ones that will engage in this way. *August 11th.*

Piece goods have advanced still further. I shall quote the prices of Such Kinds as are in market at foot. I have 15 or 20,000 Rps of Goods on account of the owners to dispose of, upon which there will be profit, enough I am in hopes to make up the loss by the Banians, this is an immense relief to me. A house here has given me some reason to hope, that they will make an arrangement, by which I Can repay in America, the loan I am indebted for. I agreed to repay it in Engld & Consign the goods as Security, but I had much rather ship to America, tho' the prospect for some articles is perhaps more flattering for shipments to England. In Consequence of this I am extending my purchases, tho' they cannot be made on any thing near so good terms as three months ago. Still there are some articles which others avoid which are yet Cheap. The bond given for the Reapers Cargo is discharged, with the Certificate you forwarded, let Captn Spooner Know this.

I have seen Mess Perkins bus Circulars sent out by EAN., from London, &a private letter recommending Consignments none of them will follow his recommendations, they had much better information than his letters gave, many months ago. I endeavour'd while Alliabad Chondogurries were 55/ @ 60/ to persuade a house to let me buy a Cargo &proceed to US as soon as Peace was made or Could be foreseen with any Certainty. I laid before them the prices of goods for ten years past, here & in America, & offer'd as far as your funds &mine would go to *guarantee them against a loss*, for which they were required to pay us from the profits, a Certain per Centage & 5% Commission. I found no difficulty in Convincing them of the truths of my Statements, but they apprehended a long Continuance of the War, &besides which, all the Agency houses are averse to Speculating, let the prospect be what it may, &especi-

ally in a branch of trade so much out of their usual line of business. E A N is trying, I believe to make an arrangement with the house of Porcher &Cᵒ, to enable them to raise funds in this Country, by Bills &c. It will not answer, it might formerly have done, when the profits were great &the Capitals of our merchants small. Bills will be 2/8 perhaps 3/. The Sales of the R's Cargo has disappointed me greatly. I thought it very low charges &well assorted, the gruff goods you were in too much haste to get rid of, they require time, &they do well, if you had look'd into an English price Current of any date, when goods were at the lowest, you would not have sold Tumerick @ 10 Cts lb nor Indigo 190¢. in the Selling the last you were probably guided by the excessive low prices yours Cost, the quality was as good as what usually costs 120/, the Same would now Sell @ 140/. Such Indigo as I sent you in the Harmony (for Owners.) would now sell @ 190/ it was of the first quality, I have the Samples by me. It is now selling at 14/ in London, I have compared it with some London musters sent me by MrWilliams. I always told you fine Indigoes would never answer in our Country, &the Sale of the Harmonys is another proof to the many I before had, there are no judges of the Article in U. S. very few in this Country, I mean of the fine sorts.

The Philadelphian keeps himself still Conceal'd, tho' we all knew what he was about, in 24 hours after he landed, he is a new man in this business, having never been this way before, his name is Comley he has not yet done anything, but look at musters &try the prices of the Contract merchants, his goods will be at least 40% higher than Mr S's. As yet only few of the Indiamen have arrived, the Captains are buying pˢ goods, it is thought there will be large exportations to England, the Company have not sent any this year, nor many for a long time past, &the demand for the Continent, West Indies &c is great, there are not more than 3000 bales in market, the Portuguese want all of them, &four ships more are look'd for, if the English ships take largely, &ours Come within 4 or 5 months, with their usual Stock, I think, indeed it is certain that cloths will be higher than for many years past, the manufacturers cannot in less than 12mos make the quantity which will be immediately required. What a prospect this for our Countrymen! ! The Indigo crop is very unpromising, but this is always the Cry. It cannot be large however. if the trade had not been open'd to the English, I could perhaps have collected Some small parcels from the natives, but there will now be so many buyers, that it will be impossible to do anything in that way.

Coffee has not yet really advanced, nominally only, there are no buyers. I have no fear. I shall ship mine if I cannot obtain 14/ @ 15/. I have no doubt all kinds of Colonial produce & especially Coffee, which Cannot be Suddenly increas'd in Cultivation, will keep up for 1 or 2 years. I think Sugar would be a good article for our country, there is not a pound of Coffee at Batavia or Isle of France, nor any Sugar, the latter article will be higher here in 3 months, it is now the Season &is plenty, but most of it is wanted for Gulph &Bombay there are several expeditions fitting for WCoast. Pepper is now about $4, it will no doubt go up to $9 @ $11 when the Americans arrive there. We expect the next fleet in a month, they were detain'd by the burning of the Custom Ho. it is probable their arrival &the private trade will raise the prices of everything, & particularly Peice goods.

I hope P T J remitted my funds before Exchange rose. I presume as soon as you heard of the Battle of Leipzick &the events which immediately follow'd, it must have advanced to par, or above.

I have nothing more to say about your business, your purchases are made, I have only to sell the amount over, & above your funds, which I shall soon do, &then Close the accounts, keeping in reserve money enough to pay for our expenses & passage to England, in case American Ships should not arrive. I shall not write you often hereafter, All Kinds of Europe Goods are low. I imagine the investments low, after the payment of all Charges from 60% @ 20%. If you have undertaken any voyage, I trust you follow'd my advice on this Subject, all the articles I recommended will do well. The Hunter, Rogers is at Madras for Condemnation. Captn Porter in a Schooner was ready to Sail 3months ago from Canton. A schr from New York got in safe, the Tammammahaa, or some such name. She was chaced by the Doris, there has been no difficulty in getting, in &out of that place, in fast sailing ships. I shall add to this if any thing new occurs.

Yours

(Sign'd) HLee

Brandy (Cognac) 3/8 pGalln ⎱ must be lower, the Consumption is not
Gin Hollands 3/8 @ 4 " ⎰ more than 50 pipes & 500 are expected.
Iron English 5/
Hoops do 3/8 @ 4 ⎱ will be lower unless the Americans buy
Swedes Iron 6/ ⎰ these for ballast.
Tar American 25/ bbl. Would Sell for 16/ for 500 @ 1000 bbls
Spars any price say for $500, 1500 Rps. if well Selected.
Copper 48/ Great quantities have been imported, but it will
　　　　　　　Sustain this rate, it has been up to 60/
Mahogany Bay 2/8 pfoot.
Wines Maderia plenty & *Cheap, &always are.*
Sugar best . . . 9/4 pmd ⎱ Will go to 12/ if the Americans should
　Ordy 7/8 ⎰ want largely, our Ships Some years have
　　　　　　⎰ taken 90,000 bags.
Tumerick 2/12 ⎱ pmd Will advance, Ginger only few hundred
Ginger 6/12 ⎰ Mds. in Market.
Goat Skins 18/ @ 20/
Pepper 13/ Will get up to 16/ perhaps 20/
Tutenague 28/
Sal Ammoniac 25/ ⎱
Shellac 25/ ⎱
Gum Copal 20/ ⎰ Will advance if English Ships Come in great
Red Wood 4/8/ ⎰ numbers
Cotton 14/ ⎰
Alliabad Chondogurry 41 by 1 7/8 83/ @ 90/
　　" Sannas 41 " 2 1/3 100/
　　" Emerties 30 " 2 70/
Bazar Baftas 24 " 1 7/8 2 60/.
Mow Sannas only few in market, Say 30/
Meergungees not a bale, nor any Coarse Mamoodies, they would sell @ 67/8 to 72/ No Coloured Goods, in market, about 25% higher on Contract than the R's Cargo. Silks none but Choppas in Bazar, they sell for 130/ like the Reapers. Merchants will not enter into Contracts, &if they would, there might be danger in trusting them.

Coarse Gurrahs   34 by 2¼ 65/ Advancing
   "   36/7 " 2¼ 75/ @ 80/ like the Reapers. All Kinds
of Cottons on the Rise, it is probable my next quotations may be 20%
higher than the above.

[written across face of letter:]
    Trowbridge saild from C G Hope
    under convy Desirèe frigate
          Dec.ʳ 3ᵈ 1814.

LETTER FROM HENRY LEE, CALCUTTA, OCT. 21, 1814, TO
SAMUEL WILLIAMS, LONDON, IN REPLY TO AN ORDER FOR
INVESTMENT IN MERCHANDISE [1]

In this letter Henry Lee assumes the rôle of a commission merchant, buying for a correspondent in England.

He had earlier, in a letter of Apr. 22, 1814, commented that "it
would be dangerous to make Contracts & advances, because of the
poverty of the Contractors, occasion'd by the long interruption in
their business." [2] Now that, in his opinion, peace was assured, he not
only made contracts for piece goods but also commenced purchasing
"Azumgur Sawns," "Donacully Seersuckers," "Choppas," "Palam-
pours," etc., from such European commission houses as Cruttenden &
Mackillop and Tulloh & Co. He continued disposing of goods previously purchased as an investment, and there are notes of his making
deliveries of indigo and pepper and selling piece goods to various
native merchants.[3]

The effect of Napoleon's abdication is indicated by the advance in
the rates for freight to England. On Apr. 11, 1814, Lee had written:
"The freight to England will not be higher than £ 18 for 50 feet paid
in England." [4] On June 6 he wrote: "The present rate of freight is

1. Jackson-Lee Papers, "Letters written in Calcutta by H. Lee from
July 1813 to March 1816."
2. *Ibid.*, Henry Lee, Calcutta, Apr. 22, 1814, to Francis Lee, Boston.
3. *Ibid.*, "Henry Lee's Calcutta Memorandum Book. — 1814 &
1815 — ." Henry Lee's "Memorandum Book January 1814," Feb., 1814–
Feb. 24, 1816, belonging to Mr. Henry Lee Shattuck, gives many details
as to prices, discount rates, arrivals, and investments by other merchants,
but little concerning Henry Lee's own transactions.
4. *Ibid.*, "Letters written in Calcutta by H. Lee from July 1813 to
March 1816," Henry Lee, Calcutta, Apr. 11, 1814, to P. T. Jackson, Boston.

£20 pton, which is as low, I am informed, as Can be afforded, payable in England. Company measurement, 50 feet for bales &boxes, 18 Cwt Coffee, 16 Cwt Pepper, other goods in proportion." [5]

Henry Lee lost no opportunity to express his detestation of the government of the United States. On Aug. 16, 1814, he wrote to a New York merchant: "I hope the present campaign . . . may be still more disastrous to our rabble armies." [6] On July 9, after expressing a hope that the British would have the opportunity of chastising "very handsomely" the "republican vagabonds," he remarked, probably in all sincerity, "Spare Mass[as]. & I care not what happens to the other states." [7]

(p[r]Cornwall)

Sam[l]Williams Esq[r]   Dup p[r] Indian Oak
                   Trip p[r].

Calcutta October 21st 1814

   London
      Dear Sir

       I received on the 8[th]inst. Yours of the 18[th]March, with the two Bills of 49,000 & 51000 Rupees, which have been accepted, &will without doubt be duly paid. I am extremely sorry to say that your order for investment, in respect to some of the articles cannot be executed at all, in others only in part. Of Bandannas there is not a case in the settlement, the manufacture of them having been discontinued for two years past, for want of buyers, except upon Contract, which requires a long time & is attended with hazard. Since advances are demanded upon very imperfect Security, Choppas are procurable, but at very high prices, &of a quality inferiour to the Companys by many degrees, large quantities of this article are on the way to England, &still greater [quantities — stricken through] will follow in the fleet of this Season. I am afraid they will fall very much. — I have not yet found any Borax, that which is produced in this Country is rather ordinary, the best comes from

---

5. *Ibid.*, Henry Lee, Calcutta, June 6, 1814, to Andrew Cabot, Boston.

6. *Ibid.*, Henry Lee, Calcutta, Aug. 16, 1814, to Peter Remsen, N. Y.

7. *Ibid.*, Henry Lee, Calcutta, July 9, 1814, to Charles Williams, London.

China &is usually high. I shall be able to get a portion of the Sal Ammoniac, perhaps one third. Goat Skins require time to collect, those on hand are wormeaten, it is doubtful if I shall be able to get them. Shellac is high & Scarce, I may get part of the quantity order'd. — Tumerick is plenty, & Ginger also, the freight however for such bulky goods is enormous, the Ships now preparing demand £25 for 16 Cwt, I will try to get them at a reduced price, allowing them to be Stow'd in places where it would be dangerous to place goods liable to water damage but at any rate they Shall be Shipped. — The remaining articles come from Persia & Arabia, the annual fleets from thence have just arrived, but the Cargoes are not yet landed, nor do I know exactly of what they Consist. I apprehend from the bad sales of Drugs for three years past, they have brought only a Small quantity this Season, I am quite Certain as to Galls, they have not a 1000 lbs, which I regret, because I think it one of the most promising things in your list. There are several parcels of Assafoetida in the Bazar, but not good enough for your market, I do not however despair of finding some of better quality. I can procure the Senna of usual quality, which is inferiour to that which Comes from Smyrna and Turkish ports in the Mediteranean — Copal is the most reasonable in price of any of the Drugs, & by garbling it, &rejecting one third, the remainder will be of good quality — I am fully aware of the frauds practiced by Drug Dealers &will attend to your Caution in Selecting them. I know too the London market requires the best qualities, &that no other will Sell. It is this consideration which will prevent my buying Several of the articles in the list, for of all the Drugs which are brought here, only a Small part are fit for your purpose. — The new Indigo has just began to Come down, the bulk of the Crop will be here the last of Novr. The proprietors expect extravagant prices &the few Sales which have been made Seem to warrant them, viz 220/ @ 230/ for fine Kinds which last Season sold for 170/ @ 180/, there are not however many Cash buyers and the Scarcity of money is great, the houses of Agency have for years past Kept up prices by shipping largely on account of their Constituents, the

planters, & they will do all they can in that way this year, but I
doubt if they have the means of doing it to that extent which
will be required to Support the present rates. I am not therefore without great hopes of being able, towards Decr. to purchase good middling Indigo at 140/ to 150/ pm^d of 74 lbs.
Such as sold at the May Sale for 8/9^d @ 10/6^d plb. I prefer
this intermediate quality to very fine, or very ordinary, because
I know that of what Sells here for very fine, a great part passes
in London only for Second Sort, &the latter when the market is
low finds no purchasers. Besides as respects fine Indigoes, I
imagine the reduction of duties on the Continent will diminish
the difference which has heretofore been made between those
and the more ordinary Kinds. — There is one circumstance
likely to influence in a considerable degree the price of Indigo,
it is said the Company have a large remittance to make for the
payment of their dividend in England, & that they will either
buy Indigo, advance money on Consignments of Merchandize,
or purchase Bills of Exchange, in either case my expectations
in regard to a reduction in prices may be disappointed. If I
can get Indigo at the above named rate of 140/ @ 150/, I shall
invest 60,000 Rs or upwards in it, the Drugs will probably Come
to 2000 Rs. the balance will be in Choppas, if I can get them at
reasonable prices &of such a quality as suits the American market, &in Baftas &Gurrahs which are now falling, & will be
lower, the two latter do not come within your order, but as I
cannot get the Band^s. nor all the Choppas, I conceive myself
justifyed in using the discretion which you probably would have
given me, had you imagined there was any chance of my not
being able to complete your order. I have a favourable opinion
of Piece goods, the Stock on hand with you, in May was less
than the Company have had for many years, &th U. S. from
whence the Continent &W Indies have hitherto received large
Supplies, cannot of course Supply any more 'till yours are Sold.
The Company last year Sent home very few, & I am told this
year they have Still further diminish'd their investments, the
private traders have taken home Scarcely any, nor do I hear of
any intended Shipments. Indeed there are no goods here hardly

fit for London markets, & very few of any Sort. I may buy a few Seersuckers if I meet with cheap ones.

You consider it of great importance that the [concerns — stricken through] returns of your adventure should reach England as early as possible. I shall make every exertion to meet your wishes. When your letter arrived business had ceased on account ofthe Holy days, &it will not recommence 'till the last of the month, when I shall proceed to the purchase of the Drugs &Ship them on the vessels which will take them cheapest, however, as most of them now under dispatch have engaged their Cargoes I shall probably be compell'd to wait for others, or for the private traders which are daily expected. The present rate of freight is £25 for 50 feet, &Same for Ginger &Tumerick. I hope to do a little better, the freight will be made payable in London. I shall inform you the the name of the Ship or Ships when I have engaged the freight, there is no probability of Your goods leaving here 'till the middle or last of Decr. It may not be amiss to remind you on account of Insurance, that this is the fair Season to Sail out of the Bay &to double the Cape Good Hope. We do not hear of any American Privateers in this quarter, nor is there any, I imagine, to the Eastward of the Cape. The Hyderally was captured some months ago, &the Jacob Jones which Sail'd with her from America, has gone on to Manilla, from whence she returns to U. S. with a Cargo via Cape Horn. The Country Ships Sail without Convoy, &generally Stop at Isle of France or CGoodHope, Sometimes both, either for water, or to land passengers, the Premium here is 6% it Should be lower in London.

I have besides the above acknowledged letter, yours of the 28th March, with a Price Current of Drugs, for which and the political information I am obliged to you. I am extremely Sorry the negotiations are likely to be protracted thro' the Summer. I was in hopes of getting home this Season in an American Ship, 'but I shall be obliged to go by way of England, I trust there are troops enough gone over to remove all obstacles in the way of Peace, &to punish the invaders of Canada.

There are 6 or 7 Country Ships of 600 to 800 tons loading for

London, their Cargoes principally Sugar, Pepper, &Cotton, only one of the private ships arrived, the PCharlotte of Bristol, we have a list of 6 more on the way. I shall write you again by some ships to Sail in 15 days.

I cannot end this letter without declaring how much I am gratify'd with the Confidence you place in me, in the important commission I am charged with, &of assuring you of my best efforts in bringing it to a profitable result. I wish the prospect was better.

I am with much regard

Yours faithfully

(Sign'd)   HLee

Borax	22/	Choppas (	135/ .. 140/
GumCopal	20/	Do (Comp^{ys})	none
Assafoetida	30/	Sugar 1st.	10/ pBazar M^d
Shellac	20/	Pepper	17/ " "
Ginger	6/8	Coffee	15/ " "
Tumerick	3/4	Cotton	15/ " "
Galls	35/	Gurrahs middling	70/ pC^o. ⎫
SAmm^c	22/	Baftas	67/8/@75/ " ⎭
Senna	10/		Sold at march sale
GoatSkins	20/p100		in London 16/ to 18/

Interest is just now 1½ to 1¾ pM^o. for the best paper &will continue So for Some months. I have no fears for any of the houses, their distress arises from the want of returns for their Shipments to Europe, &the extreme poverty of the Country, which has not Capital adequate to the business doing, what little there is the Company have, &will not pay off, 'till they can get a loan in England, on better terms, their paper is Secure, & if Bullion falls to 4/6 pDollar, I suppose the Capitalists of Great Britain will remit &buy.

If the war continues be good enough to send my letters to America by private hand, that our villianous Gov^t may not intercept them

LETTER FROM HENRY LEE, CALCUTTA, NOV. 30, 1814, TO
P. T. JACKSON, BOSTON, ANNOUNCING PLANS FOR A SHIPMENT
TO THE UNITED STATES [1]

The confidence of Henry Lee that peace had taken or shortly would take place is emphasized in a letter of the same date in which he announced: "My expenses are now a heavy charge, since I have no interest to receive, on the contrary, I am in advance to owners." [2] He had evidently invested all available funds in merchandise, which he had been steadily buying since word of the peace negotiations had reached Calcutta.

Although at the time of the letter below, Henry Lee had not yet sold his coffee, on Dec. 7 he disposed of 2,000 bazaar maunds at 15 rupees per maund.[3]

Mr P T Jackson   Calcutta Nov 30th. 1814
                                            p Camoens
          dear Patrick   via Pernambusco
                                       Copy p Mangles

I received three or four months ago, your letter of 21stOctr. the only one you have written for upwards of two years!!, I will not tell you what are my thoughts or feelings upon this mortifying subject, nor of the ill effects I have sustain'd in my property, &still more important in my health from the want of such early advices as to probable continuance of the war, as would have induced me to embark last year. — Should you however by ill fortune (which God forbid) be ever placed in my Situation, & I in yours, and refuse at your pressing intreaties to write a dozen letters, you will then probably have some idea of what mine now are. The reasons you give for not writing appear to me very unsatisfactory, &they must so to you I imagine, if you reflect upon them, but enough of this. — I shall draw on S Williams about three thousand pounds sterling, 6 mos

1. Jackson-Lee Papers, "Letters written in Calcutta by H. Lee from July 1813 to March 1816."

2. *Ibid.*, Henry Lee, Calcutta, Nov. 30, 1810, to Andrew Cabot, Boston.

3. *Ibid.*, "Henry Lee's Calcutta Memorandum Book. — 1814 & 1815 — ."

sight in favour of Cruttenden &McKillop, in payment of some goods purchased at them, I wish my friends to remit that amount immediately on receipt of this. To meet this draft — I have shipped on the Princess C for Havana&New York Indigo &Nutmegs to amount of about Rs 12,000. I have also a balance in hands of SWilliams on shipment of Indigo which may amount to 5 or £700, in addition to which are the proceeds of my adventures in R & H^y, provided they are not remitted. If these are not Sufficient I must rely upon my friends, they will not run any risk, because my property here, (not less than 30,000 Rps, including the [interlineated: remaining] proceeds of this draft), is Sufficient to indemnify them, let what will happen — The Shipment I have made in the P (C) cannot fail doing well, whether Sold in Havana or U. S. In event of wars continuing, which is impossible in my opinion, the P^s goods will be sold in Havana at any rate offer'd, &Nutmegs & Indigo Carried to London. If Captain T concludes to [continue — stricken out] pursue his voyage from Havana to US, he will take on the Indigo of course &the p^s goods Nutmegs, unless 100¢ pRupee for former & $4 for the latter can be had, clear of all charges.

I am in hopes, Captn T on hearing of Peace at Cape Good Hope when he touches for advice, will go directly to NYork, he has consulted me in all his proceedings, & I have advised him to do it. — I have not yet sold my Coffee, if I get the Batavia price only, there will be a good profit, but such is the Scarcity of Cash, & dull state of trade, in consequence of that & non arrival of foreigners &private ships, that I am afraid I shall be obliged to take less, there cannot at any rate be a loss. I hope my father nor any of you will be alarmed at my Speculations, I am as prudent as possible, &have nothing at risk, I have made no Shipment but 10,000 Rs Indigo last year, upon which I obtain'd an advance of the cost, & expect 6 @ 700 £ profit, I have gain'd several thousand Rupees on pepper &c & hope for as much more in some Nutmegs, so that my situation is better than I fear'd it might be, when I met the loss from my banians last year.

I suppose you are occupyd in your new profession, &that any

information as to markets, or what is passing in this quarter will be quite uninteresting. I would otherwise write longletters for I have nothing besides to do, except execute a Commission from MWilliams, which throws 2 or 3000 Rp^s into my pocket. All the fleet are in, Ihave no letters, except a short one from Andrew, I expected 20 in every fleet, henceforth I abandon all hopes, except from my wife, I Know if God spares her she will not fail me, I should be anxious because of no letter from her, had not Andrew told me she was well in April, he had rec^d letters constantly so that there was no want of opportunities

Yours evr

HL^e.

Tell my wife I do not write by this conveyance because I prefer another which offers as safer.   HL

Letter from Cruttenden & Mackillop, Calcutta, Dec. 3, 1814, to Capt. William Turnbull, Princess Charlotte, with Instructions for a Voyage to the West Indies and the United States [1]

Capt. Turnbull of the *Princess Charlotte* was one of the free-traders who had come out to India upon the abolition of the East India Co.'s monopoly. The Calcutta firm showed considerable perspicuity in so strongly anticipating the imminence of a peace which was not to be signed in Ghent until three weeks after the date of this letter.

The piece goods shipped on the *Princess Charlotte* were on account of Andrew Cabot and the owners of the *Reaper,* but the nutmegs and indigo, invoiced at about sicca rupees 28,000, were one-half on Henry Lee's own account.[2]

Captn William Turnbull   Calcutta Dec 3^d. 1813 [4]
   Sir
        Herewith you have an Invoice &Bill of Lading of twenty six Bales of P^s. Goods and Five Boxes of Nutmegs shipped by us

1. Jackson-Lee Papers, "Letters written in Calcutta by H. Lee from July 1813 to March 1816."
2. *Ibid.,* "Invoices of all the goods ship'd by Henry Lee during his stay in Calcutta May 1812 to March 1816."

on board the Princess Charlotte to your address. — We understand it is your intention to Call at some of the W India Islands, and also at some port in the United States of America, should peace have been reestablished between that Country &GBritain. Should you go to Cuba or any other West India Island, it is our wish you w^d sell the cloths provided One Spanish dollar p^rRupee Can be obtain'd, and four Spanish dollars plb for the Nutmegs, nett of all Charges. If these prices cannot be realized, We prefer your taking the goods to the United States, believing from very good information, they will Command much higher rates than our limits. On your arrival there, you will deliver them to the order of Mr Peter Remsen, New York.

If however from the Continuance of the American war, or any other cause, you determine upon proceeding to London from the West Indies, We would have you accept the most you can obtain for the Piece goods, as they are not suited to the English market, and three Spanish dollars perpound for the Nutmegs.

You will remit the proceeds of any Goods you Sell in the West Indies to Mr Peter Remsen of New York, provided you proceed to that place, otherwise to Samuel Williams Esqr N° 13 Finsbury Square London, to whom also you will deliver any of the Goods which may remain'd unsold on your arrival in London.

For your Compensation in the transactions of this business, we agree to allow you Five perCent on the Nett proceeds of whatever is sold by you in the West Indies, and two and an half perCent on the N^tproceeds of the piece goods &nutmegs delivered to Mr Remsen New York.

On these goods we have effected an Insurance of Rs 35000..0..0 from this port to London, with leave to touch at all intermediate ports, including the West Indies &North America, the premium is 9 perCent, with a return of 3 perCent, if you Should declare the risk off in West India or America. — From either of those places the policy covers the proceeds of the goods to London, but in that case the proceeds must be remitted in *Bullion* &not in Goods.

We enclose the first of our Bill for £3300 on Mr Remsen, refer'd to in the annexed letter to him, and which Bill you will observe is payable to Mess^s Palmer Wilson &Co on the 3^{d}Dec 1815, at the office of Samuel Williams Esqr in London. — The second third of this bill We forward to Mess^s Palmer Wilson &C^o by the direct Ships proceeding to London, &to whom we forward the policy of Insurance as it is payable there. — We inform them that you will put them in funds for the amount of the Bill from the West Indies or America, or that in Case you take the goods to the Thames, you will deliver them to Sam^{l}Williams Esqr. subject to the payment of our above mentioned Bill for 3300£.

Entreating You to excuse all the trouble we give, we remain with best wishes for your welfar &success.

dear Sir Your faithful Servants
(Sign'd)   C &McK

(Rec^d a Copy at the above WT)

[written across face of the letter:]
Copy sent A Cabot p Jane
do   do   F. Lee pPortsea
do   do   F. Lee pHewett
one Copy sent Williams pHewett

LETTER FROM HENRY LEE, CALCUTTA, JAN. 24, 1815, TO PORCHER & CO., LONDON, WITH INVOICE OF GOODS FOR SALE [1]

While waiting for the news of peace, which he correctly believed imminent, Henry Lee continued to dispose of goods which he felt would net a larger profit in Calcutta than if shipped abroad (sicca rupees 13,447, 12 annas, 3 pice worth of sugar, sicca rupees 938, 6 annas of gurrahs, etc.).[2] He was shipping goods to the United States (or, failing peace, to London) via the West Indies, and making purchases on behalf of London merchants, and was also making ship-

---

1. Jackson-Lee Papers, "Letters written in Calcutta by H. Lee from July 1813 to March 1816."

2. *Ibid.*, "Henry Lee's Calcutta Memorandum Book. — 1814 & 1815 — ."

ments directly to London. The goods shipped on the *Countess of London* were invoiced at sicca rupees 24,095, 4 annas, about a third in nutmegs and the rest in piece goods. On Feb. 27, 1815, he made a shipment to India on the *Hercules*, of piece goods invoiced at sicca rupees 31,978, 1 anna, 6 pice, two-thirds on his own account and the rest on that of his brother Francis; the shipment was consigned to Samuel Williams, for whom he had also been making extensive purchases.[3] He was not to make any further shipments on his own account for over six months. He was so encouraged by his prospects that on Dec. 19, 1814, he wrote that, though he had sustained a loss from his banians, he would "make it up in profits on goods sold, & perhaps something more."[4]

"Chuman" is an error for *chunan,* Hindustani for lime.

pC Loudon
dup^t p^r Albion. Calcutta Jany 24th1815.
Mess^s Porcher &C^o Trip^t d^{ld} A & Co.
London
    Gentlemen
      I enclose an Invoice &Bill of Lading of Sundry goods, shipped on board the Countess of London, Hammond [?] Master to your address, which you will dispose of for the most they will obtain &place the proceeds to my account. The cloths are of an excellent quality &well Suited to the Continental markets or those of the United States of America. The Nutmegs are large &sound, they are pack'd in Chuman to preserve them from worms. As it is expedient on any account that a Speedy sale of these goods Should be effected, I should imagine it will be best to have them lodged in Warehouses under your direction, instead of passing thro' the Companys hands, to wait their periodical Sales, but I leave this to your better judgment, convinced you will do every thing which my interest requires.
           [Iam Gentⁿ
             YourObtSer — stricken through]

3. *Ibid.,* "Invoices of all the goods ship'd by Henry Lee during his stay in Calcutta from May 1812 to March 1816."

4. *Ibid.,* "Letters written in Calcutta by H. Lee from July 1813 to March 1816," Henry Lee, Calcutta, Dec. 19, 1814, to Francis Lee, Boston.

I have this day drawn on you against this Consignment at Six months sight for Two thousand three hundred pounds Sterling, in favour of Mess^s Alexander &C^o. which I request you will honor

[written across face of letter:]   I am Gent^n

([Triplicates — stricken through] Your Ob^{d}Ser

Quadr^s p. Marchioness Ely)   (Sgd)   HLee

LETTER FROM HENRY LEE, CALCUTTA, FEB. 1, 2, 1815, TO FRANCIS LEE, BOSTON, DESCRIBING CONDITIONS AND PLANS [1]

In reference to the peace negotiations mentioned below, Henry Lee on Feb. 18, 1815, wrote that "the demands of the Eng^h . . . Cannot be consider'd as unreasonable." Chief among these demands was the establishment of a permanent Indian territory between Canada and the western United States; the revision of the Canadian boundary line in a manner favorable to the British; an agreement on the part of the United States to maintain no forts or armed forces along the Canadian boundary; and the relinquishment by the Americans of the right to fish in British waters and to dry their catch on British territory.

M^r F Lee   Calcutta Feby 1st1815
    dear F.

    I wrote you on 14th & 16 ulto pGen^l Hewett, Since then the Royal Geo &Cuffnells Indiamen have arrived, having left Eng^d 28th Augt. the negotiations at Ghent broken off, I was afraid the powers of our Commissions were not ample en^o to enable them to concede the demands which w^d be made. I suppose Madison will endeavour to prolong the war, unless the English should be very Successful with their land forces, yet I doubt if the nation will Support him. I am greatly disappointed in the expectation I form'd of Peace Some months ago, as you must have been. You appear'd quite certain the Gottenburgh Mission would produce an immediate Settlement. I thought so, or at least an armistice or preliminary treaty, leaving the points in dispute to an after discussion, &adjustment. — I cannot

1. Jackson-Lee Papers, "Letters written in Calcutta by H. Lee from July 1813 to March 1816."

decide (if I did, might change my mind) whether I shall wait for peace, which must come within the year, or embark in two months. I cannot bear to think of giving up the advantages which a Peace w^d bring me, incur an enormous expence in a passage to England, especially as my health is in a state which renders so circuitous & unpleasant a route very inconvenient. — You must not in any of your voyages count upon my Stay here, at least in those undertaken after this arrives. — I did not get a line from home, or Mr Williams by either of the last fleets,, 'tis very Surprizing why M^{r}Williams did not write. — Upon all your letter is a direction for Mr Hall to open them in case I should not be here. I imagine he Started from America with an intention of coming here, &that he gave up the plan for some reason or other. I hear nothing of him, all the Ships which left England to Septr have arrived Safe. — I have not Sold your 1000 M^{ds}. Coffee, it does not fall either here or in Eng^d. but there are no buyers, of my own I have Sold 2000 M^{ds}. at a gain of 10000 Rp^s. & have 2500 more on hand. I have your Nutmegs on hand, shall sell if a profit can be obtain'd, the arrival of any foreign Ships would probably create a demand. I bot some Sugar &other articles on hearing the Peace, have Sold all at a Small gain. I have on hand in p^s goods, Coffee & Nutmegs on acc^t of the Owners more than the amount due them. Upon goods Sold for their acc^t there is a gain enough to make up the loss by My banians, but my expences have been &are now, going on, without any interest to meet them. — Every thing has turn'd out So much against my Calculations, that the voyage will close to a loss. — The P Charlotte was to leave Madras about 12thulto. If She discharges in U. S. my Shipment will do well, in Havana the p^s goods & nutmegs will do, but the broken Indigo I am afraid of in London, tho' the quality is very fine. — If the P.C. goes to London from Cape, you must order the p^s goods, Nutmeg, &perhaps the broken Indigo to America. — If I had not thought Peace certain, I would not have made the Shipment. — The 1000 p^s Choppas I had made last year, I have taken to my own account & sent them to London, there was no Selling them at any price, there will be a gain of 10/

pC° at the price I allow. — I have sold a few more bales of the White goods, but have no hopes of getting rid of the remainder, there is not a buyer in town, two more Portuguese are expected daily, but they will not take Such goods as I have remaining, but for these two expected Ships, piece goods would fall very low, but a great quantity Could not be purchased without raising them. the Cloth dealers are poor, &will not make many goods 'till our ships arrive, there are no Cotton goods in Bazar but Gurrahs, Baftas, Sanda &All^d goods. — Choppas fallen from 135/ to 115/. No Band^s made. I could get them for 87/8 like the Reapers, on 4 m^os contract. — No colour'd goods made these [four — stricken through] 2 years, except such as Portuguese want, Indigo remains the Same, Crop 90,000 M^ds. will be as high or higher next year, the Scarcity of money, & diminished number of Indiamen has Kept the price 20/ to 30 Rps lower than it would otherwise have been. — There are only 7 houses of Agency, they have 7/8th of the Crop, &their plan is to Ship, unless they can get a high price. It may be bo't of the natives Somewhat cheaper, but of an ordinary quality, a good judge will sometimes get a bargain from them. — You must not count upon Indigo Such as I sent theShippers in the R. at less than 130/ pm^d. — T.H.P. has written to Palmer &C°. to buy Indigo if good quality at 100/ or under, he was led into this error by my letters I imagine, but if he had look'd into London price Currents, &noticed the quotations, he would not have imagined it could ever be so low, P &C° have Sold their best at 220/. & ordinary, 150/. Middling 170/ — If the double duties Continue, the New Orleans People will Supply ordinary Indigo cheaper than the Bengal, &fine Indigoes will now go direct to Europe. — The exportation of P^s goods to England has been less than usual, I think they will Keep up in England, as no foreigners have taken any to Europe except the Portuguese for the Brazils & Peninsula — The market for all Kinds of Europe goods continues very bad. I have often Cautioned you against Sending any thing this way, but Tar and Spars, &Copper if low, the latter article is down to 45/ but Will advance again to 50/ — We have two or three cargoes from S°America.

Mr Williams I am afraid will not Send me a letter of Credit as you requested. I wish Pat had remitted my funds. Dollars were low in Eng^d &would have made a remittance equal to 2/4^d pRupee, which with the disc^t on Bills in America would have been an advantageous transaction, besides increasing my Small capital. I intend to Ship by the first vessel 60000 Rps to SWilliams in Flags of a quality Such as used to cost 140/ Say 6000 p^s. Gurrahs &Baftas at 60/ &few Seersuckers, 2/3^ds on my account, one third on yours. I pay for the goods by Bills drawn against the Shipment at 2/9^d 6 m^o. the Gurrahs &Baftas will I think do well in London. The Hdkfs I shall order Sold at 25/ otherwise held for your orders, they will cost me 110/ C^o nett of drawback. The Same goods to America pay a duty of 7½ pC^t., So that I can send them to you via London almost as cheap as they could go direct, for besides the 12½ pC^t Saved, the price is 30 pC^t lower than they used to cost us, &15% below what they will be when our Ships arrive. The India Captains paid 130/ @ 135/ for the Same goods. I shall get them insured here. You must write M^rWilliams immediately on getting this what to do with the Hdkfs &Seersuckers, &also the Baftas &Gurrahs if unsold. — You will of course make provision for their payment. I think there cannot under any circumstances be a loss on this adventure, 18/ will Save us on the Hdkfs which is less then they ever were in the worst of times the March Sale of 1814 was 28/ to 32/ pps. & I think the demand for Continent which is great, & for Canada, will Keep them from falling below 23/ to 26/. Gurrahs sold at 25/ for Companys, mine I think will sell at 15/, &Baftas about the Same, 12/ will Save us, at which price they must answer in U. S. the quality if very good, none of the Baftas inferiour to Reapers Calliputty which Sold for $4. — The Seersuckers will bring $12 in common times in America. It is not improbable they will be wanted in London for West Indies. — Should a letter from W come forward with liberty to draw for the £2000, I shall try to negotiate on our joint account, in which case I shall have to Send the goods to London as security for payment of the Bill.

Do not lose any time in writing M^rW upon the Subject of

this adventure. I presume in any event the Hdkfs will not Sell
for less than $7 @ $7.50 in U. S. I never knew them under
$6.50 for goods of equal quality, the[y] are full 20 pCent bet-
ter than the Gullivers her last voyage, which cost 127/. I
should prefer Bands. but they are not procurable. I may get a
few hundred pieces. I shall desire MrWilliams to inform you
the prices in London of Choppas, that no time may be lost in
getting orders to him in case you think it best to have them sold
there. It will be necessary to recruit him in part, &for the balance I suppose he will be content to draw on you. — The fall of
Bullion in Engd has produced an effect here already on the
money market. Some remittances in Dollars @ 4/4½ were
recd in the last ships, &large Sums are look'd for in the next. —
All the houses of Agency are firm, there is no danger in taking
Bills upon them, &it is not worth while to pay SW a Guarantee.
— The duties are to be reduced, but will not be much in our
favour, as we pay double &get no drawbacks. — No Danes
nor French yet arrived to Eastward of the Cape, they are too
poor to commence yet. Do not Send any Ships to Java or Isle
France. Produce will be high, &we cannot make a circuitous
trade answer in competition with Cargoes which go direct to
Europe. We may in Bengal ps goods, if wanted in Medn &c
&c. — Drugs are high having been bought up for London.
There will not be any Ships Sent from hence (as I thought
probable some time ago) to U. S. the Country ships are prevented by Navigation law &new Charter, & there are no English
Ships here, nor any expected, &if they come they will return
to London. — I repeat again that Piece goods cannot be made
cheaper than the prices the Americans have paid for three or
four years past. Raw Silk is 50 pCt lower than before the opening of the Continent to English. So that Silk Hdkfs can be
afforded 10 to 15 pCt lower than the prices of 1809/ to 1812/
— American Bands like Reapers say, can be afforded at 100/.
Choppas of that cargo at 110/. — but they will be higher,
especially if there should be a demand for England, as is usually the Case. — Sugar varies from 8/ to 9/ &10/ will never be
lower than 8/ & generally higher. — Ginger 5/ to 6/8, SaltPeter

5/ to 6/8 — I mention these things for your government in your voyages here.

Feby 2^{d}1815 — I shall make a Shipment in a vessel to Sail in 30 to 40 days 1/3 on your acc^t & 2/3ds on my own. I have great hopes from this adventure. Silk Hdkfs must be wanted, tho' I dare Say the war has lessen'd the consumption. The Seersuckers I shall send are assorted, narrow &broad stripes, & check, of all colours, they used to sell for 10 @ 14 dollars. — I shall write you again via Liverpool in 15 or 20 days.

$$\text{(Sgd) Yours}$$
$$\text{HLee}$$

B Gurrahs Common 60/ @ 65/.
　do   best 75/ @ 80/

	Baftas 45/	Not many in Bazar will rise when Portuguese come P^s goods cannot again be so low as they were 12m^o since. There are not many made, & the Eng^h Ships will require some when they come in May. Some foreigners too, will no doubt be this way by Ship — One Dane is on the way.
All^d Goods	Chon^y 75/	
	Sannas 90/ @ 110/	
	Emerty 65/	

[written across face of the letter:]
p^r Albion
Copy p Marchioness Ely
care of Mr Andrews. —
sail^d from S^t. Helna — 2? July 1815.

LETTER FROM HENRY LEE, CALCUTTA, MAY 8–27, 1815, TO FRANCIS LEE, BOSTON, WITH A SKETCH OF BUSINESS POSSIBILITIES [1]

The letter below describes in detail the state of trade at the time it was written and the possibilities for it after the restoration of peace, which is announced in one of the later sections. Henry Lee evidently had no high opinion of the knowledge or efficiency of the English merchants trading with India. His account of the fate of those who, seek-

1. Jackson-Lee Papers, "Letters written in Calcutta by H. Lee from July 1813 to March 1816."

ing credit from the houses of agency, came under their control, is instructive.

"S. Cabot . . . our worthless cousin," as Henry Lee called him, was Stephen Cabot (1788–1831), a son of Samuel and Sally (Barrett) Cabot. His life made up in variety for its comparative brevity.[2]

(p Neptune)
Mr F Lee   /Dup pr Portuguese Ship Fama/
           Trip. pSwallow —   Calcutta May 8th 1815.
    dear F.

    Your last Came via Madeira, it is dated 13th & 24th June. SCabot was So thoughtless as to send it via Bombay, which besides the delay of 3 mo. put me to an expence of $5. he wrote me himself a letter of 3 lines, which I suppose was all the time he could spare from his drunken revels. — So much for our worthless cousin. — I have a letter from S W authorizing me to draw on him, Twenty five hundred Pounds. (£2500.0.0) on my own account, which I shall do. I wish the money had been re-mitted, because of the bad rate of Exchange, & the difficulty of Selling Bills — but I Suppose Pat thought it uncertain whether I should be here, he (S W) Seems to Consider the £2000, you desired him to hold to my order, as part of this Sum, I do not however, & shall draw for that also on your Sole account, & not half on my own as I before wrote you. — I have already in-form'd you by half dozen letters, of my having Ship'd on Her-cules for London, two thirds on my acct & 1/3 on yours, the following goods, consigned to S Williams.

viz 3000 ps [interlineated: (Cys)] Choppas cost 105/ Co.

"   345 " SFine Compy Bands. 125/ Co.   (*the amount insured is [it —
                                           stricken through] 2 [blot]
     600 " Seersuckers assorted patterns   26,000 Rps See letter to
          & Colours, broad yellow Stripe,   SW March 3d)
     Check blue Stripe, Narrow yellow Stripe &c. — cost 9/ pps —

The cost is about *25,000Rps upon which insurance is made, payable in London in Case of loss, & Policy transmitted to Porcher & Co. who will hand to SW on the acceptance of my

2. Briggs, *op. cit.*, vol. i, p. 228; vol. ii, pp. 598–615.

draft for £3000, in their favour, against this shipment, drawn
on M^rWilliams. — I have told SW. you would send him orders
for the disposal of these goods — In meantime, I authorize him
to accept for the Choppas 25/, Seer-suckers 40/, Band^s 35/. —
tho' I think if Peace with GBritain has been made, the adventure would terminate more favourably in U. S. The Band^s I
told you I had contracted for, will begin to come down in a
month. The Companys, such as used some years ago to cost
140/ will Stand me in 110/, &the Reapers quality which you
Sold at $7.50, about 87/8. The latter will cost delivered in
U. S. $3.30 to $3.40, the former $4.20¢, *all charges,* [inter-
lineated: except duty in America] *including, freight & insurance from London to America, & interest,* valuing them at old
prices, with the addition of the new duties, the profit will be 50
perCent upon the cost here. If sold in London at the last prices,
say of Septr Sale 1814, the gain will be Something less. — If We
get these Hdkfs to U. S. before any direct importations from
hence, I think they must do extremely well, but should Americans arrive within 6 mo^s. they Cannot undersell us. — they will,
whenever they Come, have to pay 100/ @ 105/ for my 87/8, &
an export duty of 7½%, & 125/ to 135/ for Companys, for
Choppas like mine, 125/to 130/, indeed these prices are less
than the India Captains gave last Season, & are not beyond the
cost & a very moderate profit to the Merchant, &Manufacturer.
— The reduction in raw material has never produced so much
effect in prices as I expected. — &of late it has been advancing
from 6/8 to 8/8 pseer — It has been found to Stand a competition with Italian Silk, which I did not believe it could. — As
you Seem to think Scarlets more Saleable than Chocolates, I
shall vary the Colours from what I intended, and have ☞ *
have 60 S. 30 C. 10 B &G. — I prefer Band^s because they are
more liked in U. S. &because [none — stricken through] Few
have been Shipped to London, not more than 2 or 3000 p's. —
Of Choppas great quantities are gone & going — but they Cost
125/ upon an average, & cannot be afforded under 22/ to 25/ —
The Band^s cost 135/. I shall have 6000 p's Band^s. &may buy
if I can get them cheap, 1 or 2000 p's Choppas. — My first ship-

ment will be made in 2 M^{os}. & [interlineated: will] consist of all
the Hdkfs then ready, &2000 p's Blue Gurrahs, which I am
getting dy'd, they stand me in little more than white &will be of
an excellent Quality. — I observe they sold at 22/ to 24/ last
sale, &every bale (900) put up by the Company, was disposed
of. — They are much used in all quarters, but it is the African
trade I rely most upon, — not a bale has been Sent from hence,
nor do I believe any will go in private trade. — The Company
Sent only a small investment last year, & of those 3500 *Coast*
goods, which must have comprised many of their Blue Cloths,
were burnt in the Bengal, at Ceylon. Their Shipments this year
will be small, only 8 Ships are expected. Several of which will
go to the Easter^d. last year they had 16, & two preceeding years
28 & 36!!! — I do not think it will be expedient to have the
Blue Cloths go to America in Case of Peace, they will Sell better in London, I shall limit them at 18/, only 2/ or 3/ more than
white Cloths of the Same quality would Sell for. — In addition
to these two articles, I may ship some white Gurrahs, if, as I
expect, they should fall to about 62/ for those of good quality,
they have fallen in Eng^d. but the worst brought at Sep Sale 20/,
I calculate on 15/ to 16/. They write from Eng^d. the Continental Manufactures, have been so much improved as to cheapness, &c, that Bengal p's goods will not henceforth find the Sale
they formerly did. I knew this very well, in few years when the
raw material becomes cheap, Europeans will make as cheap as
they can here, all except very heavy cloths. At present Cotton
is 2/ lb, & must continue So till our war ends. A p's of Gurrah
requires 5 lbs Cotton, at least, which is 10 Shillings Sterling,
for the raw material only. The shippers of P's goods here, when
they do ship, go wholly upon Baftas, Cossas, &Mamoodies. I
do not believe there has been 100 Bales Gurrahs sent to London
in private trade, these 3 years. The Company Send a few, and
as to the Salampores & Longcloths from the Coast, they cost so
high that they Cannot be afforded under 20/ for the most inferiour quality. Should I send any white Gurrahs, I shall
order S W to Sell them in London, they will not do to reship
to U. S. — I cannot now say what my next Shipment will

amount to, it must depend on my Band[s] coming down, probably 20 to 25000 Rp's. My third will follow in 2 more months, &will amount to about the Same. So that you may estimate the whole, including the Hercules at 75000 Rp's. of which one third for your & 2/3ds for my account. You will have to remit Mr W. in addition to the £2000, of yours now in his hands &2500£ of mine, Such further Sum as you think necessary. I hope you will be able to do this without inconvenience. If the war continues I suppose your Capital will be idle. You must not defer writing instructions to Mr W respecting these goods, under the idea, that I myself will be in London before your orders will reach him. It is probable I may be there, but the time of my departure is uncertain, &my passage will be long. I hope you wrote Mr W immediately on getting notice from me, which you must have done long ago, of this intended shipment — Having been so often disappointed in my expectations Since my Stay here. I have not entered into this Speculation without much considera-tion. I do not at present believe it is possible we can lose any-thing let what may happen — rate the goods at prices lower than they were ever Sold at in London, &still we shall gain, the very low prices they are purchased at, Saves us from loss. When I was in London, India goods were at the lowest depres-sion, I saw the most intelligent brokers, &went to the India Stores & examined goods. *Choppas* were then, in common with other goods, shut out of the Continent. Still they Sold for 19/ @ 22/ for such as I sent in the Hercules at 105/. Blue &White Gurrahs were 15/. they are of all Cottons, the most in demand, for Med[n]. Africa, SDomingo, Spain, Baltic, S[o] America &Can-ada. If the Slave trade is carried on to the extent I fear it will be, it is probable Blue Gurrahs will Sell for 24/. The French for the present must buy in London, not a bale has been ex-ported to any other Quarter. No foreign Ships have been here yet, nor are there any expected, except some Gov[t] Ships with the Officers of the Indain possessions. the fleet with those on board have reach'd the Cape, &look'd for here.

I observe the price of Indigo at Oct[r] sale is 1 @ 1/6 below the preceding one of May. I am afraid Turnbull must end his voyage then, &that my Shipment by him will give no profit. I should not have engaged in that adventure had I not tho't it nearly certain peace would have been made in time for him to go to U. S. I felt so certain, especially after getting your letters p Rambler that I regretted not having increased the sum. Indigo will continue down in London, I have no doubt the Sale about this time was very low, &that such Indigo as suits the consumption of U. S. went at 4/ to 5/6 plb, ordinary kinds at 3/5. The Sep Sale of 1815. will be still lower, for the crop now on the way is the largest ever Collected, & 30,000 M^ds of very inferiour, much of it will go at 2/9 @ 4/6 — For 2 years to come at least, London will be a better place to buy Indigo for our use, than Calcutta, especially if the Crop now on the ground should be as productive as we have reason to expect. — All agree it cannot be less than 100,000 M'ds, & if the weather holds good a month longer, there will be 130 to 150,000 M'ds. There will not be buyers for more than 30,000 M'ds, — this year, prices have been kept up by favourable accounts from Eng^d, now they are the reverse — I am of opinion good Indigo may be had next Novr. at 130/ @ 140/, Such as sold this Season at 170/, &so in proportion for other kinds. The natives will have to Sell 70/ to 100/, &it is among them a judge of the article will get bargains. The Agency houses will ship the Chief part, still some of them must also sell part. The Exporter to Eng^d gets a drawback of 5 pm^d. we pay a duty of that Amount.

There are only 2 buyers for p^s goods (2 Portuguese) the quantity at market very small, the Manufacturers have nearly discontinued making them, &converted their Capitals to Other uses, prices as I last quoted, except Gurrahs, which are rather lower, & falling. No cold goods now made, nor Band^s. Lungees or Sistersoies, nor indeed any other kinds except All^a & Tanda, Gurrahs & Luckipore Baftas, the three first for Portuguese, the latter for Eng^d. Seven ships are loading for Eng^d. 20,000 M^ds Indigo, 15000 p^s Choppas, 600 bales p^s goods — A quantity Pepper, Sugar, Salt-Peter, &Cotton make up their Cargoes. 10 or 12 more will be dispatch'd before the 1st Jan^y, with Cotton principally. There will not be many Cotton p's goods ship'd this year, the letters from Eng^d. discourage Sending them, besides which, they are not to be had.

I shall embark in Octr or Novr. If you have any business, with Mr. Stark, & in his absence, Mr Goodwin, I presume they will remain all the war, unless their employers order the goods to Eng^d. of this you will know by inquiring of them. Shold rate of Exchange on London, be favourable, I should think a remittance here might do well, to be placed at interest 12 perCent, 'till the war ended, & then invested in Band^s & Choppas, or Indigo, if good can be bought at or under 100 pm^d. M^r S will be able to buy the Hdkfs by Sending to Cossimbazar at near about the rate mine Cost, which I am about to Ship. I do not think Coarse Cottons will ever again pay a great profit, unless bo't here cheaper than prices will rise to after Peace with our country, or whenever there may be the usual demand here for them. You are aware that by New Charter, an English register'd Ship, mannd with 2/3ds English Seamen, Can go direct from hence to any port in Eastern Coast of America, North or South, or to any foreign Island in W Indies or Atlantic. Should many private traders come out in Course of 12 or 10 [?] mo's, & peace have taken place, it is not improbable some of them may adopt the plan of Captⁿ Turnbull, but this year, even if Peace takes place, I do not believe any will go to America. The English Merchants in general are far from possessing that degree of intelligence & enterprize which our's do, & of the India trade appear to me as ignorant as if it was just discovered, their vessels sail at an enormous expence, certainly double what ours do, &they make no dispatch, either here or in Europe. The freight to London is now £25 pton. A ship of 500 tons will carry 700 Measurement, &yet all agree that little or nothing can be made. They cannot supply the continent with gross goods, unless allowed to go direct. We can [not — stricken through] undersell them, even if compell'd to go first to U.S. unless more duties are imposed upon us, which I think there may be.

.With regard to owners goods, the Coffee is Still unsold, &the Nutmegs. Of the Mem^o. P^s goods I sent you Some time ago, the 2000 p^s Mow Sannas are sold at cost & interest. My expences

here, passage money to Eng^d &c &c, will diminish their property
to a very small Amount. I am not decided what to do with the
balance which may be due them. The Coffee I shall send to
London, unless sold, & also such of the p's goods as may remain
on hand, when I embark. — I have seen the Presidents message,
the Princes Speech, &the Despatches of the Commissioners to
19th. Augt. I suppose the war will continue unless the British
make Some abatement in their demands which I think not improbable. I judge from Something in a Speech of Lord Liver-
pools in a debate upon American affairs. The return of M^r
Dallas which must happen in Decr. will decide whether Peace
can result from the present negotiation. We shall hear by the
next fleet of his arrival at Ghent, &[also — stricken through]
soon after of the final issue of the negotiation, it must end one
way or another. If Peace takes place, Still I shall Send the
Hdkfs to Eng^d. I must do it or I cannot sell my Bills, as no one
would take them without a Consignment of the property as
Security, but in this Case, we shall be as well off as our Countrymen who Ship direct, except Mr S. who bought as low as I have.
There will not be any Hdkfs like my Second quality, ship'd to
America within 12 mo's after Peace, at less than 110/ to 115/
including export duty, add to this freight 11 pCt 15 m^os Interest, 8 pCt Insurance, &the price of 2^dquality will stand the importer $355 @ 350 ps. which is something more than I estimate
the cost of mine via London. With regard to Blue &White
Gurrahs, Peace cannot affect them, they will be sold in Eng^d at
any rate, or if you order them reship'd, it will be to Havana, or
some other port in W Indies — Leghorn is a good market for
White Gurrahs. I have had the worst ever imported to America,
sold there at $5½ pps. & you must remember, the worst goods
of this description sent to London by Company are not sold for
less than 20/. &that my Blue Cloths are equal in Quality &
colour, to Madras 9 Call Guineas which cost there 30/ to 33/
[interlineated: Pagodas] pC^o. —

All kinds of Europe goods, except a few eatables, such. as
Cheese, Hams &c. are low. By the new System of duties, imports in British bottoms are charged with only 2½ duty, except

Spirits &Wines, which continue as they now are. No change with regard to foreigners who Still pay 25 pCt. *Do not Send any merchandize here,* except tar & Spars, the first which comes will do well, & shipbuilding has so much increas'd that great quantities are wanted. More vessels have been built within 3 years than for the 10 preceding, & 10 or 12 are now on the Stocks, including a 74.

I shall write you again by a vessel to Sail in a month. — All the Agency houses stand firm. If property should become unsafe, as it may, in case of a long Continuance of the war, you may send it here, & have it converted into Companys paper at 6 pCt. or loan'd at 9 to 12 pCt. to the Merchants upon Collateral Security. I think Alexanders house the most solid, from their wealth & prudent way of doing business, but the others are also safe. Do not pay S W. any guarantee. If a bill should be return'd the drawers are good. The safest houses in London are those which give Bills on India, &they must, from the nature of their Concerns, always be So. —

Yours

(S'g'd)   HLee

We hear nothing of Admiral Hull, who has been expected in these Seas, with a 74 & 3 frigates — he would do much mischief. H'M'Ts Ships would not Stand an hours Contest if all collected together. there are 6 or 7 half mann'd frigates & a 74 — A privateer off the Cape has taken a Batavia Ship, the Clarendon. Dollars 204/8, 6 pCt Paper 9 pCt disc^t. Interest 12 pCt. Madeira Wine 175 Rps. charges 75 to 100 Rps 9000 pipes on hand. Brandy Cognac 3/ Gin 2/8. Copper pig 48/ pm^d. Spars $50 each for a lot of 2 or 300. — fit for topmasts &yards for ships of 250 to 700 tons.

Iron Swedes 6/8   Mahogany 2/8 foot, Small quantity broad will always
  "   English 5/8   do, if bot in U. S. at 20 ¢
  "   Hoops   "
May 12th1815
All^{d}Chondogurry (Mam^y) 40/ + 1⅞. 84/
  do Emerty   31 " 2   65/
  do Baftas   36 " 1⅞   70/

All^d Sannas	40 +	2⅛	90/ @ 110/	There may be 1500
Luckipore Baftas (Ord^y)	24/5 "	1⅞ 2	55/	bales in all of the
do fine	25 "	2	65/	various goods in
B Gurrahs best	36 "	2¼	80/	Bazar, & generally
do Middling	35 "	2⅛ ¼ 65/		of bad quality
do Ordy	33 "	2⅛	50/	
Tanda Sannas	39 "	2⅛	80/ @ 110/	
Chandpore Cossas	40 "	2	110/	⎫ Few in market, the
Meergungee Mam^y	40 "	2	75/	⎬ merchants only
do do	39 "	1¾	60/ @ 65/	⎭ bring a few down, as they are wanted.

Mow Sannas, Jal^aMamoodies, Jannah do, Baftas Patna, Moharaz Gungee Jal^aSannas, & many other kinds of Cloths have disappear'd in the Bazar, occasionally a parcel is brought down for the use of the natives, or for Country trade, & sold at high prices. —

Blue Gillas	10 in p's	32/ to 40/	No Checks or Custers made for
Sooty Romalls	15 " "	28/ (coarse)	2 years. The Americans are the
do fine	" " "	37/8	only buyers of these two, & many
Seersuckers			other manufactures.
Chintz Patna	14		

May 13th. I shall send this by a portuguese Ship for Rio de Janeiro. I have lately sold some p's goods to a SCargo of a ship bound for Lisbon, he will have 2000 bales, &he told me he should send part of them to U. S. if prices continued high there. They take principally All^d & Tanda goods, Coarse Gurrahs, Blue Gillas &Sooty Romalls. No Silk goods. — Large quantities of Salt Peter have gone to Lisbon, which will I suppose in part be ship'd to U. S. if the price is high. — If the American war Continues, a voyage from Holland to China under a Dutch flag, will do very well. Teas must Continue high in Europe, since there are no cargos Carried there but by E I Company, & they have very little to Spare, their importations are limited to consumption of GBritain, or nearly So, & besides they will not Sell without high prices. You could import direct from China to Holland, much cheaper than the London prices. I should imagine such an expedition would Suit Bromfield, if he Still retains his inclination for a Sea voyage. — The English under the new charter, are allowed to go to Sumatra, Mocha, or any other place to the Eastward of the Cape except China, hitherto

they have only Sent Ships to Batavia, by &by they will become
more enterprizing, & extend their views to other ports, but at
present they are ignorant that Such Countries exist. & instead
of going direct to Sumatra &buying Pepper at $5 picul, they
buy it here at 15/M^d. &still higher at Bombay, &for [inter-
lineated: Mocha] Coffee pay 25/. — I should think you might
do well by Sending a Ship from Liverpool, where Port Charges
are not so high as in London, either to Mocha or Sumatra, at
the former, Coffee might be procured at $10 &probably less,
pCw^t, &Pepper on W Coast at from $4 to $7 according to Circumstances, the returns might be Sold in Liverpool, or permission obtain'd to proceed to the Med^n. — You Cannot employ a
ship less than 350 tons. You may Calculate Pepper at 10^d as
the lowest it can fall to in London. 12^d will not more than save
the Shippers from hence & Bombay. It can never be sold here
for less than 10/ @ 12/ pm^d, for the expence of bringing it from
Sumatra, & duties, are half as much as charges from Sumatra
to England. — A ship fitted out in Nova Scotia or Penobscot, if
it is Still a British possession, with a load of Spars to Eng^d.
&from thence to Calcutta, would do extremely well, there is
some fear however, that the Danes &Swedes may supply the
market, & reduce prices, but as yet we do not hear of any expeditions preparing at Copenhagen, their trade will be very trifling,
formerly they carried much French &Spanish property, &thus
found employ for considerable Shippings particularly in trade
to Manilla &Mauritius. Two Russian Ships within two years
have taken cargoes Pepper from Penang &West Coast, &2 or
3 portuguese, but they do not understand the trade so well as
our Countrymen, nor where to look for Cargoes. Still they will
do well. The Russians paid 10 @ 11 doll^s, while the traders
from hence, bought at about half that price. — *Spanish dollars*
should be Sent, they will always procure Cargoes. — The Java
traders from England, bring out letters of Credit, they paid $12
for Coffee, & drew at 5/ pr dollar, which for hard dollars, the
price was $7 @ $8 ppicul — A French ship would make a good
voyage, in buying at this port, an assorted cargo for Marseilles,
which has become a free port, &will be visited by ships from all

parts of the Mede^n. the following articles, which can usually be procured here, might do well, Sugar, (Bengal) is liked better than any other, in every port in South of France & Italy. I know this from experience. You may calculate the following prices as probable cost here. 18 M^{os}. hence — A Cargo for Med^n.

2000 M^{ds}.	Fine White Sugar	8/8 to 9/8 pm'd. (83 lbs)		
1000 "	Pepper	10/	"	
500 "	Mocha Coffee	20/	"	I put down a Small
500 "	Ginger	6/8	"	quantity because it is
500 "	Tumerick	3/4	"	usually high —
500 "	Blue &Purple Indigo	135/ @ 160/	"	

300 @ 400 Bales Coarse India Cottons, say Gurrahs @ 65/. Baftas 55/ Blue Cloths 65/ @ 70/. Mamoodies 65/ @ 80/, Sannas 80/ @ 100/ they will always be wanted in Med^n. for printing, for Barbary Coast, Black Sea &c, at present the Med^n is supplied from London. By shipping direct, goods could be afforded at just about one half what they now stand the importer into Italy. To the above list, might be added Cotton, if price in Europe will warrant it. While American war continues, France must depend for its supplies, from Smyrna, &the Brazils, unless the Blockade upon our ports should be rais'd, the price therefore will continue high. Cotton will cost on board, Screw'd into Bales of 300 lbs each of 10 Cubic feet, 13/ to 15/ pmd of 83 lbs. Drugs & Gums in small quantities will sell in Med^n. &they can generally be procured here, at least, some are always to be found. they will cost as follows.

From Persian Gulph {	Copal	15/ to 25/ pm^d 83 lbs
	Assafoetida	25/ " "
Produce Bengal {	Shell lac	18/ " 22/ " "
	Sal Ammoniac	20/ " " "
do China {	Camphor (rough from China 80/ "	
	Borax do " "	10/ @ 15/ "
Malabar Coast {	Cardamoms	80/ @ 100/ "
China	Arsenic, red &white	10/ @ 15/ "

this is used in making shot, There are also to be found here, Ammoniac, Tragacanth, Gum Arabic, Benjamin, Olibanum, Myrrh &c &c. but the qualities are always bad, &it is dangerous to meddle with them. Lac lake &lac dye have of late years been exported largely to London, but they are now in disrepute. I suppose because Cochineal is again procurable, for which they Served as a Substitute. Nutmegs may be bought Sometimes at 5/ to 6/ Seer (2 lbs) *Cassia* is generally at 25/ to 30/ pm^d. Cloves are generally as low as in Bourbon, they serve as a remittance from thence, but now the Island is restored, they will be exported to France, &via here, the price for 3 years has been 2/8 to 3/4 pSeer. — Redwood which you find So troublesome, may always be had at 2/12 to 4/ pm^d. it is used in all parts of Europe, &usually Sells in London at £30 to £40 pton. Tutenague fluctuates between 22/ & 28/ pm^d. & can always be procured, it is used in Holland & I suppose in France & Italy. A Cargo of the above named goods w^d. answer equally well at Naples, &probably most of them at Trieste.

In any voyage undertaken beyond CGHope, dollars are indispensable, at same time a letter of Credit may be useful in order to increase the amount of Cargo, as Bills can be sold sometimes for money, & always in Exchange for Indigo & any P's goods which the houses may have on hand, but in these negotiations besides an unfavourable rate of Exchange, which now exists & probably will continue. You have to pay 10 to 15 pCt higher than goods are Selling for in the Bazar. — This business of this place is done by about 7 or 8 houses, & whoever is dependant upon any of them for Credit, must pay dearly for it, besides being exposed to the Knavery of their Banians &Sircars. The few traders who come from Eng^d. &those who are Settled here, are without Capital or Credit, except what they can obtain thro' the Agency houses, &for which they pay heavy Commissions & Interest. For instance, a Merchant who wishes to make a Shipment to London, has to pay Interest 1 pCt on money advanced 5 pCt on Invoice, &if the amount is repaid in London, give Bills at 2/9^d @ 2/10^d. pRupee, besides which, he is oftentimes compell'd to take his goods from the Agent, at a much higher price than he would give for them in the market with Cash. These shipments are attended with heavy charges in London, &by the time they reach the Continental markets, must be double what they would cost, if sent directly from hence. — The Merchants in England tho' they [express'd so — stricken through] discover'd So great a desire to have the trade open to them, do not Seem inclined to engage in it.

Only two ships have arrived as yet, &both without funds or Credit. few or none are expected this year. They Continue to go to Java, but will not make any thing unless Coffee Keeps up to 90/ to 100/ Short price. I certainly think there is every encouragement for [a — stricken through] French or Dutch Ship's to come this way, &the first which do, will make good voyages. —

May 16th 1815 We have this morning received intelligence of a treaty between our Commissions &those of GBritain, having been Signed at Ghent, 24th Jany, & of its ratification by the Prince Regent. Some persons in Engd. imagined our Govt would not accede to it. I entertain no Such opinion, but on contrary believe they will think themselves fortunate in getting such favourable terms. We understand that the Americans are no longer allow'd the privilege of trading to the British possessions this Side the Cape. — If our Govt think this branch of trade of any importance, they will [I suppose — stricken through] Stipulate for it in the Commercial treaty, which I suppose will follow the general one, & in that case they must give an equivalent. It is upon this principle the British have acted in regard to that article. I do not think Mr Madison, or the nation at large will regret the loss of this branch of Commerce, or make any Sacrifices to have it restored. Indeed since the general peace & the opening the trade to British merchants, the advantages it formerly offer'd are done away, besides, with regard to our principal export from hence, Coarse White Cottons, our Govt, if they wish to encourage manufacturers at home, ought to prohibit those of this Country, even if the trade is renew'd. — As to Indigo, as I before observed, it may be purchased [interlineated: in London] lower than we have usually paid for it in this market, & what we should henceforth pay, if our Ships come this way. The Agency houses will never sell their most ordinary Indigoes under 120/. Now I know by refering to public Sales for Several years past, that 1/5th to 1/4 of all that is sent to London, sells there from 3/6 to 6/ lb which includes the qualities the Americans usually buy here. You will find on Calculation, it is as cheap to buy in London at 6/ as here at 120/. The Shipments of Indigo is remittance trade, most of the shippers are content with prime cost, The freight to London is less than ours, rating ours at 10/ pCt. & they get a drawback of 5 pm^d. We pay a duty of that Amt. — Silk Hdkfs may also be supplied as cheap thro' London. — Sugar is cheaper in W Indies, or will be as soon as the Sugar Estates are reestablish'd, there are no other exports of any importance. — If we are not eventually allow'd admittance here, some English ships will be despatch'd from hence, but not immediately, at least, I do not know any as likely to adventure at present. It would not be prudent to adventure till it is known whether India p's goods will be admitted or not. They might it is true be reship'd, I suppose on that condition they would be allowed a landing.

I have Sold within a few days, the remainder of my white Goods, at about the prime cost & interest, which I consider as a fortunate thing. You have no idea of the difficulty of selling anything which must pass thro' the hands of a native, & particularly when there is only one buyer in market, as now the case. I have been trying for 9 mo's to get rid of them. — I have still on hand for the Owners, the Chintz Say 11,000 p's checks &few other Colour'd goods. I shall find it difficult to get rid of them. I have also the Nutmegs &Coffee. I am thinking of Sending the former to London, & directing S W to reship them to you, I know nothing which promises better, the quantity is rather too great. — I shall go on with my Shipments of Hdkfs to London, &you must arrange the payment of my Bills with S W. If the trade is renew'd, it will be sometime before our Ships Come, &when they do, we can sell as cheap in U. S. as they Can, if it is not renew'd, So much the better for our Speculation. If an English Ship sh^d go to U. S. I do not think they would run much upon Hdkfs. — I shall embark in Novr for Eng^d. as there is no prospect of my getting a direct passage. I wish I may however. The Merchants regret the cessation of our trade very much, &the natives still more. P's goods, when the news first arrived, began to rise, they fell again when it was understood we were not allowed to trade here any longer. — There are no Ps goods in Market except the few I I have stated, nor any expected. — The manufacturers have lost by them for 5 or 6 years &many are ruin'd. I conceive the trade in Cloths with Europe, is nearly at an end. When our Cotton shall have become more extended in its Cultivation, as it will now be, the raw material will be as cheap in Europe as in Asia, &every thing else is cheaper. I am convinced our own Cotton manufactures, will stand a competition with the Bengal, even if admitted at the Old duties, &if not now, in few years, expecially if they get into the way of making more inferiour Cloths & affording them lower — A buyer Who is poor, thinks more of prime Cost than the durability. It is this which makes India Cottons Sell.

May 18th. I do not find any of the Houses inclined to adventure to America a Cargo. Some imagine the treaty will not be ratified, others that English ships will not be admitted, while the more enterprizing who would be most likely to engage in such a voyage, have not the means. — If many private traders come out from Engd. it is not improbable one or two may go to U. S. it is ascertain'd E I ps goods will be admitted, but this cannot happen for Several months, we shall not hear of the ratification by our Govt 'till some time in Sept. I expect a despatch of Bands in 3 or 4 weeks, &shall then make up a shipment. I have purchased about 400 ps Companys Choppas @ 105/, drawback will reduce them to 100/. I have also bot 300 ps Bands at 90/. & shall perhaps be able to pick up a few hundred ps more in the Bazar, in time for the Shipment. I hope our Govt will not prohibit Silk Hdkfs, whatever they may do with Cotton Cloths, I do not think there is much hazard.

There are 8 ships loading for London. I shall write by Several of them. Remember to write S W to Invoice the goods he reships to you, at prime cost, estimating the Rupee at 2/3d. or merely to send a Copy of the Calcutta Invo. — If the new duties are, after the expiration of a year, [to be reduced, — stricken through] for the termination of the War, to be reduced to the

former rates, it might be an object not to have your goods arrive in U. S. 'till that time, but I think they will be Continued.
Our war debt will require great revenue, &there is no way so
easy in getting it, as impost on foreign Goods. — I Shall try to
get some of the houses to send a ship to U. S. but am not Sanguine of succeeding. Nothing in that way can be done till we
hear of the ratification by Mr Madison. — Coffee at Java in ✔
March 7½ to 8 Sp dollars picul. A dollar is worth there 6/
Pepper at Sumatra $6 picul

(P.S. May 25th. p Fama via Rio di   Yrs &c
Janeiro recommended a voyage from   (Sgd)   HLee
Antwerp or Marseilles [blot]
St. Petersburg)

/May 24th & 27th — Wrote Francis Lee — Americans w^d.
not be permitted by this Gov^t. to go to Chandarnagar — new
C. H. Regulations — voyage from Marseilles, Antwerp and St.
Petersburg, to Calcutta & &c

p John Bull via Port Louis
Isle France saild 24th May.

LETTER FROM HENRY LEE, CALCUTTA, AUG. 7, 1815, TO FRAN-
CIS LEE, BOSTON, ON THE ARRIVAL OF AMERICAN VESSELS [1]

Henry Lee had expected that for a time at least the British would
prohibit American vessels from trading with India and that he would
thus be temporarily protected against American competition. He had
consequently not made all the purchases he had intended — although
his memorandum book throughout the spring and summer contains
many entries concerning piece goods purchased, contracted for, or
delivered to dyers — and, at the arrival of American vessels, prices of
course immediately rose. Henry Lee, nevertheless, began purchasing
extensively, fearing prices would rise still higher. Part of the funds
which he employed was derived from the resale of goods purchased
earlier; e.g., sicca rupees 12,600 received on Sept. 7 for 770 cwt. of
Java coffee. He also disposed of 2,500 goat skins @ 22 rupees per
hundred, 900 pieces of bandannas @ 117 rupees per corge, nutmegs

1. Jackson-Lee Papers, "Letters written in Calcutta by H. Lee from
July 1813 to March 1816."

amounting to sicca rupees 7,872, 11 annas, 6 pice @ 6 rupees per maund, another quantity of coffee amounting to sicca rupees 3,064, 5 annas, 6 pice @ 13 rupees per maund, etc.[2]

The "Revolution in France" refers to Napoleon's return from Elba in Feb., 1815; Lee had evidently not yet heard whether or not the allies intended to allow the Emperor to retain his newly regained throne.

origl p Ind

Mr F Lee   via Isle de france   Calcutta Augt 7th1815

Dup Hope

dear F

I recd on 2dinst, yours of 20th Mch, & Copy of 23 Feby by the Indes, the Favorite and Hope, which arrived the same day, brought me no letters but from my wife. You will have observed from my late letters, that I did not expect our Countrymen. We were told they would be excluded by Ghent Treaty, & no one wrote, from London to Contradict this information, tho' I learn from London letters recd a few days ago, that S Williams was informed by a person who communicated with the Govt that the prohibition against our coming here, had been revoked, I wish I had known this a month ago, as we might have done, if the Agents here had not the worst Correspondents in the world. I should in that case, have extended my purchases, & made them on better terms than I now have been able to. On the day this Ship arrived I had just Concluded upon freighting an English Ship, in conjunction with an American, & going in her to U. S. The plan has been in agitation ever since we heard of the treaty having been signed at Ghent. It is needless to say that many of the advantages which such a voyage offer'd, are now done away by the trade being open'd to the Americans, but I may still do this, it will be for the advantage of the Owners, and the quickest mode of getting the goods to market. If I engage in this, I shall insure the property here, payable in case of loss, in London, at 2/6 pRupee, which is 10 pCt better

2. *Ibid.*, "Henry Lee's Calcutta Memorandum Book. — 1814 & 1815 — ."

than the rate you get in US, for a Rupee, the premium will be
5 pCt — I have always anticipated a high market here on the
arrival of our Ships, & unluckily the same tide brought in 3 rich
Portuguese, with great capitals & news of as many more just at
hand — You can hardly imagine the Sensations produced in
the minds of Europeans &Natives, particularly the last, by the
appearance of our Ships, there is not an article which has not
felt the effects, even those we [interlineated: never] deal in.
The holders of Piece goods are unwilling to sell at any prices.
There are but few goods in the Bazar, & buyers extremely eager
to get them, the holders looking for more ships are not willing
to sell, but in few days the market will Settle at Some rate or
other, No doubt a high one. — In consequence of my determination to ship for London, I had in my House a few thousand
pieces of Cloths, which I closed for immediately, before the
news was known to be true among the natives, & I made Contracts for some others which I hope will be fulfill'd — You seem
to have been quite at a loss to know what value to fix upon
piece goods on return of the Ships — I think common charged
Invoices will Sell at a moderate profit even tho' our manufactures should be found to have taken place of many Kinds, the
demand for exportation will alone take off 3 or 4000 bales annually. We can Supply the Continental nations, & certainly the
W Indies & So America cheaper than the Engh. The goods bo't
at present prices are too high, unless it may be for 3 or 4 first
cargoes, Mr Stark will however furnish a tolerable supply for
retailers who are in immediate want, & others will wait 'till
Goods fall. The Hope has I am told $60,000 in freight, she fills
up with MrStarks goods, bo't on account of Perkins, Dodge &c,
The Favorite $40,000 takes any surplus of Starks goods which
may remain from other vessels — I don't imagine any freight
can be obtaind on either of these, they talk of getting away the
Indus & Hope in 4 or 5 weeks, they are mistaken, the Indus may
clear her pilot by the 1st Octo. The Hope has something to do
with her bottom, &if she goes into dock, her departure cannot
take place earlier than the 15 Octr. — Besides the Stocks Consigned to the Captn &SuperCargoes of these Ships, MrStark

has 50,000 R. from Wigglesworth & Wm Bartlett. I understand all the Captn & SuperCargoes had orders to consult with Mr S. & get his advice as to what goods to buy &c, this is very like Thorndike, he would willingly throw the responsibility upon Mr S. & get the benefit of his experience & information, without paying for it. Some of them I hear, have orders for fine Indigo. They will not get any, tho' it is not improbable

Such as I sent you in the P C is not to be found, & the 2d quality is held at 150/ to 160/ No man should be employ'd in purchase of this article, who has not had considerable experience & Knowledge of qualities, both here & in Europe. I have been very attentive to collect information &to make myself acquainted with quality. I hope the Knowledge may hereafter be useful to us. Let me advise you not to purchase this article in W. I. to ship to Europe. You may rely upon it, the price is lower for it in London than the Amns will give for it here, unless it may be some Small lots of broken & ordinary, bo't of the natives, which cannot be rely'd upon, except to sell to retailers in U S for home use, I told you some Country Ships would probably [Stop — stricken through] touch in America on their way to Engd. the appearance of our Ships will probably discourage them from doing so, still I should not be Surprized if Some of the Agents, finding it impossible to sell their Indigoes here should make trial of our market, since they can do it without inconvenience or expence, in that case you may buy middling Indigo at low price, for none of prime quality will be Sent. I shall give you notice of any voyages undertaken while I remain here, which may be 'till Novr or Decr. — Neither of the Ships now here would give me freight, if I should fail in getting an English Ship, & if freight, they would probably reserve a passage. The Indus will be with you by the 15thMarch. The favourite about the Same time. The Hope I imagine will not make so much dispatch, they are all wooden bottoms, but sail well. — I think you acted prudently in not sending out a ship on your own account. but I am sorry you did not try for a freight, &put in $20,000 of your own I could have pick'd up 50 or 60000 [M'ds — stricken through] Rps for the Owners on good terms. tho' the

Bazar is high. Many of the goods I would have procured from
the Country, but it would have been been Still better had you remitted me 50,000 Rs some time ago, and directed it to Stark in
my absence. I wonder Since you were so ready to engage in any
desperate adventure which offer'd, you should have had so little
confidence in the plan I recommended. If you had sent that
Sum I could have taken up a ship two months ago, after the
Treaty was known, and anticipated every vessel by 3 or 4 mos.
with a Cargo which would certainly have given a great profit —
I have still on hand 1000 Mds Coffee & 30 mds Nutmegs, for the
last I am offer'd a price which will give a profit, & the former I
have good hopes of Selling when the Free traders come. 6 or 8
are on the way. — The Owners investment will consist of Blue
&White Gurrahs, Silk Hdkfs, Custers, Checks, Chintz, Blue
&White Baftas, Sooties Blue &Red Gillas & Seersuckers —
these are goods which will do either for exportation or home
Consumption, &some of them less run upon by Americans than
White Goods. At present they are Scarce &higher by 15 to 20
pCent than I gave. You must not expect so cheap an investment as if I bo't 18 mos ago, but on the other hand you Save the
interest, besides the gain I get upon the sales made last year —
I shall send nothing which will not in worst events give a good
profit, even tho' prices of goods should be lower than they were
ever known in U. S. — Of Indigo there is none on hand but a
few parcels of 2 & 3d quality for which high prices are ask'd. —
If the Amns had not come a few hundred M'ds might perhaps
have been collected in Novr. among the Natives at 90/ to 110/
but they will do better now among some of the buyers not acquainted with qualities — The Agents never will sell much below the London price, & one year with another they get more
for Ordy qualities than London sales. I have ascertaind this
fact by examination of Catalogues for 10 or 12 years past. —
It was the case the last season & it will be the coming one. The
May Sale was expected to be a bad one in Consequence of the
Revolution in France, &the Succeeding one of Octo will be Still
worse, even tho' the Allies should not make war upon Buonaparte — The Crop last Season was too great for the consump-

tion, &the the rains have carried off 30,000 m'ds this season, still the crop will be 100,000 mds. & of course keep down the prices in London for 2 years to Come. If there is a war between France & Eng^d, this among other articles of E I produce, will be enhanced in U. S. but I w^d not were I sure of this give over 100/ for midd^l quality — piece goods at the prices mine will be ship'd, I look upon as certain, tho I am aware that large importations into U S will reduce them to old prices, with the addition of the New duty. —

August 21st. Neither Hope nor Indus receives freight, Captn Orne thinks he may have Some room, but will not engage to furnish it, till he buys his Cargo, he names an exorbitant rate — dont speculate in Indigo — there must be 7 or 8000 Mds sent to U S this Season, it will be impossible for the rich ships to make up their funds without taking largely. It ought, considering prices in Eng^d. & future prospects, to be low, but the agents are very Stiff in their price, as most of them prefer shipping, to a sale here. I dont think the Am^ns will get Ord^y at less than 120/ Midd^l 140/ fine 160/ @ 170/ — All which prices are higher than the London prices of May last. The Oct^o Sale of 1815 must be a bad one. Good midd^l Indigo such as will cost here this Season140/ will be sold at coming sale in London at 5/6 to 6/1. I dont imagine any of the ships except Mr Starks three can sail earlier than Feb^y, they will make bad voyages —

✓ The Ships for Sumatra will not all of them get Pepper &those who do must pay high Say $10 picul, those who fail will I suppose go to Peru, perhaps they may get Coffee at 9 to 10 doll^s ppicul. It was higher 3 or 4 Mo^s since — Sugar is 10/8 — last year @ 8/4. I bo't a great quantity for a H^o &it afterwards went down to 7/8. Dont think of sending merchandize in American ships except Spars & Tar, which we pay 20 pCt & English only 2%. — There must be considerable loss on all the articles the Ships have brought this Season, except Tar &Spars. Liquors nearly total loss. Copper a gain — I shall write by the ships for Boston, but the letters may not reach,

Yrs &c

LETTER FROM HENRY LEE, CALCUTTA, SEPT. 2, 1815, TO SAM-
UEL WILLIAMS, LONDON, WITH A CONSIGNMENT OF GOODS [1]

Henry Lee felt qualified to compete with the "private traders from
hence" to England because "none of them," as he wrote on July 13,
1815, "understand the P's goods trade. . . . They buy thro' Houses
of Agency, & pay 30 pCt more than Bazar prices." [2]

Saml Williams Esqr Calcutta Septr 2^d 1815
    London,
        Dear Sir,
            Enclosed are Invoices of 86 bales Cotton & 13 chests
Silk piece Goods on board the Ship Mary, amounting to
S^{a}Rupees Forty nine thousand, seven hundred, ninety seven 7
annas 3 pie (S^{a}Rp^s 49797..7..3) on account of myself &M^r
Francis Lee, against this shipment I have under this date drawn
on you at six months sight, Five thousand pounds Sterling
(£5000..0..0 St^g) in favour of Mess^s Porcher &C^o. which I request you to accept. You will look for your reimbursement in
case of loss of Mary, to proceeds of a Policy of Insurance as
effected here to the amount of Fifty thousand Sicca Rupees, and
payable in case of loss in London, at 2/6 pS^{a}Rupee. The Policy
(In Triplicate) has been Sent to Mess^s Porcher &C^o. together
with the Bills Lading, to be dl^d you on the acceptance of my
draft. On the other hand, if the Goods reach in Safety, the Bill
can be provided for out of their proceeds, or in Such other way
as Mr F. Lee, who has been apprised of my intentions, may
have arranged with you. — It was my intention, had the Americans not been allow'd to come here to make some further Shipments, but their arrival has induced me to abandon it. The Silk
Hdkfs were originally intended for America but now I think
it may be for our interest, to have them sold in London. I am
afraid the B①1 @ 6 1440/n @ 105/ may be found too coarse
for Europe markets. In which case if 18/ cannot be obtain'd

1. Jackson-Lee Papers, "Letters written in Calcutta by H. Lee from
July 1813 to March 1816."
2. *Ibid.*, Henry Lee, Calcutta, July 13–29, 1815, to Francis Lee, Boston.

without delay, I wish you to reship them to any port in U. S. prefering Baltimore or Phil^a, and also ◇©◇ no 1 which are rejected goods, &some of them coarse, as to the other two parcels @ 137/8 & 118/, I leave them to your disposal. I should think they would certainly bring 22/ &probably 25/. The price here is 125/ @ 130/ &no probability of their being lower for 6 or 9 months to come. The Cotton piece goods I wish you to sell either at private Sale or at the Companys, as you may judge best, but not under the prices which are noted in Red. I imagine you will find a ready sale at considerable higher prices, if not, it is probable my brother F may direct them reship'd to Havana, or some other market, or reduce my limitations & have them Sold by you. — The Gurrahs are Such (or somewhat better) as the Americans used to export to Italy, Holland &c &c, and as they come much cheaper than the Company can afford them. I hope you will be able to dispose of them to the Continental buyers. The parcel of 400 are very Ordinary, &fit only for U. S. or W Indies. I would not expose them 'till the others are sold, as they might excite a prejudice against the other parcels, which are all good Substantial Cloths. The Hdkfs are for W Indies, S^oAmerica &c &c & I should judge from the Sales &Brokers reports, were in great request. They are very inferiour to Companys of same names, &so are the prices still more below the [prices — stricken through] Companys limitations. The Blue Cloths are of as good colour as the Madras, but I dont expect them to sell So high, — It is common to make Blue Cloths from damaged White goods, but these are new Cloths fresh from the loom & colour^d with the first quality of Indigo. The last Sales I have Seen of Bengal Blue Cloths, were for Baftas 36 + 2, 16/ @ 17/. Gurrahs should bring more. I observe some of the Shippers here, pack the A B &C in different Bales, but I have follow'd the more general practice of packing a proportion in each Bale, the A's on top & C's at bottom. For selling at private Sale, it would be best to open two or three of each lot, as one Package may happen to be a little better or worse than another. — At the India House I understand it is the practice to open every bale &reassort them. In opening the goods, the right Side of the Package facing the mark should be chosen, as it displays the best side of the goods &there is a perceptible difference — I wish you would inform M^r F Lee of the arrival of them, &what you have done, & are like to do, with the goods. — In addition to the draft for £5000, I have under Same date, drawn on you in favour of CBluney Esqr. Agent for Star Insurance Company, at 6 mo^s sight. Three hundred thirteen pounds. 10/ prm^o policy for S^aRps 50,000. And also on 1st inst payable 60 days after Safe arrival of the Mary in River Thames, for Four hundred ninety two pounds, 4/11^d in favour of J W. Tasker Esqr. in payment of freight on the Shipment in Mary. — If any of your Choppas are unsold when this reaches, I should think it might be for your interest to sell them at 25/ rather than ship to U. S. as the quantity now going direct will be large, &Mr Starks cost very low. —

The property I retain'd on account owners of the Reaper, and most of my own is invested in P's goods, purchased while they were low. I shall embark in few months for U. S. &hope the result of my voyage will compensate in Some measure for the long time I have pass'd here. — Mr Starks two vessels & the Favorite will sail in 20 to 30 days. The Emily & Kensington must be detain'd till Feb^y, &the others too which arrive within a few months. — We are looking for one ship from Phila, One from Baltimore, two from New York, &one or two from Massachusetts. —

Yours truly

(Signed)   HLee

I would thank you to inform Mr Francis Lee, the price of unrefined E I Salt peter, short price, &whether any exportation of that article from GBritain is allow'd, either to U. S. or the Continent — Immense shipments are now making from hence, encouraged by the great prices obtain'd last year. —

H Lee

[written across face of letter:]

pr Mary
Copy to F. Lee p Indus
Sep 1815
Copy pr Hope for S. Williams
via Boston
Copy to F Lee p Hope
Triplicate to S. Williams
p Lord Cathcart

LETTER FROM HENRY LEE, CALCUTTA, SEPT. 14, 1815, TO
PETER REMSEN, NEW YORK, WITH PLANS FOR SHIPMENTS TO
THE UNITED STATES [1]

In a letter of Sept. 11, 1815, Henry Lee had written: "Do not by
any means Sell my goods by the Invᵒ., if you do they will not bring
any thing like their value, in proportion to others bought since they
rose. — An auction is the best way to sell goods when they are high,
& upon a falling market — I never knew it fail." [2] Selling by invoice
was at a rate of so many cents per rupee cost. If goods were invoiced
low, there was an unwillingness on the part of the buyer to pay as
much for them as for the same quality purchased, and therefore invoiced, at a higher price.

On the *Hope*, Sept. 30, Henry Lee shipped to Boston sicca rupees
27,895, 5 annas, 3 pice in sal ammoniac, indigo, gum copal, and cardamons, and sicca rupees 6,848, 2 annas in piece goods, on the account
of himself and his brother Francis; on the *Favourite* to Boston, Oct.
15, sicca rupees 49,201, 10 annas, 10 pice in piece goods, one-half on
his own account and one-fourth each on the accounts of his brother
Francis and the owners of the *Reaper*. He also made various other
shipments solely on the account of the owners of the *Reaper* or of individual merchants.[3]

1. Jackson-Lee Papers, "Letters written in Calcutta by H. Lee from
July 1813 to March 1816."
2. *Ibid.*, Henry Lee, Calcutta, Sept. 11, 1815, to Francis Lee, Boston.
3. *Ibid.*, "Invoices of all the goods ship'd by Henry Lee during his stay
in Calcutta from May 1812 to March 1816."

Mr Peter Remsen   (p Indus)   Calcutta Sepr 14 th1815
  New York,   (Dup p Hope)
  Dear Remsen,   [Hope left the pilot about the 13thOcto-
                                 ber — stricken through]

I recd your welcome letter of 20th & 26 April by the Emily, on the 19thUlto. The information it contains, is more particular than I have received from my Boston correspondents, & I dare say more correct, for they appear'd at the moment of writing, to be in a state of great uncertainty, Doubtful of every thing, I hope they may after a while recover from that stupor which the conclusion of Peace seems to have left them. During the war there was no scheme however hazardous, which they did not readily embark in, except the only one which offer'd any advantages, the remitting funds to Calcutta to be invested by me, or by Mr Stark in my absence. — There was no risk in this, for if the war had continued, their money could have been loan'd at 12 pCt, or if invested in Cloth, they could have been sold, either last year or this to the Portuguese. — Besides the letter I now acknowledge, I have recd only two others from you during the war. — You complain of want of opportunities, & so does Mr Jackson. — Yet from some of my friends I have letters dated every month in the year, &only two or three of all they wrote, miscarried — I must confess to you there have been moments during my long stay here, when I felt extremely hurt at your forgetfulness &neglect. I should have derived a great deal of pleasure, &probably many other advantages from your correspondence, which I always counted upon, from the confidence in the Sincerity &strength of your friendship, with the utmost certainty. — The letter I have now before me, confirms me in my hopes of doing very well with the goods I am about to ship for myself &owners. — You know that the Sum I remaind here with, was very small, &it could never have been an object to have done so, had I not in first instance felt confident of a speedy peace, &afterwards indulged a hope that my friends would have adopted the plan I recommended of sending out funds for purchase of a Cargo, they did not do it, &I should make a wretched business for myself, considering the loss of 4 years of the best part of my life, &the ruin of my Constitution, had I not been aided in my plans by more friends I have acquired [by — stricken through] during my residence here. I have now a prospect of adding a Sufficiency to my little property, to enable me to live hereafter Comfortably, &to place my family beyond the reach of want. — I may be too Sanguine, but at present I can hardly imagine any event which will disappoint my expectations — Let goods be at what prices they may, even than any time since the India trade was known in U. S. Mine must give a great profit. — It is my intention to ship 200 M^{ds} Sal Ammoniac, & 150 M^{ds} Indigo, 1000 ps Band^s &some Copal, on the Hope, to Sail for Boston in 15 days. — On the Favourite, 150 bales ps Goods of various Kinds, for myself &owners, principally Blue &White Gurrahs, Checks, Chintz, Custers, Palampars, Bandannas, Choppas, Baftas, Blue &Red Gillas, Seersuckers, Andy Sannas &c &c all of them cheap & of good quality. Of the Sal Amm^c & Indigo, part will be sent you immediately, & I hope a speedy sale may be effected, as there are 100 M^{ds} on the Favourite, & the next ships will probably have a quantity. The Indigo must be sold within 3m^o of its arrival, & as there is very little in the 3 ships, I think you will easily run it off. — The ps Goods I imagine will be chiefly sold at Auction in Boston, as I have urged an immediate Sale, but Still they may find it will [interlineated: be for their interest] to send you via Sound, 2 or 3000 ps Silk Hdkfs. & any other goods which may be in great demand. — I shall make a more considerable shipment 2 or 3 mo^s hence, & accompany it myself. You may expect me at your port some time in May or June. I shall want a pretty large advance upon a valuable consignment, partly in Sp dollars &partly in Bills on London. I beg you to be prepared. I shall hereafter Send a Mem^o of some of the goods, which my investment will comprize —

Goods, as every one acquainted with the market here, foresaw, rose on the appearance of our Ships, & 6 rich Portuguese, which came in about the Same time. I don't imagine there ever was a moment within 10 or 15 years when White goods were So Scarce, &Silk Goods too, except Fine Choppas for London market — The 3 Boston ships had but few to buy, as they came for M^rStarks owners, whose goods were already pack'd &at very low prices, that speculation will turn out as I expected, immensely profitable. — We are looking for 4 more Americans, they will all make bad voyages which come within 8 mo^s. after that time, piece Goods will fall, but not extremely low. — We have many free traders come & expected, I dont know what they can find to fill up with. — There are no bulky exports but Cotton &Sugar, former will not do &the latter is too high. Piece goods wont [blot] answer in Eng^d, Indigo occupys no room. This article will be 20 pCt lower than last year, The price in London is down, & cannot recover for 2 years. The Crops are too great for consumption, formerly they averaged only 73,000 M^d. of late 100,000 M'ds. ½ the quantity will suffice. — You appear'd to think Silk manufactures would be cheap from the fall of the raw material, they did fall, &will be down again, 8 mo^s hence, but not below 100/ for Common Bandannas. — The raw Silk is up again, &has been found to answer so good a purpose, mix d in with fine Italian as to stand a competition with European Silk extremely well. It has been at 6/8 for Common, &is now at 8/8 pSeer, of 2 lbs. It will fluctuate between these two prices, & cannot be afforded under the former. — Drugs are Scarce, I find others are going upon them, &shall not buy unless at very low prices, Such as will enable me to ship them to Europe in case of need. — The prices you Sent me of Cottons at the Auction Sale, were enormous. I shall be satisfied with Something more than half. I think our home manufactures will have taken the place of many India but still there will be a sale of 6 or 7000 bales a year. — One third for Exportation perhaps, — Captn Turnbull must have done well, the Indigo I sent would suit an exporter to France, where only our flag can be admitted, as long as the war lasts, we shall have a good market open for India & Colonial produce. I hope with all my heart it may be a short one, & terrible in its effects to these restless &profligate nations, who are so eager to act the revolutionary scenes over again. — I send you a Memo of the Cargoes of the 2 Boston ships — The Emily has 350,000 Sp dollars, of which 150,000 on account of LeRoy & Bayard, she will get a dear cargo, the S Cargo has already made Some bad bargains in Indigo, instead of waiting for the new crop which would be better & cheaper, he must in order to invest his great capital, buy largely of Indigo — The E cannot get away Short of 5 mos. — The Kensington has 200,000 R's & £60,000 in Bills on London, — A Baltimore Ship from S &Buchanan is expected with some Capital, principally in Bills, which must be Sold at 2/9½d @ 2/10d. pRupee, Neither of these Ships can get their cargoes Short of 5 mos. The SCargoes of the I understand their business &will do better than the others — R Lenox's funds are not invested, he will also make bad voyages with his 2 Ships which we hear are coming — Merchandize of almost every sort is low, we cannot expect anything but Specie 'till the duties are reduced, at present English Ships pay nothing on most articles &only 2¼ on others. We pay 20 @ 25 pCt. They will be alter'd when our Commercial treaty is made — The English So far from wishing to exclude us, are desirous we should continue to trade here —

I am Sorry to find your brother Daniel has been compell'd to leave the Country for ill health, he ought to remain in a mild climate 'till it is completely restored. I found great benefit from my voyage to France, for Climate, &from eating freely of grapes & asses milk — I shall probably write you by the other ships, in mean time, farewell. —

Yours truly
Sgd)   HLee

Cargo Indus P Dodge brothers. —
1100 bales ps goods, Mr Starks
    purchase.

  300 " bot by captain
30 or 40 chests Indigo, Sugar, Gin-
    ger &c —

AllaChondogurry	40 + 2
" Sannas	40 + 2¼
" Emerty	30 + 2⅛

Hope. P Thorndikes —
600 bales Mr Starks purchases

300 @ 400 " bot by Captain

150 boxes Indigo & Sal Amm^c
([?])

Favourite
3 or 400 bales ps Goods
100000 lb Coffee
100 Chests Indigo, a quantity
of Sal Amm^c. Copal, Sugar

Ginger, Borax &c

Dols 20/6 — Bills
 Choppas fine 130/a150/
 Seersucker 30 + 2 — 12/8
2/9 @ 2/10 pRupee
 do Blue — " — 10/

All^a Baftas	36 + 1⅞	
Baftas common		
5 bales	25 + 2 —	57/
do good		
5 bales	" "	71/
Gurrahs fine	36 + 2¼	85/
Middling	35 + 2½	72/ @ 75/
Coarse	32 + 2⅛	60/ @ 65/
Mow Sannas	22 + 2⅛	40/
Tandu do	40 + 2⅛	90/ @ 130/
Mengungee		
Mam^y	40 + 2	90/
Jannah "	37 + 1¾	70/
Blue Gurrahs	34 + 2¼	75/
do Baftas	24 + 2	55/ @ 65/
Checks	13 + 1⅜	24/
do	19 + 1⅞	40/
Band^s coarse 7 ins		105/ none
do fine	" " "	140/

A Mem^o on the back of the Copy Instructions to SWilliams, respecting Shipment pMary, Sent to F Lee p^r Indus. —

Sep 15th1815   (Dup pHope)
The Mary left her pilot about the 10th or 11th inst^t, she will reach Eng^d in 5 mo^s. —

A Statement of Sums drawn on S Williams, 2/3ds on account HLee, & 1/3d on account Francis Lee, against a shipment of piece Goods made on the Hercules to

     London ⎤
A Bill at 6 mo^s sight in fav of Mess^s Alexander &C^o on ⎬ £3000.0.
   S Williams Esqr date 3 M^{ch}1815 ⎦

On the 11th March in favour of Mess^s A &C^o. (Bill for
     prem^u) on S W at 6 mo's . . .   195.0.0
3 M^{ch}. A Bill in fav^r of Fairlie Fergusson &C^o at 60
     days after the arrival of the
     Hercules in pay^t of freight   121..15..0
            £3316.15.0

Shipment pMary 2/3ds HLee 1/3d FLee —

2	in fav Porcher &Co 6 mo on SW . . . £	5000..0..0	
2	" " " CBlaney for premu 6 mo on SW	312..10..0	
1	" 80 days after arrival of the Mary, infav		
	J W Tasker, for freight, on SW .	492..4..11	

£5804..14..11

LETTER FROM HENRY LEE, CALCUTTA, DEC. 23, 1815, TO PETER REMSEN & CO., NEW YORK, WITH PLANS FOR A VOYAGE TO THE UNITED STATES [1]

For the past month Henry Lee had been making shipments to the United States: Nov. 29, on the ship *Galatea* to Boston, sicca rupees 9,868, 11 annas in indigo and piece goods; Dec. 5, on the ship *Hope* to New York, sicca rupees 48,841, 5 pice in piece goods, indigo, sal ammoniac, and cardamons; both shipments were two-thirds on his own account and one-third on that of his brother Francis. The 53 bales shipped, Dec. 18, on the *Kensington* for Philadelphia were invoiced at sicca rupees 13,802, 8 annas, all on his own account.[2] During Nov. and Dec., 1815, he had been making extensive purchases and contracts, through native merchants and sircars, in manufacturing and commercial centers outside of Calcutta; he bought colored cloths in "Barnagore" (Bonai Garh ?), gurrahs in "Modun Mohunpore" (Midnapur ?) and "Catuah" (Katwa), long cloths in "Danacully" (Dhenkanal ?), silks in Cossimbazar and "Mirzapore" (Mirsapur).[3]

By the time of the letter below Henry Lee had decided to return to the United States, bringing with him all the goods for which he could obtain funds. He was to be concerned in this voyage with the Calcutta firm of Cruttenden & Mackillop, and urged Remsen to "establish a character for punctuality" by making an advance on the value of goods immediately on their arrival.

1. Jackson-Lee Papers, "Letters written in Calcutta by H. Lee from July 1813 to March 1816."

2. *Ibid.*, "Invoices of all the goods ship'd by Henry Lee during his stay in Calcutta from May 1812 to March 1816."

3. Henry Lee Shattuck Collection, "Memorandum Book January 1814," Feb., 1814–Feb. 24, 1816; *Lippincott's Gazetteer of the World*, Angelo and Louis Heilprin, eds. (Philadelphia and London, 1922).

p Kensington Calcutta Dec 23^d 1815 —

Mess^s P Remsen &C^o   Dup p^r Rum duloll dy
  New York,   Trip " Orient.

 Dear Sirs,

  I have made a shipment of 53 bales p^s goods in the Kensington, consigned to Saml Archer Esqr. My brother F will send you a Copy of the Inv^o. If you can Send M^r A any information to aid in the Sales, pray do so — I shall send some Indigo &piece goods in the RDDay to your consignment, &draw for part of the amount — I hope you have disposed of all my goods &especially the Indigo. There is not So much going to U. S. As I expected, nor are the shipments of Cloth So large. A considerable proportion of the funds intended for Cotton piece goods only, was invested in Silk Hdkfs &Indigo because of the Scarcity & dearness of the former — I see no reason why prices with you sh^d not Keep up so as to afford a good profit, thro' the coming year, the quantity of Cottons will not be more than 2/3ds. the average importations for 15 years past, &there was heretofore, some of the old Stock remaining over from year to year — I am trying to get a voyage under weigh. If I do any thing I shall persuade the concern to consign to you. &we shall require large advances immediately on the arrival of the Ship — Keep your vaults well fill'd, &with Dollars, — I cannot trust any Bank out *ofNew England!!!* — I expect to get my Cloths 5½ to 7½ or 10 pCt cheaper upon the average than last purchasers. — Pray be prompt in remitting to Mess^s C & McK. It is important to establish a character for punctuality as I look forward to future transactions with them — The RDDay, Geo, &Orient will leave early in Feb^y, the Pickering Some time in M^{ch}. — At foot there is a Mem^o of the Cargoes of Emily &Kensington, neither of them has so much Indigo as I expected, &most of the parcels cost 130/ to 145/ for Middling. — I wish you w^d collect for Me catalogues of the Auction Sales of Calcutta goods, that I may immediately on my arrival, judge oftheir value in the different towns of U.S. — Get too what information you can of the value of Indigo in France, Holland

& Russia — I may bring with me a large quantity, tho' I shall not venture on my own account, because I think piece Goods more certain.

Dec 24th. Since the above, the voyage refer'd to has been decided upon, I have commenced buying — The time of departure uncertain. If we are not disappointed in the Ship we have in view, It will be early in March. — The Cargo will be consigned to you, &we shall require large advances immediately on arrival — Freight must be paid by Bills on London, &will amount to £ 7 or 8000£, & a further sum will be required to remit to this place in dollars. Or in Bills to London, if they are considerably under par, say 5 pCt. I have made great promises, &you must fulfill them, even tho you be incommoded for a time. — It is a great object to get quick returns, as 1 pCt is the rate of interest upon all mercantile transactions — My Cargo will consist of 700 bales Goods, some Indigo, &150 tons S P. for dead weight — I am told this is now made in U.S. I hope not under 20 cts. Try if you cannot dispos of part to Govt. Perhaps it may do for Export to France, or some other quarter of Europe. I will have among the Cargo 10,000 ps low priced Baftas, Cost 40/ — 10,000 ps Gurrahs 55/ — 10,000 ps Checks & Custers 16/ — 5000 palampores, 5000 ps Chintz, 20/ 3000 Blue Gurrahs 65/ 1000 Blue Baftas 50/. 500 seersuckers 9/8 @ 10/8 3000 ps Bands @ 90/ 2000 Compy Choppas 110/ 2000 Mow Sannas 29/. &200 bales Alld goods, if they fall 10 pCt below the prices paid for the last Cargoes — I must intreat you would not on any account, mention this voyage, & on my arrival, I wish the concern considered as mine. I have my reasons for doing this. It is not necessary to explain them in this place. It is very important to my interest &convenience, that sales be effected of all the goods I have sent you, as soon as possible — pray lose no oppy of doing so —

                              Yrs   HLee (Sgd)

LETTER FROM HENRY LEE, CALCUTTA, DEC. 24, 1815, TO
JOSEPH LEE, JR., BOSTON, WITH SPECIFICATIONS FOR A
FREIGHTING VESSEL [1]

Joseph Lee, Jr., like his father, was a naval architect.[2] The high
repute of William Rush, Philadelphia sculptor, is indicated by the
reference to him below.[3] The letter demonstrates a recognition of
non-economic motives as factors in business policy. We do not know
that any vessel answering the description below was built for Henry
Lee and the Philadelphia supercargo.

Mr Josh Lee jr   pr Kensington   Calcutta Dec 24 1815
     Dupt pRam duloll day ⎱
 Dear Jos., Trip p Orient ⎰ copies

Knowing from former experience, which has also received a confirmation by my residence here, that the business
of employing ships on freight in the Calcutta trade, may be
made safe and profitable, I am desirous of again entering into
it. I wish you wd build a Vessel of 300 to 320 tons, upon the
plan of the Emily, as she unites all the properties which can
be required, and is at the same time extremely admired by the
Southern people, which for the purpose required, is of some
importance — I have met here a phila SuperCar who has been
engaged in this trade for 5 or 6 years, &who will either continue to follow it, or be succeeded by some of his brothers.
In either case, he aprises me of his ability to procure a stock
of 200,000 to 250,000 dollars at 10 pCt, &shippers to pay
S Cargo. I have proposed to offer him half this vessel at prime
cost, in return for his freight &at same time to use my endeavours to procure shipments from Boston, &, should there
not enough offer in Phila — Should we succeed in our first
attempts, the vessel to be continued in the trade, as long as
we can get freights — We shall both arrive in July or Augt.

1. Jackson-Lee Papers, "Letters written in Calcutta by H. Lee from
July 1813 to March 1816."
2. Morse, F. R., op. cit., pp. 16, 17.
3. "William Rush," Appleton's Cyclopaedia of American Biography.

&will commence Collecting Shipments immediately — My Associate thinks the Philadelphians would prefer a Ship to a Brig, &that she should have a figure head made by Rush of Phil^a be copper'd to the bends &have large & convenient cabin accommodations, because their Ships have 2 SuperCargoes, a Surgeon, &one @ two assistants — As it is best she should be a popular ship, I think it would be worth your while to conform to these notions, tho' they may differ from your own. — We wish you to defer naming her, as we think a good purpose may be answer'd by calling her after a person in Phil^a upon whom we shall rely a good deal for getting us freight. I dare not tell you the name least from its length you should despair of contriving a stern large en^o to admit all the letters, but it is no matter, if it can be made to serve our interests. — Should we be disappointed in this object we can perhaps get up a freighting voyage from Boston, in which the philadelphian will have no concern, as it is only upon the presumption of getting a freight at phil^a, that he is to be interested. I will take a joint concern with you & Frank, or a larger share, if you prefer it. I trust my shipments will result in a way to enable me to do so, if not, of course you will not build her. — The E has a cargo which by computation I make equal to 475 tons measurement, & 20 tons dead weight. I understand she was not full, I imagine by starting among the bales, she w^d carry 550 tons dead weight &measurement — It will be well to have a port by which we can put Spars into the hold — they are always wanted, &but few of the Ships bring them. Sh^d you not incline to take any part yourself, nor Frank, You may go on upon my account, &I will pay a Com^n of 2½ pCt at any rate, & 5 pCt if I succeed in my object.

Yrs affectionately
(Sgd)   HLee

½ doz Boats for ships of 400 to 600 tons w^d Sell, very well, & 20 to 30 tons larger Size Lignum Vitae

THE PRIVATEER HERMAPHRODITE BRIG ABAELLINO ESCAPING FROM THE BRITISH BRIG PAULINA OFF SICILY, MARCH 4, 1815

LETTER FROM HENRY LEE, CALCUTTA, DEC. 26, 1815, TO FRAN-
CIS LEE, BOSTON, WITH FURTHER PLANS AND INFORMATION
FOR TRADE BETWEEN INDIA AND THE UNITED STATES [1]

Henry Lee had constantly warned his correspondents against depending upon bills on London for supplying a return cargo from
Calcutta, and against shipping to India an outward cargo of any but
a very select group of European and American goods. On Oct. 2, 1815,
he mentioned "pig copper very cheap," "cheese . . . 50 large ones
put up in tin & fresh made," "Cyder well cork'd," mahogany, "White
Champaigne," "some Old Hock & Seltzer water," and tar, as goods
which might pay. On Oct. 16 he asked Francis Lee to import "200
doz of White Champaigne, & 200 doz Burgundy" from France, since,
as he said, "I have engaged" that quantity, by which he apparently
meant that it had been ordered from him.[2]

Orig^l pRamdulollday (private)

M^r F Lee   Calcutta Dec 26 1815
(Duplicate p George)
dear F,   (pKensington)
not forwarded by this ship

The voyage is finally determined upon, & I have commenced purchasing. The principal advantage I shall derive
from it, will be in profits on my share of the concern, which
they furnish me credit for, on reasonable terms. — I shall go
to NYork, &hope to be away early in March. I mean instead
of interesting you, to offer Joseph one quarter of my share, if
he thinks it may prove advantageous — To enable him to
calculate the probable issue of the adventure, I shall send you
a Mem° of my purchases, the rate of freight &c by the next
ship. — I expect to get my goods, one Kind with another, 10
to 15 pCt less than the last cargoes, which together with some
other advantages, will, I am confident, insure us a certain,
&probably a great profit. — The arrival of the pickering has
not affected prices, but the others on the way will prevent So

---

1. Jackson-Lee Papers, "Letters written in Calcutta by H. Lee from
July 1813 to March 1816."
2. *Ibid.*, Henry Lee, Calcutta, Oct. 2, 16, 1815, to Francis Lee, Boston.

great a fall, as piece goods must otherwise have experienced. —
150 tons S P. will form part of the Cargo, look round &see what
can be done with it. I hear it can be made in the WCountry at
a moderate price, but I should think not under 20 Cts lb. &
it must be inferiour to the best of this Country, which can be
had at 6/ @ 6/8 pm^d. I shall take no Indigo, unless the price
should fall still lower than its present rate. I do not think that
which I am sending on the Ship Ramduloll Day is very cheap,
tho' I have seen only one parcel bought by the Am^{ns}. which in
my judgment will afford so great a profit, because it will be sold
where there are few or no good judges of quality — I know you
have express'd a different opinion, but your own experience, if
you will reflect a little, is against its Correctness — If you were
like Mr Gray, a large exporter, the very finest qualities w^d be
the Safest, because they will always sell in Europe. If you
want to adventure there, Sell your own, &buy Cap^{n}Skillings' —
he will not find any one to give 25 Cts higher than ordinary
Indigo whereas the price in Europe w^d be 25 to 50 pCt in favor
of the best. In buying the parcel I am Shipping, I take with it,
and payable in the Same way, a quantity of Piece goods which
are extremely Cheap, &which I shall send also by the Ramdulollday — Against this shipment, Remsen will have to remit
7 or 8000 Sp dollars to meet the payment of the purchase, ¼ of
which only, I pay here, I shall insure out &home, &leave the
policy to discharge the debt in case of loss. There is not an
article among them which is not extremely low, &that will not
in the worst events, give a great profit, Nor in any future shipments will I adventure anything without Securing a profit here,
by its cheapness. — Mess^s Burr &Foster have given up their
plan of remaining here for a second cargo. One of them returns
in the K, the other in the Benjamin Rush, they came out with
Bills on London, &have found great difficulty in disposing of
them. There was only one house who w^d take, &it was quite
accidental their doing it. Had they refused, their voyage w^d
have been ruin'd — Let me repeat to you again that it is always
difficult to sell bills, &that they should only be sent in aid of
avoyage, Not as a dependence — I have not yet sold the £1500,

which remains of the £2500, sent me by Patrick — Only in this small sum it will make a difference of $3000, between his remitting a Bill, in dollars, or sending me a letter of Credit. I dont mean by this to find fault, but to shew the loss upon the negotiation of Bills. — I observe by the papers there is a Commercial treaty with G B on foot. I imagine the duties on Eng^h goods will be diminish'd — but I sh^d imagine upon Bengal manufactures they w^d be continued. Upon Indigo &Drugs, I hope they will be lessen'd. The double duties upon goods brought here, will be reduced or repeald altogether, in which case I recommend your Shipping pig Copper, calculating upon 45 @ 50/ pm^d. Some french Wines as before mentioned, Silk Hose, Verdigrinn [Verdigris] Mahogany, Salmon, $1000 worth French Cambrics &Laces, &some other things which I defer naming till I arrive. — It was my intention to have sent my Indigo, &more piece goods by the Kensington, but was disappointed of tonnage. The next ship will be the RDDay, but the George will anticipate her arrival, if she sails 2m^o later. — The Pickering from her appearance will never make ashort passage, tho' Capt S praises her Sailing — I dont believe his account of her. — The Ellen, Douglas, has arrived at Madras, we dont know what vessel she is, or whether she comes this way. There are no Cotton piece goods shipping to Eng^d in private trade, &very few by the Company. The India Cap^ts take a few Choppas, &remainder of their funds in raw silk &Indigo, the former at 7/8 @ 9/ pseer, the latter 145/ @ 170/ pm^d — They dont expect much upon either, and they will make less than they expect. — I am confident we shall do well upon the Shipments to London, whether Sold there, or reship'd — Do not take the alarm at my extensive shipments I shall never have a second opp^y so Safe &promising, & I must improve it to the utmost. — I wish you to say I shall return in the Pickering, &make no mention of my real intentions.

Yrs

(Sgd)   HLee

The Persia has gone from Bombay to Muscat for a Cargo of Drugs &Coffee, intended for the Europe markets, she will I think make a poor voyage, unless she gets the latter article lower than I think for.

LETTER FROM HENRY LEE, CALCUTTA, JAN. 30, 1816, TO P. T. JACKSON, BOSTON, WITH ADVICE FOR A VOYAGE TO INDIA [1]

As early as July 1, 1815, P. T. Jackson announced that he was "concerned with C a p t GLee in building a vessel for the Calcutta Trade." [2] Although Jackson was at the same time actively engaged in his textile manufacturing at Waltham, which he probably had no idea of neglecting, Henry Lee seems to have regarded this revival of attention to commerce on Jackson's part as symptomatic of a design to give up, in part at least, his interest in manufacturing, of which, apparently, Lee had no high opinion. "Cutting," associated with Francis Cabot Lowell, Patrick Tracy Jackson, and others, in the Boston Manufacturing Co. was Uriah Cotting, a prominent Boston merchant of the time, whose financial standing is sufficiently indicated by the reference to him below.

On Jan. 20, 1816, Henry Lee had written to Peter Remsen: "I am vexed beyond measure when I look upon the advantages which have been thrown away, for want of that support which my frends threw away on their dangerous & absurd speculations of Sheep Keeping &c &c." On Aug. 21, 1813, Mary Lee had written to her husband with some amusement that "J. Bromfield and Frank [Lee] have been on a jaunt to Rhode Island and have returned Merino-mad. . . . Joe [Lee] is very earnest about it, and is interesting Charles [Jackson] in it. . . . I believe they are contemplating buying Hogg Island for the purpose." [3] C. A. Stephens has written entertainingly of "the Merino craze" which afflicted New England about the time of the War of 1812.[4]

The vessel which Jackson was building in the summer of 1815 was probably the brig *Hindu*, 301 t., built at Charlestown by Joseph Barker, which cleared for Calcutta, Dec. 26, 1815, under the command of David D. Pulsifer, also one of the owners, the others being

1. Jackson-Lee Papers, "Letters written in Calcutta by H. Lee from July 1813 to March 1816."
2. *Ibid.*, "Letters B," p. 203, P. T. Jackson, Boston, July 1, 1815, to Samuel Williams, London.
3. Morse, F. R., *op. cit.*, p. 198.
4. *My Folks in Maine*, Norway, Me., 1934, pp. 55–56.

Francis Lee, George Lee, and Augustine Heard.[5] P. T. Jackson was not mentioned among her owners, though he probably had an adventure on board.[6] His withdrawal from shipownership signalized that he had decided to devote his attention mainly or entirely to textile manufacturing.

p Ramduloll day

M^r P T Jackson, Calcutta Jany 30th 1815 [1816]
   dear Patrick,

   I enclose an Inv^o &Bill Lading of 4 bales p^s Goods, amt^s to Rps 366.14..2, the proceeds of a quantity of Lignumvitae rec^d from Madras. &Also an a/c balance in my favor Rps 24.14.5. — I have not allow'd any interest, becaus this among other sums was involved in the affairs of my Banians, &loss sustain'd, more than equal to the interest. I am glad to hear from Captn Bancroft that you are returning in some degree at least, to your old profession, which you are so well skill'd in as to be certain of success, while in the other line, there is much uncertainty, not to say danger — It is is no matter if Mr Lowell &Cutting lose some thousands, because they have them to spare, without any abridgement of the comforts, &all the wants which money can supply — I hear you are building a Ship, &that Captn Pulsifer is coming in charge, I hope on a freighting voyage merely. Should he come in Feb^y, I shall give him any advice he may require, &on my departure, if he does not arrive leave a letter, advising him not to take any Indigo, on your account, at any price, as it will certainly be low in Europe 2years to come, &an enormous quantity has been sent to our Country — As for any thing else It w^d be impossible for me to say what w^d be useful &if I could [as it — stricken through] it is not probable he would pay any attention, as he considers himself, & doubtless is, as well qualified for business here, as myself. — If he has Spars &Mahogany &Copper, they will do well, Piece goods will be lower in April, if no more, as only 2or 3 Am^ns should arrive.

   5. Registers, Boston Custom House, 1815, no. 512; *Columbian Centinel*, Dec. 27, 1815.
   6. *Columbian Centinel*, Dec. 11, 1816; Waters, *op. cit.*, pp. 23–24.

Cap^n Bancroft remains here 6 weeks for Goat Skins &c, after which he returns to Coromandel Coast to receive Skins — You can judge better than I can, whether this article will do. I should imagine too many had gone, there are no piece goods at Madras. the manufacture on the Coast is now confined chiefly to Consumption of the Country. I am certain we can do well in this trade, &you must not engage all your funds 'till I arrive. I want you to help me in a project I have in view, which can be explain'd when we meet — You will know from Frank what I am doing. I have only one letter since the Peace from you. Mr Remsen has been very attentive, &the information he sent me has been very serviceable. — I have put a pair of Hdkfs in a packet to my wife, I think you will like the Colour &figures — if it is not against your new principles to wear a *foreign* manufacture. —

Yrs truly
HLee —

LETTER FROM HENRY LEE, CALCUTTA, MAR. 1, 1816, TO ALEXANDER & CO., CALCUTTA, IN REGARD TO SECURITY [1]

This letter is valuable for the detail in which it describes one of the processes by which merchants endeavored to guard against the uncertainties of business.

On Feb. 1, Henry Lee had made a shipment of piece goods, muslins, and indigo, invoiced at sicca rupees 53,493, 6 annas, 8 pice, on the ship *Ramduloll Day* (named after a Calcutta millionaire) for New York, two-thirds on his own account and one-third on that of his brother Francis. He was now preparing to return to the United States on the *Portsea* and had used every means available to increase the shipment he was to make by that vessel, which was in the usual proportion of two-thirds on his own account and one-third on that of Francis Lee. He was interested one-fourth in a consignment of sicca rupees 141,101, 10 pice, for Liverpool on the *Portsea*. On Feb. 26 he also made another consignment of piece goods, sugar, shellac, nutgalls, and senna on the *Cririe* for New York, invoiced at sicca rupees 22,084, 1 anna,

1. Jackson-Lee Papers, "Letters written in Calcutta by H. Lee from July 1813 to March 1816."

2 pice, all on his own account. There were consignments on both vessels on the account of others than Henry Lee.[2]

To Mess Alexander & Co
    Gentlemen —   Calcutta
    I have deposited at your Office an Invoice and Bills Lading of one hundred ninety nine Packages of Merchandise shipped by Messs. Cruttenden and Mackillop on board the Portsea, Nicholls master for New York and Liverpool on the account and risk of myself and Mr. Frances Lee, amounting to Sicca Rupees Eighty thousand eight hundred thirty, seven annas (SaRs. 80,830..7.. —) and two Policies of Insurance upon the same "No 56" Calcutta Insurance Company" for Sa.Rs. 55,000 — No 632 "Star Office" for SaRs. 25,000 amounting together to SaRs. Eighty one thousand (SaRs. 81,000) — My Object in leaving these documents with you is to secure a remittance from New York, of thirty one thousand Spanish Dollars ($31,000) for the purpose of discharging a Balance due On account of Goods purchased from you, of SaRs. Fifty two thousand seven hundred Sixty Six — ans 15/6d — (SaRs. 52,766..15..6) and the Interest which may accrue thereon at the rate of twelve prCt per annum, together with the premium of insurance, on the Dollars from New York to Calcutta. This remittance I engage shall be made immediately on my arrival in the United States & in the event of any accident happening to the Portsea, or the returns in Dollars you will of course indemnify yourselves from the avails of the Policies. You will observe that according to the terms of the Policies, I am insured to Liverpool only. It will be necessary therefore, to come to an agreement with the Offices, to allow the Portsea, to touch at New York, which I trust can be effected without any additional premium, but at any rate, it must be done, or there would be a deviation — Before making the application. I wish you to communicate with Messs. Cruttenden & Mackillop. It is certain that the goods covered by the two Policies left with you, will be discharged at New

2. *Ibid.*, "Invoices of all the goods ship'd by Henry Lee during his stay in Calcutta from May 1812 to March 1816."

York, and as the risk is less than a direct voyage to Liverpool, I should hope you might obtain some abatement in the Premium already paid — you will make insurance on the thirty one thousand Dollars, on Ship or Ships from the United States to Calcutta, with liberty to touch at the usual places for trade or refreshment — I should wish you might defer making it for some months, in hopes that Premiums may be less than they now are. It is understood that in this transaction, I am not to be subject to any other charge on your part, [than — stricken through] besides those of Interest and Premium of Insurance & that the balance which may be left after the payment of the sum due you will be held to the order of myself or M^r. Francis Lee. March 1st. 1816.

Your, Ob^t S^v.
(Sig^d.) Henry Lee

LETTER FROM HENRY LEE, SHIP PORTSEA, MAY 14, 1816, TO GOLUCK CHUNDER DAY & RAMDON BONARJIA, CALCUTTA, WITH INSTRUCTIONS FOR THEIR CONDUCT AS BANIANS [1]

The questions which Henry Lee felt the need of asking are hardly more significant than the tone, that of a benevolent but stern uncle, which he saw fit to use with his banians. Ramdon Bonarjia seems to have been the Ramdon of Ramdon & Tillock, concerning whom Lee had such a high opinion until they absconded with his funds. Lee forgave them, after they had made restitution to the best of their ability, and continued to make use of their services. It was understandable, however, that on leaving India he should wish to have correspondents among Calcutta banians other than those who had betrayed his trust. He consequently seems to have addressed himself jointly to Goluck Chunder Day, a banian concerning whom he had not yet been disillusioned, and Ramdon Bonarjia, one of the defaulters. We are not told what had become of Tillock Bonarjia. Kissen was Ramkissen Day, later associated with Goluck Chunder Day and Ramdon Bonarjia.

Being written to natives of India this letter contains a somewhat

1. Jackson-Lee Papers, "Letters written in Calcutta by H. Lee from July 1813 to March 1816."

larger number of vernacular words than might otherwise be the case:
"dawks" are postal facilities; "Rowannah" refers to a passport, permit, or similar document;[2] and "Corah" is plain silk cloth as distinguished from bandannas which are the same pieces of silk cloth
dyed.[3]

"Mr. Burr" had been left in charge of some of Henry Lee's property, to be shipped as soon as his banians had delivered an order of
chintz. On Mar. 23, 1816, Richard Burr shipped to Henry Lee on the
brig *Alexander* sicca rupees 14,605, 11 annas, 7 pice in piece goods.[4]

(Sent Duplicate &
original to James Town)   At Sea, Ship Portsea May 14, 1816
   Goluck Chunder Day, Calcutta.

& Ramdon Bonarjia   We are now more than half way on our
passage, & expect to end our voyage in about 50 days more, I
received your letter of the 5 March, with the writing Paper,
which answer'd my purpose very well. I shall write this letter
very plain that you and Ramdon may be able to read it, without the help of an European. I do not wish to have my letters
seen. It is the custom with Banyans to shew their letters to
Americans & others. You must never do so with mine. I suppose all my goods have been shipped, I hope to find from M^r
Burrs letters, that you did my business well, &follow'd my
directions as to the Chintz &c. — I wrote you a long letter while
on the way down the river, I hope you read it often &follow'd
my directions. I expect to hear from you by every ship. It is
no matter what port you send my letters to, as we have dawks
every where in America, & letters go in few days from one town
to another, the same as in India. I want to know by every ship
the prices of all exports to America, &what the Cargoes cost
deducting Interest &Rowannah, Send me the Corah prices of
Silk Hdkfs at Cossimbazar, &Contract prices of Barnagore
Cloths, Prices of Sugar, Ginger, Sal Amm^c, Pepper, Copal, Shel-

---

2. [Siddons, Joachim Heyward], *The Oriental Interpreter* (London,
1848).

3. Balfour, *op. cit.*, vol. i, p. 808.

4. Jackson-Lee Papers, "Invoices of all the goods ship'd by Henry Lee
during his stay in Calcutta from May 1812 to March 1816."

lac, Borax, Senna, Salt peter, Opium, Nutgalls, Indigo, both Bazar & Agency house qualities, Cotton, Tin, Tutenague, Coffee, Nutmegs, Mace &c &c also Sp dollars, London Bills. Send me also prices of imports, particularly pig Copper, Madeira Wine, Mahogany, Verdigrease, Tar, Spirits Turpentine, Lignum Vitae, Spars, American Gin, Spanish Brandy, Swedes & Russia Iron, pig Lead, Bottles, Quick Silver, also prices of India Captains investments from London, & any other information you think may be useful. — send me by every ship. The Calcutta New price Current, by Mr Crow who lives with Mr Larkin, beginning from the day I left Calcutta & continuing the numbers as they come out every week, these you will send by some of the Ships bound to Boston or Salem that I may not have too much postage to pay. — Do not forget to send me a list of every cargo which is exported in the Ships for America, the expense for which as well as the price Current you shall be paid, so that you must not mind 20 or 30 Rupees, or whatever is necessary, for the information will be much wanted by me, as I mean to continue in the Calcutta trade. You will subscribe for a Directory at the Union Press, & send me a copy by some of the Boston or Salem Ships. I have one for 1816. — If there is any change in the duties on American Ships, let me know it & send me the Regulation. You can always buy them at the Govt Gazette press. — Write me if many free traders come out from Engd. &the rate of freight between Calcutta & Engd. Mr Mackillop will inform you, tell me what Cargoes they bring out &how they sell them — Inform me what Ships Kissen gets &also the other Banians. I want to know the Bazar interest for money, &what the Agency houses allow &also if London Bills can be easily sold for Rupees when I left, no one would take them, except for Indigo &Cloths. — If Mr Stark or any other American gentleman Should stay in Calcutta for a year, let me know what they are doing. — I forgot Raw Silk, send me the price of that among the other articles. — I wish you to get me ½ doz pices Mugga Lungees made, of the same pattern as before, but larger size & thicker cloth. I dont care about the cost, even if it shd be 14/ or 15/ but they must be of the best quality, send them to Boston, I do not think of any thing else I have to say. Mind all I have written, &if you wish to preserve my friendship, do what I ask of you. I shall either return to Calcutta or send some one, &if you follow my orders & do not get into bad habits, it is probable I shall do something for you. You know very well what I have done for others, & that it is in my power to serve you also, if you are worthy of it. —

Your friend &Serv[t]

(S[d]) HLee

[at bottom]
Sent it to the P. Master. James
Town S[t]. Helina by the Captain
of H. B. M. Brig Levant —
Captain Sneed.

DIVISION XIV

HENRY LEE, BOSTON EAST INDIA MERCHANT
1816–19

LETTER FROM HENRY AND FRANCIS LEE, NEW YORK, JULY 26, 1816, TO GEBHARD & CO., AMSTERDAM, WITH A CONSIGNMENT OF BENGAL PIECE GOODS [1]

The British ship *Portsea*, Capt. Nichols, with Henry Lee on board, arrived at New York, July 9, 1816, "102 days from Calcutta with 543 chests indigo, 2500 bags salt petre, 929 cases piece-goods, pepper coffee, &c." [2] Henry Lee had been absent from the United States for nearly five years, having sailed from Boston in Aug., 1811; nearly four of those five years had been spent in Calcutta. In a letter of Feb. 13, 1816, to his wife, Henry Lee had stated: "I shall make no stay at N. Y., but hasten on to meet you;" [3] but this intention, very forgivable, even in the case of a complete merchant, after a five

1. Jackson-Lee Papers, "Letter Book September 5th. 1816," Feb. 13, 1816–Oct. 30, 1817.
2. *Columbian Centinel*, July 13, 1816.
3. Morse, F. R., *op. cit.*, p. 165.

years' absence from his family, he does not seem to have carried out; for on Aug. 13 his brother wrote that he had been in New York ever since his arrival, and in a letter of Sept. 11, 1816, to R. P. Ochterlony he himself remarked: "I can give no information of yr Boston friends, as I have not yet been there — nor shall I move till the goods are all sold." Of course his wife and child may have joined him at New York, but there is no evidence that they did.

In resuming his position as a sedentary Boston merchant, specializing in the trade with India, Henry Lee found himself engaged in a form of commerce which had during his absence undergone a drastic transformation. On July 21, 1813, the East India Co.'s monopoly of British trade with India had been abolished. In consequence an eager swarm of British free-traders came into competition with the old Company and the foreign merchants in the purchase and sale of India goods. For more than a score of years, also, American foreign commerce had been affected by the series of almost continuous wars arising out of the French Revolution. French and British war ships, privateers, British Orders in Council, and Napoleonic decrees had hampered and harassed American trade with Europe during that period. These factors were now eliminated, but the changed situation was not entirely advantageous to American merchants; for the United States during most of the period of conflict had been able, as the principal neutral carrying nation, to trade with England and the Continent, even under difficulties, more advantageously than any other country. Now that Europe was at peace and all nations again on an equality, this advantage was lost, and the competition of the British free-traders in the Continental market put the Americans in an even less favorable position than they had enjoyed prior to the general European war. Finally, on Apr. 27, 1816, the United States Congress, under the influence of textile manufacturing interests, enacted a law placing a tariff of 25% on woolen and cotton goods; the most significant feature of this act was the provision that "all cotton cloths, the original cost of which was less than 25 cts. per square yard, should be deemed to have cost that sum, and pay duties accordingly." The object was "the exclusion of coarse, low-priced cotton fabrics from the East Indies," [4] which had hitherto been the mainstay of the American trade with India. It was, then, under conditions of greatly increased

4. Dewey, Davis Rich, *Financial History of the United States* (N. Y. etc., 1928), p. 162.

competition, complicated by the practical elimination from the trade of one of its staple commodities, that Henry Lee, handicapped by a five years' absence from the United States, again entered the lists as a sedentary East India merchant in Boston. These disadvantages, however, were at least partially balanced by the intimate personal knowledge of India commodities, business men, and business methods which he had acquired during his long exile.

The letter below reveals the Lees as beginning to gather up one of the commercial threads — the export trade to Holland — which had been dropped nine years before, in 1807, when the Napoleonic decrees, the British Orders in Council, and the ensuing Embargo Act cut off trade between the United States and Europe. It will be remembered that King Louis of Holland lost his throne in 1810 because of his unwillingness to co-operate in the enforcement of those decrees of his brother which adversely affected Dutch commerce. The goods mentioned below were exported largely, it is probable, because of the high duty recently placed upon East India piece goods imported into the United States. The shipment was not successful. On Feb. 18, 1817, Henry Lee wrote to Edward A. Newton: "I sent some Cottons to Holland, and lost about 10%." Nevertheless on July 23, 1817, in a letter to Gebhard & Co. acknowledging the complete account sales and mentioning the loss, Lee expressed his opinion that the Amsterdam market would once again be "a very good one for moderate quantities of coarse Calcutta Piece Goods;" since "the Company will not always continue to import, and sell at loss which they are now doing." He accordingly enquired concerning the demand not only for piece goods, but also for saltpetre, turmeric, ginger, and Bengal sugar. "We certainly can afford you these articles cheaper than you can obtain them in London." On Aug. 20 he dispatched a letter containing similar enquiries to L. J. Mertens, Messelman & Co., Antwerp.[5] A similar letter went on the same date to Grant, Pillans & Co., Leghorn, which firm was probably connected with the house of Grant, Sibbald & Balfour of that place, with which the Lees had been in correspondence as early as 1801. This letter also contained authorization for allowing buyers to measure the goods "to satisfy themselves at the moment of sale" and further included the not particularly startling information that "in packing piece goods in India, . . . the best are on top of the

5. Jackson-Lee Papers, "Letter Book from Jan[y]. 17th. 1817 to October 27. 1818."

bale, the 2ᵈ. quality in the middle, and the worst at bottom." It is of interest to note that the vessel on which these goods were being shipped to Leghorn was going thence to Calcutta. Henry Lee lost on this consignment also, because the same goods could be obtained more cheaply from London.[6]

(Original pr. Ariosto/

Mess Gebhard &Cᵒ.   New York July 26, 1816.
Amsterdam,   Gentᵗ.

We enclose an Invoice and bill of Lading of 39 Packages Bengal Piece Goods amounting to dollars Fourteen thousand four hundred seventy nine 96/100 shipped by us on board the Ship Ariosto, H Lambert Master, bound for Amsterdam on our account, and consigned to you. We have selected such goods as we understand are most suitable to your market, and the prices they are Invoic'd at, are as cheap as they can be imported direct from Bengal to your Country.

It is our wish to have an immediate sale effected, and we should rather have them disposed of at cost and charges, than kept on hand. Should prices be very low we leave it to yr. judgment whether to sell or wait for better prices Mr. Frederick Gebhard having authorised us to draw on you for three fourths the amount of Invoice — We have valued on you under date 24ᵗʰ. July for Twenty four hundred pounds sterling — four months sight, in favor of Messr. Palmer Wilson &Cᵒ. in London — which we beg you would duly honor. The shipment is insured in this Country for Fifteen thousand Dollars, in case of loss or damage — you will please to furnish us the necessary papers. — Be pleased to advise us by frequent opportunities of the arrival and sale of the goods — address'd to us at Boston, and at same time forward any information as to the value of Bengal goods (piece) both silk and Cotton, which you think

6. *Ibid.*, "Letter Book September 5ᵗʰ. 1816," Feb. 13, 1816–Oct. 30, 1817, H. Lee, N. Y., July 27, 1816, Mar. 7, 1817, to Cruttenden & Mackillop, Calcutta; *ibid.*, "Invoices," July 15, 1816–Dec. 8, 1817, July 23, 1816; *ibid.*, "Accounts Current & Account Sales," Apr. 18, 1816–Dec. 31, 1817, Nov. 29, 1816.

JOSEPH LEE, JR., 1770–1845, IN OLD AGE

may be useful in future shipments — We have still on hand considerable quantities of Cloths and Hkfs which we shall be glad to send you — if this adventure issues favorably — The balance which may be due after the payment of the twenty four hundred pounds — you will remit to Samuel Williams Esqr, London — for our accounts — You will recollect to send us a Certificate ofthe landing of the goods that we may recover our Debentures at the C H. Hoping tobe favor'd with frequent Communications from your respectable House. We remain —

Very Resp^y.

Yrfaithful Serv^{ts} —

H Lee

F Lee

LETTER FROM HENRY LEE, NEW YORK, AUG. 10, 1816, TO PACKARD & GOWEN, HAVANA, WITH A CONSIGNMENT OF BENGAL PIECE GOODS [1]

Henry Lee, as a member of the firm which also included his brother Joseph Lee, Jr., had maintained business connections with Havana, though not with Packard & Gowen, till shortly before the failure of the Lee firm early in 1811; and after his departure for India, the relationship of the Lees with Havana firms, including Packard & Gowen, had been maintained by Henry's brothers, Thomas, Francis, and Joseph Jr., and by his brother-in-law P. T. Jackson. Consequently the break in the web of Henry Lee's commercial connection with Cuba had not been so serious as the break with the Continent of Europe, nor was the work of repair so difficult.

In correspondence with Havana merchants, the "coast" usually meant the West Coast of Africa, which furnished one of the principal outlets for the brighter-hued cloths exported from India by American merchants; they were used as a medium of exchange in the slave trade. The "main" refers to the Spanish Main, a general term for all the Spanish-speaking countries bordering on the Caribbean.

1. Jackson-Lee Papers, "Letter Book September 5th. 1816," Feb. 13, 1816–Oct. 30, 1817.

Messrs. Packard &Gowen.   New York Augt. 10.1816.
Havanna   Gentn.

I enclose you an Invoice & bill of lading of 18. Bales Bengal
Piece Goods shipped onthe Brig Sea Island formy accounts and
consigned to you — The blue goods &hkfs are very high with
you, as appears by your letter toPeter Remsen &Co. for importation tothe coast — The white cloths are cheap and good,
and as few have been sent I am inhopes you may get rid ofthem
for the consumption of the Island, orfor exportation tothe main
—As for any limitations it would be useless to give them as you
are much better able to judge wht will be for my interest and
I have no doubt will act so astopromote it — I had rather however have you accept prices which will yield me the prime
Cost than keep the goods on hand perhaps some one would
take the whole for the sake of such articles as may happen to
be in demand. — The proceeds you will remit in good bills on
this place or Boston — Be pleased to advise by various conveyances directed Tome in Boston of arrival and sales, and in
case of loss or damage forward the necessary documents. I
shall be glad to be favor'd with your advices as to the Prices
of India goods particularly Bengal Cottons & all prices of
Pig copper Sugar Coffee & exchange on London — & U S A.
I shall always have India goods to dispose of and shall be glad
— to send any you advise to yr port —

Yrs truly
HLee —

Blue Cloths and colour'd hkfs are now high, &rather scarce
So that for the present your market isnot likely to receive any
great supplies from America I have sold 4000 to 5000 Ps. blue
cloths 5 & 5¼ within amonth —

LETTER FROM HENRY LEE, NEW YORK, AUG. 31, 1816, TO
SAMUEL WILLIAMS, LONDON, ON GENERAL FINANCIAL SITU-
ATION [1]

That Henry Lee made a profit on the piece goods imported in the
Portsea, despite excessive importations and increased duties, indicates the skill which he had displayed in the purchase of his cargo.
Nor did Henry Lee allow an opportunity to pass for obtaining a con-
cession in regard to the duties, and on Mar. 22, 1817, he wrote:
"Our application to Congress has succeeded in obtaining a partial
remission of duties, . . . We only obtained this indulgence by powerful solicitation &keeping the English part of the Concern in the back-
ground." [2]
The earlier custom had been to make remittances from Europe for
American goods in bills on London. To remit instead in Spanish dollars kept up the rate of exchange on London in the United States, of
course, by reducing the number of bills on London available.

Samuel Williams Esqr.   Original pr. Pacific
                            Duplicate Liverpool Trader
London, DrSir,   via Boston.
                            New York August 31, 1816.
I enclose you Robt. Lenox's Bill (1st) for Two thousand
Pounds. Stg (2000£) at sixty days sight on Messrs. Robert&
William Pulsford dated New York 29 August 1816. Payable to
yourself which you will place for Payment being received / two
thirds to my credit, and one third to the credit of Mr. Francis
Lee. — I shall shortly make a further remittance — this would
have gone sooner could I have found a good Bill — on my arrival it was a Common opinion here that Exchange on London
would immediately decline, and such was the case for a short
time, which made me desirous of postponing my Remittances
as late time as possible to meet my bills from Calcutta — Bills
are now scarce, and of those offered many are not [?] such as
I would not willingly take — many Remittances from Europe

1. Jackson-Lee Papers, "Letter Book September 5th. 1816," Feb. 13,
1816–Oct. 30, 1817.
2. *Ibid.*, Henry Lee, Boston, Mar. 22, 1817, to James Williamson, Calcutta.

have been made in Spanish Dollars — and they still come in every week, and from every quarter — this way of getting home funds must diminish the chance of a fall in the London Exchange — Business has been dull for some months — less so here than in Boston and Philadelphia — many sales are now making but at reduced Prices owing to the excessive Stocks in hand's of Importers unable to hold them — I dont imagine there will be any improvement in prices till Spring — many Persons here are embarrassed — particularly those concerned in Trade with England — no failures of consequence — Credit is worse at Philadelphia and Baltimore where they are calling in at the Banks — to resume Specie Payments — Currency has improv'd of late dollars now 2 to 3% for New York bills — in Phila 6 to 7% and prospect of near approach between Specie and Paper — The national Bank subscription has been filled [up — stricken through] and I understand the Stock in Philadelphia bears a small premium — It will go into operation immediately. I have made sale of about 2/3ds. the Piece goods in the Portsea — and at Prices — which give me a profit notwithstanding the increas'd duties we are subjected too — my other Shipments from India are disposed of at very good benefit. I would thank you to [advise — stricken through] desire Ripley Wiss &Co. to send me their Catalogues of Indigo, and Piece good sale's. every season — and any information as to the Prices India goods generally — you may probably have private conveyances either to this place or Boston — any expense wh you may be put to, you will please to pay, and charge to my account.

I beg to offer my sincere thanks to You, for your attentions while in India, and the liberal confidence repos'd in me in the acceptance of my Drafts.

Yrs faithfully. H Lee

Bills on London 5 to 6% advance.
   "   " Holland 39 cts the Guilder
   "   " Boston 3% advance.
   "   " Phila. 6%   ".
   "   " Balt. 8. "   ".

LETTER FROM HENRY LEE, NEW YORK, SEPT. 5, 1816, TO
GOLUCK CHUNDER DAY & RAMDON BONARJIA, CALCUTTA,
WITH INSTRUCTIONS AND INQUIRIES [1]

It was apparently the opinion of American merchants in the trade
with the East Indies that only through regular and vigorous scolding
could their banians be induced to function with a reasonable amount
of efficiency.

"Mr Miles" was Charles D. Miles, without much question the
Charles who had been Henry Lee's assistant during his Calcutta sojourn.

"Buxus" is an oriental term for any gratuity, complimentary or for
services rendered; in this case, a tip.[2]

Original p^r. M^r. Thorndike's Ship Columbus.

New York Sept. 5.th 1816

Goluck Chander Day
and Ramdon Bonarjia

I have written you once since my arrival, two Ships have
arrived which left Calcutta after I did the Rambler and Argonaut — and neither of them brot any letters from you. How is
this!, I desired you to write me by every opportunity, and you
promised you would in the most serious manner — I am afraid
you have done some bad business with M^r. Burr and are
ashamed to write me on that account — You may depend upon
it, unless you write and send me by every Ship such information
as I told you I wanted; I will not do any thing to serve you, or
allow any Vessel I am concerned in to employ you as Banians
— M^r. Miles will sail from here in two or three months, and
shall give him orders not to take you for his business, unless he
finds you have written me very often — for this purpose, you
must get me a receipt for every letter or keep some memorandum
or Copy of it — In your letters tell me the prices of all your *imports* and *Exports — Cotton piece goods, Bandannas & Choppas, Posacky,* Nimposacky, & Chellum Seersuckers, Chonder-

---

1. Jackson-Lee Papers, "Letter Book September 5th. 1816," Feb. 13,
1816–Oct. 30, 1817.
2. Siddons, *op. cit.,* "Bukshish."

corah &   and blue Strip'd — prices Corah at Cossimabar
— Barnogore Contract goods, such as Custers, Checks, Sooty
Romals — Blue Gillas, Kermetchers, Blue Gurrahs and Baftas.
— Chintz 9½ x 1⅞. — and all other piece goods. — also of
Sugar, ginger, Cotton, Opium, Indigo, Copal, Nutgalls, Tute-
nague, Pig-copper, Senna, Borax, Sal-ammoniac, Pepper, Nut-
megs, Salt petre, Coffee Mace &c — Iron, Sweedes & English —
Quicksilver, Mahogany, Verdigris, Madeira wine, this article I
want to know particularly — pig lead, Bottles, Gin and Brandy
— Tar and any other articles of Europe and american goods.

Send me Mr. Crow's Price Current by every Ship, and any
new Custom house regulations. Let me know too what duties the
americans now pay both on Imports and Exports. — also Prices
of London bills and dollars. Send me a list from the Custom
house of all Cargoes imported and exported in American Ships
— Let me know also if any free Traders have come out from
England, and what cargoes they bring and how much per ton
they ask for carrying goods to London, I have nothing more to
say at this time — I hope the next Ships from Calcutta, may
bring letters from you, and I shall then write again — I must
repeat again that unless you write as I directed I will not give
you any business — Tell Kissin to behave himself well and
Mr Miles may do him some service on his return to Calcutta.
The Cririe and Alexander have not yet arrived — we expect
them every Day.

Yr fd. & Sr.   H Lee

Send me the Directory for 1817. from the Mirror Press, every
year — I will send you the money for it. and also for the Buxus.
you pay the Custom house. Sircars — for a list of the Exports
& Imports — .

LETTER FROM HENRY LEE, NEW YORK, SEPT. 6, 1816, TO J. S. CARTER, LIVERPOOL, REQUESTING INFORMATION ON THE POSSIBILITIES FOR TRADE BETWEEN ENGLAND AND INDIA [1]

In the drastically changed conditions of the trade with India, Henry Lee was anxious to canvass every possibility for new commercial alignments. Copper was a commodity always in demand in Calcutta for shipbuilding and other purposes, and Henry Lee, from the questions below, evidently desired, if possible, to carry on a commerce between England and Bengal, wherein he should ship to Calcutta copper, lead, iron, quicksilver, etc., but principally the first, brought to England in the general course of trade; and should take returns, partly in sugar and saltpetre, but chiefly in cotton for the British textile manufactures. He wished to carry on this trade, using a British merchant as a cover and employing an American captain. He does not seem to have pursued the matter further, and this was doubtless merely one of many projects he considered shortly after his return from Calcutta.

J. S Carter.   Pr Pacific   New York Sept. 6. 1816.
Merchant. Liverpool   Dup pr

I wish to procure from you information of the price of Pig Copper — in your Place & London — English, Sweedish and Spanish particularly the latter — It is sometimes very cheap, & such I am told is now the case — It comes as a remittance from South America. Spanish Main and Havanna; — sometimes from Cadiz and Gibralter when the course of Exchange between those places and London is much in favor of England — as it is at this moment — I want the article on board for Exportation — I want at the same time precis English sheet. Copper, — To these inquiries I beg to add the following, how. many Ships have been dispatched to India particularly Bengal. the past year, and what freight do they procure out and home. at what rate can you get. 100 to 200 tons of lead and Iron carried to Calcutta — ? how cheap can the Liverpool Ships bring Cotton [goods — stricken through] from Calcutta to

1. Jackson-Lee Papers, "Letter Book September 5th. 1816," Feb. 13, 1816–Oct. 30, 1817.

England? at what price can they afford to sell it. allowing the cost to be 13 Sᵃ. Rpˢ. pʳ Mᵈ. of 83 lb.? How much will a good Ship fit for an Indian Voyage 350 to 450 Tons cost. and could you [early — stricken through interlineated: easily] procure a license for an Indian Voyage? what is the difference in your Place between Georgia Upland & good middling quality and Bengal of fair quality? is Surat esteemed better than the Bengal, and what may be the difference? If I should want to undertake a Voyage from Liverpool to India, could you stand as Owner and how could it be managed? Could an American Capᵗ. be employ'd or woud it be necessary to have a british Subject — they are so much inferiour to our American Masters that it would be quite an object to have an American — what can you calculate upon in Liverpool 18 months hence, for 300 Tons of goods Bengal Sugar and Salt Petre — and is the latter allowed exportation to this or any other Country — ? Your replies to these enquiries will greatly oblige me and I should wish you to add any other information relative to the trade between your Place and [Bengal — stricken through] India particularly Bengal. and forward Duplicate letters to me in Boston.

Business is dull particularly among Merchants engaged with the trade with England — who are most of them embarrassed by their Excessive ImportationS of last season — The new Tariff may help the coarse Cotton goods, but they will not be much affected till next Spring. Currency improving here and at the South — Dollars may be had here at 2½% advance — Phila 10% Baltimore 10 to 11% Bills on London. 6% advance — in Boston 2%. advance and falling The new crop of Cotton will be abundant & probably fall from it's present high Price as no one would. venture upon shipping without a prospect of great gain, as money can be employ'd with more Safety at home.

Yrˢ. truly

HLee

I would thank You to Quote the following articles net on board for Shipping — Pig lead — Bar Iron — Quick silver — & Turkey opium — and Spanish Dollars. H Lee.

LETTER FROM HENRY LEE, NEW YORK, SEPT. 8, 1816, TO JOHN
B. GREENE, HAVRE, REQUESTING INFORMATION IN REGARD TO
POSSIBILITIES OF TRADE WITH FRANCE [1]

In a previous letter Henry Lee had enquired concerning the values
in France of saltpetre, sugar, and cotton. Earlier in the century Henry
Lee and his brother Joseph had enjoyed close commercial relations
with France, and Henry had resided for nearly a year in that country,
1804–05; these relations he was now desirous of renewing. John B.
Greene had previously been associated with the Lees as supercargo
for voyages to France. He later became a member of the firm of
Welles, Williams & Greene, Havre. On Mar. 15, 1817, Henry Lee
shipped this firm "48 Boxes Brown Havana Sugar's . . . which you
will sell for the most you can. . . . Out of the proceeds you will pay
yourselves for the Goods per Factor, and for the balance I shall draw
on you or direct it remitted to London." Evidently Lee had received
some French goods of some sort from the Havre firm. To the sugar
he "added Some Tumeric" on the same conditions.[2] This consignment, invoiced at $3,264.18, resulted in a heavy loss, the gross sales
but little exceeding the invoice price, while the charges amounted to
more than one-third of the sales. Brokerage, and commission and
del credere, were not excessive, being ¼% and 4%, respectively;
freight made up nearly one-fourth and duties well over a half of the
total charges; and the rest was made up of charges for landing, hire
of tent, officers' fees, consul's certificate, "repairing Bags," repairing
cases, carriage to stores, "Storing, weighing, and delivering," "Store
Rent in Entrepot," "Weigh house fees," and interest on freight.[3]

Original pr. Active.

John B. Greene Esqr   New York Sept 8th.1816.
Havre DGrace.   Dear Sir.

As it is of some importance to get the information requested
in my last letter, I send a duplicate annex'd and another sample
of Salt petre & Sugar — I would thank you to forward dupli-

1. Jackson-Lee Papers, "Letter Book September 5th. 1816," Feb. 13,
1816–Oct. 30, 1817.

2. *Ibid.*, "Letter Book from Jany. 17th. 1817 to October 27. 1818."

3. *Ibid.*, "Invoices," July 15, 1816–Dec. 8, 1817, Mar. 19, 1817; *ibid.*,
"Accounts Current. & Account Sales," Apr. 18, 1816–Dec. 31, 1817, June
18, 1817.

cate replies to me in Boston — In addition to the enquires about Cotton — I would request your sending me a proforma sales of 1000 Bales Cotton & of 1000 bags. ofSugar that I may transmit the same to India — for the information of my friends there — who may be induced to make some shipments either direct or by way of this Country I would also be glad to have samples of Indigo Fine middling & ordinary with your remarks as to their value — It is my determination to pursue the Bengal trade and I wish to collect every sort of information which may be useful inthe management ofit — I understand your Agents sometimes make advances upon consignments from this Country by granting Bills on London. — suppose a Cargo should be imported from Calcutta of Cotton Sugar, and Indigo with a view of sending it to Havre deGrace what proportion of the value of it here would you advance, on sufficient security being offered for reimbursment in case ofloss of it on the way? If you can grant facilities of this kind — I may induce some Merchants in Calcutta to ship a Cargo upon which I could gain a good f^t. and at same time throw some valuable business into y^r. hands. — I brot with me from India 600 Chests Indigo hoping tofind a sale to the Exporters — but there being no demand we were compelled to send on 500 ofthem to London there was a shipment of Indigo made you some time since by my brother F onhis account — We have not heard of any sale or offer. Be good enough to write us on the subject as I have more ofthe same kind which I am anxious to dispose off. — Any information as to the value of East India produce with you will be acceptable & in return I shall be glad to be any way useful to you in this quarter Business is dull, and money scarce, owing among other causes to excessive importations of European goods beyond the wants of the country and to the depreciation in Europe of nearly all [an — stricken through interlineated: our] Exports. There will be much distress among Commercial men thro the winter and probably many failures — Currency has improved dollars canbe purchased at 1½%. advance. & in Philadelphia and Baltimore at. 8 to 10%.

Yr faithful Servant   H Lee.

Another thread in the web of world commerce which Henry Lee
was weaving after the War of 1812 was the shipment to India on
American vessels of goods from France, probably obtained from the
proceeds of Bengal merchandise.

On Oct. 1 he shipped to Tulloh & Co. "100 doz. of Champaign
wine — 27 pipes Sicily and 12 pipes Fayal;" on Nov. 3 he notified the
same firm that he was "about engaging pretty extensively in the Importation of . . . goods from France."

Original per. Columbus.
Duplicate "/Wm Savary/

Messrs. Tulloh &C^o.   New York Sepr. 11. 1816.

Calcutta

Dear Sirs, — I am shipping a few packages of French
manufactures onboard the Ship William. Savary for your place
consisting of Silk hose, Cambrick handk'fs which I shall consign to you on the other side you have a memorandum ofthem
— I am also sending by the same Vessel 130 Quarter Casks of
old Sherry wine which you will sell at public or private sale as
may appear most for my interest — I shall request the favor
of your advancing to Messrs. Alexander &C^o. such portion of
the probable proceeds as may be convenient, and the balance
when sales are effected. I dont Know of any other shipments of
wine from hence. Except a parcel of Sicily Madeira in the Ramduloll — It is so high in Madeira & Teneriffe that there is no
inducement to adventure, and in Spain wine ofthe quality I am
shipping cannot be had under 30 $ p^r. Qr Cask. — It is not at
all probable any other Sherry will be sent. & I should imagine
it would be prefered to the low Madeira of which the Portuguese carry so much to Calcutta — The french goods are intended as an experiment, and if found to answer I will supply
you with as many as can be sold, to do this to advantage I wish

1. Jackson-Lee Papers, "Letter Book September 5th. 1816," Feb. 13,
1816–Oct. 30, 1817.

you to send me frequent and minute information asto the value of silk hose french cambricks andCambrick hkfs. and what quantities will sell, — whether fine or coarse are most wanted the proportion of white and black, men's &women's — colours &c &c. Be good enough at the same time to give me some general account ofthe state of the bazar for European goods — particularly India market Madeira & Tenerife wine — Sweedes &English Iron — French Brandy — Gin — Tinplates — Pig lead — Quicksilver — Roll brimstone — Sheet & Pig Copper — Manchester cotton goods — Mahogany and any other articles that may come within your recollection — Business is very dull in this quarter, and there is much distress existing among the Commercial part of the world owing to excessive importations from Europe and a depreciation of almost every kind of Merchandize Cotton is high say 13. or 14^d St^g a pound — but the crop which will come to market in November is very promising &the article is expected to fall Considerably both here and in Europe.

Yrs truly   H Lee

LETTER FROM HENRY LEE, NEW YORK, SEPT. 12, 1816, TO JOHN PALMER, CALCUTTA, WITH A GENERAL ACCOUNT OF AMERICAN TRADE WITH THE EAST INDIES [1]

The profits accruing to Henry Lee from investments made during his five years' residence in Calcutta are indicated by his statement that he would be able to "pass the remainder of my life with my family;" that is to say, he had built up capital sufficient for his operating as a sedentary merchant without the necessity of again going abroad as supercargo or factor.

The book referred to in this letter, *A Statistical View of the Commerce of the United States of America,* by Timothy Pitkin, was first published at Hartford, Conn., in 1816.

1. Jackson-Lee Papers, "Letter Book September 5th. 1816," Feb. 13, 1816–Oct. 30, 1817.

John Palmer Es^q. Original P^r.Ramduloll Day.
  Calcutta   Duplicate   New York. Sep^t. 12. 1816.
    Dear Sir —
      Believing from the friendly manner you always treated
me during my residence in India, that you still continue to feel
some interest in my welfare, I have a satisfaction of informing
you of my arrival here about two months ago, in apleasant
passage of 120 days — my Cargo came to a very good market,
but the profits are much diminished by a new Tarif of Duties
which took effect afew days before our arrival. The Shipments
I made in American Vessels, previous to my departure have resulted very profitably — sufficiently so with my moderate expectations to enable me to pass the remainder of my life with
my family — Calcutta voyages generally have not ended very
successfully — owing in some measure to excessive importations of European manufactures, and to the increase of our
domestic ones — which causes combin'd with a general stagnation in business have lessened very much the consumption, and
sale of India piece goods — The most profitable part of my own
investments has been in color^d and blue Goods wh are wanted
for Exportation to West Indies, and South America — Indigo
has been without sale, except in small quantities for consumption — the Importers have been obliged to reexport it, and
upon an average have not realised the cost in India and the
charges — upon some parcels there has been aheavy loss — I
brought in the Portsea a very large quantity intending to land
it, if any offer had been made, but I found no one willing to
give the cost and charges. — [Upon some parcels there has
been aheavy loss — I brought in the Portsea avery large quantity — stricken through] and sent the whole on to England —
with exception of two Parcels —
      We have accounts from France & Holland to 3^d. August,
they are unfavorable to all sorts of East India produce except
Cotton — which still keeps up, and will remain so till our new
Crop gets to market which will be in January — It is very
promising, but many are of opinion it will be high for some

time to come — asthe consumption ofthe article is very great on the Continent as well as in England — there are many Ships now on Voyages to Calcutta principally for Sugar, ginger, tumerick, &c — and some of them for Cotton — more however, with view of employing idle Ships — than any expectation of great profits — The restoration of peace in Europe which promises tobe alasting one, has depriv'd us of the advantages which formerly made our East India Commerce so extensive and profitable — Business is very dull, and all classes ofthe mercantile world any ways engaged in active trade, are embarras'd — but we have not had many failures, and things are rather improving, from the prudential course which people have taken for some months past — all those houses in whom you can be interested in negociations of Bills &c — at least during my stay inCalcutta are yet existing and most of them in good credit — The Bill you received from me on Mess. Remsen &Cᵒ. £6614..7..8 Stᵍ. was duly honor'd, and has gone onto London for Collection — Our news papers are wholly barren of any thing which can make them worth the time, and trouble of perusing — or I should send a Packet — You will receive from Mᵣ. Herring the 2ᵈ Officer of the Portsea who returns in the Ramdulollday a "Statistical view of the Commerce of the United States" — a work of merit, and which may be useful to refer to occasionally — I beg of your acceptance of it. — , and at same time my sincere thanks for the many instances of your Kindness, and friendship, — which are still fresh in my recollection — I desire you to remember me to your Partners, and believe me with

Sentiments of Respect & Regard.

Yrfaithful Servant

HLee — .

LETTER FROM HENRY LEE, NEW YORK, SEPT. 20, 1816, TO
CHARLES J. CATLETT, ALEXANDRIA, VA., ACCEPTING OFFER
OF A GUARANTEE [1]

In view of the uncertain commercial situation in 1816 (a week
after this letter he wrote: "I apprehend many failures . . . in course
of 12 months"),[2] Henry Lee was glad to accept his correspondent's
offer personally to insure the importer against loss, on goods sold advantageously [3] by the Alexandria commission merchant, for a premium
of 2½%. Alexandria, Va., then a leading southern port, would be a
natural outlet for the coarse colored Bengal cotton cloths so extensively imported for use in clothing the slave population. The con-
cluding sentence is typical of the personal and informal character of
business relations at the time.

Dear Sir.   New York. Sepr. 20. 1816.
     Charles J Catlett Esqr,
       Alexandria,
         Owing to some mistake at the Post Office I did not re-
ceive your favor of 11th. ins^t till this morning — The sales are
very satisfactory, I have no doubt the Buyer is good. but as I
have more at risk than I can afford I will avail myself of your
offer of guarantee at 2½%. you allowing me to draw on you at
30 days — Please to say whether this will be agreable if not, at
what rate will you give me a bill on London,? I understand
from M^r. R. that you have funds there — I have directed a
shipment of 14 bales to be made you from Philadelphia by M^r
Saml. Archer — among them are some salempores, which Ihope
you may get off, as Ihave many on hand — Ishall send some
Bandannas — from here — and probably some Gurrahs,
Checks, Custers &c. We are in treaty for the whole of the

     1. Jackson-Lee Papers, "Letter Book September 5th. 1816," Feb. 13,
1816–Oct. 30, 1817.
     2. *Ibid.*, Henry Lee, N. Y., Sept. 27, 1816, to James Mackillop, Cal-
cutta (see below, pp. 1200–1204).
     3. *Ibid.*, "Invoices," July 15, 1816–Dec. 8, 1817, between Aug. 19 and
22, 1816; *ibid.*, "Accounts Current. & Account Sales," Apr. 18, 1816–Dec.
31, 1817, Sept. 11, 1816.

Saltpetre — but as we may not effect a sale I would thank you to transmit any offer which may be made, as to the quality we can authorise you to sell it as of the purest quality — It has been examined by various persons and among them Agents of Government, and that they all agree that it is the best ever imported It is found not to loose more than ¼ per Cent by Chemical examination — I am sorry for the indisposition of your child, and beg that my business may not interrupt for a moment the attentions necessary for her comfort and welfare —

Yrs truly.   HLee.

LETTER FROM HENRY LEE, NEW YORK, SEPT. 21, 1816, TO CHARLES WILLIAMS, LONDON, ON THE GENERAL BUSINESS SITUATION [1]

A little over a week before, Henry Lee had written, "we have not had many failures, and things are rather improving." [2] In the letter below he takes a different tone.

William Gray of Salem, the largest shipowner in the United States, acquired considerable unpopularity among his Federalist neighbors because of his defense of the embargo.[3]

/Orig^l. p^r Minerva/

M^rCharles Williams   New York Sep 21st. 1816.
    London,
        Dear Sir,
            Since my last to you of the 13thinst. My brother F has remitted £1563. on our account. I shall Soon send you a further Sum from hence, We suppose Welles Williams & Greene have remitted something on account of 6000lb Indigo sent them. — Mess^s Gebhard &C^o. will also in all probability have a small sum to Send from the proceeds of piece Goods sent them, & Mess^s Grant, Pillans &C^o. of Leghorn a further amount. The

1. Jackson-Lee Papers, "Letter Book September 5th. 1816," Feb. 13, 1816–Oct. 30, 1817.
2. *Ibid.*, Henry Lee, N. Y., Sept. 12, 1816, to John Palmer, Calcutta (see above, pp. 1188–1190).
3. Morison, *op. cit.*, pp. 119, 190.

Bill of £6614..7..8 which Mess^s Remsen &C^o accepted to pay at your office, will become due 25thDec. I believe, to meet the payment, my brother Frank has purchased of the New Eng^d Bank £4000.. at 60 days which will be forwarded you by Messrs Remsen &C^o. I shall take care that the balance of £2614..7..8 be sent in season also. I have seen your brothers letter to Frank of July   which is an answer to mine written at sea on the way from Calcutta. I am obliged for the information it Contains. It is an object of some importance to me, to be kept informed of the prices in London, of East India Goods, &the state of the Trade between GBritain &India. particularly that which is carried on in private Ships, for which purpose I am desirous of opening a correspondence with Ripley Wiss &Ripley. I send enclosed a letter, in which I request them to forward me Catalogues of Sales of Indigo, piece Goods & &c. &to call upon you for any expence they may be Subjected to, in procuring &forwarding them. It is probable in the fluctuations of prices here &in London, I may find Some articles low en^o to import from Eng^d to this Country. In which case their advices might be useful to them &myself. I would thank you also to Send me any information relative to the trade, which you may be able to procure without inconvenience — We have sold nearly all the goods you Sent us in the Sarah &Margaret, at very good prices Say 115 Cts prrupee upon the average, which does very well as they were principally Silks upon which the duties are only 15 pCt. Of the Portseas cargo, only about 100 bales remain unsold. It will do pretty well, notwithstanding the high duties we may have to pay. I had no concern in the Indigo. Of the 80 cases landed, all but 25 are Sold at Saving prices. Bengal Piece Goods are now very dull, as indeed are all others, except some articles of grocery wanted for Consumption. Most of the India traders have Stored their Cargoes 'till the Spring, but the quantity on the way &on hand, is So great, that I don't believe their expectations will be realized. They are Sending Ships Continually from Eastward, for Calcutta &other ports beyond the Cape. I Suppose to prevent their rotting. The loss

ofthe Capital engaged, being only a Secondary consideration.
Mr Thorndike has just Sent the Columbus, Mr Gray the Miles
Standish, Mr Forrester the Restitution, for Calcutta. Thomas
Ward &others are getting the Argonaut ready for the same destination, &Bryant &Sturgis another ship. They have also sent
the Marcellus to Batavia &a third to the North West Coast. —
MrGray I am told has only 44 Ships &Brigs. I suppose he
counts upon his friend Bona's getting back, &a return of good
old times. The Shipping Merchants in this quarter are quite
idle, &wholly at a loss for employment for their Ships. The
Cotton &Tobacco will afford business for a portion, &the others
must perish, fortunately they are far advanced to that point,
most of them having been built before the war. I could buy
vessels that cost $30,000 &in good order, from 10 to $15,000
&new ones for $20,000. Business dull, more So than a month
ago, money Scarce, &apprehensions of many failures. One
house heretofore in very good credit, Stop'd three or four days
ago. Mr R tells me they owe you nothing — Vandervorst &
Wooden for $220,000 to $250,000. I am told they will make a
large dividend. The following houses Stop'd in Phila Some
weeks ago. Smith &Morgan, G &E Morrison, C &C French,
Thomas S. &G Field, & last week B B Howell, this last was a
failure of considerable magnitude. The others were also extensive dealers in dry goods. I do not imagine Commercial men
will get thro' their present embarrassments for some time, not
'till there has been a Suspension of importations for a long
time. The Ships which have arrived this Season brought only
a few, but the Spring importations &the old Stock were So
enormous that the Quantity on hand is much too large for the
wants of the Country &the means of the holders. 2000 packages have been Sold at Auction Since 1 of the mo &upwards of
4000 are now advertized. The loss upon Some of them very
great, &upon all more or less. It is the overtrading of the
English Importers which is the principal cause of the distress
now existing their wants are So great, as to press heavily upon
all classes. I hope they may not find, for a time at least, those
facilities which have enabled them to plunge So deeply in

Speculations. The high rate of Exchange on London, &the [load — stricken through] bad State of American credit in Eng^d. will be great restraints upon them.

Yours truly

(Sgd)   HLee

Bills on London 6% advance
  D^o   Boston 1½%   "
Dollars 1 @ 2 pCt
Bills on Phil^a 7 @ 8
  "   Baltimore 8 @ 9
6 pCent 90, advancing

LETTER FROM HENRY LEE, NEW YORK, SEPT. 25, 1816, TO BABOO DELSOCK ROY, CALCUTTA, WITH SUGGESTIONS FOR FUTURE CONSIGNMENTS [1]

This letter apparently records the failure of a crafty Oriental's attempt to diddle the shrewd Yankees.

(Original p^r Argonaut/

Baboo   N York. Sepr. 25, 1816

Messrs. Remsen &C^o. have already informed you ofthe sales of your bale of Shawls — It will be many months before the money will become due — the buyers are safe men however, and will no doubt pay when the period of payment arrives . . . We are ordered by Messrs. Cruttenden & Mackillop to remit the proceeds ofthis consignment in Dollars — We shall do so and effect Insurance here I now inclose a certificate of dammage which wehave been Compelled to allow the Buyers — Many ofthe Shawls were damaged. — some torn, and others appeared as ifthey had been worn and washed — The assortment of colours was not good, and as the demand for these goods is very small in this Country — I should not advise your sending any more — but if you do, get some intelligent Supercargo to select such Patterns as are liked inthis Quarter. It is

1. Jackson-Lee Papers, "Letter Book September 5th. 1816," Feb. 13, 1816–Oct. 30, 1817.

very probable I may have a concern in a Ship to go to Calcutta in Course of two or three months — if I do I will direct the Super Cargo to call on you with such information as you may require

Yr faithful Servant
Sign'd   HLee —

To Baboo
Delsock Roy
Calcutta

LETTER FROM HENRY LEE, NEW YORK, SEPT. 26, 1816, TO PALMER, WILSON & CO., LONDON, ON SALES OF INDIGO AND SALTPETRE [1]

It is evident from the mention of overproduction of indigo that crop reduction is not a strictly contemporary agricultural theory. The references to sales of saltpetre by retail and at auction throw a thin and faint ray of light into one of the most shadowy corners in the business life of the sedentary merchant; namely, the system of disposing of goods locally. There is a wealth of letters to throw light upon shipments abroad, but only infrequently do transactions conducted face to face and by word of mouth leave records through which they may survive to the knowledge of later generations.

(Original p^rMinerva
(Duplicate p Carolina Ann)

Mess^s Palmer, Wilson &C^o   New York Sep 26 1816.
[written in margin: N°. 36 — old Jewry]
    London,
       Gent^m.
     I have Seen your letter of 22 July, to Mess^s Remsen &C^o. &notice what you say in regard to remittances on [interlineated: acc^t of] the Portseas cargo. You will have found before this reaches, that we have complied with Mess^s Cruttenden &McKillops instructions, having Sent you Seventeen thousand, eight hundred pounds, on account of Mess^s Dickson &William-

---

1. Jackson-Lee Papers, "Letter Book September 5th. 1816," Feb. 13, 1816–Oct. 30, 1817.

sons Shipment of 465 bales piece Goods &2443 bags Saltpetre. Two thousand pounds on account of M[r] Bradys Indigo, & One thousand, on acc[t] of M[r] Templetons. We have also remitted Six hundred pounds to meet the freight on M[r] Ochterlonys goods in the Portsea, making in all Twenty one thousand four hundred pounds Sterling £21400..00. The Ship Cririe has arrived & part of the goods are landed, We are order'd to remit the proceeds of both Mess[s] W &Dicksons & M[r] Ochterlonys consignment in this vessel, direct to Calcutta, in dollars. We have Sent the former Gent[n]. Six thousand Sp dollars by the Columbus on account of that Concern. &shall Send a further Sum by a Ship on the point of departure for Calcutta. This remittance is insured here at 3 pCt. As will be the others that we may make in future. Of the portsea piece goods about 120 bales remain unsold, of the M C concern, & 10 or 15 belonging to M[r] Ochterlony. We hope to bring sales of both of them to a conclusion in course of a month. M[r] Templetons Indigo is all Sold, at $150 @ $155 plb. this is doing better as we believe, than it would probably have done in London, which is all we expected when we decided upon landing it. Part was middling, some fine, &few boxes were ordinary. Of M[r] Bradys parcel of 48 Chests, 24 remain, others Sold at $1.50 which we think a great price. It was all more or less broken, or rejected, &some ordinary quality. I hope we may get off the remainder at Same rate. The article is dull, but little required for Exportation, &the shipments to Europe have issued so badly that no one will venture to buy for exportation on any terms. All the accounts we get from Holland, France &Italy, with regard to it, are unfavourable. Some Sales of Masseyks which is consider'd as good as was ever seen in France, have been made, to afford a profit on the India, but taking one parcel with another, the importers into this Country have lost 45 to 100 Rps a M[d]. It appears to me from the information I obtain'd in India, & the enquiries I have [been — stricken through] made of those who have been trading to the Continent of Europe in this Merchandize, that the produce is much too large for the Consumption, &nothing will raise the value, but a diminution of the Crop to 50,000 M^d instead of 105,000 which has been average for four years. — Of the Saltpetre we have only sold a small portion. The Gov^t are in treaty for the whole, but as yet, they have not decided. I found a very dull market on my arrival, but knowing that many cargoes were on the way, I concluded there was no improvement tobe expected, &that it was desirable to bring the Concern to as Speedy close as possible, to effect this we have been obliged to retail Some, sell others at Auction, when good prices were offer'd. We have Succeeded beyond our most Sanguine expectations. To induce purchases [blot] We have been Compell'd to give long credit, &it will yet be some months before we realize a dollar. This circumstance, connected with the general distress, among business men, want of confidence, &consequent Scarcity of money, have made it very inconvenient to raise [interlineated: such] large SumS, as we have remitted you. &for the duties which are very heavy & which will Soon become due. In the usual state of trade, it would have been Convenient to have met Mess^s C &M's Wishes to a greater extent than they have required, but now it is far otherwise, but as I pledged myself that their arrangements with you, for re-imbursing themselves for Portseas Cargo should be punctually met, we had only one course to follow. I trust all the Bills we have Sent forward, will be duly honour'd, Should they not be however, the parties here are very Solid, &will reimburse us for any which may be return'd. We shall remit further in course of two or three weeks. — Business is very dull, &many persons heretofore in good credit, are embarrass'd. Our importations, especially from GBritain, have been too great, either for the wants of the Country, or the means of those engaged in making them. We have thus far, avoided any loss by failures, but 'tis not tobe expected we shall always escape, in such extensive Sales &long credits. India goods are very dull, &would be very low but for an idea prevailing among Some of the largest holders, that they will improve in the spring, which induces them to keep out of the market. Mess^s R &myself are of a different opinion, &believe they will be much lower, as both

British & Domestic manufactures are abundant & cheap. The new Tariff by which duties on coarse goods are more than doubled, will stop further consumption of India piece goods except to a very limited extent — Cotton is yet high, but many believe it will fall very much, when the new crop which is abundant, gets to market, say in Decr. Some of our Merchants are sending their ships to Bengal for cotton, but it is more with a view of employment for them, than any expectation of great profit. I should think before their return, the article would be as cheap here, as the Bengal, making due allowance for difference of quality. — As it is important to my business to possess all the information I can collect relative to the value of India goods in London, I take the liberty to ask of you Some account of prices of piece Goods, Indigo, Cotton, Sugar, Pepper Coffee, Spices &c &c, also the rate of freight in private Ships to and from India, the number gone &their prospects, Rate of Ex with Madras &Calcutta, &any thing else upon the subject which may occur to you, in return if there is any thing I can do for you in this quarter, I beg you would command my Services

I am, with great respect,
Your faithful Servant
(Sgd)   HLee

Dollars 2 pCt adv
Bills on London 6 @ 6½ do
6 pCt Stocks 90 —

LETTER FROM HENRY LEE, NEW YORK, SEPT. 27, 30, 1816, TO JAMES MACKILLOP, CALCUTTA, WITH GENERAL ACCOUNT OF COMMERCIAL SITUATION [1]

That Remsen & Co. was a firm solely devoted to commission business; that a single indigo planter was capable of supplying "all that is wanted;" the number of failures, past and prospective, in the commercial world; the method of obtaining low-priced indigo in Calcutta; the suggested project of supplying American-built vessels for the

1. Jackson-Lee Papers, "Letter Book September 5th. 1816," Feb. 13, 1816–Oct. 30, 1817.

"country trade;" the impracticability of shipments from India to the United States in British bottoms; all these are notable items in the very informative letter below.

Henry Lee's high opinion of Samuel Williams is partially confirmed by Robert Bennet Forbes, who states that in 1820 "Mr. Samuel Williams was the principal American merchant in London." [2]

(Original pr. Argonaut/
(Dup pr R. Duloll Day/

James Mackillop Esq'r   New York Sepr. 27 1816.
My Dear Sir.

I have written you twice besides the communications from myself, and Messrs. Peter Remsen &Co. towhich I refer you for statement of sales effected, remittances made tothis date. We had a letter from Mess. Palmer Wilson &Co. few days since desiring us to remit as soon as possible at least to the extent of half the cost of Portseas' Cargo — I have written them in answer that we had done so and I should send them further sums — My Brother F will probably send you by the Argoneaut as an advance onthe Cririe's consignment a further sum in dollars — There are none oftheir goods except 20 bales of blue Gurrah's sold as yet — but we hope to dispose of part of the remainder as soon as they are landed — Business is now in a very bad state on account ofthe embarrassment of that class of men upon whom we chiefly rely for sales of Peice goods — As yet, only one buyer has fail'd and he was a debtor to me individually to a small amount — The general concern has not yet lost any thing — I am very apprehensive we shall not be so fortunate thro the whole business. We have really fallen upon bad times for our speculation I neverknew the time when it was more difficult to sell goods — or raise money — My share of advances upon this concern will occupy all my means &prevent me doing any other business for 6 months to come — I shall not mind this however ifwe get thr'o in a way to make a moderate profit for our friends and at same time to satisfy you that I have been as punctual in Remittances as you expected — It is

2. Forbes, *op. cit.*, p. 61.

natural you should feel some anxiety inpresent depressed state
of trade — and the failures which have taken place in all
quarters ofthe Commercial world — I am not sanguine enough
to believe y^t. the concern will not suffer some loss inthe disposal
ofthe goods consigned to us but as far as regards the safety ofthe
Property in our hands you have not the least to apprehend —
Mess^s Remsen &C^o. are Commission Merchants with alarge
Capital and who have no business of their own, and who never
engage in any speculations, or make advances except upon
Property in hand — my situation is equally secure, I have no
business butthe Sale of Portsea's Cargo and the settlement ofthe
concern, & all I possess is [?] on taken up in advances upon
this Consignment, or in notes ofhand for sales effected — The
shipments I made here with the exception ofthe lot of Indigo
bot of you result very profitably and will leave me when wholly
brot to a close, if not as much as I desire sufficient for my
comfort and happiness — We have already advanced so largely,
besides the duties which will in part soon become due, and to a
very heavy amount, that it may be a month or possibly longer
before we send Mess^s. Palmer Wilson &C^o. any further sums —
upon Mr Ochterlonys goods we shall make no remittances in
advance. but wait till collections are made and send the amount
in Dollars —

The fact is with regard to his concern, I did the business in
Calcutta without any emolument, or any wish tobenefit my own
interest and it affords me pleasure tothink he is likely to derive
so considerable aprofit from his adventures — but as it is extremely inconvenient to anticipate his sales, I think it would be
unreasonable to expect us to do it, and I have written him to
that effect — our Merchants continue to send their Vessels
toCalcutta principally I believe for Sugar, ginger, cotton and
other gruff goods — as to the Cotton it may dofor 9 or 12
Months to come — because the fine keeps up inthis Country —
but the new crop which will come forward in Decr. is very
promising and I imagine will reduce the price ofthe article in
Europe as soon as the first cargoes arrive there — The present
price here is 13^d to 14^d and the price is expected to fall to about

10d @ 11d — The charges of carrying to market are now very small on account of low freight &premiums say 1d @ 1½ lb besides the duty in England — I shall keep you constantly informed upon this subject asyour Constituents may be interested in it. — Our accounts from the Continent for Indigo are very bad, some ofthe shipments offine qualities from [interlineated: up] Country did pretty well but it is difficult to effect sales — of the ordinary qualities — there is such an abundance that they have no value. — The owners of the Emily — Mr. Smith Sup Cargo — told me they had exported theirs to Holland and France, and their accounts were extremely unfavorable, what little had been sold was at enormous loss, and the bulk ofit could not be got rid of at any rate

I should think there may have been about 9000 Md's imported into the Country, and that the loss would not be less than 50 to 70 Rupees a mau'd — I did very well with aparcel I bot of Alexander at 105/ and it is the only instance inwhich I have known a profit — Masseyks is liked in every market it has been sent to. he is the only man fit to make it, and his crop is quite enough to supply all that is wanted — You should apply tothe Govr. Genl. to hang all the other planters, andextend his concerns— If you get such alaw which would be wiser than many acts of yr Government *I might be tempted* to come out, & join him, or to speculate inthe article @ 100 pr Md. your crop is twice toolarge — I presume all the Bills you took have been paid trade is in such abad way and our Merchants so adventurous that I apprehend many failures will take place in course of 12 months I do not like to excite any suspicions or allude to any individuals as it is a dangerous subject to write about — but as you gain nothing by Bills but an accomodation ofyr Constituents I would caution you against Bill Transactions unless you know the Parties — One of our richest men & whom I recommended so strongly last year is tho't by many to have lost so much and is so deeply involved in shipping Concerns, wh are now very hazardous & losing, that some are of opinion his situation may change very materially unless commerce should be more prosperous than can be expected for ayear or two —

The persons trading to India are generally the richest and most prudent wehave. I would not however myself trust one half the men in business who 12 m^{os}. ago were tho't rich — the same I suppose would apply to houses in England The Americans have suffered by failures in G. Britain &other parts of Europe. Gibbs of Palermo who was tho't one of the richest houses, and one ofthe safest in the world has stopped for £500,000 St^g. *shot himself*, and will not pay any thing — O. Reilly &Young of London Cadiz are for much larger Am^t. — Anderson ofCork was another house who did much business for our Countrymen these things are alarming &have shaken very much the Confidence we used toplace in English Commission [houses — stricken through] establishments — There is one man nothing can affect — S. Williams of London, any letters of credit from him will authorise your taking bills to any extent he is without doubt one ofthe richest Individuals in Europe &probably the most prudent & most thriving — It is my intention to engage in a voyage to your place in the course of afew m^{os}. if there should be a prospect ofsugars keeping up it is at present almost the only article which promises afreight — At the close of the winter there is usually somebroken and rejected Indigo in the hands ofthe Agency houses &in the Bazar. I wish you to procure for me 100 M'ds at 55/ to 100/ p^r M^d. It is no matter how much broken but there must not be any *Fanuckabad* among it Perhaps you may find some parcels in the Bazar made by the natives, which will answer the purpose — for the payment I must get you to trust tomy share of the profits, on the Portsea's cargo, but least from some cause or other this source should fail you can send a bill Lading to Messrs. Remsen &C^o., and draw on me — or I will pay over the dollars to them. should the P's [interlineated: voyage] have ended in such a way as not to have left en^o in your hands to meet payment — You may ship it to any port in the United States & either insure inCalcutta or give me notice & I will have it done here. If you buy in the Bazar, you can either employ Ramshander Mitre or Ram Kissen day — the former is I believe the best judge of qualities. but perhaps your Brother Geo may find leisure to decide upon qualities, & let them look up parcels if you buy in the Bazar. I presume you have received long ago the return premiums on several Policies effected by me on goods from Calcutta to UStates & Specie returns — I rec^d Y'rs of 11th. March with Ramtonis papers Viz — Documents respecting aBalance due from Capt. John Higginson — as to the latter nothing can now be done as M^r. H is absent on a Voyage to China nor the first because it is necessary tohave the original bond and apower of Att^y. which I suppose Ramtono meant tohave sent but forgot it — I shall write [you — stricken through interlineated: him —] if there is time by the Ramduloll, as I shall always be interested in the Calcutta trade I cannot rely upon my native Correspondents I beg you would write me about Indigo, Sugars Cotton, & such other articles as the Ships take to Europe — the rate of Exchange. Interest of money — &further prospects for Indigo when you have reduced the Planters to 50 to 60,000 M^{ds}. We shall begin to import the article for our European trade and for Consumption — I shall send Newspapers for your Editors to you and wish in return they would send me files oftheir Papers say Mirror and Calcutta Gazette especially if M^r. Jameson has the conducting ofit — I would thank you also for any new Custom house regulations that Imay know what duties we pay — by Treaty. We should be on the footing ofy^r Ships — I have letters from London tothe 10th August. Pepper 6½ to 7^d the lb. Cotton keeps up pretty well Sugars low — Peice goods Ripley Wiss & Ripley write me are very low indeed and the Company have an immense Stock in their Warehouses. Indigo SW writes is very heavy sale and low — but your advice from London will be later and more particular. —

[written across face of letter:]
Letter p R.Duloll Day acknowledg'd 14th March.
by James Mackillop.

Continuation of letter to J Mackillop of Sep 27th.
            (orig pr R. Duloll Day/
Sepr 30th.

It appear'd to me while I was in Calcutta, that I might furnish Ships which would answer for the portuguese &Arabs, &for the Country trade, cheaper than the Rangoon &Chittagong people. Our vessels are not so durable in the hulks as Country would, but in respect to Sails, rigging &workmanship they are much Superior, &will last without any repairs from 12 to 16 years. pray let me know at what rate you could probably sell ships of 320 to 450 tons, copper'd &Copper fasten'd, well rigged &finished — What size do you think most Suitable? What rate of freight to London will enable the Calcutta people in India built Ships to carry on the freighting business? How low can the London &Liverpool [built — stricken through] Ships, take freight &make a fair profit? My brother F writes me that he has put 3600 Sp dollars on board the Argonaut, an advance on the 63 bales consigned us in the Cririe — that Ship hurried off much sooner than was expected orhe would have made up the amount to 9000 $, as I directed — we are getting onpretty well and to bring the accounts to a close which is desirable to us all we think of making an auction sale — It is the best way of selling when goods are demand I am much gratified that we are doing so well with M^r. Brady's Indigo as it would have been a mortification to have had his speculation turn to a loss. I dont recollect whether I recommended his shipping, however, I hope I did not — You desired me to say what might be expected f^m. further shipments this way — I am decided it will not be for your Interest to send any — our own People will import & as our freights & insurances are lower than yours & Interest only 6 perCent, It is impossible for your Constituents to send in competition with them — besides our own Importers are willing to reship to Europe when they cannot realise cost & charges here — this would not suit you — I would not advise shipments of either peice goods or any other article to U. States certainly not for the present. Be good en^o to send me a regular file of the Calcutta Price Currents — I send you 8 Cases containing Brandy fruits &c. marked as follows.

C & M N⁰. 3 — 2 Cases 1 doz bottles ea. Brandy fruits
     4 — 2 " 1 " do Capers.
     5 — 2 " 1 " do Anchovies
     7 — 2 " 1 " do Olives. Messrs. R &Co.

have sent you some Oysters pray let me know if they keep — and whether you like them, and I will send you a supply every season — Let me know if the fruits &c will do — as they are cheap and our Vessels having short passages — it is better getting them fromhere than from England — Send me information of value Madeira & Tenerife wines, each qualities — Pig copper — Quicksilver — Iron & any other European merchandize — Yrs truly   HLee —

you must make an Invoice or Mr. Trans [?] will charge more duties than they are worth Ram Kissen Day will get them thro' the Customhouse and save you the trouble — I send you afile of Newspapers —

           HLee

[written across face of letter:]
Letter p R. Duloll Day — acknowledg'd
14 March by James Mackillop

LETTER FROM HENRY LEE, NEW YORK, SEPT. 30, 1816, TO ALEXANDER & CO., CALCUTTA, WITH GENERAL REMARKS ON THE EAST INDIA TRADE [1]

The letter below supplements similar letters to other Calcutta merchants. The complaint that "we have lost our Carrying trade which was once so profitable" is familiar to the modern ear.

(Original prRamduloll Day)
Messrs. Alexander &Co.   NYork Sepr 30 1816.
  Calcutta   Gentle.

  Having been very much occupied since my arrival, I have not written you by the Ships which have lately saild from Bos-

---

1. Jackson-Lee Papers, "Letter Book September 5th. 1816," Feb. 13, 1816–Oct. 30, 1817.

ton — The Portsea was discharged within the time agreed upon — sail'd upon her voyage to Liverpool about the middle of August — and imagine by this has reached her destination — My Brother M^r. Francis Lee remitted on my account 8000 $, and some merchandize p^r Ship Pochahontas. I have had collected for two months a like sum which is going in afew days by the [same — stricken through] W^m. Savary from Philadelphia and about the same, or rather larger amount in Merchandize, proceeds of which will be paid over to you — It was my interest tohave sent the whole in Dollars, but as they were scarce and high, I found it so much more for my interest & convenience to send a portion in goods — I have taken the liberty to deviate from my engagement, presuming it could make no difference to you, so long as the balance was discharged — In consequence of this, I was obliged to effect insurance here — should any ofthe vessels be lost on the way — or the goods I send fall short in the proceeds. the balance should be made up by subsequent remittances I propose making — I was unfortunate in not getting here in season to escape an additional duty, which had been laid to take effect afew days before we arrived, otherwise we came to a good market — All my shipments have done well — but the new Tariff is so heavy upon coarse Cotton cloths, that we shall not import so many as we formerly did. — Indigo is of dull sale every where — Most ofthe importations into the United States from Calcutta have proved losing — we do not require much for consumption — and the prices on the Continent are too low, to afford any profit — Cotton is at about 13^d in Carolina & Georgia — The new Crop is promising and may go down to 10^d. in December — I conceive it tobe worth 20% to 33 1/3% more than the Bengal, in any part of Europe. — The Bengal shipments of this article will do well — till January or February when it must decline — but it may still be high en^o — to afford afreight — I should think it a hazardous article unless very low with you — Trade is on a very bad state, and many failures [have — stricken through] here and in England, and many more expected — We have lost our Carrying trade which was once so profitable &must depend upon our internal resources — Sugars are high in the West Indies, and may Keep up for ayear — our Journals are barren of every thing which can interest You — but I have sent a file which may do for some ofthe Editors — have the goodness to present my regards to M^r. Bracken, & M^r. Abbott — &believe me with great regard —   Y^r faithful Servant

H Lee —

Bills on London 6 % advance
   Dollars   2 % —

LETTER FROM JOHN TRACY, NEW YORK, NOV. 12, 1816, TO BARNWALL & POPHAM, ALEXANDRIA, VA., ORDERING AN INVESTMENT IN FLOUR [1]

A series of letters, from Nov. 12 to Dec. 12, 1816, are signed by John Tracy, who was evidently associated in some way at this time with Henry Lee. Probably he had been left in charge of the goods still unsold at New York during Lee's absence "to the southward." John Tracy was Mrs. Henry Lee's cousin and had served without conspicuous success as supercargo for his cousin Patrick Tracy Jackson.

Messrs. Barnwall & Popham   New York Nov. 12. 1816.
   Alexandria   Gen^t.
        A vessel arrived here yesterday after the very short passage of twenty eight days f^m. Liverpool, said to have [been — stricken through] an express from some house there, conjectured tobe Rathbon &C — immediately, large parcels offlour were bot up at 10½ & 11 $ — the report is that the crops have entirely fail'd, by all accounts from the interiour of England — and [in consequence — stricken through] a great scarcity of bread stuff in consequence is apprehended — that flour is considered an article of speculation appears tobe certain, and the true cause in course ofthe day will come out — and probably in the mean time, the conjecture asto the cause is correct — I wish you therefore immediately on receipt ofthis, to go into

1. Jackson-Lee Papers, "Letter Book September 5th. 1816," Feb. 13, 1816–Oct. 30, 1817.

your market and buy flour tothe extent ofthe draft, even before you present it, — depending that it will be duly honored, if any thing unforseen should prevent the payment of it, wh can hardly happen, you may rely on us in any way convenient to you by draft at short sight or otherwise —

I wish you toship the flour you may purchase by first safe conveyance to Boston — advising me ofthe vessel by which you ship, that I may get Insurance — You can no doubt Cash the draft if necessary.

Please write me if the Cotton goods have arrived, and what the prospect is? like wise what effect this news will have on your market, how your crops are &c — in the mean time believe me

Yr faithful friend
Jno Tracy.

LETTER FROM HENRY LEE, PHILADELPHIA, NOV. 25, 1816, TO TULLOH & CO., CALCUTTA, WITH PLANS FOR A VESSEL TO INDIA [1]

Henry Lee reveals himself as resolved on pushing a vigorous trade in European goods to India. In a letter of Sept. 27, from Boston, to the same firm, his brother Francis announced the shipment of a case of German goods in which both were concerned.

per Cordelia
"   Bramin (Duplt)

Messrs Tulloh & Co   Philadelphia 25 November 1816

Gentlemen,

I have written you at various times since my arrival with view of opening correspondence which I trust may prove mutually advantageous. — I have only to repeat my request that your information on various subjects should be very minute, and communicated very often.

I am [very — stricken through] pretty confident that a large quantity of French Manufactures, may be disposed of annually in Calcutta, and it is my wish to supply you with them.

1. Jackson-Lee Papers, "Letter Book September 5th. 1816," Feb. 13, 1816–Oct. 30, 1817.

Such for instance as Silk Hose, and half hose for Women & Men — Cambric, and Cambric Handkerchiefs — Silks and Kid Gloves — Black Silk Waistcoating — Millenary — Laces &c &c also French Wines — Champagne (does the still kind answer? Is white or red best liked) Burgundy. Hermitages — Bordeaux, Frontignac, Perfumery. Verdigrise. Olives, Brandy Fruits. Brandy Cordials &c. I can get these articles direct from France, and afford them much less than you can get from England — I am preparing a cargo for a Ship which will sail for Calcutta in 2 Months, to call at Madrass. You will do me a kindness by addressing a letter to *C D Miles*, care of Messrs Arbuthnot, and DeMont, informing him of state of Calcutta market for European Goods, especially the following.

Teneriffe Wine 1st quality. India Market Madeira, Sicily Madeiria, or Marcella. — *Hollands Gin,* Wine Bottles — Jamaica Rum, Tar, Swedes Iron, Brimstone 1st quality, Mahogany Boards, Salmon in Kegs — Verdigrise, Brandy. French Claret, Quicksilver, Champagne, Sherry Wine, Cider per dozen, Silk Hosiery, Cambrics. Crockery and Glass Ware. You will be good enough to transmit a copy of the same, in duplicate, to me in Boston — I hope the Goods per Savary came to a good market, Brandy having advanced of late both here, and in [New — stricken through] Europe — I don't imagine further shipments will be made — not any French Goods, as most of my countrymen know very little of their value in your place. There are some wines gone & going, but of Sherry only one small parcel, and a quantity belonging to me address to Messrs. Cruttenden & Mackillop of very superior quality. I shall write you by the vessel I am getting in readiness in mean time.

I remain — with great regard &c
(Signed)   H Lee

LETTER FROM HENRY LEE, PHILADELPHIA, NOV. 30, 1816, TO
JAMES WILLIAMSON, CALCUTTA, ON GENERAL BUSINESS CON-
DITIONS [1]

In this interesting letter, the description of the methods employed
in disposing of the *Portsea's* cargo, casual though it is, is worthy of
particular note. A letter of Nov. 20 to Cruttenden & Mackillop, Calcutta, is more explicit: "The Portsea's Cargo was only sold in consequence of the most unremitted attention to it, and by sending the
Goods to different places, by selling for exportation, and these having
a very good proportion of coarse goods, and coloured Goods; and the
holders of Calcutta Goods at that time generally having few coarse
and coloured Goods, and having Cargoes which cost high."

Henry Lee did not merely place his goods in the hands of a firm
and let them remain until sold or returned; he did not hesitate to
move goods from one city or firm to another as the sales possibilities
suggested. The "unremitted attention" he displayed is exemplified in
a letter of the following year, Mar. 24, in which he informed Appleton,
Poor & Miles, Baltimore, that "Messrs Schott & Co [Philadelphia]
have sold all my Humhums @ $5, and can probably dispose of more
— as this is better than you may be able to do, I request you would
send them all which remain on hand with you, and also all the Beerboom Gurrahs — and any other White Goods of which you have no
prospect of selling immediately." [2]

Per Cordelia Philadelphia 30 Novr. 1816
James Williamson Esqr.
Calcutta
My Dear Sir,
I received a few days since yours of 7th and 18th June
per Glide. The original per Cicero never to came to hand.
With the exception of few lines written in March, this is the
only communication from you which has reached me. On my
part I have not thought it worth while to write you and Mr.
Dickson, because there appeared to be no prospect of pursuing

1. Jackson-Lee Papers, "Letter Book September 5th. 1816," Feb. 13,
1816–Oct. 30, 1817.
2. *Ibid.*, "Letter Book from Jany. 17th. 1817 to October 27. 1818."

the Trade between this Country and yours to advantage, and as to the Portsea's concerns you would of course know every thing from Mess Remsen & Co's & my letters to C & M. I came here some days ago, to look after sales, which our agents have been making, and to examine into the affairs of a man who owed the concern about $4,000 and stopped payment. I am happy to say all the Goods except few Bales at Baltimore are sold, and that of the $4,000, the principal part, if not the whole will be recovered. I prepared you long since, to expect some losses by bad debts. As yet we have been fortunate, and confidence is so much restored that I do not apprehend many failures. Our payments will begin to come in, within two months. Messrs R & Co have made remittances to London of late, and will write you. In February we shall remit you largely in Dollars direct to Calcutta, in the mean time currency is improving here, and at New York, so that you gain by this delay. On my arrival Paper was at 12 @ 15 per Cent Discount, for Dollars and Bills on London, now only 6 @ 7 per Cent, and in few weeks will be 2 or 3% better. This favors our voyage very much. The Drawers of all Bills we have remitted are good, and you may count nearly with certainty that there will be no loss on those we have yet to purchase. — We have not been able to make up our account sales yet, because all are not rendered. In few weeks they will be completed. In order to get rid of our Goods speedily and at high prices, we were obliged to distribute them in various places. This has been attended with expence of transportation and Commissions, but prices are more than sufficient to repay it, as you will observe on comparing sales made in Baltimore and Philadelphia, with those effected in New York.

We gave an extra credit on Salt Petre to get rid of it, as we thought it dangerous to hold on an article liable to a great depreciation; and which is now selling in England at 40 @ 45/ Cwt. It is our intention to cash these notes as soon as money becomes plenty, by which we shall avoid the risk of bed debts, and bring the accounts to a termination. We had this in view at moment of making sale and added to the price. As to Piece

Goods they are and have been dull for Six Months. I cannot impress this fact more forcibly upon you, than by informing you that the following Cargoes remain on hand entire, except some small adventures belonging to Captains &c, and because sales could not be effected at cost and charges. — Ship George's, Christopher's, Rambler's, Ramdollody's, Cririe's, Herald's, Alexanders, Glide's, Benjamin Rush's, and half Sidneys, other half having been exported, besides these Cargoes which have not broken in upon, there are parts of others, still in hands of the Importers. Some of them arrived before the Portsea, were bought by experienced Super Cargoes, and paid upon an average, *30% less duty than we paid,* on Portsea's Goods. If under these circumstances there is profit on our Goods, you may infer they were well purchased, and that we have been successful in disposing of them. There was not an article hardly, except the *Posackies* and *fine Mow Sannas,* purchased from a Gentleman you know, but what was cheap, and adapted to the market. You remember what I thought of these goods at the time I received them. Indigo is dull sale, I have yet on hand part of an investment which arrived in the Spring, and there are other parcels unsold, besides 200 Boxes in the Rush and 350 expected in Hindu, and Scattergood. The fine sorts do pretty well on the Continent, but middling and inferior do not sell at any rate. Such are the letters from Holland, France, and Meditteranean. Cotton keeps up in all parts of Europe, and no doubts all your Shipments which reach England, by first February will do well, and probably through the year 1817. The price in Georgia and Carolina for Short Staple is now 22¢(11^d) The general opinion is that it will go a little lower in course of the season say 20 cts/10^d. Sterling) — The freight to England is 1^d per lb. Insurance 2½ @ 3 per Cent, so that in *bond,* we can afford it at about 13^d per lb, at the cost of 20 cts, last year it was 25 @ 30¢. Some of our Ships have gone for the article, and others are now preparing, among others the Cordelia, to the owners of whom, I have furnished some information relative to the cost &c &c. In case the agent of this Ship /MrNewton) should not have reached India, I have advised the

Owners to direct the Captain, to call on Messrs Cruttenden and Mackillop to furnish the Cargo, and it is probably they may do so. The duties on Ps Goods are so heavy under the New Tariffs, say 60 @ 80 per Cent, that it would be dangerous to hazard a shipment at any prices, besides the quantity now here, and on the way is sufficient for 18 months consumption of the Country. There are however some articles which are wanted for exportation, and others upon which duties do not fall so heavily, which may answer very well, provided they are of right patterns, and procured in the proper way. Our Ships continue to go in such numbers, that they may keep up prices of Piece Goods, though the quantity each wants is small, but in few months they will discontinue going, and Goods will fall among the natives. At this distance it is impossible to point out what kinds will answer, but in two months I shall, in connection with my brothers in Boston, send out a Ship which we have lately purchased. Mr. Miles. Supercargo. You will then have an opportunity of joining us, if you approve our plans, and have confidence in our management &c. By next Ship I shall write further, and perhaps propose purchasing some articles from the Country, to be ready for Shipment. As to S. P it is a dangerous article to meddle with on many accounts. We are trying to make contracts for some, in which case we will engage in the importation of a Cargo. In mean time you could be looking round, to see at what rate you can procure 6 or 8000 mds. of best sort in Calcutta, or from the Country. I think it would be prudent, not to converse on the subject, with any of the Americans who may happen to be in Calcutta, as in present state of the trade, they are looking every way for some new article of speculation, and should more than one attempt it, we should not succeed, or they might be talking on the subject, make it known to Government, and cause the detention of the Ship, or Bonds to land the S. P. in England — All that can be done my Brother, and myself can accomplish — We should have done something with Government, but for the preference given an Army Officer who was in need and favored by them. We may hereafter succeed — You shall hear further on the subject in few weeks. — I think Sugar may be procured from the Country at a price which would make it a safe and profitable article, at our low freight and insurance, of this too you shall hear further in my next.

I enclose a copy of a very Gentlemenly Letter received from Mr Ince. It is of no further consequence than as it respects my feelings, towards Messrs Alexander &Co, to whom I am under many obligations. I shall write them on the subject when more at liesure, in mean time be good enough to assure them, that what Mr I affirms is false, and that we gave all the despatch in our power, and discharged her within the time.

If this mans power of doing mischief was equal to his malice and folly, I should devote a few lines more to do away the effect of any misrepresentations he might make, but my paper will not afford it, and I trust I have said enough.

Be good enough to remember me to Mr Dickson and my other friends, and believe me ever Yours

(signed)   H Lee

(Copy)

Messrs P Remsen &Co,
　　Gentlemen,

　　I have the pleasure to forward you the Certificate which you gave Capt Nicholls to get receipted. I am extremely sorry to hear from Capt Nicholls that he did not receive that attention in regard to the despatch of the Portsea as we had a right to expect, and you may be sure that Messrs C & M will be sorry to have to pay any demurrage, but that I shall insist on it, on my arrival in Calcutta.

This has, I am aware been Mr Lees doings — I hope you have forwarded the Dollars to Messrs Alexander & Co. The Portsea leaves this port on the 16 th for Calcutta.

I remain &c

(Signed)   Wm. B Ince.

Liverpool 12 Octr. 1816

LETTER FROM JOHN TRACY, NEW YORK, DEC. 5, 1816, TO
CHARLES H. HALL & CO., CADIZ, ENQUIRING CONCERNING
COPPER [1]

During his sojourn in Calcutta, Henry Lee had learned that copper
was the chief among the very few European products which could be
trusted to achieve a good sale in India. While Henry Lee was on his
way home from Calcutta, on Apr. 16, 1816, his brother Francis
shipped on the *Agawam* for Calcutta "1830 Pigs of Copper . . . Two
thirds . . . on account of Mr Henry Lee, and one third on account
of Mr Pickering Dodge." The captain, John Wills, Jr., "in lieu of
freight and Primage, and as compensation for your Services, in selling
and paying over the proceeds," was to be "allowed . . . Two & an
half per Cent Commissions," himself — "paying the Brokerage, on
the net proceeds." On Sept. 6, Henry Lee was enquiring about the
possibility of shipping coffee from Liverpool to Calcutta; in the letter
below he considers a more direct shipment from Cadiz.

New York
[Nov^r — stricken through interlineated: Dec^r] 5. 1816.
Messrs. Ch^s. H. Hall &Co.,
Cadiz
Gent,
    I have had the pleasure to meet your. M^r. Ch^s. H Hall
inthis City, and introduced him to my f^d. Mr Henry Lee, who
was desirous of learning from him the general state of your
market for the article of pig copper — and in consequence of
the information he received — andbeing [interlineated: now
absent] on a visit to the southward, he has requested me to
write you on the subject, in reference to [your — stricken
through interlineated: the] present price for that article —
which I wish you would inform me and likewise give all the
information in your power as to the quantity your market may
at all times afford, whether it is subject to fluctuate much?,
and what may be the most profitable mode ofplacing funds
with you for the purchase of it. — how Exchange is at present
between your place and London? whether any change of im-

    1. Jackson-Lee Papers, "Letter Book September 5th. 1816," Feb. 13,
1816–Oct. 30, 1817.

portance is likely to take place with Exchange, and the events that are likely to operate upon it? — a general view of the state and prospect of your market for the productions ofthis Country — if any Cargo could be sent from this of Staves &c. that w^d. pay afreight — if the recent alarm in England on acc^t of grain is likely to operate much with you — or can you suggest any new source of Export from this that would place you in funds profitably, if aVessel should be sent out for the purpose of obtaining Copper — your replys to me in Triplicate's addressed to Boston would be doing a great favor. — if your brother was in the City I should request him to enclose this — but he is now in Connecticut with his family. I was gratified in finding him in good health, — and with good wishes for your establishment, and hoping the present may lead to advantage. I remain

Yrs &c. J^n Tracy —

P. S. It is possible that a cargo of Staves or such an one — as might be sent could be profitably bartered with the holders of Copper — as I am informed at times there are quantities, and it maybe an object for large holders to push it off, say, if any thing might be done in this way. —

LETTER FROM HENRY LEE, BOSTON, JAN. 17, 1817, TO PACKARD & GOWEN, HAVANA, ACKNOWLEDGING INVOICE OF SUGAR AND GIVING INSTRUCTIONS FOR THE SALE OF INDIA GOODS [1]

The letter below is taken from Henry Lee's "Letter Book from Jany. 17th. 1817 to October 27. 1818." This manuscript volume overlaps in time with Henry Lee's "Letter Book September 5th. 1816," which runs from Feb. 13, 1816, to Oct. 30, 1817. Most of the letters in the latter volume are written to Calcutta merchants and supercargoes, although during 1816 appear a number of letters to merchants in Havana and in various ports of the United States and Europe; the present volume contains letters to cities in the United States, the West Indies, and Europe, but none to Calcutta. The 1816 letters in "Letter Book September 5th. 1816" are written from New York,

---

1. Jackson-Lee Papers, "Letter Book from Jany. 17th. 1817 to October 27. 1818."

where the goods Henry Lee had shipped from Calcutta on the *Portsea* had been landed; those in the present volume are mostly written from Boston, to which he had returned after having disposed of most of the goods landed from the *Portsea*.

In a letter of the following day to George Knight, also of Havana, Lee acknowledged other returns in sugar, gave further instructions for the sale of his goods, and asked for samples of piece goods suitable for the market that he might order by his next vessel for Calcutta. In a letter of Jan. 29 to Peter Remsen, Henry Lee announced: "I have been retailing Havana B Sugar at 14¾, and two days ago closed sale at 14.50."

Boston January. 17th. 1817

Messrs Packard & Gowen   per Sch John F. L. O
(Havanna)   Dear Sirs

Since my last the Friendship has arrived, and I have received the 200 Boxes Sugars — I regret not to hear of further sales of Piece Goods, as I apprehend from the large shipments from this quarter that they may decline — Blue Gurrahs however are scarce, only one or two of the late arrivals having brought any. —

Should any of my Goods remain on hand when this reaches, I wish you to get rid of them on any terms that will secure the cost and charges as I am desirous of closing the sales of the Cargo to which they belong. You may remit what may be due on closing the sales either in White or Brown Sugars, whichever may appear to you most for my Interest, and send them to Messrs Perit & Cabot, Philadelphia, or Messrs P Remsen & Co., New York — I shall have more goods in few months, and shall be glad to send them to your place, if there is any encouragement.   *Yours truly*

LETTER FROM HENRY LEE, BOSTON, JAN. 18, 1817, TO PERIT & CABOT, PHILADELPHIA, WITH INSTRUCTIONS FOR SALES [1]

Henry Lee was endeavoring to sell in Philadelphia not only drugs and gum from India but also gin from Holland which had been received in exchange for India goods shipped to that country.

1. Jackson-Lee Papers, "Letter Book from Jany. 17th. 1817 to October 27. 1818."

Perit & Cabot was a wholesale commission firm, the partners in which were John W. Perit, Samuel Cabot, formerly of Hazard & Cabot, and the latter's brother Joseph.[2] The "C" was the *Cruttenden*, a vessel which Henry Lee was loading at Philadelphia for Calcutta. Stephen Cabot was the rather unstable brother of the above-mentioned Samuel and Joseph.

Boston 18th January 1817

Messrs Perit & Cabot
     Philadelphia
          Dear Sirs,
               I have yours of 11 th and 13 th. The prospect is so bad for an India Voyage that I do not want Mr MoCall's ship on any terms. — It is probable I may engage with Messrs Wheeler & Dupont for S. P some months hence, at present I can say nothing more — There are many difficulties in the way of succeeding and failure, which bring great loss upon me.

I would thank you to let me know when the C will be ready to receive Cargo. You have not sent me the dimensions and tonnage. I wish the Government entered in her papers, if it is more than Carpenters —

The Holders of Gin are confident no more importations will be made from Holland till next years harvest is in — and that it will be much higher; It sells here at 130, the large holders ask 150. — I wish you to put mine @ 150 but not refuse 140 at 3 or 4 Months Credit, of the 60 Pipes, you will sell 40 — Is there any prospect of getting rid of the Bottles, which are in better order, and the Gin at my limitations?

I wish you would try the Cardemans, Lac & Sal am — and accept any tolerable offer — if you can get $1 for the Cardemans — I would put the Lac and Sal^m. at 20 cents each — My Brother has put down 20 Barrels of Beef, and 8 of Pork for provisions for the voyage: Let me know at what rate you can get these articles, such as are suitable for the Voyage. Capt T will let you know what qualities he wants. —

Have the Goods all arrived from Baltimore? Is the Logwood purchased? If none in Philadelphia I shall send it from hence.

2. Briggs, *op. cit.*, vol. ii, pp. 556, 596.

Be good enough to let me know when you can discount the S. P. Notes at 1% per Month — The Butter proved very good [interlineated: in] deed, I would thank you for a Memᵒ. of it, as I have disposed of a portion to my friend who wants to pay me for it — On conversing with Mr Stephen Cabot, he appears to think the Madeira House will not ship any quantity of Wine for India, I hope he may be mistaken — I shall probably want 30 or 40 Pipes of Lewis' Wine at 6 Months at 120. If there is any appearance of the article getting up let me know, and I will decide whether to buy or not. —

Business is very dull, and will remain so this season. Bills on London at par, but getting down, and will go to 3 or 4% Discount. — I have 350 Boxes of Brown Havanna Sugars, and cannot sell them, I wish they had gone to your port, and if I was sure the river would keep open, I would send them round. Pray what might I expect for those of middling quality, say 200 Boxes.

Yrs truly

LETTER FROM HENRY LEE, BOSTON, JAN. 26, 1817, TO CAPT. ROBERT TURNER, PHILADELPHIA, WITH INSTRUCTIONS IN REGARD TO PREPARING FOR A CALCUTTA VOYAGE [1]

The letter below gives an idea of some of the multitudinous duties, other than navigation, which rested on the captain of a merchantman. Henry Lee's brother, described as having had "so much experience in . . . India trade," was doubtless George Lee, who from 1803 to 1812 had made four voyages to Calcutta.

Boston 26ᵗʰ January 1817

Capt Robert Turner
  Philadelphia
    Dear Sir,
        I have yours of 23ᵈ. and am glad to hear that you are satisfied with the first mate — should he not continue to be attentive to his duty, you can get another before you sail, but

1. Jackson-Lee Papers, "Letter Book from Janʸ. 17ᵗʰ. 1817 to October 27. 1818."

I hope he will give no further occasion to reprove him. — I enclose a Memᵒ. for Stores &c for the Cruttenden made out by my Brother — he has had so much experience in fitting ships, and has been commander in India Trade so often, that I have confidence in his judgment, and should wish you to conform to it —

Provisions are dear, and the less we buy the better — he has put down 20 Barrels Beef, and 8 of Pork — which you may purchase in Philadelphia — of the small stores you will purchase per Memo. Cabin furniture, Carpenters Stores, Coopers, Cooks &c you will I presume find all which are neccessary among the things purchased with the Ship; all that is wanting, you will purchase, always having in mind, that the ship may be sold in Calcutta, and therefore you will require only a 6 Month supply — There will be some Linseed Oil in Cargo — You may get the provisions and other stores ready, as soon as you find convenient, as I shall direct Messrs Perit & Cabot to commence taking in Cargo, as soon as the ship is ready —

I wish you to look at the Beef and Pork, and indeed all the Stores, that we may not be imposed upon as to qualities, and in all cases to bargain for the price before you agree to receive anything — I wish you would hurry the Carpenters, that we may be off by the 1st of March — In your next let me know how seamens wages are on voyages to India.

Your Obt Servt

LETTER FROM HENRY LEE, BOSTON, FEB. 5, 1817, TO PERIT & CABOT, PHILADELPHIA, WITH INSTRUCTIONS FOR A CARGO TO CALCUTTA [1]

The letter below gives an idea of the kind of goods Henry Lee was shipping to Calcutta in the period immediately after the War of 1812.

On Feb. 1, Henry Lee gave careful instructions as to how the vessel should be loaded. "I would have her take in some of the heavy articles where she now lies, and remainder when she is removed. . . . the

1. Jackson-Lee Papers, "Letter Book from Janʸ. 17ᵗʰ. 1817 to October 27. 1818."

Steel . . . will be useful in bringing her down by the Stern, which is the trim best suited to sailing, but it must not be stowed where any water can reach it. . . . I would reccommend the Lignumvitae, and Logwood placed as dunnage, and the Steel placed upon it, which will raise it well above the Keelson."

Boston 5th February 1817

Messrs Perit & Cabot
   Philadelphia
      Dear Sirs,
            I enclose a letter for Capt Turner, with a Memo of Cargo for Cruttenden, I hope you will get most of the Articles on board by the middle of this month. Should Ice break up it would be well perhaps to move her, otherwise take in Cargo where she now is — I wish every thing may be put in good order before shipping, — all the liquors well bung'd and tin-need, Cider Boxes nailed, Iron Hoops upon any of the Gin, Rum and Wine Casks, which may require them — Of the Gin from New York, you will ship only 20 Casks, and of the bottles, only such as are in good order, and dispose of the remainder — I wish for a Memo. of Rum from New York, and that which you purchased for me — Olives &c from P & Carter from Balti-more, Lignumvitae and Logwood — Sherry Wine bought by you — [Brimstone by Goodhue & Co. — stricken through] Juniper Spirits, Steel, Champagne Bottles bought by you, — Brimstone by Goodhue & Co — Verdigris and Whiting, and also of any other goods you have bought & may buy — If you can purchase 1500 lb more Verdigrise at 40¢, I wish you to do it or enough more for Debenture — You will also buy 1000 Galls best quality [interlineated: Linseed Oil] in good order, and 600 Galls Spirits of Turpentine the latter will require to be examined by a judge, as qualities vary very much. — I wish for the dimensions of the Ship as measured by your officers — I want 10 Tons of Campeachy Logwood if not already pur-chased, and of best quality. — I wish to know as soon as you can form a judgment how much more, than the Goods enumer-ated on the list sent Capt Turner the Ship will carry that I may

direct further purchases should any thing more be required to fill her. I wish the 5 Casks Juniper Spirits, to be put in between decks, and stand with great care that they may not leak — If the Rum purchased by Johnson & Halsey at New York can be resold without loss and trouble, I should be glad to have it disposed of — No Goods must be shipped on which Debentures expire earlier than 20th March. — You will let me know as soon as you can, if any of the holders of double debenture Teneriffe Wine will sell at low price in which case I should be induced to buy 40 or 50 Pipes — I was offered 60 Pipes Cargo Teneriffe in New York at 95 Cts, 56 cts debenture, but there would not be time to ship before the debenture expires. I should be glad of more Steel at 4¢ short, or I might give as high as 5¢ for German. You would oblige me, by sending a Memº. of the cost of the Butter sent me pr Pedlar —

If you hear of any White Silk Hose, say 2/3 White 1/3 Black, well charged and at 22 @ 23 cts franc, I should like to purchase 50 doz for Cruttenden say mens or mens & womens — I hope you will soon be able to cash the S P notes at 1 pr Cent

Yours truly

Henry Lee

LETTER FROM HENRY LEE, BOSTON, FEB. 5, 1817, TO PETER REMSEN & CO., NEW YORK, ON GENERAL BUSINESS MATTERS [1]

The letter below is valuable for its many observations on the general business situation.

Henry Lee was trying to buy bills of exchange on London in New York and Philadelphia in order to make a remittance. On the same day, he wrote James Schott of Philadelphia: "I have learnt it is the intention of your Banks to pay Specie — I imagine this determination will lower Exchange on London, if so perhaps it may be well to defer the purchase of the £2000." Banks outside New England had suspended specie payments in 1814, but in 1817, by the establishment of the Second Bank of the United States, were forced to resume specie

1. Jackson-Lee Papers, "Letter Book from Jany. 17th. 1817 to October 27. 1818."

payments.[2] This offered another means by which remittances could be made to England and decreased the demand for and the value of bills of exchange on London.

At Washington, Henry Lee's brother Francis was trying to get the *Portsea,* on which Henry Lee's most recent consignment of goods from Calcutta had been imported, placed "on footing of an American Ship" so far as the duties on American-owned goods therein were concerned.[3]

Despite the dullness of business, particularly as regards goods from India, Henry Lee on Feb. 6 wrote George Knight, at Havana, "I look to Calcutta Goods, as principal article in which I shall in future deal."

On Feb. 19, 1817, however, Henry Lee was trying, through Perit & Cabot, Philadelphia, to sell the *Prince of Orange,* a vessel he had purchased with the intention of selling it for use in the "country trade" of India, or to dispose of the *Hindu* by charter, a brig owned by his brothers George and Francis. Two days later he was suggesting that Perit & Cabot sell the *Cruttenden,* which he was then loading to sail for Calcutta by the middle of March, to Wharton & Sargent, or at least get 200 tons of freight from that firm. On Feb. 24 he wrote to Perit & Cabot: "The prospect is so bad for a Calcutta voyage, that I wish to wait 6 Months, or else send to some other part of the East Indies."

Boston 5 February 1817

Messrs P. Remsen & Co.
    New York
        Dear Sirs,
            I am obliged by the information in yours of the 1st Inst, perhaps it might be well to direct Schott to wait few days, before buying the £2000, I have written to him to that effect. I should think it would be best to accept 15/ in the pound, for Dean & Thoburn's debt. I have been engaged constantly since my return, in looking into accounts yours and others, and will let you know the result as soon as I have finished.

I shall enclose the Calcutta Accounts to Messrs C & M, and

2. Dewey, *op. cit.*, pp. 145, 151.

3. Jackson-Lee Papers, "Letter Book from Jany. 17th. 1817 to October 27. 1818," Henry Lee, Boston, Feb. 7, 1817, to Peter Remsen & Co., N. Y.

forward them by the Holoforn to sail in 15 or 20 days. I shall merely make some remarks upon currency, and leave you to write about remittances. I have explained to them the advantages to them, of our not drawing funds from Philadelphia and Baltimore while the discount was great, but that you [will — stricken through interlineated: would] soon have to do it, to comply with their wishes in remitting — It appears to me that nothing should be sent Mr. Octerlony, till you are in funds, nor the owner of the Camels hair Shawls. The Ship at Philadelphia will go about middle of March, and you can send Dollars, if you shall be ready at that time — She will stop at Madrass for few days — I suppose my brother writes you from Washington I am in great hopes he will succeed — he has made himself acquainted with the most influential men, and will succeed if any one can.

Business is more dull than ever I knew it [interlineated: at] any season. — The Shopkeepers and Importers are pressed, and of the former we have had several failures — It appears to me we shall have a dull spring. — I thought some months ago the New tariff would raise prices of Calcutta Goods — but the Stock on hand is so great, so many are on the way, that I apprehend they will be dull through the year, or at any rate till next Fall. Some of the last Ships for Calcutta have gone for Rice — had I not a certain prospect of selling the P. 'orange, I should regret having purchased her, but she is so cheap, and well suited to the Country Trade in India, that I have no doubts of a sale — I dont think any of the Calcutta Traders will buy the Copper, unless at very low price — the last sales in Calcutta did not yield more than 14 or 15 Cts, lb. in Canton it is $22 per Picul (133 lb) say 16 cents lb.

Yours truly

H Lee   (Signed)

Exchange on London ½% disct, & falling.

Flour 14 50/100, rising but no buyers for Shipping as yet.

Pepper 21 @ 22 cts but no sales.

Havanna Brown Sugars 14.50 @ 14.75 at retail no demand for exportation, as they are worth less in all parts of Europe.

I wrote Mr Octerlony on my arrival that he must not expect any remittances till you were in funds for his Goods.

(signed) H Lee

I find Mr Tracy left behind a Case of goods (Samples) of mine marked H No 1. It stood in your counting Room up Stairs, but on my going to Philadelphia it was removed into the back room — I would thank you to send it me by first conveyance, as it contains samples much wanted by me.

(Signed)   H Lee

LETTER FROM HENRY LEE, BOSTON, FEB. 10, 1817, TO JAMES SCHOTT, PHILADELPHIA, TRYING TO INDUCE AN INVESTMENT IN A CHINA VOYAGE [1]

"Mr H," the supercargo, was Henry Higginson (b. Feb. 5, 1781, m. Nancy M. Cushing, 1803, d. 1838),[2] who had failed in 1811 in London while Henry Lee was there as a supercargo, and who had thereafter himself become a supercargo as a step toward recouping his fortunes. Henry Lee, who had undergone a similar experience, was sympathetically interested in assisting a brother in misfortune, who was also a cousin twice removed. On Jan. 23, Lee had written Schott concerning this voyage: "The rate of freight for Silks will be 8%, *including commissions* payable in China — This is 3 or 4% less than you pay in Philadelphia." On Feb. 2 he had written Peter Remsen, of New York, in the same connection, adding that the rate would be "on Nankins 10%, and Teas $50 per Ton."

Boston February 10th 1817

Mr James Schott
    Philadelphia
        Dear Sir,
            I have yours of 6th [Inst — stricken through] with the sales which have been examined and found correct, As I have goods from several Invoices of same mark, and Accounts of

1. Jackson-Lee Papers, "Letter Book from Jany. 17th. 1817 to October 27. 1818."

2. "Materials for a Genealogy of the Higginson Family," *Essex Inst. Hist. Coll.*, vol. v, p. 41; Higginson, *Descendants of the Reverend Francis Higginson*, p. 31.

which are at New York, I would thank you to send me a Mem⁰. of Marks and Numbers and Names of Goods corresponding, any time within 4 or 5 days — I am glad you waited as Exchange must be more favorable in a few days. I am sorry you will not adventure — the Ship will not go short of 40 days in mean time your adventures will return. We have secured 90,000 to 100,000, and only want few thousand more — If you will ship 5,000 or 10,000 and order Silk Goods — I will engage after 6 Months if you dont then like the prospect to buy it of you, and pay cost and 6% Interest, should you be inclined to keep it on its arrival, I will either sell the Goods here free of Commission or send them to you — I have no concern in the Voyage, except the desire of promoting the views of a friend who goes out Supercargo. Some of our most shrewd men are sending, and think well of the voyage. Mr H is brother in law to Cushing of the House of Perkins & Co, and will of course have his assistance in selecting his goods. The Ship is new, coppered, and in all respects first rate. I hope you will conclude to send on this safe footing

Yours truly
(Signed)   H Lee

Business dull,
Failures   C W Greene, Ralph Haskins.
Will not your Chintz Printers buy the Humhums @ $5?

I have handed the sales you sent me, Nett Proceeds $419.05 & 1028.24 to Messrs P Remsen & Co New York, to whose order you will hold the amount when collected say fourteen hundred forty seven Dollars 29/100.

(Signed)   H Lee.

LETTER FROM HENRY LEE, BOSTON, FEB. 16, 1817, TO R. P. OCHTERLONY, CALCUTTA, WITH PLANS FOR A VOYAGE TO CALCUTTA AND THE RESULT OF THE PREVIOUS VOYAGE [1]

The R. P. Ochterlony to whom the letter below is addressed was evidently a British merchant in Calcutta; he was the son of David

1. Jackson-Lee Papers, "Letter Book September 5ᵗʰ. 1816," Feb. 13, 1816–Oct. 30, 1817.

Ochterlony, conqueror of Nepal, who was born in Boston, 1758, but went to India in 1777 as a cadet in the Bengal army of the East India Co. The war in which he subdued the Gurkhas was ended by treaty Mar. 2, 1816.[2]

Two days later than the letter below, writing to Edward A. Newton, Henry Lee expressed uncertainty as to whether he would send out the ship which he had so often announced would sail in two months. "I purchased a ship some months ago," he wrote, "intending to send her to Calcutta, but so many have gone, and prospect is so much worse, that I am now trying to sell her again, but I am afraid I shall not be able to find a buyer. If I do not she must go in about 2 Months, your friends shall know of the opportunity."

"Mr. Joy," referred to in connection with "a settlement with Government for his Georgia Lands," was doubtless Benjamin Joy (1757–1829), a Boston merchant who was "the first Consul General of the United States at Calcutta,"[3] where he had presumably met Ochterlony. An act of Mar. 31, 1814, "appropriated $5,000,000 from the proceeds of land sales in the territory, to be shared among the companies" concerned in the Yazoo land purchases.[4]

Per Holofern.
Dup^{le}.   Boston 16 February 1817

Mr R. P. Octerlony
  Calcutta
    Dear Sir,
        I refer you to my letters to Messrs Cruttenden & Mackillop for the result of your Shipments pr Portsea & Cririe. I have enclosed a/c Sales of each adventure to them — The proceeds will be remitted by Messrs Remsen & Co as soon as collected — You have already suffered somewhat by failures, and I fear may still more. There never was more difficulties among men of business, than have existed since my arrival, owing to excessive importations, scarcity of money &c.

Your shipments upon the whole will yield you a good profit,

2. "David Ochterlony," *DNB*.

3. Joy, James Richard, comp., *Thomas Joy and His Descendants* (N. Y., 1900), p. 85.

4. Haskins, Charles Homer, "The Yazoo Land Companies," *Papers of the American Historical Association*, Oct., 1891, p. 436.

but would have done much better but for the increase of duties. Some of the Goods pr Hope were short in measure, and Messrs Remsen & Co were obliged to make an allowance. I saw them opened & the allowance was just — They were of the Lots purchased of your friend Mercer — The Goods which gave the largest profit were the Blue Gurrahs manufactured by me — The Calcutta trade has been very much overdone, and the Cargoes now on the way will yield no profit, as to Piece Goods, the New [Tariff — stricken through] Duties are too high, and we shall not want any more Cottons from Bengal. I am now preparing a Ship to sail for Calcutta in about 2 Months. Mr Miles will go Supercargo. — With his experience in buying in Calcutta, and the information I shall transmit him of Prices in this quarter, I think we may collect some particular Goods which will do well — If you are inclined to adventure a moderate sum, he will be authorised to agree with you for the terms of Freight &c. If you are in the Country, and wish to do any thing, it may be worth your while to write him on the subject — Business is very dull both in this Country and Europe, and many mercantile Men have become poor by trading too much, when it is almost impossible to gain anything. I observe by the Papers, your father has brought the Gourkas to terms, I suppose you will go at the Chinese next — I hope in that case, he will allow the Yankees /his Countrymen) to continue trading with them. Mr Joy has lately improved his circumstances by a settlement with Government for his Georgia Lands — I am sorry to say that Gideon Snow, who I believe was one of your friends, has failed, he will have enough I believe to pay all, or nearly so, but will be left poor, and not find it easy to get back his money — I hope you will contrive to keep yours — You will [interlineated: now] have enough with good management to live comfortably, and I hope I may be instrumental in increasing it.

My regards to your wife [and children — erased], and believe me

Y^r friend & Servt

(signed) Henry Lee

You promised to write me, but as yet I have none of the letters. Pray do not fail, and you shall hear often from me.

H L

LETTER FROM HENRY LEE, BOSTON, FEB. 20, 1817, TO PETER REMSEN & CO., NEW YORK, ON VARIOUS BUSINESS OPERATIONS [1]

This letter suggests the complexity of Henry Lee's business life at this time. He was still trying to obtain funds for Henry Higginson's voyage to China. At the same time he was endeavoring to induce mercantile firms to allow him to invest for them through his agents in Calcutta on various conditions: he to receive half the profits, charging no commission, paying no interest; or to allow the investors one-third the profits, paying 6% interest, "perhaps 9% from the time I get the money."

He was also buying brimstone and trying to sell gin; these commodities typify the wide range of goods in which he was dealing. On Feb. 7 he had been trying to sell rum, gin, bottles, and "S Petre Notes," and to purchase "Oils," through Perit & Cabot, Philadelphia; a week later, in a letter to the same firm, he was ordering the purchase of verdigris and both the purchase and sale of steel. Evidently he wanted to dispose of steel which he could not ship "prior to the expiration of the debenture," and to purchase another lot subject to debenture. On Mar. 7 he suggested Amsterdam, Rotterdam, Bremen, or Hamburg as an outlet for his superfluous wine. On Sept. 4, 1817, in a letter to Peter Remsen & Co., he expressed a desire to purchase "20,000 feet Bay Mahogany @ 6 cts 18 to 28 inches wide, . . . also . . . 10,000 Quicksilver @ 50 cts short price." All these transactions in bottles, gin, steel, mahogany, etc., were incidental to the trade with Calcutta, these commodities being conspicuous among the exports from the United States. But his enquiry of Perit & Cabot, Aug. 15, 1817, "Would your Cabinet makers buy 20,000 or 30000 feet Birds Eye Maple 12 to 24 inches wide," can hardly be so explained.

"C. M" was Charles Miles, one of Henry Lee's supercargoes in Calcutta.

1. Jackson-Lee Papers, "Letter Book from Jany. 17th. 1817 to October 27. 1818."

Boston 20 Febr^y. 1817

Messrs P Remsen & Co
    New York
        Dear Sirs,
            Their is a balance due J Tracy from Barnewell & Popham, Alexandria of $570 12/100 which you will please to draw for at sight, and place the same to my account. Mr Tracy has written them by this mail to pay your Bill — I have yours of 17th — I have given in $10,000 to the owners of the Suffolk, as [you would — stricken through] the amount you would furnish — their Voyage drags heavily, and it would be a disappointment not to have it perhaps prevent her going. The extreme scarcity of money has prevented several of their friends this way, from sending so much as they intended.

If you think well of the voyage, I wish you would put in $10,000 your funds will be less engaged the coming season — If you don't ship, I shall be obliged to make up 5,000 or $10,000 myself, as I have been active in persuading Mr. H to go, and pledged myself to ship — In case you dont think well of the voyage, I will at the end of 6 Months take the adventure paying you 6 pr Cent Interest, and you may order what you like except nankins —

It would be a good purchase to get $15,000 in Calcutta, paying here $100 for 206 Sicca Rupees. It is uncertain how remittances could be made to China. If Charles was there he might by watching the market, do it under par, but an Agency house would not do it so well probably. If L. B. & M. will give an order for C. M to receive their $15,000. I will have it invested in Goods, and brought home at my expence, free of Commissions &c &c, taking ½ the profits — they making no charge of Interest — Goods to be sold by you on their return — or I will allow them 6% for it, and ⅓ profits — perhaps 9% from the time I get the money — See what you can do — You may buy me 20 Tons of Crude & 200 Boxes Roll Brimstone, at the prices quoted — I will tell you what to do with them few days hence. I don't want any wines at higher prices than 120¢.

for best Marcella, and 130¢. For Teneriffe. If you can sell my Gin in Philadelph^a. @ 144 deliverable there, I wish you would do it, and give an order on P & Cabot —

I think very well of Silks from China next year, but I dont want to ship, because it will take from my means of carrying on my voyage to Calcutta.

Yours &c
(Signed)   H Lee

Letter from Henry Lee, Boston, Feb. 23–Mar. 6, 1817, to Fletcher, Alexander & Co., London, on the General Commercial Situation, Particularly in the Trade with the Orient [1]

The letter below is particularly valuable for what it tells of re-exportations of India and China goods from the United States to the Continent. On Mar. 6, 1817, Henry Lee wrote to Remsen, "We have 2½ Millions of East India and China Produce now landing. . . . All must go to Europe. . . . No sales for anything." Bengal sugars were shipped to Europe because "our retailers prefer Havana, and New Orleans for home use." [2]

Via New York.

Boston Febr^y. 23^d. 1817

Messrs Fletcher, Alexander & Co
  London
    Gentlemen,
        I received from Calcutta, a few days since, your several favors to 26th March last, covering a/c^s of Nutmegs, Cloths and Hdkfs, consigned you per Countess of London. I presume the goods bought in, and the uncleared lots have long since been disposed of, if not you will have the goodness to sell them for the most they will bring, and pay over to Samuel Williams Esqr. any balance which may be due me.

1. Jackson-Lee Papers, "Letter Book from Jany. 17th. 1817 to October 27. 1818."
2. *Ibid.*, Henry Lee, Boston, Feb. 25, 1817, to Charles Williams, London.

And on the other hand, should there be a balance due from me, which it is hardly possible there can be, you will draw on me for the amount. With the accounts relative to my consignment, I received much information about India Goods in your markets, for which I am much obliged.

Our importations of China, and Bengal Goods, since the peace have been immense, of the former we have found good markets for the Teas, and Nankins, in Holland, Hamburg &c. Of the latter the Sugars, and Indigoes have been principally exported to the Continent. The Piece Goods are consumed here, and in South America & West Indies, some have also been sent to Italy, and Holland, but we find our shipments undersold by the Company Goods from London.

We are expecting many arrivals from China, Bengal and Java, most of these Cargoes will be exported to Europe. The New Tariff will prevent further importations of Piece Goods, the duties imposed by it amounting to a prohibition — The last Ships for Calcutta, will return with Cotton, and Sugars, which will be sent to Europe, Cotton chiefly to France. This article keeps up in this country, but must I think, come down in Europe, in course of few months. Our currency is now at par through the Union, and Stocks rising, money is scarce, and a good deal of embarressment exists among the trading community, and will continue to till we diminish our speculations or till they become more profitable. We are still overstocked with most articles of British manufacture so that our imports for 12 Months to come will be very small, besides the excessive duties upon Cotton fabrics, will diminish the consumption, they have hitherto formed one of our most valuable imports from your country. Exchange on London is here at par, at the South 1 @ 2% advance. It will probably decline a little, as we shall have but little to import from any part of Europe, and our Southern produce for exportation is very valuable.

Should J D Alexander Esqr., be in London you will oblige me by presenting him my respectful regards.

Your faithful Servt
(Signed)   Henry Lee.

Febry. 28th. 1817. We have no later accounts from Europe than 1st Jany., at which time, Cotton was falling on the Continent, which may have some influence on the price here, but we are governed by the English market chiefly, in regulating the price of that article — We have accounts from Calcutta to 4th Octr. I presume yours will be of later date, before this reaches. Cotton has risen, and was advancing,

(Signed)   H Lee.

Prices American Produce.

    Cotton Upland (in Carolina) 25 @ 26 Cts.
    Rice $5.50 pr 100 lb.
    Flour $14, pr Barrel.

Postscript of a Letter to Fletcher Alexander & Co dated 23d. Febry.

March 6th 1817. We have dates from Calcutta to Novr. 10th — Cotton was up to 17/ @ 18/ per M'd, and [was — stricken through] still advancing. We have 13 arrivals within few weeks, at this port, from different parts of India and from China — Teas, Sugars, Coffee, Pepper, Drugs, ⅞ of which must go to Europe — We are looking for 40 @ 50 more ships in course of 2 Months, in different parts of the States — Our dates from China are to 13th Novr. An English Frigate had committed some outrages in the Tigris, which may be attended with serious consequences to the trade — When the last ship came away, all business with foreigners had been stopped — The Company's Ships were not half loaded — Teas were scarce and high — We shall have large quantities of Black Teas, particularly of the ordinary kinds, to send to the continent — Cotton keeps up at the South to 25 @ 26 cts lb, and will not vary much till it falls in England — Rice will be high through the year. Our Stocks continue to advance — All our Banks have resumed Specie payments. Exchange on London par, at the South 1 @ 2% advance.

Yo Obt Servt
(Signed)   Henry Lee.

LETTER FROM HENRY LEE, BOSTON, MAR. 6, 1817, TO CHARLES WILLIAMS, LONDON, WITH DESCRIPTION OF THE GENERAL BUSINESS SITUATION [1]

This letter reveals the fate of various consignments of piece goods and indigo re-exported to the Continent. The piece goods, from the reference to the fact that they "fall short of the prices they were shipped at, though they do well enough at the India cost," were evidently reinvoiced before being reshipped from the United States to the Continent.

By "outrages" committed by an English frigate at Canton doubtless is meant the episode of Nov. 14, 1816, when H. M. S. *Alceste,* the vessel by which Lord Amherst had come on an embassy to China, was fired upon by war junks and Chinese forts, which latter the *Alceste* silenced by a single broadside.[2]

Via New York

Boston 6th March 1817

Charles Williams Esqr.
    London
        Dear Sir,
            I have yours of 22^d Nov^r., enclosing Prices Current for which I am again obliged to you. I now enclose the (2^d.) G & Benjamin Welles' Bill for £1000, on your brother Samuel dated Febr^y. 25th 1817 at 60 days sight — I desired Messrs Remsen & Co to remit you Two thousand Pounds, some weeks ago — they write me they had sent you £1000, and would remit the other — I presume this will pay all my drafts — I should have remitted sooner, but supposed the shipments of Indigo, to Havre and Russia, and Piece Goods to Amsterdam, and Leghorn, would have placed £2000 at least in your hands — The Indigo will come back to this Country, and the Piece Goods fall short of the prices they were shipped at, though they do well enough at the India cost, we cannot send any India Goods to the Continent; the Company sell lower in London than we can afford them at, allowing for difference of quality — I have al-

---

1. Jackson-Lee Papers, "Letter Book from Jany. 17th. 1817 to October 27. 1818."   2. Morse, H. B., *op. cit.,* vol. iii, p. 270.

ways supposed the demand on Continent for Cotton was very trifling, our people counted much on Havre for [interlineated: a] sale of the article — It goes to market so slowly and the consumption is so immense in Great Britain, that I should not be surprised if it kept up for some months, but I should imagine the importations from India, would have some effect as they will be greater than was calculated upon in England — We have dates from Calcutta to 10 th Novr. Cotton had advanced to 17/ per M^d., and was still advancing — most of our Ships will bring it — Sugars and Piece Goods were also high — We have immense quantities of Bengal Sugars, Ginger, Cassia &c. from China, and India most of which must go to the Meditteranan, and the North of Europe — The Calcutta Voyages will be indifferent some of them losing — Teas are low. China Silks will do pretty well as the quantity coming is small —

Cotton and Rice keep, and will remain high 'till they fall in England. Currency is at par all over U States — Money in this quarter very scarce — I never knew it so difficult to effect sales — at the South business is rather better — British dry Goods have advanced, but no sales of consequence have been effected —

Some voyages for China, Calcutta, and Batavia are going on, and others contemplated, but our rich men, are so much in want of money, and have such large Stocks of Goods unsold, that they will do less beyond the Cape, than last year — Sugars, and Coffee keep up in Havana — Flour has fallen to $13½ at the South, and is dull — It will not go much lower at present, as the wants of our own people, [interlineated: are great] more so than usual on account of the failure of Indian Corn — Our Stocks continue advancing. Dollars are 1% here, and 1½ @ 2% at the South. Brandies and Gin are very high, but of the latter very little is consumed. All sorts of Russian Goods remain low, and without demand — We shall not have any more ships built for 3 or 4 years to come — Freights are low to all parts of the world —

We shall have many failures among the small dealers. We have dates from Canton to Novr. 13th. An English frigate has committed some outrages in the river which may be attended with serious consequences to the trade. We don't know all the particulars, as the Canton came away few days after it happened — but all intercourse had been prohibited with foreigners by the Chinese Authorities — the Company's Ships were not half laden — We have had 13 arrivals within few weeks from beyond the Capes, and 50 more are expected at different ports in U States within two months. —

I have just received a letter from Messrs Remsen & Co, in which they say, they should remit you a £1000 — as soon as they could find a Bill —

Yours truly
(Signed)   H. Lee.

LETTER FROM HENRY LEE, BOSTON, MAR. 7, 1817, TO STEPHEN CABOT, CHARLESTON, S. C., REQUESTING PURCHASE OF A COTTON GIN [1]

On Feb. 18, Henry Lee had tried to obtain a cotton gin directly from Eli Whitney, New Haven. The machine was wanted for Cruttenden & Mackillop, Calcutta, to whom he wrote on the date of the letter below: "I applied to Mr Whitney for a machine to clean Cotton, he resides 150 Miles from here, I have no answer — I do not expect to get one as a Brother of his told me the proprietor would not allow one of them to go out of the Country, unless he could be secured part of the advantages which might be derived from it, which I of course could not guarantee, I have in consequence of this written to a friend in Carolina, to procure one if he could, at a cost not exceeding $150 — It is doubtful whether I succeed, should it be received within 6 Weeks, it shall be sent you by a ship which myself and brother, will despatch for Calcutta in about 2 Months or less." [2]

Eli Whitney was probably quite uninterested in filling an order for his famous invention. Since 1798 he had concentrated upon the manufacture at New Haven of firearms with interchangeable parts, any

1. Jackson-Lee Papers, "Letter Book from Jany. 17th. 1817 to October 27. 1818."

2. *Ibid.*, "Letter Book September 5th. 1816," Feb. 13, 1816–Oct. 30, 1817, Henry Lee, Boston, Mar. 7, 1817, to Cruttenden & Mackillop, Calcutta.

profits accruing to him from his invention having been consumed in lawsuits against infringers of his patent. In 1812 the United States Congress had rejected a petition for the revival of his patent. It was unlikely that Whitney was at this time engaged in the manufacture of cotton gins. His brother doubtless had reference to an arrangement between Whitney and the States of North Carolina and Tennessee, which for a time paid Whitney 37½ cents annually for every cotton-gin in operation within their boundaries.[3]

Stephen Cabot (1788–1831) was the rolling stone of the Cabot family. We encountered him in 1814 on his return from a mysterious voyage during which he suffered from privateers, mutiny, and shipwreck; in Jan. 1817, he was in Boston, and seems to have been interested in the wine trade. He next turns up in the West Indies some time before 1826.[4]

1st pr Mail
2d " Factor   Boston March 7th 1817

Mr Stephen Cabot
    Charleston So.. Ca..
      Dear Sir

        A friend of mine wishes to get a machine for cleaning short staple Cotton. I am told there are several sorts. I don't wish to go beyond $150. If you can buy me one which will answer the purpose, I would thank you to do it, and ship it to Philadelphia by the 1st conveyance, consigned to Messrs Perit & Cabot. I wish if possible to have it there by 15th April. Mr Whitney invented one which I believe is in general use. I applied to him to furnish one, which he refuses to do, for some reason which he does not explain. Money is very scarce, and business dull. We have many arrivals from India & China, but their voyages do not promise much.

If you have anything from Madeira, respecting freight of wine to India as proposed by Perit & Cabot, I would thank you to write me.

Yours truly
(Signed)   Henry Lee.

3. Olmsted, Denison, *Memoir of Eli Whitney, Esq.* (New Haven, 1846), *passim.*   4. Briggs, *op. cit.,* vol. ii, pp. 607, 611.

LETTER FROM WILLIAM OLIVER AND HENRY LEE, BOSTON,
MAR. 15, 1817, TO CAPT. BENJAMIN SWETT, SHIP HOLOFERN,
WITH INSTRUCTIONS FOR SALE OF WINE AT THE ISLE OF
FRANCE [1]

In this letter Henry Lee's old associate William Oliver again appears in commercial relations with him. Cruttenden & Mackillop, in a letter of Mar. 18, were instructed, in case the wine was delivered to them at Calcutta, to "allow Capt S. a commission of two and an half per Cent, on a fair valuation . . . in your market." Lee and Oliver were to draw on the Calcutta firm against this consignment for 8,000 sicca rupees at 6 months sight. Capt. Swett was further ordered, in case he proceeded to Calcutta, "to purchase, and ship on board the Holofern seventy five tons of . . . Salt Petre . . . and twenty five thousand pounds Ginger," in fulfillment of an agreement with the owners of the *Holofern* "to provide One hundred tons Cargo;" [2] or in case the exportation of saltpetre was forbidden, to ship 50 tons of sugar and 50,000 lb. of ginger.

Boston March 15th 1817

Capt Benjamin Swett
  Ship Holofern
    Sir,
        We hand you an Invoice, and Bill of Lading of 20 Pipes Sicily Madeira (Marcella) and 20 Pipes Vidonia Wine both of them are old and of the very first quality — and fit for immediate use — If on your arrival at the Isle of France — you can dispose of them at a price which will yield us One hundred and forty Spanish Dollars [interlineated: per pipe] nett of all charges, you will do it. — If you take Bills on London [interlineated: or Calcutta] be careful they are *undoubted* — Many of the Merchants and dealers in the Isle of France, are not worthy of trust for the smallest sum. If you take Bills on London in Payment, estimate them at 2/7d Stg. per Sicca

1. Jackson-Lee Papers, "Letter Book September 5th. 1816," Feb. 13, 1816–Oct. 30, 1817.
2. *Ibid.*, Henry Lee, William Oliver, William B. Swett & Co., Boston, Mar. 20, 1817, to Capt. Benjamin Swett, ship *Holofern*.

Rupee, which is their value in Calcutta. Recollect in that case to have 3 Bills, two of which you will forward to Messrs Cruttenden &Mackillop — Calcutta — the 3ᵈ. take with yourself — If you carry [thence — stricken through] the wine to Calcutta, you will deliver it to Messrs Cruttenden and Mackillop, who will have orders to pay you a commission of two and an half per Cent on the value of it, which is the Commission you are to receive on the sales in Isle of France. If you conclude to sell at the Isle of France, we reccommend your doing it immediately on your arrival, as several ships are preparing to follow you. — Whether you discharge the Wine in Isle of France or Calcutta, you will recollect to have it included in the general landing certificate, to cancel our debenture Bonds. We consider the wine as very low at our limitations, at the last dates from the Isle of France, it was worth 300 to 350 Spanish Dollars. Both the Marcella, and Vidonia, are much superior to those which are usually shipped from this country under these names — In the price demanded for the wine in the Isle of France, you must remember that usually there is great loss in getting away the proceeds to Calcutta. We mean by limiting the price at 140 Dollars, that you are to get a price, which will net the sum in Calcutta.

For the disposal of the proceeds of this shipment, we refer you to our further instructions. Wishing you a prosperous voyage

We remain

Your friends &Servᵗˢ

Wᵐ Oliver

(Sgd) Henry Lee

LETTER FROM HENRY LEE, BOSTON, MAR. 28, 1817, TO HENRY HIGGINSON, SUPERCARGO, SHIP SUFFOLK, WITH INSTRUCTIONS FOR THE PURCHASE OF CHINA GOODS [1]

On a previous occasion Henry Lee, barred by a non-intercourse act from Calcutta, a British possession, had turned to China as a stop-gap

---

1. Jackson-Lee Papers, "Letter Book September 5ᵗʰ. 1816," Feb. 13, 1816–Oct. 30, 1817.

for his trade. Now, when trade with India was much reduced by prohibitive duties on the most important of the previous exports therefrom, he similarly directed a portion of his capital and attention to the Canton trade. On the same date as the letter below, he delivered to Higginson another box of 2,500 Spanish dollars with instructions to invest in the same articles as those ordered by Daniel Remsen; that is, principally in crapes and shawls, for the rest in sarsenets and sewing silks. On the following day he handed over a box of 300 Spanish dollars to be invested in an assortment of crapes, nankeens, teas, and combs, so miscellaneous that he remarked, "You will laugh at my orders no doubt." It is unfortunate that we do not have recorded "the freight, and commission as per agreement on Bill Lading."

Boston March 28. 1817

Mr Henry Higginson
  Supercargo Ship Suffolk
    Sir
        I hand you with this an Invoice and Bill of Lading of a Box marked HL N⁰ 1. containing twenty five hundred Spanish milled Dollars, which you will invest in the following articles, and ship them on the Suffolk for my account, after deducting the freight, and commission as per agreement on Bill Lading. Vizt. One fourth the amount in 4/4 Black fringed and twilled Handkerchiefs of the low and middling qualities —
    One fourth in Sewing Silks — high colours and put up in the usual way — pound Bundles. 4 parcels in each bundle of ¼ lb each
      20 Pieces Black Sarsnets of the lowest price
      20 Pieces High coloured Sattins for Havana Market
    and remainder in low priced coloured and Black Crapes. If these articles are high you may purchase 500 Pieces Blue Nankin, low priced *Canton* dye, not to exceed 100 cts per Piece.
    Wishing you a prosperous voyage. — I am
                                    Yʳ Obᵗ Servᵗ
                                    Sgd.   Henry Lee

Mark the Goods H L
  (Sgd) H Lee

Letter from Henry Lee, Boston, Apr. 6, 1817, to Steiglitz & Co., St. Petersburg, with Samples of India Piece Goods and Sugar [1]

Henry Lee did not allow the unfortunate results of his first shipments of India goods to the Continent, after his return, to discourage him as to the possibilities of future profitable trade. The spring and summer of 1817 saw him sending letters of enquiry not only to ports to which he had not recently made shipments, such as St. Petersburg and Gibraltar, but also to countries, adventures to which had resulted in a loss, such as the Low Countries and France. On Aug. 21, 1817, he wrote to Hottinguer & Co., Nantes, and John Lewis Brown, Bordeaux, asking the prices of cotton, Bengal sugar, indigoes, saltpetre, ginger, and turmeric. He was particularly interested in knowing the possibility of his importing India goods into France in French vessels, paying only such duties as would be levied on goods belonging to a French subject. "If you have undertaken the East India trade extensively, and can carry it on with as much economy as our merchants, we cannot supply you with the produce of that country, because your own ships pay less duties —."

pGarland
dup per Lark

Mess Steiglitz & Co Boston April 6. 1817.

St. Petersburgh,

Gentlemen,

At the request of our mutual friend Mr Slade I have sent pBrig Garland a small package Cont^{g} Six sample pieces of Bengal piece goods, such as are usually imported into this Country, for the purpose of ascertaining their value in your market. Be good en^{o} to make the necessary enquiries and transmit me the result by the earliest conveyances I send also to your address two small boxes cont^{g} samples of East India fine Sugar & Refined Saltpetre Of which also, I am desirous of learning the value As I may be interested in both of them & shall send them you may if they can be disposed of advantageously. Please to

1. Jackson-Lee Papers, "Letter Book from Jany. 17th. 1817 to October 27. 1818."

state the price, demand, charges, &c. I shall at same time be obliged for any information as to the value of Ginger, Tumerick, East India Cotton

Your Ob Srv

(sgd)   HLee

Mem⁰. Samples Cottons refer'd to above.

Nº 1	—	1 Ps Chandilly Mamoody	40x2	cost say	70/
2	1 "	Beerboom Gurrah	36x2¼	" "	65/
3	1 "	Foolpore Cossa	40x2¼	" "	82/
4	1 "	Compʸ. Gurrah	36x2¼	" "	83/
5	1 "	fine Baftas	25x2	" "	65/
6	1 "	Coarse Dº	24x2	" "	50/

> [written across face of letter]
> The Sugar refer'd to in this Letter was
> first sent Double boil'd & worth here
> within $2. of Havana White common
> quality. —

LETTER FROM HENRY LEE, BOSTON, JUNE 7, 1817, TO PETER REMSEN & CO., NEW YORK, IN REGARD TO AN ALLOWANCE FOR BROKEN GLASS [1]

Claims on account of goods damaged in transit are a perpetual feature of business correspondence and are not always made in so good a temper as in the letter below. We do not know the result, but Henry Lee not only claimed allowances, as buyer; he also, as a seller, was made the object of similar claims. On Aug. 30, 1817, he wrote to Perit & Cabot objecting to an excessive award against him for poor quality of borax sold on his account, declaring that "it reduces the price to almost nothing about 5 Cts lb," whereas the merchants making the award had themselves been willing to pay 12½ cents.

Henry Lee, we learn later, had overestimated his balance with Peter Remsen & Co. by $6,000.

1. Jackson-Lee Papers, "Letter Book from Janʸ. 17ᵗʰ. 1817 to October 27. 1818."

Messrs P Remsen &Co.　　　　　　Boston June 7th 1817
　　New York
　　　Dear Sirs
　　　　Messrs Miralla & Co have shipped you on my account
61 Bags Coffee per Sch[r]. Betsey. I presume you will have the
Bill Lading. Sell it for the most you can, they call it green of
goods quality. I have to day drawn on you at 75 days date
$4000. 4 Months $4000. & 6 M[o]. $6000 more payable at Bos-
ton Bank Boston — I have money to pay my brother, and can
discount at the Boston Bank as they come round or sooner —
I wish you would let Mr R make out a sketch of my account,
on the other side I send you a Mem[o]. of a part of the Glass you
sold me. I disposed of a portion because the ship could not
take it — You will observe that of 347 Boxes sold. 105 were
broken, for which the buyers are not willing to allow me anything as yet, though they may a trifle. You may suppose a part
of this broken happened on the way to Phil[a]. but I think not as
it was carefully taken from along side the Coaster by the men
who purchased it It appeared to have been badly packed. I am
told the breakage is usually 2½ to 5% & I accordingly received
50 cts pr Box extra, and agreed to allow breakage I think you
should make me some allowance say 15% on the 497 Boxes &
I then suffer a loss of 15%. The men who bought of me are
very honest, & I saw part of it opened myself. I leave you to
act as you think right. It is true the price was low but the
sizes were bad. I wish you would send me the low priced
Palempores, I think I can get them off at about 80 or 90 cts.
　　　There is nothing doing in sales except for exportation —
　　　A Ship is fitting for Chili owned by Thorndike. Gray is
sending the Union to Calcutta & 2 or 3 Ships are going to
Batavia. Several Cargoes of Bengal Sugars gone lately to
Havre. The holders of Calcutta Goods are not inclined to sell
them under 95 to 100 cts but they make but few sales.
　　　The Columbus goes to Calcutta in 6 or 7 days.
　　　　　　　　　　　　　　　　Yrs truly
　　　　　　　　　　　　　　　　(Sg[d]　H Lee

Statement of Glass recd by J & D Elliot from Perit & Cabot
& examined, counted out and repacked by the Subscriber

12x14.	59	Boxes &	15	lights
10x12	53	" "	109	"
9x11	130	" "	78	"
8x10			152	"

242
105 broken

347. —

Philadelphia 5 Mo. 26 1817
            Sgd   Robert Stevenson

LETTER FROM HENRY LEE, BOSTON, JUNE 12, 13, 1817, TO
CHARLES D. MILES AND RICHARD CLARKE CABOT, CALCUTTA,
WITH INSTRUCTIONS AND INFORMATION IN REGARD TO THE
TRADE WITH INDIA [1]

Charles D. Miles, probably Henry Lee's clerk during his stay at
Calcutta, 1812–16, and Richard Clarke Cabot (1795–1884), son of
Samuel and Sarah (Barrett) Cabot,[2] and therefore Henry Lee's
cousin, had sailed from Philadelphia early in May on the *Cruttenden*,
probably named for the senior partner in the Calcutta firm of Cruttenden & Mackillop. This was the vessel which Henry Lee had been so
long intending to send to Calcutta. His idea was for the supercargoes
to sell both vessel and cargo in Calcutta and themselves remain as
resident agents for some time. Between Apr. 7 or 8 and June 12, 1817,
Henry Lee had been travelling to the southward of Boston, doubtless
to look after the sales of his India goods being handled by commission
merchants in that part of the country.

Ozias Goodwin, with whom Henry Lee sent this letter, is said to
have formerly "served him as clerk and supercargo" and was later
associated with him as a partner. Henry Lee had had the pleasure of
hearing through him of his wife and family, at Calcutta where Goodwin arrived in the schooner *Alligator*, May 6, 1813.[3]

1. Jackson-Lee Papers, "Letter Book September 5th. 1816," Feb. 13,
1816–Oct. 30, 1817.
2. Briggs, *op. cit.*, vol. i, pp. 53, 228; vol. ii, p. 638.
3. Morse, F. R., *op. cit.*, pp. 4, 152.

Boston June 12th 1817.

Orig^lp Ship Columbus (Sail'd 16th)

Dup. p^r. Naiad

Messrs C D Miles &

  R C Cabot

    Calcutta

      Dear Sirs

I suppose you were disappointed at not hearing from me by the Cadmus, I was at the south and my letter came too late — Let me remind you while I think of it, to send back a Box of Musters &c. and which you by mistake took with you in the C. They should be invoiced low, as we shall have to pay duties again — I send this by Mr O Goodwin, who goes out in consequence of Mr Prince having returned sick, instead of proceeding to Calcutta, where it was intended he should have remained. Mr G only remains 2 or 3 Months, long enough to sell the Cargo he carries out, and to buy a return one. I have told O that you would remain in Calcutta, 'till I sent out a vessel and then return. I don't wish anything further of our plan, should be communicated, as it might be an inducement for him to return, and do something in same way for those who now send him out, his stock will be about 90,000$. Gruff Goods — few Gurrahs Silk & coloured Goods on ½ profits — he has Merchandise, Boards, Bottles Lignumvitae, Paints, Salmon, Cordage, Iron, Brimstone &c &c.

The Brig Naiad owned by W^m B Swett & Co, and Pickering Dodge is loading with Cargo also, to sail in 15 days. Mr Gray thinks of sending the Union, but it is doubtful. I don't know of any going from the South — ½ dozen have gone [from — stricken through interlineated: to] Batavia within 5 weeks, most of which will proceed to Calcutta if they dont get Coffee — They cannot produce much effect on prices of Cotton and Silk goods or Indigo, they will take Sugars a great deal — Ginger, Saltpetre and perhaps Cotton if not higher than 16/ or 17/ per maund and small quantity of Indigo — It is probable some of the Ships now on Voyages to Europe may go from

thence to Calcutta, but not for piece Goods or at least they
will only venture [interlineated: up] on small quantities.
They are now so low, that it requires great courage to think of
facing the New Tariff. I am quite sure no voyages will be
undertaken from Baltimore, Philadelphia, nor do I hear of
any at New York. From this quarter it is probable they will
continue to go, but not so many as last year. — Piece Goods
have fallen since you sailed. They attempted to sell the Neptunes Cargo while I remained in Philadelphia at Auction, but
did not succeed. It would not have yielded more than 83 or
84 cts — It has been since offered at 90 cts on long time, there
is no speculation going on, and they only go off now and then
at retail at 90 to 95 cts they are to be sure very high charged
which is not known to the Importers but it is favourable to us,
because it has tendency to keep prices high, as few of the
holders are willing to sell at great loss; the assortments too are
bad, there [interlineated: being] but small portion of low
priced Mamoodies, Mow Sannas and other coarse goods. No
good plain Blue Cloths or wide Custers which are wanted. —
Small Sooties, Gillas, Kermitchees, Lollchees &c continue to be
dull sale, and quantity accumulating, You must not buy any
for me. — I have just seen in the New York papers, that the
Horatio is going to Batavia. You will bear in mind that all the
Batavia and Sumatra Ships, have small stocks, and will not
want Piece Goods or Indigo — I find that Choppas are more
in demand and Bandannas less so than when you left, you will
omit sending any of the latter, unless they are cheaper than
Choppas, and then only small portion. I don't want *any*
Lungees, Sistersoys, or Ringas, nor any Taffetas unless extremely low, they might do, but as we have only small stock it
is better to go upon other articles which are more certain —

As to Choppas all kinds will do Chellun, Nimposacky, Common Company and superfine Company, send such as you can
get in Bazar as soon as possible, and then get others made at
Cossimbazar — Seersuckers promise well. The Ships gone and
going have orders for some but not any great extent, but if they
buy ever so many we shall do well as you will buy 1/ or 2/. ps

less than they do. Mr Burr tells me good Chanderconah were only 11/. when he left, and Blue striped 9/8 to 10/. If you sell the C. or after she has sailed, you will have to ship the goods on freight, in articles of value say Indigo, Seersuckers, and Silk Hdkfs, don't mind the rate of freight as the charge is small — time is of more importance, nor do I care to what port you ship but prefer New York — Indigo will do well especially broken and middling native. I am not afraid of any quantity however large.

Some of the ships now going will have orders but I think most of them will take fine, because it does best in Europe. Ozias will want some, and I have given him a Bill on London, to be in part invested in fine Indigo on my account and his; shew him a muster of your fine — Mr Gray will order his captains to buy fine I imagine as he did pretty well with the Unions. If you don't find plenty of broken and middling native, I should not be afraid of 200 Mds Farruckabud at 75/ of middling quality, it will sell at 1.10cts to 120 cts. I continue to think well of Blue Gurrahs (fine) Blue Baftas — the latter it will require some time to get, go as high as 55/. This article will not be purchased by others, unless they know you are buying, it is a great advantage to have goods which others have not, as you can keep up the price I think I can sell 10000 ps or more in a year @ $3.25 ps, they are used for consumption and are also in demand for exportation —

Blue Gurrahs are lower in Havana, but there are not many in the country and good ones would now sell at 4.75 @ 5 in large quantities — Company Custers and Broad Checks are also in demand. I find Mr Gray had in the Fawn, China Custers 14 x 1½ which cost only 26/ — per Corge. I presume you will get them much less, and as they are admitted at the Silk duty they will do for consumption 18/20 1⅞ would be better dimensions —

You must be accurate in your Invoices, as they now open every 3d Bale or so at the Custom House. I wish you to ship a portion of the goods for consumption, say White Gurrahs, Mamoodies &c and in small Bales — of white Goods I think the

safest are Meergungees, Gurrahs, Coarse Mow Sannas, Chandilly Mamoodies &c &c   Of Baftas fine and coarse a
great many are yet on hand, I would not go largely unless you
find them very cheap

Don't be alarmed at buying rejected, stained, and old goods
when they are cheap. The long Chintz will certainly do when
you find any cheap cloths to make it — you must [pay —
stricken through interlineated: devote] great attention to patterns, colours and also to dying the Blue Cloths. If the Logwood answers let me know it that I may send more, It is now
only 20 $ Ton. I have no intention of sending out any vessel to
you for 6 Mos. to come — probably not till I hear of the sale of
the Cruttenden. I hope you may have disposed of her — but
don't lose any time, and if she has not already gone when this
arrives, despatch her at once. I hope you will negotiate my
Bills on London, and also the letter of credit for 50,000 Rs.
shall not have it in my power to make further remittances 'till
I get returns from Calcutta.

I am in hopes you will contrive to make Gin, if it succeeds
let me know if more sand [?] &c &c and how much of each is
wanted, I don't know that any one is sending out Gin, but you
ought to get off all your merchandise as soon as you can — The
Columbus will have 200 doz Champaign, and 4 Cases Silk Hose
owned by W Oliver & myself consigned you. Get it off as fast
as you can, through Tulloh & in any way. Some of the still kind
goes out in the Naiad, consigned Mr Swett which cost $6 pr
dozen, No hose in either ship, nor Window Glass, or Gin Cases
or Wine, nor any Linseed Oil — You ought to hurry the sales
of the Bottles, Brimstone, Verdigris, Salmon, Mahogany Cider
and Perry of the two latter articles Tulloh & Co will be able to
aid you in the sale — Most of the Americans will go to Gould
which favors us, as [most of the Americans will go to G. —
stricken through] T & Co. will devote more attention and have
the best custom — Let me know all about French Goods, particular [interlineated: sorts] colours, &c & most in demand.
The Perkins' have lately bought 400,000 lb Quicksilver, to
send to China. Enquire about the consumption of it in Bengal,

and how much will sell. Does it come best in Iron Bottles, or will the usual way of packing it answer? Let me know the value of British Pig Copper, and whether much has been imported from England, and how it is esteemed compared with Spanish Copper. Some ships are going to Chili for the latter, from thence I suppose they go to China, If the Country continues in the hands of the patriots they will succeed — our last news from Pernambuco is not favourable to the Revolutionists, but I think the Portuguese will not buy so many goods for 1 or 2 years — this will favor you — I wish you would not say anything to encourage shipments by any residents in Calcutta to this country, unless to Williamson, nor do anything with him, except on the terms I named — The Eagle arrived just in time to save the New Tariff but her cargo (1800 Bales) is not worth the cost & charges within $60,000 — The Marcellus not arrived — some accident I think must have delayed her, if she comes they must export her Cargo. There will be a loss on the Eliza's Cargo, on the Neptunes &Mentors. The Horatio made something for her owners, in freight — her Salt petre has been sold at 9 cts on long time. Gray & Perkins' hold on theirs but it will not advance. Cotton keeps up in Europe. the Malabar from Bombay has 800 Bales cost 11 cts will pay a fair profit, she will probably go again, and some other ships, her Pepper cost 9 cts I wish if the C has not sailed you would send in her 100 Bags best Rice

Let me know if you can get Saltpetre in large Crystals, [interlineated: & how soon] at what price & in what way. also about Radnagore Sugar, how much could you get in 6 or 12 Months, and the price, also Beerboom with good grain — There will not be any Whiting sent from this Country. Let me know how it answers, accept the first good offer which I think may be 5/ or 6/ per Maund, as it must be worth 3 times as much as Chalk — The Natives will use it to adulterate White Lead as our painters do. Brandy keeps up but will be lower if the Vintage is good. If any of mine remains with Tulloh & Co let it be sold — You must take great pains to get the Sherry into use — if really good there are great many people in Calcutta who will buy it, it is not probable [m — stricken through] any more will be shipped. Mr Stark did not succeed in getting freight to China, he remains at home —

The Persia has been purchased by N Bridge & others and is going for Batavia, Gentoo also for P Dodge — the Milton goes there via Holland, some ships have gone to Isle of France since you sailed from thence they proceed to Calcutta Bombay or Java. I have sent letters for Messrs C & Mackillop & Messrs Alexander & Co under cover to you deliver them in person — I hope you talk every day or two with the agency houses or at least often enough to keep up an acquaintance with them. Business has [interlineated: been] very dull. Teas are low and in [fact — stricken through interlineated: deed] almost every thing but China Silks which are selling at 70 @ 80% pr Invº. but they will fall in the Spring when the ships arrive — I send you a bundle of Newspapers, send me the Calcutta in return by private conveyance, and not through the Post Office, among the failures at New York are Potter Lovell & Co, Palmer Nicholls & Co. Halsted & Wiggin I lose nothing by them. Dennis Smith it is said will have a surplus — Scrip has advanced to 95 for 65 paid in, which adds 150000 to his estate, as he yet holds 15 @ 18,000 shares bought in at 65 and when you sailed it was only worth 85.

13th June. I have yours of 8th off Cape May, I am glad to find the Box Musters is on board the C — I was afraid it might have been lost. I hope she proved a good sailer. Let me know your opinion of Capt T that I may know whether it will do to send him back again. Give me notice when you can of intended shipments, and as much of the detail as possible of your business — I shall be very anxious to know everything, and when I think you wrong I shall have an opportunity of advising. I shall do no other business but sell the Goods you send me, and keep you advised of all that relates to your voyage — Practice economy, and keep your business to yourselves. I shall write by the Naiad to sail in 8 or 10 days — The Ellen Douglas sailed from Gibralter about the time you left the Pilot, I don't hear of any other ship going to Mr Newton. I have given your friends notice of this conveyance, and hope they will write you —

Yours truly

(Sgd)   H Lee.

(Postscript over leaf).

Postscript of Letter to Messrs C D Miles and R C Cabot, from last page —

p Columbus

Dup p Naiad

They admit China Custers at this Custom House as Silk Goods at 15% duty which is right this might not be the case at New York or Philadelphia, as they have not had any Goods of that kind, and the collectors may consider them as Cotton. You will therefore send your China Custers — Silk & Cotton Penas to this place or Salem. Seersuckers & Boglepores are admitted in all places as Silk Goods — You will Invoice the Penas and China Custers "Silk & Cotton Penas & Custers" and enter the export duty of 7½% among the charges, at foot of the Invoice. — I think from Mr Grays Custers that you will get China Custers nearly as cheap as the common [custers — stricken through interlineated: sort —] the Silk is ordinary and very little of it The mix'd Ginghams Silk & Cotton will do well, don't allow your Banians or the weavers to discourage your making them; they always oppose new things or anything which can give them the least trouble — I hope you have been able to employ Goluck [interlineated: Ramdon &] Kissen, treat them with kindness but by no means make confidents of them, you ought to keep Pran, and the Godown Sircars in good humour as much depends on them — It is better to pay them few Rupees now & then, than to wait till you are coming away, this will induce them to serve you. Keep your acc'ts with great care, and use all the caution neccessary, settle often & look well into the petty charges. Every one complains of loss of Tare in Indigo Boxes, you must take care and get fair allowance.

Send me as much information as you can, as to what others are doing, and what they pay for Goods. It will help me in my sales —

Let me know also what Portuguese are doing, what Cargoes the French Dutch and other foreign ships take away. I observe a Ship is going from Havre and one from Marseilles for Calcutta, what Cargoes do they bring and how have they answered? It is said British Ships are to be allowed to go direct [from — stricken through interlineated: to] Gibralter and Malta from Calcutta, such a regulation would injure us and they could deliver goods in Meditteranean cheaper than we could. — We hear also of some alteration of duties on American Bottoms —

Let me know any changes, and send me the mirror Directory of 1816 & 1817. if they have not been already sent — If the Cruttenden sells let me know if [any — stricken through] more ships would sell — If you don't sell her, say what offers were made, and what she may bring if I send her back. At what rate can you procure Cotton through the agents by advancing or making an engagement 12 Mos. before hand. Keep up an acquaintance with S & Robertson, they will always want to hear about Cotton when you have letters and you can give them information. You may find some cheap rejected cloths [and — stricken through] at their Godowns, and also at Fairlees, the Sircars will deal with you for them. I made more upon my rejected goods than any others. Send me always a Memo. describing the Goods such as I used to send F Lee.

It will aid me in the sale. In purchasing Bandannas you should have 30 ps to the 100 Yellow they begin to come in fashion again, but I hope you will find Choppas cheap, and will not have to buy any Bandannas for the present, some time hence they may be in demand again.

I count a great deal upon Broken Indigo, you can tell your Banian it is wanted to refine, or make Blue Cloth, this may prevent others from following you, make some arrangement with Morgan &c, [& — stricken through] to get all the rejected from the Godowns, and if you don't succeed, go to the principals and bargain first. Good rejected would do & 70/.80/. or 90/ which would be higher than it was at any time during our stay. When a person buys for London Market they sometimes throw out

¼, and it is then sold at a reduced price what remains would do for you — C & M may be inclined to make large shipment of ordinary, if it should be low, to this country such a transaction would injure our sales very much, and you must not encourage it. Mr Newton will I suppose remain some years in Calcutta I hope you will be on pleasant terms with him, but I don't wish you to have any transactions of business with him, or that you should communicate on the subject unless in a way not to expose your plans.

No one knows that you are to remain any time in Calcutta — It is not worth your while to say you shall, not even to your Banians for all you tell them goes to others, — Business is so much reduced and so many have capital to dispose of, that every [interlineated: one] is on the watch to know what his neighbour is doing, and it would interfere very much with us were there others sent out to reside & purchase such goods as we depend upon, they would follow us in everything —

If anything is to be made, it must be by great prudence, economy, and knowing something more of the trade here, and in Calcutta than most others engaged in it — I have every confidence in your disposition to follow my orders, and to effect in every possible way the object I had in sending you out, if you succeed and I continue it, I will raise the compensation you now receive.

The Jane which I thought was going to Calcutta from Gibralter goes from thence to Batavia — The Union will stop at Rio de Janeiro, and be sold there if a price offers — It is quite doubtful if she goes to Calcutta — It is thought the Sachem will do pretty well with her Cotton, it is probable she will go on to Europe with nearly [the — stricken through] same Cargo, and thence to Calcutta for Cotton Sugar, Saltpetre, Ginger &c &c, there is one thing you may be certain of that all the ships now out and all that may go within 6 Mos. will want but very few piece Goods of any sort. All together not more than [interlineated: equal to] one Philadelphia Cargo. Don't allow yourselves therefore to be alarmed, and think Goods will rise, when you hear an American announced at the

Banks Hall. If you find goods very low, I wish you to extend the sum borrowed, relying upon my remitting. If there is any want of confidence in me on the part of Messrs C & M. let me know it, and I will make some arrangement through Remsen &Co or S Williams [to — stricken through interlineated: which will] strengthen it.

If George Mackillop should discover any disposition to make a shipment, and allow me to have ½ he furnishing funds, agree to it. It is not likely he will wish to do so, as all the agents are principled against speculations [particularly — stricken through interlineated: especially] abroad — I expect to hear from you in about 7 Months &half. Don't let me be disappointed in letters by every ship.

Yours
(Sgd)   H Lee

Flour $11½ & 10½ at South
Coffee 19 cts

Havana White Sugar	18	Hollands Gin 115 Ɛ @ 120
Brown	13¼	Brandy no price fallen 80 @ 100cts
Pepper	21 cts	U S Bank Scrip 94 for 65
Teas as when you left		Six pr Cents 10 3
Nankins Yellow	84¢	Bills on London 1% advance
do Blue	190	
Calcutta Peice Goods	82 @ 87½	
British Goods low & abundant		

LETTER FROM HENRY LEE, BOSTON, JULY 8, 1817, TO PETER REMSEN & CO., NEW YORK, MENTIONING THE PRESIDENT'S VISIT [1]

The remark, "We are now all Republicans," jocular though it was, indicates to what extent the phrase "era of good feelings," referring to Monroe's administration, was actually valid. A few years before, the author of the letter below had been advocating secession, so embittered were his feelings toward the party of which Monroe was now the head. The "Essex Junto" was a phrase popularly applied to a group of merchants from Essex County, belonging to families con-

1. Jackson-Lee Papers, "Letter Book from Jany. 17th. 1817 to October 27. 1818."

nected by ties of business and kinship, who were conspicuous for their tenacious adherence to the Federalist party and their opposition to Jacobinism, Napoleon, Jefferson, and the party of which the last-named was the founder.

At one time, Henry Lee — handicapped in forming a correct opinion by his remoteness from the American scene — had urged his brother-in-law P. T. Jackson to give up his "factory at Waltham." His opinion later so changed that on July 22, 1817, he wrote to Peter Remsen & Co.: "This factory [the one at Waltham] is going to become a very profitable concern. You ought to be a Stock holder — Come this way and see it — "

Henry Lee wrote more freely and generally to Peter Remsen, New York, upon business and other matters than to any other correspondent. His opinions upon the commercial situation can be traced more readily through his letters to Remsen than in any other way, but should be supplemented by reference to his correspondence with Perit & Cabot, Philadelphia, of which firm his cousin Samuel Cabot was a member. To Perit & Cabot, on Feb. 12, 1817, referring to sales of his gin, he wrote: "I prefer Grocers to speculators, and don't give beyond 4 Months." To Remsen on the following day, in regard to "the long Credits" at New York to which some had been objecting, he wrote that the New York grocers "were the richest and safest men in the Union." On Mar. 8 he wrote Remsen that "our Grocers cannot buy unless at low prices, and on long credit." Later in the same letter he remarked that "no one here thinks of Importing Piece Goods" but rather rice, cotton, spices, sugar, etc. And on June 30 he wrote to Remsen: "Business is very dull. I don't see how we are to live by trade, at least more than half who are now engaged in it." Such was the situation at the time of the letter below.

"A. P. & M" were Appleton, Poor & Miles, a Baltimore firm, through whom Henry Lee had sold some India piece goods and endeavored to purchase others,[2] doubtless for exportation to Havana.[3] Charles D. Miles, who sailed as supercargo on the *Cruttenden* for Calcutta early in May, was a brother of one member of the firm. Henry Lee's experience with this Baltimore firm was evidently not happy, for on July 22 he wrote to his confidant, Peter Remsen, that

2. *Ibid.*, Henry Lee, Boston, Mar. 1, June 23, 1817, to Appleton, Poor, & Miles, Baltimore.

3. *Ibid.*, Henry Lee, Boston, June 9, 1817, to James Schott & Co., Philadelphia.

"they do business in a very irregular & unmercantile way and don't know how to sell or buy. I shall do no more business with them."

Boston July 8th 1817

Messrs P Remsen & Co
  New York
    Dear Sirs

I have yours of 5th & 3ᵈ. I have received an Account Current from A, P, & Miles — Ridgleys Note for $407 50/100 & Burkitts 622 2/100 which are charged in the A/C are in the hands of Messrs A P & M, the latter they say will be paid when due the former they expect to get 10/ in £, I wish you would write & have them both sent to you. I have not yet had time to examine the A/C They ought to have handed over our notes to you their not doing it alarms me a little, though I don't feel as if they were in great danger

Mr Tracy is going to Baltimore in a Packet which sails in 2 days, and what is due he will get from them, I am glad you have drawn for the $1500. I shall order the purchase of some wine to the amount of 1000$ or $1200 & some piece Goods which will offset anything that may be due.

Ridgely's Note for $407 50/100 belongs wholly to me sales of ◇ Goods. Your Blue Goods are not what I supposed them, should be 36 x 2¼ and fine, no others will sell in Havana. The Eagle's Cargo will be forced by Lippincott at low prices & get into your market, for which cause I am anxious to have my Choppas got off and also the Miltons Goods. I don't believe Calcutta Goods will advance for 8 or 9 Moˢ. to come. there are too many in the Country. A Ship will go to Calcutta in 15 days & the last for some time —

The Presidents stay has put an end to business for a week he is off to day. We are now all Republicans even the Essex Junto — Among his other visits he went to P T J's factory at Waltham.

The last accounts from Havana are unfavourable — Sugars high & imports low — White Gurrah $3 50/100 Blue 5 50/100 & dull.

Write A P & M in a way not to excite any distrust of your good opinion.

I have a regard for them & they have taken great pains to sell my goods

Yours truly

H Lee

LETTER FROM HENRY LEE, BOSTON, JULY 24, 1817, TO HILL & BLODGET, GIBRALTAR, WITH ENQUIRIES CONCERNING THE POSSIBILITIES FOR THE SALE OF PIECE GOODS [1]

The letter below is valuable not so much for its revelation of Henry Lee's intention to trade, if possible, with Gibraltar — a place with which he had not previously had commercial relations — as for its description of the chief types of India cottons and the principal markets for which they were intended.

per Geo Long

Boston July 24. 1817

Messrs Hill & Blodget

Gibralter

Gentlemen

When I had the pleasure of seeing your Mr B in New York he told me there was sometimes a demand for Calcutta Piece Goods. I notice in your Price Current of Febr^y. 5th they are quoted but in so general a way that I can form no idea of their value — The goods we import from India are generally coarse, and from 12 to 15 to 20 yds by ¾ to 1⅛ Yds wide say

Beerboom Gurrahs	34/6	x 2⅛	Cubits of ½ yard.
Mamoodies	39/40	x 2	"
Coarse Sannas	40/2.	x 2⅛.¼	"
fine do	39/40	x 2 1/16	"
Coarse Baftas	24/5	x 1⅞.2	"
fine do	25	x 2	"
Alliabad Emerties	30	x 2	"

these are all plain, white and rather coarse — We also import for the African trade. Blue Gurrahs 36 Cubits x 2¼. Chintz 5

1. Jackson-Lee Papers, "Letter Book from Jany. 17th. 1817 to October 27. 1818."

Yds. Sooty Romal Hadkfs 10 in a ps Custas 10 yds x 2, and many other coloured Goods — You will oblige me by particular quotations for these articles, or any that may happen to be known to your dealers — You will notice that the White Goods imported into this Country are inferiour to such as come to you from London called "Company" goods — Quotations of actual sales are more satisfactory than any other, and at same time dimensions should be mentioned — If the sale of Piece Goods is confined to the consumption of your own place the demand must be very limited — I should be glad to know whether this is the case, or whether large sales could be made to those who carry on the trade with Spain — A pretty large supply destined for Cadiz has been lately captured by the Patriots and carried into [Buana — stricken through] Buenos Ayres — this may have some influence on the prices of the article — I refer, to the Triton bound from Calcutta for Spain and taken off Cadiz — I am also desirous of knowing what would be the charges upon goods landed at Gibralter from a British Ship & reexported to the United States in an American Ship including your commissions for doing the business.

By a late act of Parliament British Ships are allowed to go from East Indies direct to Gibralter and Malta — Be good enough to inform me if any ships from India are expected to call at your place, and in the event of their doing so what is the probability of finding a Sale for Sugar, Indigo. Cotton & Silk Piece Goods, Ginger &c &c &c

If there is any trade with the African Coast there may be a large sale for Blue Gurrahs, of this I wish to be particularly informed —

Your reply when at leisure will oblige me and perhaps lead to our mutual advantage

Your Obt Servt
Sgd   Henry Lee

LETTER FROM HENRY LEE, BOSTON, JULY 25, 1817, TO JOHN
TRACY, BALTIMORE, ON BUSINESS PROSPECTS THERE [1]

The most significant passages in this letter are those in which the
writer enquires concerning the possibility of obtaining an advance on
goods shipped to Baltimore for sale and concerning the prospects for
opening a tea store in Baltimore.

Henry Lee was at this time trying to invest in India piece goods
not only in Baltimore and Philadelphia but even in London.[2] He
apparently preferred to buy such goods from among the large quantities in the hands of other merchants, as he needed them for local sale
or for re-exportation, rather than to take the risk of importing them
directly from Calcutta himself. He was also buying "Black fringed
Hdkfs at $12.50. 4 Mos." [3]

In view of the great quantity of piece goods on hand, Henry Lee
was concentrating upon other articles of exportation from India which
had not been so much overdone. Conspicuous among these was saltpetre. On Mar. 3 he was offering through Perit & Cabot "a contract
with Whelen for 200000 or 300,000 lb crude or refined, deliverable in
15 Months — the price he offered was 13¢ & 15¢. . . . I should like
to receive in payment an endorsed note, that I may sell it if needful,
and agree to a penalty of 2 Cts lb." Two days later he was willing to
agree to supply "100 @ 400,000 lbs . . . 12¢. for 2d. & 14¢. for 1st
quality, deliverable in 15 Months. . . . I should rather agree for
½ Cent less and have the payment made in 3 Months after delivery,
instead of 9 but am willing to say 9 if he insists upon it." On Mar. 21,
Lee offered other terms, namely, "to import 200,000 @ 300,000 lb
of Crude or refined, . . . advance the money, charging him, in lieu
of Commissions, profits & freight, 7 Cents plb payable on delivery
. . . I will agree to take a good note on 60 or 90 days with interest,
or even 4 Mos provided the Security is perfectly good." Observe how
his terms had been lowered in the letter below. One reason was doubtless that word had gone abroad that the export of saltpetre from
Calcutta, rumored to have been forbidden, would be allowed. An-

1. Jackson-Lee Papers, "Letter Book from Jany. 17th. 1817 to October 27. 1818."

2. *Ibid.*, Henry Lee, Philadelphia, Apr. 17, 1817, to Charles Williams,
London.

3. *Ibid.*, Henry Lee, Boston, Mar. 11, 1817, to Peter Remsen & Co.,
N. Y.

other was that Henry Lee wanted to import saltpetre as ballast for his vessels from India.

Boston July 25. 1817

Mr John Tracy.
 Baltimore
  Dear Sir,
   I have yours of 20th. I am sorry you have lost so much time in letting us know what you could do in buying Piece Goods. I should suppose you might ascertain in a day what they would or would not take. It does not appear probable you can buy any, or any other sort of Goods. I direct the wine if you have purchased it [be — stricken through] must be for your own account, as I should not know what to do with it as the vessel will go in few days for Calcutta — It was only in the event of their being very bad that you could feel authorised in buying it, and from your account of them and what I learn here I don't apprehend any danger for so short a time — on the whole I think you had better examine their accounts and see if they have accounted for all the Goods expecially Hdkfs, draw on them for the balance and leave the acceptances in U S Bank to be collected for account of Messrs Remsen & Co.

On your return through Phil^a. see if you can't get Schott to advance you something on your goods as I shall not have funds to meet Mr Grays note when it comes round —

Choppas are getting in demand and fine ones are worth here & in New York nearly $6. You dont say anything of the Rats or Eagles, they may be cheap at 85 cts if well charged.

Havana Brown Sugars have come in plentifully & are falling If you have not bought, don't buy unless to get off A P &M's Notes without endorsement. Enquire about Ridgley & Burke whose notes were sent Remsen & Co. they say Burke has failed which is not the case I hope. If R & Co have not drawn for the $800 desire them to pay it to you, and send it to R & Co.

I will contract to deliver Lovering or any one who is safe, Crude Saltpetre at 10 cts payable 6 Mo^s from the delivery and will engage to deliver it in 15 Mo⁵. probably it may come in 12 Months

Yours truly

(Sgd)   H Lee

Ask Mr Williams whether in case of Goods being consigned he would advance any part or allow half the value to be drawn for at 60 or 90 days. I may in 6 or 8 Months find it for my interest to send him some piece Goods & Indigo. Put the same question to Saltonstall.

Is there any one who would sell India Goods better than G W? Would not a man succeed in a Tea Store in Baltimore? Is there any one in that business, say [interlineated: to sell] by Chest and smaller package? Does Mr W appear desirous of business & does Saltonstall?

H L

Don't forget to send certificates of wine if not already sent

H L

LETTER FROM HENRY LEE, BOSTON, JULY 31, AUG. 1, 7, 9, 1817, TO CHARLES D. MILES AND RICHARD CLARKE CABOT, CAL-CUTTA, WITH DETAILED INSTRUCTIONS FOR THE PURCHASE AND SHIPMENT OF GOODS [1]

Below is a typically detailed Henry Lee letter to supercargoes — one of a series which, long and minute though they are, may be regarded as supplementary to a manuscript book given to Charles D. Miles,[2] for his guidance, at his departure. This book contains all the information acquired by Henry Lee, during his four years in Calcutta, pertinent to the purposes of the *Cruttenden's* voyage: descriptions of cotton goods, their qualities, dimensions, origin, and price limits, together with similar information concerning indigo, cotton, gums, spices, drugs, goat skins, sugar, etc.; and also invoices of the goods Henry Lee had shipped from India during his stay and a list of vessels then absent for India. Some of Henry Lee's suggestions

1. Jackson-Lee Papers, "Letter Book September 5ᵗʰ. 1816," Feb. 13, 1816–Oct. 30, 1817.
2. *Ibid.*, "Directions to C. D. Miles 1817 for purchases Piece goods, Indigo &c &c. &c."

Rajkissen Mitter, Calcutta Banian, 1838

throw light on the best business ethics of the time; for example, his information that old cloths, or cloths which had been washed, would sell for as much as new ones, but that, since the natives did not know this, a discount could be obtained, and also his instructions to pack rejected cloths in the same bales with those of better quality, taking care that a good cloth should be on top.

The reference to saltpetre is explained in a letter of July 22 from Henry Lee to the same correspondents, stating that he had contracted for "300,000 lb at 12 cts for refined, & 10 cts for Crude, payable 10 Mo^s. from delivery. 1/3 to be delivered within 12 Mo^s., 2/3 within 18 Mo^s." Henry Lee had been trying to obtain a saltpetre contract ever since his return.

Advice concerning methods of dealing with banians is a constant feature of Lee's letters to supercargoes. In a postscript of Sept. 6, ordering the purchase of "Caster Oil . . . 3000 Gallons, packed in Iron bound Hogsheads, free from hot taste, cold pressed . . . from 8/ to 15/ M'd, see that the natives don't boil it which injures the quality" and of senna "200 /Two hundred/ Maunds. preferring Country, if at 3/ less than Arabian, Dont garble it, Put it in Bales, and have them tared," he incidentally gave instructions on handling banians. "You must manage the exportation [of piece goods] through Pran, who is . . . Jessender to Campbell, Company's Examiner." He continued: "Seersuckers . . . you must get . . . from the weavers, and now and then you may find a cheap lot in the Bazar among the small dealers. . . . In your contracts, see that the Banians charge only what they give — It was long time before I could find out the weavers lowest prices — Give them (Banians) to understand that goods will not do unless at very low prices, and that you shall change for some other Banian, unless they do well — Have a good understanding with Pran, and the leading Sircars, and get as much knowledge of the language, as will enable you to converse with the Bazar Merchants, and to understand conversation between brokers &c &c &c, and Merchants, Banians &c &c — Don't confide in any one, nor make known your intentions to your Banians; nor say how long you shall remain in the Country to them, or any one else — " As to indigo, "It is among the natives you will do best, Their Broken, ill looking Boxes, often contain good qualities, and no one will buy it for European Market — Most of the Eastern people, avoid an acquaintance with the agents — I hope you visit them often, and in a way to hear all that is going on, without occupying too much of their time — They will always want to know about Cotton &c &c, which I shall always advise you about — " On Sept. 25 he wrote, "See if you can't get some cheap rejected Cloths of Colvins, Fairley & Co, or some of the other houses. The Godown Sircar or the Banian is the person to settle for you — You must allow them Brokerage — As Mr Newton has fixed upon Ruggoo Ram, it is necessary you should caution Ramdon, against communicating with Tillock." This last reference confirms our impression that Ramdon Bonarjia was the banian formerly associated with Tillock.

"Old Mr F" was doubtless Simon Forrester.[3]

Boston July 31st 1817

p Eliza Ann

Messrs C D Miles   Sailed 13 August.
  R C Cabot   /Duplicate p Nancy
  Calcutta   from Providence)
Dear Sirs,   Saild 8th Sept r

I wrote you on the 22d Inst. by a Ship from Philadelphia for Bombay she goes I presume for Cotton. This will go by the Eliza Ann Capt Park, on which I have engaged to ship Eighty Tons, in either measurement or heavy goods, you will bear in mind in making out the Bills Lading that you must reckon 2240lb to the Ton, nett of Tare which never pays freight — You will ship on my account 80 Tons of Saltpetre, refined if to be had within 3 Rs. per Maund of the Crude, but if the difference is greater then ship the best Crude — I wish you to have an extra Gunny Bag put over it and crossed with Ropes — We lost some thousands of pounds in Portsea for want of this, and you will take the same precautions in any future shipments — I wish you to see that the ship is well dunaged, before you send any on board — It would be well that a tier of Ginger should go under it, to absorb any moisture, it will not be injured, and it may save the S. P.; but if they don't do this, you must have 20, or 30,000 lb of refined, put into Boxes of 10 feet, and let them form a tier in the bottom of the ship — Be careful and have the S P as pure as can be obtained, as it will be subjected

3. Morison, op. cit., p. 119.

to an examination, and I must allow for all impurities over 7½% for the Crude, and 4% for the refined. — I hope you may have found some in large christals in which case ship it always in Boxes that it may not be broken — It will command an extra price for provision dealers use — If you can't buy in the Bazar, you may procure from the country or get it made in the City. I think C & M may put you in the way of getting it — I shall always be able to retail a considerable quantity at 3 or 4 cts more than common quality will command — Take notice if much S P. goes to England or any other part of Europe — The price in London is now 36/ @ 40/ Cwt. for Crude, and 5/ to 10/ more for refined which is not enough to induce further shipments, but the Cotton ships may be compelled to take it for dead weight — The last sale here, and in New York for Crude has been 8½ to 9½ cts lb. but an importation of 2 or 300 Tons would reduce price to 7 or 8 cts as the powder dealers are supplied or have made contracts. Mr Gray and Messrs Perkins still hold on their refined, it having cost them something more than they are offered. — Be careful to have different marks put on Crude & refined, and let one be with red paint & other Black — In my order of 3ᵈ May, I told you to prefer New York to any place, when you made shipments, but I now wish you to prefer Boston because I can sell many of the Goods myself, and distribute the Cargo where it is most in demand better than any one else I wish you to remember & keep musters of each lot you buy, and to send me also samples of the principal articles you ship say A pieces, they will help me, in the sale, and often times save the expence and trouble of opening. —

I hope you have made sale of the Merchandize at least such articles as will be likely to be shipped — The E Ann takes some Lignumvitae but not much else — No more Champaign or Silk Hose will go from hence or any part of U S — nor any sort of Wines, Verdigris — Whiting — Window Glass. Corks or Gin Cases — Gin & Brandy are both too high to ship, and will continue so for many months — Some rich glass ware made in this town is shipping on the E Ann, because they could not sell it here for any price. The E Ann's concerns are managed by W^m B Swett & Co, owned by the Captain & mate, cost only $5000, but is I imagine a safe ship — S G Perkins & Co. have conditionally engaged some freight by her say 50 or 60 Tons, she will have very little capital — may probably do her business with Ramdon and Kissen, in which case do Capt P any service you can without interfering [without interfering — stricken through] with your own interest — Should he go to other Banians you will not advise him — It makes the Banians hostile to you when they find their business watched, besides you [would — stricken through] injure those you would serve and generally get their ill will — I am pretty well convinced that no one can serve you or will serve you so well as Ramdon & Goluck & Kissen I am the more convinced of this by comparing the goods I purchased through them, with all the Cargoes shipped since the Peace and particularly Dulolls and Ruggoo Rams which in general are 10% to 15% higher than Ramshander Meties — The Stars and Eagles are excessively high charged, though purchased when the Bazar had declined a little. —

Most of the Goods now in U. S. are fine sorts and high charged, which is an advantage to us in our importations of coarse goods especially which are now wanted — I could easily run off 100 Bales Coarse & small Meergungee at $3.80 @ $3.90. and they will be worth $4 in March next. — You may go to 60/ if necessary including rejected which is higher than we paid in Portsea by 5/. *Don't be prevented buying Goods because they are very coarse, provided they are cheap in proportion, nothing can be too bad for our market, some one or other will purchase.*

I wish you would send me the prices of Madrass Goods say such as are usually sent to U States that I may know whether they can undersell me. Can anything be sold to such advantage at Madras as to make it an object for a vessel to call there on the way out? By a late act of Parliament British Ships are allowed to go direct from India to Gibralter & Malta. — Let me know if any ships have sailed for those places, and whether in that case they receive at the Calcutta Custom House, the same drawbacks as ships bound to London. — I desired you in my last to purchase for J Lee Jr^s. vessel to sail 1st Novr. for Calcutta 10,000 Good Goat Skins — You may also buy 50 Mds Senna if under 10/ pr M'd 50 Mds Copal if at or under 21/. for good 14/ for ordinary — You may buy for me at any time you can procure it 50 Mds good Assafoetida at 30/ per M'd, or even 36/ if but little has been shipped, and 100 Mds if at 25/. Put it into small Boxes, and Tin Cannisters, and ship in any vessel which you can obtain freight by. All the light freight you may have, say measurement Coarse Goods, you may reserve for the vessel J. Lee Jr will send out in Octr. or Nov^r., she will be with you in 7 Months from now — probably 6½ Months and get home as soon as the Eliza Ann — In sending Silk Goods & Indigo $10 per Ton is no object compared with the advantage of getting the goods a month or two earlier especially to one who like me has only a small capital — Give me as much notice as you can of intended shipments, and write *by every* ship. I should be disappointed if one should arrive in any part of U S without letters — I like details, they cannot be too particular —

I shall address letters to you, under cover to Messrs C & M because they go safer, and for other reasons — Many vessels have lately gone to Batavia, at foot you have a list of most of them, it is probable some of them will fail getting Cargoes and proceed to Calcutta, they have 25,000. to 40,000 Spanish Dollars, and will want Sugar, Cotton Saltpetre. Ginger. Skins some few drugs, and perhaps few Boxes Indigo & few Bales Piece Goods — The Southern ships will go to Ramduloll few to Ruggoo Ram — the Salem & Boston to Ramshander Metie, & Duggo Pesaud — Mr Clark who was out in the Mentor of New York is getting up a voyage for Calcutta, and may sail in Septr. I will send letters if they will take them. Burr & Babcock think also of sending out a ship as a remittance, if they do she will sail within 2 M^o. & I shall write — It is probable Ropes & Co and the Salem people may send out vessels in October, but not so many as last year, the inducements are less, and ships are not so plenty — freights are getting better to Europe — We have had no arrival from Calcutta since the Star — We look for the Sachem & 2 of Forresters Ships. Old Mr F died few weeks since which removes one of the largest Calcutta Traders — I think Mr Gray will decline it gradually finding it unprofitable. The Southern people have done so, & will not resume it, having better employment for their capital — Some of the new adventurers will also abandon it, so that next year we may have a better chance than now offers, though my present expectations are satisfactory.

I observe on looking over the French Papers that many Ships are advertised for Isle of France and Bourbon, some of which I presume will proceed to Calcutta, one named the Epaminondas was to sail about 1st June. of 500 Tons. from Marseilles for Calcutta and Chandernagore, one named the Brake owned by Mr Cushing sailed from that place some time in April or May, she returns to Marseilles again — I wish to know what Cargoes they brought out, & their returns, and whether they pay same duties that we do. Does a Cargo shipped at Chandernagore in a French Ship pay same as if shipped from Calcutta? Have the French any priviledges that we don't enjoy in their trade in Calcutta? Is there any considerable accession to the French population in India, and any commercial Houses established? or do they continue to employ British Agents? what rate of freight do they have per Ton in the French Ships? I am in hopes you will find French Manufactures do pretty well say Silk Hose, Gloves, Black Silk for Waistcoating, coloured for Gowns. Laces, Cambrics, Perfumery Millenary. Paper &c &c. Send me the Best information you can obtain upon this subject —

I am sending you pr E A 200 Doz Old Hock. and 200 doz Seltzer Water direct from Germany, the former from England sells for 30/ to 45/. doz. they may not like this because it does not come from London, but Tulloh & Co. will run it off and I think you should hold it high to get it into repute and say nothing of the Ship which brought it or America, the same in regard to the water, the jugs contain 1½ pint, about three times as much as Williamsons they drink the Wine & Water together

½ & ½ or less wine, as may be preferred. When the Wine & Water are put into the Glass put into them 1 or 2 Tea Spoons full of powdered Sugar which cause them to effervesce, and become lively, without doing this they would seem insipid & flat, they are much more esteemed than artificial Waters, in Countries where they are known — It is possible however that in Calcutta the Soda made there may be preferred — You must take some pains to make them known, and if you can, sell the Wine & Water together. A Bottle does not lose its goodness immediately on being opened, but may be drank as required only keeping in the Cork — Let me know how it answers, and how much of each could be sold — Would a quantity of the Jugs sell, and at what price.

August 1. The Ship Tartar has been purchased by P & Rogers for their friends in Salem, and is going to Bombay for Cotton, the Malabar belonged to the same people — she returned some weeks ago with a Cargo, and has gone to Europe with it — Let me know the price of Cotton there — I shall write you by that ship under cover to Messrs C & M care of Forbes & Co. pay them the postage, other ships will also go for Cotton to Bombay. The Sumatra Ships have done well this year; and so have the Batavia, the last dates from thence 28 March there was no Coffee so that some of the vessels must go to Calcutta for Cargoes. Let me know the season Cotton crops are gathered, and when the article comes down to Calcutta in greatest abundance. Does the high price of the article have much or any [interlineated: influence on] prices of coarse cloths? They write from France that the crop of raw silk will be bad one, both in that Country and Italy. If it is true you will know by letters from London, and the article will be effected in India — Choppas of all sorts have become quite scarce, especially good ones of the quality corresponding to A B & C No 54. which are what is called here best Company such would now bring $6 in New York you may go to 120/ on board for them if they can't be had for less, the best months to buy at Cossimbazar are from January to May & June — Such as you get made have good patterns, and Yellow & Red, but don't refuse cheap ones in the Bazar on account of patterns & colours, any sort will sell though not so readily as good patterns.

Remember to look out for rejected Choppas among the Banians who supply the India Captains — the agents now and then buy largely, and throw out 1/3d, which you may have at 6/ to 10/ less.

I don't want any shipments of Bandannas made unless they are 10/ to 15/ cheaper than Choppas of same quality, they are not in fashion, and many are yet on hand. while the Choppas have become scarce — Of Seersuckers I have as favorable an opinion as ever, if obtained at my limitations. I count more upon broken & low-priced native Indigo than any other article, if you can't find enough of this you may venture upon 200 to 300 Mds of Farruckabad even as bad as the 400 Mds. I purchased of C & M @ 105/. provided you can get it at 75/ per M'd — You must try to bargain with G. Mackillop for all his broken and rejected, his fine broken may be cheap at 100/ to 110/ per M'd —

I rely on your sending me a Memo. of all the Cargoes shipped to this Country, and also what Cargoes are shipping when you write, this you can easily ascertain from Banians. C House, and [interlineated: conversation with] Americans; my sales here will be much aided by such information.

I shall write Mr Newton by most of the Ships which go, but in a way not to discover what you are doing. It is quite essential to my interest that you do not communicate your plans. Keep a Memo Book & note in it everything you hear that may be useful. and the result of your various enquiries as to value of imports & exports &c &c &c &c. — There is no intention on part of any of those engaged in India trade of sending out a person to reside in Calcutta — Mr N will probably remain as long as he can find it profitable — I apprehend he has formed expectations which will never be realized, and that he will return much sooner than he intended — Let me know what he does. I wish you to avoid being concerned in any purchases with him or any one else. The Ships gone to Chili will get Cargoes of Copper, and some proceed to China, unless the Patriots should be driven away, at the last dates they were in undisputed possession — Give me particular information of the value of Pig & Sheet Copper. the former has got up to £5 Cwt in London for English. No Spanish there. One of the Phillippine Companys ships has lately been captured off Cadiz with 400000 lbs Pig Copper bound to India. The Revolutionists at Pernambuco have been subdued, I suppose their Bengal trade will go on as usual but it is only about once in two Years they take largely. I don't think the European Spaniards will have any trade 'till South America is quiet. The privateers from Spanish Maine, Buenos Ayres &c have increased, they are manned by Americans & English, and many of them owned by Baltimore & other Southern people. The Triton from Calcutta carried into Buenos Ayres was taken by a privateer owned by some people in Baltimore, where part of the proceeds of the Cargo has arrived.

You must have some one on board the E Ann when they get out the Wine & Seltzer Water, as the Captain & Mate are careless people & will break it if no one overlooks them. It is shipped in perfect order having been repacked by me — the landing Certificate must say 50 Hampers, and 48 Boxes to agree with outward Entry — on shipping the Saltpetre you must also see that she is well dunnaged, and have part of it put into Boxes to form a tier in the Bottom —

There will not be many American Ships in Calcutta when the E A arrives unless the Batavia Ships go there. Don't take upon yourselves the responsibility of reccommending American Bills to the agents, unless it may be to oblige Messrs C & M. — August 7th. The Restitution arrived few days ago and brought accounts to the last March, they are bad enough for export and import articles and such as will discourage from sending so many ships as went last year, the next will be still worse. I dont lose my confidence in my own plan, persuaded that you will pick up enough goods within my limits to engage all my funds and credit — I am glad to find that few white Goods are expected in the Ships now on their voyages, nor do I think they will have Stock enough to overdo Indigo and Choppas Seersuckers &c &c. It was the Southern people that run most upon these articles, and they have no ship out but Athens that can interfere with us, and she has but small funds. —

Mr Remsen writes me the Essex Junr. is about sailing from N York direct for Calcutta in charge of Mr. Clark who was in the Mentor — No one knew of it 'till within a day or two. I wrote a short letter and sent it on with hope of getting it on board. She will have small funds, and some credit and do business with Duloll. I find Indigo was low in March, the article has advanced a little in Europe but chiefly the fine sorts, the ordinary and middling are still cheap, and you will always find the agents ready and willing to sell. Goluck has sent per R very good letters, and Tillock has also written — he is still with Ruggoo Ram and you must not confide in him —

Try if possible to get on with Goluck, Ramdon, & Kissen. I am convinced they will serve you best, it is their only chance, and they are sensible of it, everything depends on your having a Banian who is manageable, and they will be more so than with me, because you will not owe them money — We have now received the return duties from C House which my brother received at Washington in all $18582 18/100 less $2200 expences incurred; of this — $9630.77/100 goes to M C — $4246 15/100 to ◇ Invoice (Mine) $2902 to R P O & $1803 to WD PWP this is great help to the Voyage, and we take great credit in obtaining it as it cost a great deal of trouble and management. You should say thus much to Williamson — No one believed we should succeed. —

Mr Clark applied for letters to C & M from Mr Remsen but he refused, he goes out upon a credit speculation and will probably take anything he can get in payment for Bills — avoid any such intimacy as will expose your transactions, neither he, nor any one you [interlineated: will meet] can give you useful information, but they may be glad to communicate for the sake of yours, and follow your shipments which in present state of the trade would be injurious. The Canton of 500 Tons is going from New York in about a month or 6 weeks, I shall write by her she will have small funds for Cotton, Sugar &c &c

Ruggoo Ram packed the Sachem's Piece Goods 251 Bales. and her Blue Gurrahs cost only 55/ to 61/. Checks 15/ to 17/. Custas same Long Checks were only 32/ say 30/ nett 19 x 2. — I infer from this those kind of Goods were low, and that you will buy still cheaper Checks @ 15/ 16/ small and 30/ for Long 19 x 2. will do very well with new duty they are lower than my limits — for Coarse checks you will find Catuah cheaper than Bernagore. They write me there is great difficulty about Alliabad and Viziers goods at the Custom House. It is no matter as they are generally dearer than Rowannah Goods.

Some of the Americans are thinking of importing Raw Silk — Don't you buy it for me nor indeed any articles but those I have reccommended or similar ones. You know I am not governed by names. I go by qualities and dimensions, and care not what goods are called so that they are cheap —

The vessel my brother will send is new, a Brig of 220 Tons, coppered and first rate, her *voyage is fixed* and she must go by 15 October or 1st Nov[r]. and be with you in 4½ Months from time of sailing, make use of this to encourage Goluck & Kissen. We shall send but little stock by her, nor shall remit 'till I hear of your arrival. The market for Piece Goods remains about same as two months ago. The Eagles Cargo goes to Philadelphia and with the Neptunes will be sold in Sept[r] or Oct[r]. at Auction, they are high charged and may bring 87 @ 90 cts nett of Comm[o]. and Auction duty, this ought to discourage further importations, because most people believe them to be well charged — Coarse Goods will be wanted in Spring and all sorts will advance by that time. The George's Cargo now looked for will go to Leghorn — there will be few Debenture Goods here of the present Stock, when your goods reach me. Common Bengal Sugars $12.50. best Benares $13½, and such Radnagore as I had in the Cririe $16½ @ $17. It will always be wanted and you must collect it as you find it in the Bazar at

12/ @ 13/ M'd. It should always be shipped in Boxes. Ginger $9. dull. Tumerick, 4 cts. Goat Skins 20 cts. good ones will always be worth 25/ [?].

Pepper 20 cts don't ship any as it comes from Sumatra. lower than Calcutta price. Java Coffee 19 cts — When you export Silk Goods or Goods mixed with Silk enter at the foot of the Invoice the particulars say Duty on China Custas, on Seersuckers &c &c naming each article and charging it at 7½%. This will convince our collectors that such Goods are considered in India as Silk.

August 9th. I have letters from Mr J Mackillop, acknowledg-[ing] mine written after the arrival of the Portsea in this Country. he appears to have been much pleased with our manner of doing her business, advances made &c &c. I think you found the house disposed to serve us. I shall write you a letter on the subject of a contract for Saltpetre in which you will offer Mr Williamson a concern, or if he refuses to Mr Octerloney —

Your friends have written you, and I forward you their letters.

If anything more occurs I shall add to this. You cannot be too accurate and particular in your accounts, nor too cautious in all your dealings with your Banians. Don't trust out any property to the natives without making them accountable.

If you did not send the Castor Oil per Cruttenden then get ready 2000 /Two thousand) Gallons for the Brig which sails in Novr.

In your Silk & Cotton Goods from Bernagore say China Custas Penas &c &c you must have them passed into town as Cotton, and you will then get Drawback instead of paying a duty.

Powdered Tobacco is the best thing to preserve Goat Skins — Business very dull, I shall do nothing but pick [interlineated: up] information for you, 'till the Cruttenden or proceeds of her and her Cargo get back I may remit 5 or $6000 per Brig. you will do the business, she will have small stock. the Commissions divide 3/5ths to Mr Miles 2/5ths to Mr Cabot which will be in addition to what I allow you. We have had some failures.

S S Newman was the last. Several in New York among them Johnson Halsey & Co by whom I lose 1000 or $1500.

I shall write you per Canton & via Bombay.

Yours truly

(Sgd)　H Lee

Bills on London 1% advance
　　Dollars　　　do
U S Bank Stock 133 for 100 paid in

[written across face of letter:]
In landing the Seltzer
Water you had better
have the Bottles taken
out and landed in
that way.

LETTER FROM HENRY LEE, BOSTON, AUG. 9, 1817, TO CHARLES D. MILES AND RICHARD CLARKE CABOT, CALCUTTA, IN REGARD TO SALTPETRE CONTRACT [1]

In tendering a share in this contract to James Williamson, Aug. 7, Henry Lee had offered to exempt Williamson from any responsibility for the "3½ cts lb penalty in case the Saltpetre does not arrive" and also to have the "Commission charged by my agents . . . to come out of the profits." The only charges to Williamson were to be "premium & interest." It was Henry Lee's hope since, as he wrote, "The trade between this Country and Bengal is now so poor," that "many now in it will decline further voyages, in which case it may improve, in mean time I believe I can make [interlineated: it] a tolerable business by attending closely to sales here, and having agents who know how to buy in Calcutta." He would have liked to have association in the saltpetre contract lead to more permanent and extensive connections.

"Messrs. Dupont & Co Powder makers" was the firm headed by the famous Eleuthère Irenée Du Pont (1771–1834), with works near Wilmington, Del.[2]

1: Jackson-Lee Papers, "Letter Book September 5th. 1816," Feb. 13, 1816–Oct. 30, 1817.
2. "Eleuthère Irenée Du Pont," *DAB*.

per Eliza Ann

Boston Augt 9. 1817

Messrs Charles D Miles   Duplicate p Nancy
  & R C Cabot
    Calcutta   Copy
      Dear Sirs
        I have made a contract through Messrs Perit & Cabot
of Philadelphia with Messrs Dupont & Co Powder makers for
Two hundred thousand pounds of Saltpetre to be delivered in
Eighteen Months from 11th July 1817 to be paid for in approved notes at 10 Months Credit from date of delivery at 12
cts for refined and 10 cts [interlineated: lb] for Crude, whichever I may deliver, impurities in the Crude not to exceed $7\frac{1}{2}\%$
and in refined, 4% all beyond that to be allowed in the price,
penalty for non: performance of contract $10,000 — I au-
thorise you to offer Mr James Williamson one half this contract, he agreeing to add a shipment of forty or fifty thousand
Sicca Rupees in Piece Goods and Indigo, to be invested by you,
allowing a commission on the purchase of $2\frac{1}{2}\%$. — 3/5ths of
which for C D Miles, 2/5ths for R C Cabot. I will on my part
agree to convey these Goods to United States, receiving, in lieu
of freight and Commission on the sale here, one half the profits
— No charge will be allowed but the Commissions paid you
and such expences as occur on sales here, the premium of Insurance he of course pays, as in case of loss of Goods. I get no
freight. I at same time agree to exempt him, from share in the
penalty, in case of non compliance of contract of Saltpetre —
These Goods will be shipped on the vessel which sails in Octo.
or November, a new coppered Brig which may be here insured
at $5\frac{1}{2}$ or 6% out and home —
This is more advantageous than the terms in other ships
where ½ profits is paid on Gruff & Piece Goods, without any
advantage of a contract, which secures a great profit on the
Salt-petre, besides having goods purchased by you who are acquainted with Calcutta market, instead of inexperienced men,
and sold here by me, who can devote all my time to making

most of the Goods — If Mr W refuses offer it to Mr Octerloney, and at any rate you may give him ¼ of the Saltpetre —
[erased: besides] shipping in same proportion piece Goods and
Indigo say 20 or 25,000 Rupees. I enclose a letter to Mr W on
the subject — open. You will not deliver it unless you think
there is a probability of doing something — If Mr W don't join
in this, he probably will not in anything, as I can never offer
him anything so advantageous. The profits of course must be
settled here, and he may make Remsen & Co joint consignees
to manage for him.

Let me know whether he will do anything. If he objects to
your Commission give it up. and I will allow 1½% on proceeds,
to be divided in same proportion as before stated. Whether
they engage with you or not, you will purchase 100 Tons of
Refined Saltpetre, if not more than 3/ p^r Maund higher than
Crude. If it is not to be had or the difference is greater, you
will buy the same quantity of the best Crude. You will have 3
Bags and crossed with Ropes, if you ship some of each have
different marks, and refined with Red paint, Crude [with —
stricken through] Black, that they may the more easily be kept
seperate — Any you may buy in large Chrystals put into
Boxes — If Mr W or Mr O agree to take a part commence buying the Piece Goods, agreeably to my Memorandums

Dont take Goods of W. unless as cheap as in Bazar, nor
allow him to overrule your opinion in any degree, nor allow
them to draw in Mr Newton or any one else — I want no con-
nexion with others. If Mr W. refuses [interlineated: this,]
you may decline doing anything, unless he should propose doing
something very advantageous. I think Octerlony will be glad
to join, and continue trading to this Country, and give me half
profits for managing. If not it is no matter, I will get on alone.
If you succeed my capital and credit will be increased, and
some of my friends will be glad to join us —

Don't communicate too freely in your correspondence, even
with Messrs Remsen & Co, as they write Newton, and there
are no secrets with Commission Merchants.

I shall probably charter a Vessel and send her out in March

next, or as soon as I hear of your arrival, but of this you shall hear more some months hence. I write Alexander & Co. Mr Palmer. and C & Mackillop by this conveyance.

Yours truly

(Sgd)   Henry Lee.

LETTER FROM HENRY LEE, BOSTON, AUG. 31, 1817, TO CHARLES D. MILES AND RICHARD C. CABOT, CALCUTTA, IN REGARD TO INVESTMENTS FOR OTHER BOSTON MERCHANTS [1]

That Samuel Cabot and the firm of J. & T. H. Perkins should leave to Henry Lee "the disposal of their £3000" indicates something of the reputation he had for knowledge of the Calcutta trade.

Despite the comment "Business dull," the references to the plentifulness of money and the rise in stocks indicate a welcome improvement in the business situation.

original per Canton

Messrs Charles D Miles &   Boston August 31st 1817.
   Richard C Cabot   Duplicate p Tartar
     Calcutta   for Bombay
Dear Sirs   Sail'd September 9th

I wrote you on the 25th Inst per Nancy copy of which is enclosed, she has not yet sailed — This goes by the Canton from New York — I also enclose a copy of a letter from Messrs S. Cabot & J & T H Perkins Jrs. and myself, relative to a credit of £3000, which S Williams will authorise you to negotiate on him, on our joint account. On this transaction you will charge a commission of 2½% to be divided equally between you. It is pretty certain I shall in conjunction with these gentlemen remit you a further sum, either direct or via London. If Messrs C & M should not be willing to purchase this Bill @ 2/6d or 2/7d from an unwillingness to be out of funds, they may be induced to do it, your Banians agreeing to advance the money for a year, or what would be the same thing, they would agree to take it and pay in 12 Mos. and then Kissen could ad-

---

1. Jackson-Lee Papers, "Letter Book September 5th. 1816," Feb. 13, 1816–Oct. 30, 1817.

vance money upon their paper — You can say that unless he is willing to facilitate your Business, he must not expect you will give or procure him business — You will find him willing enough to do this, as he runs no risk and can make as good an interest of his money in this way, as any other. From Mr Mackillop's letters I judge you will find him very friendly and willing to loan you money at fair rate, but you must negotiate my letter of credit even if you pay 12 per Cent, as without [interlineated: it] and the proceeds of the Bills, you will not have sufficient funds — Cotton Piece Goods are getting up especially coarse sorts of which there are very few in the country, say Meergungees and other low priced Mamoodies, Ordinary Mow Sannas, Ordinary Emerties, Gurrahs, coarse and middling Baftas &c &c Mamoodies under 60/ will do better perhaps than any other article would now sell at $3.75 or more, and will be worth $4 in the Spring.

Remember that a Cloth 38/40 x 1¾ 1⅞ will bring nearly as much as one 38/40 x 2⅛ that is a small Meergungee is worth nearly same as Chandilly —

Messrs S. C & J & T H Perkins have left to me the disposal of their £3000. I advise ½ in coarse Mamoodies, Gurrahs, Coarse Mow Sannas, ¼th in Choppas & Seersuckers and ¼ in ordinary and middling Indigo. These goods should be charged with a fair proportion of Godown rent, Sircars Wages &c &c have them ready for Mr Lee's Brig. I am more than ever convinced that Broken Indigo will be one of the most profitable articles you will send me even at 80/ or 90/ you may go higher if necessary, though I think you will get it for less. If you can at any time get from C & M or Alexander &Co a parcel of good broken and good middling, such as I bought at 105/. with an accommodation of a year to pay for it, you may venture upon 2 or 300 Mds at 90/ @ 110/ allowing 8 @ 12 pr Cent Interest. By looking in upon them every day or two, you may find a bargain. Ordinary Indigo will always be dull and low in London compared with the fine sorts and some of the planters had rather take any price in Calcutta, than risk a shipment, especially as they have suffered these last two or three years — Cultivate the acquaintance of all the houses particularly C & M and Alexander &Co but I rely chiefly on C &M. I don't think Mr Palmer will do any good for you. Ruggoo Ram has too much influence and his terms are always high, yet I have known them sell Indigoes extremely cheap for want of time to look at qualities. I have observed some letters forwarded to Mr Ingraham from Kip & Ingraham of N York. Don't have any concerns with him nor communicate on business Mr Miles must remember what occurred formerly in my endeavours to serve him — In making out your Invoices take for your measurement the smallest and largest dimensions, as this will be allowed at the Custom House, formerly we invoiced Cloths to their utmost dimensions now it should be otherwise perhaps the following would be about correct

Small Meergungees	36/8 x 1⅝ 1¾
Chandilly Mamoody	38/40 x 2
Long Gurrahs	34/36 x 2⅛ ¼
Middling do	33/35 x 2 1/16 ⅛
Chotah do	31/33 x 2. 2 1/16
Gaurypore Baftas	23/24 x 1⅞ or 15/16
Luckipore do	23/25 x 1 15/16 . 2.
Tandah Sannas	38/40 x 2 . 2 1/16
Alliabad Chodongery	39/41 x 1⅞ @ 1 15/16
Chandpore Cossas	38/40 x 1 15/16 2
Coarse Mow Sannas	20/2 x 1⅜
Bissuah Emerties or Guzeenahs	28/9 x 1⅞ . 2
Alliabad Emerty	28/30 x 2
Dacca Baftas	23/24 x 1⅞ . 2
Alliabad Sannas	39/40 x 2¼ . ⅜
Long Check	18/20 x 1⅞ . 2
small	11/12 x 1⅜ ½

[in margin: In next — say have Checks made of
various dimensions say 10/12 x 1⅜ ½ &c]

Blue Gurrahs & Blue Baftas as white of the same description — Baftas [of — stricken through] rather less, as they always diminish in dyeing — Seersuckers and goods paying 15%

duty as before — You must pack your short and long goods together in order that the Bales may measure as you invoice them, formerly we used to pack the short and narrow cloths in seperate Bales. In mine of 31st Ult°. I desired you to buy me 50 M'd Senna if under 10/. You may buy me 100 Md's if at 15/ or 150 Md's at 10/ of Country, if Arabian can't be had, and pack it as you buy, they will not pay for the garbled in proportion. You may also buy 100 Md's Shellac of middling quality @ 15/. or half that quantity at 18/. — These articles you will keep [interlineated: for] Mr Lee's Brig. — I shall ship by her 10000, perhaps 20,000 feet Mahogany in Boards & Logs, some Salmon, perhaps 100 doz Seltzer Water. No wine or Brandy or indeed anything else —

Say to Messrs C & M that Cotton keeps up, and will do so for some months to come, afterwards it must depend upon the Crops, and Importations into England from India — Write me by every conveyance. I forwarded some letters for R. C. C. by the Nancy & now enclose one for Mr. Miles. Six per Cents 105 and rising!! U S Bank Stock 145 — Money rather plenty — Business dull — Ship my goods *to this place,* in preference to any other — I shall request Messrs Remsen &Co to forward you some of their Boston Newspapers. If the Gentoo does not get coffee at Batavia, she proceeds to Calcutta and Mr Blanchard may do his business with Kissen in which case give him your assistance if he wants any. I am told the Nancy has no Bills, but I dare say Mr Tingley will draw if he finds Exchange will sell @ 2/7ᵈ. I advise you by all means to avoid any intercourse with him which may lead to a knowledge of your views

No arrivals since the Sachem

> Yours truly
> (Sgd) H Lee

LETTER FROM HENRY LEE, BOSTON, SEPT. 1, 1817, TO WILLIAM
G. GILBERT, NEW YORK, ON CLOCKS [1]

This letter suggests how remote from his ordinary business were
some of the activities in which a merchant of that day might find
himself involved. "Mr Willard" was undoubtedly Simon Willard
(1753–1848), the famous clockmaker of Roxbury.[2] William G. Gilbert was probably a kinsman, perhaps an uncle, of William Lewis
Gilbert (1809–90), well-known clock manufacturer of his day.[3] "Mr
Steel" was apparently an employee or associate of some kind of
Simon Willard. Henry Lee had evidently acted as Gilbert's representative in arranging for the manufacture of the clock.

Boston September 1. 1817

Mr Wm. G Gilbert
    New York
        Dear Sir
            Mr Willard has finished the Clock and calls for his
money — I shall pay him part in advance and the remainder
when you remit the money. There is due for the Clock $650 —
                        for fixing the Bell about   50
                                                        ——
                                                        700
            Premium of Insurance on $1700 & policy   88.50
                                                        ——
                                                       788.50
and some small charges which I will render you an account of
hereafter. I would thank you to remit a draft on U S Bank or in
any other way you please $800 — Mr W has received yours of
23d. Mr Steel is not inclined to adventure on his own account
any clocks as he cannot afford to take the risk of your market —
All he wants is his passage and expences paid out and home, his
board while in Washington, and wages while employed in putting up the clock, he is willing to go for $100 and his pay &

---

1. Jackson-Lee Papers, "Letter Book from Jany. 17th. 1817 to October 27. 1818."

2. Willard, John Ware, *A History of Simon Willard, Inventor and
Clockmaker* (Boston, 1911).

3. "William Lewis Gilbert," *DAB*.

expences while setting up the clock — of this sum Mr Willard will pay half if you are willing to buy of him 18 Clock's, 12 large & 6 small, this will be better for you than sending 3 dozen, as it is easier to sell a small than a large number. Mr W's object in this is to have Clock put up properly so that you may be satisfied with his work and reccommend him in your quarter, and I really think considering Mr Steels valuable services which he will lose for some months that his proposition is a liberal one — Mr Steel wishes your answer immediately — I have seen the Clock and as far as I can judge, the work appears to have been neatly and faithfully executed — It will be packed with care, but I should wish you might get Mr S to go on as you might lose your whole trouble and expence for want of a workman to fix it for you — You will see by the papers that great quantities of East India Cotton have arrived in England — In the year 1818 there will be double the quantity say 150,000 Bales, which must bring [bring — stricken through] down the Upland in price — Let me know what the prospect is in Georgia & Carolina for crop of Upland —

Yours truly
(Sgd) H Lee

According to Mr W's proposal you will have $50 to pay Mr S. and his expences and wages while at work in Washington —

H L —

LETTER FROM HENRY LEE, BOSTON, SEPT. 9, 1817, TO A. E. BELKNAP, MARSEILLES, ON THE POSSIBILITIES FOR TRADE BETWEEN MARSEILLES AND CALCUTTA [1]

Henry Lee's idea evidently was to have a French vessel plying between Calcutta and Marseilles, carrying freight for American merchants, such as himself, and commanded or at least largely manned, if possible, by Americans.

1. Jackson-Lee Papers, "Letter Book from Jan. 17th. 1817 to October 27. 1818."

Boston Septr 9. 1817

Mr A E Belknap
   Marseilles
     Dear Sir

     I think it may be useful in the business you contemplate doing between Marseilles & Calcutta, to obtain the most accurate information you can as to the value of the following articles — the produce of East Indies —

Bengal Cotton its usual value, and its value compared with Georgia Upland *Good Benares Sugar,* and its value compared with Havana Brown, & whether it is used in France, or sent to other countries — If not used in France, there will be no advantage in importing under the French Flag, as all bottoms pay alike in entrepot —

Sugar like the sample handed you — Will this be admitted at the same duty as Benares or common India Sugar,

Value of India Saltpetre, refined & crude, and the difference [interlineated: in] duty between what is imported in French, & foreign bottoms — The usual demand for the article

Ginger and Tumerick — value and demand for each —

Bengal Indigoes, the qualities & sorts most suitable for your market —

Block Tin & Tuetenague —

Demand for Switzerland & Genoa &c &c, for Bengal piece Goods — say of the following,

Beerboom Gurrahs	36 x 2¼	Cubits of ½ yard English
Alliabad Mamoody	40 x 2	"
Tanda Sannas	40 x 2⅛	
Luckipore Baftas	25 x 2	
Alliabad Emerties	30 x 2	
Blue Gurrahs	36 x 2¼	

the prices and charges they would be subjected — Ascertain the number of ships gone, and going from various ports in France for Bengal — and the amount of their Capitals — Some of the French ships which have been sent to Calcutta may have returned — It will be satisfactory to see actual sales of what they brought home, to guide us in our investments —

Ascertain if your friends can open a credit on London for 3 or £4000, for Mr Oliver, to be drawn for in Calcutta, @ 6 Mos. sight — If you think you can send out a ship, You had better write Mr. Oliver or myself immediately on your arrival by way of Havre in triplicate letters, that we may make some preparation against your arrival — I have furnished you with two pieces of Indigo, to aid in your enquiries about that article — No 1. is very fine, No 2, middling — If you engage a ship, and come out with her, it ought to be understood by the owners, that the freighters here, will not allow her to stop on the way out or home, and she ought to have a steady Captain, only two officers, no Monks, or military men —

If your laws will admit of it, it would be well to have an American master, or if that is not allowed, then American Mates and portion of the seamen It would reduce the rate of Insurance, and shorten the voyage three or four months — Perhaps Government on a representation, might grant something in your favour on this score —

Is there any trade with the Barbary powers, and would a quantity of Bengal Goods sell for that market?

The less said upon the subject the better, except to such as will engage in it with you — Let me know if any ships have lately gone from Marseilles to Calcutta, and the rate of freight per Ton — Perhaps I may order some Sugar shipped to your house, if there is time and the rate low — Write us immediately on your arrival —

Yours truly
(Sgd)   H Lee —

LETTER FROM HENRY LEE, BOSTON, SEPT. 23, 1817, TO PETER REMSEN & CO., NEW YORK, CHIEFLY IN REGARD TO SELLING DOMESTIC COTTONS [1]

The letter below is of particular interest for the information it gives concerning the cottons manufactured at the Waltham factory,

---

1. Jackson-Lee Papers, "Letter Book from Jany. 17th. 1817 to October 27. 1818."

their dimensions, price, and method of disposal. It also contains a good deal of information on general business, particularly the trade with India. On Nov. 3, 1817, writing to James Schott & Co., Philadelphia, apropos of domestic vs. India piece goods, Henry Lee remarked: "The Manufacturers in New York State are getting up a Petition to have the importation of Bengal Cotton Goods prohibited — They might spare themselves this trouble, for they are effectually prohibited by the present duty — . . . By the Invoice 100 cts is asked [per rupee], our wholesale price as you know, being generally higher, than the retail." This is a curious reversal of the usual relationship; perhaps the purchasers of goods at wholesale had to be given such long credit at this time that a price higher than retail was necessarily charged.

Lee had been intending to buy quicksilver, as well as nutmegs, for shipping to India, but on Oct. 7 he wrote to Perit & Cabot, Philadelphia, that he no longer wished quicksilver but would "take it out to India for a Comm°. of 5%, & charge no freight, or free of any charge, and pay what it may yield on the return of the Brig, say 10 Months hence." The brig to which he referred, the *Lascar,* belonged to his brother Joseph Lee, Jr., and cleared for Calcutta, under the command of Smith Knowles, Oct. 29.[2] On Nov. 29, Henry Lee offered, in a letter to Samuel Cabot, Jr., Philadelphia, to sell "20,000 lb [quicksilver] in the Lascar, . . . at 57 cts short, and give the buyer 4 Mo^s^. Credit, and charge freight only $5 per Ton, they to pay 2½% Comm°. — I will pay over the proceeds to the order of the buyer."

Boston 23^d^ Septr. 1817

Messrs Peter Remsen &Co

New York

Dear Sirs,

I have yours of 17th & 19th — J Lee's Brig will sail between the 15th October & 1st Nov^r^., certainly by the latter, and be there long before the Canton even should she go direct. Insurance can be effected at 2¾ @ 3% on Dollars — I think I can loan on Interest any Dollars you may send on for a remittance to be delivered again, 25 Octr.. I find the Perkins' and some others who want, are nearly supplied, this, together with

2. *Columbian Centinel,* Nov. 1, 1817.

the great influx of Specie may prevent their rising beyond 1½ or 2%.

I shew the Catalogue to Mr Wigglesworth — Goods will not rise much, because they are now dearer than Domestick's — Some exportations of New Tariff Goods are going on, and some sales have been made at saving prices, but they are very dull — fortunately most of our Ships will have Cotton. I am afraid my limits (16/ per Maund) are too low for Miles to buy, but I hope he will be able to sell the ship, and send home my Stock in Indigo and Silks — I hold on my adventure per Suffolk — I fear Silks will be high in China, but she will have the best chance there, and here — We expect her last of Febry. — Our friends have about $35,000 or $40,000 cost, in Silks and Nankins —

Mr Jackson has agreed to let me have 30 Bales, say 5 per week at 26 cts Cash, their lowest price has been 27 cts, 90 days, and they sell in NYork 28 cts, short credit, through V & Givan — Let me know by return mail whether you accept — If you have any doubt whether they will answer, you may put down ½ to my account — You will not mention this affair — I must pay Cash, and can draw on you, if you wish at 90 days for ½, which I can discount at U S Bank here — I don't want however any concern if you are not afraid to venture the whole. I wish you to order me to buy, my wish is to get you the agency, this may lead to it, if not now, hereafter —

There will be no Commission to pay on this transaction, as I have no trouble or responsibility — I am very desirous you should take the 30 Bales, you will readily sell them at 28¢, or higher, if you give long time. a Bale contains 25 pieces, say $200 —

I have a letter from S Williams to 11th Aug — Flour 44/ @ 48/ & falling. 6 per cents 10 — Almost every article except Corn improving —

I have seen an intelligent man (Sturgis) of house of Bryant & Sturgis who came out in last ship, he thinks prices on the continent, would not keep pace with the rise in London, and that many articles will fall again. 6th Augt Java Coffee had not advanced beyond 11½ Stivers, in Holland — The Courier has but few goods £300 freight, The importations will pay well. Bills on London 3% advance —

I enclose a letter [interlineated: open] for Mr Gilbert, I wish either you or Mr Lawrence would write him, if he has gone South that his Bill will be duly honoured, he himself pointed out that mode of payment. I like the man and reccommended him to Mr J. Forward the letter by mail if he has gone from New York. Let me know if you think he will be a good agent for buying Cotton —

I have yours of 20th. with sales crapes, I think they ought to have made an allowance in Duties for damage. I have not had a line from C & M since the letter you forwarded me, nor any from Mr Williamson, they are so busy that we shall not hear from them often — I have had only one letter from Alexander, My Banians write me that C & M were looking out for 100 Mds Indigo, which I had ordered, It will do well because none has come. I ordered Miles to buy 200 Mds positively, he will have 200 more for F & Geo. Lee, we must do well with this article — D. R. has added a note to yours of 20th. to say he could buy Roll Brimstone @ $3. I wish you to buy me 300 Boxes at that, and get it sent round as cheap as you can. I can send it free of freight, and it will do well, as it is only the cost in Italy. That per Oscar sold at $6 pr Cwt. and but little has since gone. Buy at once as others are in search of the article. I should be glad to get 20,000 lb steel at 4½ cts short price. Bills are as with you — If any one will agree to give 142 for U S B'k shares, to be delivered in 12 Mos. I think there are persons here who would furnish 1000 shares or more, But few Choppas in the last ships — Bandannas are plenty enough but they hold good ones @ 525 to 5.50 No Company in the Country — I would give $1.25 lb short price for 2000 lb Nutmegs for shipping to India — There are about 8000 lb on the way from London to your place

Yours truly

(Sgd) H Lee

LETTER FROM HENRY LEE, BOSTON, SEPT. 23, 1817, TO WILLIAM G. GILBERT, NEW YORK, ORDERING COTTON [1]

The letter below gives an idea of the extent of the textile manufacturing at Waltham, and the methods of obtaining raw material.

On Oct. 11, writing to Felix G. Gibson & Co., Augusta, Ga., apparently the "house in Augusta" to which Mr. Gilbert had referred, Henry Lee ordered an additional 150 bales @ 25 cents per lb. On Oct. 31, Lee, on Jackson's order, raised the price limit to 26 cents and on Nov. 25 to 27 cents, or 100 bales @ 28 cents. Even then Lee feared that the cotton could not be obtained within Jackson's limits and in a letter of Dec. 6 to W. G. Gilbert, Washington, Ga., remarked jocosely: "If Cotton keeps up, I expect that even your Slaves will be clothed in Silks — We must be content with exporting your produce, & supplying your luxuries." On Jan. 6, 1818, Lee wrote to Samuel Williams, London: "Our Cotton Manufacturers in this quarter have actually been obliged to buy at Liverpool prices, say 38 cts lb." However, to Peter Remsen & Co., Jan. 19, 1818, Henry Lee wrote: "I will venture to hazard a conjecture there will yet be more lost than gained by it [cotton]."

Boston Septr 23d. 1817

Mr William G Gilbert

Dear Sir,

I have yours of 12th, Mr Willard will attend to your order for potatoes &c &c, and Mr Steel will see, that the Clocks are shipped under his direction here, and at Savannah, he will be away about 10th Octr., which he thinks is soon enough to be [away — stricken through] safe from your bad climate — I will draw for the Insurance on the Clocks &c — I will not fail to mention your nephew, to any who may inquire for a Land agent in your quarter, but there are no persons in this place who are likely to be interested — You mentioned to me when here, that you had a house in Augusta which would like to purchase Cotton on Commission, and that for the payment you would draw on New York — Mr Jackson a friend of mine, & a

1. Jackson-Lee Papers, "Letter Book from Jany. 17th. 1817 to October 27. 1818."

large proprietor in the Waltham Factory, where your Cloths
were made, has directed me to request a purchase of fifty Bales
Upland, of the new Crop, the best you can find — You will ship
it from Savannah to this post consigned to Patrick T Jackson
send a B/L and Invoice of the same to him, and another per
Mail to me — I understand your Commission to be 2½% for
the whole transaction, purchasing, shipping, and drawing, which
is indeed what is paid to the Charleston & Savannah houses —
for your reimbursement you will draw at 30 days sight, or
shorter if neccessary on Peter Remsen &Co New York — Mr. J
consumes about 500 Bales a year, and in course of 18 Mo. will
want three times that quantity, he has hitherto procured it from
New Orleans & Savannah, but at my suggestion has sent you
this commission — should it be executed to his satisfaction, it
may lead to important business — I should be glad to hear
from you on this subject, and as to quality and extent of the
Crop —

   We are much interested as importers of the article from
India, from whence 15,000 Bales are expected in course of
few months, and much more next year — about 10,000 have
been already imported, and afforded a good profit. It all goes to
Europe — the article keeps up in England, on 12 th August
Georgia was higher than it had been for a year or more —

Yours truly

(Sgd)   Henry Lee —

LETTER FROM HENRY LEE, BOSTON, OCT. 9, 1817, TO WIDOW
MAURICE ROBERTS & CO., CADIZ, ON THE POSSIBILITIES FOR
TRADE BETWEEN CADIZ AND CALCUTTA [1]

   Henry Lee's intentions in regard to a trade between Spain and
India are clearly developed below. On the following day he wrote
an almost identical letter to Bloomfield & Tunis, Cadiz.

   1. Jackson-Lee Papers, "Letter Book from Jany. 17th. 1817 to October 27. 1818."

Boston October 9. 1817
[written across face of letter]
Widow Maurice Roberts &Co Original via Gibralter
Duplicate " New York
Cadiz   Triplicate per Brig Augusta
Gentlemen

Mr Timothy Williams of this place having mentioned
your respectable house, as [from one — stricken through interlineated: one from] whom, I could obtain the most accurate
information, I take the liberty to make the following enquiries,
with the request that you would reply to them, as soon as convenient in Triplicate letters —

Is it practicable to obtain from the King's Warehouses, or the
merchants 100 Tons Copper & 25 Tons Quicksilver (in Iron
Bottles) and if so, at what prices?

What is the quality of the Copper, Is it Mexican or Peruvian,
are the Pigs square or flat and round, and is there any difference between them in price?

What are the charges on each including your commission for
buying & negociating the Bills on London, if such should be the
mode of payment?

Is there any duty. If so, could not it be avoided by purchasing the articles from the Kings Warehouses?

What may be the probable value of Bills on London at 60
days, and Doubloons, say 6 Months hence?

If I should wish to make a purchase of the above articles
what mode of payment should you reccommend?

Are there any articles from this country, which might be bartered to advantage in Exchange for Copper, and Quicksilver? —

If an American Ship bound to Calcutta, should call at Cadiz,
could you secure a freight of Copper to Calcutta, and if so, at
what rate?

Would any of your merchants take up 2 or 300 Tons in an
American Vessel going to Calcutta from Cadiz, say for Piece
Goods, I agreeing to deliver them there and if so, what freight
would they allow? Your flag is now interrupted by the Patriots,
and may continue to be for some time to come —

Is the exportation of Dollars allowed free of Duty?

Is there any considerable quantity of lead to be procured in Cadiz & at what price?

Praying your excuse for the trouble I am giving you —

I am respectfully

Your Obt Servt

(Signed)   Henry Lee

LETTER FROM HENRY LEE, BOSTON, OCT. 12, 1817, TO SAMUEL WILLIAMS, LONDON, ON THE STATE OF THE CALCUTTA TRADE [1]

On Aug. 26, 1817, Henry Lee wrote to James Schott & Co., Philadelphia: "I am about ordering an Investment of some funds I have in Calcutta — , and I rely much upon your opinion as to the value of Calcutta goods — I dont think the trade will answer but it may do to import fine goods. which in case their not being wanted for home use may be exported." In a letter of Oct. 6 to the same firm Lee wrote in terms similar to those below: "Calcutta Goods are without any demand whatever, while the Domestics sell as fast as they are received and at 15% higher than last year, which is an evidence that India Cottons are done with, at least, in this quarter — . . . Our friend Archer has been buying all the Blue Gurrahs he could find in this market, within certain limits, I can't imagine what he will do with them, *unless he means to go into the Slave trade*, which I don't think would suit him — There is no sale for them in the Havana, and quantity on hand very great — " The lack of demand for piece goods in Havana was emphasized by a letter to Miralla & Co., Nov. 3, ordering that firm to "Accept any prices which will give the cost and duty." That even exportation was not a safe solution was indicated in a letter of Nov. 11 to Welles, Williams & Greene, Havre: "Cotton, Coffee & Sugars, there is not an article in your Price Current which would do from hence — " piece goods were not even considered.

1. Jackson-Lee Papers, "Letter Book from Jany. 17th. 1817 to October 27. 1818."

Samuel Williams Esqr   Boston Octr 12th 1817
   London   [written across face of letter]
   Dear Sir   Orig^l. via New York.

    The first of the within Bills have been forwarded via
New York — I have yours of 12th & 23^d August, with Price
Currents down to the 26th of that month — I am glad to find
Cotton keeps up — The Crop of Upland is very fair, but will
open at high price 26 or 27 cts, unless we should have accounts
of a fall in England — Large orders have gone on for buying
at 25 to 28¢. for Georgia, and something higher for New Orleans — We are expecting 8 or 10 Cargoes from Bombay and
Calcutta, which must do very well — In May the price in Calcutta was 17/ to 18/ M'd say 12 to 13¢ lb, on board — I imagine it will be higher the coming year, an immense number of
ships have gone, and are going for it, to all parts of India, 15
are now actually fitting, out in Salem for beyond the Cape, and
12 here, they go for Coffee, Pepper, & Cotton, with from 40 to
80,000 Dollars capital — We shall have upwards 40 ships from
China in all 1818, the prospect for silks & Nankins very good,
the early sales of green teas will also be favourable — We have
given up the Calcutta trade except for raw cotton, Manufactures will not do — The Duty on coarse Cloths under new
Tariff is from 60 to 70%, and they are lower than they were
12 Mo^s. ago the Stock on hand being very large — The Domestics now undersell them and [are] extending in all directions —
They are doing well at Waltham, now make 8,000 Yards a week
& will soon get to 20,000, which they sell as fast as they can
pack it, at 27 cts [@ — stricken through] y'd, and of a quality
which cannot be had in Manchester, under 11^d to 12^d a yard —
    The importations of British Goods have done well, and next
season we shall require very large quantities, this branch of
Trade has recovered from the effects of the excessive overtrading of last Year, and we begin to want new supplies of almost every article —
    Stocks have not varied for some time past — Exchange
steady at from 2 @ 2½% advance here, and about same at the

South — Flour is yet at $9 at the South, some are of opinion it will go down to $6 & others not below $8 to 9.

Yours truly

Henry Lee —

LETTER FROM HENRY LEE, BOSTON, OCT. 21, 1817, TO HENRY ALEXANDER, CALCUTTA, ON THE INTERNATIONAL, COMMERCIAL, AND INDUSTRIAL SITUATION [1]

At the time of this letter, business seems to have been well on its way to recovery from the sad state into which it had been thrown at the end of the Napoleonic Wars. Henry Lee ascribed the upturn largely to good crops and continued prospects for peace, which had increased confidence and consuming power. Another hopeful sign for commerce was the progress of the movement for independence in Spanish America, though Henry Lee was in constant fear that this would be checked by British intervention in favor of the royalists. Mexico, at this time, was in the throes of the desultory guerrilla warfare into which the revolutionary movement had disintegrated after the execution of Morelos in 1815; in Chile, on the other hand, José de San Martin had, on Feb. 12, 1817, defeated the royalists at Chacabuco and made his associate Bernardo O'Higgins supreme director.

In a letter to Cruttenden & Mackillop, Mar. 7, 1817, Lee gave two reasons why the "country Ships are driven out of the trade," namely, "they are too expensive to be employed in any trade, — besides Lascars, and high pay to European officers, make them sail at a dearer rate than British manned Ships."

Henry Lee's comments on the importation of British cottons into India and the necessity for restricting the production of indigo indicate his keen economic sense.

By the same vessel, Henry Lee dispatched a number of letters of a similar tenor to various Calcutta merchants; these, while they presented in the main the same information, occasionally included comments worthy of specific note. In a letter of Oct. 26 to John Palmer, referring to certain "observations upon the irregular way in which our Merchants carry on their business," Henry Lee commented:

1. Jackson-Lee Papers, "Letter Book September 5th. 1816," Feb. 13, 1816–Oct. 30, 1817.

CALCUTTA SCENE, 1792

"It has arisen in part I conceive from the nature of our Commerce during the War in Europe — the temptations to wander from one branch of trade to another, and to excessive speculation's were too great to be resisted — and tho' less safe and perhaps less profitable than a more steady course was more interesting to the enterprising tempers of our People. — Peace has made them more prudent — Those who are now engaged in extensive foreign concerns, are for the most part rich, and able without inconvenience to bear heavy losses. — This Year, as you will have heard from your London friends, will prove much more favorable to the trading World than any one could have foreseen 12 M^{os}. ago."

Turning to another cause for the recent unfortunate condition in the East India trade, Henry Lee wrote: "As to piece goods we have done with them as an article of consumption. It is found they will not bear the new duties, which amount upon coarse cloth's (the only one's we require) to 65 @ 80% — There is no prospect of a diminution — the manufacturing interest is powerful and becoming more so and they are now thriving — I happen to be nearly connected with some of the Proprietors of the largest in United States, and know that their goods can be afforded cheaper than Bengal, even at the former duties on them —I do not however believe that it is the true policy for this country to force Manufactures upon it — with such high duties — but the Gov^t. are pledged. and they are supported by that Class of People. who are the greatest Sufferers." It will be remembered that Henry Lee's brother-in-law Patrick Tracy Jackson was one of the principals in the textile mill at Waltham which is said to have been "probably the first one in the world. that combined all the operations necessary for converting the raw cotton into finished cloth;" while Francis Cabot Lowell, P. T. Jackson's associate and Mrs. Henry Lee's brother-in-law, "had been mainly instrumental in procuring from Congress . . . the establishment of the minimum duty on cotton cloth." [2] It would doubtless have been interesting to hear the discussions on free trade vs. protection which must have raged between Henry Lee and P. T. Jackson; we are, however, assured by a family historian that F. C. Lowell and P. T. Jackson "never advocated permanent high duties." [3]

2. Hunt, *op. cit.*, vol. i, pp. 562–564.
3. Morse, F. R., *op. cit.*, p. 10.

Boston October 21. 1817.

Henry Alexander Esqr   Duplicate per Independence
     Calcutta   [written across face of letter]:
     My Dear Sir (Copy)   Original pr Lascar

By the Bengal I received your's of the 27th.–30th.
March and 8th. April acknowledging the receipt of dollars and
Quicksilver per Sachem & Savary and SaRp's 10000 from
Messrs. Tulloh &Co. — If any thing was. due on the arrival of
Mr. Miles he had orders to pay you — I. am glad that you are
not dissatisfied with my remitting Merchandize altho as it turns
out, it would have been for. my interest to have sent all in dollars. — We cannot stand the competition now that your
freights are so low. — and our duties so much increased —
That opening the trade I always tho't a *bad measure.* — It
would have been better for us had John Company prevail'd —
You acted judiciously in selling the Quicksilver, as immense
shipments had been made to various parts of Asia from England and this country which must have reduced the price still
lower — You will have heard long before this reaches of the
great and favorable change in England in almost every article
of East and West India produce. As the rise has in every instance commenced in London. We apprehended that it might in
part have been the [interlineated: mere] effect of speculation
— but we find that a corresponding increase of prices /tho' not
to the extent which might have been expected/ has taken place
on the Continent and that at our last dates in September they
were still on the advance — It is probable that the staple
articles will be maintain'd, and some of them go higher — the
abundant harvest all over Europe, and the prospect of continued
peace has given confidence to trading men. and increas'd the
means of the consumer's — In no quarter has this improv'd
state of commerce been more sensibly felt than in G Britain
especially among the manufacturing interests — There was a
time when those who were disposed to entertain the most cheerful views, felt desponding, but such are the advantages which
your Nation has over the rest of Europe, in enterprize, skill,

capital and commercial policy, that they will always maintain their ascendency in peace and in War. — A long continued peace may raise up rivals in some of your manufactures — at least some who are now dependant on Great Britain may supply themselves, but there is an inexhaustible source of employment for your Capital and labor, in the increasing wants of this Country — We have our own Domestic manufactures and they are increasing very fast. but there are many articles we shall always want and always have from England . . . for instance Woolens — last year there were exported from [England — stricken through] Great Britain about £8,300000 of this prodigious sum — 3,500000 £ came to this Country — 20 Years. hence we shall require double the amount. — South America too, if You do not interfere and reestablish the old system of exclusion will be a great and increasing market. — The revolution by opening the trade, has taught them the comforts of cheap clothing &c. and they will never willingly forego them — I am afraid your Offices have sustain'd heavy losses by the capture of Spanish and Porteguese Ships — the Patriot Privateers respect no flag but the British & American — they are very numerous and active — They are manned cheifly by English and American Seamen of the most desperate characters — By our latest accounts it appears — the Royalists are gaining in Mexico and the Revolutionists in Chili, and other parts, and tho' it will be a long time before they can establish a Government of their own it is quite improbable they should ever be subjugated by Spain, unless Great Britain should take part against them, which is I conceive too much opposed to every principle of policy and justice ever to happen — This Government whatever the London Editors may say, have taken no part in the contest, tho there is no doubt their wishes are with the South American's — I suppose you are sufficiently interested in Cotton, to wish for some account of it in this market — the old Crop is gone — the new begins to come in, but not in great quantities till Decr. It is conjectured there may be 50,000 Bales more than last year — but the price will open higher than for 15 years say 28 cts. (15^d St^g.) for Upland. — I presume there is not an Individual who 12 M^os. ago anticipated so high aprice — there must have been 50 or 60,000 Bales more India Cotton than was ever before sent to Europe, and about the usual quantity from this quarter — the Brazils, & West Indies, something less than year preceeding — but the consumption has increas'd much beyond the production, and will probably go on increasing — I presume much ofthe Cotton usually sent to China from Bengal will go to Europe. and that in all 1818 — there will be something like 150,000 Bales reach Europe — from all parts of India — if such should be the case, and would infer either a further increased consumption or afall in the article — I pretend not tohave any opinion having hitherto been so wholly mistaken in my predictions of a fall — You may suppose that our Merchants believe it will keep up. or they would not send so many Ships for it to Bombay and Calcutta. — More than 40 Ships are now beyond the Cape for it, and the Coffee and [pepper — stricken through interlineated: Pepper] Ships which fail to get those articles, will proceed to India for Cotton — The Stock on hand in Europe is so small that it must at any rate keep up for 6 M^os. to come. — I am sorry to see freights so low in Calcutta. — The Country Ships must be driven out of the trade, if those from the Outports can carry even at 10 or 12 £ and we are told they can do it for £8. — This however I could very well support, but I am afraid We shall also be distanc'd in the race. — I should be glad to know what is aliving freight for the Liverpool Ships — say Cotton & Sugar. — Of Coffee and Sugar, we have a very moderate Stock on hand. — these Articles now go direct from the Islands to Europe. — nothing has been made upon Bengal. they are too high compared with the West India, at the prices they have been selling in Europe the last 18 M^os. 9/ w^d be quite enough to pay for the Best Benares — Pepper has done well, because we get it with Spanish Dollars, and carry [interlineated: it] direct from Sumatra to Europe — Our Java Ships have also done well, and ships enough have gone to take away the whole crop, and they will pay as high as $12 p^r Picul rather than come away without

Cargoes — You should have retained that Island — conquer Sumatra, China &c &c, tax us with more duties in Bengal, and then, you will have a clear field for your free traders — We have sent an unusual amount of Specie to China a large portion of which will be invested in Silk Goods which are cheaper there than in France and Italy, owing to the high price of Raw Silk in those countries The Crops have been bad for two or three years, and the consumption has increased, so that Sewing Silks which 6 or 7 years ago used to cost $3 to 3½ in Italy now come charged $5.50 — The article of Piece Goods which made [interlineated: up] so important a branch of our trade with you will no longer be imported except in small quantities for exportation to Europe, where they are very low, as you will notice by London Sales, the fact is, the improvements in machinery have enabled the British to undersell them, and you will see every year the importations of fine Cotton Goods [from — stricken through interlineated: into] India *from England* increase, and in time become a large branch of trade — I was convinced while in Calcutta, that in all the fine sorts of Cotton Cloths, and coarser kinds Muslins such as are made in Scotland, British Manufactures would undersell the India, and in time get into use among the natives. In the coarse Cloths such as we used to take, we now find, that with the aid of heavy duties our domestic goods undersell them, and are much better liked by the consumers.

On the last Cargo of Cotton Goods entered at this port from Calcutta, the duty averaged 69%. It was formerly 18% — We have yet on hand of the old stock of Piece Goods, more than half of all which have been imported since the Peace. Of Indigo but little has come, the goods did very well, ordinary will not sell at any rate, when there is any other [at — stricken through interlineated: in] market, but one time with another, prices in London are higher than here, because the market there is controled by 5 or 6 Houses who understand very well, as the agents in Calcutta do too, how to keep up prices. I am sorry to hear Mr Fullerton's admirable plan for reducing the production did not succed — It appears to me that 60 or 70,000 Maunds are sufficient for the use of the whole world, and that it would produce as much as 100,000 to the planters, but it is probable a continued peace may increase the demand, and that 90 or 100000 may be wanted. — The consumption in this country is moderate, and we get a good deal from South America. Saltpetre is lower than in London — Ginger, Tumerick & Drugs about the same — We have had a very fine harvest of Corn & in fact of every thing — Rice is high — I think the shipments made from Bengal this year will do well, the reduced rate of freights bears most essentially on that article, and will bring it more into use than formerly — Every thing is tranquil in France, they have had good Corn harvest but an indifferent Vintage — Among commercial Men we have had a trying year in this country, but have got through with fewer failures than was expected — Money is plenty and our Stocks higher than were ever known to be. Six per Cents payable in 1825. 107. United States Bank Stock 150 for 100 paid in. Bills on London 2% advance. Dollars 2½% advance, we have exported an immense amount beyond the Cape, and shall continue to do so, while there is a prospect of making any thing. I have now said everything, and much more than will interest you on business. I should have written oftener than I have done, had I supposed I could afford you [interlineated: any] useful information, or that my letters would not have come in upon you at some of those busy moments when you were burried in chits, and surrounded with Banians, Captains, Subalterns, civil servants & sircars. It would require at such a time, even more than your politeness, not to feel that so long a letter as this, is too great an intrusion upon your time. I have been very much gratified with the expressions of friendship in your interesting letters, and with the kind remembrance of Mr Fullarton and the other members of the house, to all of whom I beg in return to be presented to their recollection —

If it comes in your way to promote in any way the views of Messrs Miles &Cabot you will confer a favor on me in so doing —

Should there be any thing new, before the departure of the
Lascar. I will write again. I am

With great regard

Your faithful Servant

(Signed)   Henry Lee

LETTER FROM HENRY LEE, BOSTON, OCT. 23, 1817, TO CHARLES
D. MILES AND RICHARD CLARKE CABOT, CALCUTTA, WITH IN-
FORMATION AND INSTRUCTIONS [1]

The brig referred to in this letter, and by which it went, was the
Lascar, "owned by Mess[rs]. William Oliver & Jos. Lee Jr." Henry Lee
had "engaged to fill" all the vessel on the return voyage except 120
tons. For the purchase of the return cargo he had sent to Calcutta in
the *Lascar* merchandise, quicksilver, and mahogany, invoiced at over
$11,000, and $5,700 in Spanish dollars, and had ordered remittances
to be made from London to the amount of 57,000 sicca rupees. He
hoped that he might be able to obtain credits in Calcutta which
would bring his investment up to 120,000 rupees, which he wished
invested in saltpetre, broken indigo, and coarse cotton cloths.[2]

John Lowell, Jr., one of the young men who went out on the
Lascar "to learn Seamanship," was born in 1799, the son of Francis
Cabot Lowell and Hannah Jackson, a sister of P. T. Jackson and Mrs.
Henry Lee; the other, John Adams Gardner, was the son of John
Gardner and Sarah Jackson, also a sister of Mrs. F. C. Lowell and
Mrs. Henry Lee.[3]

[written across face of letter:]
Original p[r] Lascar
Duplicate pr Independence /Copy)

Mess[rs]. C D Miles & R C Cabot   Boston Oct[r] 23[d]. 1817.

Calcutta, Dear Sir's   As the Lascar is now almost ready
I will begin to write and note down all that is going on, which I

1. Jackson-Lee Papers, "Letter Book September 5th. 1816," Feb. 13,
1816–Oct. 30, 1817.

2. *Ibid.,* Henry Lee, Boston, Oct. 30, 1817, to Cruttenden & Mackillop,
Calcutta; *ibid.,* Henry Lee, Boston, Oct. 29, 30, 1817, to C. D. Miles &
R. C. Cabot, Calcutta.

3. Morse, F. R., *op. cit.,* p. xiii.

think may be interesting in y^r. business — It has been my intention to give some account of all the voyages beyond the Cape which I tho't might end in India, particularly in Calcutta, because they effect your proceedings there — At foot ofthis you have alist of clearances for some weeks past — those which fail in getting pepper and Coffee, will go on to Bombay and Calcutta, most of them to the latter — The Canton for Isle of France and Calcutta sail'd about 15 days ago. — The Orient of Marblehead owned by the Hoopers will go in afew days to Calcutta — her object I presume will be Cotton Sugar and some Indigo of middling quality. I dont think they will order any Cotton piece goods — The Sally owned by Sam. G Perkins &C^o. will go sometime towards last Nov^r., I dont believe she will have large funds — T Wigglesworth has advertized the Independence a Newburyport ship — their plan is — 90,000 $ stock, ½ to be invested inCotton and Sugar @ ½ profits, and ½ in p^e goods — at 10% for Cotton goods — 9% for Indigo — 8% for Silk goods. — The [Dorothea — stricken through interlineated: Bainbridge] is fitting from Phila. $80,000 Stock for an entire Cargo of Cotton @ 4 cents p^{r}lb freight — This was the Ship S Cabot Jr and myself tried to get consigned to you, but the conditions were such as we could not accept. — She was to sail early in Nov^r. I dont hear of any other Ships from the south, tho it is probable they may undertake some Cotton voyages. seeing ours have done so well. — The Bengal Richardson SupCargo sail'd 10 days ago for Bourbon for Cargo of Coffee — ifshe fails, to proceed to Calcutta &load with Cotton, and other gruff goods — The Carrier has gone. same route, but she may go [interlineated: on] to Batavia from Bourbon. The Malabar was at Cowes 1st. Sep^r. to go thence to Bombay for Cotton — All the Ships which fail in getting Cotton at that place, will probably go round to Calcutta, — Where else can they get Cargoes? — you will bear in mind, that the object of all these voyages is Cotton Pepper &Coffee — and their funds therefore small, so that in case of coming to Bengal. — they will not take piece goods and very little Indigo — This article having done well these last 6 M^{os}., many people will order it, but the whole quantity which may come cannot be very large, if it is, what you send me, will not be much effected — Many of the Importers will order fine — (high pric'd) — most that I have talk'd with, think it the safest, say 135/ to 160/. pM^d. When it comes, they will either export or keep it, unless 140 to 170 cents can be obtain'd. what you send me I shall be able to sell for less. — You must be cautious, and not allow what you are doing in this article to be known. [interlineated: so many parcels of double boil'd Sugar have been brot, that it is getting to be generally known.] Town has most ofhis Cargo of that sort and it will do well — the Beerboom too is more known and what came in Arganeaut cost ⅛ less. than Benares &sold for 1½$ more. — I think Dr Williamson might make something by procuring 2 to 3000 M^{ds}. from Country and selling it, or shipping as might happen — If you can get it at 10/8 all charges paid inCalcutta, I think you would get 13/., and you may join with him in a purchase of 3000 M'ds say Radnagore — or 2 or 3000 Beerboom of good quality at 9/. — At these prices it will be a good article for a year to come — The fine grain common Benares is still low., and will not do beyond 9/8. — The Borneo is fitting for N. W. Coast, I try'd to get 60 tons of their Copper consign'd you, and offered to take it at $5 p^r ton. but they prefer'd M^r. Newton — It is since sold to Sam. G. Perkins &C^o. and will go in Sally. — M^r. Thorndike will send back two or three ofhis Ships for Cotton & Sugar — M^r. Gray will also send some for same articles, &probably small quantity of Indigo for reexportation to Europe — these voyages as you will see dont interfere in the least with my prospects, or views — as I shall go on broken and middling Indigo for consumption — Cotton piece goods at limited prices — Silk hkf's, Seersuckers &c &c — The undress'd [interlineated: or unbleached] Seersuckers 20 x 2 have done well. — I have before mentioned them in some of my letters they cost I believe, about 5/12 to 6/8.p^s. M^r. Stark had some made — RamMohar Bonargia can tell you what they are — Send me 300 p^s on trial — the narrow stripes, and small checks still continue to be the patterns most lik'd for Seersuckers, and they will do well. I trust you have many on the way to me. — Our crop of Cotton is expected to [be — stricken through] exceed last years by 50,000 bales but the price will be higher say 28 cts p^r lb. I think the India will do well, if it dont go beyond 20/. on board or 21/. — The Benares Sugar best worth 13 — Beerboom 14 @ 14½ — double boil'd such as I had inCririe 16 to 17$ — Ginger has fallen in Europe — sells slowly here @ 9 @ 9½$ — Tumerick no sale, yields 4 to 5 cts in Europe — Most articles ofDrugs heavy sale. — but at my prices will do well — not many piece goods sold this season — they are certainly getting more out of use and the Domestics more in fashion — but such as I have ordered will do well enough for home consumption — particularly low Mamoodies — for I see in June they were below my limits — never mind quality, and pack the rejected — The sale of Blue Gurrahs has become very limited in the Havana — you need not get any more made till you hear from me again on that article nor any more blue Baftas — Taffaties, Lungees and Sistersoy's are still out of fashion, dont buy unless you are oblig'd to take them in barter for some articles you find it difficult to sell for Cash — Messrs. Remsen &C^o write me they have made a final remittance of Portsea's concerns, and sent on a/c^t. if so, you can settle for my share of the profits and [recollect — stricken through interlineated: refer] to the papers, that you may know. on what principle the account is to be settled — I pay no part of the Commission to C & Mackillop — I have written to H^y Alexander, and M^r. Palmer, and given them such information as I tho't would be interesting to them, and not injurious to us. — I shall also write M^r. Williamson — I wish you to procure at your leisure 50 p^s best Choppa Romals, and 10 P^s. Bandannas. — (chocolate), and send them to me — my friends want them they can be had at Cossimbazar @ 6 or 7/ for the Corah — must be substantial and at same time soft — I wish you to see that the payments are regularly made on my 2 shares in the Provident Society — M^r. Mackillop has them — I have sent M^r. Palmer some newspapers — he desired me to do it — I have written Ochterlony and send the letter to you open, put in a wafer before it is sent him — October 28. —

M^r. Oliver who is half Owner of the Brig has procured some shipments to say 15 or 20,000 consigned to you — to do so, he reduced his freight, and I told him I was willing you should do the business at 1½% — our knowing ones, dont believe you can buy goods quite so well as M^r. Newton, or even the Salem [interlineated: Sup] Cargoes. — I am not of that opinion — You will of course buy the goods on the best terms you can in the Bazar. — but they cannot have the benefit of your Contract goods — For the investment ofM^r. FLee & S Cabot S^r & T H Perkins Jr's you will take goods from your own Stock, the same as for me, charging in the price of them, what you may consider as fair rate for Godown hire — and other expences of the establishment — The same should also be done in all the goods you buy for M^r. Williamson & Ochterlony, otherwise I get nothing to indemnify my expences. — M^r. Oliver &M^r. Lee Owners ofthe Brig will direct you as to their concerns. — I have turn'd over to them the Goat skins, I ordered you to procure, on which must be charg'd interest & expences — they will want besides some Ginger &c to fill up with, on what you buy charge them 2½% commission — The Capt. must stay at your house but I pay none ofhis expences. — Two young Men John Lowell J^r. & J A Gardner who are in the Lascar to learn Seamanship, will stay with you if they please, and assist in the Godowns — You must give them to understand unless they work, they are not to remain on shore. They are not to have any Palanquin at my expence. — Neither of them can do any thing at accounts. nor even copy letters — Mr Newton will have 100 Tons measurement goods to go on board — the rest of the Brig save what M^r. S Cabot Jrs. W^{m}Parkman S P Gardner J Tildon &F^s. Lee goods occupy belong to me with regard to my investment & sale goods out, per Lascar, I shall address you a seperate letter — Messrs L. & O will send you two bills Exchange £500. each signed by me and W Oliver — They are for sole account the Owners. — you must negociate them on the best terms you can. — I have written M^r. Newton on general subjects and observ'd that you would send me some white goods which I expected to do well with by exporting — I must repeat my caution that

you have no concerns with him or any one else except D^r. W. R
P O. or any other Resident there on such terms as I have named
— Certainly it is impossible to conceal every thing, but you
may do so to certain extent and as much as may be useful —
There is a 14 Inch Cable not included in the Invoice Bill Lading
W^g. 44.0.2 you can sell it [for — stricken through interlineated: from] the Vessel and save the duty. — It is Russia,
but well made I believe — John Lowell has $2000 which he will
want your aid in investing — he pays $40 p^r. Ton freight on
delivery of the goods. — John Gardner pays nothing onhis $200
— It is to be invested inPiece goods or Indigo — take care and
see that Capt. K. delivers all his letters, that we may have no
complaint onhis return. I have sent some Landing Certificates
for present and future use, I have sent 2 Cheeses in Tin, one for
you, theother for D^r. W. & M^{r}Dickson and some herrings which
if good send each ofthem a box I have also sent a box of Pre-
serves, they are mark'd [the — stricken through] in names of
persons to whom they are tobe delivered — When we hear of
your arrival inCalcutta, I shall try to get aCotton Ship consigned to you — I hope you have been able to influence Williamson to join you in the terms proposed, if he will not, I am
willing to purchase one Lac — in Indigo, Choppas, & Seersuckers, Coarse white goods &c as per my Mem^o. — he to procure the money, charging afair interest, and ship the same on
our joint account, consigned to me — uniting Messrs. Remsen
&C^o. if he wishes — & to divide the profits — he at same time
will allow me, what he thinks right for sale here, &purchasing
there — Next year I shall be able to get some person here to
take a share in the business if it turns out well, unless Williamson is liberal, in which case, I shall want no one else. — I shall
send you a copy of my letter to D^r. W. — I think the prospect
very good for all the goods there may be on the way — Small
coarse col^d. goods N°. 37 to 43 are still low, &with out demand,
& many on hand — I dont want any more blue Gudgees, Blue
Gurrahs, or Blue Baftas for the present — but send any you
may have on hand, unless they can be sold at aprofit — the sale
just now is dull — tho' I shall do well enough with such as are

on the way — I still think better of lowpriced Mamoodies than any other article, but almost all white goods were at my limits in price Current in [May — stricken through interlineated: June] sent me by my Banians — now is the time for Williamson — goods are low inCalcutta, and few here ventured to order them besides myself — but next year, if mine do well, others will import — Seersuckers do best to arrive here in the Spring — still they will answer at any time [interlineated: if] cheap. — Chintzs at my prices promise well — Do give the Brig all the dispatch you can, as it is important she should return early, for sales of the Cargo — have the goods well dunnaged, & ship my Bale goods as soon as the Saltpetre is in — as they will then come rather safer. — I shall write again by Sally. she goes in 30 days. &by other opportunities — The S., touches on the Coast, I suppose for Goat skins — Col'd goods &c &c — The rage for Cotton will I am in hopes occupy the attention of our Traders for a Year to come — and give us the better chance of succeeding in our objects. —— —

Yours truly
(signed/   Henry Lee —

LETTER FROM HENRY LEE, BOSTON, OCT. 30, 1817, TO JAMES WILLIAMSON, CALCUTTA, DESCRIBING HIS BUSINESS AND SUGGESTING AN ASSOCIATION [1]

In this letter Henry Lee reveals the special qualifications which made him feel capable of continuing his interest in the trade with Calcutta, despite tariff restrictions and excessive competition. The five Lee brothers, who were at this time so closely if informally associated in business, were Joseph, George, Thomas, Henry, and Francis. Another brother, Nathaniel Cabot, had died in 1806.

1. Jackson-Lee Papers, "Letter Book September 5th. 1816," Feb. 13, 1816–Oct. 30, 1817.

Boston October 30th 1817

James Williamson Esqr.   [written across face of letter:]
                             Orig^l p Lascar
Calcutta   My dear Sir   Duplicate per Independence

Since mine of 15th October via Bombay, I have nothing
from you. On looking over yours of 9th & 10th May per Bengal, I repeat the gratification I feel that you and Mr D are
satisfied with the way in which Messrs R & Co and myself
managed the Portsea concern, they have sent on the accounts —
so they write me from N York — 10 days shorter passage would
have made it a great voyage — The Lascar is the vessel I wrote
you some months ago was coming out — I hope you have joined
Messrs M & Cabot in buying the amount Piece Goods &c &c
which I advised — All that I reccommended will do — You
should however order me to make Insurance here as it can be
done at half the Calcutta rate. The Lascar will have orders
to make great despatch in Calcutta that she may be here in
season for the Autumn Sales. The attention of our India
Traders is taken up with Cotton and will continue so for a year
to come, which gives a better chance for such goods as I have
reccommended they will all do well — As soon as I hear of
Messrs M & Cabots arrival in Calcutta and whether you enter
into my views, I can point out a Cargo to be collected which
will do very well — Indeed, as I devote all my time to Calcutta
Goods and have had so much experience in your Bazar I am
confident I can make a very good business by importing every
year a considerable amount and I am ready to do so in conjunction with you, if we can agree upon a principle of profits
&c &c The expence of the establishment in Calcutta is considerable, as they do no other business but for me — It is just
you should allow me some compensation in way of freight or
commission In the sale here no one can dispose of them to the
utmost advantage but myself — a commission house has not
leisure enough, nor sufficient knowledge of qualities &c &c
without the aid of a dealer in Ps. Goods — To get rid of them,
it is often neccessary to send them about from one port to an-

other and there is great deal of trouble in this to a busy man,
but I have no other business — With regard to my brothers, I
have four, but we are not partners, though in case of my death
or sickness, they would manage my business as well as I could
— We are in the habit of doing so for each other — I think
with you Sugar is too dear in India, 9/8 for good Benares is
enough — Our new crop Cotton will open @ 30¢ (16ᵈ Stᵍ) 4 cts
higher than last year — most people think it will keep up
through the year 1818. I am afraid of it — A vast number of
Ships have gone, and are going for it from this country and
they will run it up to 21/ or higher, unless you have double the
quantity you had last year to export — The manufacturing
Interest are going to petition Congress this session for a prohibition of Bengal Goods — I have this from one of the leading
men. I don't communicate it — I don't believe they will succeed, but such a measure would help any white Goods you may
have sent — There are some particular sorts of Cottons which
may do at my limitations, and I see they are down — I don't
think the Portuguese will send so many as formerly, the Patriot
Privateers capture them, and they are not tranquil in the Brazils
—Ince is not the man to send to South America with 8 Lacs,
he may however blunder into a good voyage, but we consider it
a hazardous trade in any hands — they are too poor to pay
for much, and too unsettled to induce purchasers to buy on
speculation — We have many ships gone to Chili &c &c, but
they are considered as voyages of adventure, and engaged in by
very rich men only — Indigo has got up in England, but the
ordinary sorts are still dull sale on the continent — In this
article we may do great things — There are certain qualities
and those not the dearest which answer our dyers and pay very
well, — M & C have samples, 1000 Mds a year may be retailed
or even more — I have written Volumes on this and other subjects to my agents — I am anxious to hear from them and you
after their arrival — this will be a good year for us, and I hope
you have many goods with them on the way — Our dates from
France are to 30th Septʳ. Ireland 27th Septʳ. and London 17th
Septʳ, no changes. Raw Silk will be dear in Europe 'till they

have had one or two good crops, the two last have been very
short —
    I have sent a new cheese for you and Mr Dickson —
Yours truly
(Sgd)   Henry Lee

LETTER FROM HENRY LEE, BOSTON, DEC. 5, 1817, TO PERIT &
CABOT, PHILADELPHIA, WITH A CONSIGNMENT OF SALTPETRE [1]

Observe Henry Lee's suggestions for avoiding all unnecessary
expense in the sale of saltpetre. Note also his desire to purchase
some Calcutta goods, for which two months before he had declared
there was no demand whatsoever.

Boston December 5th 1817

Messrs Perit & Cabot
    Philadelphia
        Dear Sirs,
            I enclose Bill Lading & Inv^o. of 206 Bags good Saltpetre,
you may sell it together with the 50 Bags, at 11 cts, on landing;
in store 12 cts 6 Mo^s.
    The weight in the Bill Lading is as I purchased, and you will
settle the freight without the expence of reweighing — In selling allow Invoice Tares, or actual weight average say of 10
Bags, and please to have it done in your store — In selling let
the quality be examined at the moment, and no allowances
afterward made —
    If not sold on landing, please to hire some cheap store, that
the charges may be as moderate as possible — As advertising is
so expensive, I wish to have it included in your general one,
and only inserted once a week — It is a bulky article, and without all possible saving, it cannot afford expence of transporting —
    Let me know what can be done, as I may buy a parcel now
looked for — I want 1000 p^s. Choppas such as cost 118/ to 125,

1. Jackson-Lee Papers, "Letter Book from Jany. 17th. 1817 to October 27. 1818."

let me know at what rate you can buy them — I want also some coarse ones, costing 95/ @ 110/, see if any can be had — 7 or 8 ships are going in few days for Calcutta — I am glad I have not ventured largely, as goods must come out high charged —

At what rate can you buy me an Invoice of Silks, in some of your early China Ships?

Yours truly
(Sgd)　　Henry Lee —

I hope you have been able to sell my Quicksilver —
Bills on London 2% advance —
Dollars 2½% do. —

LETTER FROM HENRY LEE, BOSTON, DEC. 9, 1817, TO JAMES P. HIGGINSON, BOSTON, WITH INSTRUCTIONS FOR PURCHASES IN ENGLAND [1]

Evidently the market for Calcutta goods was improving, since Lee commissioned a purchasing agent in England to invest so heavily in choppa romals, seersuckers, and such piece goods. Observe the warning concerning brokers' bias, and note the alternative offers for compensation. On Jan. 1, 1818, Higginson was ordered to invest in cloves @ 3s. per lb. if piece goods could not be obtained at Lee's limits; failing this he was to remit to Calcutta.

James P. Higginson (b. Boston, July 1791) was the youngest son of Stephen Higginson (1743–1828) by a second marriage. He married in 1813 the widow of his brother George.[2]

Boston Decr. 9th. 1817

Mr. James P Higginson
　Dear Sir,
　　Accompanying this is 1st. of Exchange, Sullivan Dorr on Thomas Wilson &Co London, for Eight hundred and twenty five Pounds 12/ Stg, say £825..12.. — dated Decr. 3^d. 1817.

1. Jackson-Lee Papers, "Letter Book from Jany. 17th. 1817 to October 27. 1818."
2. "Materials for a Genealogy of the Higginson Family," *Essex Inst. Hist. Colls.*, vol. v, p. 41; Higginson, T. W., *Life and Times of Stephen Higginson* (Boston and N. Y., 1907), p. 252.

60 days sight — With the proceeds on your arrival in London, you will make the following investment —

   2/3ds the amº. in Choppa Romals, (or Flags, as most generally called,) at not exceeding 18/ per Piece —

   1/3d in Seersuckers, at not exceeding 30/ for quality like the sample, say 13 to 14 yds by ⅞, or 36/ for those of a finer description —

Both these articles have been very low for some time past, and you may perhaps get them under the limits, which I recommend your concealing from the Broker you employ, as they are in the interest of the holders generally, and of course inclined to serve their interest in preference to yours — Ripley Wiss &Co are the principal Brokers, and well known to Mr Williams — perhaps you may deal directly with some of the India houses — If you can get the goods at the limits, I authorise you to invest a further sum of 1200 or £1500, provided you can draw on me, for the payment — For your services, I will either pay you one half the nett profits which may arise on the importation, or a commission of 2½% — You can make your election here, or in England — Please to write me in Triplicates what you can do — Ship the goods if purchased, without delay either to me, or Messrs Remsen &Co N York, whichever may be most convenient —

If Carraderies 12 to 13 Yds long, can be had at 24/, you may buy 100 pˢ., and diminish the proportion of Choppas — Please to let me know what quantities of these goods there are in the market, and at what prices they may be purchased at, as I may wish to send for further quantity — You would oblige me also for any other information you may collect, as to the value of India Goods, especially Spices, Saltpetre — Canton Silk Goods — Bengal Piece Goods, and Turkey Opium —

You have a sample for the Choppas — There may be some of a very inferiour quality, which you may buy at 15/, if those I order cannot be procured.

If neither Choppas, or Seersuckers, can be purchased, you will pay over the amount of the Bill to Mr S Williams, and desire him to remit to Messrs Cruttenden & Mackillop, Calcutta, for my account.

Please to quote in your letters to me, the rate of Exchange, on Madrass and Calcutta, and Price of Spanish Dollars —

Wishing you a pleasant voyage, and safe return, —

Make Insurance on what you ship — I am. Your faithful S^t.

(Sgd) H Lee —   Sgd   Henry Lee —

Boston Decr. 9. 1817. Received of Mr Henry Lee a letter of which the foregoing is a copy, with the first Bill of Exchange therein — mentioned —

Attest

James AHolden   J. P. Higginson

LETTER FROM HENRY LEE, BOSTON, DEC. 9, 1817, TO STEIGLITZ & CO., ST. PETERSBURG, WITH ORDER FOR THE PURCHASE OF RUSSIAN GOODS [1]

On Apr. 6, Henry Lee had written the same firm, with samples of India goods, but evidently no shipments had followed or Lee would not have instructed the St. Petersburg firm to draw on London.

"Flems." — probably short for Flemings — were a sort of sheeting.[2]

Boston Decr. 9. 1817

Messrs Steiglitz &Co   orig^l pGalen
  St Petersburg   Duplicate pr.
  Gent.   Triple per.   fourth per.

    I wish you to purchase whenever you think the market most favorable, the following goods for my account —

400 (four hundred) pieces of third quality Flems.

200 (two hundred) pieces of 28 inch ordinary Ravens Duck cheapest you can find —

500 (five hundred) pieces common quality Broad Diaper —

for the payment of the same I authorise you to draw on Samuel

1. Jackson-Lee Papers, "Letter Book from Jany. 17th. 1817 to October 27. 1818."

2. *Ibid.*, Henry Lee, Boston, Aug. 28, 1818, to Peter Remsen & Co., N. Y.

Williams Esqr. London, at ninety days sight — You will please to write me what you have done, direct, and via England — I wish the goods shipped by the earliest conveyance, consigned to me, to any port north of Baltimore, preferring N York or Boston —

I am — Your Obt Servt
(Sgd) Henry Lee —

LETTER FROM HENRY LEE, BOSTON, DEC. 11, 1817, TO HENRY MILES, c/o ROGERS, BROTHERS & CO., NAPLES, ENQUIRING CONCERNING POSSIBILITIES FOR TRADE BETWEEN BOSTON AND NAPLES [1]

In addition to suggesting the type of trade with Naples in which Henry Lee would like to engage, if possible, the letter below describes the improved state of business and mentions some of the reasons.

Henry Miles was apparently a brother of Charles D. Miles, who had gone out to Calcutta as a supercargo on the *Cruttenden*.

Boston December 11. 1817
Mr Henry Miles.   p Adriana
Care of Messrs Rogers, Brothers &Co,   Mr Harrod [?]
Naples —   Duple
Dear Sir,
I believe you have forgotten a promise you made, that I should hear from you occasionally, on your return to Naples — I am not much in the Meditteranean, or indeed any other, but the India trade, but still I should like to know what is doing in your quarter, especially in India and China Goods — I may wish to export an article now and then, when it is very low in this market — I wish more particularly to know the value, and demand, for the following articles in Dollars and Cents, and our weights—

1. Jackson-Lee Papers, "Letter Book from Jany. 17th. 1817 to October 27. 1818."

Bengal Piece Goods. say

Alliabad Mamoodies .	. 20 by 1⅛ yards		—
Meergungee "	. . 18 "	¾ "	—
Beerboom Gurrahs	. . 18 "	1⅛ "	—
Emerties	. 15 "	1 "	—

and generally Bengal White Coarse Goods, somewhat inferiour
to those called Company, which are sent to your place, from
London — What is the demand for these goods?

Bengal fine & middling Indigoes —
     do   do   do   Sugars —
Ginger, and Tumerick   —
Saltpetre, Crude, and Refined
Bengal & Surat Cotton —   Block Tin, and
Tuetenague, Pepper and Coffee — Let me know the charges
upon them, and the rate at which remittances may be made to
London, and the price of Spanish Dollars — I would thank you
also, for information as to your exports, particularly Sewing
Silks, we used to get them cheaper than from China — At present I believe the China undersell them, and also your Sarsnets,
and other manufactures, but this may not be the case when your
Raw Silk declines — We are told here that the crops for three
years have been bad — Is this really so, or is there an increased
demand for the article? — If you write me via Havre de Grace,
I shall get your letters sooner than by sea, unless vessels happen
to be coming away, direct for America — I am in expectation of
hearing from Charles in few weeks, his prospect is pretty good —
Business has been better than we feared some 12 Months ago —
Our foreign trade increasing — We have had fine crops, and
every thing is in pretty good demand — Cotton 32 Cents, Rice
$5.50 — Flour $9. — All colonial produce very dear, as you
will see by the Price Currents which you must receive by this
conveyance — I shall have many Piece Goods in few months,
and be inclined to send you some, if they will sell at a moderate
profit — Cotton Goods have advanced in England, which may
help East India fabrics —

Yours truly
(Sgd)   H Lee

LETTER FROM HENRY LEE, BOSTON, DEC. 13, 1817, TO MIRALLA
& CO., HAVANA, OFFERING TO SELL A SHIP [1]

The ship to which Henry Lee referred was the *Cruttenden,* which
arrived at New York, Apr. 8, 1818, 134 days from Calcutta.[2] On
Jan. 5, 1818, Lee was trying through Perit & Cabot, Philadelphia, to
get "a freight of flour, staves or anything else to Gibraltar or Cadiz"
for the *Cruttenden,* or to sell her for the trade with "Sumatra, Java
or any other trade, where her Cargo could be carried direct to
Europe, the duties being same as if she had an American Register —
. . . Could you get me $55 per Ton to go to Calcutta for Cotton?
say 150 Tons." On Feb. 14, 1818, he offered the *Cruttenden* to
H. & R. Osgood, Baltimore, for trade between the East Indies, the
West Indies, or South America on the one hand, and Europe on the
other hand, or for a privateer; he also enquired concerning the pos-
sibilities for a freight to the Spanish Peninsula, Teneriffe, or Rio de
Janeiro. On Feb. 23 he reminded Peter Remsen that "The Whalemen
want ships — Hicks Jenkins &Co can tell you, I would give 6 to 9
Mo[s]. credit, but shall hold her @ $18000."

Despite the lack of encouragement from Havana for the shipment
of India goods, Lee, on Dec. 20, did ship the Havana firm 4 bales of
seersuckers to be sold for at least $14, proceeds in bills at par, coffee
@ 15 cents, or brown sugar @ 14 rials, and, on Dec. 29, 17 bales of
gurrahs, to be sold for at least $3.50, proceeds in pig copper @ 19
cents on board. On June 23, 1817, Henry Lee warned the firm to
which the letter below is addressed: "When you ship Goods for me
give the preference to vessels with two decks, and avoid all ships
owned east of Boston unless better than usual."

The *rial* or *real* in Cuba was worth 12½ cents. *Vide* John Tracy,
June 12, 1818, to Miralla & Co., Havana: "14 Rials, equal to
1 75/100."

1. Jackson-Lee Papers, "Letter Book from Jan[y]. 17th. 1817 to October 27. 1818."
2. *Columbian Centinel,* Apr. 15, May 13, 1818.

VISTA DE CADIZ.

CADIZ, 1792

Boston Decr. 13th 1817.

Messrs Miralla &Co   [written across face of letter]
   Havana   Per George Beckworth
   Dear Sirs,   Dupl^e. Hero

Mr Knight when here, seemed to think it might be possible to dispose of an American ship in your place — I am expecting one in about 70 or 80 days, and as she is without American Register, I am desirous of selling her, the following is a description — 320 Tons, Coppered to the bends, and copper fastened, 11 years old, but the lower part rebuilt about six years since, and the upper works 7 or 8 Months ago, when she was new masted new rigged, including 3 or 4 Cables — her Cabin is handsomely finished with Mahogany &c, and she is in all respects a staunch, and good looking ship, and will carry say 2000 Boxes Sugar — her Copper may last 18 Months, perhaps 3 years with slight repairs, she is a fast ship, and a good sea Boat — A new vessel of this description would cost in this place 70 or 75 Dollars per Ton, say 23,000 to 25,000$ —

What encouragement can you give me to send her to the Havana for sale? If she can't be sold, could you secure me a freight to Cadiz of Spanish property? In which case she might call and take a new clearance from New York, to make the property more safe from capture by the Patriots — If freights for Spain could not be procured, is it probable that any would offer for other ports in Europe? —

Please to write me fully on the subject by several conveyances — The letters via New York or Baltimore have shorter passages at this season — If you could get me an offer for the ship which I should be satisfied with, I would agree to bring out a load of Flour, or any other merchandise, free of freight — Flour may I think be down to $7.50, if the English ports are shut against grain — perhaps lower — I have you[r] favor to Novr. 4th — and am sorry they afford no inducement to ship any India Goods — I have been trying to pick up some fine white Goods and Seersuckers, but don't meet any cheap enough — I shall have some from India in the spring — Your produce is too high, there is not a market in Europe which will give the cost and charges. I have no doubt it will fall when the new crop comes in plentifully — If you have any good offers for my goods on 6 Mo^s. credit, accept them — If there is any demand for white or coloured goods I would thank you to write me —

Yours truly
(Sgd)   H Lee

I am expecting a quantity Cloves & Cinnamon of the finest quality, which I shall send you if they keep up — I shall invoice the latter as Cassia, Mr Knight thought it would pass —

.H. L.

LETTER FROM HENRY LEE, BOSTON, JAN. 1, 1818, TO GEORGE CABOT AND JAMES JACKSON, BOSTON, WITH PAYMENT TO A CREDITOR [1]

When Henry Lee and his brother Joseph failed, early in 1811, they made a voluntary assignment of their property for the benefit of their creditors. It is evidence both of Henry Lee's comparative financial prosperity and of his scrupulous honesty that on New Year's Day, 1818, he should of his own accord make a large payment to the wife of one of his creditors. Stephen Higginson, Jr., best known as the father of the famous abolitionist, Col. Thomas Wentworth Higginson, had experienced financial reverses which had forced him in Apr., 1815, to retire to a farm.[2] This accounts for Henry Lee's making the below-mentioned payment to his wife rather than to Higginson directly; otherwise Higginson's own creditors might have endeavored to obtain possession. George Cabot and James Jackson were doubtless the former senator and the well-known physician, brother of P. T. Jackson, respectively.

1. Jackson-Lee Papers, "Letter Book from Jany. 17th. 1817 to October 27. 1818."

2. Higginson, Thomas Wentworth, *Cheerful Yesterdays* (Boston and N. Y., 1900), p. 10.

GEORGE CABOT, 1752–1823, IN YOUTH

Boston January 1. 1818

Mr George Cabot and
   James Jackson
     Trustees,
      Gentlemen.

     Having been always desirous to make some reperation to my creditors for the losses sustained by my failure, it has been my uniform intention to make such repayment to them, as due regard to my family, and the state of my [family — stricken through interlineated: affairs] would fairly permit. The period is not arrived to execute such an intention, but I think it expedient to anticipate it so far, as to advance gratuitously, the sum of Four Thousand Dollars by a draft herewith enclosed, dated Decr. 23^d. 1817. on Messrs Peter Remsen &Co N York, at six months sight on Interest, for the benefit of Mrs Louisa Higginson & her children — I am induced to take this measure by a consideration of their necessitous condition, and also by the recollection that Mr Stephen Higginson Junr. became my creditor, by paying as an endorser, I wish it to be understood however, that if my circumstances should not allow me to pay to others, this advance is irrevocable, and if I should pay to others, I shall then consider this as a substitute for payment to Mr Higginson.

        I am. Your Obt Servt.
        (Sgd) Henry Lee —

LETTER FROM WILLIAM OLIVER, BOSTON, JAN. 12, 1818, TO ANTONIO DE FRIAS & CO., HAVANA, WITH A CONSIGNMENT OF PIECE GOODS AND ORDERS FOR A RETURN CARGO [1]

     Henry Lee's Havana correspondent had been Miralla & Co., but that firm's accounts of the market in Havana had not been encouraging. Observe the writer's policy of "prompt sales . . . small profit." Note also the description of the various types of copper.

    1. Jackson-Lee Papers, "Letter Book from Jany. 17th. 1817 to October 27. 1818."

"Gallapago" is the Spanish word for turtle, which explains why "small round plates" of copper were so styled.

Boston January 12. 1818.

Messrs Antonio De Frias &Co
   Havana.
      Gentlemen,
         By advice of our friend Mr Morland who has shewn me some late letters from you, I now send you per Brig Horace James Hubbard 22 Bales Piece Goods of the finest quality which this market furnished; and which came nearest to those of which you recommended a shipment — The Comboys and most of the White Goods are of excellent quality —

The three Bales of Blue Gurrahs are common, and I send them to help out an assortment — The other kinds mentioned by you cannot now be had — The highest price in the 2^d Inv^o. are the actual cost to me, and they are lower than any goods of the same quality which have been shipped for a very long time — I have no doubt you will be able to make a ready sale of them at a handsome profit, because but few Goods of this description have been lately sent from this country —

I ask your particular attention to this adventure, and to recollect that I always prefer prompt sales at a small profit to keeping accounts open with an hope of greater gain. For these white Goods however, I am induced to think you will get high prices — Should this shipment come to a favorable issue & you recommend it to me, I should be glad to make others, and keep you fully supplied, having means to do this with peculiar advantage — Remittances to be made in Bills on this place, or its neighbourhood in preference to any articles of produce, unless they should go down to 20 Reals for the best White, and 14 Reals for Brown Sugar, or 14$ pr Quintal for Green Coffee — Or if Pig Copper can be bought so as to cost $19½ pr Qtl on board for the best kind it will be a good Remittance — The Peruvian is much better than the Mexican & the small round plates, preferable to the large square blocks — The small round plates are sometimes called Gallapagos — A considerable part

of the export duty is often saved in Havana — The price of
$19½ per Qtl on board should be for the best quality; and the
inferior kinds should cost lower in proportion.

Sgd   Wᵐ Oliver.

LETTER FROM HENRY LEE, BOSTON, JAN. 25, 1818, TO CAPT. WILLIAM FARRIS, NEWBURYPORT, IN REGARD TO TAKING HIS SON INTO LEE'S STORE [1]

The letter below gives a good idea of the kind of training to which
young men just entering business were subjected.

Capt. William Farris (b. Belfast, Ireland, 1753; d. Newburyport,
Nov. 22, 1837) was one of the leading citizens of Newburyport,
active both in commerce and in public affairs. There was a rather
tenuous family relationship between Capt. Farris and Henry Lee.
Mrs. Henry Lee's aunt, Mrs. John Tracy, was the sister (or cousin)
of Mrs. William Farris, which was probably a principal reason why
Capt. Farris thought of putting his son under Henry Lee's care.[2]

Boston Jany. 25. 1818

Capt William Farris
  Newburyport.
    Dear Sir,
      I have been on the point these six months past of writing
you on the subject of your sons coming into my store, but have
been prevented by the fear, that I should not have sufficient
employment for him — If you have no other place in view I
will receive him into my store, in course of three or four months,
possibly sooner — It is requisite he should write a very good
hand, and understand Arithmetic & Book keeping, if deficient
in either, he will have time to improve this winter — I am willing
to allow four Dollars per week for his board, and I recommend
your getting him into some family you are acquainted with, who
may feel an interest in his welfare — I wish you to understand

1. Jackson-Lee Papers, "Letter Book from Jany. 17ᵗʰ. 1817 to October 27. 1818."
2. Currier, *Newburyport*, vol. ii, pp. 202–203; *ibid.*, *"Ould Newbury,"* p. 579; Lee, T. A., "The Tracy Family of Newburyport," p. 67.

that I do not obligate myself to keep him, if from ill health, or any other cause. I should be compelled to diminish, or abandon my business, and further, that in case he should be disinclined to business, or acquire any habits which may unfit him for it, I shall return him to you immediately — Perhaps it may have a good effect, before he leaves home, if you read to him, this part of my letter — It may be a restraint upon his conduct on some future day should it be necessary — I shall require his attendance early and late during the whole year — It is probably you may have occasion to come to town in course of two or three months, when we will have some further conversation on the subject — In mean time it might be well to secure him a boarding place, such as I have described, as it would be a means of guarding him against many temptations which young men are exposed to, more especially when absent from their friends & parents.

Please to let me know your determination as soon as you can with convenience —

I am

Your friend &Servt

(Sgd)   Henry Lee —

LETTER FROM HENRY LEE, BOSTON, JAN. 26, 1818, TO PETER REMSEN & CO., NEW YORK, ON MISCELLANEOUS MATTERS CONNECTED WITH THE INDIA TRADE [1]

Henry Lee's jocose instructions on how to sell indigo were probably also at least semi-serious, and perhaps were intended to reflect on the practices of some of his competitors. Note his comment on owning ships. In a letter of Apr. 16, 1818, to Peter Remsen & Co., he vehemently declared: "I hope never to own another stick of timber if I live 1000 years."

"Mr N" was probably Edward A. Newton and "Mr T," John Tracy, Jr.

1. Jackson-Lee Papers, "Letter Book from Jan[y]. 17th. 1817 to October 27. 1818."

Boston 26 Jany. 1818.

Messrs Peter Remsen &Co
  New York
    Dear Sirs,
      I have yours of   & 22ᵈ. I believe there is
nothing unsold but the Indigo and Baftas. I suppose the former
is bad, but if you will put it into your darkest room, swear it is
good, & *ask a high price,* I have no doubt it will sell — It has I
am sorry to see by my Price Currents fallen in London but that
ought not to affect my small parcel, as no more can come 'till
Cruttenden arrives and it is uncertain if she brings much — I
hope you will get the ship for M &C and pick up some freight
from some of your friends, I am told you found no difficulty in
doing this for Mr N & I suppose you have the same confidence
in M &C. at any rate I will pledge myself their goods will come
as well charged as any other — I have a prospect of getting
freight for the Cruttenden from Philᵃ., but I believe I shall let
you sell her if fair price offers, and take up a new Brig of J Lee's
on freight to be launched in May — I am not rich enough to
own ship timber. I wish you would ship on the Edward $4000
for me, consign them to order in B/L, and endorse the one you
forward to Messrs C D Miles & R C Cabot, both or either of
them — take 4 Bills. Mr Burr writes me the freight wᵈ. be 1%
perhaps they may take ½% as she don't go direct. This may be
considered as an advance against the Spices — Mr T desired
Mr Williams to enter them as Merchandise that the quantity
might not˙ get into the Price Current — In such an article it is
important not to have the quantity known, nor do I wish them
advertised as coming from London, as Mr T has sent for more
Cloves &Mace and they promise very well. — If you could get
10 or $20000 consigned to M &C by the Edward for Indigo &
Pˢ. Goods on 1/3ᵈ profits or on commᵒ. only, I should be glad,
I will get the goods here as I can, and engage if they will allow
me to give the orders to buy the adventure 6 Months hence or
any time after at 6% pr annum — Perhaps Rankin & Hyer
might engage, or some of the rich grocers. —

I advise the owners of the Calcutta ship not to put Zinck on, the Persia's was corroded like a honey comb in 3 Mos., and taken off before she sailed from here —

Yours truly
Sgd.   H Lee

Your Sales Hdfs are exd. & found correct.

LETTER FROM HENRY LEE, BOSTON, FEB. 13, 1818, TO HOTTINGUER & CO., HAVRE, WITH PLANS FOR A DIRECT TRADE BETWEEN CALCUTTA AND FRANCE [1]

This was not the first time that Henry Lee had written to European merchants suggesting the advantages of direct trade by American merchants between Calcutta and European ports, but the letter below is probably the clearest and most detailed expression of his views on the subject.

Brig L'Eucharis via Nantz.
Duple.   Boston February 13th 1818

Messrs Hottinguer &Co
    Havre
        Gentlemen
            I am favored with yours of the 9th October, & 21st. Novr., and thank you for the information they contain — It is very evident to me, from the result of the shipments made to your country from hence since the peace, that we can no longer supply you with East & West India produce under our flag, while the duties are so much in favor of your own, more especially the articles of Coffee, Sugar and Pepper — Believing this to be the case, and at the same time hoping that our experience in the India trade, may for a few years at least, give us some advantages over your Merchants, I am desirous of making shipments of Sugar, Cotton, Ginger, Indigo &c &c, direct from Calcutta to your port, or any other you may recommend — In order however, that it may be profitable, there should be sev-

1. Jackson-Lee Papers, "Letter Book from Jany. 17th. 1817 to October 27. 1818."

eral moderate sized ships of 250 to 400 Tons; sailing at different seasons, between Havre and Calcutta, under the command
of steady, and experienced commanders, they should go, &
return direct, without stopping at any port on the way, that no
time may be lost, and that Insurance may be effected on the
lowest terms — The rate of freight should also be low, that
these adventures may not be undersold by shipments from here,
or from England — The rate from Calcutta to London for two
years, has been from £6 Stg. to 8£ for 2240 lb dead weight, and
the same for a Ton measurement of fifty cubic feet — The
rate from Calcutta to this country has varied, but ships can
now be chartered at $35 @ 40 pr Ton 2240 lb dead weight, or
40 cubic feet measurement — It is probable that you cannot
sail your ships quite so cheap as ourselves, and the English —
If you can furnish tonnage say 40 Cubic feet to the Ton, &
2240 lb dead weight, for two hundred & fifty francs payable on
delivery of the Goods, without any primage, I would engage to
procure shippers for a vessel of 300 to 400 Tons; such a ship if
full built, would carry 450 to 550 Tons, say in Sugar, Cotton,
Ginger &c &c, and make the voyage in 12 Mos., ours do it in
10 Mos. frequently — The shippers who would furnish the
cargo, have agents in Calcutta; so that no Supercargo would
be required — If you could induce any of your ship owners
to engage in this business, it might be profitable to them, and
furnish your friends here, with an opportunity of pursuing a
profitable trade —

I am myself entirely devoted to it, and have agents established there, through them I could get consignments to you from
some of my Calcutta friends — If however it is too troublesome to engage these vessels in the trade, I should be glad to
have you hire for me, 100 Tons dead weight, 2240 lb English
to the Ton, @ 250 francs in some ship to sail after the 1st July,
or such time as notice of the engagement would probably reach
me — I presume shipments made in my name in French Bottoms, would pass at the same duty as if shipped and owned by
a French subject — You will please to let me know immedi-

ately whether you can procure the freight, that I may write to my agents to get the goods in readiness —

If your Government would allow Americans to command these ships it would give confidence to our people, and they would procure freights with greater readiness, &make shorter voyages — Raw Silk at your quotations would pay a handsome profit — the cost during my stay in Calcutta, was 8 to 12 Rupees pr Seer of 2 lb, say $2 @ 3. lb It has probably advanced this last year — It is an article which requires more experience than I possess, to give me sufficient confidence to deal in it, besides one or two good crops in Italy would I presume reduce the price very much, in mean time this country [would — stricken through interlineated: will] get her supplies of silk fabrics from China, whh may make some impression on prices in Europe, though not much — Our importations of silks this year from Canton (manufactured) will not be less than two millions of Dollars cost, — Their sewing silk which is inferiour however to Italian, can be afforded at $4.50, though it now sells at higher price — I imagine your people who want to import Raw Silk, would do better in China, than Bengal — If your government would allow an American ship with her crew to assume your flag, I could provide one on this side of the water, but I presume they would not consent to this — I should be glad to hear from you on this subject as soon as convenient, and to have proforma sales of Sugar, Cotton, Indigo &Ginger for consumption, coming from this country under our flag, and from India under your flag — I shall then be able to see how much is saved by employing a French Bottom — If the idea of employing 3 or 4 vessels regularly [interlineated: in the trade], strikes you as practicable, and not likely to afford you more trouble than advantage, I should like to correspond with you on the subject; or what might be more satisfactory to you, confer with any confidential agent you may have in this country —

I have considerable quantities of Sugar, Indigo, Ginger &Saltpetre on the way from Calcutta, but it is impossible to send them to your port while duties are so much against foreign flags; there has not been an article of colonial produce for 18

Mo^s. past in our market, which would bear shipping — We must employ your flag, or abandon the trade — I am very respectfully

Yr Obt Servt
(Signed)   Henry Lee

From the low prices at which Sugar, Cotton, Indigo &c, can be afforded in India especially Bengal, I am confident the European trade, will continue to be great & even extend beyond its present rate — Sugar can be cultivated for less than in any of the West India Islands, and Cotton for 8 to 9 cts lb, which is only half what it costs our planters, formerly they could afford it at 12 @ 13¢. but Slaves Lands &c, have advanced so much, that it cannot be afforded under 16 or 17 cents. —

H. L. —

LETTER FROM HENRY LEE, BOSTON, APR. 8, 1818, TO PETER REMSEN & CO., NEW YORK, ON SALES OF CHINA GOODS [1]

The goods mentioned below were in the return cargo of the *Suffolk,* in charge of Henry Higginson, supercargo, whom Henry Lee had so greatly assisted in getting an outward cargo. It is pleasant to learn from a letter of Apr. 7 to James P. Higginson, London, that "H H makes a very good voyage for himself, owners, and shippers."

Messrs. Peter Remsen &C^o.   Boston April 8 th 1818
    Dear Sir's.

I have yours of 2^d & 3^d — The Silks did well. I have disposed of ½ or more of my Invoice per S. at about 92% advance. I shall get off the whole at average of say 85% which is better than they would yeild with you. Our Market has advanced since the Auction sale about 1 $ p^s. on Crapes. & Sarsnets and 2 @ 5% on other articles — F Lee has sold his Invoices @ 70% — I am retailing M^r. Lowell's & shall get about 80% — Lyman will hold on his Silks unless great prices are offered — Our people think they will sustain their present prices, full ½ of

---

1. Jackson-Lee Papers, "Letter Book from Jany. 17th. 1817 to October 27. 1818."

Suffolks have been sold & distributed. Smith has not I believe made any large parcels, he may buy at 70% perhaps — I shall probably send you some Sewings and Sarsnets — I return D M^c. Gregors Bill accepted — they would not do it in any other way — I should be glad to have the C's gruffs goods sold as landed, at the prices of [interlineated: in] mine of 1st April, but I had rather not try an auction, the charge is heavy, and the prices never go beyond private sale, generally below — On a high & falling market, an auction may be the best mode of selling, and generally here where the charge is only ½% — There is not an article in C's Cargo which is falling — The oil is very good — Most of the Indigo here will be exported — Mr Gray's will sold be to the Grocers for consumption, as it is only common I imagine — I shall make a shipment per Cririe — I wish you to collect me $5000 not exceeding 4% and if you think they will fall before she goes, perhaps it may do to wait, but I fear they will rather advance. as our people here, are paying 4 @ 4¼ — I shall remit tomorrow — It has raised since Thursday & continues too so that D R's silks will not be landed for 2 days at least — I can tell by your sales of M^r. H's goods on the way, whether you can do better than I can here for silks.

I am willing to reduce the Baftas 25 cts p^s. but if they don't go readily at that have them put away 'till they advance as they will between this & Oct^r. — Teas are considered worth 10 cts lb more since the sale with you, & some sorts pay a little profit — I shall come on when I hear of my ship she ought to be hear but the winds were light in Bay of Bengal — and stormy on the Coast — Some of our fast ships are still out longer than she is — I got something done on profits yesterday @ 3% — Fawn makes a great voyage — Canton Silks are retailing as follows.

Blk Sarsnets	20 @ 21.	
Changeable do	22 " 22½	
Blk Sinchaws	27	
do 4/4 Hkfs	11⅜	
Canton Crapes	12½ @ 13	
Nankin do (22 yd)	25 " 26	

| Blk Florentines | 20 — |
| Sewings assorted | 5.50 @ 5.75 asked — no sales — Blk has been bot on speculation by T &Bumstead |

Exchange ½% @ 1% adv^e.

Dollars 4¼. —

Yours truly

Sgd   H Lee

M^r. Tracy has sold his Mace @ $4¼ send him a Case more —

LETTER FROM HENRY LEE, BOSTON, APR. 13, 1818, TO PETER REMSEN & CO., NEW YORK, ON DIFFICULTIES IN REGARD TO ADMITTING THE CRUTTENDEN [1]

The *Cruttenden,* though American owned and flying the American flag, was British built and therefore had no American register. The collector of customs at New York had taken advantage of the latter circumstance to make difficulties in regard to entering the vessel. He may have been partly moved by a Democratic New York desire to make trouble for a merchant of Federalist Boston. Lee, at any rate, was convinced that the *Cruttenden* would meet no difficulty at the latter port.

Peter Remsen &C^o.   Boston April 13th. 1818 —
                                            Monday

    Dear Sirs

        Yours of   is received the Construction put upon the act of 1st March is a very singular one. It is meant to apply only to British & Swedish vessels and only to former coming from W India ports or such as our ships a[re] prevented going to. our Vessels go freely to Calcutta and of course the law does not apply to [him — stricken through] them The act is however worded in such a way to make it obscure tho there can be no doubt that it was the intention to admit vessels situated as mine is I am unwilling to place myself in the power of your Collector nor do I wish any thing said of the matter that may induce your Custom house to apply to Government in this case — you will

1. Jackson-Lee Papers, "Letter Book from Jany. 17th. 1817 to October 27. 1818."

therefore order her round to this place. without delay. unless she is allowed an entry. paying foreign duties I have written to M^r. Crawford Sec^ry. of the treasury and shall get an answer by the time she arrives here. This is much against my interest and convenience but I am afraid of your Custom house Officers —

I hope to hear she is entered without difficulty

Yr's

HLee

I beg nothing may be said about the cause of her coming this way —

LETTER FROM JOSEPH LEE, JR., APR. 16, 1818, TO PERIT & CABOT, PHILADELPHIA, OFFERING A VESSEL FOR CHARTER [1]

The brig owned by Joseph Lee, Jr., frequently appeared in Henry Lee's letter books during the process of construction. She was the *Archer*, 274 t., built by Isaac Sprague at Medford, and registered June 10, 1818.[2] On Jan. 3, 1818, Henry Lee had offered the brig to Richard Burr on the following conditions: "for Indigo & Piece Goods 8% in Calcutta, or if you like better, $45 pr Ton paid in Calcutta, instead of $55 paid here." Then on Feb. 17, Henry Lee suggested to Peter Remsen that, if the latter could obtain an investment of $70,000, he would "engage she shall run between Calcutta & New York — You may take 1/3^d or not as you like if you determine to take 1/3^d. now and alter your mind hereafter, J Lee has no objection — His wish &mine is to get a ship in the trade from N York — If you conclude to do this . . . I pledge myself to bring you consignments . . . to value of $70000." Apparently some sort of arrangement was made with Burr, for on June 8 Henry Lee wrote to Peter Remsen & Co. that "J. Lees Brig will sail as soon as Mr Burr is ready say — 15 or 20 th." On the same day he wrote Perit & Cabot ordering them to "invest . . . in Spanish dollars not exceeding 4%, or American dollars or ½ dollars, at not exceeding ½% — please to let me know, if the dollars can be had, by return mail & what the Coasters will ask to bring them round — I want to ship

1. Jackson-Lee Papers, "Letter Book from Jany. 17th. 1817 to October 27. 1818."

2. Registers, Boston Custom House, 1818, no. 130.

them by J. Lee's Brig." The brig *Archer* cleared from Boston for Calcutta and Madras, June 13, under the command of Abel Coffin.[3]

Messrs. Perit & Cabot

(Philadelphia) If Mr. Burr will give me 42½ Dols per ton weight & measurement & *give me as much salt Petre or Sugar,* as will answer for ballast, & pay one quater part of the freight, say in ten days after her arrival, the remainder in a good Note at sixty days, I will let her go, & sail from this on the first day of August, lay days in Calctta to be thirty, & no Cabin stores & no "Charges on shore to be paid by me" as he proposes," it being also understood, that I may fill all the breakages with ginger in bulk, or gingerbread as I please, & I wish to reserve 20 to 40 tons room if he has no objection — I will give room for a SuperCargo out, as much as he wants — home, only just enough to live My Vessel will [interlineated: sail] well — shall be well fitted shall not be spoken with short of wood, water or provisions — these terms are [interlineated: not] so good to me as 40 dols from this place, but I will accept them provided she is not engaged before I get his answer, & I will defer accepting any offer that I may have it, — *if I can* till I can hear from you — If we agree & Mr Burr should want before he goes any Change to be made I will accommodate him with pleasure, he paying the extra expence — My Vessel can be ready by the 20th. June, of course I loose by Keeping her till August —

(Signed)   Yours Jos Lee Jr.

I will agree to build & furnish another Vessel upon the same terms to sail in 4 or 6 Months as he may wish. —

LETTER FROM HENRY LEE, BOSTON, MAY 21, 1818, TO GEORGE MILES, BALTIMORE, DESCRIBING LEE'S SITUATION [1]

Evidently the Baltimore firm of Appleton, Poor & Miles had failed. This would not have surprised Henry Lee, who had always had a poor

---

3. *Columbian Centinel,* June 17, 1818.

1. Jackson-Lee Papers, "Letter Book from Jany. 17th. 1817 to October 27. 1818."

opinion of the firm's way of doing business. We learn from the letter below something of the extent of Lee's failure in 1811 as well as of his commercial condition at the time of the letter. His wife, writing to him in 1814 and expressing her agreement with his wish "that we should, as opportunity offered, pay the whole or part of your portion of the debts," went on to say that "as far as I have learned I believe you have paid 16/ in the £ — if you never pay another cent we have nothing to reproach ourselves with — all that could be done we did, and I believe even those who were sufferers thought so." [2]

We learn from a letter of Mar. 31, 1818, to Peter Remsen, that Charles D. Miles had "a Brother to aid him" in Calcutta. It is agreeable to read Henry Lee's statement that "Mʳ Miles . . . is doing as I expected, the goods in the C are well charged."

Boston May 21ˢᵗ. 1818

Mʳ. George Miles
   Baltimore
      Dear Sir
         I avail myself of the first moment of my return home to acknowledge yours of the 8th Inst and a note by Mʳ. Appleton — The letters enclosed to my care shall be forwarded — I have also a letter from your Brother William — With regard to his application for his employment were I in want [of any one — stricken through] I have several near relations who are in want, and whom I should be obliged to prefer — Your Brother Charles found so little to do that he sent home Mʳ. Cabot who accompanied him — I have [in — stricken through] formed no establishment in Calcutta having no object in view but the purchase of 2 or 3 Cargoes for myself &friends — I shall in course of few months send out a vessel for his return — I have not yet received your first letter referred to in yours of 8th containing an application for 500$ on your Brothers and my account — I have no funds of his save the profits not yet realised on an importation of goods from Calcutta, and as to myself I am wholly unable to afford the aid having yet upwards of $40000 of old debts which though legally discharged from I

2. Morse, F. R., *op. cit.*, p. 209.

am bound in honor and conscience to pay, and have already begun to do it — I sincerely lament the misfortunes which have come upon you, and hope you may be able to resume your business or some other which may prove more successful than your late concerns — Your brother has done my business very well, but there is so much loss on the outward cargo, and on the ship that the voyage will not end very profitably — The trade to Calcutta is now almost confined to Sugar &Cotton, and no longer affords those advantages to me which it would have done had not the duties on Piece Goods been increased, they are not used in this country and the demand for exportation is limited — Opportunities for Calcutta offer every month, and I shall always be glad to forward your letters

Yours truly
(Sgd)   Henry Lee

LETTER FROM JOHN TRACY, BOSTON, MAY 28, 1818, TO WILLIAM & N. WYER, NEW ORLEANS, WITH A CONSIGNMENT OF PIECE GOODS [1]

During the period of the embargo, the trade with the West Indies being cut off, Henry Lee had turned to New Orleans as a market for his India piece goods. Now, since the American trade with India was hampered by high duties and increased competition, he once more turned to the southern port. Tracy was evidently writing on Lee's account.

The goods shipped were doubtless from the cargo of the *Cruttenden* which arrived at Boston, May 12.[2] For some time thereafter Henry Lee was engaged in disposing of India goods. On May 30 he wrote to James P. Higginson: "Mr Tracy & myself have done very well in spices, but they have fallen here. . . . Bengal piece goods are very low." He found it necessary to make an allowance for saltpetre sold in Baltimore which did not come up to the sample. His comment was that "they have us in their power and you must allow ½ cent." [3]

1. Jackson-Lee Papers, "Letter Book from Jany. 17th. 1817 to October 27. 1818."

2. *Columbian Centinel,* May 13, 1818.

3. Jackson-Lee Papers, "Letter Book from Jany. 17th. 1817 to Octo-

Other articles were also a disappointment. To Peter Remsen & Co. he wrote June 13: "I hope as this experiment of Castor Oil has cost me $1000 you will not quote it or Seeds for 6 Mo^s. to come as 2 or 3 persons having it would reduce the price to nothing."

Messrs. W^m. & N Wyer.   Boston, May 28th 1818.
   New. Orleans.   Dear Sirs.

Enclos'd you have Invoice & Bill lading five Bales uncommonly fine goods which I think may prove well suited for consumption in your market — and hope to have some encouragement to ship you occasionally, as I may find any Bengal piece goods cheap in this market; — for this object you will do me afavor to write particularly regarding white & col'd piece goods of the following names and dimensions — viz —

		cubits		yd
Mamoodies	38 @ 40	x 1⅞ @ 2 or	"	19 x ⅞ to 1
Cossas	— —	40 x 2⅛ —	"	20 x 1 1/16
Mow Sannas.	— —	21 x 1⅜ —	"	— 10½ x 1 1/16
Gurrahs	— —	34 x 2⅛ —	"	— 17 x 1 1/16
Checks	— —	12 x 1½ —	"	— 6 x ¾
Custas	— —	12 x 1½ —	"	— " " "
do	— —	20 x 2 —	"	— 10 x 1
Chintz	— —	10 x 2 —	"	— 5 " "

Choppa Romals 7 in a piece
Blue Gurrahs 34 x 2⅛.

Seersuckers, particularly the last article — in regard to Paturns best lik'd. I think y^t. the Broad stripes are most valued, and that the Soosies will prove a good article

You are getting to have a great trade and fewer manufactures to interfere with imported Cottons, than is the case here, which must give some opening, for good sales to be occasionally made — formerly we had sales made in your Port at considerably advanced prices from their value here — the Sale of cottons for Consumption has almost ceased in this quarter of the Country — but a good demand now and then for Export — M^r. Lee

---

ber 27. 1818," Henry Lee, Boston, June 10, 1818, to H. & R. H. Osgood, Baltimore.

will always import more or less, & if you keep us well advised of the State of your market I have no doubt he will feel a wish to consign You —

We have never had a Correspondent in your place who was industrious en° to give a just account of the market

The Seersuckers Invoic'd $15 are higher cost, and finer than the others. As I wish to make Sale on arrival of the Vessel you may accept $13. for those Inv^d. $15. and for those Invoic'd $14 you may accept $12 if no more can be obtain'd.

The Soosies you may sell for the most they will bring. giving a particular acc^t. of the estimation in which they are. held by the Purchasser compared with Seersuckers.

I have forwarded by the Vessel aCopy original Invoice, Certificate for Debenture &c. and taken every precaution that we [interlineated: may] not be embarrassed by the Custom house. as any such difficulty may occasion the loss of a Sale for the season.

In any Remittances you make I. should prefer bills on this place if to be had at par or Specie Dollars would be better.

Wishing to hear from you regarding prospect of sale. and future shipments

I am

Yr^s. truly

Jn° Tracy.

Letter from Henry Lee, Boston, June 13, 1818, to Perit & Cabot, Philadelphia, in Regard to Difficulties over the Du Pont Saltpetre Contract [1]

In July, 1817, Henry Lee, through Perit & Cabot, had made a contract with the Du Ponts to furnish them 200,000 lb. of saltpetre, to be paid for in approved notes, with a penalty of $10,000 for nonfulfillment. A Mr. Vaughn stood surety for the Du Ponts in this agreement. Unfortunately for all parties, "in March, 1818, five powder mills exploded, destroying almost the entire plant and over

1. Jackson-Lee Papers, "Letter Book from Jany. 17th. 1817 to October 27. 1818."

eighty-five thousand pounds of powder. The actual loss was about thirty thousand dollars."[2] Henry Lee's comment on this disaster, Mar. 30, 1818, was: "I am afraid Dupont's credit will suffer, the loss of money and time is very serious affair, his agents must of course give me satisfactory security, or we can't deliver the S. P —" He added: "If Dupont is in a situation not to require his S P. I am ready to release him from the first 100000 lb — It will be very injurious to me if when it does arrive he fails in giving good security, for under present circumstances I should not deem it prudent to deliver it without first rate names in addition to his own —" Du Pont delayed in deciding whether he wanted the first installment or not, and, when he finally decided to take it, would not at first give what Henry Lee regarded as proper endorsements. Lee declined, for example, on June 11, to accept Irenée's brother Victor as a proper endorser "as he is same concern with the other Dupont one of the Company — or if not a member of the firm, is under responsibilities to other D's." Lee offered as a further compromise to "accept $5000 in lieu of 10,000 & rescond the contract," $10,000 being the original penalty for non-fulfillment, or to "diminish the quantity about 20,000 lb" from the original first installment of 100,000 lb. As a matter of fact, he had hardly enough on hand to make up the full 100,000 lb. In the letter below he suggested other possibilities. Fortunately, according to a letter of July 6, "the business with Dupont" had by that time been "amicably arranged," partly by Perit & Cabot themselves offering to guarantee the payment of the notes. Henry Lee, however, remarked on July 31: "It appears unjust to me, that Dupont's Notes should not be dated at the time the Saltpetre was first offered him — a portion was ready for delivery in May — & it was his fault in not giving the security agreed for, that it was not deliverd — I hope on a representation of the case, they will consent to alter the dates." Lee desired the notes to be "sold @ 1% per Month . . . which is a great loss to me — if that can't be done — I accept your offer of guarantee @ 2½% — on the whole amount."

During all his difficulties with the Du Ponts, Henry Lee was steadily engaged in trying to make contracts for and sales of saltpetre to various powder manufacturers: the Aetna and Bellona com-

2. Du Pont, B. G., *E. I. Du Pont de Nemours and Company: A History, 1802–1902* (Boston and N. Y., 1920), p. 54.

panies through H. & R. H. Osgood, Baltimore; Whelen and others through Perit & Cabot, Philadelphia. By Sept. 29, 1818, he was all out of saltpetre save for 90 bags which he had "kept to retail . . . at 10 @ 11 cts" but which on that date he shipped to H. & R. H. Osgood, Baltimore, requesting that firm to make an agreement for a contract with a powder manufacturer. On Oct. 1 he wrote to Peter Remsen & Co.: "I think you will get 11 Cts for the Saltpetre — I believe there is not a Bag for sale in U. States."

Boston June 13th. 1818.

Messrs Perit &Cabot
    Philadelphia
        Dear Sirs,
            I have yours of   with Bill Lading — I can't imagine upon what pretence D can refuse us an endorser — I shall not take any paper, unless good enough to get off @ 1% per Mo., I am willing to allow 2½% for a good guarantee, rather than have a contest in law — I hopeMr. Whelen will lend you enough to make up 100,000 lb — I would allow him interest 'till returned if he requires it — I shall have a parcel early in July —
    If you could get off the S P. for good paper, the difficulty [interlineated: with D] could be got rid of — I must trust to your taking all the proper steps to give me my rights — Mr Chauncey should be consulted — Cannot I attach Duponts property in this state on account of my demand against him? I shall be satisfied with the penalty in the Bond, or you may proceed and sell at Auction for [interlineated: a/c of] whom it may concern and buy it in for my account if under 9¼ cts.
    This is a serious business to me, and one I did not anticipate, from your representations of the character of Dupont, and Mr. Vaughn — I should have thought the latter had more regard to character, than thus grossly violate his agreement — If this thing is not settled justly I shall take great pains to state the particulars, and Dupont may in the end and Vaughn too find themselves sufferers — I hope you may get through without resort to law — If you choose referees, get such as are in

no way under the influence of D & V if they should decide that Victor Dupont is a safe endorser it would be worse to me than an abandonment of the contract — If D does not want to use the S. P. he might give what name he pleased, and let it remain with you 'till the note is paid or sold —

Let me know as soon as possible whether Whelen will loan you enough to make up 100 th — The C's departure will be too soon for any agreement for importations unless I get your letters immediately — I can lend the shippers $10000 in Specie for 15 days, whatever you do, I should look to you for a guarantee that engagements would be performed.

Yours truly

Have you any return from Dr Cooper   (Sgd)   H Lee
HL

LETTER FROM HENRY LEE, BOSTON, JUNE 26, 1818, TO GRANT, PILLANS & CO., LEGHORN, WITH AN INVOICE OF GOODS [1]

Despite his poor opinion of the prospects for the sale of piece goods either in the United States or in Europe, Henry Lee continued to import them into the one and re-export them to the other. On July 1 he shipped to Hill & Blodget, Gibraltar, "171 Bags Ginger" to "yield net of freight and other charges $7.50 Cwt." Evidently the reports from Gibraltar in regard to piece goods had been so discouraging that he did not choose to venture even an experimental consignment. By a letter of July 23, 1818, to A. E. Belknap, Marseilles, we learn that Henry Lee saw no chance of making a profit by shipping goods to that port unless he "could secure freight at a moderate rate say $50 ton," when he "should like to make shipments of sugar, cotton &c &c," but he had not "the means of purchasing & owning ships even here, much more in a foreign country." Lee had evidently given up hope of trading directly between France and Calcutta in his own vessels.

1. Jackson-Lee Papers, "Letter Book from Jany. 17th. 1817 to October 27. 1818."

Boston, June 26th 1818

origl. p Amsterdam Packet sailed 8th July

Messrs. Grant Pillans & Co

Leghorn

Gentlemen,

Since I last had the pleasure of writing you I have been favored with your various letters to 30 th Jany. — The sales of Bengal goods from this country must have been attended with a heavy loss more especially the George's Cargo which were under the average cost in Bengal for 10 years — I am well convinced that there will no longer be any considerable consumption of coarse India Piece Goods in Europe — they have ceased to be used here. in any quantities — I now enclose you an Invoice and Bill Lading of small shipment of Piece Goods made in the Amsterdam Packet more as an experiment to ascertain the state of your market than any expectation of profit, the Mamoodies & [interlineated: Beerboom] Gurrahs are coarse, the Surool are very good — All sorts of Piece Goods have come out unusually thin and coarse since the rise in Cotton in Bengal — You may sell the coarse Gurrahs &Mamoodies at a price which will yield nett of all charges 2¼ Spanish Dollars, and the fine Surool Gurrahs $2¾ do. I presume however bad the state of your market, they must command these low rates — The Saltpetre at any price offered — I am afraid the direct cargoes from Calcutta will in future prevent our doing anything to advantage in Bengal goods to Italy — Please forward Certificate of Landing, and remit the proceeds to Samuel Williams Esqr. No. 13 Finsbury Square London

Your Obt Servt

(Signed) Henry Lee

LETTER FROM HENRY LEE, BOSTON, JULY 25, 1818, TO H. &
R. H. OSGOOD, BALTIMORE, ON SALES OF SALTPETRE AND PROS-
PECTS FOR THE SALE OF GUNPOWDER [1]

The Baltimore firm was taking its place beside Perit & Cabot as one
of Henry Lee's leading agents for the sale of saltpetre. Observe the
suggestion of making part payment for saltpetre in gunpowder — a
variation on the old custom of paying the miller in flour. On July 3,
Lee had questioned Miralla & Co., Havana, concerning the prospect of
selling "30,000 lbs powder in 25 lb Kegs."

But the Baltimore firm also handled piece goods for Henry Lee,
whose associate, John Tracy, on Aug. 11 remarked: "yours is the
best, and almost the only market for India piece Goods at this time.
our advices from Havana afford no encouragement but I hope that
market will be better in the fall." However, writing to Miralla &
Co., July 3, Lee had said that there were very few "India piece
goods — . . . in this Country especially coarse white goods."

Messrs. H & R. H. Osgood   Boston 25th. July 1818
    Baltimore
        Dear Sir's
            I have yours of 21st. inst. It is true the Saltpetre sold
by you on account of Mr. P. is as good as the L. but it is refined & worth more than the common crude — I am willing to
supply all crude @ 10 cts. payable in cash 9 Months or best
refined @ 12cts — I think you will find them disposed to come
to our terms in course of 2 or 3 months I am offered 11¢ and
13 cts by a Philadelphia concern — powder in payment for
half, @ 6$ Cask — I think I shall do better with this concern
than the offers of the Aetna Company — The prospect of
Spanish war & the success of the Patriots in South America will
help the Sale of S. Petre, in course of few months — The British Government have issued an order in Council, prohibiting
[interlineated: the] export powder & arms to South America.
which will oblige them to look wholly to us for supplies — I
believe you are under engagements on my behalf to the Aetna

    1. Jackson-Lee Papers, "Letter Book from Jany. 17th. 1817 to Octo-
ber 27. 1818."

Company for 200 to 300 Bags. deliverable first October —
having been at New York at the time, — I wrote some of the
letters on this subject, I have not retained copies of all of them
— Please to let me know the quantity & time — Perhaps you
may find some of your small dealers inclined to contract for
refined at 12 cents 6 Months from delivery — say like that you
received from Philadelphia — Severing may want — as he is in
high credit, as I understand, I would give him 10 Months time
& supply crude of fair quality @ 10 cents say 100 M.

Yours truly
(sgd)   Henry Lee

Bills on London par

Spanish dollars 3% premium

U. States Bank Stock 128 falling — our people would buy
largely @ 120 — I am looking for 500 ps. Brown Sheeting by
an early arrival from Russia — What is the prospect for them
with you?

H.L

It will be more convenient if you would note at foot of your
A/Sales the average time at which they fall due

LETTER FROM HENRY LEE, BOSTON, SEPT. 12, 1818, TO STEIG-
LITZ & CO., ST. PETERSBURG, ORDERING CHEAP RUSSIA GOODS [1]

Henry Lee had evidently shipped some turmeric to the St. Petersburg firm, though we have no record of his having done more than
enquire about the possibility of its meeting a sale in Russia. Evidently, however, Lee had made no large consignments to St. Petersburg or he would not have needed to instruct Steiglitz & Co. to draw
on London for the amount of the Russian goods.

With Russian manufactures, as with India goods, Lee preferred
to handle the cheaper qualities.

1. Jackson-Lee Papers, "Letter Book from Jany. 17th. 1817 to October 27. 1818."

Boston, Sept. 12th. 1818

Messrs. Steiglitz &Co
  St. Petersburg   (origl. prGarland/
    Gentlemen
        I am favored with your several letters of 19th. Feby. 7th
May and 4th. June, and thank you for the information they
contain. If the Tumerick should remain unsold when this comes
to hand, I think you had better dispose of it, for the most it will
command — I have reason to be very well satisfied with the
manufactures sent me by the Thomas — I am desirous of making an other small importation the coming year & would thank
you to procure me either on contract or any other way, you
judge most for my interest, the following articles —

    300 pieces Sheetings narrow & of the most ordinary qual-
           ity as they are intended for a market, where ordinary
           sell better in proportion than the fine —
    300 pieces narrow and coarse Ravens Duck wanted for the
           same market.
    300 pieces Broad Diaper of common quality
    200   do narrow do.   do.   do.
    100   do Drillings do.   do.   do.

and 50 pieces of the most inferiour sail cloth — If goods of
the description wanted cannot be procured in the market, it is
probable they may be manufactured — It is quite an object to
have them of cheapest sorts — I have agreed with Mr. Slade to
pay him £500..0..0 here on account of this order & to place funds
in London in the hands of Samuel Williams Esqr. for the Balance say to be drawn for by you, in March, at 90 days sight. I
should have been glad to have made a remittance per Garland
in Merchandize, but our market affords just now. nothing but
India Cotton which I am apprehensive will not answer. I wish
the goods ship'd on board first Vessel which will take them, to
any port in United States north of Virginia, to my address —
You will please to write me via England, what you may do &
at same time communicate any information relative to the value
of East and West India produce which you think may be in-

teresting in this quarter — There will be heavy importations of Bengal Indigo, Rice, ginger Sugars &c &c and if any of these articles promise well, I shall be inclined to make a shipment, in the next years ships. our people will not import many sheetings next season, unless they go lower with you, as they are considered too dear for Consumption at any thing beyond $16. for those of fair quality. There will be a loss on this years importation of Russia manufactures — as well as Hemp and iron — I am respectfully

Your Obt Serv[t].

(sgd)   Henry Lee

LETTER FROM HENRY LEE, BOSTON, SEPT. 12, 1818, TO PETER REMSEN & CO., NEW YORK, ON PRICES OF A NUMBER OF COMMODITIES [1]

The India goods shipped to the New York firm doubtless came on the brig *Lascar*, Joseph Lee, Jr., owner, which arrived at Boston Sept. 5, "125 days from Calcutta." It had been found impossible to sell the *Cruttenden*, which had arrived at Boston, May 12, because of her British registry, so she had cleared again for Calcutta, June 27.[2] On Sept. 26, Lee wrote to Peter Remsen & Co.: "W. Oliver & S. Cabot Jun[r]. have purchased the Lascar & she goes to Calcutta."

Lee was continuing not only the importation of piece goods directly from India but also their purchase in London.[3]

The reference to the want of letters from Calcutta is at least partly explained by a remark in a letter of Sept. 19 to Peter Remsen & Co.: "If poor Miles had lived I should probably have had a small importation in the next ships." It will be remembered that Charles D. Miles had sent home his fellow supercargo, R. C. Cabot, because there was not work enough for two, disregarding one of the principal reasons for sending supercargoes to Calcutta by twos rather than singly — the heavy casualty list of unacclimated Europeans and Americans in that unhealthful tropical city.

1. Jackson-Lee Papers, "Letter Book from Jan[y]. 17th. 1817 to October 27. 1818."   2. *Columbian Centinel,* May 13, July 1, Sept. 9, 1818.

3. Jackson-Lee Papers, "Letter Book from Jan[y]. 17th. 1817 to October 27. 1818," Henry Lee, Boston, Sept. 18, 1818, to Samuel Williams, London.

Observe the reference to the decline in the use of coffee. During the War of 1812, tea drinking suffered a similar declension.[4]

Boston, Septr. 12th. 1818

Messrs. Peter Remsen &Co
      New York
            Dear Sir's,

I enclose Invoice Bill Lading and Certificates of Sheetings — Ravens Duck & Diaper you may sell the Ravens @ 11½ if you think best — the Diaper may now be dull sale at 5. but so few have come they will go at that & Sheetings ought to bring $17 — all I have sold here has been at $16 50/100 & most of holders ask $17 — I have yours of 7th. & 8th. Sept. I am not surprised you got no letters from Calcutta. I have had none by any of the late arrivals. they are very negligent in this way. Cotton cost on board including commission 11 @ 11½ Cts lb & when Canton arrives it may not I think be worth more than 12¢ to 13¢ short — If she takes rice and sugar the owners will save themselves — most of her Cargo will be on freight at $20 ton — Sugars are as scarce as with you, have been through the year worth ¼ @ ½ $ more here than any other market as most of our importers export, as they arrive — My Choppas are best patterns that have come for some time quality rather better than Cruttendens I have sold 1 Case at 5¼ & shall get 5⅛ to 5¼ for the rest — you must get me 5½ — My white goods are very good — I am sending you some — I shall send you 200 Bags excellent crude & 20 Boxes refined Saltpetre you must get me 11¢. & 13¢. what is wanted here will sell for 10¢. & 12¢. I shall sell part & rest deliver on account contracts — If De Wolf would agree to take 200 Bags now & 100 on or before 1st. January & 2 @ 300 March to June. I might let him have Crude @ 10½cts 6 Months — If I send you a Draft at 60 days on Philadelphia for 5 or 6000$ more on acc^t. Balance Due you. Can you get the money on without any loss? I have money due there at that time & in Baltimore also & find it difficult to get it here without a loss of ½ to 1% — Pepper is better acc^{ts}. from

4. Porter, *op. cit.*, vol. ii, p. 591.

Havre & Antwerp favorable — It will I think sell for 22 Cts long — Teas have been purchased by our large Grocers — Hyson worth 120¢. Skin 65 — no more Coffee consumed, except by the rich & extravagant — Midas carries out say 250 ^{m}. owned by Dodge of Salem. Williams & Pratt send 30 ^{m}. E Francis 20 ^{m}. Sawyer 10 ^{m}. &c &c. M^r. Gray will I think send out a ship to China & Thorndike also. It will not be so profitable as last year —

J. Lee J^r. has had very good offers for the Lascar, I am in hope he will sell her — she does well for M^r. Oliver & himself & for all the freighters — Large or orders have gone on to your place for dollars F. Lee & myself are getting 175 for the little Indigo we have in the Lascar

Yours truly
(Sgd) Henry Lee

You have some Arsenic of mine on hand I wish you would sell it even @ 20 Cts, if no more can be obtained — H L

Sept. 14th. I enclose Invoice of 22 Bales p^s goods — I think you will get my prices for them, but rather than lose a sale. I would have you accept prices in red. I think if you can get your dealers to look at them they must sell, as my prices are no higher than you got for W to sell the goods at auction within 10 @ 15 cts p^s of my limits

LETTER FROM HENRY LEE, BOSTON, SEPT. 28, 1818, TO JAMES SCHOTT & CO., PHILADELPHIA, ON THE VALUE OF BUFFALO ROBES [1]

The letter below is rather more interesting than important, though it does show Henry Lee's willingness to handle goods outside his usual line. Buffalo robes were at this time by no means the important article of commerce which they later became. They do not appear in the existing records of John Jacob Astor's fur trade till during the War of 1812. In the year before the letter below, Astor "sold by can tract 1000 Boffolo Ropes to young M^r. fawler of Albany at 4$ to be Delivrd to him." In 1834 they were the same price.[2]

1. Jackson-Lee Papers, "Letter Book from Jany. 17th. 1817 to October 27. 1818." 2. Porter, *op. cit.*, vol. i, p. 270; vol. ii, pp. 1165, 1227.

Boston Sep^t. 28th. 1818

Messrs. James Schott &Co
    Philadelphia
        Dear Sir's,
            I have made many inquiries to ascertain the value of
Buffaloe Robes & should imagine they might bring $4.50 to 6$
according to quality — From the nature of the article, it is not
easy to ascertain their worth without having them, on hand —
If the price would answer it might be well to send 200 on trial &
by the sale you could see exactly what they would bring — I
hope in day or two to hear of arrival of my goods — I would
thank you to render me account Sales of Choppas & Bandannas
as soon as completed —

Yours truly
(Sgd)   H Lee

LETTER FROM HENRY LEE, BOSTON, OCT. 21, 1818, TO PETER
REMSEN & CO., NEW YORK, ON FINANCIAL STRINGENCY [1]

The straitened condition of finance mentioned below was the result
of the policy of contraction adopted by the United States Bank in
Aug., 1818. On Sept. 28, 1818, writing to Peter Remsen & Co., New
York, Henry Lee had remarked: "Dollars are 7% @ 7½, & none to
be had — our people must diminish their trade beyond the Cape, or
pay 10% for dollars." On the following day, however, he wrote to
Miralla & Co., Havana: "Business is very good, as most articles of
import are in fair demand at good prices." The Baltimore branch of
the United States Bank went to smash in Jan., 1819, with a loss of
$3,000,000.[2]

1. Jackson-Lee Papers, "Letter Book from Jany. 17th. 1817 to October 27. 1818."
2. Dewey, *op. cit.*, p. 152; Rezneck, Samuel, "The Depression of
1819–22, A Social History," *The American Historical Review*, vol. xxxix
(Oct., 1933), p. 29.

Boston, October 21st. 1818

Messrs. Peter Remsen &Co
   New York
      Dear Sir's
         I have yours of 17th. I shall not draw before 29th. for
Balance due on P & C's acceptance — & not then if you find it
inconvenient to pay, I have been afraid of difficulties at the
South for some time & have been getting funds this way — have
lately received Drafts on Salem from Baltimore & expect more,
if they don't come I shall be glad to get acceptances collected
through you — I have nothing coming round there for 3 or 4
Mos. scarcity of money has commenc'd here & will be severe
some time this winter. It will with price of dollars 9% stop the
India Trade in a great degree — Our greatest India merchants
will fell the presure more than any other Class — I have drawn
on you to day for 2500$ 90 days I believe I have only before
drawn for 3500$ — on account of the late shipments — Keep
my Bengal ps. goods in the paper — some of your exporters
may want & I am very anxious to have them sold — Your
Eastern friends will be calling for money in few weeks. the presure will I am afraid be of long continuance & produce bad
effects south of you — The Osgoods say their Baltimore Banks
will not stop payment, as they did during the war, but will call
in & distress their customers very much —
                                          Yours truly
                                          (Sgd) H. Lee

Marcellas goes to Canton to morrow 400,000 Dollars, 2/3ds. or
3/4 on freight the rest for Teas for a Cargo —
There is freighting voyage getting up for Silks & Teas, but I
am not at liberty to name vessel or Supercargo, You will probably see him in New York — a 3d. ship is going owned by the
Doors for teas &c —

LETTER AND PRICES CURRENT FROM GRANT, PILLANS & CO., LEGHORN, FEB. 3, 6, 9, 1819, TO HENRY LEE, BOSTON, DE-SCRIBING MARKET FOR INDIA PIECE GOODS [1]

In almost every case, the surviving business papers of a merchant of a century or more ago give but a one-sided view of his operations. Usually it is only his letter books and account books which have come down to us. We consequently know from the former what he thought of business in general and, in particular, what he thought his goods should bring; but we get only occasional hazy glimpses of what his correspondents thought, and of the reasons, according to them, that his consignments did not bring so much as he had hoped. The reason for this incompleteness of material is simple. Letters to a mer-chant needed to be kept by him only until the transactions mentioned therein were completed; then they might be, and frequently were, de-stroyed. In some cases, however, they were assorted according to some rough and frequently inconsistent scheme, and the neat bundles, each with a paper collar inscribed in India ink, and bound with a pink tape, were stowed away in shelf or drawer or chest. But house clean-ings and removals frequently disturbed their repose; fires, accidental or inspired by a passion for clearing away rubbish, sometimes caused their destruction; they mouldered away in the damp of cellars or in the drip of leaky roofs; in minute fragments they furnished comfort to countless generations of mice. The compact, heavy, sometimes rather handsome, leather-bound letter books and ledgers, however, presented no such challenge to the fanaticism of the "redder-up" and, though succumbing readily to any general conflagration, offered much greater resistance than would unbound papers to the other elements and to the teeth of rodents. It is consequently not so much a matter of surprise that so few specimens of letters to sedentary merchants from their commercial correspondents are to be found among their business papers, as it is a matter of congratulation that some few have survived. Chief among the few loose letters to Henry Lee in the Jackson-Lee Collection is a bundle belonging to the year 1819, in which merchants in various European ports and in Havana describe the fortunes of East India goods shipped to them for disposal. Through these letters we see, if only briefly, an aspect of Henry Lee's

1. Jackson-Lee Papers.

business life as it appeared not to himself but to his foreign correspondents.

During the year 1819 Henry Lee was apparently more zealous in cultivating the Leghorn market than that of any other foreign port. A dozen or more letters from the Italian port, similar, in a general way, to that below, give an account of sales; mention the impossibility of disposing of goods at Lee's invoice price, which it is assumed is marked up; describe the types of textiles most suitable for the market; usually refer to claims for allowances because of damaged goods; and in most cases — though not in the letter below — complain of the inferiority of the goods in texture, color, and dimensions.

A letter from the same firm on Mar. 8 gave word of a remittance of £300 for the sawns, baftas, and gurrahs in another consignment, by the *New Packet*. The emerties and mamoodies remained, but the Leghorn firm did not doubt that they would soon be profitably sold. Another letter of Apr. 7 announced sales of the remaining goods by the *New Packet* and of a new consignment by the *Acorn*. Here, for the first time, Grant, Pillans & Co. complained, and that in most vigorous terms, of the quality of the goods shipped to them by Lee. The gurrahs were of "wretched quality" and "but for the prevalence of the plague in Barbary . . . we hardly know how they would have been got off;" the need for winding-sheets helped the sale. The goods by the *Acorn* sold, but at a heavy loss on invoice, increased by demands from buyers for allowances because of damaged goods.

Henry Lee did not confine his consignments to any one Leghorn firm; on June 1, Reed, Bell, De Yongh & Co. announced the receipt of a consignment by John Jacob Astor's famous brig *Pedler*. The firm gave discouraging reports of the prospects for checks, custers, comboies, seersuckers, romals and bandannas — indeed all handkerchiefs — all Madras goods, and Patna sannas and baftas. On the other hand there would probably be a ready sale for "Blue Sallempores and Blue Guinées — Necannias . . . Chapelas Blue . . . Neganepauts," and long cloths. But in general the prospects were poor. "We never knew this Market more dull." On June 29 the same firm gave in detail the objections to the goods by the *Pedler*, which in most cases were found too narrow, short, and coarse, but which had nevertheless mostly been sold, though at low prices. On July 24 the firm, now known as Bell, De Yongh & Co., announced the sale, still at low prices, of nearly all the remainder of the consignment.

Prices had suffered a decline and were unlikely to rise, the briskness of the demand for piece goods being counterbalanced by the abundance of the supply.

There follows a run of letters from Grant, Pillans & Co. A letter of July 27 agreed with the other Leghorn firm that there was no market for sannas, handkerchiefs, or Madras goods, but that blue Surat goods were suited to the market. Another of Aug. 23 announced a remittance to London of £1,000 and the receipt by the *Spartan* of 60 bales of piece goods, which, despite earlier warnings, were not well assorted, containing a large proportion of handkerchiefs, "Checks & Custahs," which were almost entirely unsalable. Blue gurrahs and mamoodies would not "answer at all." Blue baftas, once sold for use on the Guinea Coast in the slave-trade, were no longer "consumed in africa at all." The Leghorn firm, however, modified the earlier ban on all handkerchiefs by excepting "Sassergaties" and "Masulipatam & Vintopolam . . . deep red." On Sept. 11 they announced the sale of the *Spartan's* "Gurrahs — the largest single article of the Shipment" at pezzas 2⅛ to 3⅛ "leaving in the face of your invoice a very heavy loss, — we hope & must believe not so heavy in reality as it appears — for we do assure you that we have Gurrahs by the same vessel — too many unfortunately . . . — invoiced from 47 R^s. up to 56 & 60. certainly superior to yours which we see set down from $2.40 to $2.75." Since a rupee was roughly equivalent to 50 cents, this means that gurrahs invoiced at 60 rupees per score cost about $1.50 per piece in Calcutta. The cost price of Henry Lee's gurrahs, apparently reduced to dollars per piece, was thus far higher than the highest of those of his competitors. On Sept. 18, Grant, Pillans & Co. again complained of inferior goods. Such phrases as "very poor light goods," "too narrow . . . for printing," "the most ordinary goods we ever saw," appear again and again. The blue baftas were "absolutely stained as it were from the wretched dying." There was also "almost uniformly a considerable quantity of pieces more or less stained & damaged."

According to a letter of Sept. 18, Webb & Co. found 15 bales shipped to them to be no better. Their "very inferior quality" caused the Leghorn firm to dispose of most of them at public auction. A ray of improvement, however, appears in a letter of Sept. 26 from Bell, De Yongh & Co., who sold 23 bales by the *Minerva* "at . . . prices . . . higher than any lately made, and above what We *expected to*

HENRY LEE'S HOUSE, 4 BEDFORD PLACE, BOSTON

get." But here, too, are complaints that goods are "badly woven," "of short measure," "narrow." Cossas and Koyrabad mamoodies were given a clean bill; Jalapore sannas were good but dear.

These letters indicate that Leghorn was a good market for properly assorted India piece goods but that Henry Lee had been shipping to that port inferior goods and colored goods better suited to the west coast of Africa, for which destination the goods he had principally handled before the War of 1812 had been intended, rather than white goods of reasonably good quality and suitable dimensions. As a result, his goods had to be disposed of at a large loss on the invoice and certainly at little if any profit.

In the letters from Leghorn there are frequent references to quarantine. Italian cities, because of their early trade with the plague-ridden Orient, were the first to prescribe a probationary period for vessels arriving at their ports before intercourse with the shore was permitted. Goods to be landed were placed on shore in lazarettos for inspection and fumigation.[2] There is mention in letters and prices current of goods "being admitted to prattick" or "pratteek;" this last word is a corruption of *pratique,* meaning a license granted to the master of a vessel for communication with the shore.

Rates of exchange are frequently given in letters from Leghorn, on London and sometimes on other commercial cities. "£800 at 53⅛ in p 3614.2.4" means that £800 stg. was equal to 3,614 pezzas, 2 sols, and 4 deniers, inasmuch as 1 pezza, about $1, would purchase 53⅛d. in exchange on London. Later in 1819, the pezza declined relatively till in October it would purchase only 49d. in bills on London.

Leghorn 6 February 1819

Boston. Henry Lee Esqre
Sir

The annexed is copy of our respects of 30 ulto. advising the arrival of the Eliza Hailey and our remittance for your account to Saml. Williams Esqre in anticipation of your shipment p New Packet. — £800 at 53⅛ in p 3614.2.4.

---

2. M'Culloch, J. R., *A Dictionary . . . of Commerce and Commercial Navigation,* 2 vols. (Philadelphia, 1847), vol. ii, p. 370.

LEGHORN PRICE CURRENT
GRANT, PILLANS & Co.

The 3. Feby 1819

Reduced into American Weight & Currency — calculating the Spanish Dollar at Livres 6. 1/3 all Leghorn charges deducted on Imports; — Exports free on board. Where two prices are quoted, the reduction is made on the highest.

IMPORTS		LEGHORN PRICE from	to	per	Net proceeds in Spanish Dollars exclusive of freight & insurance		per
Bark Jesuits	Livres	1	10	lb	1	73	lb
Cassia Fistula	Pezzas	6	7	lb 100	8	31	cwt
Lignea	"	36	38	"		37 1/4	lb
Cinnamon	Ducats	240	270	lb	3	27	"
Cloves	Livres	4 1/4	5	"		87 2/5	"
Cochineal black	"	{35	37	"	6	34	"
Silver	"						
Cocoa Caracca	Pezzas	30	32	lb 100	35	62	cwt
Trinidad	"	18	20	"	22	26	"
Maranham	"	13	1/4	"	15	02	"
Coffee fine	"	29	30	"		31	lb
good middling	"	27	28	"		29	"
middling	"	25	26	"		27	"
ordinary	"	24	—	"		25	"
Mocha	"	27	28	"		29	"
Corn Indian	Liv. eff.	10	11	Sack		79	bushel
Cotton Fernambucco	Pezas	40	42	lb 100		43 1/3	lb
Louisiana	"	30	32	"		33	"
Georgia	"	26	30	"		31	"
Dyewoods Logwood	Ducats	15	17	lb 1000	42	50	ton
Braziletto	Pezzas	16	18	"	40	73	"
Fustic	"	12	14	"	29	85	"
Nicaragua large&solid	"	{20	40	"	90	80	"
middling & rough	"						

REMARKS

Our market has been, for most articles, in a state of uncommon dulness for the last fortnight or three weeks. We are less detailed on each separate article than usual, & quote prices with difficulty, having no real operations to guide us. The last sale effected of SUGAR (150 Hhds English crushed) was, in a manner, forced on the market at Pezzas 18 with extra allowances that reduce it to about Pezzas 17½ — the quality was equal to the general run of Havannahs. Some good Jamaica COFFEE was sold, under the same circumstances, as low at Pezzas 25. With firmness on the part of holders, however, & no disproportioned accession to our actual deposit, we should think prices may recover;— though we really question whether they are likely soon to rise again to our December quotations, which we have accordingly reduced in our present price current by 3 @ 4 per %. —

CASSIA LIGNEA None in first hands.

IMPORTS	LEGHORN PRICE from	to	per	Net proceeds in Spanish Dollars exclusive of freight & insurance.		per	REMARKS
Fish salted Codfish Engl. .... *Pauls*	50	63	lb 160	5	03	cwt	FISH. The price we quote only obtained for small quantities. A cargo
Salmon .... Eff. — *Pezzas*	40	50	tierce	41	38	tier.	of Labrador Fish was sold a few days ago at 50 Pauls.
Flour .... "	7	8	barrel	6	36	bar.	
Ginger black .... "			lb 100			lb	GINGER. Depressed beyond all precedent by sales at public auction at
white .... "	4 3/4	5	"		5 1/2	"	Pezzas 4 1/2 @ 3/4.
Hides Buenos Ayres .... "	5 1/2	3/4	hide		15 1/7	"	
Brazil salted .... "	3 1/2	3/4	of lb 40		9 4/5	"	PIECE GOODS we have run off 100 bales during the last month to a fair
Indigo Guatimala .... *Livres*	6	12	lb	2	10	"	profit, & have now on hand 96 more,
Caracca .... "	10	12	"	2	10	"	chiefly Mammoodies Sannahs & Gurrahs which we hope to place to equal
Bengal .... "	7	11	"	1	48	"	advantage.
Nankeen E.I. long pieces .. *Liv. eff.*	9 1/2	10	piece	1	48	piece	
Short .... "	5	1/3	"	1	78 1/2	"	
Nutmegs .... "	7		lb	1	21	lb	TOBACCO continues quite neglected.
Pepper .... *Ducats*	12 1/4		lb 100		14 1/4	"	The arrivals from the United States America since the 1st ult.o are
Pimento Jamaica .... *Pezzas*	19	20			20	"	The Brig New packet, Thacher, from Boston.
Piece Goods Baftaes .... "	2	3 1/2	piece	2	85	piece	— d.o Strong, Cocklin from Baltimore.
Calicoes .... "	5	5	"	4	08	"	
Cossaes .... "	4 1/2	3 1/2	"	4	85	"	— d.o Harriet, Dimond, from d.o
Emerties .... "	2 1/2	4 1/2	"	2	67	"	— d.o Eliza Hailey, Woodberry from Boston.
Gurrahs .... "	2 3/4	4	"	3	26	"	
Humhums .... "	3 3/4	11	"	3	99	"	— d.o Dispatch, Shimmons from d.o
Longcloths .... "	9	4	"	8	26	"	— Ship William & Henry, Pierce, from d.o
Mammoodies .... "	3 3/4	5	"	3	08	"	
Salampores .... "	4 1/4	4	"	4		"	and the importations by them are
Sannahs .... "	3 1/4		"	5		"	800 boxes Havannah.— 500 bags, 66 boxes Calcutta Sugar.
Rice Carolina .... *Liv. eff.*			lb 100		14 1/2	cwt	200/m lb. Coffee.
Rocoa .... *Livres*	1	1/4	lb	1	02	lb	300 bags Pepper.
Rum West India .... *Liv. eff.*	6	7	Gallon		72 1/2	Gall	4000 Quintals Codfish.
New England .... "	4	5	"		57	"	
Salsaparilla Portuguese .... *Pezzas*	50	55	lb 100		37	lb	
Spanish .... "	20	35	"			"	

LEGHORN PRICE CURRENT (Continued)

IMPORTS	LEGHORN PRICE from	to	per	Net proceeds in Spanish Dollars exclusive of freight & insurance.	per	REMARKS
Sugar Havannah white ...... "	18 1/2	20	lb	15 40	cwt	80 Tons Logwood.
brown ...... "	14 1/2	15 1/2	"	11 96	"	900 Bags Cocoa.
Martinique whites ...... "			"		"	160 Bales Piece Goods.
Common ...... "			"		"	and other minor articles. The Leopard
Tetes ...... "			"		"	from Boston arrived on 6.th ult.o & proceeded on to Smyrna.
Brazil white assorted ...... "	17	18	"	13 82	"	
brown ...... "	12	1/2	"	9 63	"	
Vera Crux white ...... "	—	—	"	— —	"	Our actual deposit of Sugar & Coffee is
brown ...... "	12	1/2	"	9 63	"	Of Sugar 1023 Hhds Crushed.
Muscavadoes ...... "	15	16	"	12 19	"	2423 Boxes Havannah white.
East India white ...... "	14 1/2	15	"	11 51	"	1051 " d.o brown.
usual assortment ...... "	10 1/2	11	"	11 —	"	2041 bags } East India / 175 boxes }
Tobacco Virginia leaf ...... lb	7	8	lb 100	— 8	lb	479 Hhds. Of Coffee
Maryland ...... "	30	33	"	— —	"	1530 Bags.
Wax Bees yellow ...... Ducats	—	—	lb	— 38	"	70 Barrels.
white ...... Livres	2 1/4	1/2	lb	— 41	"	100 Packages.
Wheat Odessa ...... Liv. eff.	17	—	Sack	1 17	bushel	

EXPORTS	LEGHORN PRICE from	to	per	Free on board exclusive of freight & insurance	per	REMARKS
Almonds Sicily sweet ...... Liv. eff.	82	84	lb 100	20 51	cwt	
bitter ...... "			"			
Anchovies ...... "	25	26	per barrel	4 25	bar.	
Argol white ...... "	42	45	lb 100	10 90	cwt	
red ...... "	38	42	"	10 16	"	
Berries Juniper ...... Pezzas	9	—	bale 1.170	1 34	Gall.	
Brandy Neap.n oil proof ...... Pezzas	8 3/4	9	1 1/2 g.	72	"	
Holland ...... "	6 1/4	1/2		52	"	
Spanish oil proof ...... "					"	
Holland ...... "					"	
Brimstone rough ...... Liv. eff.	8	1/4	lb 100	1 87	cwt	
in rolls ...... "	11 1/4	1/2	"	2 77	"	

LEGHORN PRICE CURRENT (Continued)

EXPORTS	LEGHORN PRICE from	to	per	Free on board exclusive of freight & insurance		per	REMARKS
Cheese Parmesan .... Pezzas	19	21	"	—	25 1/5	lb	
Cream of Tartar "	11 1/2	12 1/4	"	—	14 3/10	"	
Essences Lemon .... Livres	} 19	20	lb	4	23	"	
Bergamot "							
Lavander .... Liv. eff.	3	—	"	—	67 1/3	"	
Elephants teeth .... Pezzas	60	90	100	1	08	"	
Fruit. Currants .... Pauls	81	—	"	—	10 1/6	"	
Figs "	40	42	"	—	5 3/5	"	
Raisins Smyrna "	60	—	"	—	8	"	Our exports in general have undergone no material variation since our last. — OPIUM. Continues very scarce & what small supplies drop in are eagerly purchased at our quotations. — [Two lines stricken through]. — RAGS. Also keep high, owing to the large demand for England. — STRAWHATS. The demand for this article is beyond all former precedent & prices have risen full 15 per %.
Lipari "	—	—	"	—	—	"	
Sultana "	—	—	"	—	—	"	
Galls blue .... Pezzas	39	40	"	53	40	cwt	
mixed "	24	25	"	33	38	"	
Gum Arabic "	30	35	"	—	42	lb	
Assafoetida "	30	55	"	—	66	"	
Benjamin .... Livres	1 1/2	3 1/2	lb	—	70	"	
Copal .... Pezzas	15	30	lb 100	—	60	"	
Myrrh "	20	50	"	—	60	"	
Sandarac "	24	25	"	—	30	"	
Styrax. in drops .... Livres	5	—	lb	1	02	"	
Tragacanth .... Pezzas	50	70	lb 100	—	84	"	
Hats Chip pressed with bands L. eff.	80	100	doz.	16	57	doz.	
Straw d.o from n.24 to 42. "	108	504	"	82	80	"	
" 40 to 60. "	432	2880	"	473	14	"	
Ipeccacuanha .... Livres	9	10	lb	1	90	lb	
Liquorice Paste Calabria .... Pezzas	13 1/2	14	lb 100	18	62	cwt	
Sicily. "	11 1/2	—	"	13	29	"	
Manna in flakes .... Livres	3 1/4	1/3	lb	—	68	lb	
sorts "	1	1/6	"	—	23 2/3	"	
Magnesia "	—	—	"	—	82 2/3		
Oil eating 1/2 chests .... Pezzas	4	—	1/2 chest	5	21	1/2 ch.	
Box of 12. bottles .... Liv. eff.	5 1/2	3/4	box	3	29	box	
Gallipoly "	20	21	b. of lb. 88	—	—	tun	

[1355]

LEGHORN PRICE CURRENT (Continued)

EXPORTS		LEGHORN PRICE from	to	per	Free on board exclusive of freight & insurance	
Levant	"	68	71	"	3 32	"
Opium	Livres	22	23	lb	4 56	lb
Quick Silver	Pezzas	49	50	lb 100	67 76	cwt
Rags Tuscan 1. sort	Liv. eff.	30	—	"	7 76	"
2. "		19	20	"	5 07	"
Rhubarb	"	4	10	lb	2 23	lb
Saffron	Pauls eff.	68	70	"	10 32	"
Senna Alexandria	Pezzas	32	35	lb 100	47 43	cwt
Tripoli in sorts ..	"	14	15	"	20 32	"
Shumac Sicily	Livres	18	20	"	4 83	"
Soap Leghorn white ..	Liv. eff.	72	73	"	17 93	"
marbled	"	63	67	"	16 45	"
"	"	60	65	"	15 96	"
Candia & Levant	Pezzas	40 50	120	"	1 62	"
Spunges	Liv. eff.	59	60	"	15	lb
Tallow	"	68	69	"	17	"
Candles	"				—	
Wine Corsican	Pezzas eff.	22	23	{ 425 Litres	26 21	{ Pip. of 115. G.
Marsala		85	90	Pipe	86 62	Pipe

Besides the above Articles great quantities of Florentine wrought silks are exported from Leghorn, but the qualities, lengths & breadths are so various that they cannot well be comprised in a general Price Current. We have likewise in the vicinity considerable paper manufactories where paper of all kinds can be had on very moderate terms.

Goods in general are bought and sold for Silver money, betwixt which and the money in which Bills of Exchange are bought, there is a difference of 7 per cent (*Agio*) against Silver i e 107 Dollars in Silver are equal to 100 in Gold.
On Goods bought or sold there is generally speaking a discount of 3 per cent. On all Cotton manufactures 4 per cent.
On Goods bought or sold in effective money there is no discount.
Charges on sales including Commission & delcredere are generally from 6 @ 7 per cent. On Fish 8 @ 9 per cent.

MONIES

Pezza of 8 rials	6 Livres or 9 Pauls long money
	5¾ Livres or 8⅝ Pauls effective money.
Ducat	7 Livres long money.
Livre	1½ Paul or 20 Sols of 12 deniers each.
Spanish Dollar	9½ ditto or Livres 6⅓ a medium valuation.

Accounts are kept in Pezzas of 8 rials sols and deniers.— 20 sols make a Pezza, 12 deniers a sol.

WEIGHTS and MEASURES

lb 100 of Leghorn are equal to	lb 77 English " 69½ Amsterdam " 108 Genoa	lb 70 Hamburg " 62½ Trieste " 85 Marseille	155 Braces of Leghorn equal to 100 English Yards. 4 ditto ditto one Cane. 380 Sacks are equal to about 100 English Quarters.

The English cwt is equal to lb 145 Italian, but from the difence of tares and allowances, it seldom renders, excepting in a very few Articles, more than lb 140 @ 142.

N. B. Freights when expressed simply *in Pounds Sterling* are payable in silver money — To authorise the payment in gold or the money necessary to purchase a Bill of Exchange the freight must express *payable in gold money or in a good Bill of Exchange on London.*

We come now to advise the sale of your 28 cases piece goods by that vessel as follows.

500	pieces	Choud^y. Mamoodies	at p	3	7/8
480	"	Alliabad Emerties	— " —	2	5/6
840	"	" — "	— " —	2	3/4
90	"	Johntilly Sawns	— " —	3	1/3
550	"	Barilly Mamoodies	— " —	3	3/4
180	"	Janda sawns	— " —	4	3/8
210	"	Luckon Cossacs "	— " —	3	

pble the 30th June.

You mentioned in your letter of 26 Novr. that these goods as well as those p Eliza Hailey had been examined in Boston, and found free of damage. We regret to state that without any external appearance of damage on some of the bales, and very little on others, we shall have to make an allowance on nearly 300 pieces p New Packet — some more, some less, injured, and that from the view we have taken of the 52 bales still at the Lazaret, there appears in these also a considerable number of pieces in a damaged state. Every deduction made however, the New Packet goods should net very little short of Invoice Cost, which we presume, may be considered a very fair profit. The Mamoodies the largest article in your Invoice must do well for we have since sold a parcel of 30 bales received from London at the same price which remits a net profit of 14 @ 15 p: on the Company's price. You will remark that the difference of price obtained here between your Choud^y. Mamoodies and the Barilly, is less by a great deal than that of the cost, so that the latter article which is equally saleable with us, is at all times to be preferred if to be had so much lower than the former.

Mamoodies in general are much run upon at present — these you have p Eliza Hailey will help us greatly with the whole parcel as will the Emerties, for both articles are much in demand, and indeed they are of all others those we would most recommend 60 @ 70 bales of each would not be at all be too much at a time. For the single bale of Tandah p New Packet we got it is true p 4⅜ which leaves a profit on your $3¼, but the Eliza Hailey's are invoiced at $3.70 @ 60 and even $4 prices which be the quality what it may we can never expect to realize at this market. The Gurrahs may do well and if a return of $2¾ @ ⅞ perhaps 3 p peice, all charges deducted, leaves as it should seem a fair profit we would recommend 30 @ 40 bales by an early vessel. We have just sold a parcel of Companys at p 4¼ to a profit of 10 p% on the London cost. Baftas are some how or other out of repute with our dealers just now, and for the present we would recommend your avoiding them. — We shall return on the subject another day after retiring the Eliza Hailey's goods, adding only in the meantime that we are inclined to think favorably of the shipment on the whole, notwithstanding the exceptions which for your future government, as well as your present information, we have made in our review of the Invoice — We enclose landing certificate of the New Packets goods, the a/ sales will follow as early as possible, & a further remittance to Mr Williams when money gets a little plentier.

We refer to our P Current & remain very
We have sold a parcel of Foolpour Cossacs. 38 @ 40 + 2⅛ at p 3⅝, and from that to 3½ could run off a large quantity.

Leghorn 9th febry 1819

Sir
We confirm & beg your reference to the preceeding Copy of our respects of 6th instant per New Packet via Messina In addition to the articles of your Invoice by that vessel which we found well adapted for the market, we may mention Luckipore Emerties. They are equally Current as the Alliabads invoiced ¼ of a dollar higher whereas the difference in the price obtained here is not, you will mark much more than 3 p%. — The John tilly Sawns we would recommend your leaving out altogether — Indeed, Sawns, in general, had better be avoided or [interlineated: rather] sent only in very small quantities; &we may correct a mistake in our last respecting Foolpore Cossacs which do very well, as we then stated, but *not*, as we added to a great extent. Ten to twelve bales are at any time quite enough for the market. Your Lucknore Cossacs are equally current with the

Alliabad Emerties & may always be safely sent with or substituted for them if to be had on the same terms. In the instance of the New Packet's you will even remark that the
Cossacs sold [for — stricken through] a fraction higher — We
have seldom seen the demand for any regular steady article
fall off so much [interlineated: as] that for Baftaes: & for the
present they should form but a small proportion of any shipment this way. We have a parcel of Company's on hand (12
yards) invoiced from 8/2 to 9/, for which we hardly expect
to do more than cover cost & Charges. — We repeat our hopes of
an immediate & we trust advantageous sale of your Goods p
Eliza Hailey whenever they are admitted to prattick. And with
reference to what we shall have the pleasure of writing you on
that subject at an early day we remain, Sir,

> Your obed^t Servts
> Grant, Pillans & Co

[Addressed]
C B & Co
(1163)
Henry Lee Esqre
Boston
via
New York p Ja^s Monroe

[Postmarked]
PACKET SHIP
NEW-YORK   SHIP 39
[Endorsed]
A
Grant Pillans & Co
3 & 9 Febry 1819.

sales goods p N. Packet
remittance to 800. —
Rec^d. 11 April 1819.—
by a vessel which saild
from Eng^d 1st. March
Rec^d. April 11th. 1819.

LETTER FROM WILLIAM C. GOWEN, HAVANA, MAY 14, 1819, TO HENRY LEE, BOSTON, ADVISING AGAINST FURTHER SHIPMENTS [1]

The information in the letter given below is considerably more encouraging than that in other letters of about the same time and from the same place.

On Jan. 23, Packard & Gowen could not "advise any further sales of . . . India Goods . . . in consequence of their being all of qualities at present without demand." Had there been some desirable goods, such as blue gurrahs or long checks, in the consignment, the Havana firm might have been able to work the others off; in other cases they had "obliged the purchasers to take other & inferior parcels" in order to obtain blue gurrahs, etc., "thus making the finer qualities facilitate the sale of the more inferiors." A letter of Feb. 1 from Miralla & Co. was more encouraging only by the hopeful remark: "The white goods will no doubt go off as Spring approaches." Even when sales were actually made they were not always final. Miralla & Co. on Feb. 9 announced that they "had effected sale of the Carrideries at $7.32 [?] but on opening them, the purchasers refused to take them, being as they say damaged, but which we Contend is not damage, but is the defect in the manufacture of the goods. In the Same peice there is 3.4 & more different shades; and in some the blue is faint in spots, and in none are the colours clear. We . . . shall if possible make the purchasers receive them, as we consider it a handsome sale." From a note by Henry Lee to the effect that said goods "cost about ⅝ R^s p^s." there is little doubt that from the seller's viewpoint the sale was a "handsome" one; but the buyer's description of the goods indicates what was to be expected in goods bought from native weavers, working without supervision and thus producing merchandise which fell far below the standards insisted on by the East India Co. It also, taken in connection with the comments in the letter below on silks, suggests that Henry Lee had not yet accommodated himself to changing conditions in the export of East India piece goods from the United States. Previously Henry Lee's slogan had been: "It matters not how inferior the goods so they be cheap." This watchword had been shrewd enough in the days when the larger proportion of piece goods shipped to Havana

1. Jackson-Lee Papers.

had been intended for the slave trade, but in 1817 Spain had "abolished the trade north of the equator . . ., and promised entire abolition in 1820;"[2] and, however ill-enforced the agreement, it could not but have decreased the demand for the inferior colored goods from India. It should have been Henry Lee's aim, in view of the changing situation, to endeavor to supply and to stimulate a desire for a better quality of East India piece goods among the inhabitants of the West Indies and Europe. This he had apparently not sufficiently taken into consideration.

The situation did not improve throughout the year. On Oct. 13, W. C. Gowen announced that "fine Seersuckers only are wanted in this market; and that the narrow blue stripe; and the purple stripe, . . . are now most enquired for — the broad stripe & the cross bar having gone out of fashion." In the final letter of the year from Havana, on Nov. 20, James Drake & Co. announced the sale of 136 pieces of seersucker @ $11.50, the highest offer which could be obtained since they were all yellow instead of an assortment of greens, blues, reds, etc.; and of "251 Pieces Lungee Hkchfs at 5$ Cash;" but he added that "India Goods, for the African Trade, continue a drug;" that "Bills are not to be had;" and that "Produce keeps above your limitts."

Mͬ Henry Lee   Havana May 14. 1819
   Boston
      D Sir

      I have the pleasure to acknowledge recͭ. of your esteemed Letter of 21 apͭ. which reached me a few days since.

      I have already advised you of the sale of the goods p John Howe from Philadelphia at $ 6 p pce — they were much liked by the dealers & I could have disposed of a much larger parcel at the same price — still however the Market is so full of Goods that I cannot with safety recommend anyfurther shipments — .

      Besides oftheir abundance, we have another powerful cause for the dulness of these articles — They are only shipped to the southward of the Equator to which quarter the voyages

2. Du Bois, William Edward Burghardt, *Suppression of the African Slave-Trade to the United States of America, 1638–1870* (N. Y., 1896), p. 135.

recently at an end have terminated very badly, while those running North, tho' acting in open violation of the Treaty have got clear & made enormous profits — Arms, ammunition, Iron, rum &c &c are therefore the principle articles now shipped —

Your Silks [interlineated: Cuttanies] p Betsey are in store but I fear are too glaring to suit the tastes of our good folks here, who are not in the way of furnishing their Houses with Curtains, sofa covers &c — they would answer extremely well for the Coast if not so high charged. Business is extremely dull & I think our produce must decline. Coffee is worth $ 22 @ 24 — Sugars White $10 @ 11. Brown $7 @ 8. Bills on the States 2 @ 2½ pC^t pm.in demand. on London par to 1 pC^t pm. heavy. Molasses 9 @ 9½ r^{ls}. American produce generally is dull.

I remain   D^{r}sir

Y^r. Ob^{t}S

W^m.C. Gowen

[Addressed]
SHIP   12
M^r. Henry Lee
Boston
[Endorsed]
W. C. Gowen
May 14th. 1819. —
Sale Bejutipauts —
Cuttanies will not sell.
But w^d do for the African trade
at low prices.

FRAGMENT OF A LETTER FROM GRANT, HEPBURN & CO., TRIESTE, MAY 28, 1819, TO HENRY LEE, BOSTON, ON PROSPECTS FOR EAST INDIA PIECE GOODS[1]

In addition to many large consignments to Leghorn, Henry Lee shipped a few bales of piece goods to Trieste, then under Austrian rule. We have no evidence that he was encouraged to push the trade

1. Jackson-Lee Papers.

to that port, though a letter of Aug. 3 mentioned an improvement in the market.

The "average" on damaged goods mentioned below was the minimum percentage of partial loss for which the underwriters agreed to be responsible, usually 3%.[2] The £250 stg. remitted to London was doubtless in anticipation of the sales of the shipment. "Exchange at f 9.8" means that it took 9.8 florins (1f. = 2s. 1½d. stg.)[3] to purchase £1 stg. in bills of exchange on London.

Trieste 28 May 1819

Boston
Henry Lee Esq[r]

Sir,

By arrival of the Caroline we were favored with your much esteemed letter of the 17 Feb, with Invoice & bill of loading of 8 Bales Piece Goods, for which commencement of a correspondence we are very much obliged to you, and we shall do all in our power to render the result of this shipment satisfactory — Having requested M[r] Trueman to inform you of the Caroline's arrival, we deferred writing to you until she had completed her quarantine & discharged your Goods — 5 Bales proved to be damaged; we have had them surveyed & you will find a note of the result at foot — The damaged pieces are to be sold immediately by auction, and if the loss amounts to an average we shall take care to forward you the necessary documents to recover from your underwriters — As there is no direct opportunity of forwarding letters to the United States at present, nor any early prospect of one, we shall send a general landing Certificate of the Caroline's cargo to Sam[l] Parkman Jr Esq[r], to whom you will have the goodness to apply to get your bonds cancelled — we do this to save you the heavy additional expenses of portage & consul's fees.

On the 21st. ins[t]. we remitted to Samuel Williams Esq at London, on your account,

£250 Stg, which we placed to your debit at the exchange of

2. M'Culloch, *op. cit.*, vol. i, p. 59.
3. *Ibid.*, vol. ii, p. 678.

f 9.8 . . . inf 2283.20 — With your sound Piece Goods we have not yet been able to do anything, but we hope ere long to send your account Sales, altho' we are sorry to say there is no chance of our covering cost p Invoice & Charges, in consequence of the low rates at which Company's Goods received from London are selling — Regarding your Emerties we cannot at present give a decided opinion, because they are the first we have had of the Kind — but we think they will do for some of our buyers —

Your Comp^ys Gurrahs are good; but if we procure f 7 [inter-lineated: = $3.20 Nett P'ds] for them it will be the utmost we can expect, in consequence of the cheapness of Salampores rece'd from London, which can be afforded at about that price for finer quality. Company's Longcloths or Guineas 9/8 36 & 37 yds are also much preferred by the buyers who consume this description of PceGoods, and they can be had at 15½ af ¾ at present = $7.10 @ 7.22 NettPds Your Moorabud Sawns are well adapted for our buyers from the Morea & those parts — they prefer this width, but we have frequently procured better proportionate prices for the same quality a little narrower, say about 2 1/16 @ 2 3/16. We consider the present value of these goods about f 5½ @ 6 — = $2½ @ 2¾ nett but the market for Cotton Goods is at this moment in so critical a state that any opinion about prices is very uncertain. —

Your Beerboom Gurrahs are too ordinary — these very ordinary goods are only saleable when the plague is raging in Albania &those parts, and then it is better they should be Baftas 1⅞ @ 2 by 24/25 Cubits, because the object is to have an entire piece for a very small sum, a custom of the Turks requiring the dead bodies to be wrapped up in a piece of cloth — Humhums full 1½ yard wide by 12 yards, of fine quality are much wanted — we have never had any of them ourselves, but buyers are so continually asking for them, that we think a trial well worth while. We have also never had any blue Salampores orGuineas here — but we think they would answer, because we find a considerable part of the Long cloths & Salampores received from London are died blue &black here — Our dealers tell us the colors should be well fixed, so as not to rub off or dirty the hands when touched — Colored E. I. Cambrics & Nickanies are not known here; if blue or black & of finer quality than the Salampores & Guineas we would recommend a trial. — Salt Petre should not be sent here — it is a royal Monopoly to refine it, and we believe the crude is found in the Country — At all events Government have now so ample a stock on hand, that they are endeavoring to sell but find few or no buyers. Ourmarket forColonial Produce is very much depressed, we enclose our last price Current — Today we quote white Havannah Sugars f 30 af 33 —— yellow &bro. f 23. 24 — Brazils are quite Nominal — & so or nearly so are E. I. — Coffee — f 50 was offered the other day &refused for 1000 Bags of St Dom^o. — 400 bags commanded f 52 yesterday — holders Seem inclined to ask higher prices. —

[Endorsed]
Grant, Hepburn & Co
Trieste
28 May 1819 —

E. I. *Peice goods* from
London of fine quality undersell
the I. goods from U. States — Remarks on
my ship^t. p Caroline —

Letter from John Berenberg, Gossler & Co., Hamburg, June 18, 25, 1819, to Henry Lee, Boston, with Commentary on the Unfitness of Lee's Consignment [1]

Once again, from the letter below, Henry Lee learned that the piece goods he was shipping to Europe were too inferior in quality and too high in price, in comparison with the standard goods of the East India Co., to meet a good market.

The prices given in the letter below are unusually confusing. The reference, in giving the price of sugar, to "10½ d. equal to 46/— d. sterl^g." is evidently to the rix-dollar banco, normally worth 54⅔d. stg. On the other hand, "£200 . . . at the Exchange of .34/4^d." in

1. Jackson-Lee Papers.

B^{co}My 2575" means that 34 schillings and 4 pfennigs, Hamburg currency, would purchase £1 stg. in exchange on London, and that £200 stg. in exchange on London could be purchased for 2,575 marcs banco in Hamburg currency. One marc contained 16 sols or schillings, and the sol or schilling was divided into 16 pfennigs; £1 stg. normally was worth 13 marcs, 2.7 schillings banco. The symbol _ℳ_, used in the letter below, may prove puzzling to the modern reader; it was used in Germany to represent the marc banco, about 18d. stg.,[2] until the latter part of the 19th century. Why the sign _ℳ_ should be used to represent a marc is no more clear to the average business man than why $ stands for dollar and £ stands for pound.

Duplicate

Henry Lee Esqr. Boston

Sir!   Hamburgh 18th. June 1819

We hand you annexed Copy of our last respects 3rd. Inst. and have since examined thouroughly the 13 Bale Piece Goods p^r. Milo; besides the damage of 130 p^s. mentioned in our last, we have found in the other Bales 33 p^s. more, but old damage which cannot have happened on this last journey, at foot is a note on which Bales they were found. We should with the greatest pleasure comply with your request and furnish ample details and remarks about the quality and its more or less suitableness for this market, but we regret we must comprise the whole in one general and unfavorable remark, viz: that they are altogether unsuitable and of a much too coarse quality, far inferior to brittish Comp^y Goods, and deficient in breadth & length to what they are, but even the most sellect Comp^y Goods of the descriptions you sent, would be incurrent; this we have expressed in the remark of our prices Current stating Gurrahs, Salempores, Longcloth &c of _fine quality_ as the almost only saleable sorts and since a twelve month this remarks has been thesame in all our prices Currents. The only chance to clear these Goods off is a public Sale, which we have advertised p^r. 21 Inst; and as the result of this small trial cannot be improved by delay, we shall let them go to the highest bidder requesting

2. M'Culloch, _op. cit._, vol. i, p. 725.

you only to be prepared, that the result will be most miserable. An assortment of abt. 90 Bales similar Goods were imported last year from Copenhagen, a public Sale was tried with them, but no higher offer than 5-£ 8s. to 6-£ being made, the Goods were withdrawn; such however is the depreciation since, that the holders now offer to sell at 4-£ without being able to find any body disposed to listen to this price. To meet your desire we annex a complete prices Current of piece Goods, which from the measurement you will find is what we call Comp^y. Goods, and deviates on the Baftas and some other Goods from your statement, we reduce the prices in sterling for your better oversight and though superior qualities of the descriptions before mentioned may be more current than other sorts, yet we cannot in good faith encourage you to even a shipment of them, unless you can afford to sell them considerably below our quotation, for we apprehend that piece Goods will grow more and more difficult of Sale because the brittish Cotton Goods, since the depreciation of raw Cotton, have experienced a very material depression in price, especially common Goods. If not in this, we wish you may find an opportunity of doing something in some other E. I. Articles. The Cadmus is just arrived from Manilla with 6000 Bags of Sugar 52 Bales Cotton & 54 Chests Indigo The Sugars are disposed of already the whites &yellow at 10½ d. equal to 46/- d. sterlg. the brown at 8¾d equal to 38/4d. The true American is arrived from Canton with Teas and some Sugar which we expect will sell at abt. our quotations. We annex our Prices Currt. inwhich you will not find any alteration except in Coffee which has improved and Sugars are also a trifle higher. Believe us very regardfully etc.

P. S. What you call Comboics & Nickannas are not known under that denomination here.

Note

In the Bale ⟨C⟩ #776.	are 3	Pieces old damaged	#538. 1	Piece	D⁰	together
" 621.	" 1	" " D⁰	" 549. 1	"	D⁰	
" 622.	" 6	" " D⁰	" 550. 9	"		33 Pieces
" 792.	" 12	" " D⁰				old damaged.

Hamburg 25th. June 1819.

Referring to foregoing Duplicate of our respects of the 18th. we now hand at foot a Note of sale of your Cotton Goods, which we are sorry to say went off at miserable prices indeed, but as before intimated we do not think it would have been adviseable to protract the sale, as it is very likely, such low qualities have not yet seen their lowest —

We remit to day to Sam¹. Williams Esqʳ. London for your Account

£100 — pr 12 Septʳ. on John Browing &Son
"100 —   13   do.   " Sir P. Pole Burt. &Cᵒ
£200 —   which we place to your Debit at the Exchange of
·34/4ᵈ. in BᶜᵒMy 2575. .   As soon as the Goods are all delivered, we shall make up Account sales, and remit the + Balance for account to same friend — .

We are Very respectfully
Sir   Your obt. hble Sts.
John Berenberg Gossler & Co

Exch. on London 34/4d. 2M

Note

Lot	1.	95	Pᶜᵉˢ.	Baftas Barille @	3-₰ 7/
"	2.	94	"	do	3-₰ —
"	3.	58	"	Cossas	3-₰ —
"	4.	99	"	do	3-₰ 3/.
"	5.	94	"	do	3-₰ 2/.
"	6.	100	"	do	3-₰ —
"	7.	100	"	Mamoodies	4-₰ —
"	8.	12	"	do	3-₰ 8/.
"	9.	99	"	do	3-₰ 13/.
"	11.	88	"	do	4-₰ 12/
"	12.	100	"	do	4-₰ 7/
"	10.	91	"	do	3-₰ 11/
"	13.	94	"	Goldh. Cossas	5-₰ 1/

1127
163
1290
damaged.

Lot: 14.	1	Pˢ.	Baftas Barille @	2-£5/
" 15.	21	"	Cossas	2-£6/.
" 16.	21	"	do	2-£ —
" 17.	7	"	do	2-£3/
" 18.	28	"	Mamoodies	2-£9/
" 19.	28	"	do	3-£7/
" 20.	32	"	do	3-£12/
" 21.	10	"	do	3-£10/
" 22.	12	"	do	3-£7/
" 23.	3	"	Goldhead Cossas	3-£14/
	163			

[Addressed]
Henry Lee Esqʳ.
Boston

[Endorsed]
John. Berenberg Goslier
&Cᵒ. Hamburgh June,
18. th. 1819. & 25th.

Cʳ 200 Augᵗ. 23ᵈ. 1819 —
Bengal pˢ goods coarse will
not answer & Company's are
also very low —

LETTER FROM PALMER, WILSON & CO., LONDON, JUNE 29, 1819, TO HENRY LEE, BOSTON, ON THE PRICES OF AMERICAN AND INDIA COTTON [1]

Henry Lee, of course, did not consider shipping India piece goods to England, but he was interested in the extent of the English trade with India because of the effect it might have on his own shipments to the Continent, and he was particularly interested in the prospects for the sale of American cotton in England in competition with cotton from Bengal. "The *upland* or *bowed* Georgia cotton forms the largest and best portion of the short stapled class. All the cottons of India are short stapled." A glance at the statistics will easily convince any one that America was not "driven from the trade" by any improvement in India cotton.[2]

1. Jackson-Lee Papers.
2. M'Culloch, *op. cit.*, vol. i, pp. 518, 522.

London 29 June 1819

Henry Lee Esq
    Boston
Sir —

We are duly favored with your letter of the 1st. instant &shall be happy to afford every information in our power upon the subject more immediately referred to. — The stock of indigo in this market is nearly the same which has existed for some years past (22000 chests) but in consequence of the stagnation in all commercial concerns both here & elsewhere the Holders are more disposed to sell than formerly & the prices are consequently materially lower than they were some time back. The import we imagine will not much if any thing exceed 10000 Chests from Bengal during the present year which not being much more than half the quantity of former year's may probably occasion a material advance towards the Spring sale of next year in the want of our general commercial prospects improving towards the Autumn of the present — if we are disappointed in that expectation we shall not see any improvement in the market &from the very large stocks of other goods including Cotton which the Agency Houses are forced to hold we can hardly calculate upon their adding Indigo to the burthen, but will principally sell as the half yearly sales are brought forward. As far as our information extends the prices now obtainable in the Continental ports cannot give the prime cost to the Proprietors. —

With respect to Cotton we can hardly think it possible for the American cultivator with a Negro population to afford Cotton under 17 to 18 Cents. if a lower price would have afforded a remunerating profit for his labour we should surely have seen the cultivation doubled or trebled in former years when the price continued so long in this market from 16d. to 22d plb — at any rate untill the fact is *positively ascertained* that 13 Cents *will pay* the Grower &that the American cultivation continues at that price, we do not imagine that the present Holders of E. I. Cottons will ever consent to accept 3½ or 4d

plb. There is every reason to expect a continued improvement
in the quality from India & which we know can be afforded on
board ship at Calcutta for little above 4ᵈ plb. if therefore
the improvement we look for does take place &the quality shall
hereafter equal Bowed Georgia: we apprehend America will be
driven from the trade — all this however is mere speculation at
present &never can take effect untill the quality is *very materially* improved — in the mean time India Cottons will never
command an extensive sale in Europe except when Bowed
Georgia: are sold above 13 or 14ᵈ plb Stg in this market. —
Our I[ndia] private trade is greatly   ] diminishing
at present; about ½ of the preceding years tonnage may perhaps be going round the Cape, but even that reduced quantity
will bring back but little if any profit unless a material advance
in prices takes place within the next twelvemonths —

We are Sir
Your faithful Servᵗˢ.
Palmer, Wilson & Co

[Addressed]
Henry Lee Esqʳ.
Boston —
[Endorsed]
Palmer Wilson &Cᵒ.
London, 29ᵗʰ June 1819.
Indigo and Cotton &c

LETTER FROM J. L. MERTENS, MOSSELMAN & CO., ANTWERP,
JULY 2, 1819, TO HENRY LEE, BOSTON, WITH PRICES[1]

The letter below and a similar one of July 24 and Aug. 13 contain less general business information than any others of the year.
Their writers confine themselves to a bare mention of prices, which
are given in florins, each equal to about 1s. 8¾d. stg., and in stivers
(20 stivers = 1 florin).

Exchange in London is expressed as 39 schillings and 5 stivers per
£ stg., 1 schilling being equal to 6 stivers. The exchange on Hamburg

1. Jackson-Lee Papers.

is probably expressed as 35 11/16 grotes Antwerp equalling 1 marc Hamburg. Since accounts in Antwerp were simultaneously kept in florins (divided into sous and cents) and in pounds Flemish (divided into rix-dollars, florins, schillings, stivers, grotes, and pfenings), and since accounts in Hamburg were kept in marcs (divided into sols, or schillings, and pfenings) and in pounds, schillings, and pence Flemish, this gave opportunity for a bewildering variety of exchange relationships.

The references to entrepôt originate from the fact that in Antwerp goods could be warehoused *en entrepôt* and exported on paying a charge of ½% ad valorem.[2]

Antwerp July 2d. 1819.

Henry Lee Esqr.
    Boston
  D Sir!

      We had last this pleasure on the 17th. ulto. p Minerva, Bates, sailed from Flushing afew days ago —

The Miles Standish, Carver, arrived here on the 30th., we are happy to say. all well — We will take particular Care of the consignmts youhave been pleased to make us by hr & follow with it the directions contained in your favor of the 26th. May —

We cannot say what the Choppa Romals are worth, before we see them — they will be landed to morrow — the price varies from frs. 10 to frs. 27 — . p pce. — Sale depends a good deal on the quality — We'll advice further on the Subject —

Blue Salempores 18 . 1⅛ at present worth frs. 19. fr. 20 — [interlineated: in Entrepôt] and Nicanias 13 . 1, which may be quoted frs. 12. to frs. 14.— are generally in some demand —

The Sale of Blue guineas 18 . 1⅛ at present noting frs. 36 — frs. 40 — in Entrepot & neganepauts, 17 . 1. at fr. 16. fr 17 — is not quite so regular —

We could not ascertain the value of Camboies —

Chelloes, 17½ . 1 are in demand at fr. 16. frs. 17. Entrepot, as are Blue Byrampauts, 17 . 1. at frs. 17 — ditto —

White goods have not varied since our last dates — The prices

2. M'Culloch, *op. cit.*, vol. i, pp. 47, 727.

quoted, to be sure, were low — but we did not like to raise expectations, without a probability of their being realised — It is our opinion that for a parcel of some importance, due publicity given to a Sale by auction, would bring forward purchasers from different parts of the Interior —

Ginger & Tumeric are dull & low articles —

We believe that Saltpetre will sell readily — Prices as plast — refined 6 . 6¼ St: — crude 4 to 4¼ st — we observe what you say about the quality & will examine it —

Indigoes are scarce & wanted — little or none in the Interior —

Bengals at 50 to 105 St: ⎫
Manilla " 45 " 80 " ⎪
Caraccas ⎫ ⎬ would sell very readily at
& ⎬ " 50 " 110 " ⎪ present —
Guatemalo ⎭ ⎪
& . . . . ⎭

Rice has been heavy for the last weeks —

Cotton seems to get a little steadier —

Sugars in some demand —

Coffees have got up rapidly in London — we hope the advance may bemaintained — here, 14 to 14¼ st: paid for Dom⁰. & good and [?] Chribon in Consumption —

Hides firm

Spices without activity —

Teas are abundant, but good fresh quality always enjoy a preferency.

As you wish a remittance, on arrival of the Miles Standish, &we See no probability of the Exchange declining soon, we sent Mr. S. Williams London, for your acct, this day:

£700 .—. due 10 dte at 39/ — Exf 8190 —— to yourdebit which please book in

Landing Certificates will be attended to,

We are Respectfully, Dsir! Yrobedtservts
JL.MertensMosselman&Co

[The below is a printed form. Commodity prices and exchange rates are inserted by hand.]

ANTWERP, (2ᵈ July 1819)

107½ lb. Antwerp weight are equal to 112 lb English.
212 11/16 "   "   "   "   100 kilograms.
  1 Guilder Exchange money is 20 Stivers Exchange.
  2 Dg. or grots "   "   1   "   "

SUGAR ...	Jamaica brown 100 lb.	F	22	24
	Mart. and Guad. brown	—	20	23
	— — clayed	—		
	Havana .... brown	—	26	28
	— .... white.	—	31	37
	Brazil .... brown	—	22	25
	— .... white.	—	26	32
	Batavia in Canisters	—	24	26
	East India in Bags.	—	16	26

COFFEE ...	Moka .... lb.	S	14	15
	Bourbon	—		
	Brown Java	—	15	16½
	Cheribon and pale Java	—	13	14¾
	St. — Domingo	—	13	13¼
	Surinam and Demerara	—		
	Martinique and Guadel.	—		
	Jamaica and Havana..	—	12¾	13¼

[In margin opposite coffee and sugar prices: free of consumption duty]

INDIGO ...	Bengal	—	50	100
	Caraccas	—	55	105
	Guatimalo	—		

COCHINEAL .	.... lb.	F	15	17
COCOA ...	West-India	S	8	8½

COTTON ..	Pernambucco ...... lb.	Dg		
	Georgia sea Island	—		
	— Upland	—	26	29
	Louisiana	—	26	30
	Surat and Bengal	—	13	18
	Macedonia	—		

TEA	Imper. and Gunpowder	S	55	65
	Hyson	—	50	60
	Hysonskin	—	23	30
	Young Hyson	—	36	43
	Tonkay	—	23	28
	Pecco	—	65	80
	Souchong	—	22	35
	Congo	—	20	27
	Camphoi	—	21	28
	Bohea	—	12	16
TOBACCO .	Virginia	—	6½	10
	Maryland	—	10	13
	Georgia and Carolina..	—	5½	7
	Kentucky	—	5	6
	Varinas	—	70	80
	Porto-Rico	—	7	10
RICE ...	Carolina ...... 100 lb	F	14	15
	Bengal	—	7½	8½
	Brazil	—	9	10
LOGWOOD .	Spanish cut	—	5.10	6
	Jamaica	—	4.10	5
FUSTIC		—	6	7
HIDES ...	Buenos-Ayres ..... lb.	S	7	10½
	Brazil	—	7	9½
	Bull hides	—	7	8½
PEPPER	.... lb.	S	7¼	7¾
PIMENTO ...	.... 100 lb.	F	42	44
CINNAMON ..	.... lb.	—	6	7.10
CASSIA LIGNEA	.... lb.	S	12	22
MACE	.... lb.	F	5	5.5
GUM	Arabick .... 100 lb.	—	30	40
	Senegal	—	35	45
	Barbary	—		
ASHES	American Pot	—	25	27
	Russia .. "	—	23	24
	Dantzick "	—	22	24
	American Pearl	—	26	28

QUERCIT BARK	.... —		9.10	10.10
MAHOGANY ..	.... Foot	S	5	20

NANKEENS	Long .... Piece.	—		75	80
	Short	—		36	38

ENGLISH SUGARS in Bond	LOAVES .	Double refined . 100 lb.	F	
		Single — 6 @ 8 lb.	—	
		10 @ 14 "	—	
		16 @ 18 "	—	
	LUMPS .	....	—	
		Crushed	—	

ANTWERP, 2ᵈ. July 1819.

Paris short. parr	London short. 39/5
2 mo.s ½% loss	2 mo.s 39/2
Amst.m short. 1½ . 1⅝% advᶜ.	Hamb.g short. 35 11/16
2 mo.s ¾% "	2 mo.s 35½

[Addressed]
Henry Lee Esqʳ.
Boston.
pMercury —

[Endorsed]
J L Mertens Mosselman
&Cº. July 2ᵈ. 1819.

E. I. Piece goods. — Madrass &
Surat. —
Cʳ. £700 Aug 23ᵈ. 1819.
Recᵈ. & forwᵈ. by Y M. O. S.
T.S. Carter &Co
L'pool 7ᵗʰ. July
— 1819 —

LETTER FROM SOLOMON TOWNE, PALERMO, JULY 9, 1819, TO
HENRY LEE, BOSTON, ON GOODS ADAPTED FOR THE SICILIAN
MARKET[1]

Henry Lee tried the experiment of sending a consignment of sugar
and East India piece goods to Leghorn by the way of Palermo, but

1. Jackson-Lee Papers.

the piece goods, "large and small Checks Custers & Blue Salampores," would not answer, "white East India piece Goods" being "best adapted" for the Palermo market. Accordingly, after selling a quantity of sugar, Solomon Towne proceeded on the *Galatea,* with the piece goods entrusted to his care, to Leghorn.

The phrase "Average of ~~OZ~~ 8. pr Cantar Net Sales $ 12.. 33½ pr 112 lbs" means that the "442 Bags of Brazil — and 229 Bags of Manilla sugar" were sold at an average net price of $12.33½ per cwt. of 112 lb. and at a gross average price of 8 oncie per cantaro. The oncia was equal to 3 ducats of 3s. 5 2/10d. stg. There were two cantari, the cantaro grosso, equalling 193 lb. avoirdupois, and the cantaro sottile of only 175 lb. avoirdupois.[2] Since the net price of the sugar was almost exactly 11 cents per lb., the gross price per lb. should be somewhat more. At 8 oncie per cantaro sottile the price per lb. figures out to 11.3 cents, which leaves hardly sufficient leeway between net and gross price to pay the charges.

Palermo July 9 th 1819

Henry Lee, Esq[r]

Sir,   I have the pleasure to Inform you of my safe arrival at this port after a passage of 32 days; in 21 days we passed Gibralter. —

on my arrival I was put under quarantine for 14 days, I, immeditely Applied to James Rugg Esq[r] (with whom I, have done my Business here) Gave him a Memorandum of my Cargo and requested that He would not loose a moments time to see what Could be done,

He Observed that this was the best market in this quarter for the moment — the Prices at Leghorn were very much depressed and Sugar beyond measure. He presumed I, might sell a part of my Cargo here (say for 20 pC[t], more than there. India Goods a ready sale if of a Good quality —

having Exhibited the Samples of E. I. piece Goods you gave me in Boston Consisting of large and small Checks Custers & Blue Salampores I, have to inform you that they will not answer this market as there is no Consumption of this Kind of Goods in Sicily

2. M'Culloch, *op. cit.*, vol. ii, p. 263.

white East India piece Goods best adapted for this market are 12 y^d. Baftas Long cloths 36 y^ds. & Salampores 18 y^ds. the Consumption is very Considerable those Goods are Generally imported from London and sell according to quality from $8 @ 12 per piece of 36 yds — Other white goods such as Mamoodies, Cossas and Gurrahs are not less Saleable if of a Good quality. I, am sorry that I Could not Effects a sale of your 15 Bales at the Limits — which Could have Easily been done if they had been of a Better quality — the most of the East India Goods Imported here are Companies from London, I, have sold 442 Bags of Brazil — and 229 Bags of Manilla sugar at The Average of O̶Z̶ 8. pr Cantar Net Sales $ 12.. 33½ pr. 112 lbs

finding nothing more to be Done here I, have Closed my Business and am on the point of sailing for Leghorn,

I, am with Sentiments of Esteem
Your Obt srv^t
Solomon Towne

[Endorsed]
S. Towne. Palermo July 9. 1819
Galatea Goods unsold
_____
East India p^s goods.
Calcutta common goods
not wanted mine pr
Galatea are common
sorts.

LETTER FROM GEBHARD & CO., AMSTERDAM, JULY 16, 1819, TO HENRY LEE, BOSTON, ON PROSPECTS FOR THE SALE OF EAST INDIA GOODS[1]

In Amsterdam the demand for piece goods was not sufficient to make a profit probable. The situation had not changed by Oct. 5.

Note the promise of immediate remittance on the prospective sales of indigo.

Prices are given in florins of 1s. 8¾d. stg.[2]

The curcuma mentioned at the foot of the price list is another name for turmeric.

1. Jackson-Lee Papers.   2. M'Culloch, *op. cit.*, vol. i, p. 38.

Boston
Henry Lee Esqre.   *Amsterdam July 16th. 1819*
            Dear Sir

We have the Pleasure to acknowledge the receipt of your esteemed favors of 13th. & 26th. May via Antwerp and to give You our Quotations of Piece Goods with some Remarks on the same at foot. The Duties here are too high and we do not believe they will leave any Prospect of Profit to this Market. The Transit duty is 3 pct ad Valorum but it must be expressed in the B / lad^g that the Goods go transit. Indigo's & Saltpetre would readily sell at the quoted Prices — but of Ginger & Bengal Turmeric our Market is over stocked and not the least Inquiries made for them. —

The Ohio has not yet arrived — we duly note that Messrs. Peter Remsen & Co. NYork have sent us by her for your Acc^t. 5 Cases Bengal Indigo of which we shall procure the most advantageous Sales remitting the Proceeds to Saml. Williams Esqr. London. As soon as we have an Invoice so as to be able of ascertaining the Quantity we shall make an immediate remittance of 2/3^ds. of its Value, according to your Desire. You will please observe by our Quotations at foot that Coffee's have improved and it is believed this Article will maintain its present rate.

We remain respectfully,
                    Dear Sir
The Entry duty here on   Your obed Servants
Silkhdkerchiefs from Bengal is 4% —   p Gebhard & Co.
                    17th. July

We just got Intelligence of the safe Arrival of the Ohio at the Texel.

Memorandum of Piece Goods.

Blue Gurrahs 17½ 1⅛ y^d. ..	f 7. 7½ p p^ce.	⎫ Sales, seldom
" Guineas 36.	" 20. 22 "	Current and
" Salempouris 18	" 10. 11 "	Realisation
Silk hdkerchiefs equal to those⎱		very slow.
p Ariosto.⎰	" 7.9 p p^ce. of 7 p^ces.	inferior Quality
d^o Superior equal to the English		quite unsale
C B A N ... .. 13..14. — p D^o.		able. —

The Madras & Malabar Piece Goods are in no Demand, on Acc^t. of their
not suiting our present Manufactures, nor those in Germany —
the Prices of White Bengal Piece Goods are:

Gurrahs	18. 1⅛ y^d.	......	f 7½ @ 8½ —
Baftas	12. 1 "	......	" 5½ " 6.
Callipatty	— —		" 6 " 6¼
Emirties.	14. 1 y^d.	......	" 5½ " 6.
Mamoodies	20. 1 "	......	" 6 " 7.
Sannas.	20. 1⅛ "	......	" 9 " 9½
Hamans	12. 1½ "	......	" 7½ " 8½
Cassas	20. 1 "	......	" 7 " 8.
d°	20. 1⅛ "	......	" 9 " 9½
Guzinahs	14. 1 "	......	" 4¾ " 5¼.

Exportation of all kind of Piece Goods to the West Indies very limitted.
Saltpetre f 26. 28 p 100 lb
Curcuma Java f 14. 16 p D°.
  " Bengal " 12. — p D°.

                    [Addressed]
                    Henry Lee Esqre.
                    pthe *Johnes Boston*
                    [Endorsed]
                    F^r Gebbard &C°. Amsterdam
                    July 16. 1819.
                    ―――――――――――――――――
                    E. I. Cotton & silk goods
                    duty as transit goods.

LETTER FROM STEIGLITZ & CO., ST. PETERSBURG, AUG. 1, 1819,
TO HENRY LEE, BOSTON, ON PRICES OF EAST INDIA GOODS[1]

Henry Lee had in the previous year ordered some duck and other
Russian manufactures and had also shipped some turmeric, etc., to
St. Petersburg. He now tried the experiment of sending a few bales
of piece goods. In a letter of July 1 the St. Petersburg firm acknowledged the information that the captain of the vessel by which the
goods had been shipped was to co-operate in their disposal and to
receive 1% for his trouble; this letter also notified Lee that the importation of dyed cotton goods was prohibited.

The letter below stresses the necessity of sending only fine piece
goods and indigo to Russia. It will be remembered that Lee had
consistently urged his supercargoes to specialize in the inferior quali-

1. Jackson-Lee Papers.

ties of both — the piece goods to be sold eventually in the West Indies and Africa, the indigo to be disposed of in the United States where the better qualities were not appreciated. Henry Lee had not yet learned to accommodate his purchases to his new markets.

Prices in the letter below are given in rubles — paper rubles worth about 11d. stg. The weights of coffee, sugar, indigo, etc., are in poods of about 36 lb. avoirdupois. The same seems to be also true of Gallipoli oil. The price of rum, however, seems to be given in ankers of about 10 gal.[2]

The rates of exchange at the end of the letter below are, per ruble: London, 10 1/4d.; Hamburg, 9 1/16 sols; Amsterdam, 10 stivers; Paris, 106 centimes.

Henry Lee, Esqre.
Boston.

St. Petersburgh 1st. August 1819.

Sir!

Since our last Respects to you, dated the 1st. July, a Copy of which we enclosed, we are come into possession, not only of the 12 Bales of E. I. Piece Goods and 20 Chests Indigo p the Fame, but Captain Barker has also communicated us your letter of 29th. April, of the Contents of which we have taken due notice. We have the satisfaction to inform you, that the George, Captn. Saml. M. Holland also reached Cronstadt on the 24th. July, by which opportunity we received your Favor of 9th. June, covering Invoice and Bill of Lading of afurther consignment of 12 Bales E. I. Piece Goods made us by her. The disposal you are pleased to give has also been noted, and shall strictly be followed. Regarding the Sale of the whole of these Goods, nothing could possibly be done untill yet, because our Country buyers had left this for Nishney Novogorod's annual fair, before any thing could be cleared and received from the Customhouse. Sales are consequently for the present confined solely to the Consumption of this town, untill accounts respecting the issue of the said Fair are received.

As soon as more Buyers reappear, we shall not suffer an opportunity to Slip in effecting Sales for you if possible, and we

2. M'Culloch, *op. cit.*, vol. ii, pp. 290, 293.

hope then likewise to succeed in disposing of your Indigo, although not acknowledged here as fine, but only to be of a good middling Sort.

In point of the white Goods, we much regret, to be forced to say; that most probably they will not be got rid off without considerable loss, because their cost is much too high, considering the low quality, the greater part of them consist off. — For instance; such Sannas like the T N⁰. 7, 9 & 10 [in margin: Fine Jalalpour cost 109 / —], which even at the exchange of 4/6 & 11ᵈ. stand in at abᵗ. 25¾ R⁰, would now hardly be saleable at 20 R⁰. at 6 & 7/n. Credit. — The Gurras [interlineated: (good Comp'y)] N⁰. 22 to 24 by the same calculation cost abᵗ. 23¾ R⁰, and in all probability will not fetch above 18 or 19 R⁰, likewise the Beerboom Gurras SIV. N⁰. 38/39 [interlineated: good quality cost say 15/], which cost abᵗ. 20¼ R⁰, we think would find no Buyer even at 17 R⁰. — The Callipatty Bafftas calculate at abᵗ. 18½ R⁰. /: N⁰. 51:/ [interlineated: very fine] and are valued at 14½ @ 15 R⁰. only, and those p N⁰ 53 scarcely at 13½ @ 14 R⁰. —

In general we advise you: infuture to send less Gurrahs, because they are not abundantly used here, and above all no ordinary, but rather fine Sallempores, measuring 18 to 18½ yds, which latter goods would just now fetch from 23 to 25 R⁰, also fine Baftas, and Sannas of a quality similar to the 2 Bales SW. N⁰. 90/91. [in margin: They refer to E. I. C⁰ goods from London of very Superiour quality. —] In order to insure a ready Sale at the Market prices, it is requisite a Parcel of 1000 pᶜᵉˢ. should be assorted nearly as follows: abᵗ. 400pˢ. Sallempores, 200 pˢ. Sannas, 300 pᶜᵉˢ. Bafftas 12 to 12½ yds, & abᵗ. 100 pᶜᵉˢ. ditto of 14 yds; above every thing no glazed stiff Lots, nor ordinary Goods, because they are not only of a difficult Sale, but an unproportionate difference being also made in the price against the finer qualities.

For the same reason alledged, you will do well, to sellect your sendings of Indigo to this place in such a manner, that the whole as much as possible, consists of as much, real fine qualities.

Shortly after the date of our last letter to you, such Goods were paid for Nishney Novogrod's Market, up to 400 Rᵒ. at 6 & 7/m Credit, and most probably at this moment they would fetch 380 Rᵒ; when fine and good middling Sorts are not to be quoted above 350 to 330 Rᵒ [in margin: My Indigo p Fame was bo't by E. A. Newton & was first quality Blue. —]

The Speculation on Coffee has been but short, and has been succeeded by a calm: Ordinary Goods might likely sell from 54 to 57 Rᵒ, good middling 60 to 62 Rᵒ, & fine middling 64 to 66 Rᵒ.

Fine Coffee is buying by Single Casks & paid from 74 to 75 Rᵒ Fine white Havanah Sugars are somewhat higher, having been paid from 30½ to 31 Rᵒ Term 5 & 6/m; for inferior Sorts not above 26 Rᵒ. are offer'd. On the other hand, white Brazil Sugars have got lower; a middling Sort sold at 25 Rᵒ. 4/m; and for a Parcel of fine white, 27 Rᵒ. on 6 month Credit have been offer'd yesterday.

East India Cotton quite neglected at present, so that no price at all can be quoted. Some Georgia Cotton has been lately sold at 40 Rᵒ. — Best new Campeachy Logwood at 35 Rᵒ. 2 & 3/m; inferior however at 32 Rᵒ. with 6/m Credit. Nicaraguawood & Fustic without demand, which is also the case with Ginger & Turmeric. Cassia Lignea has been by degrees taken out the Market, & paid from 90 to 100 Rᵒ, according to quality. —

You will perceive, that fine black Cocheneal advanced very materially; It is paid from 1325 to 1350 Rᵒ., and we have to add, very little remains for Sale in our Market. — Carolina Rice has lately been paid at 13 Rᵒ at 3 mᵗʰ. Credit.

Although our Stock of Gallipoli oil has lately been increased by some arrivals, yet prices remain Steady from 32 to 34 Rᵒ., & in our opinion will yet go higher, provided the Autumn Supplies are not too large. We have been much less supplied with Rum, than was generally expected! New England is in consequence risen to 70 Rᵒ., & fine Jamaica paid in proportion higher.

Inclosed one of our latest General Import Lists, likewise our price Current of this day. You will notice in the latter; that clean Hemp is quoted higher, manufactured Goods on the contrary have declined, against the general expectation, owing no doubt to the unusual small exportation, which to all the Ports in the U.S. is confined to 7226 p^ces. SailCloth, 5790 p^ces. Raven-ducks, &. 3322 p^ces. Flems.

To the same destination there has been exported to this day, about 58,000 pood Iron, & about 55600 P^d. clean Hemp. —

We should have been glad to second your views regarding remittances by way of anticipation, but the exchange is so very disavantageous at present, that a more favourable turn must be waited for, which no doubt will meet your approbation.

We observe that you have paid to M^r. Slade the Sum of £500.. — . — on account of the purchases of manufactures directed by you in autumn last. We have credited you at the exchange of 3^d. May, 11 3^d/16, in R^o. 10726..26¢. which please book to our conformity.

Certificates of the Russian Consulate are no longer requisite, but an exact Specification of the Weights and measure together with the proper signature is rigidly demanded, for which reason we shall have some expences to charge you with on the 12 Bales p the George.

We are respectfully
Sir.
Your most obed^t. Serv^ts.
Stieglitz&Co

London 10 1/4
Hamburgh 9 1/16
Amsterdam 10
Paris.   106.
Inscriptions. —

[Material immediately below is in Henry Lee's handwriting.]

[Endorsed]
Stieglitz &Co 1 August 1819

Remarks on Bengal p^s goods p^r.
Fame & Ge^o. & an assortment
that will answer — duties
have been augmented since
this date, so that no facts will
any longer answer —
H.Lee 1821 —

LETTERS FROM F. & E. DELIUS, BREMEN, AUG. 4, 20, 1819,
TO HENRY LEE, BOSTON, ON THE PROSPECTS FOR EAST INDIA
GOODS[1]

The letter below is written in a rather desultory style. Such remarks as "Coffee in very good demand . . . Sugar not very brisk . . . East India Cotton more demanded than it was . . . Spices . . . very saleable" are useful in their way but compare unfavorably with the almost meticulous analyses of price situations found in the reports of certain other merchants. The signs for price, quantity, etc., are unusually cryptic and potentially deceitful. There is reference to exchange on London which looks very much as if it were saying "got up as high as 605%;" this is of course impossible, and probably the cipher was intended for an @. Prices are given in rix-dollars, worth 3s. 2d. stg., and grotes (72 grs. = 1 rd.); but the signs attached to numerals to express the prices of saltpetre and of hyson tea, though a comparison with an Antwerp price current of the same day shows that they must be intended for an "r," standing for rix-dollars, are no more like that letter than they are like several others, and at first glance closely resemble "sy." The second letter, written in a hand unlike the first, is equally confusing. The sign employed for the reader's confusion here is "gC," which, being the sign of a unit of value, would seem to stand for the groschen, worth about 2 cents, but here again comparison with prices in nearby ports at the same time indicates that "gC [?]" is probably an eccentric version of "grs," standing for grotes.[2]

[written across face of letter:]　Orig[l] p Governor Carver,
　　　　　　　　　　　　　　　　Dup[e]　　Boston
Henry Lee Esq[re].　　　　　　　Bremen 4th. Aug[st]. 1819.
　　Sir,
　　　　We had the honor of writing to you last on the 3[d]. ult[a]., to which letter we beg to referred. We then advised you of our Remittance of £ 300. — . stlg to our mutual friend; S[l]. Williams Esq[re]. of London, &have since not placed any further funds in his hands, the exchange having got up as high as 605% [?], which makes Remittances unfavorable just now; we shall wait however any turn the exchange may take, &shall not fail to remit, when it can be done to advantage,

1.　Jackson-Lee Papers.　　　2.　M'Culloch, *op. cit.*, vol. i, p. 244.

The sale of your East India Goods, we are sorry to say, goes
on but very slowly, & as yet we have not disposed of any more
of them. We are in treaty however for the whole, that now
remains undisposed of, &shall advise you shortly of what we
have been able to accomplish. The pieces are invoiced much
too high to answer here, & unless you can afford these Goods
cheaper, we can not recommend their being shipped to this
market

The Saltpeter, we are happy to say, has all been sold at 11½
& 12r [?], though we only obtained the latter price for a very
small [parcel—stricken through] quantity — We shall hand
you the Account Sales very shortly, &give you credit for the
half of the Proceeds; the Saltpeter is not yet delivered, or they
should be forwarded with this opportunity.

Our markets generally speaking, are improving. Coffee in
very good demand, & although prices are lower than they were,
there is yet much speculation, & the opinion tends to a rise.

Sugar not very brisk, but prices are the same, &we do not
think they will be lower

Teas are wanted. We had a public sale of a small Cargo very
lately, which went off very well, &this has taken the greater part
of our stock out of the market. Hyson Tea &fresh Congo are
very much in request, &would sell immediately to a profit.
Hyson may be quoted 1r [?] 24 grs, but then the quality must
be very good; good fresh Congo 38 grs. —

Indigo goes off very readily at the currency, &we have just
sold all we had on hand. The good middling Bengal sorts are
brisk of sale. —

East India Cotton more demanded than it was, but must be
shipped extremely low with you to answer. The prices here
may be quoted 12 to 17 grs. North American Cottons of all
sorts are very much wanted, and a few hundred Bales would
prove a good article just now.

Spices are always very saleable, if not imported in too large
quantities. The conditions of sale here are very simple &charges
extremely moderate; the duties are quite trifling on all
articles; this being a free port, & goods being only subject
to a river due at Elsfleth.

There is every appearance of the prices of Produce now remaining pretty steady, &we think that confidence is reviving a good deal.

We enclose a Price Curr^t and remain &c

Bremen 20 Aug^st. 1819

Sir

The preceeding is copy of our last respects of the 4th. Instant to which we beg your kind reference. The Ganges being on her departure for Marble head we have again the pleasure of addressing you, but are sorry to say that we have not been able to dispose of any more of your Piece Goods, though we might have sold them them all at 1..42gC on an average, this however was too low a price. We shall wait a little therefore and see what is to be done, more over the Leipsig Fair is again coming round, and we may perhaps then [may be — stricken through interlineated: find] a purchaser.

The Mow Sannas are much too narrow, if you could ship them of the same quality and much broader, they might do better. The Mamoodies however are more suited to this market and are higher in proportion — We shall be watchful for your interest in endeavouring to dispose of these Piece Goods & advise occasionally of what has been done.

The Account Sales of the Saltpetre we shall forward very shortly.

In our market there is no great variation except in Coffee which has advanced to 25 gC for the good and y [?] Qualities.

Sugar without alteration.

Indigo in demand and there are pretty ready sales at the currency.

Teas scarce and but a small stock on hand. Cotton very brisk and improving a good deal —

We inclose a price Current and are very truly,

Sir

Your very ob^tServants

F. & E. Delius

LETTER FROM WELLES, WILLIAMS & GREEN, HAVRE, OCT. 21, 1819, TO HENRY LEE, BOSTON, DISCOURAGING THE SHIPMENT OF INDIA COTTONS TO FRANCE AND ENCLOSING A MEMORANDUM FROM A FRENCH MERCHANT ON BLUE GOODS FOR AFRICA [1]

During the years since his return from Calcutta, Henry Lee had been investigating the possibilities for his carrying on a direct trade with India from various European ports, including Havre. On May 15, William Rollins reported discouragingly on the prospects for direct trade between France and Calcutta. Failures of French houses and heavy losses on voyages to Calcutta had caused a decline in the trade and decreased the likelihood of an American's obtaining tonnage at a low rate in French vessels, none of which were then fitting out for Bengal. There were prohibitive duties on the importation of saltpetre, and of sugar in a foreign vessel. Ginger, turmeric, goat skins, Bengal rice were out of the question as articles of importation into France. On the other hand, "Blue & colored goods are Sometimes wanted for Senegal." The letter below, however, tells why it would not do to import India piece goods for that purpose.

On Aug. 18, Welles, Williams & Greene announced the sale of 9 cases of Bengal indigo, shipped them by Henry Lee, at 10f. 97½s.

Of all the many samples of India piece goods mentioned in Henry Lee's correspondence only the one described below has come down to us. The swatch is a coarse, rough, loosely woven piece of goods, dyed a dark unattractive blue, and would seem ill-calculated for sale even on the west coast of Africa, not to mention in France. It is not surprising, then, that on Nov. 18 the Havre firm strongly discouraged the shipment to Bordeaux of "any description" of Bengal cotton goods.

Havre Oct⁰. 1819 — *Blue Cloths*

Les toiles bleues, nommées Guinées, doivent être de Pondichery pour convenir au commerce du Senégal — Les marques préferées Sont celles DIDM &. D2DM. Mais ce sont celles de la compagnie Anglaise et il n'est pas a presumer qu'on puisse en trouver ailleurs qu'a Londres — Il faut donc S'attacher a celles privileges dont les marques ne sont point déterminées.

1. Jackson-Lee Papers.

Les Balles contiennent 60 ou 80 pieces. Les Pieces sont de 17½ @ 18 Yards de long sur 1⅛ @ 1¼ Yᵈˢ. de large. —

Le tissu le plus fin & Regulier, est le plus estimé; mais il faut que le bleu Soit bien cuivré, déterminé de couleur de gorge de pigeon, ayant un apprêt gommé qui lui donne par l'effet du Cylindre, un luisant evide — comme le sont les étoffes des Indes appellées cirsacas —

La Consomation du Senégal est de 20 m pieces — par années au plus l'an dᵉʳ. il est arrivé un navire directement de Pondichery au Senégal, ce qui a porté un coup funeste a la Colonie puisque ces 9000 pᶜᵉˢ. ont fait Caisser l'article de 40 = % —

La bonne guinée courante vaudrait ici 35 f la piece au plus — & 60ˡᵇ. Gomme au Senégal en y faisant crédit de 3 a 4 mois sans Reglement a des gens qui ont peu de Moyens —

Toutes les autres toiles bleues d'autres dimensions & qualités c a d. plus inferieures ne pourraient convenir qu'a la traite des negres

The above is a note given to us by one of our Neighbours who has been in the habit of buying blue Cloths here for the African trade. —

duplicate

Havre 21ˢᵗ. Octʳ. 1819

Henry Lee. Esqʳᵉ.
    Boston.
        Dear Sir

We have your favour of the 21ˢᵗ. Augᵗ. which we partially replied to on the 10ᵗʰ., Since which we have made full enquiry relative to the articles of *Blue Gurrahs* & *Salempores,* of the quality you describe. — The result of which is that they will not answer to be sent to this place. —

The high prices that were obtained last year for blue Guineas, Caused a good Many to be sent here and they are difficult to Sell, as few expeditions are making from hence to the Slave Coast, and our Rouen Manufacturers have got to make blue

Cotton Goods that answer perfectly well for the Senegal market,
The Blue Goods that Sold best last year were those marked

D 2 DM	} Long Cloths	
N 5 DTM		
D 12 B	Succatoons	Measuring 18¼ Yds.
D 1. M	} Salem pores	by 1⅛ Yds.
D 2. M		

This description of Merchandize his Sold as high as 55 fr. p .
piece of 18¼ by 1⅛ Yds. — We have endeavourd to obtain a
Sample of these Goods but have not Succeeded — They are
better than the Sample enclosed of a darker blue, and a Shade
enclining to Copper Colour. —

The inferior qualities, Such as you describe are particularly
ill suited to this market and we Cannot recommend your shipping even the Best, or any Kind, either of *blue* or *white* Cotton
Goods. The latter are not admitted in the french colonies and
no Sale Would be found for them here. —

We are glad that the sale of your Indigos was made at the
time & at the price we advised — If it had remained on hand
untill this time we certainly Should not have done better.

The prices of Indigo remain about the same it has rather
declined a little if anything, and the quantity at Market is Much
more considerable. — these Supplies have Come in from England, as our prices are materially better than theirs —

Please to refer to our friends Messˢ J & B Welles for a Note
of all the actual sales, as we keep them furnished with a regular
list. —

Always at your service we are
Dear sir
Your friends & Servants

We have no advices yet from ⎫
Bordeaux relative to Blue   ⎪
cloths — when they are rec^d. ⎬
we will send them to You   ⎭

> [Endorsed]
> Havre 21 Octob^r. 1819
> E. I. Blue & White
> piece goods — W. W &
> Greene.
>
> ———————————
> with sample Blue Cloths
> enclos'd. —
> Welles, Williams &Greene — Havre
> Octo 21. 1819
> Blue Goods

LETTER FROM THOMAS W. LANGDON, SMYRNA, DEC. 28, 1819, TO HENRY LEE, BOSTON, ON SALES OF EAST INDIA PIECE GOODS[1]

The chief importance of the letter below is its very existence, for it completes the picture of Henry Lee's shipments to Europe of East India goods during the year 1819. These shipments extended from the Baltic, through the North Sea and the English Channel to the Mediterranean; and, in the Mediterranean, through the Tyrrhenian, Ligurian, and Adriatic seas, to the Aegean.

In the price list given below, such entries as "CP 28 — 80 — Cossas — 87/8 — 28½ p p^s." are to be thus interpreted: CP (owner's mark), 28 (number of bale), 80 (number of pieces), Cossas (type of goods), 87/8 (cost price in rupees and annas), 28½ p ps (sales price in piastres per piece).

The reference to the methods of remittance to London is of interest. The piastre fluctuated greatly in value.[2]

1. Jackson-Lee Papers.
2. M'Culloch, *op. cit.*, vol. i. p. 461.

Smyrna 28th. decr. 1819

Mr Henry Lee
   Dear Sir,
      My last was under date 14th. decr. to which beg your
reference. — The Messenger arrived on the 27th. to a very
excellent market for her Coffee & Indigo. — The peice Goods
will not interfere much in the Sale of ours that remain unsold. —
   I now enclose the prices of those already sold — Vizt.

				piasters			
RCC	7 @ 8	240 ps. —————	14	p ps. —————	3360 —
	15 ——	80 " —————	24	" " —————	1920.—
	16 ——	75 " —————	24½	" " —————	1837.50
	28 ——	75 " —————	24	" " —————	1800 —
35 @ 37	——	210 " —————	25	" " —————	5250.—
THp Jrs					
	5 ——	120 " —————	18	" " —————	2160.—
	6 ——	120 " —————	14	" " —————	1680 —
	11 ——	80 " —————	24	" " —————	1920 —
	12 ——	75 " —————	24	" " —————	1800 —
	14 ——	80 " —————	25	" " —————	2000 —
SC					
2 @	3 ——	160 " —————	26	" " —————	4160 —
4 "	5 ——	170 " —————	23	" " —————	3910 —
8 "	9 ——	200 " —————	17	" " —————	3400 —
10 "	11 ——	200 " —————	24	" " —————	4800 —

   21 Bales   p   39997.50

CP 28 — — 80 Cossas — 87/8 — — —	28½ p ps.
38.36.40.39 321 Gurrah 58/ — — — — —	25 " "
62.67 — — 200 — 69/10 59/10 — Baftas —	19 " "
64 — — — 100 — — 64/10 — Ditto —	18½ " "
58 @ 59 160 — — 70/ Gurrahs — — —	26½ " "
B — — 8 — — 80 Cossas 71/15 — — — —	27¼ " "
EL — — — — — 44 @ 49 — — — — —	19 " "
FL 17.35 — Mow sannas 25/ — — — — —	8 p ps. not Saleable
34 coarse — — — — 23/ — — — — —	8½ — — — — do.
38 — — — — Gurrahs 70/ — — — — —	26½
39 — — — — — " — — — — — —	26 —
CRC 17 — — — Mamoody 57/8 — — — —	26½
26½ — — Ditto — 65/ — — — — — —	27

making 41 Bales sold and the prices are considered good for the different kinds. — I regret very much that I have not a little more discretion left me in making remittance — Dollars can be shipped from hence to America at 7¼ piasters ea which makes the piaster nearly 13¾ Cents ea, while Exchange on England is 36 p £ Stg which makes the piaster 12½ a diffirence in favor of remitting dolls of quite 10 pC^t. — A small saving can be made by remitting dolls to Eng: &the neat remittance on y^r. acc^t. will probably be in this way &shall advise Mr Williams respecting Insurance. — We are now in treaty for a few more Bales of the India Cottons & I am in hopes in the course of a fortnight or 3 Weeks to close sales entirely &forward acc^t. Sales by the Washington that sails in 20 to 30 d^s. —

I am

Dear Sir

very respectfully

Your M^o. Obd^t Ser^t.

Thos. W Langdon

Mow Sannas are unsaleable all over the world — they bring a pezza at Leghorn down to ⅞ — 7 to 8 piastres in Smyrna white goods cost only double some bring nearly 3 times the price. they are too narrow — & very coarse.

[Addressed]

Henry Lee Esqre.

Merchant

Boston

N America

[Endorsed]

T. W. Langdon Smyrna

Decr. 28th. 1819.

Sales part of goods

Sales p^s goods p^r. *New Packet*

DIVISION XV

HENRY LEE AT THE END OF HIS BUSINESS LIFE
1840–44

LETTER FROM HENRY LEE, BOSTON, OCT. 31, 1840, TO JONES, GIBSON & ORD, MANCHESTER, ON PRICES OF COTTON GOODS[1]

A few years after the War of 1812 there appears in the Jackson-Lee Papers and associated collections one of those lacunae which almost inevitably harass historical students dependent upon so perishable and particularly so combustible a material as the papers of a particular family or firm. After 1819 the business papers of Henry Lee completely vanish to reappear more than a score of years later, near the end of 1840, when Henry Lee had largely withdrawn from active business. It is necessary, then, in order to follow Henry Lee's business life up to the time of his retirement, to seek information thereon in the more general records. But the most important of these potential sources of information, the Boston customs records, have, save for the ships' registers, been completely destroyed. This leaves us dependent upon the advertisements and marine notes in the Boston newspapers, but this information, fragmentary and terse at best, is rendered particularly one-sided by the character of Henry Lee's business after the War of 1812. Before their failure in 1811, the Lees and their associates had owned not only most of the vessels in which they imported goods from Calcutta but also some of those on which a portion of these India goods were shipped to the West Indies and the Continent. During that period, then, even in the absence of Lee business papers, at least a general idea of their commerce could have been derived through observing, in the newspapers, the movements of their vessels, the names of which are ascertainable from the registers in the Boston Custom House. But after the end of the War of 1812 and his return from Calcutta in 1816, Henry Lee never again owned a controlling interest in even a single vessel, although on Dec. 16, 1825, he was recorded as one of 19 owners of the ship *Courier,* 293 t.[2] We are consequently dependent solely upon

1. Jackson-Lee Papers, "Letters 1840–41. Henry Lee," Oct. 30, 1840–Dec. 21, 1852, p. 2.   2. Registers, Boston Custom House, 1825, no. 300.

such information as the newspapers may deign to give us, and this resolves itself into a matter of imports, a subject interesting alike to customs officials and other local merchants, whereas no mention is made of outward shipments by individual Boston merchants. We thus know, in a rough and general way, at least a minimum of the imports made to Henry Lee, but know nothing whatever, directly, of the exports he may have made, save as imports may suggest, in some cases, an attempt, at least, to keep the trade balance level with corresponding exports. Whatever general and fragmentary knowledge we may build up of Henry Lee's business life during the years 1820–39 inclusive must be based upon the newspaper accounts of the character and sources of his imports and upon the evidence of his own business papers immediately before and after this period of obscurity.

During the three years (1816–19), immediately following Henry Lee's return from Calcutta, for which we possess manuscript sources, fragmentary though they are for much of the period, Henry Lee's business centered about the importation of goods from Calcutta (and to a much slighter extent from Canton) and their sale in Boston or other cities of the United States, or their exportation to the West Indies or the Continent of Europe.

A greater number of importations from Calcutta to Henry Lee is recorded in Boston newspapers, 1817–43, than from the four ports next in order together. These importations, 82 in all, are not, however, spread evenly over the twenty-seven years from Henry Lee's return from Calcutta to his final complete retirement. From 1817 to 1820, inclusive, from 1 to 3 importations per year are recorded. Then, from 1821 to 1827, inclusive, Calcutta drops out of the list entirely, partly because during most of 1821 and part of 1822 Henry Lee was on a voyage to Calcutta. No particular tendency is seen in the importations during this period, in which were represented ports in the United States, the West Indies and South America, Great Britain, and northern Europe, the first two much more conspicuously. In 1828, however, and for more than a decade thereafter, both Henry Lee's trade in general, and his attention to Calcutta, demonstrate steady strength. This was concomitant with the association in business of Henry Lee and Ozias Goodwin, which began about 1826, the first year in which Ozias Goodwin is recorded in the Boston directory as having his office at 39 India Wharf, where Henry Lee was first registered in 1821. From 2 or 3 importations annually in 1828–30, the count rose to 7 in 1831 and 10 in 1832, fell off to 1 each in the next two years and then oscillated for the next seven years between 4 and 12 importations annually. After 1841, Calcutta invoices cease to come to Henry Lee, Sr. Henry Lee's interest in Calcutta after the War of 1812 thus lies in two periods, 1817–20 and 1828–41, the latter being out of all proportion the more important. The disproportion is not, however, so great as might appear from a comparison merely of the number of invoices in each period. Just after the War of 1812 the shipments from Calcutta to Henry Lee were nearly all rather large ones, representing most of the bewildering varieties of goods characteristic of the Calcutta trade: indigo, saltpetre, hides and skins (buffalo, cow, goat); drugs, gums, and spices, such as senna, sal ammoniac, borax, turmeric, safflower, sumac, shellac, gum copal, lac dye, sage, ginger, and curry powder; cotton goods (choppas, gurrahs, mamoodies, sannas, salempores, etc.); silks; and a miscellaneous assortment of such merchandise as hemp, jute, gunny bags, twine, rattans, linseed, red paint, horn tips, wine, etc. A typical advertisement for that period offers for sale: "Eighty bales Mamoodies, Gurrahs, Checks, Chintz, Palempores, Blue Baftas, and Mizapore Carpets. 800 pieces Flag and Bandanna Handkfs. 13 cases 4–4 black fringed and twilled Silk do. 2 do. Sewing silks. 1 do. colored crapes, 1 do. Levantines, 10000 lbs. refined Saltpetre, 5000 large size Goat Skins, 490 bags Tumerick, 15 quarter casks India Sherry Wine, Mace and Cloves."[3] In the second period such invoices as the following continue: "38 cases shellac, 26 do lac dye, 40 do indigo, 57 do choppas, 23 do bandannas, H. Lee; 99 cases shellac, 30 do lac dye, 40 bales cow hides; 14 bales buffalo hides, 13 bales goat skins, 34 cases silk goods, 503 bags salt petre, 19 cases indigo, H. Lee and O. Goodwin." But references to such invoices as "1 case cashmere shawls," "13 bales hides," "20 bales gunny cloth," etc., increase.[4]

Calcutta, although the principal, was not the only far eastern port from which shipments were made to Henry Lee. Five invoices from Canton were both widely scattered and small; 2 appeared in 1818, the others in 1832, 1835, and 1837. Those of which the content was specified consisted of 29 cases merchandise, 15 cases silk, 46 cases and 2 boxes merchandise, 6 cases silks, etc.;[5] evidently the China

3. *New England Palladium*, June 5, 1818.

4. *Boston Daily Atlas*, Nov. 7, 1837, Aug. 27, 1838; *Boston Daily Advertiser*, June 1, 1840, Aug. 21, 1841.

5. *New England Palladium*, Mar. 31, Apr. 3, 1818; *Boston Post*, Apr. 26, 1832; *Boston Daily Atlas*, Mar. 11, 1835, Aug. 21, 1837.

trade was then, as previously, of but little importance to Henry Lee.

The only other far eastern region with which Henry Lee had commercial relations — Batavia — was of even less importance to him. The 2 consignments therefrom, in 1831 and 1832, consisted of "221 bags coffee, 311 pigs tin" and "263 bags coffee," respectively.[6]

The trade with the Continent having been so long under restriction incident to the Revolutionary and Napoleonic wars, Henry Lee now showed a particular interest in that part of the world, and made, or enquired concerning the prospects of, consignments to a dozen ports evenly divided between northern Europe — St. Petersburg, Hamburg, Bremen, Amsterdam, Antwerp, Havre — and southern Europe and the Mediterranean — Cadiz, Gibraltar, Leghorn, Palermo, Trieste, Smyrna. He also continued shipments to Havana and kept up his correspondence with merchants in New York, Philadelphia, Baltimore, and New Orleans, in London, and in Liverpool.

An examination of the Boston newspapers for the same period (1816–19) will reveal their inadequacy as a source of mercantile information, for, though 6 importations from Calcutta and 1 from Canton are recorded, the only other foreign port mentioned is Havana; in the United States, New York and Salem are noticed. The reason is simple. Most of the ports to which Henry Lee shipped oriental goods made returns not in merchandise but in exchange, and consequently are not mentioned in the lists of imports. Havana, with its staples of molasses, sugar, and coffee, was a conspicuous exception, and most of the other ports to which Henry Lee made shipments occasionally furnished returns in the form of merchandise. Continental ports, however, appear but infrequently as furnishing goods to Henry Lee.

Such continental imports as there were, came in larger proportion from northern than from southern Europe. Gothenburg and Hamburg ran neck and neck, each making, however, only 4 shipments during the entire period. Those from Gothenburg occurred in the years 1823, 1832, and 1833, and consisted entirely of iron; the last 3 importations were to the firm of (Henry) Lee & (Ozias) Goodwin and amounted to 1,387 bars and 658 bundles, 3,745 bars and 289 bundles, and 87½ tons of iron, respectively.[7] This iron was probably intended for use in railroad construction (Henry Lee's brother-in-law P. T.

6. *Boston Daily Advertiser*, Nov. 7, 1831, Nov. 21, 1832.

7. *Boston Daily Advertiser*, July 28, 1823, Feb. 26, Nov. 19, 1832; *Boston Commercial Gazette* (semi-weekly), Feb. 28, 1833.

Jackson was importing iron definitely for that purpose, 1832–37), and Henry Lee's importations may have been unrelated to any previous shipment to Gothenburg of Calcutta goods.

The 4 shipments from Hamburg occurred in 1825, 1830, and 1831. The first 2 were of miscellaneous dry goods, linen, etc.; the others, to Lee & Goodwin, consisted of 500 and 1,000 demijohns, respectively.[8]

Next in order came 2 shipments from Cronstadt, both to Lee & Goodwin and both in 1831; these typical Russian invoices were 164 bales flems, 60 bales ravens duck, 300 packs sailcloth, and 21 bales broad diapers, 91 bales brown flems, respectively.[9]

Next, in 1831 and 1832, came 2 shipments, from Stockholm and from Stockholm and Copenhagen, both to Lee & Goodwin; they consisted of 11,754 bars and bundles iron and 13,526 bars iron,[10] doubtless intended for the same use as that imported about the same time from Gothenburg.

The only importation mentioned from Amsterdam was a miscellaneous one of gin, steel, and other merchandise, in 1830.[11] No importation from Le Havre occurred till 1843; it consisted of "2 cases mdse" which may have been returned Calcutta goods.[12]

From the above items, brief and casual though they are, we learn that, particularly in the early 1830's, Henry Lee and his partner Ozias Goodwin were engaged in importing iron from Sweden, glassware from Hamburg, linen and canvas from Russia, and miscellaneous merchandise from Hamburg and Amsterdam. To what extent, if at all, these importations were the result of shipments of merchandise by Henry Lee to the above ports, or whether, on the contrary, they were independent of other mercantile operations, there is no way of learning.

During 1816–19 Henry Lee was interested in southern Europe, particularly the Mediterranean. Any continuance of this interest is but feebly reflected in the newspaper items of importations during the twenty years following. Smyrna leads the list with 3 importations, 1831, 1832, and 1835. In 1831 arrived 3 cases opium, but the other

---

8. *Boston Courier*, Apr. 15, 1825; *Boston Daily Advertiser*, June 11, 1830, Sept. 6, Oct. 5, 1831.

9. *Boston Daily Advertiser*, Aug. 12, Oct. 11, 1831.

10. *Boston Daily Advertiser*, Sept. 27, 1831; *Boston Post* (morning) Feb. 3, 1832.

11. *Boston Daily Advertiser*, July 28, 1830.

12. *Ibid.*, Aug. 30, 1843.

2 invoices, in 1832 and 1835, "1 box mdse" and 10 cases indigo, were both probably returned goods; the latter was explicitly so.[13] In 1832 "2 qr. casks wine" from Malta and Gibraltar and in the same year 2 additional boxes of opium arrived from Constantinople. The only other shipments from the Mediterranean, 5 cases lac dye from Palermo in 1838 and "1 trunk mdse" from Leghorn in 1842, were both probably of returned goods, the former certainly so.[14] Here again it will be observed that Henry Lee's connection with these Mediterranean ports, so far as the newspapers reveal, was almost entirely in the early 1830's. Importations therefrom were insignificant, a few boxes of opium only; but the references to goods probably or certainly returned from that region as early as 1832 and as late as 1842 indicate that during that period, as certainly shortly after the War of 1812, Henry Lee was using the Mediterranean as an outlet for Calcutta goods. Probably very rarely were goods ever actually returned to the United States from such a distance; the references to goods thus returned are therefore indicative of a much larger quantity shipped and sold there.

The largest outlet for East India goods was probably the ports in Latin America, although, when newspaper items alone are used as a basis of comparison, the fact that most of these countries produced commodities eminently suitable for remittance to the United States may give an overemphasis to their importance in this connection. Cuba (with 19 consignments from Havana and 3 from Matanzas) appeared more frequently among the Latin American countries from which goods were shipped to Henry Lee than all the other West India and South American regions together. These consignments ran with occasional lapses from 1819 to 1841 inclusive, the years 1821–23, 1826–29, 1833–34 being the ones not represented. There are definite tendencies observable in the types of Cuban goods imported: from 1819 to 1825, 2 consignments from Havana and 2 from Matanzas, consisting almost entirely of molasses, sugar, and coffee; then in 1830 a consignment of 53,000 cigars from Havana, followed in the next year by 3 consignments of sugar, 1 from Matanzas, 2 from Havana, 291, 400, and 158 boxes, respectively; in 1832 and 1835–38 the Havana consignments were of cigars exclusively, but in the years

13. *Ibid.*, Jan. 19, July 21, 1831, July 10, 1832; *Boston Daily Atlas*, Feb. 16, 1835.

14. *Boston Daily Advertiser*, Feb. 9, Sept. 7, 1832; *Boston Daily Atlas*, May 17, 1838; *Boston Daily Advertiser*, Oct. 19, 1842.

1839–41 all the Havana invoices, save a small one of cigars in 1841, indicate Henry Lee's gradual withdrawal from business, consisting, as they obviously do, of returned East India merchandise.[15]

Next to Cuba, Henry Lee enjoyed the most extensive relations, among Latin American countries, with Venezuela, though these extended over comparatively few years. In the years 1832, 1840, and 1842, 5 consignments came to Henry Lee from Venezuela, 3 from La Guayra and Puerto Cabello, 1 from Puerto Cabello alone, and 1 from Maracaibo. These invoices consisted of coffee and a few hides. Just after Venezuela came Brazil with an invoice of tobacco from Bahia in 1831 and 3 of coffee from Rio de Janeiro in 1839 and 1841. Rio was to divide with Calcutta the attention of the firm of Bullard & Lee which succeeded to the business of Henry Lee, Sr.

No other Latin American country or port, so far as the newspaper records go, shipped as many as 2 consignments to Henry Lee. Coffee from Port au Prince, 1823, hides and horns from Buenos Aires, 1824, cotton goods (returned) from St. Thomas, 1832, more merchandise (also returned) from Trinidad, 1836, and "151 bars copper" from Guayaquil and Valparaiso, 1837, tell the story.

The most striking aspect of Henry Lee's trade with Latin America was the slight extent to which it had changed during the last 30 years of his active business life. He had traded with Havana and Rio de Janeiro as early as 1810, with La Guayra as early as 1811 — in each case within a year or two of the actual opening of trade; his father had traded with Haiti and the Danish West Indies. Henry Lee, it is evident, took little advantage of the opportunity to press the trade with the other newly independent Spanish American countries, such as Argentina and Chile, and even his commerce with Venezuela could hardly, it would seem, be called extensive.

Henry Lee's relations with ports in the United States are at once complex, confusing, and comparatively unimportant. We have record of 21 consignments to Henry Lee from 8 United States ports, 1819–37: 7 from New York, 3 each from Charleston and New Orleans, 2 each from Salem, Philadelphia, and Mobile, and 1 each from Marblehead and Baltimore. The 7 from New York occur during 1819–32, and 6 of these, 1819–25, are described in only the most general way as "merchandise;" the exception was "1 bale hides." It is probable that this "merchandise," and also the hides, were goods imported by

15. *Boston Daily Advertiser*, Sept. 15, 1830, June 27, July 6, 12, 1831.

Henry Lee, probably from Calcutta, and shipped to New York for a better sale, which not materializing, they were returned to Boston.

The 3 consignments from Charleston occurred in 1828, 1832, and 1837, and consisted of "sundries," "4 cases mdse.," and "17 bales bagging," in all cases, no doubt, goods returned by Charleston commission merchants as not meeting the limits set by Henry Lee. The 3 consignments from New Orleans all occurred in 1832; 2 of them consisted of 50 bales of cotton, the third of "8 cases silks," doubtless returned. The cotton was probably in payment for East India goods. Two consignments from another southern port, Mobile, were received in 1839; one consisted of "60 bales cotton," the other of "41 bales domestic goods." The cotton was doubtless in payment for an earlier shipment, perhaps of a consignment of "domestic goods" which met with a better market than those later returned. Henry Lee was evidently being forced into shipping to the South not only imported East India textiles but also the domestic goods which by dint of technology and high tariffs were ruining the market for the Calcutta cottons.

Two shipments from Philadelphia, in 1826 and 1828, of coffee and "220 chests, 200 half do tea," hint at another aspect of Henry Lee's business. It is possible that coffee imported by Henry Lee from Cuba may have been shipped to Philadelphia for sale, and then returned, but Henry Lee, so far as we know, had not imported any tea for years before 1828. It is possible that he may have ordered tea from Canton to be shipped to him by the first vessel to any northern port, but it is more likely that some Philadelphia importer sent him this tea for sale on commission. The same possibilities arise in connection with the sugar and saltpetre received from Salem in 1819 and the "156 cases indigo, 13 cases lac dye, 7 cases silks" in 1832. As to the latter, it is probable that Lee & Goodwin had ordered the consignment from Calcutta and instructed that it should be shipped to any northern port; this probability is increased by Salem's proximity to Boston, by the size of the consignment — somewhat large for a shipment to be sold on commission — and particularly by the fact that Lee and his partner were then actively and extensively engaged in the Calcutta trade.

A shipment of coffee from Marblehead in 1827 may have been goods returned or a consignment for sale on commission. In 1828 "2 cases dry goods" from Baltimore were doubtless goods returned.

The most we can say of Henry Lee's relations with other ports in

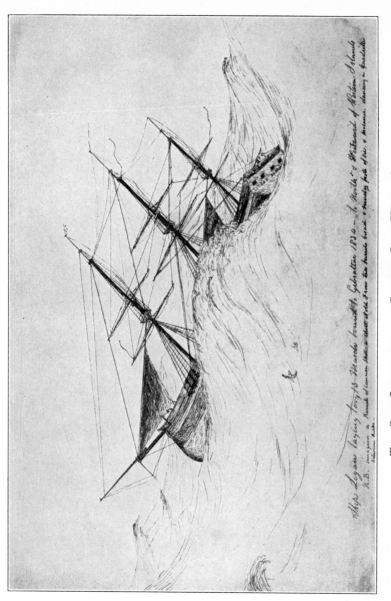

Ship Logan laying too 13 March bound to Gibraltar 1834 — to Northing Westward of Madeira Islands

N.B. see piece a French Clamour that is shoot at the 8 too ten hands but a twenty five of No. & Mizzun shewing a Guadalite between two.

THE SHIP LOGAN OFF THE CAPE OF GOOD HOPE, 1834

the United States, as revealed in the newspapers, is that he probably sometimes imported goods by way of ports other than Boston; that he sometimes sold, on commission, goods imported and sent to him by merchants in other cities; and that he undoubtedly shipped goods to other United States ports for sale on commission. These shipments were some of them certainly on his own account, some probably on that of other merchants, particularly British. A portion of the consignments, of course, did not meet a good market and were consequently returned; when sold in the South, they were sometimes paid for in cotton.

So far as the newspapers indicate, the greatest change in Henry Lee's business life after the War of 1812 came in his relations with England. The four leading ports which made shipments to Henry Lee, 1818–43, were Calcutta, Liverpool, Havana, and London. It will be observed that the second and fourth were English ports.

The 39 consignments from Liverpool occurred 1825–39. They are for the most part referred to non-committally as "dry goods," "mdse.," etc., but sometimes there is a specific reference to "30 tons hemp, 3 casks ale," "2 bundles vises," "186 brs flat 465 do. round iron," "100 boxes guns," "55 bales cotton bagging," "25 tons pig iron," "36 bales woollens," [16] etc. The "bales," however, in which the quantity of the unspecified merchandise was usually given, doubtless in most cases consisted of English cotton goods, which we know Henry Lee a little later was importing to lend variety to the East India and American cottons in which he dealt. Some of these goods may have been shipped to Henry Lee for sale on commission.

The 14 consignments from London, 1824–40, were also usually referred to casually as "merchandise," but those which are described more exactly differ considerably from the Liverpool invoices. Among them were "61 tons hemp," "50 tons hemp, 420 mats," "77 tons hemp," "200 boxes tin plate, 44 chests shellac," "11 chests indigo, 2 cases silk goods, 13 bales cotton goods," "4 hhds. ale, 13 bales salempores," [17] etc. A strong East India aroma is perceptible about these goods, wafted from the hemp, shellac, indigo, silks, and cotton goods. It is probable that many of the "chests" and "bales" from London contained indigo or shellac or consisted of cotton goods. We

16. *Boston Daily Advertiser,* Mar. 8, 1831, Oct. 5, 1832; *Boston Daily Atlas,* Sept. 16, 21, 1835, Jan. 18, Sept. 6, 1836, Jan. 28, 1837.

17. *Boston Daily Advertiser,* Feb. 5, 1831, May 5, July 7, 1832; *Boston Daily Atlas,* Aug. 15, Dec. 31, 1838, May 23, 1839.

know that in 1817 Henry Lee was taking advantage of the lowered prices, resulting from increased competition following upon abolition of the East India Co.'s monopoly, to purchase Calcutta goods in London; we know that in 1840 he was selling, in America, East India goods, particularly indigo, on commission for London houses. It is impossible to tell which of these invoices were imported on his own account and which were being shipped to him for sale on account of others.

Importing of British textiles from Liverpool and of East India goods from London and the sale on commission of East India goods for London houses are among the principal developments of Henry Lee's business during the last twenty-five years of his active commercial life. Again a cycle had been completed. Before the Revolution the American merchant had imported all oriental goods from England, because banned from the direct trade with the Far East. Now, after a period during which all, or nearly all, oriental goods had been imported directly into the United States, the American merchant was finding it profitable to deal also in far eastern goods which had reached the United States by way of London. He was also importing British factory textiles which were low-priced imitations of Calcutta hand-woven cotton goods. The letter below is to a manufacturer, among other goods, of imitation India cottons.

On Nov. 5, Henry Lee reconsidered and decided to "order a few more bales of goods," 500 pieces plaids, 750 pieces neganepauts, 1,000 pieces bejutipauts, 750 pieces chilloes, 1,000 pieces Nickannas, "by way of helping the sale of some East India." [18]

The "party . . . now coming into power" was the Whig Party; Van Buren, leader of the opposing party, was a staunch believer in "hard money."

Mess Jones, Gibson & Ord.   Boston. Octo 31. 1840
                    Orig p Acadia
    Manchester.
        Dear Sirs,
            I am obliged to you for your attention to my little order, but the prices do not seem to have fallen for former rates, though

18. Jackson-Lee Papers, "Letters 1840–41. Henry Lee," Oct. 30, 1840–Dec. 21, 1852, p. 3, Henry Lee, Boston, Nov. 5, 1840, to Jones, Gibson & Ord, Manchester.

the raw materials, cotton & indigo are 25 @ 33 1/3% lower and wages & profits also to their lowest point. Here on the other hand prices of cotton fabrics are 25% below those of 12 months ago, and not likely to advance much, while such is the case, the export demand will be supplied from our home made articles to a greater extent than formerly. Checks 30 @ 40 inches wide of nearly double the weight of your 28 inches are selling 8 @ 9¢ p yard and coarse ones lower. Drillings 1/3 lb in weight p yard 30 inches 8¢ @ 8¼¢ p yard made of prime New Orleans. I thank you for the "Glance" and shall be glad of the annual one. By Feby, when our crops are realised, currencies, sound, and elections completed, we shall have a *very active business,* through the Union and probably a spirit of speculation excited that may induce over importations, still with our 900 banks badly as the are managed, I think there are causes in operation, which will carry us 2 & perhaps 3 years before we come to another suspension. An entire paper currency, or what amounts to it, is the party cry of the men now coming into power,

Yours &c

(Signed)   Henry Lee

LETTER FROM HENRY LEE, BOSTON, NOV. 9, 1840, TO DE CONINCK & SPALDING, HAVANA, EXPRESSING HOPE FOR SALES OF COTTONS[1]

Henry Lee had begun shipping India cottons to Cuba in 1809 and now after more than thirty years he was still shipping to Havana "India Long Cloths" and "Blue goods," to which, however, he was now adding "American domestics," as doubtless he had been doing for a score of years past. In 1840, as in 1810, coffee was one of the principal products in which returns from goods shipped to Cuba were made.

Henry Lee continued to write the Havana firm at more or less frequent intervals, urging and acknowledging sales, announcing a prospective rise in textiles, enquiring concerning the trade with Africa,

1. Jackson-Lee Papers, "Letters 1840–41. Henry Lee," Oct. 30, 1840–Dec. 21, 1852, p. 5.

ordering cigars, and, finally, urging that the goods on hand be either sold at certain limits or returned; by May 17, 1843, the Havana firm had rid themselves of the last of Lee's cottons by sale or return.[2]

We may infer from items found in Boston newspapers that the West Indies and South America ranked third among the sources of Henry Lee's importations during the quarter-century after the War of 1812, trailing far behind the Far East and even the British Isles, but running a considerable distance ahead of United States ports, northern Europe, and the Mediterranean. Among West India and South American ports Havana was incomparably superior; it furnished more invoices to Henry Lee than all the others together, 19 from 1819–41 — in fact, there may have been more than that number. Of these importations at least 4, all during or after 1839, were apparently goods returned unsold; of the others, 11, all between 1830 and 1841, consisted entirely of cigars, in one instance totalling 110,000; while the other 4 consignments, 1819–31, consisted of molasses, sugar, and coffee. Matanzas, a port to the west of Havana, in the years 1821, 1825, 1831, furnished 3 consignments of molasses, sugar, and coffee.

Mess De Coninck &Spalding.   Boston. 9 Novr. 1840.
     Orig p Sophia & Eliza
Havana.
  Dear Sirs.

   Your last letters have not been acknowledged as they appeared not to require any particular answer. I was in hopes from what you wrote about India Long Cloths, that they would have met with a ready sale. I have, however, no doubt your exertions have not been wanting to effect a sale and I hope soon to hear of one as also of the Blue goods and the American domestics, for though not of the heaviest description they are of good quality. I shall be glad of any advices as to change in your markets for Cotton goods such as I have on hand with you, as I also have a stock here of similar goods, which I shall be glad to send you if there is a fresh demand for them. When you

  2. *Ibid.*, pp. 46, 53, 119, 140, 145, 154, 175, 178, 186, 187, 198, 200, 210, 279, 288.

write let me know the prices of coffee and how your crop is as
compared with the last.

Yours truly

(Signed)   Henry Lee

LETTER FROM HENRY LEE, BOSTON, NOV. 9, 1840, TO W. P.
FURNISS & CO., ST. THOMAS, COMMENTING ON LACK OF DE-
MAND FOR COTTON GOODS [1]

St. Thomas, one of the Danish West Indies, had evidently been
used not only as a market for some of the East India textiles which
Henry Lee was still importing but also as a center for distributing
such goods through the West Indies. The reference to the decline in
"the Coast trade" was doubtless called forth by the slump in the
trade with the west coast of Africa, produced by the outlawing of the
slave trade which had been its mainstay; some trade with the coast
of Africa continued, however, as the natives still wished rum, calico,
and muskets and there were merchants willing to supply them in exchange for palm oil, gold-dust, and white — rather than black —
ivory. How long Henry Lee had been trading with St. Thomas is not
known. Seven bales of unsold cotton goods had been returned therefrom on Mar. 5, 1832 [2] — the only reference to the trade with that
island in Boston newspapers; returns from St. Thomas were evidently not made in the products of the island.

On Jan. 30, 1841, Lee ordered that his goods at St. Thomas should
be returned to him unless they could be sold at once at from $1.40
to "$2⅛" per piece; on Apr. 9 he repeated the order, lowering the
prices slightly. On Oct. 1, 1842, Lee acknowledged receipt of sales.[3]

Mr W. P. Furniss &Co Orig p Kanahaw Boston. 9 Novr. 1840
St Thomas.

Dear Sirs.

I am favored with yours of the 4th Septr and regret to
find my goods do not go off. I am aware the Coast trade is of

1. Jackson-Lee Papers, "Letters 1840–41. Henry Lee," Oct. 30, 1840–
Dec. 21, 1852, p. 4.

2. *Boston Daily Advertiser,* Mar. 6, 1832.

3. Jackson-Lee Papers, "Letters 1840–41. Henry Lee," Oct. 30, 1840–
Dec. 21, 1852, pp. 48, 60, 122, 250.

small extent compared with former years, still I find goods do occasionally sell in Cuba and at the same time some of those you have of mine are, I hope, fine enough for the consumption of the Spanish Maine, Porto Rico &c. Be good enough to say if in your opinion there is a pretty good chance of a sale in the course of the coming 4 or 5 months. There is here a demand now and then on the continuance of which I can rely in case there is no hope of your selling,

Yours truly,

(Signed)　Henry Lee

LETTER FROM HENRY LEE, BOSTON, NOV. 10, 1840, TO JAMES CULLEN, CALCUTTA, WITH INFORMATION ON SALES OF INDIGO AND GENERAL BUSINESS MATTERS [1]

Henry Lee was evidently selling indigo and other goods on commission for the Calcutta merchant. In letters of about the same date to other Calcutta merchants he gave various reasons for dullness in both the London and the American markets: the diversion of consumers' earnings to investment in "preparatory war measures" resulting from the tension caused by France's support of Turkey's vassal, Egypt, against her overlord, and England's support of Turkey; and the intense interest universally felt in the "Tippecanoe-and-Tyler-too" election.[2] By Jan. 28, 1841, the indigo situation had so changed that Henry Lee commented to the same Calcutta merchant: "The ships now absent on voyages to Calcutta have not orders or means of bringing us half our consuming wants . . . of indigo and I therefore recommend shipments." The American market, he wrote, would have been without indigo had it not been for parcels from London.

From his first entrance into business Henry Lee's chief interest had been in the trade with Calcutta, an interest which, as supercargo, merchant, supercargo again, agent, and again merchant, he had continued up to the year of the letter below. Boston newspapers, 1817–

1. Jackson-Lee Papers, "Letters 1840–41. Henry Lee," Oct. 30, 1840–Dec. 21, 1852, p. 7.

2. *Ibid.*, p. 5, Henry Lee, Boston, Nov. 7, 1840, to Cockerell & Co., Calcutta; *ibid.*, p. 6, Henry Lee, Boston, Nov. 9, 1840, to Charles Huffnagle, Calcutta.

41, record a minimum of 83 importations to Henry Lee from Calcutta — the largest number from any single port — consisting of sugar, ginger, hides, indigo, horn tips, saltpetre, hemp, gunny sacks, drugs, gums, rattans, silks, etc., etc., in which, however, cotton piece goods, once the staple of the trade with India, took a subordinate place, because of high protective tariffs on cheap cottons and technical advances in the European and American textile industries. During 1821–27 the newspapers reveal no Calcutta imports to Henry Lee. But during those same seven years they mention only 17 imports to him from other ports.

James Cullen Esq.   Boston, 10 Novr. 1840
           Orig p Mary &Susan sailed 16th
  Calcutta.
    Dear Sirs.
      I have nothing from [interlineated: you] for some time. I have sent the house sales of the Indigo for which remittances have been made. The Oude netts   d more than the gross valuation in London and if you take the charges off, the result is a favorable one as compared with what it would have been in London if sold even at the April sale or the January, but I should have done much better but for the extraordinary bad turn which money matters took on the suspension of the United States Bank and all the other banks south of New York in October. To that unexpected event may be attributed a fall of prices equal to 20% on Indigo and Silk goods beyond what could have taken place had it not occured. The advance in prices of Indigo at the Octo sale appears to have been unexpected every where and in no place more than London judging from all the letters I have had & seen from there for some months past. I do not, however, consider the advance as founded on sound calculation, but as forced and artificial and in the face of facts and circumstances which ought to have lowered prices and would have done so, but for the extraordinary conduct of holders in withdrawing and stopping the sale of all but about 4000 out of 11.000 Chts. In this way prices of any articles may for a time be maintained and raised far

above their natural value. It has in the case of indigo suceeded sometimes but the effect is to accumulate production and decrease consumption and in the end agents, planters, London consignees and speculators all suffer and such I think will be the end of the *"holding on system"* pretty generally. The only specious reason for the withholding 6000 Chts was the reported falling off in the estimates of the crop as p 10ᵗʰ Augᵗ statements which were rec'd just before the sale, but taking them at the lowest which is 115.000 Mds there is no good reason to look for an advance that can long be sustained, since with the increased stock and 12 mos supply there can be no scarcity of the articles if the 2 or 3 coming crops should fall off to 90 @ 110.000 Mds. On the 30 Sept the stock in Europe was 29.346 Chts against 24.433 the same period last year and that will soon be increased by the arrival in Holland of the Java crop now not to be overlooked as formerly in the estimates of the value of this staple. There does not appear to have been much if any advance realised in the low qualities. The London house were disposed to send me 100 Chts of a quality of Oude somewhat below yours, for which I remitted 4/8¼, upon the supposition I could remit them ⅜ lb, but were discouraged by the apprehension I might not do so well as that. The state of the money market Mr J. Mackillop writes me, is not favorable to prices, nor does he seem confident that commercial matters will improve or ever remain in as favorable position as they now are.

The bank with only £4.145.000 of bullion against liabilities £23.993.000 which is about 1/6ᵗʰ metal reserves instead of 1/3ʳᵈ which they profess to keep and which they expected to have if the grain harvest proved abundant which turns out to be the case. This critical state of the currency has already induced a curtailment of loans and circulation which in 1 month had amounted to nearly one million, but as the exchanges were not favorable enough to bring in coin to the extent wanted there is reason to suppose there will be a further contraction and its consequent action upon prices. We shall also want coin from England when we resume and when our crops are shipped we shall the means of procuring it and that as in former years will be the cause of trouble to the London money market. It is these expansions and contractions dependant not upon the great interest of trade, but the will of a few individuals here and in England, which are ruinous to all the regular operations of prudent men, but I see not how they are to be avoided, without the substitution of paper, almost an entire metal currency, and though that will not be done in England yet I think the Bank of England will be put under better management for the public at the renewal of its charter, than it now is, at least I hope so.

I have nothing to add to former letters in respect to Hdfs. there will be nothing done in them till February, when I look for an improvement in prices, None of your staples will pay a profit except hides and cotton bagging, both of which do very well. Indigo also will do well [interlineated: as] compared with London, & also upon the prices which I am told you were paid for a parcel of Oude sold the Supercargo of the "Rouble," but I can better judge of that when I see the samples. I do not expect a supply of over 2/3 or 1/2 our usual wants in the ships which arrive in 1841 and consequently I think money will be made on shipments.

Our Cotton crop is estimated at 1.700.000 to 1.800.000 bales against 2.177.000 last year prices have advanced about 10% but there has not been a corresponding one in England, nor do I think prices ought to advance, since a crop of 1.800.000 bales is enough in the face of a stock in Europe, on the 30 Septr of 846.652 bales against a stock in 1839 of 653.215 bales, but if the article be *hoarded* like indigo prices may advance, as in 1838 when the agents of the United States Bank in Liverpool held upwards of $10 @ 12.000.000 of Cotton for some months and with the aid of a superabundant money market suceeded in raising prices and for some time maintaining them, but when they fell the losses to shippers and consignees of our crop were enormous. One Liverpool house is said to have made reclamations for *over advances* to the extent of $2.000.000 a very considerable portion of which was supposed to have been lost to them. If then there should be a rise in the prices of cotton, beyond the October Liverpool prices, I do not think it will stand on even so good a footing as the advance in the prices of Indigo. I will, however, give you from time to time the fluctuations with the extent of the crop, and in the prices here, and in the prices here, in accordance with the wishes of Mr Mackillop. The bill of £ 1000 drawn by Mr H. Sock for the acct of Mr S. Austin jr has been collected and remitted the London house.

In cases where you wish to buy American bills, but feel a want of confidence if you will take a B/Lading as collateral, and send it to me to collect, I will do it with pleasure without any expense either to you or the other party, but generally, authorised bills can be taken with safety, as events, in spite of disastrous times, have shewn to be the case,

Yours truly

(Sig'd)   Henry Lee

LETTER FROM HENRY LEE, BOSTON, NOV. 10, 1840, TO JAMES MACKILLOP, LONDON, WITH REFLECTIONS ON THE GENERAL STATE OF BUSINESS, PARTICULARLY THE MONEY MARKET AND THE EFFECT OF WAR ON CONSUMPTION[1]

The following is one of the long, leisurely, philosophical letters, more intent on dealing with general conditions and the broad reasons therefor than on conveying immediately pertinent commercial information, which become increasingly typical as Henry Lee approaches and passes the time for his retirement from active business. It reveals him, however, as selling on commission not only indigo shipped directly from Calcutta to Boston but also consignments which, after being sent to England, were thereafter transported across the Atlantic to seek a better market.

Henry Lee's reflections on the respective conditions of labor in England and the United States are of interest, as is his comment on the frontier as the dominant factor in maintaining wages in the latter country. Even more interesting is his finding a measure of comfort in the "break down of the U. S. Bank" which "put an end to this vast over trading," of which he complains. The United States Bank and others, he complained a little later, had engaged in speculations

1. Jackson-Lee Papers, "Letters 1840–41. Henry Lee," Oct. 30, 1840–Dec. 21, 1852, pp. 9–12.

in cotton which had caused such a high, though temporary, price expansion that advances made during the boom by British commission houses exceeded the amount for which the cotton could finally be sold.[2] Jonathan Jackson, Henry Lee's father-in-law, before the Revolution, had similarly complained to British merchants of the undue credits which they were granting to American traders, to the detriment of the more conservative and reliable element among colonial business men.

During the years since Henry Lee's return from India in 1816 his relations with London, as far as revealed by importations mentioned in the newspapers, had ranked after those with Calcutta, Liverpool, and Havana, but ahead of all other ports. In the years 1824, 1829, 1831–33, 1838–40, 14 vessels with goods from London for Henry Lee had arrived at Boston. These goods were usually referred to noncommittally as "merchandise," but were sometimes specified as hemp, mats, tin plate, shellac, indigo, silk goods, cotton goods, and ale. It will be observed that all these goods, except the tin plate and ale, are typical products of the Far East, and it is probable that the various bales and chests of undescribed "mdse." consisted of textiles and indigo from the same region. These goods probably were being shipped by British merchants to Henry Lee for sale on commission, as was the indigo mentioned below, and were not being imported on Henry Lee's own initiative for sale on his own account.

Orig p 13th packet.

James Mackillop Esq.   Boston, 10 Novr. 1840
   London.

   Dear Sir.

   I have yours of the 19th ulto, you seem to think I had too low an opinion of the parcel of Oude Indigo consigned by the house, and the sales of which lately went to you. The valuation was the one you sent me of a brokers report upon 4 sample cakes I sent you. I have also seen samples of 3 or 4 parcels on which London reports were made of the prices generally at the April & July sales. I am surprised at the advance at the Octo sale and presume all must have been in England except those

2. *Ibid.*, p. 71, Henry Lee, Boston, Jan. 26, 1841, to Colvin, Ainslie, Cowie & Co., Calcutta.

who knew that the holders would not sell without an advance but withdraw or bid in. The advance has had no effect here because it is not considered as a legitimate one and therefore not likely to be maintained. With a stock in Europe of 29.345 Chests against 24.443 last year and a crop estimated at 115.000 Mds by some and at 120.000 Mds @ 130.000 by others, and commercial & manufacturing concerns by no means in a prosperous condition, with an increased expenditure in war preparations, abstracting greatly from the means of the great mass of consumers of paying for goods. What is there to authorise an advance in the price of a staple which with a 12 mos supply, would not be scarce if the coming 2 or 3 crops should not exceed 90 or 100.000 Mds especially when you take into consideration, the increased and increasing crop of Java? Again, you advert to the bad state of the money market and the circumstance, [interlineated: is] dwelt upon largely in letters from France as well as from England. Your bank has, it would appear by an inference drawn from the last average returns, only about £ 3.500.000 bullion against £ 23.993.000 of liabilities and with a tendency to a still worse state of matters from the demand for coin for the continental markets, How you are to get right and remain right, without a further reduction in the prices of your exports so as to bring commercial balances more in you favor, I am at a loss to conjecture. There is too, another bad point in the case, namely, the unsettled political condition of Europe, Asia &c. I do not apprehended a war, but as long as such a feeling does exist, it has an important bearing upon consumption and especially on all articles which may not come under the class of prime necessaries of life. In 1830, the year of the last French revolution it fell off from 73.991.093 lbs to 45.797.545 lbs nor was any of this deficiency made up in succeeding years, as within two subsequent years it only advanced to 75 to 76.000.000 lbs so that consumption was actually decreased by that event and the fears of a counter revolution, 40%. The export of tobacco to France in 1829 was 6835 hhds against 1673 in 1830 and 7007 in 1831. There may have been some other causes to influence this great change though I am not aware of them, and at any rate the principal one was the decreased demand and consumption in France owing to the political inquietude existing and the apprehensions of what might follow. I do not believe even among the most intelligent persons a true notion exists of the extraordinary effects on consumption growing out of the causes to which I have referred. I certainly was much surprised at them on looking into the facts as connected with Sugar, Cotton Coffee and other leading staples. Mr Mackensie may regret that I did not hold on to his Indigo longer, since it has risen, but in the first place I had no reason to expect such a rise and, 2nd I had no encouragement from him or from you to look for a favorable change, but the contrary, 3rd If I had held on I could not now do any better than I have done. As to the 77 Chests it is all on hand nor do I expect at present to obtain his limits. The future value here will be ruled by the prices on your side which are not expected to be maintained unless the coming crop is below 110 @ 115.000 Mds. I shall be glad of a continuance of your advices as to its future value and to have your opinion which will always influence me. Attempts have been made to raise the prices of Cotton under an anticipation of a crop of 3 @ 400.000 bales, short of last years, and they have advanced about 10%. If the commercial, political & pecuniary state of Europe was favorable to high prices, I think a spirit of speculation in this staple might have been created with the aid of the suspended banks at the South and their extended issues, but the accounts from Europe and the embarrassments at home, from the discredit or ruin of many of the banks out of New England & New York, has checked the favorable feeling and the new crop will open lower than was expected. The outturn of the last crop was greater than I ever estimated. The returns give 2.177.835 bales and about ¾ths are from the "Gulf states" where the bags average 420 @ 450 lbs. I call the average of the crop 385 instead of 370 lbs as formerly. This gives 838.466.475 lbs allowing the consumption of England for 1840 to be 450.000.000 lbs. U States 100.000.000 lbs and of the Continent of Europe 250.000.000 lbs besides the yarn sent there from England say 80 @ 90.000.000 lbs the aggregate would be

800.000.000 lbs. If I am correct there will be the imports from Egypt, Brazils, India &c in excess of consumption. They amounted, to Great Britain, the first 6 months of the year, to 145.773 bales which would give 291.000 bales for the year which is not far from the average of several past years in addition to what may be imported into France & the other parts of Europe. As a majority of those bales are India, which average, according to the Manchester estimate, 363 lbs, it may be reasonable to call them 300 lbs making about 90.000.000 lbs to which add the excess of our crop over consumption of 38½ millions there would be a superfluity of 128.500.000 lbs beyond the largest consumption of Europe and this country. This is a discouraging view to those who are disposed to speculate on advanced prices because of a falling off from our last crop even though it should be to the extent of 25%. The truth is the last crop was an excessive one, & as I have shewn, too great for the wants of consumers even when the raw material and the manufactured commodity are at lower prices than were ever before known — too low, no doubt, for the manufacturer to obtain a remunerating compensation for his capital, while wages every where but here are down to *bread & water* rates, nor do our manufacturers save themselves from loss though wages have been reduced to lower rates than they can be maintained. Here the low prices of land and the disposition of the manual laboring classes to emmigrate to the new states, the moment employment slackens, is a check to the fall of wages nowhere else existing and prevents our successful competition with you in manufactures where the expense of manual labor is a principal element of cost. In Cotton goods we have water power versus steam to do most of the labor, and female labor principally which is about as cheap as yours considering the superior efficiency of ours as compared with the unhoused, unclothed & unfed operatives of Manchester.

There is another point which I had forgotten. The stock of Cotton by late returns from Europe has greatly and suddenly increased, being on the 30 Septr 846.652 bales against 653.215 last year, 7/8ths of which is American and consequently largest sized bags. It is thought, too, there is a larger stock of yarns, goods and of raw material in the hands of the manufacturers than there usually has been while you have reason to expect a *diminished* demand for goods for China and the countries about Turkey, Egypt &c, nor shall we be in want of so many cotton goods, as your manufacturers appear to be counting on, our own fabrics being below what similar ones as substitutes can be imported for, even with a disposition to forego all profit. The importations from England for the past 7 or 8 years, with the exception of 1838, when you would not trust us and our currency was in a state of contraction, though not too much so, have been based upon artificial values, viz upon prices beyond what would have existed had our currency been in a sound and natural state, and consequently on a level with the countries with whom we trade. The usual corrective of a superfluous currency a demand for coin, was not applied, because in 1834 to 1837, the foreign balances were paid or postponed by a reliance on our borrowings and our credit abroad from mercantile houses. The last over importations of 1839 being $162.092.-132 against exports of $121.028.416 shewing an excess of $41.063.716 were for a time provided for, by the sales of state and bank stocks and other contrivances to borrow money and to borrow credit and in both cases that of 1834 to 1837 & 1839, the foreign exchanges were kept so much in favor of the country that no coin was called for and consequently there was no check to the issue of bank paper. If you had gone on buying and loaning we should in 1840 have got our imports up to $200.000.000. There were in 1836 within $10.000.000 of that sum with a population upwards of 2.000.000 below the existing number & crops not so valuable as this year by at least $100.000.000. The break down of the U. S. Bank and the hundreds of others acting on the same principle and many of them sustained by her funds & credit put an end to this vast over trading in connection with our discredit in England which was the main cause of the discredit here. The popular belief, however, among us and which is encouraged by the party now about to come into power, is, that the fall of prices was not necessary, and the leaders have pledged themselves to manage the banks & the currency, as far as they have influence and control, in a way to restore former prices. This of course can't be done without an inflation of currency, and that can't soon be accomplished, and long maintained without a concurrence on your side, viz without a free demand for state bank and railroad stocks, an extended mercantile credit &c that will enable us to keep the foreign exchanges in our favor and thus give the bank free scope for unlimited paper issues, free from the apprehension of being called upon for coin, or if called upon, they may have the public feeling manifested as in 1837 & 1839 in *favor of a suspension.* If one intelligent man in 100 or 1.000 in England among that class, upon whom American credit depends entertained similar opinions to mine upon the folly and danger of repeating the transactions in money matters which occurred in 1836 to 1840. We might count on this side upon a postponement of another suspension for some years to come, but there is so much credulity, judging from the past, on your side, and so many contrivances to deceive on ours, that I fear you will not be strict enough in your future dealings; still the machinery for inflation, overtrading &c is, for the present so much deranged, that I am in hopes with all the efforts of party, acting upon the ignorant notions prevalent here upon the subjects of bank and currency, there will be a prosperous course of business for several years to come, and though in the interim our 26 currencies may some of them be in disorder, yet we shall get on without a suspension in the chief ports and places of business. The U. S. Bank wants to borrow 2.500.000$ of our banks to enable her to resume. It is doubtful if she obtains it, as our own community would suffer by the transference of so much capital at a time when the foreign exchanges are getting somewhat unfavorable to the country. What is the intention of that Bank? Mr Jandon, who is on the way to London, can better tell, than I, or any one out of the Direction. The opinion I have expressed in regard to the value of its stock is unchanged, but at the same time, I must say that the majority of persons differ from me, & think better of it than I do, while there are others who think much worse of it.

In respect to the samples of the 128 Chts of Oude Indigo, I think there is some misapprehension on your part or some mistake on mine as [interlineated: to] the samples sent you. My intention was to say there was one sample of washings that would not answer. The arrival of the 12 cases in the President will enable me if they are samples of the lot to give you more accurate information and in the meantime you may be able to obtain an advance consequent upon the late improvement at the Octo sale. Be good enough to shew this letter to Mr Mackensie as containing all I could say to him on the subject of Indigoes. I shall write him by the next steamer and in the meantime I hope to hear further from him as to how low I may sell his 77 Chests.

Yours truly

(Sig'd)   Henry Lee

LETTER FROM HENRY LEE, BOSTON, NOV. 17, 1840, TO MACKAIGHEN & GOLDING, LA GUAYRA, EXPRESSING HOPE FOR THE SALE OF BLUE GOODS[1]

Havana and La Guayra were the Caribbean ports with which the Lees had begun earliest to trade, before the War of 1812; Henry Lee's interest in both continued. It will be remembered that at about this time India goods were not selling well in Havana or in St. Thomas, and the same situation seems to have existed in La Guayra. Note that Lee fixed no limit on the price of the goods, evidence probably both of his desire to get rid of them and his confidence in his correspondents. Early in 1841, however, Lee heard of some sales in La Guayra and expressed the opinion that the rise in the price of raw cotton would stimulate the textile market.[2]

Among ports in the West Indies and South America from which Henry Lee imported goods after his return from Calcutta in 1816, La

1. Jackson-Lee Papers, "Letters 1840–41. Henry Lee," Oct. 30, 1840–Dec. 21, 1852, p. 12.

2. Ibid., p. 69, Henry Lee, Boston, Feb. 2, 1841, to Mackaighen & Golding, La Guayra.

Guayra and Puerto Cabello to the eastward (both in Venezuela) ranked next after the Cuban ports — but a long distance after. In 1832 there was a shipment from La Guayra and Puerto Cabello, and another from the latter port alone, to Henry Lee, and in 1840 and 1842 there were 2 shipments from La Guayra and Puerto Cabello. These shipments consisted mostly of coffee, but also included some hides, from Puerto Cabello.

Boston 17 Novr. 1840

Mess MacKaighen &Golding, "orig p Black Hawk"
    La Guayra
        Dear Sirs.

        I am favored with yours of the 18 Septr & 6 Octo. I am sorry to find your market so unfavorable for Blue goods, but as you anticipate an improvement soon, I hope they may have been sold before this arrives. I give you no limits, but wish you to do the best you can with them. I have a further supply which I shall be glad to send you, when your market requires them,

Yours truly
Signed   Henry Lee

LETTER FROM HENRY LEE, BOSTON, NOV. 20, 1840, TO OGDEN BROTHERS, MOBILE, OFFERING TO SELL GUNNY SACKING[1]

Observe the conditional sales agreement mentioned in the letter below. Gunny sacking was used in baling cotton.

Boston newspapers reveal no great amount of trade carried on by Henry Lee with Mobile. In fact, we find mention of only 2 consignments from that port to Henry Lee, both in 1839, the first consisting of cotton, the other of "domestic goods," doubtless being returned.

Boston, 20 Novr. 1840

Mess Ogden Brothers   Orig p Mail
    Mobile.
        Dear Sirs.

        As the Exchanges have improved and are improving I would thank you to remit the small balance due me in a good bill

---

    1. Jackson-Lee Papers, "Letters 1840–41. Henry Lee," Oct. 30, 1840–Dec. 21, 1852, p. 13.

on Boston or New York and if to be had 2% lower, on Baltimore, Phila, as their currencies are improving. I may have 500
ps of India Bagging 2¼ lbs x 43 @ 44 inches wide, for sale in
10 @ 20 days. It is sold if the vessel arrives within a limited
period @ 25¢, but she may not come within the time and in that
case I may have to ship it, Perhaps you can sell it receivable
here, cash, in which case I will submit to a lower price than your
quotations which are 32¢, I think. Will not this article greatly
advance if the Cotton crop is 2.000.000 bales? What may be the
value of Rio Coffee prime to common, and is yours a great market?

Yours &c

(Sigd)   H. Lee

LETTER FROM HENRY LEE, BOSTON, NOV. 28, 1840, TO WILLIAM
WADDELL, MADRAS, WITH INSTRUCTIONS FOR PACKING AND
SHIPPING GOAT SKINS[1]

Hides and skins, particularly after 1816, were a large element in
most of the cargoes to Henry Lee from India. Lee, however, so far
as the newspapers show, received no imports from Madras after the
War of 1812. Apparently any goods shipped to him by Madras merchants came in vessels from Calcutta which stopped at Madras en
route to the United States, or were goods which had been sent to
Calcutta from Madras for reshipment.[2]

Boston. 28 Novr. 1840

William Waddell Esq Orig p Britannia
    Madras.
        Dear Sir.
            I have received a few days since yours of the 11th June
& 11th July. In respect to the preserving of Goat Skins, I apprehend there is no difficulty as the bulk of what comes from your
place &Calcutta arrive here in good order. The only exceptions,

---

1. Jackson-Lee Papers, "Letters 1840–41. Henry Lee," Oct. 30, 1840–
Dec. 21, 1852, pp. 20–21.

2. *Ibid.*, p. 209, Henry Lee by W. S. Bullard, Boston, Mar. 7, 1842, to
William Waddell, Madras.

or nearly so which have come under my notice are parcels sent here by Hall & Bainbridge and which were ruined for want of care in the packing. they were not well beaten & dried. If on packing them it is done in dry weather and you throw a quantity of tobacco dust among them they will be certain to come safe & if you can procure spirits of turpentine without much expense dip a small brush into it & draw it across the hair side two or three times. The effect of such operations is, to kill the worms & destroy the eggs of worms. You may then venture on shipping with a due attention to the precautions recommended without apprehension of damage and even if a little injured by worms, our dealers will take them with a very small abatement, especially when unpacked here & beaten, which is my custom when the skins exhibit any signs of having suffered. If you rub them with salt it might improve the skin. As to sizes all will answer, but if an undue proportion of kids it is usual in India to get an allowance in the price.

The prices I quote are for average sizes, say bales containing smallest up to largest, and all sizes should be mixed together and not be packed in seperate bales. The more you press the bale the better & they will appear better if the skin is not folded, though that is not essential. There is I have no doubt good deal of labor in collecting, but it is worth your while to encounter it, as good deal of money can be made upon them with a very small outlay of capital as you may count on remittances from here immediately on their arrival so as to meet bills drawn against the shipments at 6 mos sight or 12 months date. There are at least 500.000 shipped from your place annually, from Hall & Bainbridge some years 100 @ 105.000 have been shipped for their own account & for others. I notice one ship in Calcutta in August had 140 bales of them (70.000) and they will pay a fair profit on a cost of 30 Rupees p 100 on board, exchange 2^s/1^d & freight @ $20 p ton. The price is now 25¢ with a tendency to advance. In my letter of 23 July, overland, I recommend you to go to 25/ and I now advise you to ship 50.000 if you can ship them direct from Madras at 28/ p 100 all charges on board and the same via Calcutta where freight can usually be had at $20

MADRAS, 1792

p ton. If, however, you will authorise me to take up 50 tons for
you or more I can occasionally do it here at $16 p ton. I am not
aware of any vessels gone this year that will call at Madras, nor
probably will there be any in 1841, since Blue Salempores are
no longer an article of import having become uncurrent everywhere at almost any prices, nor do I think prices can be raised
high enough to cover the cost of 8 kall, 5 lbs @ 76/ p Corge.
The supply in England is heavy, prices low & will be lower. I
cannot recommend your sending me any at any prices. Indigo
will pay well as compared with the London prices especially for
low qualities. I have just rec'd a parcel from London charged
at 2s/9d on which I expect to remit a profit of 25 @ 30 p%
though the charges of importation are as great as from India.

The lowest qualities pay the most profit. As this quality and
all low qualities of Indigo are now at very low prices in London.
I suppose prices may be very low with you and if you can ship
it so as to pay well at a remittance of 3s/6d plb for the lowest
qualities. I recommend your shipping it. Bear in mind that in
shipments of Indigo or any goods but Goat Skins, the Invoices
should be accompanied with an affidavit of the shipper of the
goods, sworn to before a Magistrate & certified, specifying the
actual cost or market value of the goods, such a document is
required by the Custom House, the duty on Indigo being an
advalorem one. The forms which are necessary can be learnt
by inquiring of any of the houses who have done business with
Americans. I do not think it possible to get any one to go to
India & reside there under the chance of finding the employment
to which you refer and as to preserving hides and skins the art
is as well understood in Calcutta as here at least as far as in
necessary to put them into a state for shipping to this country
& England   Of hides nearly 2.000.000 now go annually from
Calcutta to Europe and this country and there has been a great
profit on them this year, though the Invoice cost prices have
been unsually high. I can receive & sell goods in Phila: to as
great an advantage to you as here. The communication by mail
is but 24 hours. If that market is best they can be sold there,
otherwise they can be brought here at very small expence or

to New York at still less. I will soon write you again. My correspondents in Philadelphia are Mess Bevan & Humphreys.

Yours truly
(Sig'd)   Henry Lee

If you will say what hides can be had in Madras, their weight, usual prices, & whether saltted or dry, I will say if they will answer to ship to me. I notice you direct your letter to me in this country. Please send them in future to the care of your own correspondents in London, or to mine Mess Palmers, Mackillop, Dent &Co, as in such case they will be certain to reach me.

LETTER FROM HENRY LEE, BOSTON, NOV. 30, 1840, TO WILLIAM EDMOND, LIVERPOOL, DISCOURAGING THE IMPORTATION OF COTTON BAGGING INTO THE UNITED STATES[1]

Note Henry Lee's description of his own business, particularly that he considered himself primarily a commission merchant.

Next to Calcutta, Boston newspapers report a greater number of shipments to Henry Lee from Liverpool than from any other port. During the years 1825, 1829–32, 1834–37, 1839–40 there is newspaper mention of 39 shipments from Liverpool to Henry Lee, usually referred to as "mdse," "dry goods," or so many "bales," "boxes" or "bundles," but sometimes specified as hemp, ale, vises, iron, guns, cotton bagging, woolens, and specie. We do not know whether these were sent to Henry Lee for sale on commission or imported on his own account, but probably the former.

William Edmond Esq   Orig p Brittania   Boston 30 Novr. 1840
  Liverpool.
    Dear Sir.
      I was favored early in the month with yours of 3rd ulto. I am glad you have found anything useful in my correspondence & now you are settled at Liverpool, I shall be glad to continue the correspondence hoping if it does not lead to any business transactions, there may be information gained of mutual bene-

1. Jackson-Lee Papers, "Letters 1840–41. Henry Lee," Oct. 30, 1840–Dec. 21, 1852, p. 22.

fit. My line of business is chiefly the sale on commission of the products of India & more especially Indigo Saltpetre, Hides, Goat Skins, Lacdye, Shellac, Raw Silk, Ginger &c, Information as to the state of the Liverpool & London market of the stocks & value of these staples will always be acceptable.

Mr Lindsay called when I was absent from the city, but it is probable I may meet him in New York or here sometime hence. I shall always be glad to be useful to him in any way I am able. Mr Lindsay obtained almost all the information he wanted from my associates in the Compting House. Cotton Bagging & its value was one of Mr Lindsay's subject of inquiry. This article we use to the extent of from 10 @ 12.000.000 yds according to the amount of the Cotton crop. Formerly we relied much on the Dundee of late years & under a heavy protecting duty of about 25 @ 33 1/3% on the varying cost of it in Europe & India we have been almost wholly supplied from Kentucky where a much better quality is made, than what we have heretofore had from Scotland. It measures 44 to 46 inches & weighs 1¾ @ 2 lbs yd & has been selling for 2 @ 3 years in the Cotton states at 20 @ 25¢ up occasionally 28 @ 30¢ yd. It can now be afforded @ 22 @ 23¢ yd and lower when (Hemp) of home growth is at low price within 4 or 5 years we have commenced importing it from India from whence goes a heavier fabric than we make, 44 @ 46 in wide & 2¼ lbs yd, made of jute, at a price that can be sold in the cotton ports @ 25¢ yd & in Boston 21 @ 22¢. Mr Lindsay I understand reckons the cost of jute Bagging in Dundee at a rate which would enable us to import it and sell it at a profit at 23 @ 24¢ yard in New York or here. If such be the case I don't see that you can compete with the Kentucky or the India, since yours to command the price should weigh not less than 2 lbs p yard 44 to 46 inches as I am an importer of this article from E. I. I shall be shall be glad to hear from you as to the cost of the Dundee made of Jute @ 2 @ 2¼ lbs p yard 44 inches & also of the common quality of 1½ to 2 lbs p yard made of flax or hemp. The prices of all sorts of bagging have fallen owing I suppose to heavy supplies of Kentucky caused by a sudden advance in price about 4 mos ago. Our Cotton crop opens at 7½ to 10% in advance of previous prices on the expectation of a short, but as none of the estimates place it below 1.800.000 bales I do not think the rise is a legitimate one. The last one was an excessive one & therefore a moderate one will be sufficient to meet the consumption. The stock in Europe on the 30th Septr nearly 200.000 bales more than 1839. Our last crop was 2.177.835 @ 385 lbs is 838.446.475 lbs. I can't make out a larger consumption for Europe & the U. States than 800.000.000 lbs this would give a surplus of 38.500.000 together with the entire import from India, Egypt, & Brazils. The extension of the cultivation in India & improvement in its quality under the expectation of competing with us is I think a dangerous enterprise. I will write you more fully on this head.

Yours truly,

(Sig'd)   Henry Lee

LETTER FROM HENRY LEE, BOSTON, DEC. 23, 1840, TO SAMUEL ETTING, BALTIMORE, ON THE MARKET FOR INDIA GOODS AND THE AFRICAN TRADE[1]

The letter below reveals Henry Lee's continued interest in supplying goods to African traders, even after at least nominal abolition of the slave trade. Colored goods from India were evidently still proving an object of importation, despite the competition of British and domestic cottons.

Mr Samuel Etting   (Orig p Mail)   Boston Decr 23. 1840
Baltimore.

Dear Sir.

I have yours of 14.16 & 19th. I hope soon to hear of the sale of Indigo. The limits are low and it is a cheap article compared with Manilla &Carraccas. I have a large supply of Bengal and shall have more and be able to furnish all you can sell through 1841 & shall therefore wish you would keep your eye upon it. The Cotton Bagging is all sold but I expect more. It is held here at 21¢ and sells readily at 20¢ & was worth 60 days

1. Jackson-Lee Papers, "Letters 1840–41. Henry Lee," Oct. 30, 1840–Dec. 21, 1852, p. 33.

ago 25¢ and it is probable it may again advance. If any demand write me. I have few bales of Blue Salempores in New York p Champlain same as you sold for me but I fear to send them on to you least I should lose a sale in New York. They go off gradually there and at better prices. If you can sell them say 200 ps *@ 3⅛ 8 months, cash 4% off & you guarantee commission you may do so on condition if on hand & write Mr Sale. I will write Mr Sale to send you strips as samples.

I have some colored & Blue goods suited to African trade say Blue Sannas, Mamoodies & Neganepauts. A Mr Hall called to see them of your city who has been to Africa, who is I suppose from what he said preparing a cargo for that market & promised to call & see me when he was ready to buy. I believe he is called Dr Hall & Mayhew &Co sold him some Blue goods last winter for me. I have written to them but they do not know his movements. I wish you would see what can be done with him, if he wants the goods I will send on samples. There are also some Liberia traders who now and then buy. I have an assortment and shall always be glad to supply — the checks & stripes are 14 x 28 cheaper the home made & better colours & patterns. The Gunny Bags will do better than you quote.

* I find on reference to my N. Y. letters that Mr Sale is negotiating for the 200 ps B. S. & till he has done he will not send any samples. He will send you samples of some Blue Baftas & Sannas which may do for your exporters

I have sent you by Mr Hamden samples of Blue Goods

Nº 1 — 300 ps Blue Baftas 11½ x 33 @ $2.

    2 — 300 " Bengal B. Salempores 18 x 38 @ 2¼

    3   300 " B. Mamoodies which Dr Hall liked 19 x 35 @ 2⅜

    4   250 " Neganepauts 14 x 28 @ 1.20

    5   250 " Chilloes   "   @ 1.20

    6   250 " Bejutipauts   "   @ 1.20

Yours &c
(Sig'd)   H. Lee

LETTER FROM HENRY LEE, BOSTON, JAN. 13, 1841, TO STETSON & AVERY, NEW ORLEANS, ENQUIRING CONCERNING THE PROSPECTIVE DEMAND FOR BAGGING [1]

It is interesting to observe the continuity of Henry Lee's business career. Forty years earlier he had entered the India trade, which was then largely a matter of importing textiles from Calcutta to the United States. High duties had ruined the textile importations, so Henry Lee was now importing from India bagging to be used in baling cotton to supply the mills of Manchester and the Merrimack which had destroyed his earlier commercial specialty. Some connection with India and with textiles seemed essential to Henry Lee's business life.

In 1832 newspapers record 3 importations from New Orleans to Henry Lee; 2 of these were of cotton, the other was several cases of silks, doubtless returned. Although shortly after his return from Calcutta in 1816 Henry Lee had been active in purchasing cotton for his brother-in-law P. T. Jackson, to be used in the latter's textile mill, newspapers, at least, reveal little interest in the purchase of cotton thereafter, probably because the mills began to take the purchase of cotton into their own hands; a consignment from Mobile in 1839 completes the tale. Henry Lee, Jr., and his partner William S. Bullard, on the other hand, during their first three years in business, showed as much interest, as far as newspapers are valid evidence, in the importation of cotton as Henry Lee, Sr., had displayed over the preceding twenty-four years.

Mess Stetson & Avery   Orig p Mail   Boston. Jany 13. 1841
    New Orleans.
        Dear Sirs.
            I have written you several times to remit the balance due me & as exchange is favorable on New York & Boston, I have been hoping to hear from you. If you have not already remitted please do so on the best terms you can, in duplicate bills on New York or Boston, or on Phila: if to had at $1\frac{1}{2}\%$ lower than New York or Boston. I give you no limits as to the rate, but want it because I am precluded drawing, as I could have done at 1%

1. Jackson-Lee Papers, "Letters 1840–41. Henry Lee," Oct. 30, 1840–Dec. 21, 1852, pp. 47–48.

discount, had I not ordered it. Your letter to HLee jr quotes bagging low. I am in hopes the price will advance in the spring. I shall be glad to be kept informed as I have 2000 ps on the way from India expected in few weeks. I am told that in April there is a demand and your cotton crop may perhaps come up beyond present estimates. Will it not do in your opinion to count on a sale 12 months hence at 22¢. The Scotch cannot come in competition and I should think, 2¼ lbs India would when better known take preference of Kentucky which you told me was 1¾ lbs. I shall be glad always of any facts in reference to this article, and as I shall have consignments from India as long as the article will sell. What in your opinion will the Cotton crop prove to be? It is of importance to know as regards future value of bagging

Yours truly

Sigd   Henry Lee

LETTER FROM HENRY LEE, BOSTON, JAN. 15, 1841, TO JAMES HILL, CALCUTTA, OFFERING TONNAGE[1]

Fourteen bales of buffalo hides and three of cow hides shipped by the Calcutta merchant had already been sold, Dec. 28, 1840,[2] and the entire consignment had been disposed of Jan. 28, 1841. Note Henry Lee's offer of the refusal of tonnage at a lower rate on condition of being the consignee; "ship owners," however, Henry Lee later stated, "are seldom willing to make conditional engagements as in case of rejection they are put to a disadvantage."[3]

Orig p 19th packet

James Hill Esq   Boston. Jany 15. 1840 [41]
   Calcutta.   Dup p Acadia
    Dear Sir.

         I wrote you on the 28thDecr since which not much progress has been made in the sales of your Hides. The prices are

---

1. Jackson-Lee Papers, "Letters 1840–41. Henry Lee," Oct. 30, 1840– Dec. 21, 1852, p. 50.
2. *Ibid.*, p. 41, Henry Lee, Boston, Dec. 28, 1840, to James Hill, Calcutta.
3. *Ibid.*, pp. 62–63, Henry Lee, Boston, Jan. 28, 1841, to J. Mackey & Co., Calcutta.

so much in advance of former ones that buyers are cautious of supplying themselves, still as the quantity expected is small and the cost high I am in hopes I shall succeed in getting my prices, but if I were to give way the market would suffer and I might not get rid of them as the season is too late and too early for the usual demand. The rivers are frozen and internal conveyances high and difficult.

The ship Albion will sail from hence for your place on the 15 Feby and by her a remittance will be made you in corn on account of the hides but I fear the sales cannot so soon be closed without forcing a sale to your disadvantage. I shall direct the Captain to offer you 50 tons at the rate of $18 p ton for any goods — measurement which you may be willing to consign me. I have done this because it will probably be some time before any other ship goes to Calcutta & of hereafter to be despatched most of them have all their room engaged here or if not they would require a higher freight a heavy charge on so coarse an article as hides and goat skins. I think you will do well to send Cow hides, say Hoskolly 4½ to 6 lbs — 6½ @ 7 lbs dry and 7 @ 8 lbs salted and as many Buffaloes as you can secure. Goat Skins will do at the usual prices of 16/ @ 20/ for Patna and 22/ @ 24/ for Cawnpoor. At foot you have a memo of sales of Hides.

Yours truly

(Signed)   Henry Lee

On the 1st Jany I remitted Mess Mackey Holt &Co a bill for £ 300
and on the 5th a further sum of 250

making   550 as

the proportion of the Nett pro sales of Hides which you desired might be remitted Mess Mackey Holt &Co. Since writing you on the 28th ulto I have sold 2 bales green salted @ 125¢. 6 mos & I hope as the season advances to close what remain on hand. You would oblige me by informing me, in event of further shipments, concerning your insurance, where effected &how, whether an average on each bale or not.

[written across face of letter]
Enclosed to Mackey, Holt & Co.

LETTER FROM HENRY LEE, BOSTON, JAN. 28, 1841, TO CHARLES HUFFNAGLE, CALCUTTA, ON CHANGES IN THE DEMAND FOR INDIA GOODS [1]

British-made colored handkerchiefs (appealing to Indians, Negroes, frontiersmen) were then defeating the India-made variety, just as at present Japanese bandannas are dominating a similar market. The preference for British and domestic handkerchiefs over those from India was not entirely a matter of price; Henry Lee refers to the printing of "a good many China Pongees with brilliant colours and handsome patterns and they are prefered to the ill looking India figures." [2]

On Feb. 6, Henry Lee offered to obtain for the Calcutta merchant tonnage at less than the usual rates and to "make liberal advances in coin, or by remittances to London" for articles which Huffnagle might ship at Lee's suggestion.

Charles Huffnagle Esq   Boston, 28 Jany. 1841
Orig p "Albion"
Calcutta
    Dear Sir.

      I have none of your favors to answer since my respects of the 9 Novr. I suppose your Phila friends continue to advise you fully, still you may be glad to hear from me also and the more so as I have not yet had any letters from Phila to forward to you. In India goods some improvement. Hdfs is the worst article. They have gone out of fashion to a great extent in consequence of the substitution of British printed Corahs and Spitalfield manufacture which come in free of duty and of Pongees which

1. Jackson-Lee Papers, "Letters 1840–41. Henry Lee," Oct. 30, 1840–Dec. 21, 1852, p. 61.

2. *Ibid.*, pp. 62–63, Henry Lee, Boston, Jan. 28, 1841, to J. Mackey & Co., Calcutta.

are printed here and sold at $3.50, for 7 hdfs in ps and interfere with the Mediums. I consider India Choppas and Bandannas as no longer a staple and they ought not to be sent even at 120/, for prime qualities. Of the old importations one half remain of 1839 and 1840. Gunny cloth was 25 is now dull at 20¢. Kentucky having fallen 33 1/3% within 90 days and the stock is so heavy that India may go down to 16 @ 17¢ or even lower during the summer — Saltpetre — 600 bags I have just sold at 5⅝¢. The prime is worth 5¾ @ 6¢ — Ginger held @ 4¢. Indigo, we get more from London than from Calcutta —Prime 1.80 @ $2. — ordinary and middling 120 to 150 — Shellac 10 @ 16¢. Lac-dye good 20 @ 22¢ — common and ordinary 16 @ 18¢ but hard to sell. Hides 8 @ 9 lbs 125 @ 130¢ — dry 7 lbs. 80¢ Buffaloe 10¢ salted, but @ these extreme prices they get off so slowly and prices can't be maintained when the cargoes on way and soon expected arrive. We have resumed specie payments in most of the Atlantic ports and I hope we may go on for 2 years and perhaps longer, before we again suspend. In Phila one half their bank capital at least including U. S. Bank has been sunk in speculations of cotton, stocks &c, and the United States Bank &Girard may have to suspend again as they are rotten and in bad hands. In the loans they required here and in New York, there two banks were not trusted.

There will be, I suppose, the usual number of ships sent to Calcutta, but I do not see any strong inducements unless on the part of ship owners who can procure $20 @ 25 p ton. Cotton crop estimated at 1.700.000 bales, prices about 15% in those of last year.

Yours truly

(Signed)   H. Lee

LETTER FROM HENRY LEE, BOSTON, FEB. 6, 1841, TO COCK-
ERELL & CO., CALCUTTA, ON THE FAILURE OF THE BANK OF
THE UNITED STATES[1]

Note Henry Lee's pleasure at the bank's suspension; also his
description of the function of Philadelphia and Baltimore in American
commerce, as compared with that of Boston and New York.

Mess Cockerell &Co   Orig pr Albion   Boston 6 Feb 1841
    Calcutta   Dup pr Rouble
      Dear Sirs
         The suspension of the U S Bank took place three days
ago. It was an event which by many was looked for though it
came somewhat sooner than was anticipated. It may cause
some temporary inconvenience in Philadelphia and some of the
states, but not in New York or New England, where the banks
are prudent and strong and will in any event maintain specie
payments. In this state and New York, about 2/3^{ds} of the foreign transactions are now carried on and Philadelphia has become with Baltimore places of distribution chiefly instead of
importing or exporting to any great extent. The failure of the
U S Bank is the best thing which could happen for the stock-
holders, provided its affairs are taken out of the hands of its
present incompetent and unworthy managers. About 5⁄8 of
the loss will fall on Europeans. there being stock holders to
extent of half and have also loaned on its shares on a higher
valuation than they will probably be worth on the winding up
of its affairs which will require 10 and perhaps 20 years. Some
of the Anglo American houses will lose heavily on this stock and
many others and stock holders of state stocks (American) are I
fear in danger of suffering to an enormous amount. This stock
gambling has done infinite mischief to the regular and *honest*
operations of trade in both countries and could the losses be
apportioned among the wealthy bankers, brokers and gamblers
concerned in promoting it, there would be less cause of regret

1. Jackson-Lee Papers, "Letters 1840–41. Henry Lee," Oct. 30, 1840–
Dec. 21, 1852, pp. 79–80.

than there now is, knowing as I do that a greater portion of the suffering goes to the middle classes of property men who have been tempted to investments by the high rates of interest which were offered and for some time obtained. The U S Bank has paid 8 pr ct for many years but for the last 4 or 5 years the dividends probably were paid out, not of the earnings but the capital though the directors represented a surplus fund of upwards of $5.000,000 even after the suspension of 1839 in October. Cotton continues to advance in price based as calculations are upon 1.600.000 bales. I think it may come up to 1.800.000 and so do many well informed persons, but the certainty cannot be known for some months to come. by which time 3/4ths or more of the crop will have passed into second and third hands.

Yours truly

(Sigd) Henry Lee

LETTER FROM HENRY LEE, BOSTON, FEB. 15, 1841, TO JAMES MACKILLOP, LONDON, WITH A SURVEY OF BANKING AND FINANCE [1]

Observe Henry Lee's verdict on Baltimore and Daniel Webster. Webster opposed the independent treasury plan and was a national bank advocate.

Boston Feb 15th1841

James Mc Killop Esqr   Orig pr 19th packet

London   Dup p Columbia

    Dear Sir

      I wrote you on the 6th inst in relation to the suspension of the U S Bank. I then expressed a hope that the other banks of that city might have courage and strength and inclination enough to persevere in specie payments but I have been disapointed. That the majority of them are well disposed to do their duty I have no doubt, but they are weakened by loans to the U S Bank, and by committals with some of the weak banks (local ones) and all of them have loaned largely to the

1. Jackson-Lee Papers, "Letters 1840–41. Henry Lee," Oct. 30, 1840–Dec. 21, 1852, pp. 83–84.

state of Pensylvania. The Baltimore banks suspended as soon
as they had news of the Philadelphia suspension — But little
was expected of them. The City of Baltimore is poor — deeply
in debt and among its community the least enlightened perhaps
of any in the Atlantic seaports, the standard of action is not
very high. They stopped as a matter of gain whereas the Philadelphia banks stopped from necessity or an apprehended necessity. That city has probably sunk 30 or 40.000.000 by bad
banking, canals, roads &c but still is very rich. and as the really
honest portion who have heretofore been too quiescent in the
matter of currency &C are begining to see and to feel the injurious consequences of being dishonest & of relying on an
irredeemable paper currency. I think, though they have suspended, that a majority of the Banks will contract their loans
and issues and prevent their currency from depreciating more
than 2 or 3 or 4 prCt, & gradually while under suspension, so
reduce it as to make it worth par. This was the course of Boston
& NYork in 1837, where currencies come to par some months
before the resumption took effect. The banks in Virginia hold
out, as I think they will do, in all the Atlantic ports south of that
state. Mobile may not resume for many years as the whole or
nearly so of the bank capital of Alabama has been already lost
or is involved in doubtful and unavailable securities. New-
Orleans banks are partly sound — have coin enough, but have
thus far not resumed, assigning no reasons, but as is well known,
from the fear of reducing the prices of Cotton and of being compelled to pay heavy debts due in NEngland & NYork in good
money. In most of the Western States the currencies are not
likely to recover for some time. Perhaps Ohio will be an exception. N England however with her 2.500.000 population &
NYork with as many more will sustain specie payments & be
ready and able to [interlineated: assist] and furnish the other
States as are able & willing to resume. In this section N E
& NY about half the capital of the 26 states is owned and the
policy of sustaining the currency has worked so well, that other
states will certainly strive to fall in with us, and especially
Pensylvania with her 1.800.000 people and the neighbouring

states under her control of 500.000 more. The suspension independent of its immediate bad effects, will be salutary as the currency south of NYork was in excess, and but for the contractions which is now taking place in NY as well as in the suspended states our prices would have got up — too many goods would have been imported and in 1843 we would have suspended under worse circumstances perhaps, than at this moment. We have already laid the foundation I fear of too large an import of British & French manufactures the Losses on which however, will somewhat reduce the remittable amount; This belongs I presume chiefly to foreigners who will inundate us at all times with dry goods, though for 7 or 8 years they have not in the aggregate got 15/ for their proceeds. State stocks continue to fall, partly in consequence of the suspension and partly &principally because the more they are investigated the worse they appear. Even Pensylvania can not command 60 for any great amount She owes 38.000.000 & wants 10 or 12.000.000 more to complete the works and render them available and then the income may not much exceed the expenses. The only thing to sustain them is a tax of $2000.000 to 2.500.000 to be continued till the works are productive enough to take care of themselves, but I fear the people of that state will not submit to it. nor any legislature dare recommend or impose it. So in other states the works were built on the anticipation of their being productive enough to support themselves, but in 8 cases out of 10 such is not the result. I hear of only one state which has confined itself to pofitable works and that is Masstts. & her credit is good because of that fact and her 5 pr Ct are worth as much here as they sell for in London, but it is more popular to borrow abroad than at home, and for that reason the stock was sent to you. There will gradually be more bank failures & the sooner the better. South of NYork more than half the banks are ruined and in NYork state all the free banks but 3 or 4 will have to wind up or fail. They are and have been a nuisance & were got up merely for the sake of banking upon property which is inconvertable into money at any time and especially in a pressure, and valued at 2 to 10 times its market value. We have no failures here, but sales are dull and may so continue for some time as we do not know how to deal with most of the states who buy of us because of the uncertainty of the currency. In NYork some of the the stock gamblers have stopped and pretty much the whole of the Wall Street jobbers in stocks are in danger on account of the great fall in the value of their stocks and the probability of a still greater decline in their value. Congress will come together probably in June or July but they have no power over the states in the worth of banking and currency and can do no good, besides the opinions entertained by Mr Webster and other leading men of the New Administration are so erroneous in my opinion, that all they will recommend will be wrong. What they really want to produce is an enhancement of prices now above those of Europe — and that can't be done but by over issues of paper which would end in another revulsion and they can't have their own way as the whole Van Buren party are opposed to it on *party* grounds and all honest and intelligent whigs upon higher principles. The only compensating effect of this bad state of things is the certainty I think of preventing our States and coporations from borrowing any more money and as I hope for 10 years to come. There is Capital enough to borrow at 5 prCt for the investment, if as much as can be laid out in improvements that will produce 5 or 6 per Cent, The Rail Roads in this state sell at par up to 4 pr Ct premium as far as they have been completed and even such as are not only are excepted, The suspension will probably keep cotton from rising higher because the U S Bank and others connected with her have no longer the means to speculate in it or to aid others in so doing. I call the crop 1.800.000 bales but generally it is estimated at 15 to 1.600.000 bales.

Yours truly
(Signd)   H. Lee

LETTER FROM HENRY LEE, BOSTON, FEB. 21, 1841, TO WILLIAM
E. MAYHEW & Co., BALTIMORE, OBJECTING TO SALES AT TOO
LOW A PRICE[1]

Merchants selling on commission were, if of a shortsighted nature,
under constant temptation to sell below the owners' limits. Apparently the goods sold by the Baltimore merchant were some which had
been shipped to Lee for sale and which he had sent on to Baltimore.
On July 3, 1844, Henry Lee ordered Alexander Turnbull & Co. to
send any unsold silks of his to New York by railroad, and on Aug. 26,
1845, Fisher, Miller & Co., also of Baltimore, announced sale of a
final bale of seersuckers, which Lee had ordered sold for what they
would bring, May 10.[2]

Boston newspapers reveal only 1 shipment from Baltimore to
Henry Lee and this, in 1828, consisted of dry goods, doubtless returned.

Boston Feb 21st 1841

Messrs Wm E. Mayhew &Co,
    Baltimore,
        Dear Sirs,
            I have yours of the 17th, — I cant but hope you have
quoted the sales wrong; as I have never authorised a sale of
those goods at anything near the price of $4.50. on the other
hand — I have refused to sell in Philadelphia @ $5 or even 5¼
— I hope therefore if the goods are not delivered, you will induce the buyer to surrender them. I now wish you to refrain
from selling any more of the handkerchiefs at any prices at
present. I am under limits for these goods, I shall have to lose
the difference between $4.50 and a price that will cover the cost,
and charges. As to Seersuckers I wish you to hold them at $6 —
and not sell under, till I give limits.

Yours truly
(Sig^nd)   H Lee

1. Jackson-Lee Papers, "Letters 1840–41. Henry Lee," Oct. 30, 1840–
Dec. 21, 1852, p. 85.

2. Ibid., pp. 336, 350, 351.

LETTER FROM HENRY LEE, BOSTON, FEB. 24, 1841, TO THOMAS
THORNELY, LIVERPOOL, ON THE TARIFF AND THE FINANCIAL
SITUATION[1]

The letter below is not a business letter but a general survey of
the economic situation, such as becomes increasingly prominent in
Henry Lee's letter book as he withdrew farther and farther from active business. Such letters are interesting as revealing the opinions
of a man with forty years of active business life behind him, a craving
for exact information, a philosophical turn of mind, and the inclination and leisure for setting down his observations in permanent form.

Henry Lee was an importer who had stubbornly refused to turn to
manufacturing, although he was intensely interested in the subject
and held, as trustee or guardian for his children, a number of textile
factory shares, and perhaps a few of his own.[2] But his main, and almost his only, business interest was importing, and as an importer he
was inevitably a free-trader. He had already signalized his devotion
to the cause of free trade by the preparation and publication of two
pamphlets, *Report of a Committee of the Citizens of Boston and
Vicinity, opposed to a Further Increase of Duties on Importations*
(Boston, 1827) and *An Exposition of Evidence in support of the Memorial to Congress . . . prepared in pursuance of instructions from
the Permanent Committee appointed by the Free Trade Convention*
(Boston, 1832). These pamphlets won him South Carolina's vote for
the vice-presidency in 1832. In 1830 he had run, unsuccessfully, for
Congress as a free-trade candidate, opposing Nathan Appleton, who
was associated in textile manufacturing with Henry Lee's brother-in-
law, Patrick Tracy Jackson. Where the tariff was not concerned,
Henry Lee was more successful politically, and in Nov., 1834, was
elected as a state representative from Boston, on the Whig ticket. He
may on this occasion have received a few votes, normally Democratic,
from Irish Catholics, and may have lost a few Yankee Protestant
votes, because of his membership on the committee, appointed Sept.
12, 1834, to protest against the burning of an Ursuline convent in
Charlestown by a Protestant mob; he stood among the first twelve

1. Jackson-Lee Papers, "Letters 1840–41. Henry Lee," Oct. 30, 1840–
Dec. 21, 1852, pp. 86–88.

2. *Ibid.*, p. 346, Henry Lee, Boston, Oct. 28, 1844, to P. T. Jackson,
Boston.

of those elected in the number of votes received.[3] In 1845, Henry Lee was to publish a thick free-trade volume entitled *Considerations on the Cultivation, Production and Consumption of Cotton, . . . addressed to the Cotton Manufacturers of Massachusetts*. But despite the efforts of Henry Lee and other free-traders, "the tariff act of 1842 was highly protective." [4]

Henry Lee, as a business man, was also, of course, interested in banking. In 1834 he had been appointed, with Nathan Appleton, P. T. Jackson, and others, to a committee which drew up a memorial protesting against the withdrawal of government deposits from the second United States Bank, and also to a delegation to go to Washington to remonstrate with President Jackson and "to do what could be done towards a renewal of the charter of the Bank." On their way to Washington, however, "they had an interview with Mr. Biddle, the president, whose policy of violently contracting the currency," in order to exert pressure upon the public toward the renewal of the bank's charter, "they disapproved and protested against." Henry Lee took the lead in drawing up in 1836 a document entitled *An Exposition of Facts and Arguments in Support of a Memorial to the Legislature of Massachusetts, by Citizens of Boston and Vicinity, in favor of a Bank of Ten Millions*, which bank was intended "to relieve the pressure in the money market and the general distress which followed" the expiration of the United States Bank's charter by doing "the business which had been done by the Branch Bank of the United States." [5] Nothing, however, resulted from this proposition.

It will be observed that though Henry Lee advocated in 1834 the renewal of the United States Bank's charter, he now opposed the establishment of a national bank. This would seem, by a process of elimination, to suggest a tacit approval of Van Buren's independent treasury, which the triumphant Whigs repealed Aug. 13, 1841; but although Henry Lee might criticize Nicholas Biddle ("who laid the foundation of all the mischief"),[6] he could not, as a loyal Whig, be

3. Morse, F. R., *op. cit.*, pp. 5–9, 57; *Evening Mercantile Journal* (daily), Sept. 30, Oct. 1, Nov. 7, 13, 1834.

4. Dewey, *op. cit.*, p. 238.

5. Morse, F. R., *op. cit.*, pp. 8–9; *Evening Mercantile Journal* (daily), Mar. 7, 1834; *Columbian Semiweekly Centinel*, Apr. 12, 1834.

6. Jackson-Lee Papers, "Letters 1840–41. Henry Lee," Oct. 30, 1840–Dec. 21, 1852, p. 92, Henry Lee, Boston, Feb. 24, 1841, to James Colvin, London.

expected openly to favor any proposal of the Democratic archenemy Van Buren.

Thomas Thornely Esq   Orig p Columbia   Boston 24 Feby 1841
  Liverpool
    Dear Sirs
      I have nothing from you, nor am I disappointed at all your long epistles, however gratified I always am at hearing from you. I know you are much occupied in public matters &c. I see an extract of my letter in the M. C. The fact presented to the public through that popular organ of national feeling and public opinion will have some effect on intelligent minds, but there are hundreds which might be adduced of similar import and I wish they were spread through the nation. I trust the day is not very remote when the Corn Laws will be a test at every election a no man supported who will [not ?] advocate their repeal, or at any rate a modification. Mr Tooke, in one of his works, shews clearly, to my mind that taking a range of years and allowing for the effect of occasional suspension of the law as in some former years, that the landholders are not so well off as with a free trade in Corn or a low duty. I have no doubt such is the case taking into consideration all the collateral and remote consequences incident to such a change, though in some particular cases it might be otherwise. The Tariff may be discussed to some extent at the extra session of Congress, if we have one but it will not be finally settled till next winter, when they usually sit 6 or 7 months, time enough for each member to deliver *some acres* of speeches, most of which are mere repititions of what has been before said and addressed rather to the Constituents of each delegate than to the Assembly to which they belong.
      The disposition is to set aside the Compromise Tariff of Mr Clay by which duties on all articles paying of 20%, was to come down to that rate and lower if Congress thought best, the goods to be valued in the places of landing. This will probably be commuted for an addition of 5% to the 20% making it 25%. The Administration for the most part, friends to the *protecting*

policy, that is to say to lay such duties as will prevent foreign goods from coming in competition with such as we can produce at home. As the Southern men on the side of the Administration and without whose support the Government can't maintain their majority in Congress, have declared they will not vote for higher duties than the Compromise, it may be difficult for the Tariff party to carry out their works and intentions and more so as the most inteligent of our Cotton Manufacturers say they can do with 25 prCt, to which add 15 @ 20 prCt for other charges, affords a protection of 40 to 65 prCt, and that they are therefore content to let the Compromise rates be the permanent ones: — Such I hope may be the issue of the contest for I do not like the policy of attempting to constrain other nations into a liberal policy by discriminating duties unless it be quite certain that such will be their effect — Time and reflection and bad seasons, and money pressures, and commercial and monetary revulsions, all of which are occasioned by, or aggravated in their consequences by the restrictive & prohibitary system, will compel good and influential men to unite their efforts for a gradual and a prudent abandonment of their basis and regulations which now stand in the way of the welfare of the two nations, I trust the report will furnish you an occasion to speaking freely & strongly on the subject it so well elucidates & discourse and to illustrate the importance of changes in your laws by their unfavorable bearings on the interchange of commodities between this country & yours. Give us a free trade or a moderate duty on Corn and Timber and our imports would soon get up 25 @ 33 1/3 — to 50 pr ct beyond what they now are. Thus far the cultivation of wheat is limited or so intended to be — to our consumption and our average export of about 1.000.000 barrels of flour. The surplus of this and last years is the over plus of two or three abundant crops. If however our farmers were sure of an entrance to your market at 5/ or 10% they would at once enlarge their grain growth, and we should have an excess for export of some lbs 3.000.000, or more as your wants might seem to us to require — The U. S. Bank as you will have heard is a complete wreck and the proceedings of its managers have inflicted a disgrace upon the country, which is more to be lamented than can be measured by pecuniary estimates, and so have the acts of States and other corporations — Somebody in the present aspect of our financial concerns will have to lose 50 — 75 or perhaps $100.000.000 by the delinquency of states who thus far seem determined not to tax their constituents for the means of paying the accruing interest. In states where the money has been expended in productive improvements matters will go well, but such is not the general character of the works constructed by the aid of foreign loans, and even where such is the case as in New York, there is a disposition to go far beyond that point, and if such be the fact even the stocks of that wealthy common wealth will be insecure, for when the debt for her works shall amount to 50 or $60.000.000 & as large a sum as I have named may be required to carry out the scheme already acted upon — why there will be a heavy tax required to meet the interest, and if many of them are un-productive, taxation must follow, My hope is that the difficulties in which some 8 or 10 other states are involved may discourage the imprudent enterprise of N York before she proceeds too far. Pensylvania owes about $35.000.000 for improvements and 10 or 15.000.000 more may be requisite to complete her roads, canals &C. Last year the *net income* was only about $200.000. She requires a tax of $1500.000 to $2.000.000 to meet her deficiencies, but as yet there is no disposition to levy it — nor do I believe the Legislature will come to it. The people of all the states when they authorised the issue of stocks, were told that the income of the works would pay the interest on the debt — and enough more to redeem the cost of them. Such not being the result they are willing to borrow money to pay interest, but not to submit to taxation. I hope something from Pensylvania because she has the ability to pay which is hardly true in respect to Maryland, Illinois, Alabama, Mississippi, Indiana, Michigan, Florida Louisiana &C. Some of these states are growing rap-idly, but a road which has no income will soon doubble its cost, at 6 to 8 pr ct pr anum, the rates which our weak states have

paid for their borrowings. I hope as matters have now indicated the actual state of our States and Corporations — at
least in some instances — that you will stop loaning us & by
increasing our debt, diminish the small chance you have of
getting the value or half of it. There is some chance I think
that the bankrupt & embarrassed states may have strength
enough in few years if not sooner to compel the Goverment to
assume their debts — in exchange, perhaps for their rights to
the public lands, which however do not bring in over $3.500.000
pr. an Such a plan has been suggested, but as yet the leading
party men are not ripe for a movement in it. Our politicians
are so selfish & as unprincipled as in all countries and they will
do in this matter, or in any other matters — what they believe
will promote their popularity and power. There are exceptions
but too few to have much influence in public affairs. The men
coming with power have more talents and character as I think,
than those who are retiring, but the action of our Goverment,
will be I fear as little conformity with public interest & public welfare and public honor — as it has been the past 12
years. The machinery is the same, though it may be made of
better stuff, and more polished — but it will move for the
benefit of the office holders and their partisans, and not in accordance with the great interest of the nation. There is a call
for a National Bank, but I hope it will not prevail — confident
as I am that it will be founded on bad principles & be ad-
ministered on still worse ones. Mr Biddle was the model of
bankers, and though he is admitted to have been unlucky, yet
the principles on which he acted are as popular as ever, and will
be followed and are now followed by nearly all the Bankers
in the country. The U S Bank has made her dividend for some
4 or 5 years, not out of earnings but out of capital. It must
be so because the foundation of its ruin was laid more than
5 years ago. Of the 800 or 900 remaining banks, 200 perhaps
have failed, and 2 or 300 more are in the condition of the
U S Bank. We shall hold out here, and in NYork, in specie
payments & so they will in the Carolinas, Virginia and Georgia.
I am in hopes too that the Philadelphians will do their utmost

to resume within 12 months, and in the mean time to keep down their issues, and not allow their bank paper to depreciate below 2 or 3 pr ct. Baltimore is poor, and in all respects we don't expect she will do so well, as she stopped avowedly for profit. It will cease to have much foreign trade. Their city debt alone requires a tax of 2 pr ct on all its capital to pay the interest of her debt, and her ordinary expenses. If this be levied, her citizens will transfer their concerns to other places. Our Cotton Crop I estimate at 1.800.000. bales, though many persons act on 1.600.000, and prices are in accordance — 4 years out of 5 prices are too high to make a remittance.

Yours truly

(Signd)   H Lee

LETTER FROM HENRY LEE, BOSTON, MAR. 13, 1841, TO CRAWFORD, COLVIN & CO., LONDON, ON IMPORTATIONS FROM CALCUTTA, CHANCES OF WAR, ETC.[1]

The indigo and shellac mentioned below had evidently been shipped directly from Calcutta to Henry Lee on the London firm's account. It seems questionable that at this time Henry Lee was importing any goods on his own account; he was certainly operating primarily as a commission merchant.

It is something of a surprise to learn that at this time rum was being shipped from India, though there is no reason why Bengal, which, like the West Indies, was a sugar-cane raising area, should not have manufactured this liquor. India, while producing excellent timber for the hulls of vessels, could not supply satisfactory spars, which consequently were shipped from the United States; evidently wood for the manufacture of casks was also lacking in India.

Relations between England and the United States were somewhat strained at this time because of both the northeast boundary dispute and the recent indictment of a Canadian for murder of an American citizen on American soil, in a border fracas. Henry Lee was correct, of course, in scoffing at the idea of war, the Canadian being acquitted that fall and the boundary dispute settled the following year. On the day before the letter below he had written to a friend in Liverpool:

1. Jackson-Lee Papers, "Letters 1840–41. Henry Lee," Oct. 30, 1840–Dec. 21, 1852, pp. 106–107.

"I have no apprehension of any serious difficulty with your country; but if you want to *increase the peace securities* take off the duty on wheat, and then you will have 5.000.000. of Corn-growers, who will feel the same strong *pecuniary* interest in preserving peace with the consumers of it, that the Cotton planters now have, who depend on you for the purchase of 50,000,000 lbs. of their products." [2] In regard to the prospects for war, or the lack of them, it seemed to be Henry Lee's opinion that patriotism, according to Samuel Johnson "the last refuge of a scoundrel," was also the first refuge of a politician.

Orig pr Britannia

Messrs Crawford Colvin &Co   Boston 13th March 1841

London

Gentlemen

The indigo pr Potomac & Harrison, has been examined. The Scinde charged at 80/ is a very poor quality, and I fear will not bring the cost and charges. The 150/ cost is good enough for our customers as is the parcel costing 171/, but both are higher charged than some parcels lately received from Calcutta of corresponding qualities. There is no sale just now for any thing without a sacrifice of price in consequence of the uncertain state of the currency, south of NYork, where half of our goods must be consumed. There is no want of means of paying for goods, but prudent men whose business it is to distribute these goods, for the ordinary profits of business, will not buy freely while it is so uncertain what they shall get in return for their sales. I am in hopes matters at Philadelphia may soon become more settled. If the Legislature of that state (Pennsylvania) act prudently, the currency in that quarter will improve and if so business will proceed on a better footing since the conduct of that state will influence the movements of some half dozen others. I am sending you by this steamer samples of the Indigo p "Potomac" and shall be glad to have the brokers valuation and also your opinions as to the future probable value of this staple based on a crop of 120 @ 125.000 Mds, the latter

2. *Ibid.*, p. 105, Henry Lee, Boston, Mar. 12, 1841, to Thomas Thornely, Liverpool.

being as I learn from Calcutta and infer from what I hear the probable extent of the crop.

The Shellac is well charged and will, I think make a good remittance, though at present I do not expect to make sales of much of it. I have made contracts for the sample casks and expect to receive & ship them in the course of 50 or 60 ds. I perceive that shipments of rum are made from India to a great extent and it appears to me that there could be no risk in your ordering a larger quantity at the low prices they cost here in comparison with the cost in India and elsewhere of casks fit for the conveyance of liquors. There appears to be various points of difference between your Government and ours, still the evils of a war are so manifest and so enormous to both parties and more especially to us that I do not apprehend any serious result to any of them. The difficulty of obtaining money without annoying the people who must be taxed for it is here a greater restraint on popular leaders, and no other can hold power with us, than all the moral considerations which could be presented to the minds of our rulers and such, I suppose, may be the case on your side. Well we now owe on the part of the nation about $25.000.000. The revenue is unequal to our lowest peace expenditure and we will submit to no other taxes than *indirect* ones which are on imports and in case of War with you 2/3rds of that would vanish.

As to loans, such is the distrust on the part of capitalists of the power of the government to raise taxes to pay even the interest on them, that the most prudent would refuse any terms that could be offered, nor do I believe government in case of war could raise 50.000.000 on any terms, nor 20.000.000 under 8 or 10% unless it was under the expectation of reselling the stocks on your side. The foolish speeches made in congress in a war like time came from men who are quite pacific and who want not war but popularity for the patriotic sentiments which cost them nothing to utter, at least nothing beyond the derision and contempt of sensible men whose opinions, however are of little consequence in the minds of such persons. You may rely upon [it] the administration do not [want] war, for who ever leads us into it will be sure in the end to lose their popularity and their power, while at the same time they will find it hard work to procure the means of prosecuting it. Your ministers have fewer obstacles to encounter as their constituents have a better *habit* of bearing taxation

Yours &c

(Sig'd) Henry Lee

LETTER FROM HENRY LEE, BOSTON, MAR. 15, 1841, TO FORBES & CO., MACGREGOR, BROWNRIGG & CO., EDMOND BIBBY & CO., REMINGTON & CO., BOMBAY, ON THE COTTON SITUATION[1]

Cotton was one of the subjects upon which, together with the tariff and banking, Henry Lee most loved to hold forth. The letter below is one of courtesy and commercial discourse rather than of business, strictly speaking.

The casual reference to "correspondence . . . overland" as preferable to "correspondence by ship" reveals the great advance in transportation and communication which had been achieved since Henry Lee's latest previous surviving letter book, some twenty years before. "Until 1835," writes an historian of the British post office, "all our mails for India were carried around the Cape of Good Hope, and the approximate time occupied was four months." The time from the North Atlantic Coast around Cape Horn was at least as great. "In that year," however, that is, in 1835, "a change was made, and the mail was sent *via* Egypt." A futile petition in 1832, from various merchants concerned in the East India trade, for regular steam transportation from Alexandria to Malta, describes the India–London route. After reaching the Red Sea there seem to have been two possibilities: to go westward overland from Kosseir [Cosseir, Qoseir] to the marked eastward bend in the Nile just opposite, and down the river; or to go on up the Red Sea and the Gulf of Suez and across the Isthmus, the advantages of which route, we are told, compared with that around the Cape of Good Hope, "even before the opening of the Canal, were . . . obvious."[2]

1. Jackson-Lee Papers, "Letters 1840–41. Henry Lee," Oct. 30, 1840–Dec. 21, 1852, pp. 108–109.

2. Bennett, Edward, *The Post Office and Its Story* (London, 1912), p. 214; "Steam Communication with India," *Annual Register for 1832*, chronicle, pp. 137–140.

"Capt. Bullard" of the barque *Brighton* was probably Stephen H. Bullard, W. S. Bullard's brother, who was acting as supercargo of Bullard & Lee. On Jan. 1, 1844, his entrance was announced into that firm, henceforward to be known as Bullard, Lee & Co.[3]

   Orig pr Brighton   Boston 15th. March. 1841
Messrs Forbes &Co
 " MacGregor. Brownrigg &Co.
 " Edmond Bibby &Co
   Remington. &Co.

       [written across face of letter]
       enclosed to
       J B Higginson
  Bombay.
    Gentlemen.
      You will recognise in my signature a correspondent, who at the request of your London friends, wrote you some years ago upon the subject of Cotton. and availing myself of so slight an acquaintance, I have taken the liberty to give an introduction to you, on behalf of Capt Bullard. who goes to your place, on commercial objects and may therefore have occasion to transact some business with you or to call on you for advice & information, which I doubt not, will be readily offered him. I discontinued my correspondence by ship conveyances. because the later dates. overland would, I know, deprive my letters of all interest & utility. If however, you desire to hear from me upon the subject of Cotton, through London, I will with pleasure, write you. This staple must now have an increased importance in the eyes of the East India agents, because of the attempts to raise it, and extend the former cultivation, under a belief that your producers can compete successfully with our planters for the supply of the Europe markets. Such, however, is not my opinion, believing, as I do, that this is the country, of all others where this staple can be

3. Jackson-Lee Papers, "Letters 1840–41. Henry Lee," Oct. 30, 1840– Dec. 21, 1852, p. 312, W. S. Bullard and Henry Lee, Jr., Boston, Jan. 1, 1844, to Henry Miller and Fletcher Alexander & Co.

raised cheapest. The rapid progress made in planting here, while it has receded in the Brazils. Egypt & West Indies, is one evidence of our superior capability in underselling those countries. As to India, you have only made money in shipments, when our prices have been *unnaturally high* owing either to short crops, or to over issues of currency, and its action on prices. For the past years our crops have sold low enough, to enable us to lay down Cotton uplands at 4¾ to 7ᵈ. and at those rates, cotton planting will be the best employmen for southern capital, and labor, At such comparative prices. India Cotton. would give a very bad result, unless the cost of production shall have been diminished, or my information is incorrect. In 1820, and 1821, our crops of cotton average 138.000.000 lbs. The crop of 1839/1840 season ending 30 Sept 1840 amounted to 838.446.475 lbs. The last crop I consider as super abundant, and *not likely* to be exceeded even under an increasing growth, for some years to come, and especially at the present moderate prices. There, facts shew what can be done with cotton, though for several years during this period prices were within ½ᵈ above, in England, as they now are. As to Cotton lands, they are beyond any assignable quantity and can be had for the expense of surveying or somewhat above it, and between the United States, and Mexico there are also Cotton lands enough to supply mankind with cotton for ages to come. The present crop of cotton has been usually rated at 1.600.000 to 1.650.000 bales. I estimate it at 1.800.000. and more likely to exceed than to fall below. I consider existing prices in England quite as high as can be sustained, at least till our crop of 1841/42 is at hand, when if it should prove a short one, prices might advance. Our currencies, south of NYork, are depreciated, and in disorder, but measures are in progress which, I think, may tend to restore it to a specie value. There are many remarks in our news papers, and speeches in Congress &C. which indicate serious difficulties with England, but I have no apprehension they will lead to a war, an event which both countries are so strongly disinclined to, upon every principle which can operate upon the minds, and feelings of both nations. I shall be glad to learn what success is met with, in improving the qualities of your cotton, and upon any other subjects you may chose to teach.

> Your Obt St
> (Signed) Henry Lee.

LETTER FROM HENRY LEE, BOSTON, MAR. 29, 1841, TO WILLIAM WADDELL, MADRAS, WITH SUGGESTIONS FOR TRADE BETWEEN THEIR RESPECTIVE PORTS[1]

The suggestion for "a very profitable business . . . without the employment of much capital, or indeed any" is of interest. The technical advance of the American textile industry is illustrated by Henry Lee's suggestion that American textiles might be a profitable shipment to India, which a quarter of a century before had been America's principal source of cheap cotton goods.

  Orig pr Brighton   Boston March 29th. 1841
William Waddell Esqr.
 (via Calcutta)   Madras.
care of I. M. &Co   Dear Sir,
         I have none of your favors to acknowlege since my last respects of the 15 Jany. The ships lately arrived from Calcutta, have brought out a large quantity of Madras Goat Skins, but the prices have not been reduced below rates which afford the importers a very good profit, and I am inclined to the belief that we shall not have a full supply for the season. I can recommend shipments with confidence now, and at all times when a good skin can be had at 30/, containing a proportion of the small sizes, they being sold here without any solution of sizes at an average price. I would again call your attention to the necessity of having them well beaten and dried before they are packed, and some tobacco dust or pepper dust mixed with a little spirits of turpentine scattered on the hair side of each skin, The ship Brighton, by which this will go, will on application to the house to which she is consigned, let you have

---

1. Jackson-Lee Papers, "Letters 1840–41. Henry Lee," Oct. 30, 1840–Dec. 21, 1852, pp. 112–113.

tonnage for such goods as you may wish to send me. She returns
to New York, but I can as well sell the goods there as here, and
it is often times a better market than this. If you are inclined
to make shipments to me I can secure tonnage here on lower
terms than the $20, usually paid by shippers in Calcutta, and
a few dollars pr ton bears considerably on the results of so bulky
an article. Hides still continue high notwithstanding the fall of
prices in London, and the opening the B. Ayres trade, and I can
safely recommend shipments at moderate prices. There is so
much low quality Indigo in this country, and in London that it
will not answer from your quarter except at the low limits I have
named in some of my letters. In about 3 or 4 months a vessel
will leave here for Calcutta. on board which I will endeavour to
engage some tonnage on low terms, which may be filled or not,
as you deem for your interest, but this cannot often be done,
as the ship owners usually prefer disposing of all their room
here, rather than taking the chance of getting rid of it in Calcutta. — With care in collecting Goat skins, and economy in
transporting them, I believe a very profitable business may be
done, between this place, and yours, and without the employment of much capital, or indeed any, since by having your insurance done in London, and drawing on your agents there
against consignments, the principal portion of the cost of the the
goods, could in that way be anticipated, and I shall always
be ready to make the necessary advances to meet those bills
at the usual date of 12 months, or at 6 months sight. As persons
at a distance are some times disinclined to trust their concerns
to a single life on account of the inconvenience which may result from death or indisposition. I should have informed you
that I am connected in my business with two others who have a
respectable capital, and long experience in the management of
the sales of India goods having been connected with me for some
past years, namely Mr Wm. S Bullard & Mr Henry Lee Jr. on
them in case of necessity will devolve the care of my concerns.
and I now have their aid in the disposal of my goods. The currencies of N England and NYork are in a sound state, & I do
not apprehend they will become otherwise. All kinds of India

Cotton goods Blue as well as White, are utterly without demand, superceded by cheaper imitations, nor will there in my opinion ever be a revival of the demand so long as Cotton is as low as it now is, say 4 to 7ᵈ lb. and at those prices, our planters can afford to carry on the cultivation. So also of Madras & Vantepollam Hdkfs, they are also superceded by goods made here, and in G Brittain at about ¼ of the cost of the Madras. The American drillings, a cloth which you may have seen in the Madras market, is now a profitable article of remittance to Calcutta where it sells at 4 to 4½ annas a yard. It is worth more with you, and perhaps it may be an object worthy of your attention, in the way of remittance for such goods as you may send me. It is 30 inches wide, wove with wale, and weighing a pound to 3 yards, made of the best N Orleans Cotton, and sold in the unbleached state chiefly, but it can be had in the bleached state. at about 7 or 8 pr cent addition to the price of the brown. There are also many of our other products, and of foreign products to be had here lower than in England which usually pay a fair profit in Calcutta, and whose prices are still higher with you, because of the more limited supplies you receive, namely, pine boards, deals, tar. spirits of turpentine, tobacco, pig copper, flour, when as now, it can be had at 9 Rupees a barrel of 200 net lbs., beef, pork, soap, spars, bread, crackers, and other articles, which have often times been sold by ships calling at your place on their way to Calcutta, at a handsome profit. A vessel can generally be induced to call, on the way out, if any considerable quantity of freight can be had either out or home. Till within these 2 or 3 years some of the residents in Madras have been in the habit of collecting skins &c. and shipping to this country; at this moment, they have ceased to do so. I have had many consignments from there, on nearly all of which there was a good profit.

Yours truly
(Signed)   Henry Lee.

LETTER FROM HENRY LEE, BOSTON, MAR. 29, 1841, TO J. MAC-
KENZIE, LONDON, ON THE EFFECT OF DEPRECIATED CURREN-
CIES ON PRICES[1]

In a letter of the same date to a Calcutta firm, which had sent him
bagging, Henry Lee commented that "prudent men who must re-sell
the principal part of the goods they buy. in states where the currency
is depreciated, and on 6 to 9 months credit — will not buy, as none
can conjecture, where the depreciation will end . . . Independently
of the currencies. the country is well able to buy & consume." [2]

Orig per Caledonia.   Boston March 29th. 1841
J. Mackenzie
   London   No 90.
      Dear Sir.
         Annexed you have a dup of my last respects, since which
I have yours of the 3d. The state of the currencies out of NEngland & NYork has so discouraged men who buy for distribution
in the depreciated states, that sales have become limited &
prices of every thing have fallen. On the arrival of your indigo,
had I been at liberty to sell. I should probably have close[d]
the whole, on better terms than now can be done, but you required an advance on your Invoice out. By your subsequent
letters, you desire me to sell at my discretion. if I think supplies
will come in, beyond what our market will bear. Such has been
the case in arrivals of several parcels from India one of which
is offering at low prices, besides several small parcels from
London, which are also offered very low. In addition to this
one of our largest holders, who has good deal on the way from
Calcutta, besides a heavy stock, but who was firm in his asking
prices, has lately come into market at low prices, and cut us
off from sales, we expected to make, while our cotton & wollen
manufacturers, discouraged at the fall in the prices of cotton &
wollens, have shortned work, and do not buy half the quantity

---

1. Jackson-Lee Papers, "Letters 1840–41. Henry Lee," Oct. 30, 1840–
Dec. 21, 1852, pp. 116–117.
2. *Ibid.*, p. 117, Henry Lee, Boston, Mar. 29, 1841, to Mackillop,
Stewart & Co., Calcutta.

of dye which they was expected to purchase. Under those circumstances, I have accepted for an article a lot of ⟨A⟩ 30 Chests @ price lower than I have before obtained namely. $1..60 cts. on 10 mo Credit [interlineated: ½% off 9 Mo.]. It is not delivered, and though the buyer regrets his purchase, yet I dont think he will refuse the goods, as he examined them pretty thoroughly. This will not cover your Invoice cost, but I fear it is better than I can do with what remains, and I can assure you it is good profit on the cost of some parcels imported from London by one of our dealers according to the statement of what he reported. If the article improves in London it may not go lower here. I shall try to run off the balance, and in mean time I shall probably get an answer to this before the whole is closed. Our business concerns are in a miserable state owing to currencies &c, and a heavy pressure on the money market, every where out of New England, and here it is not easy, nor could I have sold so large a lot as 30 chests, without giving an extra long credit. I cant recommend shipments this way, till our financial concerns. currencies &c are in a more settled condition. No further sales of Madras.

Yours truly

(Signed)   Henry Lee.

LETTER FROM HENRY LEE, BOSTON, APR. 17, 1841, TO T. S. FIELD & CO., PHILADELPHIA, WITH INSTRUCTIONS FOR THE SALE OF INDIA TEXTILES, SOME DAMAGED [1]

Philadelphia had long been one of the best markets for India goods imported by Boston merchants, and the firm to which the letter below was addressed constituted at this time the principal channel whereby Henry Lee disposed of goods shipped to the Pennsylvania metropolis. On Apr. 7 he had shipped them "6 Cases superior quality Choppas" to add to other India goods, including twine, which he had sent them earlier.[2] As is mentioned below, some of the bandannas were spoiled en route. On June 2, Henry Lee expressed the conviction that, in the

1. Jackson-Lee Papers, "Letters 1840–41. Henry Lee," Oct. 30, 1840–Dec. 21, 1852, p. 132.
2. *Ibid.*, p. 121.

season just arrived, such goods as seersuckers should be in demand,[3] and on Aug. 5 mentioned that the "new duty of 20% on silk goods from India instead of 10% & 20% European Silks which were before free of duty must enhance the prices of silk goods some 10 or 15%."[4] But, over a year later, these expectations had not been fulfilled, as is indicated by a letter of Oct. 19, 1842, suggesting that the Philadelphia firm should "try a few of the silks at auction" and that choppas, originally priced at $"5⅛" per piece should be let go "if you can get 3¼."[5] These goods were being sold for correspondents of Henry Lee, as is indicated by the latter's remark on Nov. 5: "The goods had better be distributed at your auction sales as they may happen. We consider it unfortunate that we should be called upon to force these goods, but such is the order from those interested. Nothing doing here."[6] The goods were finally sold "so very low, that," Henry Lee wrote Dec. 5, "were I not under most peremptory orders to close — I would not accept — but let them go if you cannot do better. I hope you may induce him to advance a little on his offer — "[7]

On Aug. 3, 1843, Henry Lee sent on "10 Cases Silks . . . to help your assortment . . . to sell at the prices prefixed."[8] But about a year later, July 3, 1844, he ordered "all the silks they had on hand, into the hands of Mr W. C Langley New York — "[9] Thus ended Henry Lee's sales in Philadelphia through commission merchants.

Boston April 17th. 1841

Mess T. S. Field &Co
   Philadelphia,
      Dear Sirs,
         I have yours of the 14, & 15, you had better take out all the spoiled pieces of Bandanas, and make one Case by itself with others, and then resell the good @ 5.50, and the damaged for the most you can. It is the only complaint I have had. If you can close them without selection @ 5¼ — do so — I hope soon to hear of sale of the 2d quality Bands. & the Childrens, & also the Seersuckers.

      Mess Crocker & Sale have sent you samples of the Blue

3. *Ibid.*, p. 153.   6. *Ibid.*, p. 262.   8. *Ibid.*, p. 294.
4. *Ibid.*, p. 177.   7. *Ibid.*, p. 275.   9. *Ibid.*, p. 336.
5. *Ibid.*, p. 254.

PHILADELPHIA, BEFORE 1754

Baftas. I hope you will not forget them. Bagging is all bought up here @ 20 cts 6 months save our lot, and one more, which we hold @ 23¢ 6 months. If you can get a price that will *nett* that deliverable in Boston, may do so, if on hand when your order reaches, provided the offer reaches me in course of 7 days. It has got up in N Orleans, and last year we got 25, and it may soon go to that. If your only demand is among southern buyers. I fear you can't do better than we can, as they usually buy here, and there are 4 or 5 persons who are now buying if to be had @ 20 Cts.

Yours truly.

(Signed)   H. Lee

LETTER FROM HENRY LEE BY W. S. BULLARD, BOSTON, APR. 29, 1841, TO JOHN H. MASON & CO., PROVIDENCE, WITH AN INVOICE OF INDIGO[1]

Providence, as one of the earliest and most important textile manufacturing centers, was a natural outlet for indigo imported into Boston. Note reference to "to days cars," and the commission for sale and guaranty. Henry Lee did not, however, confine to dyestuffs his shipments to Providence, and on Dec. 24 sent the Mason firm "15 Bales Bombay Senna." [2] Another letter, of May 31, 1842, explains why the letters of this period are signed by W. S. Bullard for Henry Lee. "Please have the check payable to W S Bullard," Bullard wrote, "Mr Lee is living out of town [in Waltham], & may not be in for several days." [3]

Henry Lee also sold indigo to A. & W. Sprague, who did not, however, so far as is known, sell for him on commission.[4]

1. Jackson-Lee Papers, "Letter Book 1840–41. Henry Lee," Oct. 30, 1840–Dec. 21, 1852, p. 136.

2. *Ibid.*, p. 196, Henry Lee by W. S. Bullard, Boston, Dec. 24, 1841, to J. H. Mason & Co., Providence.

3. *Ibid.*, p. 226, Henry Lee by W. S. Bullard, Boston, May 31, 1842, to J. H. Mason & Co., Providence.

4. *Ibid.*, p. 123, Henry Lee by W. S. Bullard, Boston, Apr. 12, 1841, to A. & W. Sprague, Providence.

Boston April 29th. 1841

Mess John H. Mason &Co
    Providence
        Gentlemen.
             Your favor of 27th. with note for bill sundries, due 14/17 Oct. Amtg to $413154. is recd & passed to your credit.

    By to days cars I send you 2 Case good quality Indigo (English Cases) which I hope you will find saleable. I also send you Samples (cont^d in Case No 21 Ⓑ) of some Common Indigo for which I shall be glad to get an offer.

Your obt St

(Signed)   H Lee by

Sell the Indigo at
Invoice price,

W. S Bullard

I understand you are to sell & Guarantee for 5 pr Ct. Please have this property covered by fire insurance.

LETTER FROM HENRY LEE, BOSTON, JULY 21, 1841, TO B. & H. P. UPTON, SALEM, DESIRING TO SELL GOODS FOR THE AFRICAN TRADE [1]

Supplying goods for the African trade was one of the earliest and most important methods by which Henry Lee had disposed of colored cottons from Calcutta. Now, at the end of his commercial career, he was still interested in the African market.

Boston 21 July. 1841

Mess B. & H. P. Upton.
    Salem
        Gentlemen,
             I notice you have a vessel from Africa. I have an assortment of Checks. Plaids, Stripes, and Blue goods, suited to the markets of that country. & shall be glad to supply any, you may want, and at prices much below the price of domestic goods.

1. Jackson-Lee Papers, "Letters 1840–41. Henry Lee," Oct. 30, 1840–Dec. 21, 1852, p. 176.

I have sold the most of the African traders, for some years past,
& have reason to believe that the buyers have made money.

I am Gentlemen,

respectfully

Your ObtSt,

Henry Lee

No 39 India Whf

LETTER FROM HENRY LEE BY W. S. BULLARD, BOSTON, OCT. 4,
1841, TO BEVAN & HUMPHREYS, PHILADELPHIA, ON INSUR-
ANCE, ETC.[1]

In the early years of the century the Lees had shipped large quantities of goods imported by them to Philadelphia for sale there. At
the time of the letter below, Henry Lee and the Philadelphia firm,
with which his cousin Joseph Cabot (1790–1878) was connected,
were furnishing mutual assistance in the disposal of goods and in
other business functions. The inadequacy of newspapers as a source
of information particularly for coastwise trade is clearly brought out
by the fact that none of the shipments from Philadelphia to Boston
mentioned immediately below is included in the marine news of contemporary Boston papers. In fact, during the entire post-war period,
1817–43, only 2 shipments from Philadelphia to Henry Lee are mentioned, coffee in 1826, tea in 1828. There is of course no way of
knowing whether these consignments were from Philadelphia merchants to Henry Lee for sale on commission, or were purchased by
Henry Lee from Philadelphia merchants, or were consignments from
the Orient made on Henry Lee's account by way of Philadelphia, or,
perhaps, shipments from London merchants by way of Philadelphia,
on Lee's own account or for sale on commission.

The horse hides, from Buenos Aires, were badly worm-eaten, but
by Nov. 16 Henry Lee had managed to sell them. Late in November,
Lee was awaiting consignments of cotton goods and wool from the
Philadelphia firm and on Feb. 9, 1842, he requested them to dispose
of a cargo of coffee coming from La Guayra.[2]

1. Jackson-Lee Papers, "Letter Book 1840–41. Henry Lee," Oct. 30,
1840–Dec. 21, 1852, p. 185.

2. *Ibid.*, pp. 120, 175, 191, 204, W. S. Bullard for Henry Lee, Boston,
Apr. 5, July 31, Nov. 16, 26, 1841, Feb. 9, 1842, to Bevan & Humphreys,
Philadelphia.

The insurance Bevan & Humphreys desired was on a vessel and cargo from Philadelphia to Sidney by way of New Zealand and Manila and back to the United States. Lee had been able to obtain it "at 5½%, for the whole voyage or 5% pr annum. Should the Ship deviate, the Office will charge for such deviation at the rate of 5% p annum." [3]

The immediate danger of war at this time was in the trial then in progress of Alexander McLeod, a Canadian. While in a state of intoxication on the American side of the border, he had boasted of having taken part in the capture in 1837, in American waters, of the steamer *Caroline,* in the service of Canadian rebels, which had been sent in flames over Niagara Falls; in this action, McLeod asserted, he had shot and killed an American citizen. His conviction and execution would have meant a definite possibility of war, but the jury acquitted the defendant as a drunken braggart. [4] There still remained the controversy over the Maine boundary. Henry Lee's comments on this question are original and interesting: "The Maine dispute is not yet settled &itmaynot be on account of the folly of some of our Commissioners, but it can't lead to war nor can other questions — We are too poor, too divided &too helpless agt. foreign invasion to [?] a war with Engd — & on points of no real importance — The slave states the most belligerent could be revolutionized by 20 black regiments from the W. Indies — nor could the Northern & free states affordthem any aid — they know this & will act in accordance not withstanding war orations — " [5] This judgment was not that of an abolitionist, for in 1835 Henry Lee and his brother-in-law P. T. Jackson had been members of a committee which called a meeting of "citizens of Boston . . . who are opposed to the proceedings of the advocates for the immediate emancipation of the slaves of the South." [6]

3. *Ibid.,* p. 182, Henry Lee by W. S. Bullard, Boston, Sept. 29, 1841, to Bevan & Humphreys, Philadelphia.

4. McMaster, *op. cit.,* vol. vi, pp. 610–623.

5. Henry Lee Shattuck Collection, Henry Lee, Sr., Waltham, July 10, 1842, to Henry Lee, Jr., Paris.

6. *Boston Daily Atlas,* Aug. 18, 1835.

Boston Octr. 4. 1841

Mess Bevan & Humphreys
    Phila
        Gentlemen,

I have yours of the 1st. In regard to insurance on property to New South Wales. I can only say that our offices stand at present very well, but it would be impossible for any one to say that they could meet all their losses in the event of a war. They are *now* willing to write without inserting the War Clause, but the news by the steamer hourly expected, or the tendency of the evidence about to be developed in Mc Leod case may change their views.

The Horse Hides Shall be sold in a few days, & the sales shall be forwarded as soon as they are mad up & the Hides delivered.

If M^r Mc Gregor has not paid you the small sum of 133^{88}. you will oblige by sending for it.

                    Your Obtsts
                        H. Lee by
                        W. S. Bullard.

I regret to hear from Mr Robertson
that your Mr Cabot is unwell,
is he seriously indisposed?

LETTER FROM HENRY LEE BY HENRY LEE, JR., BOSTON, OCT. 28, 1841, TO L. SHARPLESS & SON, PHILADELPHIA, WITH ACCOUNT OF EXPENSES FOR ENTERING GOODS[1]

Henry Lee occasionally took charge of entering and forwarding goods which merchants in other cities had imported by way of Boston. For this service he charged a percentage upon the expenses involved, a commission proportionately the same as that which he would have charged on selling goods to the amount of the expenses.

1. Jackson-Lee Papers, "Letters 1840–41. Henry Lee," Oct. 30, 1840–Dec. 21, 1852, p. 188.

Boston 28 Octr. 1841.

Mess L. Shapless &Son
Philadelphia.
Gentlemen

I received your letter of 25 th inst yesterday and immediately entered the three cases goods pr Columbia as therein requested.

The goods were examined this morning by the appraisers. and are now on their way to Phila^{da}. pr Rail Road &steam Boat, as you requested despatch.

I subjoin a list of duties, charges, and expenses upon them.

Duties pr Co; house returns	$171.09
Co; house fees for entry	.20
Truckage to & storage at Co House	.75
Truckage to R Road &labor	1.—
postage on your letter	.75
	$173.79
Comss 2½%	4.33
	$178.12,

Specification of duties

Damasks &Rattinetts — £77. — . 9				
	@ 4.80 — $369.78. —	20% —	$73.96
Cassimeres		£53. 5, —		
	@ 4.80 . $255.60.	38%	97.13.
				171.09
		Fees		20
				$171.29

The amt you will remit, as you can do so
at a better rate than I can draw.
You will please find enclosed the recept for the goods
Your ObtSt.
(Sig^d) Henry Lee by
H. Lee jr

LETTER FROM HENRY LEE, BOSTON, DEC. 21, 1841, TO BIRK-
HEAD & PEARCE, BALTIMORE, IN REGARD TO THE PAYMENT OF
A DRAFT IN DEPRECIATED CURRENCY [1]

On Dec. 8, Henry Lee had sent to the Batlimore firm "Crawford
Colvin &Co draft .$2200. on John Glenn, London 17 Novr. 1841. en-
dorsed to me. & by me to you, which please collect & remit to me. . . .
This sum should be paid in specie . . . or drafts on N. York. or
Boston at par. . . . If not take Baltimore & remit to same before
your currency grows worse. . . . it should be done under protest. so
as to give claim against him hereafter, or to exonerate me from all
blame." [2] Glenn, however, as Henry Lee on Dec. 15 informed Crawford, Colvin & Co., "declines paying on those terms, & I have therefore written on to Bal^e to accept the local currency though at a
depreciation of 3½ to 4%. . . . first, because it may happen that
M^r. Glenn made his collection in it, 2^d. because by delay, the currency . . . , which rests wholly on institutions, which have a great
portion, & perhaps all, their capitals invested in worthless securities,
may soon decline in value." [3] Glenn was enraged by Lee's attempt to
obtain payment for the English firm in specie and seems to have
threatened to refuse in the future to pay any drafts transmitted to
him through the Boston merchant. The general inconvenience and
loss caused by the existence of different currencies could hardly be
better indicated.

Boston 21 Decr. 1841.

Messrs Birkhead & Pearce.
  Baltimore:
   DearSirs,
    I have yours of 17th. I thank you for your attention to
my business. M^r. Glenn has no cause to be offended. It was my
duty to protest in order to justify myself to my employers, &
I withholding that measure I act on my own, responsibility.
since the payment made by M^r. G. is not in correspondence with
his agreement to pay, namely it is not the payment of 2200 Dollars, but that sum less 4%. Suppose your currency had been

---

  1. Jackson–Lee Papers, "Letters 1840–41. Henry Lee," Oct. 30, 1840–
Dec. 21, 1852, p. 195.
  2. *Ibid.*, p. 192.   3. *Ibid.*, p. 193.

50% would it have been right for me to accept $2200 @ 50% disct?

The payment is not a legal one as M^r. G. knows. though I don't pretend to say that he is morally accountable for the loss on the currency.

Pray say this much to M^r. G. His mode of revenging himself would not be a very severe punishment to me, since the service done my London correspondent is a gratuitous one. In saying that he would pay no more bills through the same source, indicates however some more than bad temper. namely bad morals. For by what right does he mean to dictate to his principal. through what channel he must collect money due him? If the order comes through me. I shall however teach Mr G. his duty if he dont understand it, provided your courts are as honest & independent as I suppose them to be.

Your banks should resume now or they never will,

Yours truly

(Sig^d)   H. Lee

LETTER FROM HENRY LEE BY W. S. BULLARD, BOSTON, FEB. 12, 1842, TO BEACH & CO., HARTFORD, CONN., ANNOUNCING A CONSIGNMENT OF INDIGO [1]

In his anxiety to close up his business, Henry Lee was pushing the sale of consignments earlier made to him, not only in the principal mercantile centers but also in such smaller cities as Hartford. Early in the previous fall the Hartford firm had sold 3 cases of indigo and was ordered to "disct the sale & remit . . . the nett proceeds at your earliest convenience." [2] On Feb. 15, 1842, Lee, through Bullard, was enquiring concerning the possibilities for selling raw silk in Hartford. On June 15, 1842, Bullard curtly instructed Beach & Co.: "Sell the few remaining cases Indigo you have on hand for what you can get. Meet the market." [3]

1. Jackson-Lee Papers, "Letters 1840–41. Henry Lee," Oct. 30, 1840– Dec. 21, 1852, p. 205.

2. Ibid., p. 180, Henry Lee by W. S. Bullard, Boston, Sept. 16, 1841, to Beach & Co., Hartford, Conn.

3. Ibid., p. 233, W. S. Bullard, Boston, July 15, 1842, to Beach & Co., Hartford, Conn.

Messs. Beach &Co   Boston 12th Feby 1842.
    Hartford
        Gentn.

Your favor of the 10th is recd. with the sale of 1 Case Indigo $386.68 to your debit. The a/c is correct. You will oblige me by making a remittance for the pro of the 3 Cases at your earliest convenience.

By this mail I have ordered my N York agents to send you 2 or 3 Cases more of the same description of Indigo, you have just closed, You will please make your remittance payable to the order of W. S. Bullard. as Mr Lee, who has retired from business. is now absent from the City. There appears to be a large falling off in the weight of the last 3 Cases Indigo .. pr sales rendered, showing an aggregate loss of 39 lbs. This is partly owing to the increased tare, but mostly in the Gross weight. I call your attention to this fact.

Hoping to hear soon of the sale of what you have now on hand.

> Yours truly
> (Sig'd)   H Lee by
>   WS Bullard

LETTER FROM HENRY LEE BY W. S. BULLARD, BOSTON, MAR. 4, 1842, TO J. MACKEY & CO., CALCUTTA, IN REGARD TO A DAMAGED SHIPMENT OF HIDES, WITH A CERTIFICATE FROM A COMMITTEE OF MERCHANTS AS TO THE CAUSE OF THE CONDITION [1]

It must have been a disappointment to Henry Lee that, after his minute instructions to the owner of these hides as to the proper method of preservation and packing, the first invoice should arrive in such a damaged condition.

1. Jackson-Lee Papers, "Letters 1840–41. Henry Lee," Oct. 30, 1840–Dec. 21, 1852, pp. 206–208.

Orig pr. *"Farwell."*   Boston March 4th 1842

Mess J. Mackey &Co.   Dup pr "Sophia.

Calcutta.

Gent

I am in rect of your esteemed letter of the 8th Octr covering Invoice & B/Lading for 12 bales Bullock & Buffalo Hides & 40 Bales Goatskins pr Ship "G^l Harrison". for sale on account of Wm Waddell Esqr. of Madras.

The G^l. Harrison arrived about 30 days since & I regret to say. that in consequence of the Hides & Skins being shipped wet. they were landed in almost a rotten state.

They were so badly damaged, that I was somewhat apprehensive that they would not produce enough to pay the freight & expenses. I have a cert that they were well stowed, & although the coverings were badly stained & in some instances rotten. yet there was no appearance of water. & the part of the ship where they were stowed was perfectly dry. as will be seen by the Copy of certificate, the original of which I shall send Mr Waddell.

I sincerely regret the bad result of this first shipment from Mr Waddell. the more so, as the adventure would have resulted in a very handsome profit.

A survey was called on the Hides &skins & the result was a strong recommendation to put them up at auction & sell them for the most they would bring

This being in accordance with my own judgement they were sold & the nett proceeds will be about £180. The Hides are well adapted to our market & will always do at the price of Mr W^s Invoice, viz 100/ pr 100 hides & the Goatskins @ 18 @ 22/ will always be safe. The quality of the Skins was, as far as I could judge from their damaged condition, very good. heavy & fresh

Our skin dealers value Goat Skins now, according to their weight, this must be remembered in any shipts to this country, 625 @ 635 lbfor 500 skins. is considered fair weight.

Hides are just at this moment dull. the stock is not very large, but we look for a good supply through the year. & I do not look for any improvement in prices. Good heavy green salted Patnas

7½ @ 8 lbs @ 1.05. @ 1.10. 6¾ @ 7¼ — 95 @ 1.00 Dry 6
@ 7 lbs 67 @ 80. Good heavy Madras Goatskins 21 @ 22¢

We have ample supplies of all description of goods from your
quarter & there is not an article that can be named that will
cover cost & charges.

Indigo. common to good 1.10 @ 1.50. Lac Dye. good 12½
@ 15. common & ordinary unsaleable. Shellac, Liver & Orange.
good 7½ @ 12¢. S. Petre 5 @ 5½¢ the latter price for the best.
Gunny Cloth. costing landed from Calcutta 20¢. is now worth
15 @ 16. according to quality. Linseed $1⁸⁰. pr bushell of 52
lbs.

The prospects for the coming year. are very discouraging &
I hope you may not be interested in any Mdse on the way to this
country.

Your Obtst,
(Sigd)   HLee by
WSBullard.

P. s. Mr Lee is now absent from the city. He will write you by
the next Vessel. The B/Lading of the shipt of Skins & Hides
having been accepted deliverable in salem, I was compelled to
receive them at that place & to pay the expenses of getting them
to Boston.

(Sig^d)   HLee by
WSBullard.

[written across face of letter]
1st. pr Sophia.
Mch 31. 41.

Nothing doing in mdse. Calcutta produce is
very much depressed. The Gentoo. Bazar. Brighton &
Massasoit have just arrived. & increased our stock to a
very heavy supply. Every thing is unsettled & it will
be some months before there can be any improvement.

Yours
(Sig)   HLee by
WSBullard

Copy of certificate sent Mr Waddell. Madras

Orig pr Farwell   Boston Feby 16th. 1842.

Dup pr Overlandmail.

April 26.

We, the undersigned. Merchants, residing, & doing business in the City of Boston. hereby declare that at the request of HLee we have examined ◇w 1/12. Twelve bales Buffalo & Bullock hides. & ◇w# 1/40 Forty bales containing 20.000 Madras Goatskins, purporting to be imported at Salem, pr Ship "General Harrison" from Calcutta & landed here from Sloop "Nile" from Salem & we found them very badly damaged. *rotten,* & *sweated.* & otherwise much injured by wet & dampness.

It is our opinion that they were shipped wet. which is the principal cause of their present damaged condition. We are further of the opinion, that they were imperfectly cured — with *Marine salt,* which attracts moisture & gives them a red tainted appearance.

We are well acquainted with Hides & skins, having been Dealers for several years in them & we recommend their being sold at public auction, as being the fairest way of obtaining their value.

(Sigd) George Higginson. (Sigd) Joseph Southwick
(Sigd) J. C. Rogers,   (Sigd) Wm B. Spooner

It is my opinion that the Hides. & skins. mentioned on the other side, were shipped while damp, which is the principal cause of their present damaged state.

(Sigd) Henry Poor

Inspection cert. page 208.

Copy of Cert. sent. Mr Waddell. Madras pr *"Farwell"* sailed Mch 8. 1842

We, Daniel Bray Jr. Inspector. of Customs, and Wm C. Smith & Wm Burbeck, masters of vessels, called on a survey of Ship "Gl Harrison," LeCraw Master, now lying in the Port of Salem (there being in this port, no portWarden) hereby certify

that we were present at the opening of the Hatches of said Ship
"Gl Harrison, which were well &properly secured. caulked &
battoned. We were also called to examine the stowage of Hides
& Goat skins marked ⟨w⟩. & found them well stowed, and every
precaution appeared to have been made to prevent damage, and
although some of the above goods were damaged it was in our
opinion occasioned by the internal condition of the Bales and
the action of the salt upon the Hides & not from any remissness
in stowing them. the goods immediately above, below & around
them, being in perfect order. We also examined the stowage of
the Goatskins marked TW & EW a few of which were slightly
                    A   A
stained, & found them well &properly stowed & dunnaged.
   Salem Feby 10th. 1842.

                       (Sigd)   Daniel Bray Jr Inspector.
                         "   Wm C. Smith
                         "   Wm Purbeck.

    Witness
  (Sigd)   H M. Brooks.
      [in margin: Dup pr Overland
                pr GWestern
                sailed
                April 26th '42]

LETTER FROM HENRY LEE BY W. S. BULLARD, BOSTON, MAR.
23, 1842, TO WILLIAM J. DUBBS & CO., MARACAIBO, REQUEST-
ING A REMITTANCE [1]

   Henry Lee had last written the Venezuela firm, Dec. 10, 1840, on
which date he had already "for a long time been without any of your
favors." [2] His interest in receiving a remittance after so long a time
is understandable, as is his desire to receive payment in a draft rather
than a shipment of coffee. It is also quite understandable that Dubbs

   1. Jackson-Lee Papers, "Letters 1840–41. Henry Lee," Oct. 30, 1840–
Dec. 21, 1852, p. 214.
   2. *Ibid.*, p. 27, Henry Lee, Boston, Dec. 10, 1840, to J. Dubbs, Maracaibo.

& Co. should prefer to pay in a shipment, and this they probably did, since Henry Lee on June 17, 1842, received 64 bags of coffee on the brig *Rienzi* from Maracaibo.

Orig pr via N. York.   Boston Mch 23rd. 1842.

Messrs. Wm. J. Dubbs &Co.

Maracaibo.

Gentlemen.

Your favor of the 3rd. July last with sales 3 Bales Blue Salempores came duly to hand & I have been for some time looking for a remittance of the nett proceeds due pr Sale 31st Decr last. $706.31.

Please send this sum forward in a good bill on the U.S. payable in New York or Boston. under your guarantee. or if this mode of remittance is not practicable — then in Coffee. on the best terms you can. I should prefer a draft. to a shipment, but leave it to your good judgement. Hoping soon to hear from you.

I remain   Your Obdtst

(Sigd)   HLee by
WSBullard

LETTER FROM HENRY LEE BY W. S. BULLARD, BOSTON, MAY 31, 1842, TO WILLIAM BRANDT & CO., ST. PETERSBURG, ACKNOWLEDGING SALES OF INDIGO [1]

The only letter to a St. Petersburg merchant in the present letter book is printed below. Henry Lee, so far as newspaper accounts show, had made few importations from Russia since the War of 1812; 2 invoices from Cronstadt in the fall of 1831 consisted of flems, ravens duck, sailcloth, and "broad diapers." Other consignments had probably come from the St. Petersburg firm or Henry Lee would not have owed a balance to them after they had sold the indigo he had shipped them. Doubtless, too, Henry Lee had made other shipments to Russia which had been paid for not in merchandise but in bills of exchange.

The world market for indigo was evidently in a bad way at the time.

1. Jackson-Lee Papers, "Letters 1840–41. Henry Lee," Oct. 30, 1840–Dec. 21, 1852, p. 233.

pr "Acadia." Boston May 31st. 1842.
Dup pr "Britannia" sailed July 2nd. 1842.
Messrs Wm Brandt &Co.
St Petersburg
Gentlemen.

Your favor of the 25th. March with sales 9 Cases
Manilla Indigo came duly to hand. The result shows a loss of
75% on the cost, but I have no doubt you did all that could
be done for my interest.

The balance of your account I have paid to Mr Storer. your
agent of this place in the sum of $8135¹. equal to S Roubles
1067⁶⁷. or £169.17.6 @ 38¾d pr Ro — all which I presume is
correct. I shall be obliged to you for your acknowledgement of
this balance through your Agent. Mr Storer, who has promised
to inform you that this settlem't had been made, by the last
steamer.

Your Obdtst.
Sigd HLee by
WSBullard.
directed to care Messrs. E. H. Brandt's Son &Co. London.

LETTER FROM HENRY LEE BY W. S. BULLARD, BOSTON, JUNE 9,
1842, TO WILLIAM C. LANGLEY & CO., NEW YORK, TAKING
EXCEPTION TO CERTAIN CHARGES [1]

New York, at the time of the letter below, was, as it had been before the War of 1812, one of the principal United States markets for
oriental goods, even those imported through Boston. Newspapers reveal more than twice as many shipments from New York to Henry
Lee, 1817–43, as from any other United States city; totalling, however, only 7. These consignments, 1 in 1819, 4 in 1824, 1 in 1825,
and 1 in 1832, were all more or less vaguely "merchandise" except the
last, "1 bale hides," which was probably being returned to Henry Lee
as unsalable. The other shipments may have been either returned
goods, or merchandise being shipped to Lee for sale on his own account
or on commission.

1. Jackson-Lee Papers, "Letters 1840–41. Henry Lee," Oct. 30, 1840–
Dec. 21, 1852, p. 231.

When Lee shipped the New York firm 9 cases of silks, Sept. 30, 1841, he was careful to remark: "I understand your commissions and guarantee to be five per cent and no more and also that you are not to allow 1% p month discount for shortening notes as in some instances in your sales as the prices for the goods will not bear such deductions."[2] However, as will be seen below, Langley & Co. were able to keep within the letter of Lee's injunction and yet make charges open to question.

In his instructions to the New York commission firm, Lee had not only specified price limits and commission charges but had also, on Mar. 17, 1842, prescribed the order in which goods should be sold. "I wish you to put by the coarse goods . . . as . . . they cannot be sold without an almost total loss, when the fine goods are sold, they may improve . . . The increased duty on silks," he added, "& a further addition to be made will help all silk articles, but I have no expectation of doing much in the present depressed state of matters."[3] The price of silks had already advanced the preceding year, "because of the interruption of the China trade"[4] resulting from the Opium War. A year later, on Apr. 7, 1843, Lee acknowledged the sale of some "small choppas & Bandannas" but ordered that silks should be held for a rise.[5] On Aug. 3, 1843, Lee sent "By todays Steamer . . . 16 Cases Silkps. goods . . . to sell . . . on 8 mos credit" [6] and in a final letter, May 10, 1845, Lee stated: "I shall be glad to have the Hdkfs. on hand sold within the course of the season, for the most which can be obtained." [7]

Henry Lee's only other New York correspondent for the sale of India goods, Mar. 9, 1841–Aug. 4, 1843, was P. H. Frost. Lee's communications to him were chiefly confined to warnings not to sell below the limits.

2. *Ibid.*, p. 183, Henry Lee by W. S. Bullard, Boston, Sept. 30, 1841, to W. C. Langley & Co., N. Y.

3. *Ibid.*, p. 214, Henry Lee, Boston, Mar. 17, 1842, to W. C. Langley & Co., N. Y.

4. *Ibid.*, p. 177, Henry Lee, Boston, Aug. 5, 1841, to P. H. Frost & Co., N. Y.

5. *Ibid.*, p. 285, Henry Lee by W. S. Bullard, Boston, Apr. 7, 1843, to W. C. Langley & Co., N. Y.

6. *Ibid.*, p. 294, Henry Lee by W. S. Bullard, Boston, Aug. 3, 1843, to W. C. Langley & Co., N. Y.

7. *Ibid.*, p. 350, Henry Lee, Boston, May 10, 1845, to W. C. Langley & Co., N. Y.

Boston 9th.June 1842

Messrs. Wm C Langley &Co
  New York
    Gentlemen.

Your favor of the 4th inst reached me in due time covering a/c Sales of 15 cases silks. & memo of marks & nos of 15½ Cases remaining on hand with you unsold.

I feel compelled to make exception to your list of charges especially if they apply but to the 15 cases sold. The item of 61.15 purporting to be expenses of advertising. & Fire insurance. This charge is excessive. The charge of cartage & labor is also large — 39.13. this item may however include Storage on the whole 30 Cases. if so it cannot be objected to. although it is 50% more than it would be here.

There is another part of your a/c. which I have before mentioned. & which involves a principle not recognised in any other a/c ever recd. by me. Viz. considering Comss &Guarantee as due before the sales average due. & this I think on reflection you will admit to be wrong. Your Comss &Guarantee are charged — due June 1.st instead of the time. when the sale becomes due. making a difference of 5 ms or 2½% on $211.52 =$5.29.

These points I mention for your consideration. & I shall be glad to have your views. Let me know also if the charges in sale apply to all the goods say 30½ cases. — or only to the 15 cases sold.

truly yours.
(Sigd)   HLee by
WSBullard

LETTER FROM HENRY LEE BY W. S. BULLARD, BOSTON, JUNE 16, 1842, TO D. LANDRETH & D. S. MUNNS, PHILADELPHIA, ANNOUNCING SHIPMENT OF GOODS TO INDIA ON AN ICE SHIP [1]

Henry Lee occasionally took charge of the shipment from Boston of goods belonging to merchants in other cities. We have no record of his charges for this service, but see letter of Oct. 28, 1841, to L. Sharpless & Son, above, pp. 1461–1462.

The description of the method of loading this ice ship is of interest.

Boston June 16th. 1842.

Messrs. D. Landreth. &D.S.Munns.

Philadelphia,

Gentlemen.

I am this day in rect of your favor of the 14th. inst. Finding that the ice taken by the "Franklin" was closely caulked down in the lower hold, & that a considerable quantity of dry lumber had been laid on the 2nd. Deck. I shipped the packages. apprehending that they will be as free from moisture as on board any ship bound from here to Calcutta. The vessel will sail early next week — & will stop a few days on her outward passage at Madras.

Enclosed are Bills Lading — I have effected the insurance requested by you on this ship't & also on that, made by the "Sophia." Annexed is bill of charges, which you will please pay over to Messrs. Bevan & Humphreys. to be placed to my credit. A bill of expenses on ea. parcel of goods has been forwarded to Messrs. Huffnagle. &Spry. as you requested.

Your ObtSt.

(Sigd)   HLee by

W S Bullard

1. Jackson-Lee Papers, "Letters 1840–41. Henry Lee," Oct. 30, 1840–Dec. 21, 1852, p. 234.

LETTER FROM HENRY LEE, BOSTON, JUNE 17, 1842, TO JOHN
HORSLEY PALMER, NEW YORK, ON COMMERCIAL STAGNATION [1]

John Horsley Palmer (1779–1858) in 1802 entered into partnership with his father, his elder brother George, and a certain Capt. Wilson as an East India merchant; references to the firm of Palmer, Wilson & Co. have been frequent in the preceding documents. During 1830–32 he had been governor of the Bank of England. He had recently married, as his second wife, the daughter of Samuel Pepys Cockerell,[2] the father doubtless being connected with Cockerell & Co., of London and Calcutta. Palmer, at the time of this letter, was apparently a member of Palmer, Mackillop, Dent & Co., of London, an East India firm of which Mackillop, Stewart & Co. was the Calcutta representative; he was in the United States for the purpose of selling silk goods, some of which had been earlier consigned to Henry Lee. The conditions which made it impossible for Henry Lee satisfactorily to dispose of these goods are effectively reflected in various private letters written about this time by relatives and friends of the Lees. Only a month before, Henry Lee had expressed the opinion that "Matters are improving. . . . Factory goods . . . go off better." [3] Two months after this optimistic judgment he declared that "the stagnation in sales of all goods but provisions is greater than ever but," he added, "the season soon will come where goods will be wanted, tho' I dont think prices will improve much. . . . We have too much shipping by 200,000 tons & the owners are suffering heavily — Too many ships going to Calcutta considering the *over supply* of goods on hand & on the way — there will be great losses . . . the *factories* have so many goods unsold & so many bad debts that all will pass the [?] dividends — save perhaps the Merrimack — & I hope the Locks & Canals may divide something." [4] His tone a week later was but little more encouraging: "Business generally is beginning to be favourably affected by the arrival Spring purchases of goods tho' no great advance in prices has taken place nor likely to do at least

1. Jackson-Lee Papers, "Letters 1840–41. Henry Lee," Oct. 30, 1840–Dec. 21, 1852, p. 235.
2. "John Horsley Palmer," *DNB*.
3. Henry Lee Shattuck Collection, Henry Lee, Sr., Waltham, May 13, 1842, to Henry Lee, Jr., London.
4. *Ibid.*, Henry Lee, Sr., Waltham, July 10, 1842, to Henry Lee, Jr., Paris.

for several months. . . . The consumpt of coffee at the North is greatly reduced as you may suppose when beef, pork, hemp, cotton &c &c. have fallen 50%. . . . Some 50 more failures within 4 weeks but none of any interest to you." [5] Near the end of the year Henry Lee wrote: "The losses by fall of prices have been universal & ruinous to many & many men feeling as if they had something to rely on — will find when they have sold & paid up debts &c that they are poor & destitute [?]. Multitudes who depended on facty dividends are witho [ut ?] income or nearly so & are selling Lowell shares — 750 to 850 each & best *bank stocks* at 80 to 95 — Ships have depreciated about 20% — too much tonnage by 100,000 tons. . . . Nothwithstanding the bad state of business — there is some compensation in believing as I do that, we shall when we get thr'o the effects of our revulsions, over tradings, over manufacturing &c. have all kinds of business transacted on safe principles & that persons of capital & prudence who are now ruined by the competition of *mere gamblers* will then do a safe & thrifty business — " [6]

A couple of weeks later, on the last day of 1842, P. T. Jackson, Jr., wrote to his cousin Henry Lee, Jr.: "I pass my day amid the dull routine of business, or rather waiting for something to do, my greatest excitement arising from the sale of a few bales of goods or the failure of some large debtor." [7] The mother of Henry Lee, Jr., stressed the social effects of the business stagnation by a reference to "an elegant subscription ball . . . for the benefit of Papanti. . . . Not one of our family subscribed. but us. . . . We had 2. to spare but Minot or C. Jackson or the P. T. Jacksons would not avail of them, as they had from economical motives refused the subscription I hear you say pshaw, but you can hardly realise how poor people feel. — " [8]

A month later Henry Lee announced one of the usual seasonal upturns: "There is some improvement in business consequent upon the return of Spring and the importations of coin serving to supply a Currency in the States where from failure of the banks there is no bank paper in circulation — the severall importations of European goods

5. *Ibid.*, Henry Lee, Sr., Boston, July 18, 1842, to Henry Lee, Jr., Paris.

6. *Ibid.*, Henry Lee, Sr., Boston, Dec. 16, 1842, to Henry Lee, Jr., Paris.

7. *Ibid.*, P. T. Jackson, Jr., Boston, Dec. 31, 1842, to Henry Lee, Jr., Paris.

8. *Ibid.*, Mary Lee, Boston, Mar. 30, 1843, to Henry Lee, Jr., Paris.

has also had some effect — . . . the banks have largely extended
their issues." State and bank stocks were rising, and domestic cottons were being sold to exporters, though at low prices.[9]

By early fall business had once again begun to flow freely. The
highly protective tariff of Aug. 30, 1842, had now, a year after its
passage, taken its full effect; importers at least knew the worst.
"Father desires me to say," Mary Lee wrote, "that the Lawrence
factory has just made a semi annual dividend of five per-cent — The
Locks & Canals are to have a meeting on Tuesday, & are expected to
make a good dividend, & that business affairs are in a good state.
Thus things change for ever & ever, & why should we distress ourselves & croak so much . . . All that business men can do it appears
to me are to keep themselves always prepared for the horrid
revulsions whh. as far as my observation goes come at about stated
periods & this can only be done by moderation at all times."[10]
P. T. Jackson, Jr., later in the month, gave a vivid description of the
fashion in which business, a stagnant pond eight months before, had
now become a rushing torrent — its motion exhilarating but a little
too rapid to be safe. "Business has improved wonderfully; the factories are making money *too* fast. So we do for a time & then;
'hurrah boys, stand from under.' The mills cannot make less than
10 @ 15% unless there is a great change. . . . An active man could
make his fortune in a very short time. Everything is rising, and
prices that seem high one day are too low the next. In our line [cot-
ton textiles] it is impossible to keep up with the demand, and everything indicates immense profits for the next year or so. But this
expansion will of course be followed by a corresponding contraction &
then look out. It is a great temptation to leave one's regular business,
when so much money is to be made by speculation, but my first rule,
upon entering into business, was not to go out of my regular line."
It seems somehow appropriate that in the midst of this description of
alternate despair and hope, apathy and wild excitement, in the business world, should suddenly appear this comment: "The Miller doc-
trine is spreading fast."[11]

9. *Ibid.*, Henry Lee, Sr., Waltham, Apr. 30, 1843, to Henry Lee, Jr.,
Paris.

10. *Ibid.*, Mary Lee, Waltham, Sept. 12, 1843, to Henry Lee, Jr., Paris.

11. *Ibid.*, P. T. Jackson, Jr., Boston, Sept. 14, 29, 1843, to Henry Lee,
Jr., Paris.

J. Horsley Palmer Esqr.   Boston 17th June 1842.
    New York.
        DearSir.

Being absent from the city, where I reside during the summer months I did not get yours of the 10th June in Season to answer it before the "G. Western" sailed. Mr B. has sent you the memorandum of the goods on hand. The Indigo will go off by the case in few weeks probably. but it can't be forced even at a discount on prices we are getting, if I was to reduce 10 — 15 or 20%. There is no selling any articles, save those of prime necessity — provisions &c &c. except as they are wanted, unless at an enormous sacrifice, & such has been the state of our market for a long time past, & had I forced the goods to a conclusion, the proceeds would have been 20 or 30% below what I have been realizing. by retailing as wanted.

In respect to the silks, the new duty — which will no doubt be imposed, when there is a new tariff — of at least 10 or 15 prCt. in addition to the present rate — will help that article, in the mean time no sales can be made but at extreme low prices, The stagnation in general sales is greater than I ever remember, & it is the reaction of a some 5 or 6 years of over importation over consumption of superfluities: — over banking. & of every kind of excess in trade, which could be committed with the aid of over 800 banks foreign loans &c. &c. The result. has been the ruin of about ½ the men in trade while those still operating, are to a great extent in doubtful circumstances.

I regret as much as the parties interested can do, the prolonged sales of the silks &c, but the delay has been unavoidable. & has lessened the loss. which had the goods been forced would have been increased.

If you would like to see me. & obtain personally more information. as to the business in hand, than I can afford in a letter, or upon any other matters, I will come to New York. where perhaps the business you have come to this country upon, may render it inconvenient for you to leave.

                            Yours truly,
                        (Sigd)   HLee.

LETTER FROM HENRY LEE, BOSTON, AUG. 24, 1842, TO LIEUT.
COL. H. G. JACKSON, HALIFAX, N. S., IN REGARD TO A PASSAGE
TO INDIA [1]

Although not a business letter, the document below, in addition to
giving a good idea of the passenger service from the United States to
India, conveys some incidental information on commerce with that
part of the world: the number of vessels sailing annually; their tonnage; and, particularly, the fact that Boston was the port from which
they principally sailed.

It is not clear just what Henry Lee meant by his "8 passages to &
from India." Only three voyages to India, made by Henry Lee, are
known. In 1802 he went to Calcutta on the *Caravan,* returning the
following year; in 1811 he sailed for Bristol and Calcutta on the
Reaper, returning to the United States in 1816 on the *Portsea;* and
in 1821 he went to Calcutta on the *Palmer,* returning the following
year. His movements between 1802 and 1822 seem fully accounted
for, but it is, of course, at least possible that he made another voyage
to India either before or after the above period. Assuming that this
is the case, Henry Lee doubtless means that he made eight passages
to *or* from India, rather than "to & from."

So far as we know, Lieut. Col. H. G. Jackson was not related to
Mrs. Henry Lee (Mary Jackson).

Boston 24th Aug 1842.
Lieut Colo. H. G. Jackson.
  Regt. Artillery
    Halifax. N.S.
      DrSir.
        I was favored a few days since with yours of the 13th.
inst accompanied with a note from Mr Jas Colvin. It will afford me pleasure to aid you in securing a conveyance for your
son to India. and in the accomplishment of any other object
you may have in view. where my services may be thought useful to you.

There are annually sent to Calcutta from the U. States from

1. Jackson-Lee Papers, "Letters 1840–41. Henry Lee," Oct. 30 1840–
Dec. 21, 1852, pp. 243–244.

20 to 25 Ships, nearly all from this port. They depart in all months of the year but more go from Feby to July than at any other period.

The sizes of these Ships vary from 300 to 500 tons. As a class of ships, they may be deemed equal to any merchant vessels in the British service. Ships sailing from Feby to July make their passages in 120 to 130 days, occasionally few days shorter. & some times longer. As it is no part of their business to transport passengers, they have not such convenient, & elegant accommodations as are usually found on board of large British Indiamen, or in the line Ships from N. York to G. Brittain, still they are quite comfortable, & usually sail faster than the ships trading from England to India.

The passage money has not in any instances where I have had occasion to enquire exceeded $250, sometimes it may be as low as $200. A state room is allowed, but no bedding. nor any furniture beyond a chair or two, nor am I aware that any other articles will be necessary save Trunks. for clothing towells &c. The Ship will find provisions, & of a quality, which, a person in usual health can have no reason to complain of. taking into view the compensation allowed. No wines or liquors of any kind are supplied by the ship. I have at various times made 8 passages to &from India & in no instance was I incommoded for the want of good fare. The expense of bedding, & such sea clothing as may be necessary, may be from 20 to 30$ up to $50. according to the varying wants of individuals. If wines are required there will be an additional expense though they can be had much cheaper, than in England. As there are no voyages made up, more than 4 or 6 weeks in advance of the sailing of ships, it is not practicable to engage a passage for any particular day, or month. but you may count with certainty upon my finding a conveyance between the 1st.April. & the 1st. June. If it is important that he reach Calcutta as early as the 1st. Octr. I think he should embark by the 15th. May. I would suggest also whether it may not be well for your son to be here by the middle of April. or first of May. that there may be less uncertainty as to his seasonable embarkation. provided I am unable to secure a passage for about the 15th. May. — Again — some of the ships may decline passengers, or may not be of the first class consequently a few spare weeks to accommodate that matter may be requisite. I think too. that 130 days should be allowed for a passage. though the chance is in favor of 120. From 1st. Mch to 15th. May is the best period to sail for India from UStates for short & pleasant passages. & as you probably are aware Octr is a healthy season for a stranger to the climate of Bengal. to reach that country.

I believe all your enquiries are answered, but if further information is required be good enough to write me for it. If you conclude to send your son here for the object in view, you may rely on my utmost services to carry his wishes, & yours into execution.

> I am dear sir
> Your Obdtst.
> (Sigd)   HLee.

LETTER FROM HENRY LEE BY W. S. BULLARD, BOSTON, OCT. 27, 1842, TO ROBERT BROOKHOUSE, SALEM, OFFERING BLUE GOODS[1]

The goods offered for sale in the letter below apparently belonged to Henry Lee and were not merely being sold by him on commission. The goods had to be exported before a certain date in order for the shippers to collect a debenture from the government. We do not know that the Salem merchant made any purchases at this time but he seems over two years later to have bought a large quantity of remnants, from a letter of Dec. 28, 1844, in which Lee writes: "I have packed *all* the pieces &fragments of goods you bought yesterday into Cases &Bags — and congratulate you upon the bargain you have made." [2]

In 1819 and again in 1832, Henry Lee had received a consignment of India goods from Salem, in the former year, sugar and saltpetre, in the latter, a large quantity of indigo, lac dye, and silks. It is unlikely

1. Jackson-Lee Papers, "Letters 1840–41. Henry Lee," Oct. 30, 1840–Dec. 21, 1852, p. 255.

2. *Ibid.*, p. 349, Henry Lee by H. Lee, Jr., Boston, Dec. 28, 1844, to Robert Brookhouse, Salem.

that these shipments were of goods which had been unsuccessfully sent to Salem for sale and were being returned; more probably goods had been sent from India — or London — to Henry Lee by way of Salem, on his own account or for sale on commission. Salem's commerce with India had not yet come to an end, but seems to have been declining, or else Henry Lee would not have thought of finding a market there for India goods imported through Boston.

Mr R. Brookhouse,   Boston Octo 27th. 1842
    Salem
        Dear Sir.
        I had hoped to have heard from you respecting the Blue goods at which you looked a few days since. As an arrangement is proposed to me, by which they may be disposed of, my object in writing is to know if you have concluded to purchase.
        There are 1000 ps Blue Gurrahs, which I will sell to you at $1. — short price. 10 Ms. note to be dated when you take them away, provided the time does not exceed 60 days & agreeing that they shall be exported before 1st. March. next.
        I have also, 1 bale Bengal Salempores. 17 yds. by 36 @ 37 in. 2 bales Mamoodies 16ops. 19 yds by 35 inches, which I will sell at $2. — pr ps. & 1 bale English salempores 15x32 in 125 ps @ 1.50. 10 mo Cr. These with the exception of a few bales Bengal Blue Salempores are all the Blue goods I now have, or ever shall have, I shall be glad to have an early reply.
                                                            YourObdtst.
                                                Sigd   HLee by
                                                        W. S. Bullard.

LETTER FROM HENRY LEE BY W. S. BULLARD, BOSTON, APR. 29, 1843, TO MUDENEN MOHUN BHOSE AND HOLLADHER BHOSE, CALCUTTA, DENOUNCING QUALITY OF INDIA GOODS [1]

    Calcutta baboos seem to have been much addicted to shipping inferior goods to the United States and being caught at it by their correspondents and the purchasers.

    1. Jackson-Lee Papers, "Letters 1840–41. Henry Lee," Oct. 30, 1840–Dec. 21, 1852, pp. 286–287.

¡For at least two years many or most of the letters in this volume had been signed "H Lee by W S Bullard" or "W. S. Bullard for H Lee" but it is clear, from the occasional letters signed "H Lee" only, that Henry Lee was keeping in close touch with the business and that Bullard was expressing, in the letters signed by him for Henry Lee, the latter's opinions.

R. C. Mackay and J. S. Coolidge, 16 Union Wharf, constituted at this time one of the leading Boston firms trading with Calcutta.[2]

Baboos   Boston April 29 1843
Mudenen Mohun Bhose   "Dup pr Woodside"
& Holladher Bhose   D sirs
                     Since my respects 12/29 Nov. last I have nothing from you

Enclosed are A/Sales of the 20 Cases Choppas &Bands pr Chilo [?] Nett pro 689⁰⁹. due 9th Nov 1843. This amt less the interest & c will be sent to you by the 1st ship bound direct to your port.

The result of this shipment is a most loosing one, but I could not do any better for the owners. The quality was infamous, they should never have been sent to this country, & had there not been a very high duty imposed on all new importations. I could not have sold them for months to come, & then at not more than half of what I have obtained for them. Since the sale was made & the a/c closed, I have been called on to make an allowance for the worthless hdkfs found in the interior of some of the ps. I have made one deduction of 8²⁵. which I felt bound in justice to do. & this sum will be deducted from the am't to be remitted to you. Calcutta Goods of every description, are very dull. The loss on nearly every article will be from 15 @ 25%. Good quality *large Choppas* are worth about 4⁷⁵. duty 2¹⁰. pr ps covering a cost of about 75/ @ 80/ corge

Hides having been sold at less than the Calᵃ cost leaving a loss of the freight & charges

Mess Mackey & Coolidedge have a ship called the Adabaran

2. *Other Merchants and Sea Captains of Old Boston* (State St. Trust Co., 1919), pp. 42–45.

[Aldebaran ?] which they are fitting out for India, but she may not go direct to Cala. if she does your specie shall be sent by her

Yours

HLee

by WSBullard.

LETTERS FROM HENRY LEE BY W. S. BULLARD AND HENRY LEE, JR., BOSTON, MAY 5, 1843, JAN. 13, 19, 1844, TO P. BRADY, PHILADELPHIA, OBJECTING TO UNDULY HIGH COMMISSIONS [1]

These letters reveal not only what commissions were regarded as unusually high but also what was considered the norm. The 6% charged for sales commission and guarantee does not sound so strange as the $2\frac{1}{2}$% commission on the value of goods not sold but merely delivered to another merchant. Doubtless the Philadelphia merchant felt that he no longer had a motive for meeting the commissions of other competing merchants, since Henry Lee had not only withdrawn goods from his hands but had also virtually retired from business.

Boston May 5 1843

P. Brady Esq
    Phila.
        Dr Sir
            Your letter of the 3^d inst with sales silks — Nett pro. $ 351 11/100 due 27 Decr 43. is recd. The sale is correct. I notice your continue the charge of 6% Com^s. & Guar., this charge I cannot pay. I consented to pay this extra guarantee, when there were many failures, money high, & but little confidence. All my other correspondents have returned to the usual rate of 5%, & one of the largest houses in your city have sold & guaranteed for me @ 4%.

Let me know your views on this point
Please remit me notes for the amt sales

Your obtSt

W.S. Bullard

for HLee —

1. Jackson-Lee Papers, "Letters 1840–41. Henry Lee," Oct. 30, 1840–Dec. 21, 1852, pp. 287, 311, 314.

P. Brady Esq   Boston 13th. January 1844
    Phila
    Sir
        Your letter of 11th inst is before me enclosing A/Ct bal-
ance in your favor of $8675. which includes a commission of
2½% upon value of goods delivered Mr Paul —
I have referred to several of your correspondents in this city,
and other merchants who deal with Phila. Commission Houses.
they agree with me that to charge a com^s. of 2½% upon goods
unsold is unprecidented & exorbitant — Another highly respectable House in Phila who have had goods of mine on hand these
two years, hesitated to charge 1% coms, without any account
being made of storage & fire &insurance —
    I should be glad to hear from you respecting this matter
                                        Your obtSt
                                        HLee by
                            (Sigd)   HLee jr

                                Boston January 19th 1844
P. Brady Esq
    Sir
        I have this day recd your letter of 15th. maintaining the
reasonableness of your charges
    I have this day paid your draft for $8675. altho my opinion is
still, that taking into consideration the amt of business you have
done for me &the length of time these goods have been on hand
that the commission is unreasonable
    If you change your mind, and think well to remit any portion
of the charges, you will please pay over the amount to Mess
Bevan &Humphreys a/c Bullard Lee &Co
                            Your obtSt
                    (Sigd   [Bullard Lee &Co — stricken through]
                    HLee by HLee jr

LETTER FROM HENRY LEE, BOSTON, JULY 12, 1843, TO JOHN
MACKENZIE, LONDON, EXPLAINING THE RESULTS OF INDIGO
CONSIGNMENTS [1]

The letter below throws considerable light upon the state of business at this time and Henry Lee's relation thereto. Mackenzie had
evidently sent Lee various consignments of indigo for sale on commission, some of the more recent of which had resulted unfavorably.
The canny Scot therefore suggested to Henry Lee a "return [of] commissions." The latter pointed out his own losses in these transactions
through making cash advances to the shipper at an interest much less
than current; through becoming concerned in exports which turned
out unprofitably, in order to make a sale; and through dividing his
"com^s. with two other persons." These and other losses since 1837
had deprived Henry Lee "of ¾ of my property." Lee also pointed
out how successfully he had handled Mackenzie's consignments in
earlier and better days. But at the close of this discussion Henry Lee's
rather hypersensitive commercial conscience got the better of him and
he made the flourish of surrendering to Mackenzie the balance due
from him, $360.18,[2] which probably astonished the Scot as much as
it pleased him. This rather unnecessary gesture helps to make understandable the traditional remark of Henry Lee, Jr., "Father, if you
don't retire from business, I will!" [3] The "two other persons" with
whom Henry Lee had divided the commissions were probably William S. Bullard and Henry Lee, Jr., the business address of each of
whom had been 39 India Wharf, since 1837 and 1840, respectively,
the same as that of Henry Lee, Sr.[4]
To the end of 1845, Henry Lee, Sr., continued to correspond with
some regularity, either upon business in general or in regard to consignments which were still in process of being disposed of. For the

1. Jackson-Lee Papers, "Letters 1840–41. Henry Lee," Oct. 30, 1840–
Dec. 21, 1852, pp. 290–291.
2. *Ibid.*, p. 289, Henry Lee by W. S. Bullard, Boston, July 1, 1843, to
John Mackenzie, London.
3. Morse, John T., Jr., *Memoir of Colonel Henry Lee* (Boston, 1905),
p. 15; Joseph Lee [Henry Lee's grandson], 96 Mt. Vernon St., Boston,
Apr. 8, 1935, to Kenneth W. Porter, Soldiers Field, Boston; Perry, Bliss,
Life and Letters of Henry Lee Higginson (Boston, 1921), p. 341.
4. *Boston Directory*, 1821, 1837, 1840.

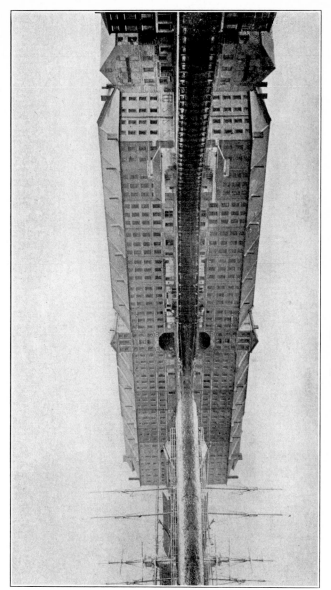

INDIA WHARF, ABOUT 1860

next few years his letter book contains an average of about three letters per annum, all written in his own extremely illegible hand; the last letter is dated Dec. 21, 1852. His retirement from business left Henry Lee, Sr., free to pursue economic research, long his dominating interest. The first fruit of his newly acquired leisure was *Considerations on the Cultivation, Production and Consumption of Cotton,* published in 1845, a thick volume on which he had been working for about three years. He never again undertook such an ambitious project but continued to acquire and dispense economic information for the benefit principally of his English correspondents. Two of his scrap books still exist [5] — old memorandum books on the Calcutta trade into which have been pasted newspaper clippings. The trend of his interests is clearly developed: at first the items have to do with the tariff, mints, coinage, the precious metals, banking and the money market, population, the death of friends, bankruptcy laws, cotton raising and manufacturing, state debts, import and export statistics, the post office, railroads, bread prices, the whale fisheries, and the sugar crop; only items on the Oregon boundary question, the admittance of Texas to the Union, and the make-up of Congress betray interest in "politics" per se. But about 1850 the items change and an interest in "humanitarian reform" movements becomes dominant: there are articles on a peace convention, anti-usury laws, a strike riot, manhood suffrage, communism, etc., though these manifestations are dealt with in a hostile spirit. Finally, items in regard to slavery, the slave trade, the Fugitive Slave Law, abolition, and the Nebraska Act become dominant, and more space is probably occupied by the attack on Senator Sumner than by any other single subject.

In 1850, Henry Lee, Sr., came into possession of a country place in Brookline and from then on became devoted to horticulture [6] — that occupation which seems to have such a fascination for those who have followed the sea, as is notably demonstrated by Henry Lee's own father and his brothers George and Thomas. Gardening seems to have usurped the place in his affection formerly held by economic research; it is notable that though his descendants insist that he was "in heart a scholar, not a business man," [7] his pamphlets on economic subjects were written while he was either actively engaged in business or still quite close to its operations.

5. Jackson-Lee Papers.

6. Morse, F. R., *op. cit.*, pp. 297, 307–308, 315–323.

7. Joseph Lee, Apr. 8, 1935, to Kenneth W. Porter.

Henry Lee died in Boston, Feb. 6, 1867, two days after having attained the age of eighty-five,[8] and about twenty-five years after his retirement from active business. Forty of the preceding years had been occupied with operations in the East India trade and it is with the earlier part of these forty years that the preceding documents have chiefly dealt.

Boston July 12 1843.

J Mackenzie Esq
  Dear Sir

    I have yours of the 25th. May I have refrained from writing for sometime because I had nothing to say in regard to your concerns & as respects mercantile matters generally I am clear of them having for several years withdrawn from new operations & have not had further connection with trade than closing up old concerns. I have found it difficult to close up the Long Cloths from the fact that ever since they were received the article has ceased to have any currency. I doubt if 10.000 ps could be sold for export to S. America &c at over $1⁵⁰. ps. Nor have I ever refused an offer since the goods came to hand such also is pretty much the case with Blue Salempores, they are superseded by cheaper goods & would not sell to nett 4/ ps — Cotton at 6 cts lb with prospect of going lower, will prevent the sale of Asiatic fabrics on any terms. I regret most sincerely the bad results of your last shipments but I feel as if I had done all in my power to render them profitable. It is true the coms. on your business have been large, but I had a great deal of trouble in selling the goods, & the heavy advances of cash at 6% & while money was for most of the time, one & sometimes two percent month has been a great drawback. I could indeed have gained more by leaving the money advanced you at the current rates of interest. than I actually gained on your consignments Again I have divided my coms. with two other persons & on one occasion in order to induce an exporter to buy a large quantity of the Manilla Indigo for which he paid much more than I could sell it for, for home consumption I

8. Morse, F. R., *op. cit.*, p. xii.

took an interest of 1/3 on which I lost £500. I made also a
similar arrangement in respect to some of your Blue Salempores,
in order to induce purchasers to take them in which I suffered
& I have also lost something on my guarantee account. I also
lost on the Carraccas Indigo shipped by your order & which
I agreed to take half to my own account, on the other hand
the general run of my business since 1837 owing to bank sus-
pensions commercial revulsions &c have deprived me of ¾ of
my property. I am not then in a condition to accede to your request in the matter of return commissions, whatever might
be my feelings in that respect, under more fortunate circumstances. You speak of heavy losses but such is not the case in
respect to the general results for I have remitted you about
2150 £ beyond the invoice cost of your goods, & some of the
Indigoes were charged at much higher prices than were current,
as far as I could — — from the importations from England, in
the London market when you shipped your goods. Again the
loss you sustained was on the last large shipments of Indigoes
they however were not made under my advices but some 4. 5 or
6 months later. only one invoice came at the time I recommended
&on that I obtained a great profit. when however the Indigo
arrived you put me under limits which prevented sales at nearly
or quite saving prices This Indigo you purchased for resale in
London & it did not come to me, the loss on the resale in London
must have been much greater than it was actually [erased:
found] to be. If you take this view of the matter, your operations with me cannot be said to be unfortunate. The truth is
that on falling markets & during commercial revulsions which
have existed ¾ of the time I was acting for you. money will
generally be lost. In this country more than half of the
mercantile men in good credit in 1837 have been utterly ruined
& nearly all that have escaped that fate have been greatly im-
poverished. I imagine the merchants in England have not been
much more prosperous than ours have been. I will however
as an evidence of good will more than from the importance of
the sum to you, surrender the balance of the account due you
& consider the account between us squared —

A commerce between this country & Bombay can hardly be said to exist, there are no goods in Bombay wanted in this country & if we send vessels to Bombay it will to get rid of our products & a principal article will be Cotton goods which we can now ship at from 5½ to 6 cts pr yard, for light up to heavy goods, the latter ⅓ lb to yd & such as would now cost 3½ d in Manchester. We this year shall send say 30000 bales to Manilla & China & perhaps 10.000 bales to India altho in Cal^a. we pay 10½ % more duties than are paid on British goods.

I take a strong interest in the production cultivation & prices of cotton the staple of Western India. I shall soon be able to send you some statements on that subject, by a direct conveyance, if I can find one drawn up by me, that may be interesting to you & perhaps useful

MrBullard who has charge of my books & has been concerned with me in all your business will answer your enquiries as to some of the charges. With by best wishes for your health on your voyage & a prosperous course of business

I am Dr sir

Yours truly

(Sigd) Henry Lee

DIVISION XVI

A GLANCE AT HENRY LEE, JR., AND WILLIAM BULLARD
BOSTON COMMISSION MERCHANTS AND FACTORS
IN THE TRADE WITH CALCUTTA AND
RIO DE JANEIRO
1840–44

LETTER FROM HENRY LEE, BOSTON, DEC. 10, 1840, TO MILLER, LE COCQ & CO., RIO DE JANEIRO, ON THE COFFEE TRADE [1]

The letter below, though written by Henry Lee, Sr., is primarily concerned with the recently established firm of Bullard & Lee, in

1. Jackson-Lee Papers, "Letters 1840–41. Henry Lee," Oct. 30, 1840–Dec. 21, 1852, pp. 28–32.

which Henry Lee's son and namesake was junior partner and which succeeded to the elder Lee's business. Henry Lee had long been interested in the importation of coffee and, from 1819 to 1840, at least 15 consignments had come to him from Havana, Matanzas, Port au Prince, Batavia, Puerto Cabello, La Guayra, Calcutta, Rio de Janeiro, Philadelphia, and Marblehead. Only one of these, however, in 1839, had come from Rio de Janeiro, although this was to be followed in 1841 by two more and in 1842 by two others from La Guayra and Puerto Cabello and from Maracaibo. (William S.) Bullard & (Henry) Lee (Jr.) were, however, to make importations of coffee from Rio de Janeiro one of their chief interests. Out of 23 importations to Bullard & Lee mentioned in Boston newspapers, 1841–44, nine were of coffee from Rio de Janeiro and nine of goods from Calcutta, the rest being from ports in the southern United States, principally of cotton. Henry Lee, Jr., who was graduated from Harvard in 1836 and entered his father's business immediately thereafter, had gone to Rio de Janeiro as a supercargo in Sept., 1838, an experience which probably turned his mind to that port when he settled down as a sedentary merchant two years later.

This letter is worthy of note for its detailed examination of the coffee trade and the influences affecting it and for its description of the methods employed by supercargoes and merchants obtaining a cargo for Rio. A supercargo or captain, with some funds of his own and with relatives or friends willing to adventure some of their capital in a shipment of coffee, would go to a commission house and offer to furnish part of a cargo, if it would charter a vessel and supply funds for the rest of the cargo, in return for the consignment of perhaps half the cargo. The commission house chartering the vessel would sometimes require the Rio house, through whom the coffee was purchased, to ship on its own account part of that portion of the cargo for which the American house had originally agreed to be responsible. All concerned were primarily interested in commissions and aimed to supply as little of the necessary funds as possible. A supercargo with funds could cause American commission houses to bid against one another for the privilege of participating in the voyage and selling, on commission, his share of the cargo; supercargoes, on the other hand, must bid against one another in order to induce a commission house to furnish the remaining necessary funds for the charter and other expenses; Rio houses, similarly, would compete for the privilege of supplying, on commission, the cargo of coffee. The supercargo's commission was paid on all the funds committed to his charge; his risk lay in the coffee he was forced to ship on his own account. The American commission merchants were paid a commission only on coffee sold through them; their chance of loss lay with the coffee they themselves imported. The Rio house would have liked to supply all the coffee in the cargo and to be concerned in none of it. All parties were engaged in a seesaw between the risks of participation and the profits of agency.

The letter below is hardly a business letter, and others which follow are even less so, resembling rather reports which a commercial and financial agency might release to its clients. They include, of course, valuable information, as for example, a comparative description, Feb. 1, 1841, of New York, Boston and Baltimore as markets: "The market here has been decidedly better than that of New York for 2 or 3 years past. To N. York go many cargoes on a/c Rio houses and commission houses in N. York, who must realize on arrival in order to remit and thus they often force their cargoes at moments when the demand is slack and over supplied. When however that market happens to be better than this, the intercourse is so easy (18 hours) that a sale can be made there to their dealers and at very small expense. The prices in Baltimore are usually ½¢ higher than ours, but that is owing to their depreciated currency, but if their currrency was as good as ours, which it is now nearly so, there seems to be no way of getting rid of large quantities unless at auction — 3/4^{ths} to 9/10ths of their cargoes are sold in that way at an extra expense of at least 2 to 3% all which must be charged to a concern. Here on the other hand if an auction is expedient the charges are not over 1½%." The advance in the rapidity of communication which had been attained since the development of steam transportation becomes clear when we remember that immediately before and after the War of 1812 the distance between New York and Boston was normally from three to six days.[2]

On June 21, 1841, Henry Lee compared British and American textiles as to qualities and prices. "It appears to me . . . that in such articles as Drillings, Osnaburghs & plain 30 inch cottons, we can undersell the British manufacturer unless he is willing to sell at 15/ in £ for sake of clearing off surplus stock. . . . There is too another point in favor of our best and heaviest goods, they are made of a

2. *Ibid.*, p. 75, Henry Lee, Boston, Feb. 1, 1841, to Miller, Le Cocq & Co., Rio de Janeiro.

better material . . . than the Manchester manufacturer can afford to use, & that will always secure a sale for a portion of goods. We now send the drillings to Calcutta & other ports in British India, paying a duty of 12%. while goods from England pay but 2½% & yet we get a small profit." [3]

Boston. 10 Decr. 1840
Orig p Brothers   sailed 25th. Decr

Mess Miller, Le Cocq &Co.
   Rio de Janeiro.
      Dear Sirs.

I was favored a few days since with yours of the 22 Septr. In respect to the few remaing cotton goods of mine I must leave them to your judgement. I think it may be as well to hold on now they are so low rather than sell them for almost nothing. I have still few Bales Madras Salempores and may have a consignment of more and shall therefore be glad to be kept informed of the value & demand for them either direct or through Mess W. S. Bullard & H. Lee jr. I shall read your letters to Mess B & L. which they will answer. I am glad they appear to have your confidence which I have no question they will merit and that the intercourse will be eventually advantageous, as, I understand from them that the trade with your place will be one main branch of their business. The commerce between the states and your country must extend rapidly, first because when our currency is not in an inflated state we can supply you with some staple articles cheaper than any other country and among them b[r]ead stuffs, lumber, naval stores, candles, soap, coarse furniture &c. We can also undersell the British manufacturers in some staple cotton fabrics, plain & coloured and as we have now got a footing with them, and the Brazilians have experienced their superior qualities. I am pretty confident there will be an extended sale for them, as indeed we now find to be the case in comparaison with what we sold some years ago. It is true there is only a small profit but that is all which is expected,

3. *Ibid.*, p. 171, Henry Lee, Boston, June 21, 1841, to Miller, Le Cocq & Co., Rio de Janeiro.

the best part of the business being the returns, though on them, in an open trade carried on with credit, only a moderate profit can be expected, in fact that is the prominent characteristic of all staple branches of commerce and if there be a very low degree of risk, then it is just [interlineated: what] should be desired by prudent men. There is now and then a year of over trading & speculation like 1836 & some former ones when all trade is dangerous & it is expedient to desist, but in 9 years out of 10, I think well conducted coffee importations from Rio to this country will be safe and moderately profitable. This market is no doubt the best market for your and when you have remittances to make in this commodity for your correspondents in Europe. I am confident the results will be more favorable here than in any port in Europe. In England the consumers appear to be more and more disaffected to the flavor and quality generally of Rio coffee, while here the contrary is the case. In the Western states it has for some years been favorite article and it is becoming more in favor in the Middle & Eastern states will become more so. Coffee being a free article as well as a favorite one the consumption is enormous as compared with that of any equal population. In Gr Britain your coffee pays 9d lb via C G. Hope, the expense on which is ½ @ ¾d lb more than by a direct conveyance. Such an enormous charge on an article shipped @ 4d @ 5d lb must of course discourage consumption & accordingly with a population in the United Kingdom of 25 millions the consumption varies from 22 to 26.000.000 the last being the maximum while with our population of 16 @ 17.000.000 the consumption ranges for the few past years from 76 @ 92.000.000 lbs, averaging for 1835 @ 1838 — 82.079.201 lbs & in 1839 the consumption was 88.593.063 lbs. The price here by the bag is from 9 @ 12¢ lb & it is retailed out by the few pounds at a very small advance. In England the price is from 13d to 16d for middling & 2/ for prime W. India so that with a consumption 3 times as large as Great Britain, the consumers pay less money than they do in England. There they consume about 1 lb a head, here 5 lbs a head. Of the import of coffee in 1839 48.694.249 lbs came from Brazils & 26.181.489 lbs from

Cuba, but at 10 @ 15% higher cost in comparison with qualities,
than the Brazils. Formerly the proportion from the Brazils
was much smaller. The consumption of coffee is much affected
of late years by the temperance societies, who have induced the
laboring classes to substitute coffee for spirits wines &c, again
by its cheapness, & I apprehend you will see a rapid increase of
your export to this country till at no distant day we shall require half your crop. I consider the cost of cultivation lower
with you than in any other country to which we have access
and as an evidence of it, your crops augment rapidly while in
most other countries they are stationary or receding. I presume
that your planters are well remunerated at the prices of the
past few years and that the cultivation will go on extending
somewhat in the ratio that it has here tofore done, while to most
of the West India islands and under the emancipation system,
cultivation will decrease, as was the case in St. Domingo after
it was liberated from French domination. In 1789 the island of
Hayti exported about 70.000.000 lbs coffee, now not over
50.000.000 lbs though it is their only exports whereas in 1789
she exported hhds of sugar. These facts show that the negro
when left to himself, will not labor beyond the supplying the
means of providing the meanest subsistence. Java is perhaps
the country of all others that would rival you in the low cost
of production of coffee, were it not that the Government tax
the farmers enormously and the India Company have a monopoly of it and thus the exportable price is perhaps double
what it would be were the business in a free and natural state,
consequently we only import from Java about 2 @ 3.000.000
lbs costing very high and only used by the more wealthy classes
on account of its dearness. We also import a small quantity of
Java from Holland at a high cost. Another point which bears
favorably on our trade, viz the unexampled increase of population which for the last 10 years has gone on in an increased
ratio & is at the rate of at least 4½%, which at 17.000.000 we
now have or nearly so, is 765.000 p annum, a small portion is
by immigration. Now these at 5 lbs @ head adds nearly
4.000.000 lbs p annum of consumption. Add to this, when our

market is overloaded it soon finds relief from re-exportation and as freights from the Northern Atlantic ports are very low we can lay down the article in Europe at a small addition to the expence of a direct exportation to Europe from Rio, as to the commercial revulsions growing in part from the bad mangement of our currency, & partly from a spirit of speculation prevalent in Europe as well as here, they do not seem to affect consumption, except for very short periods & especially for articles like coffee which is not with us, as in Europe deemed a superfluity, but a common comfort of like within the reach of all the industrious classes whose means of support are never much impaired as they are in a great degree independent of the effects of monetary revolutions which embarrass & ruin so many of the trading community. Indeed as regards the general result of all these crises which appear abroad so ruinous, there are in this country so many natural sources of prosperity that they are but slight abatements of the general welfare which do not arrest the increase of population and the accumulation of national wealth. We have good crops of everything 9 years out of 10, and all the great branches of navigation, commerce, the fisheries, manufactures and the mechanic arts, are for the most part & all the time in as flourishing condition as agriculture. All the facts & circumstances are in favor of pursuing a staple branch of import trade in this country & they are more favorable than exist in any other nation. In respect to currency we have gone through the process of contraction and may not be disturbed again for some 3 or 4 years. The profits on the Eunomus cargo were lost mainly by the contraction of our banks, which took place at the time of landing or before and by raising the rate of interest from 6 @ 7% to 18 & even 24%, of course acted strongly on prices, but for that, there would have been a fair profit, though the quality as I have often written you, was very bad as compared with the Old Colony's. Now the Banks in all the principal states have resumed specie payments or will soon do it & Phila & Baltimore currencies are within 1 @ 1½% in favor of the country & likely so to continue through the year, because our imports have been small, probably below the value of our exports, nor is there any expectation of an over importation for 1841. There is too another circumstance favorable to an increased consumption of coffee which will operate for some time to come, at least, viz the interruption of the China trade, which has gradually advanced the prices of teas in this country from 50 to 100% beyond the usual rate when that trade was open and unobstructed and this of course will induce tea drinkers of the poorer and middling classes to turn off to coffee to a greater or less degree and somewhat in proportion to the augmented rate of teas. The annual consumption of teas is about $3.500.000 @ 4.000.000 cost in China, now an advance of 50% in former rates is an addition to the cost of consumption of about $2.000.000 and this of course must lessen the demand for it. Up to this time but little effect has been produced on the prices of coffee, because it is only of late we have heard of the blockade of Canton, but it will have some effect in the course of time & shortly I think. On the whole I am of opinion the coffee trade with your place if conducted with prudence will always be a saving one and generally a profitable one and the more so since the gambling houses which ruined in 1835 & 1836 have either been ruined or their credits withdrawn & foreign agents who supply letters of credit have become much more cautious than heretofore.

You say in your letter to Mess W. S. B. & H. L jr "We observe that the freight on the coffee on the Messenger is to be ¾¢ & 5% primage which we confess is rather high more particularly as the freight by other vessels could now be readily obtained at ½¢ lb. We however, allude to the subject, that you may be aware of the saving that could almost always be made by giving the preference to European vessels in port, and at the same time avail ourselves of the opportunity that independent of shipts of coffee on adventures originating with you, by the usual mode of placing funds in this place arising from the sale of cotton goods &c, some good business might occasionally offer, were we furnished with letters of credit to be availed of if coffee could be obtained at certain safe limits warranted by the state & prospects of your market, as first class Danish vessels are always obtainable at a rate of freight more favorable than others from ½ ¢ lb to $1 p bag "&c You will no doubt have a reply to what is here said from Mess B & L but in the meantime I beg leave to make the following observations. The voyages undertaken by Mess B & L are not on their own account but with a view of securing commission business and in order to effect that, they are willing to take the trouble & responsibility to hire a vessel & to load a portion of her, but in all cases they wish to have as small an interest as possible, their main purpose being agency business, but such is the competition for it here as well as in Rio that houses are compelled sometimes to participate in adventures as the only means of extending or preserving their business. Such is also the case in your quarter where most of the houses who do business for Americans take shares or surrender what may by some be considered an equivalent, in a return of commissions. The voyages then originate here on the part of a Supercargo or captain who may wish for employment and a commission and to ensure it, is willing to load a part & to get his friends to load another portion & on that basis and a offer of a commission on the returns of perhaps half a cargo he goes to a house to obtain credit & to furnish the balance of a cargo. The amount of it is that the undertaker gets a commission on half a cargo by agreeing to provide the other half and to relieve himself of that responsibility the house which engages the vessel and supplies credit to the Supercargo requires as in your case the person who buys the coffee to load a portion of what he has engaged to supply. Such was the plan of the Messenger's voyage & such also was the Eunomus. The portion you fill, however, pays no commission to Mess B & L inasmuch as they have to pay the Supercargo 2½% on the amount you ship, which nearly counterbalances what is charged in the way of sale commission on your portion of the cargo. You perceive by this what a moderate advantage Mess B & L get for the trouble of hiring a ship, finding credit for a Supercargo & being in advance some months on the return of the vessel, charging but 6%, when the money market is in a state, frequently, to make it worth 8 to 12%.

You are the only party who gets a full commission & without any advance of capital beyond your portion of the cargo and that only for 3 or 4 months. It is obvious then, that the plan of depending on hiring tonnage in Rio will not answer and it is rarely that a first rate safe carrier, that will not damage & of a moderate size vessel, can be had under ¾¢ lb. Shipowners prefer going by the run or by the month but that is an unsafe footing. You say, however, ¾¢ is high compared with transient ships. I have within 8 or 9 years had some 20 or more consignments by transient vessels and in no instance for less than $1 p bag is 62/100ths of a cent instead of 75/100ths. In a bag the difference would be 20¢ which would be lost or nearly all of it in the *extra* insurance that would generally be required in an unknown ship while it is always difficult to insure a foreign one at our best offices without a much higher rate, still to say nothing of delay in passages & damage too little to give us an average, but frequently enough to pay half the freight. I imagine with this explanation you will be satisfied that those who undertake voyages to Rio on the footing Mess B & L do, have a very moderate benefit for their share of labor, responsibility & employment of capital & credit and that a reduction below ¾¢ lb freight is not to be expected & it is not always practicable to obtain a 3000 bag ship at so low a rate, while a larger one is difficult to fill up. On the terms you are now acting with Mess B L. I have no doubt there will be a good & safe business done and to a handsome extent when goods are on a safe a natural basis & prospects for the sale of coffee fair & promising. As I feel an interest in your trade though disengaged from it. I would thank you to send me the "Rio Circular" with an abstract of imports & exports for 1840. I have one June 5 monthly and it contains much useful and interesting information. Are hides a profitable export to the States? I believe most of what you export go to Europe. You remark that a longer time than 30 days stay in Rio would be expedient. I believe it can't be obtained and if it could the disadvantage of delay might not be compensated by a better purchase of coffee, for the price might rise or it might fall. All the information you can at any time afford as to the extent of the coffee crop or the prospects for it will be useful in the pursuit of the business you have in view and particular facts as to the sale & demand for domestic cotton goods . . Are not the goods which come to your market & made in the factories of this state and some of the neighboring ones, say drills, blue & brown, osnaburghs, Denies, Stripes &c superior to what you usually get from Baltimore & Phila and which are manufactured in that quarter?

Yours truly
(Signed)   Henry Lee

LETTER FROM HENRY LEE, BOSTON, JAN. 26, 1841, TO JAMES B. HIGGINSON, CALCUTTA, DESCRIBING GENERAL SITUATION OF COMMERCE AND THE PLANS OF BULLARD & LEE [1]

This letter, which also has to do with Bullard & Lee rather than with Henry Lee's own activities, is uniquely valuable for its analysis of shipping conditions at the time when it was written, as compared with those during Henry Lee's own early years in business. The golden age, when a young supercargo with a reasonably large circle of relatives and friends could, from commission and privilege and with almost no capital, accumulate through one or two successful voyages sufficient funds to set up for himself, was now conclusively over. The supercargo must now not only have a large circle of friends and relatives but should also be possessed of capital. Robert Bennet Forbes mentions that in 1837 he was approached by a "young gentleman" who "said that he could get a situation as assistant supercargo in a ship going to China, provided he could furnish a credit for £2,000." [2] And, after all these requirements had been satisfied, the supercargo must still be satisfied with comparatively small compensation. The merchants who, as owners or charterers, furnished the vessels and expected to sell the return cargoes also suffered through the difficulty of finding shippers or supercargoes to furnish the funds. All this resulted from the trade's having been forced into narrower limits, and competition consequently increased, by the rise,

1. Jackson-Lee Papers, "Letters 1840–41. Henry Lee," Oct. 30, 1840–Dec. 21, 1852, pp. 66–69.

2. Forbes, Robert Bennet, *Personal Reminiscences* (Boston, 1882), p. 141.

assisted by high duties, of American cottons. Competition with England was also severe. The only persons who could now carry on the trade with India were either merchants with large capital or young, energetic, experienced men who were willing to work hard for small returns. In many respects the Calcutta trade was in the same state as that with Rio de Janeiro, particularly as regards the necessity of supplying funds before being allowed to earn a commission, as supercargo or for the purchase or sale of goods.

James Babcock Higginson (1809–55), to whom this letter was addressed, was the younger brother of George Higginson (1804–89), who had married Mary Cabot Lee, Henry Lee, Sr.'s, daughter, in 1832,[3] and was associated in business with Henry Lee, Jr. George Higginson was later one of the organizers of Lee, Higginson, & Co. "Mr [Joseph] Peabody & J[ohn] L[owell] Gardiner [Gardner]," who were among the "few men" who Henry Lee believed would soon be pursuing the trade, were evidently among the leading Boston merchants of their time. Joseph Peabody (1757–1844) "built and owned eighty-three ships, which, in every instance, he freighted himself,"[4] and John Lowell Gardner (1804–83) was "largely interested in the East India and Russian trade."[5]

Orig p "Acadia" Boston. Jany 26. 1841
Dup p "Albion"

James B. Higginson Esq.

 Calcutta

  Dear Sir.

   I have your several letters to the 6th June all relating to the Dalmatia's voyage. I have been expecting to hear what had been done with the uninvested portion of the £2.000, letter of credit I sent you from Mess Baring Brothers &Co which, under limits you were authorised to invest in Raw Silk &Gunny Cloth. I presume the former was too high and for the latter you could not get tonnage. The Dalmatia's voyage for Mr G. Higginson ends well and would have done much and would have done much better in respect to one article, Gunny Cloth,

3. Higginson, *Francis Higginson*, pp. 31, 34–35.
4. Hunt, *op. cit.*, vol. i, p. 380.
5. Gardner, Frank Augustine, *Gardner Memorial* (Salem, 1933), p. 148.

had she arrived 15 or 20 days sooner, it having been sold @ 25¢ provided it was delivered by the 1st of Decr. It fell to 18¢ by the time it arrived and would not now command over 18 @ 19¢ the cotton crop having fallen 500.000 bales below last years. As you may hereafter have something to do in matters of business with Mr W. S. Bullard & HLee jr, who succeed to my business, I only retaining an interest in the consignments from old correspondents it may be satisfactory for you to learn from me something of their pecuniary condition and the principles on which they mean to do business, in order that you may feel that degree of confidence in them which will be useful and agreeable to you in case you may find it for you interest to operate with them. They commenced about 18 mos since with a handsome cash capital considerably increased with a respectable share of commission business. They are under no pecuniary liabilities having had no occasion even to issue a note of hand, but raising the means of advancing on consignments &c out of their capital and the notes they receive on sales of goods consigned them. Their united experience in everything which concerns qualities, sales of India goods is greater than that of almost any persons now in the trade and on the whole they have I think the power to pursue the Calcutta on as good, if not better terms than any person now in competition with them. The "Albion"s voyage has been undertaken in connection with Mr George Higginson who participates in the benefits though to what extent I know not, though to what extent I know not though I dare say he will communicate to you. I think it the best business G. H. can do when acting in connection with a house who have capital and credit and whose attention to business on hand is not led away by too miscellaneous concerns, but on the other hand is confined to business on hand in which they have ample experience. The success which they, I mean the three persons, have met with in filling up the "Albion," is, I think, an evidence of their skill in managing the business, since they commenced under discouraging prospects of obtaining shippers. The trade to Calcutta has of late years changed its character. Formerly a ship with a competent Supercargo, found no difficulty, in procuring independent shippers, and the owner was not obliged to furnish any stock, nor the Supercargo, indeed the latter usually had a privilege of 2% @ 3 or 4% of the ships tonnage and that was all he occupied in the vessel. At that period competition was not so great as now and the adventurers were pretty certain to obtain 10.15 or 20% profit on their adventures and sometimes more. On my last voyage in 1821 I gave them 60% down to 40% according to their articles and the freight was equal on the average to $60 p ton. It fell off in profit and rates declined to $40 . 35 & $25 and then to $20 p ton. It then fell into the hands of shipowners without much capital, who would not allow a Supercargo to go without filling about ½ the tonnage at $20. They would hire a ship that would carry 1000 tons and charge the Supercargo nearly enough for his 500 tons to pay the whole of the expences or nearly so and procure independent shippers to fill the balance or failing of that occupy it on their own account. the freight was free, which on gruff articles was a great profit even when they undersold the $20 shippers. By this arrangement ship owners grew rich and in that way was laid the foundation of some half dozen or more fortunes. The independent shippers who paid $20 lost and most of them withdrew and Supercargoes had to find among their relations and friends persons to take off part of their $20 tonnage. This caused heavy losses and it has now become extremely to make up voyages since Supercargoes who have 500 tons at $5 p ton more than it is really worth in order to get consignment of $60 @ 100.000 do in fact *buy* their voyages too dearly and many of them have suffered greatly. Formerly too when we use to import 150.000 ps of hdfs and 2 @ 3000 Chests of Indigo and Cotton goods, a stock of $150.000 @ 200.000 be made up and thus $4 @ 5000 commissions earned by a Supercargo enabling him to risk some loss on his own tonnage. Now hdfs are almost entirely out of use, superseded by those printed here and by British printed Corahs and the stock now here will last 2 years and when exhausted 20 @ 30.000 ps p year will be enough. Cotton goods are done and as to Indigo the last 10 years — 8 of them have been losing ones, so that with the exception of Mr Peabody. I doubt if any orders go out save now and then for manufacturers. The agents ask the London prices and more and generally speaking we can get our supplies lower from London than here and shipments are now made from that place on consignment. The import trade is now reduced principally to gruff goods and the best article hides, is now so much for by British and French traders than we can no longer expect to gain much upon it or to import ½ our former quantity. As to freights our smallest shippers want tonnage at $14 @ 16 p ton and that will prevent our Supercargo from doing much and the trade will be pursued by few men like Mr Peabody & J. L. Gardiner in their own ships and on their own account with a few Supercargoes who will prevail on their friends to aid them in a business where loss is pretty nearly certain and consequently not much can be done in that way. Now you are aware that such voyages cannot benefit you, as Supercargoes will always be used but the small inducements to go into the trade will enable Mr B. and his associates to get up ships to you with such aid as you may be inclined to afford and such shippers as they can secure here at to freights. In fact it can only be pursued where it is in the hands of experienced, active and young men who are willing to work for a very small compensation, and at the same time stand ready to fill tonnage on their own account to some extent if they can't get rid of it, and also to supply credit to others who will fill tonnage as they do in the case of the "Albion" and as was done in the case of the "Dalmatia," and in all the ships where I have had an interest. The very bad condition of the trade then favors consignments to you, and now and then, there will be periods when from the few ships going, an increased capital can be had. Orders too may perhaps occasionally be procured from manufacturers for Indigo, though usually they are given to some of the connections or acquaintances of the Lowell agents or propietors on the spot to solicit them not with reference so much as to their skill in buying as to favor individuals as you know very well from your acquaintance with the bad principles on which Corporations are managed. I see nothing to encouraged the persons who have usually engrossed the Calcutta freighting trade to go largely into it believing as I do, that they can't get Supercargoes to aid them, nor free shippers on any terms to much extent and even then they must submit to low rates. I believe therefore that Mr Bullard and his associates will be able to get up another voyage as soon as the "Albion" is off and within 3 or 4 months a third one and on such terms as will secure them a moderate commission and you also with a moderate certainty of neither of you losing on such goods as you may be compelled to ship in order to complete the lading. If therefore you should have purchased any goods under the overland, and any accident happen to the "Albion," they can come in the next ship.

Pursuing the business on the principles here pointed out will afford some advantages over Supercargoes who only remain 40 to 60 days (and longer would not be agreed to at such low rates of freights as are now paid). One of them will be that you will have more time to pick up goods. 2nd By giving you 30 days notice overland, many of the goods will be ready on arrival and thus the vessel be despatched in ½ the usual time and it will enable them to hire vessels on more favorable terms. 3rd If you have leisure enough to attend to the details of business as much as our Supercargoes do and must do, as you know, in order to get cheap purchases, you will be able to *under purchase* them and to get favorite articles greatly in demand which they may not have time to collect. 4th The low rates of freight which the concern here are willing to accept though it reduces their profits to a small sum will break down the business of those who have been overdoing the trade and it will become better and more of it will come to you. Therefore the persons carrying it on and getting nearly enough for ½ a ship to pay the whole of one would go to any extent without regard to prospects and now they are stopped. Two houses on one Wharf (India) sent off 9 ships or 10 within 14 mos on this principle though they did not secure so large portion of the freight. This year they can do but little unless they choose to load their own vessels and that they are too prudent to do, and at any rate, do what they may will not prevent the success of the voyages got up in connection with you. In what I have here said I do not consider myself as interfering with the connection between you an Mr Dixwell, as I learn from various and proper quarters that he is willing your business should be done by others and not in any way incommoded and were it otherwise it is only resuming a business prosecuted by Mr G Higginson, before Mr Dixwell had anything to do with you and in the last of which Mr Bullard and myself joined and it could not have proceded without our aid. Mr Dixwell is fully worthy of your confidence and I have no doubt you will continue to act with him and he with you where both of you can be mutually beneficial. Without saying, however, or meaning anything to the disparagement of your agents here I am confident that the three young men, who are now engage in this business of getting up voyages have the means of doing more for you than any one individual and especially as G. H. can devote all his time and the two others most of theirs, and I hope for your sake as well as theirs that you will fall into their views and see what will be the result. The country is now growing so rapidly that the import trade of gruff goods will grow and that is favorable as a glut of goods is so soon get rid of and when it is necessary to hold them for a market it can be done. We are now 17.000.000 increasing 33 1/3% every 10 years. We consume of Saltpetre 2/3^{rds} the amount of Great Britain Ginger more. Lacdye &Shellac 3/4^{ths} to 7/8^{ths}. Hides more. Goat Skins all that can be exported from India. Indigo 1500 to 1800 Chests besides Manilla &Carraccas. In 10 years consumption of each will increase 33 1/3% to 50% and when we have a surplus we get rid of it by exportation as in England even though sometimes at a loss. The most needy holders preferring that convenient method of closing goods to a similar sacrifice by a forced sale at home.   Our currency is getting right and as our exports exceed our imports by $27.000.000 we are clear of our stock of foreign goods and have reason to look forward to a safe and fair business for 18 months to come.

Cotton crop estimated 1.600.000 @ 1.700.000 bales against

2.177.000 last year. Prices 10 to 15% higher than last year with prospect of a further advance. U. S. Bank 54. I fear it is more than it will prove to be worth. It is in bad hands. Of the 900 banks in existence when you left, about 200 have failed — 2 @ 300 more are in discredit and it is to be hoped, will failed and if the others could be reduced to 5 or 10 in each state we should go on pretty well, as they are now managed we may go on for 3 years more before we may again suspend. The state debts are all below par but Massachusetts and she owes but little. The others are selling for 65 up to 90 and New York & Ohio — 92 to 96. We have had no failures of any importance for 6 months in the Atlantic cities, but of the men in trade a large number are in slender credit and would easily break down in any pecuniary crisis. Manufactures in Cotton doing well. I mean the best factories but 2/3rds of them are losing money for want of skill &c

Yours truly
(Signed)   Henry Lee

LETTER FROM HENRY LEE, BOSTON, MAR. 27, 1841, TO J. B. HIGGINSON, CALCUTTA, ON GENERAL BUSINESS [1]

To J. B. Higginson, resident in Calcutta and associated with Henry Lee, Jr., and the latter's partner, W. S. Bullard, in their trade with that port, Henry Lee, Sr., wrote in greatest and most informative detail not of business in general but of that in which his son and himself were actively engaged. It is clear from letters which follow that J. B. Higginson was about as poor a Calcutta agent as Bullard & Lee could have chosen. In the following year Henry Lee, Sr., wrote to his son: "J. B. H. . . . is more & more out of favor with all who have employed him — The business can be pursued with super cargoes to more advantage than thro a man so little to be trusted in as J. B. H. all the Americans from Calcutta say he is wholly unfit for employment, & he will probably end his days there in the service of some of the English houses. . . . I always had a poor opinion of him in all respects latterly He is modeled on the character of his two

---

1. Jackson-Lee Papers, "Letters 1840–41. Henry Lee," Oct. 30, 1840–Dec. 21, 1852, pp. 110–112.

uncles John & Harry — both of whom were a disgrace to their family." [2] The two unfortunate Higginsons pilloried with James Babcock in this condemnation were the mysterious Capt. John Higginson (1765–1818) and Henry Higginson (1781–1838), [3] who had failed in London in 1811 and toward whom Henry Lee had at one time manifested no unfriendly feeling. In this and other similar connections a remark by Mary Lee may prove useful: "when the zeal is up you know the extravagance in yr. father's manner." [4]

The increased specialization in the Calcutta trade is well brought out in this letter. Lee & Bullard were not for the most part importing and exporting on their own account but rather acting as brokers, bringing shippers and shipowners together, disposing of cargo space for the latter and selling the goods imported by the former, receiving returns in the form of commissions, etc., rather than as profits; they were confining themselves principally to one type of business. Henry Lee himself was confining his own business to even narrower limits. He wrote about this time to a Calcutta firm: "I did retire about 15 months ago [that would be at about the end of 1839] from all concerns of business, but I have concluded to hold on to my commission concerns in India, and I am aided in the sales by two young men [Henry Lee, Jr., and W. S. Bullard], who have for a long time been with me. so that in case of indisposition or otherwise, your interests, & others entrusted to me will always have attention." [5]

Orig pr Brighton   Boston Mar 27. 1841

J. B. Higginson Esq
   Calcutta,
      Dear Sir.

     I wrote you pretty fully on the 26th. Jany. in respect to the circumstances of Mr W. S. Bullard & Mr H Lee Jr, who are acting in conjunction with George Higginson in getting up voy-

2. Henry Lee Shattuck Collection, Henry Lee, Sr., Waltham, Aug. 31, Oct. 30, 1842, to Henry Lee, Jr., Paris.

3. *Essex Inst. Hist. Colls.*, vol. v, pp. 40–41; Higginson, *Francis Higginson*, p. 31.

4. Henry Lee Shattuck Collection, Mary Lee, Boston, Feb. 26, 1843, to Henry Lee, Jr., Paris.

5. Jackson-Lee Papers, "Letters 1840–41. Henry Lee," Oct. 30, 1840–Dec. 21, 1852, pp. 117–118, Henry Lee, Boston, Mar. 29, 1841, to Colvin, Ainslie, Cowie & Co., Calcutta.

ages to Calcutta, a business which I think they have greater advantages in pursuing with the aid you can give them, than any persons now concerned in the India trade; Since they have had more experience than most of them, and their attention & capital will be almost exclusively confined to that branch of business. Their purpose is to embark as little as possible of their own property, but to find a compensation in a gain on the tonnage, and in the commissions on the sales of such goods as may be consigned to them, — while you will find a compensation for your trouble in the commissions on the purchase of the return cargoes and on the sales of such goods as their vessel may carry to Calcutta, and which is likely to become of more importance than heretofore. Thus far their management has been fortunate, for in the sales of the Dalmatia's goods they have obtained extreme market rates, while they have closed before the market had become somewhat depressed by the fresh arrivals from Calcutta, I have my doubts whether a like parcel of goods as those pr Dalmatia, could now be sold within 7½ @ 10 pr ct of what they obtained. The Bazar goes consigned to Mess Bagshaw &Co — that being the condition on which the credits are granted by the agent of F. Alexander &Co — the old plan of forcing business when there is little or no capital to bear losses, and which has ruined so many houses in this country & Europe. and which will injure all who act on than plan. Such business might be secured to you, on such. terms, but it would not be worth your having, Gunny Cloth. Linseed & Saltpetre, will comprise ¾ of the cargo of the Bazar, and also of the Sophia, taken up by Mr Saml Austin Jr. The Gen Harrison is taken up by Chandler, Howard &Co. and will also take a good deal of seed for Mr Peabody's oil works in Salem, A duty is now levied on Bagging. and that will discourage some voyages which were in contemplation, but it will not prevent what has been ordered in the Albion & Brighton from paying a fair profit, orders will go by the steamer of 1 April to the consignees of the Bazar, to purchase Bagging. and probably seeds, so than any you may not have secured for your correspondents may be somewhat affected in prices.

Some few weeks since there was a disposition to go largely into the Calcutta trade. but the sudden dulness of business, and the difficulty of realizing goods, arising in a great degree from the uncertain state of the currency every where south of N York, has caused a more prudent feeling, and as I apprehend some who have undertaken the voyage, now in fact regret their engagements I am inclined to the opinion that we shall not have more ships in the Calcutta trade this year than will afford a supply of goods, and the prospects of the Albion & the Brighton, are better than any other on account of their having anticipated the Spring fleet. Some months hence, I think another voyage may be undertaken on safe terms. The country having for the past 3 years had fine crops, is in an excellent condition to consume, and to pay for goods, and but for the disordered condition of the currency there is no doubt we shall have had a very active business this spring. There will, I think, be a revival of business in August, for let the currency be as it may, people will have goods if they have the means of paying for them. The universal feeling in N York & here is that New England & New York, will, in any event maintain specie payments. and that Philadelphia, though she may not resume for 12 months, will not allow her banks to issue largely, so as to depreciate the value of their paper, below its present rate of 4 pct. There have been but few failures the past 15 months, and as goods, here, too low to fall much, and as the trading community have been prudent, I do not look for many failures this year, and more especially here, and in New York. Some of the London houses, who have loaned largely on American Bank & State stocks may be ruined, and still more, be greatly injured. and I hope as prudent men of capital must see the danger of furnishing credits to men without capital, that trade will henceforth be on a safer, and more stable footing than it has been since 1834.

There is good deal said about a war with England in the papers, but in the opinion of the most intelligent men, I see — there is no danger of such an event. England would be averse, and so are we on general principles. and more especially. as regards the enormus cost, such a state of things would involve. and the bad financial condition of the U States.

Our National debt, when the accounts are settled may be 20 or 30.000.000, while our usual revenue, will be for 2 years to come 5 and probably $10.000.000 below the *peace* expenditure. There is an aversion to raising the duties, or imposing any new ones, and the extra session of Congress is called mainly for the purpose of creating a loan for $20.000.000. to pay the current expenses of the government. I have given up all concern in business, save an interest in consignments of India goods. If you can throw any in my way, or in the way of W. S. Bullard & George Higginson &C. I hope you will do it. We are prepared to make free advances on all current articles, and if there are persons, who will ship hides & other gruff articles, & will authorise me to secure tonnage here, I can do so at a saving rate of 3 to 4$ ton which on coarse goods is a profit, Salt petre is 6 @ 6¼ for prime, not likely to be any higher, Hides are falling. Shellac 11 to 14¢ for liver, and ordinary orange. and 18 to 20 for Campbells. Lacdye 18 @ 25¢ — stock heavy and prices lower in England than in Calcutta. Ginger 4½ stock heavy. Gunny Cloth 19 to 20 cts, will probably advance in August, — Indigo 130 to 185¢ — no prime here. Our sales of this article for the past 12 months have been very large. principally received from London. The Java now interferes in Europe with E India, and will still more so as the cultivation is rapidly extending and the quality found to be excellent. None comes this way, but Holland & Germany use it freely.

Yours truly

(Signd)   H. Lee

LETTER FROM WILLIAM S. BULLARD, BOSTON, JULY 1, 1842, TO HENRY LEE, JR., LONDON, WITH DESCRIPTION OF GENERAL BUSINESS CONDITIONS, THE RESULTS OF PAST VOYAGES, AND PLANS FOR A VOYAGE TO RIO DE JANEIRO [1]

Henry Lee, Jr., junior partner in the firm of Bullard & Lee, had sailed from New York, Apr. 11, 1842,[2] on a belated grand tour of Europe; he had the good fortune on the voyage of making the acquaintance of Washington Irving, who was on his way to represent the United States at Madrid. During his absence, his father Henry Lee, Sr., and his partner William S. Bullard frequently informed him on the general course of business, the prices of stocks and merchandise, the results of earlier voyages, and the plans for others still in prospect.

In a letter of Apr. 30, Bullard compared the results of several previous voyages. The loss on a recent cargo of coffee imported from Rio de Janeiro and bagging shipped to New Orleans would probably equal "the profit on the Albion," which had apparently earlier brought coffee from Rio. At Calcutta there was a loss of about $1,200 on cotton goods shipped to that place and a probable loss of $800 on copper. "The Charlemagne's outward Cargo" — apparently on a voyage to Calcutta — "was disposed of without loss — & she has a freight of about 4000$ profit." There would probably be a loss of about $2,000 on her return cargo of saltpetre, gunny cloth and gunny bags, hides, ginger, etc. Of the *Brighton's* cargo, recently arrived from Calcutta, only a few hides had been sold. "No demand for Cal[a]. goods."

Each voyage in which Bullard & Lee were concerned involved multiple possibilities for both loss and profit. The outward cargo might sell at a loss and so might Bullard & Lee's goods on the return cargo, and yet the voyage as a whole be successful because of freight and commissions on goods consigned to the Boston firm. On May 16, Bullard wrote: "The Oaks Voyage has resulted in a heavy loss — on your 200 bags $941.95 — on my 309 bags 1455.[33] on the Albion — the profit on freight to your credit is 1,400[60] . . . The *goods* p Brighton will leave some loss, but the freight will exceed 6000$ — which will leave a nett profit of at least 4000$—" On July 18, 1842,

1. Henry Lee Shattuck Collection.
2. *Ibid.*, Mary Lee, Boston, Apr. 11, 1842, to Henry Lee, Jr., London.

Henry Lee, Sr., wrote: "W. S. B. has got rid of 2/3 of his coffee most of it for cash & at prices that will save nearly or quite all your com-[missions] Stephen has not yet reached N. O — prices not quite so good as here but they may improve & save S. & W. S. B. whose comm is small." The references to profit on various voyages in the letters below must be considered in the light of the above remarks.

The proposed voyage to Rio by J. C. Rogers was to be made on the *Robin Hood*. "Young H. Oxnard," jocularly referred to as "the victim," was evidently to go on the vessel and was to ship 700 bags of coffee, receiving his passage as one of the compensations for furnishing this proportion of the funds for the cargo. Bullard & Lee were going to have to furnish a part, but, they hoped, only a small part of the return cargo and were to have the privilege of selling, on commission, a much larger number of bags to be shipped by others. On Aug. 3, Henry Lee, Sr., announced: "He [Bullard] has embarked in Rogers' voyage to Rio ships 500 or 700 bags for a consignment of 3000 — "

Bullard & Lee hoped to be able to avoid the necessity of furnishing any goods for the outward cargo to Rio, which probably consisted for the most part of cotton textiles. A principal reason for the voyage to Rio, we find below, was the fact that Bullard & Lee were in advance both to Miller, Le Cocq & Co., of Rio, and to J. C. Rogers, the prospective supercargo of the *Robin Hood*; a voyage would place in the hands of Bullard & Lee coffee belonging to the Rio firm and Rogers' commissions as supercargo, which property could be used to liquidate debts due to Bullard & Lee. The comment of Henry Lee, Sr., on Aug. 3, was that Bullard "will have Rogers' comss on 4000 bags say $2000 — to increase the security ag^t any loss by over advances on his former voyage — you participate in the voyage as in all the business undertakings since you left — " The belief of Henry Lee, Sr., three months later, Oct. 30, was that the "Rio voyage of Rogers," which was not to terminate for six weeks, "promises to be a saving one."

Henry Lee, Sr., also commented on the Calcutta side of Bullard & Lee's business, which had apparently been badly mishandled by J. B. Higginson. On Aug. 16, Bullard wrote: "The Copper in Cal^a has been sold by brother Higginson @ 27/ — what think you — loss about 1,250 with [?] 300 more — instead of a profit of 1000$ which we sh^d. have realized had the 1st offer been accepted." Higginson, Henry Lee, Sr., reported in a letter of July 18, had "left

Calcutta for up country. So much the better for all who did business with him — Bullard is getting rid of his Calcutta goods — A loss of perhaps $1500 (½ G[eorge] H[igginson]'s) on the Areatus voyage — Commiss on goods & on Woods goods will more than make up the loss to you — "

On Aug. 3, Henry Lee wrote: "You [Bullard & Lee] have a consignment of about $3000 from J. P. Higginson — Calcutta goods & on the whole your comss. acc^t. will I think stand well at the end of the year." Bullard's comment on the same subject, Nov. 1, was: "We have . . . a consignment of goods from M^r. J. P. H. — who rec^d. them from J. B. H. but Mr J. P. apprehending that the cash duties & the advances would be more than convenient for him to make — solicited our taking the consignment. The goods belong to A Day, C Day Bux & c. & 510 bags S Petre to Gisborne & C — The bulk of the goods have been sold — &we shall have 9 or 1,000 dolls in Com^s & guarantee — provided we lose nothing by bad debts."

On Oct. 30, Henry Lee, Sr., wrote: "W S B has closed up many concerns — losses of 10 20 or 25 % which is well. He could not now do so well by 5 or 10 % on many articles — your profits less than I expected still I dont believe there is a comss house in Boston who on the same scale has done so well — a good deal of the loss on the Calcutta concerns — in abatement of profits often may fairly be ascribed to the negligence and incapacity of J. B. H. but you will soon be clear of him — & he will be clear of his own business — having incurred the distrust or dissatisfaction of all who have employed him . . . The *Areatus* will finally earn a small sum for you & you will gain $2000 on comiss on consignments in hand or sold in on the way of Woods & others — "

It will be observed that W. S. Bullard, unlike his former partner Henry Lee, Sr., inclined to the protectionist side of the tariff controversy; he was confirmed in this attitude by the fact that he had on hand a quantity of coffee, the price of which would be raised by a duty.

My dear Harry,   Boston, July 1.st 1842.

Thanks for your letter of the 31^stMay. I am glad tolearn that you have enjoyed so much pleasure in the acquaintance of Mr Irving & thro' him, that of so many other distinguished & agreeable persons.

I hope you may continue tofall in with those who will add

toyour pleasure &instruction. A mind &heart [interlineated: like yours] must find in almost every spot in England something of interest and sympathy. for has not almost every inch of ground its story? Stephen is at home — at the Co House — He desires me to thank you for y^r. rememberance ofhim — &wishes me to give you his best regards., He is uneasy but Ihope in bods tosee my way clear for a Voyage to Cal^a. for him

At present our plans are few — a voyage to Rio forRogers has been proposed &the conditions are such as will make it safe &profitable for us towrite in — Young H Oxnard is the victim in this case — He is toship 6to 700 bags. in lieu of passage money. we shall have tofurnish some funds but not en^o. toembarrass us. we shall get the consignment ofabout 2000bags with ample security against loss. The last acc'ts from Rio show a heavy stock of Coffee low prices &some improvement in Cottens.

The prospects are fair for an outward Cargo. but Ishall not, as a rule of action, take any interest in it if it can be avoided — It is possible we may be toa small extent implicated. but rather than go to a larger am't than 2 @ 300 bags Ishall abandon the Voyage. Ihave consulted with your father — on y^r a/c. &he thinks rather more favorably of it than I do. &is willing tointerest you, which Ishould not have done without his consent. There are some considerations that toa degree influence me [somewhat — stricken through] in undertaking this operation — We have advanced largely toMiller &Co on their shipts ofCoffee — &altho they might &undoubtedly w^d. be, ready torefund any deficiency that may accrue on winding up their consignments, it w^d be as well tohave a further shipment from them the proceeds of which might be applied with the most perfect propriety — In regardto Rogers — I have for a long time been of the opinion that there w^d. be, without circumstances should happen ofa character much more favorable for his interest than can reasonably be anticipated, a balance due us of from 1000to1,500 $. Should this voyage go on Roger's com^s will come into our hands say 7 or 800 $ nett, which may be appropriated towards paying any loss there me [?] be on winding up our accts with him, — Orders will be given for the best description of Coffee as I am inclined to think that the losses on shipments to N Orleans the last year have been so great &the houses that have operated have been so crippled & dismasted, that but few voyages will be undertaken to terminate at that quarter. There are but few Houses left in N Orleans. None of them have credit. Stetson &A have been reported to have stopped several times — Some of their paper is now unpaid. Their credit is gone — none here w^d trust them — They are deeply involved. have lost a great deal of money &many think they are ruined — Our G Cloth is not yet sold. S & A have written that it will probably improve in the fall &say they will hold it if we will refund the advance made by them, which I have agreed to do to the extent of 4,500 making our whole liabilities with them 8000

How do you feel? "Never was there known so much commercial distress," is a hackneyed sentence. but it is as true if not truer now than it ever was before. I am free to confess that I have never experienced so unsettled. dull confused. state of Commercial affairs — as have existed for the last 60days. There is a want of confidence in the Value of Mdze that cuts off all purchases except but for immediate use — To force goods on the market is to throw them away. There have been many failures — some large — in N Y Bal & Phila & here Since I wrote to you last — S. F. Nain — (col^e.) Mack Healey Wm Tucker &Sons. H Blackfield — S H Babioch. J. Houghton &Co & others of less note. The dividends will be small indeed — Houghton &Co have involved Capt Heard, it is said to the extent of 60, or 70,000 $. I do not vouch for the accuracy of this report, but the sum is large &he must lose heavily We have not as yet had a single blow — &are as smug as can be — Our prospects with all are fair. The Charlemagne has arrived &her cargo has been dischg^d — We shall make on our share of the fright 2,800 $ — Brighton about 2800 more — The prospects for the Areatus are excellent — we shall save as well as can now be calculated, about 3000, — Our Rio business will yield at least 2500 — &Woods consignments will give 1500 more — in all for the next

10 Mo say 12.600 $. It would be unreasonable not toexpect some losses — but if we make an allowance of 2800$ still we have a very handsome sum. Should the voyage in contemplation to Rio go on our gains will be increased, — There is great uncertainty in turning over so much property, but Ithink you may be assured that your profits will be equal toyour expenses in Europe & this I think sh^d Satisfy you — taking all things into view. I am not at present anxious todo a large business — Our Credit would be more or less affected by it — but if any good oppy offers for a safe operation Ishall not hesitate tounder-take it. Out of the Charlemagnes Cargo we have sold about 6000$ worth of goods. at fair prices — Some ofthe Hides &SPetre prBrighton have also been disposed of — We have rem^g about 35.000 Cost ofCal^a. goods — The chances are in favor of better prices than are at present obtainable &we shall wait till Congress has adjourned — Nothing can be done in way of sales till then — Isend you a Courier Cong all the com^l & polit-ical news ofthe day. You will notice that President Tyler has vetoed the bill proposing toextend the rates of duties existing in June tothe 1 Augt — The accts were rec^d this m^g — The popu-lar voice is extravagant with abuse — I do think this course was uncalled for — but I am not sure but that the effect will be *be good* — If the bill hadbecome a law for 30days — it might have been extended for 6mo. or longer — Cutting off all hope ofarevenue bill Commensurate with the wants ofthe gov't & leav-ing Tea & Coffee free — Ihope now, that the necessity of a revenue is becoming more &more apparent — that the numbers will be willing for the sake of doing something yield some of their party prejudices & unite in making a law that at the same time it will protect toa reasonable extent the man^g interests — /now languishing & breathing short breaths/ will give an income equal tothe Govt expenses — We look for reasonable things. but they came not — our hopes fail us &the heart grows sick — Ifeel discouraged — I confes about our Coffee &that after all there will not be a duty.

By this conveyance Ihave sent to F A &Co a letter of credit by which you can at any time overdraw the am't in their hands

£200 — This I have thot it well toget toserve in case Ishould send a bill that may prove tobe a badone, or you should unexpectedly want funds, which you may do, if you get into any of the *"Hells"* either in *London* or Paris — were I you — Ishould not hesitate tolook into the infernal regions £10 spent in this way will do no harm. Your father was in town yesterday & left the enclosed letter. While upon the subjectoffunds Ishould have mentioned that in addition tothe balance of 38 £ left with F. A&Co the last date — Iremitted 3 packets since a bill for 110-£ 10ds sight — leaving a fund of 148.£ todraw against — By the 16th*inst* packet Ishall send 100 £ more — as it is my intention that youshall not have tocall on F A&Co for a shilling in advance. The Cr is sent toserve in caseof accident — but you will understand that this contigency is not the condition of the credit — you *Can* use it if you please at any time — I notice what you say of Kerr — He is of a crabbed disposition — at least Ithink there were Several instances of it while he was in this Country — The House have lost largely by their banking a/c Healy Owes them 80,000 — but it is thot there is ample security — did I mention that Healeys debts were 500,-000 — The factories have 20.000 —

Young Chadwick &George Gardner have united with J Read& formed a concern — G.G is a special partner &has put 30,000 in cash — Chadwick &Readare gen'l partners &c has put in 30,000 more making a handsome capital of 60,000 — It is a poor arrangement — MrRead cannot succeed with his speculative disposition. & chadwick cannot influence him. C's notions of business must be too extensive — having been brot upin a concern selling 3 or4,000.000 p an — he will think 500,-000 a small matter — I must close — How do you like *Pats* engagement toMiss Loring.   Sincerelyours   W.S.B

[Addressed to:]
pr Brittania Steamer
Mr Henry Lee jr,
Care of Mess Fletcher Alexander&Co,
London.

LETTER FROM WILLIAM S. BULLARD, BOSTON, JULY 16, 1842, TO HENRY LEE, JR., PARIS, WITH AN ACCOUNT OF THE DEATH OF THE WRITER'S BROTHER ON THE WEST COAST OF AFRICA [1]

Although the episode, a description of which occupies most of the letter below, has no direct relation to the commerce of the Lees, it is nevertheless interesting as a revelation of one of those major hazards in the African trade which made that form of commerce so highly speculative, and helped deter cautious merchants, such as the Lees and P. T. Jackson, from participating in it directly. It was under the menace of such a fate as overtook Capt. John Bullard and six of his crew, that African traders disposed of the colored cottons which P. T. Jackson and the Lees imported from Calcutta and Madras.

The last paragraph of the letter below contains further details concerning the prospective voyage of the *Robin Hood* to Rio.

My Dear Harry,   Boston 16July 1842

I wrote to you by the Steamer ofthe 1stinst. since which no letters have been recd from you — altho we hearindirectly — thro MrMackillop — that you were probably at Glasgow about the last of June — I hardly know how to fill my sheet with matter tointerest you — Since my last I have recd one ofthe heaviest blows that could possibly fall on me — the intelligence ofthe death of my brother John on the Coast of africa — at the port of Angola — After leaving Rio he had a violent attack ofthe Dysentary — which lasted till he arrived at Benguela the 1stport on the coast towhich he was bound.

In the weak state he was left by the dysentary — he over exerted himself on shore — [blot] a violent fever [interlineated: set in] which endedin the black vomit — his liver was much affected & all his organs more or less badly diseased — Before leaving Benguala he had in some measure recoverd his strength tho' not his health — While on the passage from Benguela to Angola — he was well enough towalk the deck — On his arrival at Angola — he had a relapse. &he was confined on shore about 10days. with the object of having medical attend-

1. Henry Lee Shattuck Collection.

ance, such as could be got. Finding that there was no chance of recovery — he was carried on board the ship — where he lived about 10days — The fever had consumed him — He died on the 7th May last — His sufferings were great — both in body &mind The mate & crew were sick — 6 ofthe latter died — 2 of 11 passengers died on board & 3 or4 more on shore The last few hours of his life — he was perfectly rational cheerful &resigned — No complaint was known — to escape him — other than that of asking in prayer tobe taken into the arms of his Saviour — just after this exercise he desired the mate tomove him &while he was in the act of lifting him, his headfell over on his shoulder & his spirit fled — no groan — no struggle — no more.

He was buried at Angola — The ship returned to N York immediately after discharging her cargo in accordance with instructions given tothe mate by John before he died — This was most judicious as all the papers were in his name — with discretionary orders — which could not have been properly executed by the mate — The crew were sick — The mate the only navigator on board &his health very poor — Under these circumstances it was thot by him proper to order the Vessel home — The owners are satisfied that this was the best course to pursue — The 1stintelligence was by the Ship with the news of the Capts Death in the paper — Never did I feel so completely in the dust as then — His death, is not so distressing tomy mind as the tho't that he may have sufferd from wantof attention in those many little things — which when administerd by a friendly hand — &asympathizing heart relieves both Soul &body — these arethe thoughts that contain the poison — On the other hand — these [interlineated: are] reflections of comfort — the condition of life is death — he has sufferd & died — &is now happy — far happier than he could have been on earth — He has left a good name — respected by those who knew him best. & a memory dear tohis brothers &intimate friends —

Stephen has been quite unwell — is gaining strength slowly — He has been troubled with the Summer Complaint — So

soon as he is a little stronger Ishall try toinduce him togo down
to Phillips beach for a week ortwo torecruit — Your father was
in town a few days since — he has had a bad headache — but is
now much better — By this steamer Iremit to F A &C 100£
more for your a/c — making in all 348£ against which you have
advised me of having drawn 100£. By the last steamer Ifor-
warded to F A &Co a letter of Credit in your favor for 200£
which you could draw for at any onetime after taking up the
whole am't standing to our credit. Rogers will go toRio in
the [R H — stricken through] Robin Hood — We shall have
the consignment ofabout 3000 bags — we may be compelled
to take 3 or 400 bags on our own a/c — we may get rid of
it —   Sincerely yours
                                              W.S.Bullard
              [Addressed:]
              Mr Henry Lee junior
              Care of Mess Rothschild Bros &Co
              Paris.

LETTER FROM WILLIAM S. BULLARD, BOSTON, APR. 1, 1843,
TO HENRY LEE, JR., PARIS, DESCRIBING THE RESULTS OF
VARIOUS VOYAGES [1]

The *Robin Hood,* J. C. Rogers, supercargo, had arrived from Rio,
Dec. 17, 1842, and the bark *Wave,* Stephen Bullard, supercargo, returned from Rio by way of New Orleans, arriving at Boston, Jan. 8,
1843.

The *Areatus,* from Calcutta, had arrived, Jan. 20, 1843. "Mr J P H's
funds that had been appro for the pur of 200 tons goods — had been
misapplied — &we consequently are *'in for it'* to that extent — We
shall not lose by the Voyage *on the whole* — the profits on charter
will meet the loss on the goods — we shd have saved something had
she left Cal — prior to 1 Spt — she sailed on the 15th. & consequently comes under the high tariff (25$) ton [on jute] in spite of
which Higg has put on bd *240 tons for us* we have sold it to arrive @
60$ s[hort?] price — which will give us 500$ frieght for 240 tons.
say 2$ p ton — The cash duties on the por cargo [interlineated: to

1. Henry Lee Shattuck Collection.

us] will be *6,000$*. Charter — 15,000 — &c." [2] By the time of the letter below, it seems a total loss of $1,000 was expected.

The ship *Sophia* had arrived from Calcutta, Feb. 21, 1843.

Observe that in all the below-mentioned voyages the commissions on goods handled for others outweighed the losses on goods which they imported and sold on their own account.

My dear Harry;   Boston, 1st April 1843.

Your pleasant letter of the 23 Decr /the last [in margin: but not the last date Yr financial letter was recd on the 20 Feby] I have recd from you/ reached me on the 2 ndMch. I am glad you are not much troubled at the prospect of losing money — at least yr letter would indicate as much — but I suppose most of us *feel* what we are not disposed sometimes to express. It is undoubtedly unsatisfactory & discouraging — but the losses to you in yr commercial interests will not be greater, if so great, as the depreciation of Stocks — of which you are unfortunately the holder —

My own impression is that we shall more than hold our own — Our severest loss will be on the shipt. G Cloth to Stetson — say 4.500 — Sales of the bulk have been made @ 13½¢ — &they write in a letter to us recda few ds since that for the remg 40 bales on our a/c — they do not expect to get more — altho the article [here — stricken through] is worth here 15¢ — We sold a few days ago at that price — &expect to get more for the balance of what we purchased 2 mos ago on speculation — out of which we shall save 300$ —

We have Woods's &Ballards's goods p Sophia on hand. the gross sales of which will am't to say 30.000$ — we have also about 5000$ on Consignment from the Clerk of the sophia (Adams) — The Areatuss a/cts are not yet made up — the aggregate loss will be about 1000$ — a fair result for so large a transaction — Our Coffee operations have resulted as well as could be expected —

The loss to Miller&C prR Hood — was about 2% over the

2. *Ibid.*, W. S. Bullard, Boston, Jan. 1, 1843, to Henry Lee, Jr., Paris.

Com^s chargedby them on their own shipt — leaving them with nearly ¾ of the whole Com^s on sales ofgoods outw^d & investment homeward

Rogers loss — 450 — Matchel 180$ — ours 430$ — Onthe other hand we get from Rogers — 1900 Com^s. togo tohis Credit in a/c — our own Com^s &guarantee — onthe whole voye say 2100 — less loss — is 1.670$ This is well — The accts have been made up &the balance due M&C remitted — The Wave's. Voye has not yet been closed — We have remg 700 bags — ona/c Miller Stephen& ourselves — there will be some loss on the sales tobe made hereafter — what has been sold leaves a profit. The article has declined fully ½¢ lb within 30ds — Wehave been lucky in our sales — Shaw has nearlyall the Coffee p "Morleans" on hand — & I am afraid it will remain for some time. The abundance of money & the improvement in Stocks &some indications of amendment in commercial matters generally may have the effect of Carrying up prices of Mdse & Coffee may feel the general improvement —

Miller &Co have expressed their satisfaction ofthe management oftheir coffees p I S W & M.O. toS Higginson &also to us — I am inclined tothink that badas [was — stricken through] the result was — their shipts to Europe showeda heavier loss.

Our Com^s &guaranteea/c is now in the aggregate 4.900$ from which we should deduct say 2000$ forall baddebts — Etting BroderCo — Townsend&c) — to accrue on sales ofgoodson hand — fully — 2000$ — say Com^s &guar 6,900 — less 2000 losses by bad debts — against this a/c — we have thelosson GCloth in No. Areatus a/c 1000$ — If we make both ends meet shall we not do pretty well? — It is possible we may save the int on our capital — togo toward our Expenses —

Since I last wrote toyou Ihave effected anarrangement with W^{m}H Foster to furnish him with funds tothe extent of 2/3rd the Value of property he may put into our hands — further toact as agent for him while he remains in Cal^a. He sailed from onthe 29 Mch in the Sophia — as super cargo — His desire is to establish himself at Cal^a. &as he has Character &capacity & *capital* to the extent of 15 @ 20.000$ — he will be a safe person to act with — We are authorized totake for him an interest of ¼ — in vessels that will gotohis consign't — &the condition is that the room we secure for him is tobe filledwith goods to our consign't — We are not under obligation to ship a dollar — but oftentimes there may beoccasions when it w^dbe proper for us to embark moderately.

He must have an assistant —♀ this is necessary to insure that confidence in the adventurer orship owner who may bedisposed to sendto him — that the business will be attended to even in caseof death to Foster& for this purpose we propose to sendI. C. Rogers out in about 6ods as super cargo — *jointly with M*^r*F.* if R joins F — if not — then Rogers will take the whole-risk of S Cargoes portion & allthe Com^s. We have not fully matured all the details oftheplan — We have furnished £3.500 for investment pSophia — to our consignment on a/cof others — ample security against any deficiency —

Stephen is on his way home from N.O. with HOxnard & Son — may be here in 10ds — He will lose about 75¢ bag on his interest toNo — say 200$ — onthe Wave — say 200$ more — Com^s may amt to1.400 — will leave him nett about 1.000$ — this is as well as he could havedonein any other business — &much better than mostof the supcargoes this year.

His coffee onhis &my a/c — 470 bags — has been sold — &remitted pr this was done by Stephen before he left N.O — The losses on Cargoes toarrive from Rio will be heavy — say 1½ @ 2¢ lb — We thinkof setting up another voyage —!—

Have you an *idea* ofwhen youshall be on yr way home? I donot like towritetoyou abouthe details ofbusiness — as it will beofno Int of use toyou — & consequently youwill pleaseconsider the above remarks as indicating the general features of our operations — allwell YourstrulyW.S.B [written across face of letter] Since y^r. letter ofthe 29 Jany — showing abalance infavrF. A&C — of 78.2.10 — which included your dftfor 60 £ — we have remitted to F A&Co — £ 390..= this will Isuppose

be as much as you will require — at any rate Ishallnot remit
further ony^{r}a/c till Ihear from you

> [Addressed]
> M^{r}Henry Lee jr
> Careof Messrs Rothschild Brothers
> Paris.

[Stamped] Packet Letter
[Postmarked] J 16AP16 1843

LETTER FROM WILLIAM S. BULLARD, BOSTON, JULY 15, 1843,
TO HENRY LEE, JR., PARIS, WITH DESCRIPTIONS OF VOYAGES
IN PROGRESS [1]

The voyage to Calcutta by the *Woodside* had been considered since
at least Apr. 1, on which day Bullard mentioned his intention of
sending out J. C. Rogers, as supercargo, to join William H. Foster,
who had sailed for Calcutta on the *Sophia*. Foster and Rogers were
doubtless expected to act as agents for Bullard & Lee in the place of
the inefficient J. B. Higginson. Observe that American cottons were
being shipped to Calcutta.[2]

A reorganization of the company and the countinghouse force had
been outlined in a letter of Apr. 30, 1843, from Bullard. "My desire
is, that he [Stephen Bullard] should, after going another voye (shd
we see our way clear to save Com^s.) come into the Co H. & be interested in the business of the concern — Ch^s. [H. Bailey] is inclined
to go to India — altho he agreed to remain with us 1 Year @ 500$ —
from last Jany — & he may go in the winter or Spring of '44 —
Stephen can take charge of the Books & attend to the internal concerns of the CoHo — You will do the Correspondence with the
London India Houses & other things too numerous to mention at this
time, details — details, & I will 'beat the bush' — what do you say —
I know you are too sincere not to speak plainly on this subject —
Let me hear from you — I feel it to be my duty to assist Stephen —
I think he will be of use to us — & that his services will be valu-
able . . . You can think of this proposition &when you come home
we can easily arrange it — what say you to a regular firm B.L. & Co —

1. Henry Lee Shattuck Collection.
2. *Ibid.*, Henry Lee, Sr., Waltham, May 15, 31, June 15, 1843, to
Henry Lee, Jr., Paris.

we know each other pretty well. There are some inconveniences about our present business connection — w'h by making afirm w^d be wholly obviated."

On July 31, Bullard announced the dispatch of the *Lion* to Rio for coffee. "Our interest is very small say 250 bags we get the consign^t of 750 — Some profit on Millers shipt in f't — We have executed an order for Cottons from M & Co am^g to 10,200 $ — The goods have been sent out in the L — & the proceeds of the cottons will be used safely — so that the risk is small — Wm Perkins & Shaw & Co take 2/3^{rds} of the vessel home — M & Co & ourselves the balance. . . . Our next operation will be to Cal^a. Not immediately however."

The ship *Sidney* sailed for Calcutta late in October with Charles H. Bailey on board as supercargo; the vessel and cargo were consigned to Foster & Rogers.[3]

Boston 15thJuly 1843 —

My dear Harry,

Your letter of the 24 apl & 1 May — also that of 1st June date — came duly tohand — The 1st giving a very interesting account of the ceremonies ofthe Church ofRome during Holy Week. This letter has been read by many of y^r friends &they have expressed their gratification — HowlandShaw among the number. The last letter had attached toit a mem^o. of sundries — shipped or tobe shipped tothis country — amtg to 150$ — pr Co Ho — actual cost you state tobe more — Ins has been effected with general liberty valuing the amt @ 250 $ — V or Vs [?] — from one or more port or ports in Europe toU.S. When these articles arrive your directions shall be carefully compliedwith — For yr kind attention to my request, in purchasing the Cameos I thank you — I have no doubt they are well selected — in good taste — &perhaps beautiful — Ishould feel certain that they were had not you named the very low prices at which you bo't them — Let me know in yr next by what vessel you send the packages that we may be on the look out for them — The manner in which you appear toentertain

3. *Ibid.*, William S. Bullard, Boston, Oct. 16, 1843, to Henry Lee, Jr., London.

my proposition to have Stephen join us is very grateful tome —
There will be no difficulty in making our arrangement that will
be satisfactory & beneficial toall concernd — In regardtoour
business operations — which is the only subject on which I
can — with any interest toyou — write — Most of our under-
takings look well prospectively — The Woodside sailed on the
22 Ulto — outward freight about 4000 $ — profits on charter
— about as much more — say 8000 $ in all — & her prospects
are good — The outward cargo Mdze amt^d to 78.000 $ — of
which we shipped $ 36.000 in Copper Drills — ColoredCottons
Mahogany Candles &c — There is no reason why with our
Com^s &c we should not make $ 10,000 on this voyage — My
dear Harry you may think me over sanguine — but these
figures are the result of an elaborate calculation of Com^s.
chances prospects &c — The details w^d not be agreeable toyou
toread — or for me towrite about — The copper ab't 90.000
cost but *16^{ct} — 3%* off — Drills — 6¼ — 4½% off —
&othergoods in proportion — The prospects for the Sophia are
good — we shall have goods [interlineated: by her] that will sell
for fully 40.000 $ — on which we shall get a Com^s &guarantee
5% — Stephen left here for Rio in the Bg Ottawa — on the
7th inst for a cargo of Coffee — 4000 bags — to return here —
We charterd the vessel for 2,550 $ — Miller gives us 1000 $ for
1000 bags — leaving say 1600 $ — for freight 3000 bags —
which we have orderd on our owna/c — You may deem this
risky — Stephens interest in the whole voyage of this [ship —
stricken through] Vessel as well as the *Woodside* — in the fitting away of which ship he was of great use tous — is as follows
— We pay his actual expenses (*board*) at Rio — He turns in
all his Com^s togeneral a/c — & takes such interest in thefinal
result as may be hereafter agreed on — guaranteeing that it
shall not be less than 1/5th. The idea is that he shall have the
same interest in these voyages as he may hereafter have in our
general business — The truth is I considerd it ofgreat importance tohave the cargoCoffee well selected & I think he under-
stands it pretty well — We have just made up all the Waves
accounts — The loss on Stephen' & our interest — in all 600

bags — is but 13 \$ — *2¢ p* bag & we get Com^s on Millers 575 &
the 600 — say in all \$ 624 — this is doing pretty well — it is
the best *result ofCoffee* since the Messenger — Our market is
now bare ofCoffee & a cargo would do well — We have pro-
videdfunds forthe Ottawa \$ 16,000 in gold — doubloons —
\$15.73 — last quotation at Rio M R 31.900 — less than 50¢
M R — We hadsome notes 6 & 8 Mo — which we got disctd @
the rate of 4% p an!!! All the charges. including freight *insurance* out &home & 12 Ms interest will not exceed 13⁰.¢ bag
— this is very low — the guarantee sh^d be added — 1⁶⁰. in
all — E Austin has offerd me 1¢ lb — for freight — *ins out &
home* — on 500 bags which I have refused — the prospects are
such as give a reasonable hope that we shall make 1½ @ 2¢ lb
on the Rio Cost — Since the ottawa sailed this market has been
swept of Rio — with the exception of about 900 bags held by
Gardner — 7½ @ 8¼ — are the rates for fair & prime — I
wish we were to receive 10.000 bags this fall &next spring

Your Father has grown prudent — or I have grown very imprudent — he thinks our prospects good forthe coming 12 Mo —
We have forwarded all our accts toRio &made all our remittances — [Most of — stricken through interlineated: All]
the goods we have rec^d on consg't from Cal^a. [interlineated:
Houses] [in margin: we mean consignments from Calcutta
Houses] have been sold & we shall make the final remittances
by the Gentoo tosail on the 20th. We have on hand about 100
bales Hides on Woods & Ballards a/c — theywill go off during the fall & at fair prices — tho' not at the cost — our 12
Months work w^d have resulted — on the whole very well —
hadit not been for that infernal shipt G Cloth to N Orleans —
4.800 loss on 137 bales G Cloth!!! A good lesson has been
taught us. altho we have paid dearly for it — No matter — we
shall get our living which is much better than many of our
neighbors will do — The loss of the Columbia has caused some
excitement — All who had an interest in the passengers should
be thankful for their escape — Hadthe weather been heavy the
ship w^d have gone to p's at once. &all would have been lost —
We are told the ladies (M^r. Mrs &Miss Lawrence as you will

have been informed were on board) — actedwith great courage &bore their sufferings with fortitude — Whether MrLaurence with his Wife &daughter will proceedin the "Margaret" — the spare Halifax steamer — or no. I have not yet learnt — Amory Appleton died about 15 days ago — F Jackson is at his Works with his family — I have seen yr. portrait — by Gam (Somebody) — it is excellent with one or two exceptions — too dark. It is much admired —

G. Higginson is now here, will remain 6 or 8 days is connected with Sale who will do the work in NY &G H will be here much of the time to pick up consignments I hope they may make a good living — I am told Sale is poorer now than when Crocker & Warren joined him —

Pro — Longfellow was married toMiss Appleton on the 13th.

Truly yours
W.S.B

Fletcher &Co write on the 17 June as Follows
We anex Dup. of our last letter & have now to acknowledge your favors of 30th Ulto. & 1st Inst the latter enclosing a remittance on a/c of HLee jr of £ 100 by a bill on ourselves which is in order. Previous to rect. thereof we had at, Mr Lee's request given him a credit for £ 227. the then balance & following the spirit of your present instructions. We have likewise placed the amt of the remittance now made at his disposal, the two above named amts, with £ 40 drawn for by Mr Lee independently of the same, will together amt to near the sum you mention viz £ 370 —

☞ Shall I remit more

[Addressed]
Mr Henry Lee jr
Care of
Messrs De Rothschild Frerés,
Paris
P *Hibernia*

LETTER FROM FRANCIS LOWELL LEE, BOSTON, OCT. 14, 1843,
TO HENRY LEE, JR., LONDON, DESCRIBING A COUNTINGROOM
ON INDIA WHARF AS SEEN BY A RECENT HARVARD GRADUATE [1]

At this time it was the custom for a young man of good family,
desiring to enter a mercantile life in Boston, to be graduated from
Harvard and then spend a year or two as clerk in the countingroom
of a relative or of a family friend, acquiring a general knowledge of
business which he would later utilize as supercargo on some vessel
belonging to the concern which he was serving — all this as part of
the process of working up to the position of junior partner and so on.
Robert Bennet Forbes has left an interesting and amusing account
of his employment in the countinghouse of "S. Cabot and James &
Thomas H. Perkins, Jrs.," in 1816. "My duties . . . ," he wrote,
"were to sweep out, make the fires, close and open the store, copy
letters into a book in a very indifferent manner, collect wharfage
bills, run errands," etc. Among his other memorable activities were
the measuring out to truckmen of oats and shorts (brought from
Philadelphia), catching the rats which these articles attracted to the
store, and making ink of powder and water — sometimes to the
detriment of his clothing — but even such compensations as the
pocket money acquired through selling the "sweepings" of coffee,
sugar, and pepper, the sampling of sweet Malmsey when the *Hampden*
was in from Madeira, and such a rare experience as the unpacking,
washing, counting, and repacking of $300,000 of specie from the
Canton Packet which had grounded and taken fire — extra duty
made lighter by lobster and cherry-bounce from Julien's — did not
make a clerk's life interesting to young Forbes and in 1817, as he
writes, "I cut short my connection with oats and shorts, collecting
wharfage bills, catching rats, and copying letters in a very bad hand"
and became a ship's boy on the restored *Canton Packet*.[2] The duties
of Frank Lee a little over a quarter of a century later were probably
not materially different, though it is difficult to imagine the young
Harvard exquisite sweeping out the store and, even worse, sorting
the semi-rotten hides stripped from the carcasses of diseased Indian
bullocks.

It was only with considerable reluctance on his own part and on

1. Henry Lee Shattuck Collection.
2. Forbes, *op. cit.*, pp. 27–28, 31.

that of his relatives that Frank Lee had decided to enter the mercantile profession. His father probably offered him the same advice later urged upon Henry Lee Higginson and other grandchildren: "Don't be merchants; anything else is better!" [3] Frank Lee's mother seems to have been the moving spirit in introducing her son into a countinghouse, against the advice of some relatives and the passivity of the candidate. "Pat [Patrick Tracy Jackson, Jr.] . . . ," Mary Lee commented, "happened to hear something of Frank going into a store & really entered a most earnest protest against it — he was puzzled for an answer when I asked what he shd. do? & said be a Physician — but how can you expect him to study said I? he has himself said he could not venture to trust himself — no he must be a merchant & trust to becoming interested in the science of his profession at some future period." [4] Thus the mercantile profession — and how little of a profession it was is indicated by the above comment — became the residuary legatee, *faute de mieux,* of those young men of the commercial classes who were not strongly interested in anything in particular, performing the same function as did bond salesmanship in the pre-depression period of our own time.

Early in the fall of 1843 the decision was finally made and on Sept. 12, Mary Lee wrote to her older son: "Frank is going, (I believe) at Bullard's suggestion; at all events with his consent into your store, for a few months until some other place presents." [5] Frank Lee's own announcement was: "I am just packing up my *things* to go into town. I go into No. 39 India Wharf on Monday to remain there till you get home and then to find another store if I decide upon a mercantile life I must say that I cannot contemplate a mercantile life with any great pleasure at present, but my ideas may change. I would certainly study Architecture, but that it is not, at present, a regular profession Next to that, my taste leads to Medicine, but I fear that some parts of the study would be too dry, to overcome my natural laziness." [6]

The letter below indicates that Frank Lee was not overworked in the Bullard & Lee countinghouse and was able to derive considerable amusement from his situation. Allowing for the fact that in his liter-

3. Perry, Bliss, *op. cit.*, p. 65.

4. Henry Lee Shattuck Collection, Mary Lee, Waltham, May 30, 1843, to Henry Lee, Jr., Paris.

5. *Ibid.*, Mary Lee, Waltham, Sept. 12, 1843, to Henry Lee, Jr., Paris.

6. *Ibid.*, Frank Lee, Waltham, Sept. 29, 1843, to Henry Lee, Jr., Paris.

ary style he strives for picturesque facetiousness rather than for bold realism, his description of an India Wharf countinghouse on a rather dull day is of unique value in opening a window briefly on a scene in a vanished mercantile era.

It is unnecessary, even were it possible, to identify the other persons mentioned in the letter below. Since one of the principal duties of young clerks was the copying of letters, Frank Lee's fears that he would soon know to whom W. S. Bullard was writing were doubtless well-founded. C. H. Bailey, from the fact that he was engaged with the countingroom books and was to go out as clerk on the *Sidney* to Calcutta, was evidently close to completing his term of service as a countinghouse clerk. J. W. Boott, the clerk other than F. L. Lee engaged in private letter writing, was the brother of Mrs. Francis Henry Jackson, formerly Sarah Boott.[7] Those who have had the task of deciphering business letters of this period will appreciate young Lee's reference to the "most distressingly thin paper" on which J. W. Field was writing.

After only about eight months in the countinghouse, Frank Lee was sent as supercargo on the barque *Sophronia* to Rio de Janeiro. Among his duties was one committed to him by his father: "to see what can be done in respect to the claim on Mr Gardner . . . the brother of that Gentleman has for two years or more been urgent for me to settle the matter by a payment of 20 per cent."[8] The Gardner on whom Henry Lee had a claim was presumably George Gardner, younger brother of John Lowell Gardner, who became a member of his brother's firm in 1838,[9] but nothing is known concerning the residence in Rio implied in the above commission nor what, if anything, Frank Lee succeeded in accomplishing in the matter.

Francis Lowell Lee did not, it seems, remain connected with the commercial world for long. By 1848 he was married and settled at Westport, N. Y., where he was engaged in farming.[10] In the Civil War he served as major of the Fourth Battalion, Massachusetts Volunteer Militia, and as colonel of the 44th Massachusetts Infantry, retiring, at the conclusion of the conflict, to his farm, where he died

7. Putnam and Putnam, *op. cit.*, p. 30.

8. Jackson-Lee Papers, "Letters 1840–41. Henry Lee," Oct. 30, 1840–Dec. 21, 1852, pp. 334–335, Henry Lee, Boston, May 30, 1844, to Miller, Le Cocq & Co., Rio de Janeiro.

9. Gardner, *op. cit.*, pp. 161–162.

10. Morse, F. R., *op. cit.*, pp. xv, 287–293; Putnam, J. J., *op. cit.*, p. 370.

in 1886.[11] With his withdrawal from commerce the first strand in the cable of tradition which anchored the Lee family to ocean-borne commerce was snapped.

Frank Lee's heart had never really been in commerce, but by 1852 Henry Lee, Jr., had been independently engaged in foreign trade for a dozen years; the latter's withdrawal from commerce in that year is thus of considerably greater significance. His brother-in-law George Higginson, who had spent many discouraging years in commerce and had occasionally been associated in voyages with Bullard & Lee, finally withdrew from merchandising completely and formed with John Clarke Lee cousin to Henry Lee, Jr., the banking firm of Lee & Higginson. In 1852, Henry Lee, Jr., deciding that foreign trade was played out and feeling no interest in manufacturing, joined his brother-in-law and cousin. For the first time in well over a century the Lees were definitely withdrawn from foreign commerce.

After his withdrawal from foreign trade, Henry Lee, Jr., devised, and was the proprietor of, the Union Safe Deposit Vaults, opened Jan. 1, 1868, the best and about the first of their kind in the country. He was an investor in railroad and mining stock, including the Chicago, Burlington, & Quincy and the Calumet & Hecla. Aside from business his main interests were historical, architectural, artistic, horticultural, and musical — in fact, he seems from all accounts to have absorbed in one way or another most of the extra-business interests of all his recent ancestors. His death took place Nov. 24, 1898.[12] Although his activity in foreign trade covered only sixteen years (1836–52) at the most, this period, nevertheless, presented special characteristics, a knowledge of which is essential to an understanding of Massachusetts commerce in the early nineteenth century.

Boston. Oct 14th. 1843.

My dear H.

I *snatch a moment from the hurry of business to compound* a letter for your perusal; what the devil I snatched the moment for, I don't know, for I have nothing to say in it.

I must draw you a picture of *the* counting-room. At the table, W.S.B. Esqr (in a mercantile dishabille, that is an old

11. *New Eng. Hist. & Gen. Reg.*, July, 1922, p. 215.

12. Morse, F. R., *op. cit.*, pp. xiv, 280, 394–402; Morse, John T., Jr., *Colonel Henry Lee,* pp. 15, 18–19.

seer-sucker coat $\frac{CO}{E}$ i.e. confoundedly out at the elbows.) writing letters to — I know not whom! (heigho) though I fear I shall. In the corner, at the aristocratic desk, CH. Bailey [interlineated: costume the same] lost in the intricate mazes of the Ledger & Journal, into which I see by the writing you once wandered. Onthe opposite side of the large desk sits J W Boott. inditing a letter to my last flame Mrs. F. H. Jackson. Costume rather more rowdy. On the same side with myself Mr. J W. Field is copying a letter upon most distressingly thin paper. I have just been off on wild goose chase down Central Wharf in search of Mr John Foster whom I found at the head of the wharf, after having made a fruitless search to the very extremity. No language can describe the lovely scenery by which we are surrounded. Curtain rises (windowc. of course) and discovers a group of truckmen dancing round some raisin boxes, fancifully disposed among groups of grape kegs, barque Emily Wilder in the back-ground, farther on is the good ship Sidney "for Calcutta; with Despatch" "for freight or passage apply to W. S. Bullard or *H Lee jr.*" MrBailey goes out as clerk in this ship. I must say that I don't think a store-life the most exciting in the world, however, I take for granted that it is exceedingly *useful*, and thereby console myself. I am keeping bachelors hall just now in our exceedingly cheery looking basement room, Bell is my factotum and I find it an exceeding pleasant mode of life. I wonder whether, I have told you of the goods that have arrived from you a lot bronzes, casts & engravings & also a beautiful little painting which came out in good condition. I received the other day a delightful letter from you, in which I was much amused by your description of the heart of a susceptible person traveling in Europe. I almost fell in love with the "Lady of the Torrent" from imagination. I agree with you entirely upon the subject of travelling. A man just brought in small scrap of paper, which stated that you promised to pay 1068 dollars 88 cents, and handed it to me. It is rather horrible to be subject to such insults on your acc't. The City Greys have a new uniform, very beautiful & neat. Bell-crowned black beaver cap with white pompon. [sketch]

Grey coat or rather coatee and I think grey pants /silver mounted). H J. Bigelow M. D, has, I believe arr^d. this morn^g. Today, I go out to Waltham the last time this summer to our house as they move in next Tuesday. Mother will tell you, I presume, in her letter of Aunt Harriet's sad sickness, w'h is the reason ofour moving in so early.

LIST OF MANUSCRIPTS REPRODUCED

LIST OF MANUSCRIPTS REPRODUCED

PART II. FIRST GENERATION: JOSEPH LEE, 1774–1827

PART IV. SECOND GENERATION: PATRICK TRACY JACKSON, 1802–24

Division IX. Patrick Tracy Jackson, Calcutta Supercargo, 1802–06.

LIST OF MANUSCRIPT COLLECTIONS

LIST OF MANUSCRIPT COLLECTIONS

A. In Private Hands

I. Papers in the possession of Mr. Henry Lee Shattuck.

(a) Jackson-Lee Papers.

Papers relating to Jonathan Jackson.

Letters

"Letterbook, 1765." Jonathan Jackson and Jackson & Bromfield, Newburyport, Feb. 13, 1765–Apr. 29, 1774.

"Letter Book, 1774." Jackson, Tracy & Tracy and Jonathan Jackson, Newburyport, Feb. 11, 1774–Dec. 22, 1780.

Accounts

"[Acc^t.] of Goods taken . . . 23^d Feby. 1729/30." Relates to the business of Jonathan Jackson's father or grandfather.

Jackson & Bromfield invoice book, Aug. 4, 1764–Dec., 1771.

Journal, John Bromfield and Bromfield & Jackson, Apr. 24, 1765–Sept. 15, 1768.

Shop Money Account Book, Apr. 12, 1766–Sept. 15, 1768.

Papers relating to Joseph Lee, Sr.

Letters

Loose letters to and from Joseph Lee & Co. and Lee & Cabot, Aug. 31, 1777–Sept. 9, 1790.

Accounts

Miscellaneous loose papers and letters of the Cabots and the Lees, principally the latter, 1744–1851.

"J x L 1767. Ledger A," Jan. 8, 1767–Jan. 31, 1792.

"I x L & Co. 1773. Waste, &c 1773," Aug., 1773–Apr. 6, 1793.

"Blotter. J. Lees & Co., 1773," Beverly, Aug., 1773–Mar. 9, 1786.

"J. Lee & Co.'s Distilly Ledger," Aug., 1773–Aug. 1, 1793.

"Cash Book Octr. 1773,"–May, 1778.

"Account Sales of Sundry Merchandize belonging to Brig^t. O. Cromwell's Prizes acc^t. the Owners," Aug. 14, 1777–Aug. 21, 1779.

"Waste Book of Joseph Lee & George Cabot Administrators

to the Estate of the Late Eliz^th. Cabot dec^d. Began Decr. 6th. 1781." Ended May 14, 1789.

"Wast and Ledger — for Wharf & Warehouse belonging to Mess Brown & Thorn'k George Cabot Esqr. & myself —." Beverly, Mar. 25, 1784–Dec. 9, 1786.

"Ledger B. J. Lee 1785," Jan., 1785–Dec. 31, 1810.

"Journal. J. Lee. 1785," Beverly, Jan. 9, 1785–Boston, Dec. 31, 1810.

Blotter, Beverly, Dec. 1, 1785–Feb. 8, 1788.

"Journal. L. & C. 1785," Beverly, Dec. 1, 1785–Jan. 26, 1802.

"L & C," daybook, Beverly, Dec. 1, 1785–Jan. 26, 1802.

"Ledger, L & C," Dec. 22, 1785–Jan., 1802.

Loose Lee & Cabot business papers, 1787.

"Waste Book January. 1^t. 1796," Beverly, Jan. 2, 1796–Boston, Dec. 21, 1808.

"Cash Book January, 1^t. 1796 —," Jan. 2, 1796–Dec. 31, 1805.

A few loose stock receipts, 1803–27.

Papers relating to Patrick Tracy Jackson.

Letters

"Letter Book begun in Calcutta Novr. 17th, 1802 — Ended in the Cape of Good Hope March 27th 1806 — including voyages, per the Ship Hannah, Ship Pembroke & Brig Rio."

"Letter Book — From 17 June 1806 to 14 July 1807."

"Letter Book From 27 July 1807 to 16 Decr. 1808."

"P. T. Jackson — Letter Book A," Boston, Jan. 1, 1810–Feb. 21, 1812.

Letter book relating to the *Vancouver*, Nov. 10, 1810–May 19, 1814.

"Letters B," Feb. 21, 1812–June 20, 1826.

Accounts and memoranda

"John Tracy Jr's Book 1810." Memoranda on India goods for guidance of a supercargo.

"Journal. P. T. Jackson," Boston, Jan. 1, 1836–Sept. 13, 1847.

Papers relating to Joseph Lee, Jr., Henry Lee, Sr., and Henry Lee, Jr.

Letters

Miscellaneous loose papers and letters of the Cabots and the Lees, principally the latter, 1744–1851 (already once mentioned above).

"Letter Book. Clos'd on 19th. November 1806." Began Apr. 6, 1793.

"Letters written in France during my voyage 1804 — ," N. Y., July 5, 1804–Malaga, Mar. 3, 1805.

"Letter Book Finished Dec[r]. 1808," Boston, Nov. 20, 1806–Dec. 31, 1808.

"Letter Book," Boston, Aug. 19, 1810–May 30, 1811.

"Bristol letter Book, orders from Shippers in Brig Reaper 1811 — voyage to Calcutta," Boston, Aug. 15, 1811–*Reaper*, Jan. 17, 1812.

"Letters written in Calcutta from May to August 1812."

"H. Lee's Letters from Calcutta from August 1812 to June 1813."

"Letters written in Calcutta by H. Lee from July 1813 to March 1816."

Henry Lee's letter book, N. Y. and Boston, July 26, 1816–Oct. 30, 1817.

"Letter Book from Jan[y]. 17th. 1817 to October 27. 1818."

Bundle of letters labelled "1819. Letters about E. I. Goods — ," Feb. 11, 1818–Dec. 28, 1819.

Loose letters written by Henry Lee, Jr., from New Orleans, Rio de Janeiro, St. Louis, Cincinnati, Washington, D. C., Colbrook, N. H., Lancaster, N. H., Plymouth, N. H., New Lebanon Springs, N. Y., Mar. 9, 1838–Aug. 4, 1844.

"Letters 1840–41. Henry Lee," Oct. 30, 1840–Dec. 21, 1852.

Miscellaneous loose letters to or from Henry Lee, Sr., and Jr., 1828, 1845–51.

Accounts and memoranda

"Invoices," 1799–1812.

"List of Vessels clear'd for America from Calcutta," 1800–12.

"Foreign Sales on acc[t]. of J. & H. Lee from 1803 to 1810."

"Memorandum of Sales of E. I. & other goods 1818 &c &c — ." Contains accounts, May 20–Aug. 1, 1807, price memoranda, Jan.–Dec., 1818, and a "Letter about Cotton 1822."

"Memoranda, Prices Current E. I. Goods — Imports & Exports &c &c," Jan., 1810–Feb. 20, 1816. Also contains "Arrivals at China during the season 1809–10" and a list of vessels clearing from the United States for the Orient, Feb. 25, 1809–Jan. 29, 1810.

Henry Lee's account book, London, Sept. 30, 1811–Calcutta, Mar. 1, 1816.

"Invoices of all the goods ship'd by Henry Lee during his stay in Calcutta from May 1812 to March 1816."

Account book, Calcutta, Sept. 20, 1813–Feb., 1816. Transactions in India goods made by Henry Lee while in India.

"Henry Lee's Calcutta Memorandum Book. 1814 & 1815," Aug. 6, 1814–Mar., 1816, July 30, 1821–Feb., 1822.

"Accounts Current. & Account Sales," Apr. 18, 1816–Dec. 31, 1817. Also: "Invoices," July 18, 1816–Dec. 29, 1817.

"Directions to C. D. Miles 1817 for purchases Piece goods, Indigo &c &c. &c."

Two scrapbooks of newspaper cuttings, 1846–60, mostly related to economic activity. The books used for this purpose were originally entitled "Directions to C. D. Miles . . . 1817" and "Statements Cotton & Indigo exports imports and other Memorandums of a useful nature."

Papers relating to various relatives and associates of the Lees.

Ledger, probably of Capt. Thomas Lee (1741–1830), Oct. 24, 1769–June 13, 1817.

"Journal 1796 Wm. C. Lee. N. L." Mar., 1796–Feb., 1800.

"Henrico. Thomas Lee, Jr." Ship's log, Apr. 30–Dec. 18, 1824. Boston, Falmouth, Copenhagen, Gibraltar, Lisbon, Boston.

"Journal kept on board ship Logan bound to Gibraltar and Canton." Mar. 4, 1834–Aug. 10, 1834. Evidently kept by Thomas Handasyd Cabot who illustrated it with several pencil drawings of the ship.

"Notices of the Life and Character of the late John Bromfield — written at the request of Hon. Josiah Quincy; to aid him in compiling a Memoir of that great man," by Henry Lee, Sr., and in his handwriting.

(b)   Henry Lee Shattuck Collection.

Loose letters from Jonathan Jackson, Dec. 27, 1762–Feb. 27, 1792, to John Lowell.

Patrick Tracy Jackson Papers. Loose letters to Patrick Tracy Jackson, July 26, 1810–Oct. 9, 1814.

John Bromfield Papers. Loose letters from and to John Bromfield, Nov. 26, 1807–Jan. 20, 1811, chiefly between the Lees and himself.

"Memorandum Book January 1814," Feb., 1814–Feb. 24, 1816. Henry Lee, Calcutta.

Loose letters from relatives, friends, and business associates to Henry Lee, Jr., London, Paris, and Boston, Apr. 11, 1842–Jan. 20, 1845.

II. Papers in the possession of Mr. Patrick Tracy Jackson, Jr.

Papers relating to Jonathan Jackson's ancestors.

Memorandum book, containing prices of materials and labor expressed in "Silv^r" and "Pres^t Cur^{cy}," 1710, 1724, 1728, 1730, 1745, 1751. Probably kept by Jonathan Jackson (1672–1736) and his son Edward.

"1727/8." Alphabetical list of goods in stock with prices, perhaps drawn up by his father Jonathan.

"Memorandum Book N 2. relat^g to ye first Cost of Slitt^g Mill &c Began Sept^e 1728." Evidently kept by Jonathan Jackson (1672–1736).

"Acc^t. of Goods taken 16th. Feb^r. 1742." Evidently relates to the business of Edward Jackson (1708–57).

"Acc^t. of Prize-Goods I rec^d out of ye Jesus, Maria & Joseph Sept. 1748." "I" was Edward Jackson (1708–57).

"A List of Debts for Year 1755 and [Year] 1756."

Papers relating to Jackson & Bromfield.

"Waste Book belonging to Jackson & Bromfield," Mar. 1, 1766–Mar. 1, 1767.

Jackson & Bromfield ledger. Mar. 1, 1766–Mar. 1, 1772.

Jackson & Bromfield journal, Apr. 29, 1766–Dec. 23, 1771.

Shop Money Account Book, Sept. 15, 1768–June 18, 1771.

Also: cash book, Mar. 11, 1772–Mar. 1, 1774. Also: Jonathan Jackson's invoice book, Aug. 1, 1779–July 20, 1782.

Jackson & Bromfield ledger, Mar. 1, 1772–Jan. 4, 1791.

Papers relating to Jackson, Tracy & Tracy.

Jackson, Tracy & Tracy ledger, Apr. 11, 1774–Aug. 9, 1787.

Jackson, Tracy & Tracy blotter, Jan. 5, 1775–Dec. 17, 1776.

"The Sloop Game Cock to Sundry Adventurers as a Privateer," Feb., 1776.

"Profit & Loss in J T & T's Ledger."

Papers relating to Jonathan Jackson and the Tracys.

Blotter, Newburyport, Jan. 1, 1781–Jan. 3, 1783.

Privateering account book, June, 1781–May, 1783.

Stock and invoice book of Nathaniel and John Tracy, Mar. 20, 1784–Oct. 8, 1785.

Papers relating to Jackson & Higginson.

"N° 1. — Trial Balance Book for Ledger belonging to Jackson & Higginson began 13th May 1784 — date of first Entry —"

"Trial Balance Book N° 2. beginning with date of 31st Augst 1785."

Miscellaneous papers.

Loose papers relating to Jackson & Bromfield, Jackson, Tracy & Tracy, and Jackson and the Tracys individually.

Papers relating to Patrick Tracy Jackson.

P. T. Jackson's account book. Cape of Good Hope, Feb. 20, 1805–Dec. 27, 1806.

"Ledger A From 27 April 1807 to 31 Augt. 1809," and "Alphabet to Ledger A."

"Waste A From 27 April 1807 to 31 August 1809."

"P. T. Jackson, Note Book," Apr. 27, 1807–June 20, 1815.

"Ledger" and index, Sept. 1, 1809–Dec. 31, 1835.

"Waste A," Sept. 2, 1809–May 24, 1811.

"Journal A folio. 1 to 278," Sept. 1, 1809–Jan. 14, 1812.

"Account Current A," and index, Aug. 12, 1809–Feb. 17, 1813.

"Accounts at Madras of the Brig Vancouver's Cargo," July 20, 1811–Nov. 20, 1811.

"Cash Book A," Jan. 1, 1810–Dec. 31, 1819.

"P. T. Jackson," Jan. 10, 1810–Dec. 31, 1832.

"Waste B," May 25, 1811–Apr. 20, 1815.

"Waste C," Apr. 21, 1815–Dec. 31, 1816.

"Journal B fol. 279 to 563," Jan. 15, 1812–Dec. 31, 1819.

"Journal," folio 563 to 809, Jan. 1, 1820–Dec. 31, 1835.

"Day Book," Nov. 2, 1820–Jan. 1, 1837.

"Cash Book," May 1, 1822–Dec. 31, 1829.

Cash book, Jan. 1, 1830–Dec. 29, 1835.

"Disposal Book."

"Trial Balance A," folios 1 to 294.

"Trial Balance B," folios 295 to 793.

"Journal" of Union Canal Lottery, July 15, 1815–Apr. 22, 1819.

"Ledger" of Union Canal Lottery, July 15, 1815–June 15, 1821.

Memorandum book on textile manufacturing companies, Aug., 1828–Oct. 19, 1829.

Memorandum book relating to various textile mills, 1839–45.

Bundle of letters on iron works in Pennsylvania, 1835–36.

Papers relating to the Concord Railroad Corporation, July 7, 1836–Jan. 4, 1841.

"Executor's accounts of Estate of Jon^a. Jackson — deceased —"

Papers relating to the "Estate of S. Cabot," 1813–17.

Papers relating to the "Estate of Anna Cabot," 1814.

"Accounts made out from Books of F. C. Lowell deceased," 1814–17.

Memorandum book relating to the "Estate of F. C. Lowell." "Mem⁰. of Debts and other property held by the Executors of the will of Francis C. Lowell . . ." Dec. 11, 1820–Oct. 9, 1822; "Inventory of the estate of Edward J. Lowell . . . ," July, 1819–Dec. 20, 1825.

"Accounts of F. C. Lowell Estate." Also contains "Accounts as settled with the proprietors of the Boston & Merrimack Manufacturing Companies."

"Account of expenses paid by P. T. Jackson for Francis Cabot & Edward Jackson Lowell, minors John Lowell Esqʳ & said P. T. Jackson Guardians 1819."

"Transactions by George Cabot and James Jackson, relative to their trust for the benefit of Mʳˢ. Louisa Higginson & her Children," Apr. 10, 1817–June 11, 1834.

"Mem⁰. respecting C. R. Lowells affairs," 1836–40.

"Patrick T. Jackson New Eng. Bank N⁰. 2 —" Sept. 1, 1815–Apr. 21, 1818.

"Bank," New Eng. Bank, Nov. 1, 1815–Jan. 2, 1819.

Cash at Boston Bank, Feb. 1, 1816–Jan. 4, 1819. Also includes account of P. T. Jackson as agent of Boston Manufacturing Company in the Suffolk Bank, Aug. 1, 1818–Dec. 17, 1818. Also includes a few miscellaneous memoranda.

"Patrick T. Jackson Suffolk Bank," Apr. 27, 1818–June, 1822. 2 vols.

Suffolk Bank, Jan. 1, 1819–Dec. 3, 1821. Also includes cash in pocket from Jan. 1, 1819–Dec. 31, 1821.

"P. T. Jackson. Columbian Bank," June 19, 1822–Feb. 1, 1828.

Money in bank, Jan. 1, 1822–Jan. 8, 1824. Also includes money in pocket for the same period.

Cash book, Jan. 1, 1820–Apr. 30, 1822.

"Farm Book Waltham Mass. 1834."

"P T J 1844–45." This is a cash book.

"P. T. Jackson Jr. Private Cash," Jan. 1, 1873–Dec. 31, 1896. 6 volumes.

Three diaries.

III.   Austin H. Clark Collection.

Letters from Jonathan Jackson, principally to his brother-in-law and sister, Mr. and Mrs. Oliver Wendell. Dec. 23, 1760–Sept., 1798.

IV. George R. Minot Collection.

Jonathan Jackson's letter book, London, July 10–Dec. 31, 1784.

Jonathan Jackson's letter book. Port au Prince, Sept. 1–Aux Cayes, Oct. 26, 1787.

V. James Jackson Collection.

Two small trunks or boxes filled with papers relating almost entirely to Dr. James Jackson, but including a Latin oration delivered by Jonathan Jackson, July 2, 1757, on graduation from the Boston Latin School, and an account of adventures to the Orient made by Dr. James Jackson with his brother P. T. Jackson.

B. IN PUBLIC DEPOSITORIES

Massachusetts Historical Society.

Lee-Cabot Papers. 21 vols. of letters, accounts, bills, receipts, etc., relating to the Cabots and Lees, 1707–1893.

English Shipping Records, pt. iii, Entrance and Clearance, 1756–63, and Massachusetts Shipping Records, pt. iv, 1756–65. Photostats. Some of the clearances and entries go back as far as 1753.

Bowdoin & Temple Papers. A few references to the Tracys.

Pickering MSS. A few references to Cabots, Tracys, and Lees.

Thomas Lee, Jr., Papers, 1802–65. Letter books, ledgers, invoices, etc. This material was not used.

Letters of Henry Lee, Sr. Two portfolios of letters, 1813–17, chiefly from Calcutta. These letters furnished the principal basis for *Henry and Mary Lee: Letters and Journals,* Frances Rollins Morse, ed. (Boston, 1926), and were therefore not carefully sifted a second time.

Boston Custom House.

Registers, 1802 — . Indexes go back as far as 1795.

New York Historical Society.

Rufus King Papers. Contain a single highly interesting letter from Joseph Lee, Jr.

Gallatin Papers. One or two references to the Lees, of little importance.

Baker Library.

Joseph Lee, Sr., receipt book, 1780–1831.

Heard Papers. Important in themselves but have little to do with the Jacksons or Lees.

Boston Manufacturing Company Records. For P. T. Jackson after withdrawal from commerce.

Beverly Historical Society.
    Beverly Historical Society Papers, vol. i. References to Joseph Lee, Sr., and Cabots.
    "Records — Naval Office. Beverly. 1784–1800, vol. xii. Import & Export Bonds. 1784–1789." References to Joseph Lee, Sr., and the Cabots. "Port of Beverly — Entries. Imports and Imposts — 1787–1789." References to Joseph Lee, Sr., and the Cabots.
New England Historic Genealogical Society.
    Bromfield Papers. Account books, 1729–82, letter books, 1771–73. Examined only casually and not used.
Widener Library.
    Commodore Tucker Papers. Papers of Nathaniel Tracy's ship *Cato*, 1784, vol. ii.
    Jackson, James. "Notes of the life and character of the late P. T. Jackson, Esq," with some of P. T. Jackson's correspondence, 1810–11 (typewritten).
Boston Public Library.
    Chamberlin Collection. Letters of Jonathan Jackson, John Tracy, and Patrick Tracy Jackson, interesting only as autographs.

INDEX

INDEX

INDEX

Words italicized refer to either ships or newspapers; in the cases where it has been impossible to differentiate between ships of the same name, separate entries have been made. When a word indexed appears more than once in a letter, reference is commonly made only to the first occurrence in the introduction to the letter or in the letter itself.